PEASE RECORD.

In Two Parts.

PART I.

Eng.ᵈ by J.J. Pease.

David Pease

THE PEASE RECORD

An Essential Genealogical Reference on the
Pease Family of New England, Comprising

*A Genealogical and Historical Record of the
Descendants of John Pease, Sen.*
Last of Enfield, Conn.

Compiled by
Reverend David Pease
and
Austin S. Pease
as Associate Editor

and

*The Early History of the
Pease Families in America*
by
Austin Spencer Pease

HERITAGE BOOKS
2009

HERITAGE BOOKS

AN IMPRINT OF HERITAGE BOOKS, INC.

Books, CDs, and more—Worldwide

For our listing of thousands of titles see our website
at
www.HeritageBooks.com

A Facsimile Reprint
Published 2009 by
HERITAGE BOOKS, INC.
Publishing Division
100 Railroad Ave. #104
Westminster, Maryland 21157

A Genealogical and Historical Record of the
Descendants of John Pease, Sen.
Originally published Springfield, Massachusetts
Samuel Bowles & Company, Printers, 1869

———

The Early History of the Pease Families in America
Entered, according to Act of Congress, in the year 1869, by
Austin Spencer Pease,
In the Clerk's Office of the District Court of the District of Massachusetts

International Standard Book Numbers
Paperbound: 978-0-7884-1300-1
Clothbound: 978-0-7884-8276-2

INTRODUCTION.

WITH kindred esteem, the compiler presents this work to the living descendants of JOHN PEASE, (known in Salem, Mass., and in Enfield, Ct., as John Pease, Sen.,) a Genealogical Record of his posterity. The writer has not been induced to engage in this labor in expectation of sharing some great estate which had no legitimate heirs in the Fatherland to claim it—as has been frequently hinted; neither has he anticipated adequate compensation for the time, labor and expense incurred in accomplishing it; but rather from a desire to see a more certain, complete and permanent Register of our family name in this country—especially of those springing from our ancestor of the Enfield branch—thus bringing to each other's acquaintance a large circle of relatives which time and circumstances have scattered throughout our wide domain, and in other parts of the world; also as a tribute of respect to the memory of those whose pioneer lives, hardships and privations, and whose patriotism and piety, have procured and bequeathed to us a rich inheritance of civil and religious liberty. Furthermore it seemed important that the names and deeds of our ancestors and kindred, many of whom have bravely fallen in battle or died in camps, in the early and later wars of our country, should not be lost to future generations. Again, it appeared desirable and appropriate, that one who had seen and conversed with three and taken active part in religious worship with one of the grandsons of John Pease, Sen., should speak of the fathers to the present and coming generations. These considerations have led the writer to comply with a request to prepare for the press a genealogical record of the descendants of John Pease, Sen. It appeared, at the time this request was made, quite possible that, with what had been done, the object could be accomplished with convenient dispatch and in a short time. In this we have been disappointed.

By way of apology to our subscribers for the long delay in the appearance of this volume, we desire to say that its preparation has involved a much greater amount of historical and genealogical investigation than was anticipated at the commencement, resulting in important changes, and thereby hindering our progress; while professional and domestic duties have diminished the amount of time necessary to be devoted to it.

It may not be out of place here to notice some things leading to the changes referred to in our work. When the compiler's attention was first called to the subject, he was ignorant of the fact that an attempt of the kind had been made. He had been a resident of Central New York for many years, but upon the sad event of sudden death his home was made desolate. In this solitary state, he returned to New England to visit the places of early life. Some forty years had made great changes; but few youthful associates were to be found among the living; therefore the resting-places of the dead were visited, and their silent mementos were read with deep interest. Among the well cared for cemeteries in the towns of Enfield, Suffield and Somers, the grave-stones and monuments of the Peases were numerous and ancient, which revived a desire to examine their early history. After spending some time in searching town records and conversing with aged people, an attempt was made to arrange the facts collected in order, when, for the first time, the writer heard of the work of the late F. S. Pease, Esq., which he found in four numbers of the New England Historical and Genealogical Register, in the hands of Hon. Oliver B. Morris,* of Springfield, Mass. Subsequently

---

* Judge Morris is a descendant of John Pease, Sen., through Margaret Pease, who married Josiah Colton, (see Part I., page 6, No. 11.) He stood prominently as a lawyer in Hampden County for many years, and was afterwards Judge of Probate for the same County. He is now living in retirement with his son, George B. Morris, Esq., at the advanced age of nearly eighty-seven years.

he was favored with the reading of Hinman's History of the Pease Family, in the Hartford Athenæum, furnished by Dr. John C. Pease. It was readily seen from records and personal acquaintances, that there were many individuals and families omitted in that valuable beginning. Hence what had been done was an inducement to proceed and gather up what was left; also to make an advance to the next generation.

As it was the design of the compiler, at that time, to collect for the use of some one who might hereafter publish, the plan adopted was to arrange a Pease Register, in alphabetical order, giving a genealogical and biographical sketch of those of the name. In the prosecution of that plan, there have been registered between three and four thousand persons bearing the name of Pease, of the posterity of John Pease, Sen., tracing them through all the links of the genealogical chain, from our first ancestor in this country to the tenth generation.

Wishing, however, to see a more consecutive record of the descendants of our Enfield ancestor for immediate use, and one, too, that could be seen at a glance, a Genealogical Tree was first thought of, by which to represent the branches and families. But we were too numerous to be fully and clearly presented by that common genealogical figure; therefore, a Pyramid was selected as a more convenient device combining two objects, a Record and a Monumental Memorial of the Pease family.

This design having been brought to satisfactory completion, it was- suggested that it would be an improvement to have short sketches of the families to accompany the Monument. Upon this, the compiler turned his attention to that object, following the order of Mr. F. S. Pease, and had made some progress previous to the request to furnish a copy for the press. We, however, did not feel all the certainty we wished of the parentage of John Pease, Sen., viz., that he was the son of " John who came over in the *Francis* from Ipswich, 1634, aged 27, and whose name appears among the inhabitants of Salem, 1637." Yet, as we then could find nothing more certain, we adhered to the supposition of our predecessors, and so continued until after a correspondence with Mr. F. S. Pease, who had become satisfied that Robert, and not John, was the father of John Pease, Sen., of Enfield. Upon this the compiler agreed with his associate editor, that a thorough examination should be made, to settle, if possible, the question who was the father of our Enfield ancestor, whether John or Robert, and to obtain information on other points left uncertain by those who had preceded us. The age of the compiler not allowing him to engage in so active and laborious service, Mr. Austin Spencer Pease, his earnest and efficient coadjutor in this work, was requested to take the task of visiting Salem, our ancestor's first residence, and other localities where needful information could be obtained. The result of his mission may be seen in the Appendix and Second Part of the Pease Record.

These changes and efforts have not only caused a delay, but greatly increased the amount of printed matter contemplated at the beginning, which has compelled us to omit the Monument. We think, however, the additional historical information contained in the second part of the volume will be an equivalent for the omission.*

We do not expect this Record will be found without errors. Some blanks have been unavoidable, as we have been unsuccessful in our efforts to obtain the desired information about families, names, and dates: there are also many ways for mistakes to occur. But whatever defects may be found in this work, we wish to remind our kinsmen that we have designed to make it a reliable basis by which all the descendants of our Enfield ancestor, John Pease, Sen., may trace themselves, in an unbroken line, back to

---

* The projector has spent much time and labor in bringing the device and arrangement of the Monumental Memorial of the Pease Family to his satisfaction and the approval of those who have examined the plan, and regrets the necessity of its omission. But we find, to make the engraving what it should be, in dimension and ornament, and to engrave more than three thousand names, puts both objects (that is, Book and Monument,) beyond our present reach. Should we, however, find one to execute the design to our mind, and suitable encouragement be given, it may yet be done.

England; and if there should be any stray family or individual who has not been registered in this Record, the appropriate place can be found, and the names placed in lineal order.

It remains for the writer to express his gratitude to those who have, in any way, aided us in this labor, while we assure them their correspondence and acquaintance has awakened a kindred feeling which will be pleasant to cherish, and an ardent desire for the present and future good of those to whom these pages are devoted.

DAVID PEASE.

ASHFIELD, MASS., *August*, 1869.

B

PREFATORY REMARKS.

BY THE ASSOCIATE EDITOR.

It was with some hesitancy, and not until after the earnest solicitation of the compiler, that the undersigned consented to have his name placed on the title page. As the entire plan of the work, and the arrangement of the information until within four years past, was made by Rev. David Pease, the writer did not think his name worthy of so conspicuous a place.

Our acquaintance began and continued some time by correspondence; and the writer furnished the compiler with considerable information before seeing him. Since our personal acquaintance began, our interviews have been very limited, and no time was afforded the writer to make a thorough examination of the work until about four years ago, when a copy of it, which had been prepared for the printer's use by direction of Rev. Mr. Pease, was placed in his hands. He then saw it was not as complete, in all respects, as was desirable. This incompleteness was consequent to the length of time the work had been in preparation, and the impaired eyesight with which the compiler had been laboring for many years, which rendered a large correspondence difficult. A much larger proportion of names were without dates of birth and places of habitation, and a much larger number of blanks were observable then than now. No histories of any of the eighth generation were given, except some dates of births, and a few comparatively of marriages and residences.

As the final publication of the work depended entirely upon the number of persons pledging to take copies of it, and the duty of obtaining the requisite number had been placed, in a large measure, on the writer, he thought that while a correspondence was instituted to obtain subscribers, efforts should be made also to supply the deficiencies above named.

As the canvassing progressed, by means of printed and written correspondence, additional names of members of our numerous family, and fuller
information concerning others, not before obtained, began to pour in. Our
labors resulted, within the past four years, in obtaining over four hundred
names of persons belonging to the male descent of John Pease, Sen., of the
sixth, seventh and eighth generations, which had not been before obtained,
a larger proportion of whom were subscribers than from any other source.
Within this time, the writer has enlarged the biographies of many of the
seventh generation, and prepared all the biographical histories of the eighth
generation, including, with a few exceptions, all that has been said of those
engaged in suppressing the rebellion.

It "was appropriate that one who had seen and conversed with three and
taken active part in religious worship with one of the grandsons of John
Pease, Sen., should speak of the fathers to the present and coming generations." Hence the writer left this field undisturbed to the senior compiler,
except in some cases where he added such facts as have been recently
exhumed from the ancient records of the counties in Massachusetts* and the
towns of East Windsor and Stafford.

There are doubtless many who would gladly have furnished us complete
records of their own and their fathers' families had they received the letters
addressed them. It would have been especially gratifying to the Rev. Mr.
Pease and the writer, could we have learned the names of all the noble sons
belonging to the family who shared the dangers, toils and sufferings of our
soldiers in the late war for the defense of the Union. We have yet to learn
that there was one of them who fought to destroy this Union at that time.

We expect many of our readers will find errors in dates and names in their
family records. Some of them we have discovered; others have been pointed
out to us. We have made so many amends in our table of Errata, that it
appears too large for respectability. Part I. has been a long time in preparation, and much of it has been re-arranged and re-written at various times,
and by several persons, one of whom was not specially careful in writing
names legibly. This has been one fruitful source of mistakes.

The compiler and his associate by no means assume the entire responsibility
of mistakes. In making out names and dates from a manuscript, persons
cannot be aided by their association with other words in the sentences.

---

* Prior to 1749 the towns of Enfield and Somers belonged to Massachusetts.

Hence, unless they are written in a legible hand, (as often they are not,) the copyist and the proof-reader are liable to make mistakes for which they should not be held responsible. Sometimes when we have failed to receive information concerning families from their own members, we have been obliged to resort for it to friends and acquaintances, who supposed they were rightly informing us, but were not. In other cases, persons sending information concerning their own families made serious errors, either then or when they attempted to correct advanced sheets which had been sent them. One individual, in correcting the date of his marriage, made it just six years later than his legible letter had told us a few years previous. Another, in pointing out four slight errors in the printed records of his numerous family of children, showed that two of the errors were of his own making.

The writer regrets that he has had no more time to spare from his private duties, that he might have done better what he has attempted to do for the Pease Record.

Many thanks to those who have cheerfully aided us with information for the work. I trust they will find themselves amply repaid in the perusal of its pages.

AUSTIN S. PEASE.

SPRINGFIELD, MASS., *August*, 1869.

CARD FROM EXECUTIVE COMMITTEE.

LATE in the Fall of 1864, Rev. David Pease signified to one of the under-signed that he had completed his history of the descendants of John Pease, Sen., last of Enfield, Ct., and that if any were desirous of having it printed, they had only to raise funds sufficient to pay the necessary expenses of pub-lication.

After some deliberation and correspondence with friends of the enterprise, it was thought advisable to call a public meeting at Springfield, Mass., of those interested in the work, for the purpose of devising means for publish-ing what Rev. Mr. Pease had prepared.

Pursuant to a public notice, a meeting was held at the Police Court Room, March 17, 1865. Mr. R. Ashmun Pease was called to the chair, and Dr. Loren H. Pease (page 168, Part I.,) was chosen Secretary.

Rev. Mr. Pease was present, and exhibited his plans to the meeting. · He proposed to have his work published in two forms. One was to be a litho-graphic Pyramid Chart, with the names of the descendants of John Pease, Sen., to be engraved on it. This was to be accompanied by a book to be called the Pease Directory. It was to include the names found on the Pease Pyramid, and to give their genealogical history.

From the estimated cost of a lithograph Chart, as given by Rev. Mr. Pease, it was thought a sufficient number of five dollar subscriptions for a copy of each of the two works could be obtained to pay the expenses of the publication of small editions of them. Accordingly the plans of the com-piler were accepted, and a committee was appointed, styled the Executive Committee, who were to procure the necessary·subscriptions, and otherwise assist Rev. Mr. Pease in his proposed publications. The Committee ap-pointed at that meeting were Austin S. Pease, Chairman, Luke H. Pease, Treasurer, ·R. Ashmun Pease, John R. Pease and Dr. Loren H. Pease. Mr. R. Ashmun Pease has since deceased, and Mr. John R. Pease, though exhibiting much interest in the enterprise, has declined to act with the Committee.*

A circular sent out by the Chairman of the Committee, soliciting subscriptions for the two works, was responded to, not only with names of persons as subscribers, but also with names in a much larger ratio of persons whose records had not been before obtained. The accession of names of the descendants necessarily demanded a larger plan for the Pyramid Chart. But when Mr. Pease had finally completed his plan to include these additional names (many of whom were subscribers,) the committee found a lithographic chart could not be had without an expense doubly exceeding the estimates which had before been given to Rev. Mr. Pease.

On comparing the number of subscriptions which had been obtained after a lapse of nearly two years from the time the circular was issued with the probable cost of both publications, the Committee judged that their publication would greatly exceed the amount pledged, or that could probably be obtained. They therefore concluded that either the whole enterprise must be abandoned, or the Pease Pyramid must be dropped, and the Genealogical and Historical Record be published alone. They saw that either plan would be a disappointment to Rev. Mr. Pease, who originally had thought of publishing a Pease Monument alone. But the Committee felt that his Genealogical and Historical Record, published without the Chart, would be a monument of his labor and toil which would be appreciated by the present generation, and prized by thousands of our name yet unborn.

The Pease Record is a much larger work than the Pease Directory would have been. All the information in the Appendix and in Part II. is new, except a portion of Chapter V. This has been prepared for the Record, and would not have appeared in the Pease Directory.

The Steel Engravings add interest to the Record, and were not contemplated for the Directory. The Committee judge that the original subscribers to the other works are receiving in this a work equal in value to the others. On comparing the Pease Record and its price with many others of a like character, they know that the subscribers are obtaining it at a reasonable price.

* Mr. John R. Pease has had much of his time and attention engrossed within a few years past in bringing to completion a history of Enfield, which was left in manuscript by his late father, Dr. John C. Pease. It includes a history of the families originating there, and its publication is looked forward to with considerable interest by many whose ancestry can be traced to that town.

They return their thanks to the individuals who have enriched the work by adding their own or their friends' pictures to it. We feel ourselves very fortunate in having secured to do our work, the services of the only artist in the United States who produces steel engravings by aquatint process, as all the pictures, except those opposite pages 141 and 143, are done by that process, and by our kinsman Joseph Ives Pease, Esq., of Stockbridge.

The Committee, in behalf of a numerous family, express their thanks to the association of gentlemen who cheerfully consented to be assessed the expense of a visit to Salem, that the ancestry of John Pease, Sen., might be settled beyond dispute. Had the work been printed with John Pease instead of Robert at the head of the generations, as was first contemplated, and was done by others, the mistake would have been one of serious regret.

AUSTIN SPENCER PEASE,
LUKE HALL PEASE,
LOREN HOWARD PEASE.

SPRINGFIELD, MASS., *August*, 1869.

EXPLANATORY REMARKS.

(*a*) The father of John Pease, Sen., being the pioneer to America, is placed at the beginning of Part I. as Generation I., and John Pease, Sen., is made the Second Generation.

(*b*) As the work progresses, the given names standing in the parenthesis, which immediately follow the name whose history is given, indicate the ancestry of the individual.

(*c*) The small figures at the right of such names denote the generation to which the persons belong.

(*d*) The posterity of the male descent of John Pease, Sen., is made into five grand divisions. Each of the sons, who had posterity, stands at the head of a division, and his posterity is said to be of that descent, as the descent of John,[3] etc., to descent of Isaac.[3]

(*e*) Each descent is subdivided into as many families as there were grandsons of John Pease, Sen., who are known to have had children. The descent of John[3] is divided into three families; Robert,[3] into four; Jonathan,[3] into two; James,[3] into one, and Isaac, into seven families.

(*f*) This work, with two exceptions, extends only to the eighth generation from Robert Pease, Sen., the American progenitor. The exceptions are, the names of those who early signified their intention of becoming subscribers to this genealogical work, and those who were engaged in the late war for the defense of the Union.

(*g*) The names of the children of the females belonging to the descent of John Pease, Sen., who married out of the family, are not given in this work, except children of the seventh generation whose parents subscribed for the work before it went to the press, or such as were in the late war. The posterity of Miriam (No. 66, page 13, of Part I.,) was included in the Pease Family by the late F. S. Pease. Her posterity, so far as can be ascertained, will be found in Part II. of the Pease Record, Chapter V.

(*h*) The figures on the margin standing at the left of the names of the children in the families, are consecutive numbers which run through the whole of Part I.

(*i*) The marginal or consecutive numbers are also indexical, and are found at the right of the same name in the Index of Given Names, and at the head of each man's family in the next generation, except the last.

(*j*) The large or full-faced marginal or consecutive figures stand against the names of such males as are known to have married. The same sized figures are opposite to the same names in the Index of Given Names.

(*k*) In a few instances, names have been inserted into the body of the work since completing the consecutive numbers. In those cases, the number preceding the inserted name or names has been repeated with another small consecutive number little above and at the right of it. (For an illustration, see page 158). The double numbers are also found in the Index. There are about 75 double numbers in Part I., and about 100 marginal numbers which have no names against them, making in all about 3,100 names from the male descent of John Pease, Sen., counting seven generations from him.

(*l*) When the name of Enfield or Somers is mentioned in this work, if no State is mentioned, Connecticut is intended.

(*m*) A character ——o——, when placed after a family, denotes that the person standing at the head of it is first cousin to the one following; ——oo——, second cousin; ——ooo——, third cousin; ——oooo——, fourth cousin.

STATISTICS.

The three thousand one hundred names in Part I. are divided as follows :

DESCENT OF JOHN.[3]

FAMILY OF JOHN.[4]— Fourth generation, 3 ; fifth generation, 7 ; sixth generation, 35 ; seventh generation, 85 ; total, 130.

FAMILY OF JAMES.[4]— Fourth generation, 6 ; fifth generation, 13 ; sixth generation, 26 ; seventh generation, 35 ; total, 80.

FAMILY OF JOSEPH.[4]— Fourth generation, 4 ; fifth generation, 21 ; sixth generation, 67 ; seventh generation, 124 ; total, 216.

Whole number of Descent of John,[3] 434, or about 14 per cent. of the whole.

DESCENT OF ROBERT.[3]

FAMILY OF ROBERT.[4]— Fourth generation, 13 ; fifth generation, 25 ; sixth generation, 67 ; seventh generation, 139 ; total, 244.

FAMILY OF SAMUEL.[4]— Fourth generation, 9 ; fifth generation, 41 ; sixth generation, 93 ; seventh generation, 178 ; total, 321, it being the largest family except one.

FAMILY OF DANIEL.[4]— Fourth generation, 5 ; fifth generation, 15 ; sixth generation, 27 ; seventh generation, 42 ; total, 89.

FAMILY OF EBENEZER.[4]— Fourth generation, 6 ; fifth generation, 7 ; sixth generation, 23 ; seventh generation, 30 ; total, 66.

Whole number of the Descent of Robert,[3] 730 or about 23 $\frac{54}{100}$ per cent. of the whole number.

DESCENT OF JONATHAN.[3]

FAMILY OF JOSIAH.[4]— Fourth generation, 1 ; fifth generation, 5 ; sixth generation, 10 ; seventh generation, 16 ; total, 32.

FAMILY OF PELATIAH.[4]— Fourth generation, 5 ; fifth generation, 15 ; sixth generation, 37 ; seventh generation, 76 ; total, 133.

Whole number of the Descent of Jonathan,[3] 173 or 5 $\frac{6}{10}$ per cent. of the whole number.

DESCENT OF JAMES.[3]

FAMILY OF JOSEPH.[4]— Fourth generation, 12 ; fifth generation, 21 ; sixth generation, 36 ; seventh generation, 41 ; total, 110.

Whole number of Descent of James,[3] 118 or $3\frac{8}{10}$ per cent. of the whole.

DESCENT OF ISAAC.[3]

FAMILY OF ISAAC.[4]— Fourth generation, 8; fifth generation, 37 ; sixth generation, 80 ; seventh generation, 159 ; total 284.

FAMILY OF ABRAHAM.[4]— Fourth generation, 14; fifth generation, 66 ; sixth generation, 130; seventh generation, 178; total, 388, it being the largest family.

FAMILY OF ISRAEL.[4]— Fourth generation, 10; fifth generation, 29 ; sixth generation, 69; seventh generation, 125 ; total, 233.

FAMILY OF BENJAMIN.[4]— Fourth generation, 8; fifth generation, 4; sixth generation, 10; seventh generation, 34 ; total, 56.

FAMILY OF EZEKIEL.[4]— Fourth generation, 11; fifth generation, 21 ; sixth generation, 98; seventh generation, 169, total, 299.

FAMILY OF TIMOTHY.[4]— Fourth generation, 12; fifth generation, 21 ; sixth generation, 31; seventh generation, 17; total, 81.

FAMILY OF CUMMINGS.[4]— Fourth generation, 10; fifth generation, 39 ; sixth generation, 134; seventh generation, 110; total, 293.

Whole number of the Descent of Isaac,[3] 1644, or 53 per cent. of the whole.

It is probable that had the descendants of the daughters been obtained, they would have been found equally as numerous as those from the male descent.

CONTENTS OF PART I.

xxiv CONTENTS.

PART I.

GENEALOGICAL AND HISTORICAL RECORD

OF THE

DESCENDANTS OF JOHN PEASE, SEN.

LAST OF ENFIELD, CT.

FIRST GENERATION.

ANCESTRY OF JOHN PEASE, SEN.

ROBERT PEASE,[1] the progenitor of the Salem and
Enfield Peases, and father of John Pease, Sen., the ancestor of the Enfield (Ct.) Peases, is supposed to have
been the son of ROBERT and MARGARET PEASE of Great
Baddow, Essex County, England. He came to this country in the ship Francis from the port of Ipswich, England,
the last of April, 1634, and landed at Boston. He was
accompanied by his brother John, and eldest son Robert.
His wife Marie, and other members of the family, probably came in a later ship.

He settled at Salem, Mass., where he died, 1644, aged
about 37. For other particulars of this ancestor, see
"Early History of the Pease Families in America," in Part
II. of this work.

1

SECOND GENERATION.

HISTORY OF JOHN PEASE,[2] SEN.

JOHN PEASE,[2] (ROBERT,[1]) the ancestor of the Enfield Peases, was the second son of ROBERT and MARIE (   ) PEASE, first of England and last of Salem, Mass. He was probably born in England, about 1630, and came to this country when a lad. The first notice we have of him is found in the court records at Salem, in the settlement of his father's estate, under date of August 27, 1644. From that time until his death we have no difficulty in tracing his history.

He appears to have been a favorite of his grandmother, MARGARET PEASE, as shown by her will* which was brought into court, soon after action was taken in the settlement of his father's estate. It seems probable that he may have been adopted by his grandmother, before his father's decease. She doubtless had full authority for placing him in the care of Thomas Watson, to dispose of him as his own child, rendering it unnecessary for the court to take any action in relation to his custody, as in the case of his older brother.

He married, first, Mary Goodell, daughter of Robert Goodell,† of Salem, who died January 5, 1669, three days after the birth of her fifth child. He married, second, Ann Cummings, daughter of Isaac Cummings,‡ of Tops-

---

*See Appendix D.   † See Appendix E.   ‡ See Appendix F.

field, Mass., December 8, 1669, who died at Enfield, June 29, 1689. He settled as a "yeoman," in that part of Salem called "Northfields," which is now within the city limits, although in a farming district.

We find this ancestor's name frequently in the Essex County and Salem Town records, as grantee, grantor, or a witness, in deeds, overseer of wills, constable, etc.

He was made freeman, April 29, 1668, by the General Court, and took the oath before the County Court, June 30, following. He joined the First Church at Salem, to which his father and grandmother had belonged, July 4, 1667. "October 6, 1681, on sacrament day, John Pease and wife, had a letter of recommendation granted to the church at Springfield."* Not far from this last date, it is supposed he with his family, his two eldest sons' families and numerous neighbors removed to Fresh Water Brook, then a part of Springfield, where he and his two oldest sons had had land granted them, July 23, of the year previous. We find him back at Salem, November, 1682, when he sold his "house, barn, and out-buildings, and parcels of land," and acknowledged the deed before a Salem justice of the peace. He says in the deed, he was "late of Salem, now of Enfield." He was again there, February 26, 1683, to give evidence in a suit at law, involving a boundary line of land once owned and laid out by his "father-in-law, Goodell." He then stated he was "aged about 53 years." In September, 1684, he was appointed administrator on the estate of Lot Killam, a townsman of his when in Salem, and one of the first persons, it is said, who died at the "new settlement."

His relation to the church on his removal to Enfield, was an active one, and he stood foremost to assist in maintaining the worship of God on the Sabbath, in the town of Enfield, after it became incorporated.†

---

* Church Records.   † See Appendix G.

Our ancestor sickened in the midst of making prepara-
tions for building, and died "suddenly," July 8, 1689.*

Death made sad havoc in this family in a short time;
taking first the mother, ten days after the father, and one
day after that a daughter.†

His children were: ‡

1. 1. JOHN, b. at Salem, May 30, 1654.
2. 2. ROBERT, b. at Salem, May 14, 1656.
3. 3. MARY, b. at Salem, October 8, 1658.
4. 4. ABRAHAM, b. at Salem, June 5, 1662.
5. 5. JONATHAN, b. at Salem, January 2, 1669.

BY SECOND WIFE:

6. 6. JAMES, b. at Salem, December 23, 1670.
7. 7. ISAAC, b. at Salem, July 15, 1672.
8. 8. ABIGAIL, b. at Salem, December 15, 1675.   d. at Enfield, July 9,
        1689.

---

* See Appendix H.

† Some supposed facts mentioned in his history by others, are omitted here. For
explanation, see Appendix I.

‡ It will be observed that some of the dates of births in this family, do not agree
with those given by others. For explanation, see Appendix A.

THIRD GENERATION.

DESCENT OF JOHN.³

1.

JOHN PEASE,³ (JOHN.² ROBERT,¹) eldest son of JOHN, Sen., and MARY (GOODELL) PEASE, some time of Salem, Mass., last of Enfield, Ct., born at Salem, May 30, 1654; married Margaret Adams of Ipswich, Mass., January 30, 1677.

He was apprenticed at Salem to one John Symonds, who was probably a carpenter and joiner. Symonds died soon after. In his will he assigned his apprentice to his son. James "during the term of time in the indenture, paying £40 in four years, £10 per annum." It seems probable he continued the occupation of his apprenticeship until his removal from Salem, as evidenced by the sale of his "land, house and shop." He and his brother Robert are said to have gone to Enfield in 1679, two years before they removed their families there, and lived the first winter in an excavation in the side of a hill about forty rods from where the first meeting-house stood. In 1685, they had extra land given them because they had been the "first cummers."

It was undoubtedly this son "John Pease" who is named in the deed as one of the commissioners who made the purchase of the larger portion of the town of Enfield in March, 1681.*

He was one of the most prominent men in the history of the town of Enfield; was indefatigable in his efforts to

---

* See Appendix J.

promote and advance its prosperity when an infant settlement, and after its incorporation as a town. He was appointed "land measuer" by the town; was one of the
first selectmen chosen by the town, and was the first captain of the first militia company in Enfield.

He died at Enfield, 1734, aged 80 years.

His children were:

9.   1. John, b. at Salem, April 22, 1678.
10.   2. James, b. at Salem, 1679.
11.   3. Margaret, b. at Enfield, January 24, 1683.   m. Josiah Colton,
            1709.   d. 1775.
12.   4. Jonathan, b. at Enfield, January 29, 1687.   Probably d. infant.
13.   5. Ann, b. at Enfield, October 29, 1685.   m. Jeremiah Lord of East
            Windsor, Ct.
14.   6. Mary, b. at Enfield, May 24, 1688.   m. Thomas Abbe, 1714.
            d. 1746.
15.   7. Sarah, b. at Enfield, September 27, 1689.   m. Timothy Root of
            Somers, 1710.   d. 1750.
16.   8. Joseph, b. at Enfield, March 10, 1692.
            [Salem and Enfield Town, and Essex and Old Hampshire County
                Records, and New England Genealogical and Historical
                Register.]

DESCENT OF ROBERT.[3]

2.

ROBERT PEASE,[3] (John,[2] Robert,[1]) second son of
John, Sen., and Mary (Goodell) Pease, born at Salem,
May 14, 1656; married Abigail Randall, December 16,
1678, and first settled at Salem in the "*Northfields.*" He
shared with his elder brother the enterprise of leaving
the sea-coast to seek out and make ready new homes for
himself, his relatives and neighbors, in the Connecticut
Valley. To which place his family removed in 1681.

He is said to have been one of the first constables
chosen by vote of the town of Enfield.

He died at Enfield, 1744, aged 88 years.

His children were:

17. 1. WILLIAM, b. at Salem, September 26, 1679. d. at Enfield, 1688.
18. 2. MARY, b. at Salem, March 11, 1681. m. Israel Phelps, 1703.
19. 3. ABIGAIL, b. at Enfield, 1682. m. Nathan Hayward.
20. 4. ROBERT, b. at Enfield, "February 2, 1684." *
21. 5. SAMUEL, b. at Enfield, December 30, 1686.
22. 6. EPHRAIM, b. at Enfield, April 9, 1689. Probably d. an infant.
23. 7. DANIEL, b. at Enfield, May 23, 1692.
24. 8. HANNAH, b. at Enfield, June, 1694. m. Daniel Miller, 2d. m.
    Gersham Sexton.
25. 9. MARGARET, b. at Enfield, December, 1695.
26. 10. EBENEZER, b. at Enfield, 1699.
    [Salem and Enfield Town Records.]

FAMILY OF ABRAHAM.³

4.

ABRAHAM PEASE,³ (JOHN,² ROBERT,¹) third son of John, Sen., and MARY (GOODELL) PEASE, was born at Salem, June 5, 1662; married Jane Mentor, and settled in Enfield. He and his three younger brothers were appointed administrators on the estate of their father. He died 1735, without issue. [Old Hampshire County Records, and New England Genealogical and Historical Register.]

DESCENT OF JONATHAN.³

5.

JONATHAN PEASE,³ (JOHN,² ROBERT,¹) fourth son of John, Sen., and MARY (GOODELL) PEASE, first of Salem, last of Enfield; was born at Salem, January 2, 1669; married Elizabeth Booth,† October 11, 1692, and settled in Enfield.

Although a minor he appears to have presented the inventory of the estate of his deceased father at court,

---

* It is probable he was born in 1685, new civil year. See Appendix A.

† Probably the daughter of Simeon Booth, who came to Enfield in the year 1680, and had a large family, was a native of Wales. [Hinman.]

August 30, 1689, and gave bonds in the sum of £300 for securities of the estate, "to give accompt of their administration on the said estate." He died in the early part of the year 1721, aged 53.

His children were:

27. 1. REBECCA, b. at Enfield, July 22, 1694, who m. John Pierce, 1730, and settled in Enfield.
28. 2. JONATHAN, b. at Enfield, 1696. We have no history of him after 1726. His name is mentioned in the settlement of his father's estate, and on the 7th of January, 1726, he had letters of administration granted to him on the estate of his brother, John Pease. It is probable he had no family.
29. 3. DAVID, b. at Enfield, 1698.
30. 4. SAMUEL, b. at Enfield, 1700.
31. 5. JOHN, b. at Enfield, 1702. It appears he was in the French and Indian war, and was killed near Fort Dummer, now Putney, Vt., September 28, 1725. Capt. Dwight of Fort Dummer had sent out a scout of six men westward. On their return, they sat down to refresh themselves, and were surprised by a body of Indians and overcome. The Indians killed two men in the encounter, carried off three as prisoners, and one escaped. Those killed were John Pease of Enfield, and Bodurtha of Springfield.*
32. 6. JOSIAH, b. at Enfield, 1706.
33. 7. PELATIAH, b. at Enfield, 1709.
34. 8. ELIZABETH, b. at Enfield, 1712. m. Ebenezer Chapin.

DESCENT OF JAMES.[3]

6.

JAMES PEASE,[3] (JOHN,[2] ROBERT,[1]) son of JOHN, Sen., and ANN (CUMMINGS) PEASE, and half-brother of the preceding, was born at Salem, December 23, 1670; married Hannah Harmon, October 18, 1695, and settled at Enfield.

* From Massachusetts Historical Society's Collection, Vol. V., 4th Series, and Hall's History of Eastern Vermont.

He was not nineteen when his father died, yet he had a " lot " on which his father had performed labor valued at £2. In March following, we find him not only assisting in common with his brothers as to the equity of the division of his father's estate,* but in another instrument (which was allowed in court), he binds himself to be satisfied with certain tracts of land as his share after deducting (to use his own language) " the labor on my lot at £2." † He died at Enfield, 1748, aged 78.

His children were:

35.   1. JAMES, b. at Enfield, 1697.
36.   2. HANNAH, b. at Enfield, 1699.   m. Benjamin Terry, 1721.
37.   3. ELIZABETH, b. at Enfield, 1703.   m. Benjamin Meacham, 1722.
38.   4. MARY, b. at Enfield, 1706.   m. Jacob Terry, 1730.
39.   5. ABIGAIL, b. at Enfield, 1708.   m. Nathaniel Collins, pastor of the Separate Church in Enfield, 1735.
40.   6. SARAH, b. at Enfield, 1710.   m. Jonathan Terry.
41.   7. JOSEPH, b. at Enfield, 1713.
42.   8. JEMIMA, b. at Enfield, 1716.   m. Lot Killam, 1739.

DESCENT OF ISAAC.³

DEACON ISAAC PEASE,³ (JOHN,² ROBERT,¹) the sixth and youngest son of JOHN, Sen., and ANN (CUMMINGS) PEASE, born at Salem, July 15, 1672. He married Mindwell Osborn, 1691, and settled in the north-eastern part of Enfield, not far from what is now the Shaker village. He appears to have been an extensive landholder, and was among the first holding the office of Deacon in the Congregational Church in that town. He died July 9, 1731, aged 59 nearly. His grave and tombstone are to be seen in good condition in the burying-ground, north of the central meeting-house in Enfield.

---

* Appendix H.   † From Old Hampshire County Records at Northampton.

2

His children were:

43. 1. ISAAC, b. at Enfield, May 2, 1693.
44. 2. ABRAHAM, b. at Enfield, 1695.
45. 3. MINDWELL, b. at Enfield about 1697.
46. 4. ABIGAIL, b. at Enfield about 1699. d. August 28, 1723.
47. 5. ISRAEL, b. at Enfield, 1702.
48. 6. ANN, b. at Enfield, February, 1705. m. Nathaniel Prior.
49. 7. BENJAMIN, b. at Enfield, 1707.
50. 8. EZEKIEL, b. at Enfield, June 20, 1710.
51. 9. TIMOTHY, b. at Enfield, 1713.
52. 10. CUMMINGS, b. at Enfield, November 15, 1715.

FOURTH GENERATION.

DESCENT OF JOHN.³

FAMILY OF JOHN.⁴

9.

JOHN PEASE,⁴ (JOHN,³ JOHN,² ROBERT,¹) eldest son of
JOHN and MARGARET (ADAMS) PEASE of Enfield, Ct.,
was born at Salem, Mass., 1678; married Elizabeth Spen-
cer of Hartford, Ct. He died at Enfield, 1761, aged 83.
[New England Historical and Genealogical Register and
Salem Town Records.]

His children were:

53. 1. ELIZABETH, b. at Enfield, 1717. m. Dea. Cummings Pease.
54. 2. SARAH, b. at Enfield, 1724.
55. 3. JOHN, b. at Enfield, 1726.

FAMILY OF JAMES.⁴

10.

JAMES PEASE,⁴ (JOHN,³ JOHN,² ROBERT,¹) second son of
JOHN and MARGARET (ADAMS) PEASE, was born at Salem
1679, and removed with his father from Salem to Enfield,
an infant. He married Mary Abbe, daughter of Thomas
Abbe, 1710, and settled in Somers. He seems to have
commenced operations in Somers by way of improvement,
as early as 1713, and is said to have spent his summers
there, and his winters in their old settlement at Enfield,
until 1717. He was one of the first settlers, if not *the*
first, of what is now Somers, and died there.

His children were : *

56. 1. MARY, b. at Enfield, 1711.
57. 2. JAMES, b. at Enfield, 1713.
58. 3. MARGARET, b. at Enfield, 1715.
59. 4. RICHARD, b. at Enfield, 1717.
60. 5. HANNAH, b. at Enfield, 1722.
61. 6. JOHN, b. at Enfield, 1725. d. July 25, 1730.

[Somers' Record.]

FAMILY OF JOSEPH⁴ (OF JOHN.³)
16.

JOSEPH PEASE,⁴ (JOHN,³ JOHN,² ROBERT,¹) third son of JOHN and MARGARET (ADAMS) PEASE, was born at Enfield, " March 10, 1692–3;" married Mary Spencer of Hartford, Ct., January 13, 1727. He lived in Enfield, and died there in 1757. [Enfield Town Records.]

His children were :

62. 1. JOSEPH, b. at Enfield, August 10, 1728.
63. 2. STEPHEN, b. at Enfield, February 2, 1730.
64. 3. MARY, b. at Enfield, 1734.
65. 4. JONATHAN, b. at Enfield, September 11, 1740.

DESCENT OF ROBERT.³
FAMILY OF ROBERT.⁴
20.

ROBERT PEASE,⁴ (ROBERT³, JOHN,² ROBERT,¹) eldest son of ROBERT and ABIGAIL (RANDALL) PEASE, of Enfield, Ct., was born at Enfield, February 2, 1684. He married, first, Hannah Sexton, February, 1711. She died November 8, 1711, leaving one daughter. He married, second, Rachel   ; married, third, Elizabeth Emery. He re-

* It will be seen that some of the dates are subsequent to the removal of Sergt. James Pease (as he was called,) to what is now called Somers. Some of the births were at Somers, previous to the incorporation of the town, and while it was all Enfield. There is a record of the death of his wife: "Died, Mary Pease, wife of Sergt. James Pease, November 28, 1763."

sided awhile at Andover, Mass.; was there in 1717, and a part of the year 1711. It is probable he married his third wife there. He afterwards settled in that part of Enfield, which is now Somers, where he died November 17, 1766.

His children were:

BY FIRST WIFE:

66. 1. MIRIAM, b. at Enfield, 1711. She m. Nathaniel Pease, eldest son of "latter" Robert Pease* of Enfield. Among her children were some of the most enterprising and energetic the times produced.

BY SECOND WIFE:

67. 2. JEMIMA, b. at Enfield, 1712.

BY THIRD WIFE:

68. 3. ELIZABETH, b. at Enfield, 1718.
69. 4. HANNAH, b. at Enfield, 1720.
70. 5. ABIGAIL, b. at Enfield, 1722.
71. 6. ROBERT, b. at Enfield, December 19, 1724.
72. 7. EMERY, b. at Enfield, 1727.
73. 8. JANE, b. at Enfield, 1729. m. Thomas Buck, 1749.
74. 9. ANN, b. at Enfield, 1730.
75. 10. BATHSHEBA, b. at Enfield, 1732. m. Joseph Hunt.
76. 11. MARY, b. at Somers, July 3, 1734.
77. 12. ABIAL, b. at Somers, January 24, 1736.
78. 13. NOAH, b. at Somers, June 28, 1739.

FAMILY OF SAMUEL.⁴

21.

SAMUEL PEASE,⁴ (ROBERT,³ JOHN,² ROBERT,¹) second son of ROBERT and ABIGAIL (RANDALL) PEASE, was born at Enfield, Ct., December 30, 1686, and married Elizabeth Warner. He settled in Enfield where he died, 1770.

His children were:

79. 1. MEHITABEL, b. at Enfield, 1712.
80. 2. SAMUEL, b. at Enfield, 1715. d. in infancy.
81. 3. ELIZABETH, b. at Enfield, 1716. m. John Allen.
82. 4. SAMUEL,² b. at Enfield, 1718.

*For a history of "latter" Robert and his posterity, see History of the Pease Families, Chap. V.

83. 5. EPHRAIM, b. at Enfield, 1719.

84. 6. JOANNAH, b. at Enfield, 1722. m. Benjamin Root.

85. 7. MARY, b. at Enfield, 1723.

86. 8. AARON, b. at Enfield, May 4, 1726.

87. 9. NATHANIEL, b. at Enfield, September 29, 1728.

FAMILY OF DANIEL.⁴
23.

DANIEL PEASE,⁴ (ROBERT,³ JOHN,² ROBERT,¹) brother
to the preceding, was born at Enfield, May 23, 1692;
married Abigail Fletcher. He early settled in Somers,
and was one of the earliest settlers in Stafford, the town
next east of Somers. He had land allotted to him in
Stafford, November, 1722. He was living there the year
following, and some time afterwards. It is probable several of his children were born there. It is said he died
at Somers.

His children were:

88. 1. DANIEL, b. at Enfield, 1718.

89. 2. WILLIAM, b. at   d. before July 8, 1746.

90. 3. ASA, b. at

91. 4. REBECCA,* b. at   m. Ebenezer Jones, 1748.

92. 5. OLIVE, b. at Somers, March 10, 1736.

93. 6.

FAMILY OF EBENEZER.⁴
26.

EBENEZER PEASE,⁴ (ROBERT,³ JOHN,² ROBERT,¹)
youngest son of ROBERT, and ABIGAIL (RANDALL) PEASE,
of Enfield, was born at Enfield 1699, and married Mindwell Sexton, November 20, 1717. He died at Enfield
1743, aged 44. [Enfield Town Record.]

---

  * Her name and marriage are found on the Somers Town records, and there are
reasons for supposing she may have been the daughter of Daniel Pease.⁴ But
there is no positive evidence of it. Dr. John C. Pease placed Parker Pease in this
family. There is evidence to show he did not belong to it. Parker Pease lived in
Somers; married Hannah Staple 1755, and had a son Parker, born at Somers 1756.
The family afterwards joined the Shakers and lived with them for a time. It is
said the family has become extinct.

His children were:

94. 1. HANNAH, b. at Enfield, 1718. m.   Geer.
95. 2. EBENEZER, b. at Enfield 1719.
96. 3. MINDWELL, b. at Enfield, 1722. m. ·   Bull.
97. 4. JAMES, b. at Enfield, 1724. He d. 1746, in the French War, at
      Cape Breton, aged 21.
98. 5. ABIGAIL, b. at Enfield, 1727. She m. Benjamin Hall.
99. 6. CATHERINE, b. at   1729.

---o---

DESCENT OF JONATHAN.³

FAMILY OF DAVID.⁴

29.

DAVID PEASE,⁴ (JONATHAN,³ JOHN,² ROBERT,¹) second
son of JONATHAN and ELIZABETH (BOOTH) PEASE of Enfield, Ct., and first cousin to the preceding, was born at
Enfield, 1698. The only recorded history we can find of
this person is that of his birth, his appointment as one
of the administrators of his father's estate, and a creditor
of said estate. The late Dr. John C. Pease, in his manuscript history, said "he removed to the Southern States."
It seems probable he only went as far south as New Jersey,
and there had a family. For farther remarks, see History
of the Pease Families, Chap. VI.

FAMILY OF SAMUEL.⁴

30.

SAMUEL PEASE,⁴ (JONATHAN,³ JOHN,² ROBERT,¹) third
son of JONATHAN and ELIZABETH (BOOTH) PEASE, was born
at Enfield, 1700. No other trace of this person can be
found in the Enfield Town or Hampshire County records.
There was a Samuel Pease living at Mendon, Worcester
County, Mass., in 1738. From the fact that Josiah,
brother of the above, was living then at Upton (near
Mendon,) we have thought the Pease at Mendon may
have been the Samuel Pease in question. But he has no

family records there, and as no other mention of his name can be found among the Worcester County records, we have reasons for supposing he may have finally removed to New Jersey. (See Chap. VI., as above.)

FAMILY OF JOSIAH.[4]
32.

JOSIAH PEASE,[4] (JONATHAN,[3]) JOHN,[2] ROBERT,[1] fifth son of JONATHAN and ELIZABETH (BOOTH) PEASE of Enfield, and brother to the preceding, was born at Enfield, 1706; married Elizabeth   . He appears to have resided at Enfield in 1730, in 1732, in Newton, Middlesex County, Mass., and two years later, at Hopkinton of the same county. In 1737 he was residing in Upton, Worcester County, Mass., and he is supposed to have resided afterward in that town until his death. He and his wife Elizabeth were living at Upton in 1782. He was a farmer; had one child.

100. 1. JOSIAH, b. at   about 1737.

[Old Hampshire and Middlesex County and Upton Town Records.]

FAMILY OF PELATIAH.[4]
33.

PELATIAH PEASE,[4] (JONATHAN,[3] JOHN,[2] ROBERT,[1]) youngest son of JONATHAN and ELIZABETH (BOOTH) PEASE of Enfield, and brother of the preceding, was born at Enfield, 1709; married Jemima Booth, December 16, 1736, and lived in Enfield, where he died, 1769, aged 60 years.

His children were:

101. 1. PELATIAH, b. at Enfield, 1738.
102. 2. JEMIMA, b. at Enfield, May 11, 1740. m. Eldad Phelps.
103. 3. JONATHAN, b. at Enfield, November 22, 1741. d. at Schenectady, N. Y., 1760, about 19 years old, on his return from the Indian and French War.
104. 4. SAMUEL, b. at Enfield, June 26, 1746.
105. 5. JOHN, b. at Enfield, January 2, 1748.
[Enfield and Family Records.]

————o————

DESCENT OF JAMES.³

FAMILY OF JOSEPH⁴ (OF JAMES.³)

41.

JOSEPH PEASE,⁴ (JAMES,³ JOHN,² ROBERT,¹) youngest son of JAMES and HANNAH (HARMON) PEASE, and first cousin of preceding, was born at Enfield, 1713; married first Sarah , second Prudence Olds, and settled in Enfield, where he died, 1800.

His children were:

106. 1. ALEXANDER, b. at Enfield, 1731, probably d. young.
107. 2. LUCY, b. at Enfield, 1732.
108. 3. WAREHAM, b. at Enfield, 1734.
109. 4. NOAH, b. at Enfield, 1736. He went to Canada in the French and Indian War, and never returned. Is supposed to have been slain.
110. 5. ABIGAIL, b. at Enfield, 1738.
111. 6. URIAH, b. at Enfield, November 13, 1740. He was also in the French and Indian War; was lost in the wilderness and died from starvation.
112. 7. SARAH, b. at Enfield, July 26, 1742.

BY SECOND WIFE:

113. 8. JAMES, b. at Enfield, November 26, 1749.
114. 9. JOSEPH, b. at Enfield, December 18, 1751.
115. 10. GIDEON, b. at Enfield, August 2, 1753.
116. 11. HANNAH, b. at Enfield, March 9, 1757.
117. 12. EBENEZER, b. at Enfield, May 8, 1760.

DESCENT OF ISAAC.³

FAMILY OF ISAAC.⁴

43.

ISAAC PEASE⁴, (ISAAC³, JOHN², ROBERT¹,) eldest son of DEACON ISAAC and MINDWELL (OSBORN) PEASE of Enfield, and first cousin of the preceding, was born at Enfield, May 2, 1693, and married Amy French, November 8, 1722. He settled in Enfield, where he died, 1757, aged 64. [Enfield Town Records.]

3

His children were:

118. 1. EMMA, b. at Enfield, 1724.
119. 2. ISAAC, b. at Enfield, August, 1727.
120. 3. PHEBE, b. at Enfield, 1729.
121. 4. JACOB, b. at Enfield, 1731.
122. 5. ABNER b. at Enfield, 1733.
123. 6. ANN, b. at Enfield, 1735. m. Ebenezer Hall, 1753.
124. 7. NOADIAH, b. at Enfield, 1737.
125. 8. LUANA, b. at Enfield, January 23, 1739. m. John Gains, 1755,
        and settled in Granby, Ct.

FAMILY OF ABRAHAM.[4]

44.

ABRAHAM PEASE[4], (ISAAC,[3] JOHN,[2] ROBERT,[1]) second
son of DEACON ISAAC and MINDWELL (OSBORN) PEASE of
Enfield, and brother of the preceding, was born at
Enfield, 1695; married first, Mary Booth, December 3,
1719; second, Widow Abigail Warner of Springfield,
August, 1733. He died at Enfield, 1750, aged 55. [En-
field and Springfield Town Records.]

His children were:

126. 1. ABRAHAM, b. at Enfield, 1721. d. an infant.
127. 2. MARY, b. at Enfield, 1722. m. William Lord, 1752.
128. 3. JOHN, b. at Enfield, 1725.
129. 4. ABRAHAM, b. at Enfield, 1729.

BY SECOND WIFE:

130. 5. MOSES, b. at Enfield, 1734.
131. 6. LEMUEL, b. at Enfield, 1735.
132. 7. SAMUEL, b. at Enfield, 1736.
133. 8. JOEL, b. at Enfield, 1738.
134. 9. NATHAN, b. at Enfield, January 18, 1740.
135. 10. DESIRE, b. at Enfield, August 16, 1741. m. Nathaniel Parsons.
136. 11. GIDEON, b. at Enfield, August 8, 1744.
137. 12. JOSIAH, b. at Enfield, September 7, 1745. d. infant probably.
138. 13. WILLIAM, b. at Enfield, December 29, 1746.
139. 14. ZEBULON, b. at Enfield, November 2, 1749.
        [Enfield Town Records.]

FAMILY OF ISRAEL.⁴

47.

ISRAEL PEASE,⁴ (Isaac,³ John,² Robert,¹) third son of Deacon Isaac and Mindwell (Osborn) Pease, and brother of the preceding; born at Enfield, 1702; married Sarah Booth, 1726. He lived and died in that town.

His children were:

140. 1. Israel, b. at Enfield, 1726.
141. 2. David and ⎫
142. 3. Sarah,   ⎬ b. at Enfield, 1727. Sarah d. infant.
143. 4. Sarah, b. at Enfield, 1729. m. Jeremiah Lord.
144, 5. Hezekiah, b. at Enfield, 1732.
145. 6. Alice, b. at Enfield, 1736. m. Thomas Root.
146. 7. Jesse, b. at Enfield, 1738.
147. 8. Bathsheba, b. at Enfield, February 2, 1741. m. David Winslow.
148. 9. Mindwell, b. at Enfield,   m. Ebenezer Terry.
149. 10. Nathan, b. at Enfield,

FAMILY OF BENJAMIN.⁴

49.

BENJAMIN PEASE,⁴ (Isaac,³ John,² Robert,¹) fourth son of Deacon Isaac and Mindwell (Osborn) Pease, and brother of the preceding, was born at Enfield, 1707; married Abigail Rose, April 19, 1739; died at Enfield, 1768, aged 61.

His children were:

150. 1. Abigail, b. at Enfield, December 1, 1739. m. Zaccheus Prior, 1759.
151. 2. Benjamin, b. at Enfield, 1740. d. January 20, 1741.
152. 3. Lucy, b. at Enfield, December 29, 1741. m. Reuben Perkins.
153. 4. Benjamin, b. at Enfield, May 10, 1744.
154. 5. Sharon and ⎫
155. 6. Rose,   ⎬ b. at Enfield, June 2, 1746.
156. 7. Rosa, b. at Enfield, December 2, 1751. m. Daniel Kingsbury.
157. 8. Damaris, b. at Enfield, May 29, 1753. m. Edward Collins.

FAMILY OF EZEKIEL.[4]

50.

EZEKIEL PEASE,[4] (Isaac,[3] John,[2] Robert,[1]) fifth son of
Deacon Isaac and Mindwell (Osborn) Pease, and brother
of the preceding, was born at Enfield, June 20, 1710;
married Hannah Chandler, daughter of Henry Chandler,
one of the early settlers of Enfield, February 10, 1732.
He was a man highly esteemed as a citizen and Christian;
a man of prayer and consistent life.   He was by occupation a tailor and school-teacher;—for some fifteen years
Town Clerk, and was known by the title of "Master," and
"Clerk" Pease.   He settled in the eastern part of the
town of Enfield, near "Scantic River;" died there, with his
son Isaac, in 1799, aged 89.   [Town and Family Records.]

His children were:

158. 1. Hannah, b. at Enfield, January 11, 1733.   m. Job Gleason.
159. 2. Ezekiel, b. at Enfield, August 18, 1734.
160. 3. Abiah, b. at Enfield, August 11, 1736.   m. Samuel Gowdy.
161. 4. Henry C., b. at Enfield February 11, 1738.
162. 5. Eleanor, b. at Enfield, March 15, 1741.   m. Mr. Holt.
163. 6. Jane, b. at Enfield, August 13, 1743.   m. Obadiah Hurlburt.
164. 7. Mehitabel, b. at Enfield, September 23, 1745.   m. Edward
          Parsons.
165. 8. Sarah, b. at Enfield, February 2, 1747.   m. Jehiel Markham.
166. 9. Abigail, b. at Enfield, March 15, 1749.
167. 10. Isaac, b. at Enfield, June 1, 1752.
168. 11. Oliver, b. at Enfield, September 6, 1754.   He probably died
          in the Revolutionary Army at Cambridge, Mass., 1774.   From
          an old account book of Pelatiah Pease, in possession of his
          grandson, the late Mr. John Pease of Ashfield, we learn he
          had an apprentice named Oliver Pease, and that he died as
          above.   As two brothers in this family named sons for their
          younger brother soon after the death of the person mentioned
          in the account book, it is safe to presume their brother did not
          die far from the time of the births of their sons, and that he
          died in the army.

FAMILY OF TIMOTHY.[4]

51.

TIMOTHY PEASE,[4] (ISAAC,[3] JOHN,[2] ROBERT,[1]) brother of the preceding, was born at Enfield, Ct., 1713; married Mary Chandler, daughter of Henry Chandler, December 22, 1736. He settled in the east part of Enfield, about half a mile north of Fresh Water Brook, where he died 1794, aged 81. He was a soldier in the old French War.

His children were:

169. 1. TIMOTHY, b. at Enfield, 1738.
170. 2. MARY, b. at Enfield, June 12, 1739. m. Wareham Parsons.
171. 3 MARTHA, b. at Enfield, May 10, 1741. d. young.
172. 4. DEBORAH, b. at Enfield, December 5, 1742. m. Gideon Pease.
173. 5. EDWARD, b. at Enfield, September 7, 1744.
174. 6. JAMES, b. at Enfield, April 9, 1746.
175. 7. ABIGAIL, b. at Enfield, November 25, 1747. m. David Terry.
176. 8. LYDIA, b. at Enfield, June 21, 1749. m. Ezekiel Pease.
177. 9 DORCAS, b. at Enfield, March 19, 1751. m. Isaac Pease.
178. 10. MINDWELL, b. at Enfield, January 8, 1753. m. Samuel Hale, and settled in Greenwich, Mass.
179. 11. HEPZIBAH, b. at Enfield, January 4, 1755. m. Benjamin King.
180. 12. BEULAH, b. at Enfield, November 2, 1758. m. Fregrace Hancock.

FAMILY OF CUMMINGS.[4]

52.

DEACON CUMMINGS PEASE,[4] (ISAAC,[3] JOHN,[2] ROBERT[1]) youngest son of DEACON ISAAC and MINDWELL (OSBORN) PEASE, and brother of the preceding, was born at Enfield, November 15, 1715; married, first, Elizabeth, daughter of John Pease of Enfield, about 1737; second, Sarah Hale of Springfield, Mass., September 25, 1755, and settled in Enfield. His farm was on Fresh Water Brook, about two and a half miles east of what is now Thompsonville. He became a subject of hopeful piety when about 30 years of age, and after a long and painful struggle in his mind about a practical duty in making a profession, he yielded to his conviction of Scriptural teaching, and, notwithstanding he stood alone in his views, was immersed upon the profession of his faith. This was the beginning of a Baptist church in the east part of Enfield, of which he was a Deacon. This church continued until broken up by the movement of the Shakers in that part of the town. He died in East Longmeadow, 1808, aged 94.

His children were:

181. 1. CUMMINGS, b. at Enfield, 1739. d. an infant.
182. 2. ELIZABETH, b. at Enfield, June 29, 1740. d. a child.
183. 3. LOVE, b. at Enfield, October 21, 1742. m. Jacob Hill.
184. 4. CUMMINGS, b. at Enfield, November 27, 1744.
185. 5. ELIZABETH, b. at Enfield, January 7, 1746. d. young.
186. 6. EBENEZER, b. at Enfield, December 23, 1748.
187. 7. ASA, b. at Enfield, January 18, 1750.
188. 8. RUTH, b. at Enfield, January 7, 1753. m. David Hale of Enfield.

BY SECOND WIFE:

189. 9. HEMAN, b. at Enfield, 1757.
190. 10. DAVID, b. at Enfield, April, 16, 1760.

FIFTH GENERATION.

DESCENT OF JOHN.³

FAMILY OF JOHN.⁴

55.

JOHN PEASE,⁵ (John,⁴ John,³ John,² Robert,¹) only son of John and Elizabeth (Spencer) Pease of Enfield, Ct., was born at Enfield, 1726; married Bathsheba Jones, daughter of Thomas Jones, one of the early settlers of Enfield. He was a large farmer in the eastern part of Enfield. His location was part of the share which was assigned to his grandfather in the distribution of the land at the first settlement of the town. [New England Historical and Genealogical Register.] Died at Enfield, 1810, aged 84.

His children were:

191. 1. John, b. at Enfield, March 15, 1753.
192. 2. Thomas, b. at Enfield, May 29, 1754.
193. 3. Elizabeth, b. at Enfield, May 29, 1756. m. for a third husband, Joshua Giddings of Hartland, Ct., and was the mother of Hon. Joshua R. Giddings. She d. in Ohio at an advanced age. [New England Historical and Genealogical Register.]
194. 4. Gideon, b. at Enfield, November, 18, 1757.
195. 5. Bathsheba, b. at Enfield, 1760. She m. Eli McGregory and removed to the State of New York, where she d. at an advanced age.
196. 6. Sarah, b. at Enfield, May 16, 1762.
197. 7. Simeon, b. at Enfield, August 22, 1764.

———o———

FAMILY OF JAMES.[4]

57.

JAMES PEASE,[5] (James,[4] John,[3] John,[2] Robert,[1]) eldest son of James and Mary (Abbe) Pease of Somers, Ct., and cousin of the preceding, was born at Enfield, Ct., 1713; married Abigail Ford, 1737. [Somers Town Records.] He lived in Somers, and appears to have died there in the year 1760, aged about 47.

His children were:

198. 1. Elizabeth, b. at Somers, September 17, 1738.
199. 2. James, b. at Somers, February 27, 1739.
200. 3. John, b. at Somers, June 12, 1742.
201. 4. Abigail, b. at Somers, June 10, 1744.
202. 5. Margaret, b. at Somers, October 10, 1749.
203. 6. Tilton, b. at Somers, September 21, 1751. d. March 15, 1753.
204. 7. Joseph, b. at Somers, September 26, 1753.
205. 8. Joseph,[2] b. at Somers, August 24, 1755.
206. 9. Keziah, b. at Somers, October 12, 1757.
207. 10. Joel, b. at Somers, November 2, 1760.

59.

RICHARD PEASE,[5] (James,[4] John,[3] John,[2] Robert,[1]) second son of James and Mary (Abbe) Pease of Somers, Ct., was born at Enfield, Ct., 1717; married Elizabeth Parsons, 1753, November 1. He lived in Somers when he died.

His children were:

208. 1. Keturah, b. at Somers, September 19, 1754.
209. 2. Samuel, b. at Somers, August 26, 1756.
210. 3. Richard, b. at Somers, October 20, 1758.
[Enfield and Somers Town Records.]

FAMILY OF JOSEPH.[4]

62.

JOSEPH PEASE,[5] Esq., (JOSEPH,[4] JOHN,[3] JOHN,[2] ROBERT,[1]) eldest son of JOSEPH and MARY (SPENCER) PEASE of Enfield, Ct.; born at Enfield, August 10, 1728; married Mindwell King, daughter of Lieut. Josiah King, July 28, 1756. He was a successful merchant; a zealous advocate for liberty, and suffered much in the struggle for Independence. He stood high in the confidence of his townsmen whom he often served in a public capacity. [New England Historical and Genealogical Register—Enfield Town Records.] He lived at Suffield, Ct., where he died, October 16, 1794, aged 66.

His children were:

211. 1. AUGUSTINE, b. at Suffield, May 18, 1757.
212. 2. ZENO, b. at Suffield, February 2, 1759.
213. 3. OLIVER, b. at Suffield, July 27, 1760.
214. 4. ROYAL, b. at Suffield, April 16, 1762.
215. 5. SETH, b. at Suffield, January 9, 1764.
216. 6. MINDWELL, b. at Suffield, March 16, 1765.
217. 7. JOSEPH, b. at Suffield, September 11, 1766.
218. 8. CALVIN, b. at Suffield, August 22, 1768. d. 1775.
219. 9. MINDWELL, b. at Suffield, August 31, 1770. m. Gideon Granger, Postmaster-General, under the administration of Thomas Jefferson, January 14, 1790.
       [New England Historical and Genealogical Register.]
220. 10. WILLIAM, b. at Suffield, June 22, 1772.
221. 11. CALVIN,[2] b. at Suffield, September 9, 1776.

63.

STEPHEN PEASE,[5] (JOSEPH,[4] JOHN,[3] JOHN,[2] ROBERT,[1]) brother of the preceding; born at Enfield, 1730; married Elizabeth   . He appears to have first settled in Somers, Ct.; died at "Sixteen Acres Mill," Springfield, Mass., 1816, aged 86.

4

His children were:

222. 1. *PETER, b. at Somers, February 23, 1760.
223. 2. ELIPHALET, b. at Somers, February 2, 1762.
224. 3. ASAPH, b. at Somers, August 14, 1763.
225. 4. MATTHEW, b. at Somers, May 31, 1766.
226. 5. AMOS, b. at Somers, June 1, 1770.

65.

JONATHAN PEASE,[5] (JOSEPH,[4] JOHN,[3] JOHN,[2] ROBERT,[1]) brother of the preceding, was born September 11, 1740; married Mary   .   He removed from Glastenbury Ct., about 1780, and settled and died in Ellington, Ct., 1824.   [New England Genealogical and Historical Register and East Windsor Town Records.]   He is said to have been a deacon.

His children were:

227. 1. MARY, b. at   .   m. Israel Pease and settled in
             Middlefield, Mass.
228. 2. HANNAH.
229. 3. SARAH.
230. 4. DAVID, b.   1772.
231. 5. RUSSEL, b.   1789.

——oo——

DESCENT OF ROBERT.[3]

FAMILY OF ROBERT.[4]
71.

ROBERT PEASE,[5] (ROBERT,[4] ROBERT,[3] JOHN,[2] ROBERT,[1]) eldest son of ROBERT and ELIZABETH (EMERY) PEASE, first of Enfield and last of Somers, and second cousin of the preceding, was born at Enfield, December 19, 1724; married, first, Hannah Sexton of Somers, September 4, 1746.   She died in 1795.   He married, second, Submit Davis.   He removed to Blandford, Mass., about 1780, and lived there for a short time where he lost most of his wealth by the

---

* This name is found on Somers' Records as " Pelton," whether by mistake, or was subsequently changed to " Peter," is not ascertained.

depreciation of "continental money" which he had received in payment for a farm. He returned to Somers where he died, 1805.

His children were:

232.   1. ROBERT, b. at Somers, September 3, 1749.
233.   2. HANNAH, b. at Somers, August 29, 1751.
234.   3. ABIAH, b. at Somers, 1753.   m. Levi Pease, 1775.
235.   4. STEPHEN, b. at Somers, July 4, 1755.
236.   5. ABNER, b. at Somers, November 9, 1757.
237.   6. ERASTUS, b. at Somers, 1759.
238.   7. ALPHEUS, b. at Somers, April 16, 1762.
239.   8. CHARLES, b. at Somers, 1764.
240.   9. SARAH, b. at Somers, September 28, 1766.   d. young.
241. 10. HANNAH, b. at Somers, November 29, 1769.
242. 11. MIRIAM, b. at Somers, September 25, 1771.

72.

EMERY PEASE,[5] Esq., (ROBERT,[4] ROBERT,[3] JOHN,[2] ROBERT,[1]) brother of the preceding, was born at Enfield, Ct., 1727; married Mary Horton, January 9, 1755, and lived in Somers, where he died in 1796, aged 69 years. He was a man held in high esteem, a justice of the peace, and was one of the first to rally at the call of his country to defend its liberties. He marched to Boston at the first alarm in the Revolution at the head of seventy volunteers from his town, and was more or less engaged as a captain of a militia company during the Revolutionary struggle.

His children were:

243.   1. DAVID, b. at Somers, August 24, 1755.
244.   2. EMERY, b. at Somers, August 26, 1757.
245.   3. AUGUSTUS, b. at Somers, July 19, 1759.
246.   4. SYLVANUS, b. at Somers, October 3, 1761.
247.   5. MARY, b. at Somers, January 19, 1764.
248.   6. ELIZABETH, b. at Somers, August 7, 1766.
249.   7. GAIUS, b. at Somers, December 1, 1768.
250.   8. MARGARET, b. at Somers, June 1, 1772.
251.   9. MATILDA, b. at Somers, April 24, 1774.
252. 10. INDEPENDENCE, b. at Somers, August 27, 1776.   m. Gen. David Mack of Middlefield, Mass.

77.

Col. ABIEL PEASE,[5] (Robert,[4] Robert,[3] John,[2] Robert,[1]) third son of Robert and Elizabeth (Emery) Pease, was born at Somers, January 24, 1736 ; married Esther Cooley of Springfield, Mass., May 12, 1757 and settled in Somers, Ct., where he died 1806, aged 70 years. He was an officer in the Revolution, probably in the militia; was a warm patriot, and highly esteemed in his day. He had but one child, a daughter.

253. 1. Esther, b. at Somers, February 3, 1758. m. Seth Dwight.

78.

Lieut. NOAH PEASE,[5] (Robert,[4] Robert,[3] John,[2] Robert,[1]) youngest son of Robert and Elizabeth (Emery) Pease, was born at Somers, June 28, 1739 ; married Mary Ward, 1762; second, married Dorcas Arnold, widow of Samuel Arnold of Somers, and daughter of Deacon John Hubbard of Ellington, Ct. He was a respectable farmer, living in the center of the town of Somers. Died July 20, 1818, aged 79.

His children were :

BY FIRST WIFE:

254. 1. Giles, b. at Somers, April 13, 1763.
255. 2. Noah, b. at Somers, September 30, 1765. d. a child.
256. 3. Hannah, b. at Somers, July 17, 1769. m. Calvin Pitkin, Esq., of Somers.

—o—

FAMILY OF SAMUEL.[4]

82.

SAMUEL PEASE,[5] (Samuel,[4] Robert,[3] John,[2] Robert,[1]) eldest son of Samuel and Elizabeth (Warner) Pease of Enfield, Ct., was born at Enfield, 1718, and married Zeruiah Chapin, and lived and died in Enfield.

His children were :

257.   1. ZERUIAH, b. at Enfield, May 4, 1745.
258.   2. LUCY, b. at Enfield, March 22, 1747.
259.   3. ELI, b. at Enfield, November 2, 1749.
260.   4. LUCY,² b. at Enfield, January 26, 1751.
261.   5. ELIAS, b. at Enfield, September 28, 1754.
262.   6. EDWARD, b. at Enfield,
263.   7. TRYPHENA, b. at Enfield, September 28, 1758.   m. Ephraim Lord of East Windsor, February 5, 1777.
264.   8. MEHITABLE, b. at Enfield, October 31, 1760.
265.   9. EDWARD,² b. at Enfield, February 22, 1763.
266.   10. PETER, b. at Enfield, January 12, 1767 ; probably never married. He was one of those who established a community of Shakers at Union Village, Ohio.

83.

EPHRAIM PEASE,⁵ Esq., (SAMUEL,⁴ ROBERT,³ JOHN,² ROBERT,¹) brother of the preceding, was born at Enfield, 1719; married Tabitha Abbe, May 29, 1740; died in Enfield, 1801, aged 82 years. He was a merchant and contractor in the time of the French War, acquired a large estate, and was a magistrate in the town.

His children were :

267.   1. EPHRAIM, b. at Enfield, December 23, 1741. He was a merchant, and died in the prime of life unmarried.
268.   2. PETER, b. at Enfield, February 12, 1743. He died while a student at Yale College.
269.   3. OBADIAH, b. at Enfield, June 16, 1746. He died soon after graduating at Yale.
270.   4. TABITHA, b. at Enfield, December 18, 1749. d. young.
271.   5. SYBIL, b. at Enfield, May 20, 1754. m. Rev. Elam Potter, the third minister settled in Enfield.
272.   6. NANCY, b. at Enfield, September 2, 1756. m. Augustus Diggings, and d. young.
273.   7. AGNES, b. at Enfield, February 6, 1760. m. Rev. Nehemiah Prudder of Enfield.
274.   8. ANNA, b. at Enfield, February 6, 1760.

[Enfield Town Records.]

86.

AARON PEASE,[5] (SAMUEL,[4] ROBERT,[3] JOHN,[2] ROBERT,[1])
brother of the preceding, was born at Enfield, Ct., April
1, 1726; married, first, Ann Geer, 1751; second, Mary
Terry, September 6, 1764; lived in Enfield, where he
died. He was, by occupation, a blacksmith.

His children were:

275. 1. AARON, b. at Enfield, June 3, 1752.
276. 2. LEVI, b. at Enfield, June 22, 1754.
277. 3. SARAH, b. at Enfield, December 2, 1756.
278. 4. STONE, b. at Enfield, January 11, 1759.
279. 5. ANN, b. at Enfield, November 6, 1761. d. child.
280. 6. EPHRAIM, b. at Enfield, 1763.

BY SECOND WIFE:

281. 7. ELAM, b. at Enfield, June 5, 1765.
282. 8. ANN,[2] b. at Enfield, September 27, 1767. m. Capt. John Ford
         of Somers.
283. 9. ELAM,[2] b. at Enfield, August 26, 1770.
284. 10. MARTHA, b. at Enfield, May 6, 1775.

87.

NATHANIEL PEASE,[5] (SAMUEL,[4] ROBERT,[3] JOHN,[2] ROB-
ERT,[1]) youngest son of SAMUEL and ELIZABETH (WARNER)
PEASE, was born at Enfield, September 29, 1728; married
Eunice Allen, April 24, 1755. He appears to have left
Enfield soon after the birth of his third or fourth child,
between 1760 and 1764, and is said to be among the first
settlers of the town of Norfolk, Ct., where he died, March
28, 1818, aged 90 years. His wife died March 21, 1807.
[Enfield Town Record, and New England Historical and
Genealogical Register.]

His children were:

285. 1. PHINEAS, b. at Enfield, June 9, 1756.
286. 2. CALVIN, b. at Enfield, September 14, 1757.
287. 3. LOUISA, b. at Enfield, December   , 1760. m. Giles Petti-
         bone of Norfolk, and died 1835.

288.   4. ALLEN, b. at Enfield, October 12, 1762.

289.   5. NATHANIEL, b. at Goshen, October 22, 1764.

290.   6. OBADIAH, b. at Goshen, November 21, 1766.

291.   7. DUDLEY, b. at Norfolk, February   , 1768.   d. in infancy.

292.   8. EUNICE, b. at Norfolk, June 29, 1770.   m. Edmund Akin of Norfolk.   d. October 3, 1806.

293.   9. ELECTA, b. at Norfolk, July 20, 1772.   m. Abijah Pettibone of Simsbury.   d. August 3, 1843.

294.   10. BETSEY, b. at Norfolk, July 21, 1744.   m. Azias Pettibone of Granby, Ct.   d. 1819.

295.   11. FLAVIUS, b. at Norfolk, October   , 1776.   d. young.

296.   12. EARL P., b. at Norfolk, July 30, 1778.

297.   13. MARTHA, b. at Norfolk, May 5, 1781.   d. March 5, 1784.

——o——

FAMILY OF DANIEL.⁴

88.

DANIEL PEASE,⁵ (DANIEL,⁴ ROBERT,³ JOHN,² ROBERT,¹) eldest son of DANIEL and ABIGAIL (FLETCHER) PEASE, first, of Enfield, Ct., last, of Somers, and first cousin of the preceding, was b. at Enfield, 1718 ; married Hannah Jones of Somers, daughter of Benjamin Jones, November 9, 1749. First settled in Somers, subsequently he removed to Canaan, Columbia County, N. Y., where he died, February 4, 1798.

His children were :

298.   1. ELIZABETH, b. at Somers, May 24, 1750.   m. Daniel Dean.

299.   2. WILLIAM, b. at Somers, October 23, 1751.

300.   3. DANIEL, b. at Somers, February 11, 1754.

301.   4. HANNAH, b. at Somers, May 18, 1756.   m. D. Green, Pompey, (Green's Corners,) N. Y.

302.   5. ELEANOR, b. at Somers, April 9, 1758.

303.   6. ELEANOR,² b. at Somers, June 8, 1760.   m. Dea.   Deane, one of the first settlers of Cazenovia, N. Y., where she died.

304.   7. CHLOE, b. at Somers, April 30, 1763.   m. Joseph Atwell of Cazenovia, where she died.

305.   8. EPHRAIM, b. at Somers, June   , 1796.

90.

ASA PEASE,[5] (DANIEL,[4] ROBERT,[3] JOHN,[2] ROBERT,[1]) brother of the preceding, was born at   , and is said to have married   , had a family, and finally to have removed to Hamilton, Madison County, N. Y.*

———o———

FAMILY OF EBENEZER.[4]
95.

EBENEZER PEASE,[5] (EBENEZER,[4] ROBERT,[3] JOHN,[2] ROBERT,[1]) eldest son of EBENEZER and MINDWELL (SEXTON) PEASE, and first cousin of the preceding, was born at Enfield, 1719; married Mary Terry, November 29, 1739, and settled in Enfield.

His children were:

306. 1. AZUBAH, b. at Enfield, July 7, 1740.
307. 2. EBENEZER, b. at Enfield, October 17, 1742.
308. · 3. AZUBAH,[2] b. at Enfield, November 2, 1744.
309. 4. EBENEZER,[2] b. at Enfield, May 8, 1747.
310. 5. MARY, b. at Enfield, September 14, 1749.
311. 6. JAMES, b. at Enfield, December 14, 1754.
312. 7. PETER, b. at Enfield, October 14, 1763. .

———

DESCENT OF JONATHAN.[3]

FAMILY OF JOSIAH.[4]
100.

JOSIAH PEASE,[5] (JOSIAH,[4] JONATHAN,[3] JOHN,[2] ROBERT,[1]) " beloved son and only child" of JOSIAH and PEASE, first of Enfield, Ct., and last of Upton, Mass., was

---

* There was an Asa Pease living in Springfield, Mass., from 1762 to 1776. His children born there by wife, Lucy, were: Lucy, b. 1762; Roxalina, b. 1768, and Asa, b. 1765. It is probable he was Asa Pease.[5] [Springfield Town and Old Hampshire County Records.]

(probably) born at Upton, about 1737; married Lydia and settled in Upton, a farmer. He died about 1813. His will was proved at court, September 6, 1814.

His children were:

313.   1. ABIGAIL, b. at Upton, May 5, 1759. m. William Hall, and settled in Marlboro', Vt.
314.   2. MARY, b. at Upton, January 21, 1763. m. John Heywood, and settled in Marlboro' Vt.
315.   3. AARON, b. at Upton, November 15, 1770.
316.   4. JOSIAH, b. at Upton, May 25, 1774.
317.   5. STOWELL, b. at Upton, April 23, 1778. He left home when about 20 years of age and is supposed to have died at sea.
[Middlesex and Worcester County and Upton Town Records.]

FAMILY OF PELATIAH.[4]

101.

PELATIAH PEASE,[5] (PELATIAH,[4] JONATHAN,[3] JOHN,[2] ROBERT,[1]) eldest son of PELATIAH and JEMIMA (BOOTH) PEASE of Enfield, Ct., and first cousin of the preceding, was born at Enfield, Ct., 1738. He left Enfield and is said to have settled at Alstead, N. H.; married and had a family.

His children were:

318.   1. PELATIAH,
319.   2. JONATHAN,
320.   3. NOADIAH,
321.   4. OLIVER,

————o————

104.

SAMUEL PEASE,[5] (PELATIAH,[4] JONATHAN,[3] JOHN,[2] ROBERT[1]) son of PELATIAH and JEMIMA (BOOTH) PEASE of Enfield, Ct., first cousin to the preceding, was born at Enfield, June 22, 1746; married Hannah Booth of East Windsor, November 10, 1768; married, second, Elizabeth Sexton, June 15, 1786. She died 1814. He married a third wife.

5

His children were :

322.	1.	Samuel, b. at Enfield, September 6, 1770.
323.	2.	Hannah, b. at Enfield, August 30, 1774.
324.	3.	Sabra, b. at Enfield, May 28, 1776.
325.	4.	Jonathan, b. at Enfield, June 10, 1778.
326.	5.	Osee, b. at Enfield, December 5, 1781. d. at the age of 15 years.

BY SECOND WIFE:

327.	6.	Elizabeth, b. at Enfield, September 14, 1787.
328.	7.	Persis, b. at Enfield, February 27, 1789.

105.

JOHN PEASE,[5] (Pelatiah,[4] Jonathan,[3] John,[2] John,[1]) youngest son of Pelatiah and Jemima (Booth) Pease of Enfield, Ct., was born at Enfield, January 2, 1748; married Beulah Booth. He lived in Enfield.

His children were :

329.	1.	Beulah, b. at Enfield, May 8, 1774. m. Ebenezer Chapin.
330.	2.	John, b. at Enfield, August 13, 1777.
331.	3.	Asher, b. at Enfield, September 21, 1780.
332.	4.	Lyman, b. at Enfield, May 26, 1784.

———oo———

DESCENT OF JAMES.[3]

FAMILY OF JOSEPH[4] (OF JAMES.[3])

108.

WAREHAM PEASE,[5] (Joseph,[4] James,[3] John,[2] Robert,[1]) son of Joseph and Sarah ( ) Pease of Enfield, Ct., and second cousin of the preceding, was born at Enfield, 1734; married Jerusha Kent, and settled in Suffield, Ct.; died there, 1789, aged 55 years.

His children were :

333.	1.	Justus, b. at Suffield.
334.	2.	Silas, b. at Suffield, 1760.
335.	3.	Titus, b. at Suffield.

336.   4. GROVE, b. at Suffield, December 12, 1780.
337.   5. JERUSHA, b. at Suffield.
338.   6. ROXANNA, b. at Suffield.
339.   7. ELIZABETH, b. at Suffield.
340.   8. WAREHAM, b. at Suffield, 1784.

113.

JAMES PEASE,⁵ (JOSEPH,⁴ JAMES,³ JOHN,² ROBERT,¹) son of JOSEPH and PRUDENCE (OLDS) PEASE of Enfield, Ct., a half-brother to the preceding, was born at Enfield, November 26, 1749; married Sarah Colton, and settled in Somers, Ct., where he died 1830, aged 81 years.

His children were:

341.   1. PRUDENCE, b. at Somers, February 22, 1774.   m. Asa Williams of Shutesbury.   She settled there.
342.   2. MARGARET, b. at Somers, July 2, 1776.   m. Solomon Terry of Enfield, Ct.   She was the mother of Rev. James P. Terry, some time pastor of the Congregational Church at Somers.
343.   3. JAMES, b. at Somers, December 13, 1779.   d. young.
344.   4. JOSIAH, b. at Somers, September 9, 1783.

114.

JOSEPH PEASE,⁵ (JOSEPH,⁴ JAMES,³ JOHN,² ROBERT,¹) brother of the preceding, was born at Enfield, December 18, 1751.   He married   , and settled in Western Pennsylvania, where he died.

He had but one child, a daughter, who married and removed to the West.

345.   1.

115.

GIDEON PEASE,⁵ (JOSEPH,⁴ JAMES,³ JOHN,² ROBERT,¹) brother of the preceding, was born at Enfield, August 2, 1753; married Deborah Pease, daughter of Timothy Pease, 1776; married, second, Eunice Cooley; and married, third, Deborah Talcott, June 13, 1811.   He died at Enfield without issue.

117.

EBENEZER PEASE,[5] (JOSEPH,[4] JAMES,[3] JOHN,[2] ROBERT,[1]) youngest son of JOSEPH and PRUDENCE (OLDS) PEASE, was born at Enfield, Ct., May 8, 1760; married Sarah Root of Great Barrington, Mass., July 29, 1784, and appears to have settled, first, in Canaan, N. Y., where his children were born. He also appears to have enlisted in the Army of the Revolution, and was taken a captive by the Indians, and carried to Niagara, in 1781, and remained in captivity among the Indians about two years. He is supposed to have died in Pennsylvania.

His children were:

846. 1. JESSE, b. at Canaan.
347. 2. EBENEZER, b. at Canaan.
348. 3. JAMES, b. at Canaan.
349. 4. GIDEON, b. at Canaan.
350. 5. STEPHEN, b. at Canaan.
351. 6. NOBLE, b. at Canaan.
352. 7. RHODA, b. at Canaan.
353. 8. LOVINA, b. at Canaan.
354. 9. LAURA, b at

DESCENT OF ISAAC.[3]

FAMILY OF ISAAC.[4]

119.

ISAAC PEASE,[5] (ISAAC,[4] ISAAC,[3] JOHN,[2] ROBERT,[1]) eldest son of ISAAC and AMY (FRENCH) PEASE of Enfield, Ct., and second cousin of the preceding, was born at Enfield, August, 1727; married Rachael Hall of Somers, January 13, 1748. He lived in Enfield.

His children were:

355. 1. JEHIEL, b. at Enfield, May 3, 1750.
356. 2. SOLOMON, b. at Enfield, September 14, 1751.
357. 3. ISAAC, b. at Enfield, June 14, 1753.

358.   4. RACHEL, b. at Enfield, July 9, 1755.
359.   5. RUFUS, b. at Enfield, May 17, 1757.
360.   6. ABIGAIL, b. at Enfield, January 3, 1760.
361.   7. SYBIL, b. at Enfield, September 20, 1763.   m. Emery Pease of
       Somers.
362.   8. GEORGE, b. at Enfield, October 13, 1776.

121.

JACOB PEASE,⁵ (ISAAC,⁴ ISAAC,³ JOHN,² ROBERT,¹) second son of ISAAC and AMY (FRENCH) PEASE, was born at Enfield, 1731; married Mary   , and settled in Enfield. After the birth of his eighth child he removed to Vermont with his whole family. He is supposed to have settled at Andover, Windsor County, 1776, as his name is found there among the first settlers.

His children were:

363.   1. JACOB, b. at Enfield, February 9, 1757.
364.   2. JACOB,² b. at Enfield, March 7, 1759.
365.   3. LOVISA, b. at Enfield, February 16, 1761.
366.   4. RHODA, b. at Enfield, March 16, 1763.
367.   5. AMY, b. at Enfield, March 19, 1765.
368.   6. ELISHA, b. at Enfield, April 11, 1767.
369.   7. ELIPHALET, b. at Enfield, November 1, 1769.
370.   8. GAIUS, b. at Enfield, October 21, 1771.
371.   9. CHESTER, b. at

122.

CAPT. ABNER PEASE,⁵ (ISAAC,⁴ ISAAC,³ JOHN,² ROBERT,¹) third son of ISAAC and AMY (FRENCH) PEASE, was born at Enfield, 1733; married Elizabeth Farrington, January, 1763. [Somers Town Records.] He married, second, Lovisa Allen. It appears he first settled in Somers, Ct., but subsequently removed to the eastern part of the State of New York. He held the office of deputy sheriff, in what was the county of Albany, in 1777, and came near losing his life in the discharge of his duty, while apprehending riotous Tories. He joined the Shakers, which congregated near New Lebanon, N. Y., in 1780, and died in that connection at his residence in Stephentown, N. Y., in 1784, of small pox, aged about 51 years.

His children were :

372. 1. ABNER, b. at Somers, 1763.
373. 2. JAMES, b. at Canaan, N. Y., October, 1771.
 374. 3. DANIEL, b. at Somers. d. a child.
375. 4. JOHN, b. at
376. 5. SAMUEL, b. at
 377. 6. SALLY. m. Richard Hayes.
 378. 7. SYBIL, b. at Cannan, 1767. married Elisha Kibbe of Somers. married, second, John Henry of Norwich, N. Y., and married, third, Joseph Powers of Worcester, N. Y. [Enfield and Somers Town Records; New England Historical and Genealogical Register.]

124.

NOADIAH PEASE,[5] (ISAAC,[4] ISAAC,[3] JOHN,[2] ROBERT,[1]) youngest son of ISAAC and AMY (FRENCH) PEASE, was born at Enfield, Ct., 1737; married Tirzah Smith of Glastenbury, Ct., April 21, 1763, and first settled in Enfield, from which place he removed to Sandisfield, Mass., 1782, where his first wife died, 1789; married, second, Sarah Couch. He was, by occupation, a tanner and shoemaker. He was in the expedition against Ticonderoga, under Gen. Abercrombie, in the French War, 1758. He was at Deerfield at the time the Indians were committing their depredations there. [Family Record; New England Historical and Genealogical Register.] He died at Sandisfield, March 26, 1822, aged about 86 years.

His children were :

 379. 1. ROXANNA, b. at Enfield, April 22, 1764. m. Eben Ames of Brimfield and died soon after.
380. 2. NOADIAH, b. at Enfield, September 6, 1765.
 381. 3. ELISHA, b. at Enfield, June 17, 1767. d. young.
 382. 4. TABITHA, b. at Enfield, May 14, 1769. d. young.
 383. 5. PHILENA, b. at Enfield, February 25, 1771. m. Obadiah Chapin of Enfield, and died soon after 1795.
 384. 6. TIRZAH, b. at Enfield, February 5, 1773. d. young.

385. 7. WALTER, b. at Enfield, December 23, 1774.
386. 8. ASAPH, b. at Enfield, October 16, 1776.
387. 9. ACHSA, b. at Enfield, December 20, 1778. d. young.
388. 10. PERSIS, b. at Enfield, July 24, 1781. d. unmarried, aged 46 years, at Sandisfield.
389. 11. ERASTUS, b. at Sandisfield, November 4, 1783.
390. 12. ALVAH, b. at Sandisfield, December 7, 1786.

BY SECOND WIFE:

391. 13. SIMEON, b. at Sandisfield, December 3, 1792.

———o———

FAMILY OF ABRAHAM.⁴

128.

JOHN PEASE,⁵ (ABRAHAM,⁴ ISAAC,³ JOHN,² ROBERT,¹) son of ABRAHAM and MARY (BOOTH) PEASE of Enfield, Ct., and first cousin of the preceding, was born at Enfield, 1725; married   Wright, and settled in Suffield, Ct.; married, second, Priscilla Hale, and for a time lived with her in Enfield, but after her death, returned to Suffield, where he died with his son Levi, between the year 1780 and 1790. He was known as "one-armed John," to distinguish him from other John Peases, there being no less than five of them. His children were by his first wife. He was a butcher and lost his arm by accident in the business.

His children were:

392. 1. JOHN, b. at Suffield.
393. 2. LEVI, b. at Suffield, 1761.
394. 3. JEMIMA, b. at Suffield.
395. 4. DESIRE, b. at Suffield.
396. 5. HANNAH, b. at Suffield.

130.

MOSES PEASE,⁵ (ABRAHAM,⁴ ISAAC,³ JOHN,² ROBERT,¹) son of ABRAHAM and ABIGAIL (WARNER) PEASE, was born at Enfield, 1734; married Jemima Booth, November 24, 1757, and settled in Enfield, where he died, January 25, 1822, aged 91 years.

His children were:

397.   1. Moses, b. at Enfield, October 27, 1758.
398.   2. Benjamin, b. at Enfield, July 15, 1760.
399.   3. Jemima, b. at Enfield, April 8, 1762.   m. Elijah Allen, and settled in Enfield.
400.   4. Lemuel, b. at Enfield, December 6, 1763.
         [The above names from Enfield Town Record.]
401.   5. Abigail, b. at Enfield, February 8, 1764.   d. August, 1850, aged 86 years.
402.   6. Mehitabel, b. at Enfield, October 18, 1769.   m. Reuben Hall, and removed to Ohio.
403.   7. Electa, b. at Enfield, March 18, 1772.   m. Reuben Pease, and settled in East Windsor.
404.   8. Jedediah, b. at Enfield, February 13, 1774.   d. May 13, 1783, by falling from a tree.
405.   9. Benjamin,[2] b. at Enfield, March 13, 1776.
406.   10. Huldah, b. at Enfield, February 11, 1778.   m. Joseph Hall, and settled in Somers.

132.

SAMUEL PEASE,[5] (Abraham,[4] Isaac,[3] John,[2] Robert,[1]) brother of the preceding, was born at Enfield, 1736; married Tryphena Bancroft, November 27, 1760. Lived and died in Enfield.   [Enfield Records.]

His children were:

407.   1. Abiel, b. at Enfield, August, 1761.
408.   2. Chester, b. at Enfield.
409.   3. Augustus, b. at Enfield.
410.   4. Josiah, b. at Enfield.

133.

JOEL PEASE,[5] (Abraham,[4] Isaac,[3] John,[2] Robert,[1]) brother of the preceding, was born at Enfield, 1738; married Lois Warner, 1761, and lived in the north part of East Windsor, Ct.

His children were:

411.   1. Lois, b. at East Windsor, January 7, 1763.
412.   2. Joel, b. at East Windsor, November 6, 1764.
413.   3. Joanna, b. at East Windsor, September 12, 1766.

414. 4. EUNICE, b. at East Windsor, July 10, 1769.
415. 5. ENOCH, b. at East Windsor, November 13, 1773.
416. 6. ELAM, b. at East Windsor, August 13, 1776.
417. 7. LUCY, b. at East Windsor, October 30, 1780.

134.

NATHAN PEASE,⁵ (ABRAHAM,⁴ ISAAC,³ JOHN,² ROB-ERT,¹) brother of the preceding, was born at Enfield, January 18, 1740; married Hannah Potter, January 24, 1762, and first settled at Enfield. He subsequently removed to Wilbraham, Mass., where he died.

His children were:

418. 1. HANNAH, b. at Enfield, October 6, 1763. d. a child.
419. 2. NATHAN, b. at Enfield, June 5, 1765.
420. 3. JUSTUS, b. at Enfield, November 24, 1766. d. at the age of 21 years.
421. 4. ESTHER, b. at Enfield, November 22, 1769. m. Amasa Ainsworth.
422. 5. SUSANNAH, b. at Enfield. m. Dea. Bela Bennett.
423. 6. HANNAH,² b. at Enfield, March 20, 1774. m. Solomon Firman.
424. 7. AMOS, b. at Enfield, February 16, 1776.
425. 8. NATHANIEL, b. at Enfield, 1777.

136.

GIDEON PEASE,⁵ (ABRAHAM,⁴ ISAAC,³ JOHN,² ROB-ERT,¹), son of ABRAHAM and ABIGAIL (WARNER) PEASE, was born at Enfield, August 8, 1744; married Sybil Markham, April 4, 1764; married second, Deborah Meacham. He first settled in Enfield, but subsequently removed to Monson, Mass., where he died.

His children were:

426. 1. GIDEON, b. at Enfield, May 20, 1765.
427. 2. SYBIL, b. at Enfield, May 11, 1767. m. Aaron Lampheare, and lived in the State of Ohio.
428. 3. PRUDENCE, b. at Enfield,   . d. young.
429. 4. DAN, b. at Enfield, December 11, 1771.
430. 5. EXPERIENCE, b. at Enfield, January 31, 1774. m. Henry Gardner and removed to Chautauqua County, N. Y.

6

431. 6. URBANE, b. at Enfield, June 8, 1778.

432. 7. JERUSHA, b. at Enfield,   . m. Ariel Lampheare, and settled in Monson, Mass.

433. 8. IRA, b. at Monson.

434. 9. ABRAHAM, b. at Monson.

435. 10. SALMON, b. at Monson, 1788.

436. 11. SAMUEL, b. at Monson.

437. 12. DEBORAH, b. at Monson. m. Joseph Dwight.

438. 13. ADAH, b. at Monson. m. Joshua Williams.

439. 14. PRUDENCE, b. at Monson. m. Gideon Bliss, and removed to Wisconsin.

440. 15. EUNICE, b. at Monson. m. Austin Bliss, and settled in Monson.

138.

WILLIAM PEASE,[5] (ABRAHAM,[4] ISAAC,[3] JOHN,[2] ROBERT,[1]) son of ABRAHAM and ABIGAIL (WARNER) PEASE, was born at Enfield, 1746; married Martha Webster; died at Enfield, the place of his residence, March 27, 1822, aged 76 years.

His children were:

441. 1. WILLIAM, b. at Enfield, 1780.

442. 2. DAVID, b. at Enfield.

443. 3. WARREN, b. at Enfield.

444. 4. MARTHA, b. at Enfield.

445. 5. ELIZABETH, b. at Enfield.

446. 6. MARY, b. at Enfield. m. Amos Pease.

447. 7. SARAH, b. at Enfield.

448. 8. CHARLOTTE, b. at Enfield. Married, and settled in Pennsylvania.

139.

ZEBULON PEASE,[5] (ABRAHAM,[4] ISAAC,[3] JOHN,[2] ROBERT,[1]) youngest son of ABRAHAM and ABIGAIL (WARNER) PEASE, was born at Enfield, November 2, 1749; married Hannah Rugg, of Hadley, Mass. He settled in Enfield, where he died about 1829, some 80 years old; was by occupation, a house-joiner.

His children were:

449. 1. ZEBULON, b. at Enfield, 1780.
450. 2. AGNES, b. at Enfield, November 24, 1781.　m.　　　　Knight.
451. 3. CHARLES, b. at Enfield.
452. 4. JABEZ, b. at Enfield, August 6, 1786.
453. 5. SAMUEL, b. at Enfield, July 29, 1787.
454. 6. MORRIS, b. at Enfield, April 24, 1789.
455. 7. HANNAH, b. at Enfield. m. James Marshall.　Lives in Enfield.
456. 8. HARVEY B., b. at Enfield, February 4, 1798.
457. 9. CIDNIE, b. at Enfield, August 31, 1802.　m.
　　　　Johnson.

———o———

FAMILY OF ISRAEL.⁴

140.

ISRAEL PEASE,⁵ (ISRAEL,⁴ ISAAC,³ JOHN,² ROBERT,¹) eldest son of ISRAEL and SARAH (BOOTH) PEASE of Enfield, Ct., and first cousin of the preceding, was born at Enfield, 1726; married Ann　　　　. First settled in Enfield, but ultimately removed to Middlefield, Mass., where he died.

His children were:

458. 1. SIMEON, b. at Enfield, February 7, 1758.
459. 2. ASENATH, b. at Enfield, October 19, 1761.　m. Stone Pease,
　　　　September 15, 1780, and lived in Enfield.
460. 3. LOVISA, b. at Enfield, December 8, 1763.　m. Alexander Vining
　　　　of East Windsor, 1786.
461. 4. ISRAEL, b. at Enfield, February 27, 1766.
562. 5. ABIGAIL, b. at Enfield, March 27, 1768.
463. 6. GAD, b. at Enfield, January 10, 1771.
464. 7. DAN, b. at Enfield, April 25, 1773.

141.

DAVID PEASE,⁵ (ISRAEL,⁴ ISAAC,³ JOHN,² ROBERT,¹) second son of ISRAEL and SARAH (BOOTH) PEASE, was born at Enfield, 1727; married Olive Prior, August 21, 1755. He lived and died in Enfield.

His children were:

465.   1. OLIVE, b. at Enfield, March 16, 1756.   m. Alexander Vining, of East Windsor, 1774.
466.   2. ABIGAIL, b. at Enfield, November 8, 1762.
467.   3. DIADAMA, b. at Enfield, June 9, 1765.
468.   4. DAVID, b. at Enfield, March 24, 1767.
469.   5. MEHITABEL, b. at Enfield, January 8, 1770.
470.   6. MIRIAM, b. at Enfield, June 4, 1772.
471.   7. LEVI, b. at Enfield.

144.

HEZEKIAH PEASE,[5] (ISRAEL,[4] ISAAC,[3] JOHN,[2] JOHN,[1]) third son of ISRAEL and SARAH (BOOTH) PEASE, was born at Enfield, 1732; married Mary Crandal, January 1, 1752; married second, Hannah Meacham.   He lived in Enfield.

His children were:

472.   1. MARY, b. at Enfield, February 24, 1755.
473.   2. SARAH, b. at Enfield, May 25, 1756.
474.   3. ELIZABETH, b. at Enfield, September 29, 1759.
475.   4. PENELOPE, b. at Enfield, September 5, 1762.
476.   5. ALICE, b. at Enfield, September 29, 1764.
477.   6. HEZEKIAH, b. at Enfield, October 10, 1768.   Slain in battle with the Indians in Ohio.   Had no family.

BY SECOND WIFE:

478.   7. HANNAH, b. at Enfield, November 26, 1770.
479.   8. LEMUEL, b. at Enfield, January 7, 1772.
480.   9. ELECTA, b. at Enfield, April 26, 1774.
481. 10. SETH, b. at Enfield, June 4, 1779.

146.

JESSE PEASE,[5] (ISRAEL,[4] ISAAC,[3] JOHN,[2] ROBERT,[1]) fourth son of ISRAEL and SARAH (BOOTH) PEASE, was born at Enfield, 1738; married widow Martha Ducet, 1785.   He first settled in Enfield, but subsequently removed to Ashfield, Mass., and finally to Groveland, in the State of New York.

His children were:

482. 1. MARTHA D., b. at Enfield, November 5, 1787.
483. 2. JESSE, b. at Enfield, December 28, 1789.

149.

NATHAN PEASE,[5] (ISRAEL,[4] ISAAC,[3] JOHN,[2] ROBERT,[1]) fifth and youngest son of ISRAEL and SARAH (BOOTH) PEASE, was born at Enfield; married   Root. He lived at Enfield where he died.

His children were:

484. 1. ACHSAH, b. at Enfield,   . d. young.
485. 2. NATHAN, b. at Enfield, April 1, 1782.
486. 3. MARTHA A., b. at Enfield.

———o———

FAMILY OF BENJAMIN.[4]
153.

BENJAMIN PEASE,[5] (BENJAMIN,[4] ISAAC,[3] JOHN,[2] ROBERT,[1]) son of BENJAMIN and ABIGAIL (ROSE) PEASE, of Enfield, Ct., was born May 10, 1744; married Margaret Prior, January 3, 1765. He had no children. He joined the Shakers in an early part of their history. The Shakers speak of him as a man much noted and of very respectable character—a man of influence and property. He was the chief deacon and trustee in the Shaker Society and church, for some ten years. He died among the Shakers in Enfield.

154.

SHARON PEASE,[5] (BENJAMIN,[4] ISAAC,[3] JOHN,[2] ROBERT,[1]) son of BENJAMIN and ABIGAIL (ROSE) PEASE, of Enfield, Ct., was born at Enfield, June 26, 1746; married Mary Prior, October 23, 1766. Hinman says he died at Hartford, Ct.

His children were :

487. 1. MARY, b. at Enfield, May 2, 1767.
488. 2. ABIGAIL, b. at Enfield, November 21, 1768.
489. 3. SHARON, b. at Enfield, October 3, 1772.
. 490. 4. BENJAMIN, b. at Enfield, October 3, 1774. He never married.

---o---

FAMILY OF EZEKIEL.[4]
159.

EZEKIEL PEASE,[5] (EZEKIEL,[4] ISAAC,[3] JOHN,[2] ROBERT,[1])
cousin to the preceding and oldest son of EZEKIEL and
HANNAH (CHANDLER) PEASE, of Enfield, Ct., was born at
Enfield, August 18, 1734 ; married Jemima Markham, January 23, 1755. He first settled in Enfield, but removed
from there to Weston, Vt., previous to the Revolution,
where he died, 1807, aged 73 years.

His children were :

491. 1. EZEKIEL, b. at Enfield, March 22, 1756.
492. 2. HANNAH, b. at Enfield, December 22, 1757.
493. 3. RHODA, b. at Enfield, May 11, 1764.
494. 4. OBADIAH, b. at Enfield, September 8, 1766.
495. 5. ELIJAH, b. at Enfield, July 13, 1770.
496. 6. AMBROSE, probably born at Weston, Vt.

161.

HENRY C. PEASE,[5] (EZEKIEL,[4] ISAAC,[3] JOHN,[2] ROB-
ERT,[1]) brother of the preceding, was born at Enfield, February 11, 1738 ; married Ruth Chapin. He first settled
in Enfield, but removed from there to Sandisfield,
Mass., 1763–4, where he died, September 1812, aged
75 years.

His children were :

497. 1. RUTH, b. at Enfield, August 16, 1761. m. Richard Adams.
498. 2. ABIGAIL, b. at Enfield, October 22, 1763. m.
        Atwater.
499. 3. ELIZA, probably b. at Sandisfield. m.   Baker.

500. 4. TABITHA, probably b. at Sandisfield.   m.   Dowd of
Sodus.
501. 5. MEHITABEL, probably b. at Sandisfield.   m.   and d.
at Colebrook.
502. 6. HENRY, b. at Sandisfield, 1772.
503. 7. OLIVER, b. at Sandisfield, 1777.

167.

ISAAC PEASE,[5] (EZEKIEL,[4] ISAAC,[3] JOHN,[2] ROBERT,[1]) brother of the preceding, was born at Enfield, January 7, 1752; married Submit Spencer, daughter of Hezekiah Spencer, of Somers, December 19, 1776; married, second, Mrs. Rachel (Brooks) Williams. He settled in the east part of Enfield, called Scitico, where he died, 1820.

His children were:

BY FIRST WIFE:

504. 1. OLIVER, b. at Enfield, September 5, 1777.
505. 2. ISAAC, b. at Enfield, March 27, 1778.
506. 3. JAMES, b. at Enfield, March 27, 1779. d. in infancy.
507. 4. DANIEL, b. at Enfield, October 3, 1780.
508. 5. REUBEN, b. at Enfield, December 28, 1781.
509. 6. SUBMIT, b. at Enfield, October 3, 1783. d. in infancy.
510. 7. CALVIN, b. at Enfield, April 13, 1785.
511. 8. ABEL, b. at Enfield, May 16, 1787.

---o---

FAMILY OF TIMOTHY.[4]

169.

TIMOTHY PEASE,[5] (TIMOTHY,[4] ISAAC,[3] JOHN,[2] ROBERT,[1]) eldest son of TIMOTHY and MARY (CHANDLER) PEASE, of Enfield, and first cousin of the preceding, was born at Enfield, 1738; married Ruth Hale, and settled in Enfield.

His children were:

512. 1. TIMOTHY, b. at Enfield, July 30, 1760.
513. 2. ABIEL, b. at Enfield, November 13, 1764.
514. 3. TIMOTHY, b. at Enfield, July 30, 1766.

515. 4. RUTH, b. at Enfield, August 5, 1768. She joined the Shakers and died among them.
516. 5. LEVI, b. at Enfield, August 15, 1771. He died a leading man among the Shakers in 1832 aged 61 years.
517. 6. JONATHAN, b. at Enfield, August 23, 1774.
518. 7. JUSTIN, b. at Enfield, 1780. d. among the Shakers. (Killed by lightning.)

173.

EDWARD PEASE,[5] (TIMOTHY,[4] ISAAC,[3] JOHN,[2] ROBERT,[1]) son of TIMOTHY and MARY (CHANDLER) PEASE, was born September 7, 1744, at Enfield; married Abigail Hale, November 19, 1783, and lived and died in Enfield. He died December 30, 1817.

His children were:

519. 1. TIMOTHY, b. at Enfield, October 25, 1784.
520. 2. EDWARD, b. at Enfield, December 18, 1786. d. in Enfield, unmarried, 1852, aged 66 years.
521. 3. HEBER, b. at Enfield, June, 1788.
522. 4. ABIGAIL, b. at Enfield, May 9, 1789. m. Henry Killam.
523. 5. DEBORAH, b. at Enfield, 1790.
524. 6. DEBORAH,[2] b. at Enfield, July 19, 1793. m. Josiah Allen, and lived in Enfield.
525. 7. REBECCA, b. at Enfield, September 29, 1795. d. unmarried.

174.

JAMES PEASE,[5] (TIMOTHY,[4] ISAAC,[3] JOHN,[2] ROBERT,[1]) brother to the preceding, was born at Enfield, April 9, 1746; married Mary Larkham, 1773, and lived at Enfield.

His children were:

526. 1. MARY, b. at Enfield, March 20, 1774.
527. 2. JAMES, b. at Enfield, February 28, 1776.
528. 3. MARTHA, b. at Enfield.
529. 4. CLARRISSA, b. at Enfield.
530. 5. RHODA, b. at Enfield.
531. 6. LUTHER, b. at Enfield, February 28, 1788.
532. 7. JACOB, b. at Enfield, November 7, 1792.

FAMILY OF CUMMINGS.⁴

184.

CUMMINGS PEASE,[5] (Cummings,[4] Isaac,[3] John,[2] Robert,[1]) eldest son of Dea. Cummings and Elizabeth (Pease) Pease, of Enfield, Ct., and first cousin of the preceding, was born at Enfield, November 27, 1744; married Thankful Clelland, June 12, 1780; first settled in Enfield, but subsequently removed to Wilbraham, Mass., thence to the east part of Longmeadow, Mass., and died at Chicopee, with his son, Roswell Pease, June, 1822, aged 79 years.

His children were:

533.   1. Roswell, b. at Enfield, 1781.
534.   2. Elizabeth, b. at Enfield, 1782. m. Samuel Mills, Chicopee, Mass.
535.   3. Helen, b. at Enfield, June 10, 1783. m. Moses Parsons of Enfield, and removed to Ohio.
536.   4. Wilder C., b. at Enfield, October 4, 1784.
537.   5. Elseba, b. at Enfield, April 9, 1786. m. Hosea Bronson, and removed to Pennsylvania.
538.   6. Nancy, b. at Enfield, October 9, 1787. m. Luther Pease, and removed to Ohio.
539.   7. Abion, b. at Enfield, August 5, 1789.
540.   8. James C., b. at Enfield, April 4, 1791.
541.   9. Shubel, b. at Wilbraham, 1796.
542. 10. Edna, b. at Wilbraham. m. Jeremiah Bumpstead of Monson.

186.

EBENEZER PEASE,[5] (Cummings,[4] Isaac,[3] John,[2] Robert,[1]) son of Dea. Cummings and Elizabeth (Pease) Pease, was born at Enfield, December 23, 1748; married Rebecca Hill. He first settled in Longmeadow, and soon after the close of the Revolutionary War, left that place, and ultimately settled in Vermont. He died in the town of Georgia, Vt., Franklin County, aged 92 years. He was three years in the regular Continental Army, in the Revolutionary War; was a devoted professor of the Christian faith, having embraced religion in early youth,—was baptized and became a member of a Baptist church at the age of 18 years, and continued a devoted Christian through his long life.

His children were:

543.   1. EBENEZER, b. at Longmeadow, August 20, 1773.
544.   2. ENOCH, b. at Longmeadow, November 15, 1775.
545.   3. ENOS, b. at Longmeadow.
546.   4. ABEL, b. at Longmeadow, 1784.
547.   5. REBECCA, b. at Longmeadow. m. Obadiah Hill, and lived in Whitestown, N. Y.
548.   6. ACHSAH, b. at Georgia, Vt.,   m.   Hill, and lived in Genessee, N. Y., and died there.
549.   7. DELIVERANCE, b. at Georgia. m. Simeon Hill, and died at Georgia, Vt., in 1836.

187.

ASA PEASE,[5] (CUMMINGS,[4] ISAAC,[3] JOHN,[2] ROBERT,[1]) son of Dea. CUMMINGS and ELIZABETH (PEASE) PEASE, was born at Enfield, January 18, 1750; married Bathsheba Meacham, daughter of Rev. Joseph Meacham, of Enfield, Ct., 1773. She was a grand-daughter of Isaac Meacham, the King's surveyor. He settled first, a short distance west of the Shaker Village, subsequently on the farm originally owned by his father, where he died. He was generally known in the community as *Lieut. Pease.*

His children were:

550.   1. ELAM, b. at Enfield, April 22, 1778.
551.   2. ASA, b. at Enfield. d., aged 10 years.
552.   3. GAIUS, b. at Enfield, 1780.
553.   4. ALPHEUS, b. at Enfield.
554.   5. BATHSHEBA, b. at Enfield, August 30, 1788. m. Lemuel Kingsbury, and died at Enfield.

189.

HEMAN PEASE,[5] (CUMMINGS,[4] ISAAC,[3] JOHN,[2] ROBERT,[1]) son of Dea. CUMMINGS and SARAH (HALE) PEASE, and half-brother to the preceding, was born at Enfield, 1757; married Hannah Ward, daughter of Benjamin Ward, of Somers, Ct., July 10, 1783; married second, Roxanna Davis, of Longmeadow, Mass. He first settled in Enfield, but subsequently removed to Longmeadow, where he died. He served in the Revolutionary War, in the capacity of a musician.

His children were:

555. 1. HEMAN, b. at Somers.
556. 2. PLINY, b. at Enfield, October 20, 1787.
557. 3. LUCINA, b. at Enfield, May 12, 1788. m. Elam Combs, and settled in Enfield.
558. 4. HANNAH, b. at Enfield, September 26, 1790. m. Arphaxad Wardwell, and settled in Enfield.
559. 5. CHAUNCEY, b. at Enfield, February 26, 1792.
560. 6. ASA, b. at Enfield, October 24, 1794.
561. 7. ACHSAH, b. at Enfield.

BY SECOND WIFE:

562. 8. ROXANA, b. at Longmeadow, November 9, 1815. m., first, George Hills, 1835; m., second, George Tufts, in 1847, and settled in West Longmeadow.

190.

DR. DAVID PEASE,⁵ (CUMMINGS,⁴ ISAAC,³ JOHN,² ROBERT,¹) youngest son of Dea. CUMMINGS and SARAH (HALE) PEASE, was born at Enfield, April 6, 1760; married Jerusha Spencer, of Somers, Ct., January 29, 1783, and first settled in East Windsor, but not long after removed to Simsbury, Ct., from thence to Enfield, his native town, where for a time he practiced physic. His last residence was New Shoreham, R. I. He died, November, 1803, aged 44 years. He did military duty in the Revolution; was on Long Island at the time of our defeat, then 16 years old; also, in a battle at White Plain. Near the close of the Revolutionary War he commenced his study of medicine with Dr. Asa Hamilton, of Somers, Ct. His widow married James Lusk, of Enfield, July 7, 1805, where she died, February 21, 1815, aged 51 years.

His children were:

563. 1. David, b. at East Windsor, November 9, 1783.

564. 2. Sarah, b. at Somers, Ct., March, 1785. m. William Earl of Troy, N. Y., where she died, January 8, 1811, aged 26 years.

565. 3. Jerusha, b. at Enfield, February 8, 1788. m. William Earl of Troy.

566. 4. Elizabeth, b. at Enfield, February 8, 1788. m. Daniel Sweatland, and died, August 3, 1809, at Longmeadow, aged 22 years.

567. 5. Jonathan S., b. at Washington, Mass., April 13, 1791.

568. 6. Pamelia, b. at New Shoreham, R. I., 1793.

569. 7. Asa, b. at New Shoreham, R. I., March 22, 1796.

570. 8. Pamelia,[2] b. at New Shoreham, R. I., June, 1799. m. Amos Brooks of Sandlake, and died at Troy, N. Y., 1834.

571. 9. Dorothy, b. at Somers, March, 1802. m.   Purdy of Troy, and died there.

John E. Pear

SIXTH GENERATION.

DESCENT OF JOHN.³

FAMILY OF JOHN.⁴

191.

JOHN PEASE,⁶ (John,⁵ John,⁴ John,³ John,² Robert,¹) eldest son of John and Bathsheba (Jones) Pease of Enfield, Ct., was born at Enfield, March 15, 1753; married Charity Thompson, February 8, 1781, was designated "John Pease, 3d;" resided in Enfield, was a farmer, and did service in the Revolutionary War. Died at Enfield, 1843, aged 90 years.

His children were:

572. 1. John C., b. at Enfield, January 1, 1782.
573. 2. Walter, b. at Enfield, March 29, 1784.
574. 3. Lorrain T., b. at Enfield, April 7, 1788.
575. 4. Dorothy, b. at Enfield, August 22, 1790.
576. 5. Martha, b. at Enfield, May 15, 1793. m. Harvey Pease, 1819.
577. 6. Polly, (Mary,) b. at Enfield, August 29, 1795.
578. 7. Charity, b. at Enfield, August 27, 1797.
579. 8. Nancy, b. at Enfield, August 6, 1800. m. John Stratton, Esq., of West Swanzey, N. H.

192.

THOMAS PEASE,⁶ (John,⁵ John,⁴ John,³ John,² Robert,¹) second son of John and Bathsheba (Jones) Pease, was born at Enfield, December 17, 1754; married Mercy Hall of Somers, Ct., February 2, 1778; first settled in Enfield, but subsequently removed to Ellington, Ct., where he died, 1815, aged 61 years. He was a farmer.

His children were:

580. 1. THOMAS, b. at Enfield, 1778.
581. 2. MERCY, b. at Enfield, October, 1780. m. William Reed of
        Tolland, Ct., February, 1815.
582. 3. THOMAS,[2] b. at Enfield, 1782.
583. 4. SALMON, b. at Enfield, April 10, 1784.
584. 5. WILLIS, b. at Ellington, February, 1786.
585. 6. BATHSHEBA, b. at Ellington, September 5, 1789. m. Rufus
        Pease of Enfield, October 28, 1813.
586. 7. CALVIN, b. at Ellington, May 12, 1797.
587. 8. SARAH, b. at Ellington, June 24, 1799. m. Cooley Pease
        and resides at Somers.

194.

GIDEON PEASE,[6] (JOHN,[5] JOHN,[4] JOHN,[3] JOHN,[2] ROB-
ERT,[1]) third son of JOHN and BATHSHEBA (JONES) PEASE
of Enfield, Ct., was born at Enfield, November 18, 1757;
married Prudence Sexton, daughter of Asahel Sexton of
Somers, Ct., September 11, 1783. He removed to Vermont and settled in Weston.

His children were:

588. 1. HORACE, b. at Enfield, 1784.
589. 2. MARTIN, b. at Enfield, May 30, 1786.
590. 3. PRUDENCE, b. at Enfield, March 24, 1788. m.   McIntire.
591. 4. LOVISA, b. at Enfield, 1790. m. Freeman Lyon.
592. 5. RUTH, b. at Weston, May 27, 1794.
593. 6. RHODA, b. at   1796.
594. 7. WARREN, b. at Weston, February 25, 1799.
595. 8. PATIENCE, b. at Weston, February 8, 1802. m. Orrin Cook
        of Manchester, Vt.
596. 9. NELSON.
597. 10. ASAHEL, b. at Weston 1808.

197.

SIMEON PEASE,[6] (JOHN,[5] JOHN,[4] JOHN,[3] JOHN,[2] ROB-
ERT,[1]) youngest son of JOHN and BATHSHEBA (JONES)
PEASE of Enfield, Ct., was born at Enfield, August 22,
1764; married Susan McGregory, daughter of Ebenezer
McGregory, January, 1787, and died at Hartford, 1827,
aged 63 years.

His children were:

598.   1. ORRIN, b. at Enfield, 1788.
599.   2. HARVEY, b. at Enfield, April 15, 1790.
600.   3. SIMEON, b. at Enfield, August 16, 1792.   d. young.
601.   4. SUSAN, b. at Enfield, January 19, 1795.
602.   5. THEODORE, b. at Enfield, March 15, 1797.
603.   6. NORMAN, b. at Longmeadow, May 9, 1799.
604.   7. AMANDA, b. at Suffield, May 2, 1802.   d. 1805.
605.   8. ELIZABETH, b. at Hartford, June 15, 1805.   d. an infant.
606.   9. SIMEON, b. at Hartford, August 9, 1807.

———○○○———

FAMILY OF JAMES.⁴
200.

JOHN PEASE,⁶ (JAMES,⁵ JAMES,⁴ JOHN,³ JOHN,² JOHN,¹)
second son of JAMES and ABIGAIL (FORD) PEASE of
Somers, Ct., and third cousin of the preceding, was born
at Somers, June 12, 1742; married Zepary Coy in Somers, October 6, 1768. His grandson, Aaron Pease of
Marlboro, Vt., says he was one of the volunteers who
joined the colonial troops in 17—, in an expedition with
Great Britain, which was at war with Spain, for the purpose of taking Havana, Cuba. Only two, out of a number of sixty persons who went from Somers, survived the
expedition, and it is supposed he was one of them. He
seems, first to have settled in Somers, Ct., where his eldest
child was born. From thence, he removed to Stafford,
Ct., where he lived some years. He finally sold his farm,
took his pay in continental money, which became almost
worthless. For a time after this he appears to have lived
among the Shakers. Subsequently he returned to Stafford, where he resided until about the year 1820, when
he removed with most of his family to Marlboro, Vt.,
where he died.

His children were:

607.   1. ELIJAH, b. at Somers, February 12, 1770.
608.   2. JOHN, b. at Somers, 1780. m.   , lived
in Marlboro, Vt., and died without issue, May 10, 18   .

609. 3. Aaron, b. at Somers, March 6, 1786.
610. 4. Polly, b. at Somers.
611. 5. Lois.
612. 6. Miriam.

207.

Capt. JOEL PEASE,[6] (James,[5] James,[4] John,[3] John,[2] Robert,[1]) brother to the preceding, was born at Somers, November 2, 1760; married Lovisa Meacham. He appears to have first settled in Somers, Ct., and was for some time a resident of Wilbraham, Mass., but removed to the State of Vermont. He married a second wife. He was a soldier in the continental army, which he entered at the age of 16, and was captain of one of the militia companies in Somers.

His children were:

613. 1. Lucy, b. at Somers, January 28, 1786.
614. 2. Joel, b. at Somers.
615. 3. James, b. at Somers.
616. 4. Frederick M.

209.

SAMUEL PEASE,[6] (Richard,[5] James,[4] John,[3] John,[2] Robert,[1]) eldest son of Richard and Elizabeth (Parsons) Pease of Somers, Ct., was a cousin of the preceding. He was born at Somers, August 26, 1756; married Sarah Root, daughter of Timothy Root of Somers, 1786; lived with Rev. Seth Parsons of Somers, whose farm and homestead he inherited. Died, July 20, 1842, aged 86 years.

His children were:

617. 1. Sarah, b. at Somers, April 16, 1787.
618. 2. Cynthia, b. at Somers, October 22, 1788. m. Charles Cook of Somers, May 3, 1809; lived at Rodman, N. Y.
619. 3. Dorothy, b. at Somers, October 31, 1791. m. Timothy Hurlburt, 1818, and settled in Somers.
620. 4. Ruby, b. at Somers, May 13, 1794. m. Chauncey Hurlburt, 1817, and lived at Somers.

621. 5. SETH, b. at Somers, August 7, 1796.
622. 6. SAMUEL, b. at Somers, January 20, 1801.
623. 7. SOLOMON, b. at Somers, November 3, 1804.

210.

CAPT. RICHARD PEASE,⁶ (RICHARD,⁵ JAMES,⁴ JOHN,³ JOHN,² ROBERT,¹) brother of the preceding, was born at Somers, October 28, 1758; married Sovier Parsons. He settled in Somers, about two miles south-west of the center of the town. He was one of the seventy men who turned out from Somers at the first alarm of hostilities, and marched to Boston under the lead of Capt. Emery Pease, and continued actively engaged in the service of his country during the revolutionary struggle for liberty. He was esteemed as a man of strict integrity and sound judgment. He died at Somers.

His children were:

624. 1. RICHARD, b. at Somers, September 30, 1789.
625. 2. LUKE, b. at Somers, April 9, 1793. d. unmarried.
626. 3. WALTER, b. at Somers, July 4, 1795.
. **627.** 4. ORRIN, b. at Somers, June 10, 1797.
628. 5. ALPHEUS, b. at Somers, July 18, 1799.
629. 6. SOVIER, b. at Somers, September 18, 1801. m. Joseph Montague, and settled in Granby, Mass.
630. 7. AUSTIN, b. at Somers, March 8, 1804.
631. 8. AZARIAH, b. at Somers, May 22, 1806.
632. 9. ABIGAIL, b. at Somers, August 21, 1808; d. June 7, 1810.

———oo———

FAMILY OF JOSEPH⁴ (OF JOHN.³)
211.

AUGUSTIN PEASE,⁶ (JOSEPH,⁵ JOSEPH,⁴ JOHN,³ JOHN,² ROBERT,¹) eldest son of JOSEPH and MINDWELL (KING) PEASE of Suffield, Ct., and second cousin of the preceding, was born at Suffield, May 18, 1757; married Mary Austin, daughter of Seth Austin, October, 1781. Died at Nash-

8

ville, Tenn., April, 1791, aged 37 years, nearly. [New England Historical and Genealogical Register.]

His children were:

633.   1. MARY, b. at   , March 5, 1782.
634.   2. NANCY, b. at   , March 1, 1784.

212.

ZENO PEASE,[6] (JOSEPH,[5] JOSEPH,[4] JOHN,[3] JOHN,[2] ROBERT,[1]) second son of JOSEPH and MINDWELL (KING) PEASE, was born at Suffield, February 2, 1759; married Hannah Leavitt, December 13, 1781; died of dropsy at Suffield, February 3, 1809, aged 50 years.

His children were:

635.   1. ZENO, b. at   , December, 1782. d. an infant.
636.   2. CHARLOTTE, b. at   , January 25, 1784; lives in Suffield, Ct.
637.   3. HANNAH, b. at   , April 9, 1785.   m.   Rising; d. in Suffield.
638.   4. HENRY, b. at Norwich, January 14, 1787.
639.   5. LYDIA, b. at   , June 23, 1789; lives in Suffield, unmarried.
640.   6. CYNTHIA, b. at   , November 28, 1790.
641.   7. CHAUNCEY, b. at   , February 1, 1793.
642.   8. ADALINE, b. at   , August 29, 1801.   m.   East-man, and died in Baltimore, M. D.

213.

DR. OLIVER PEASE,[6] (JOSEPH,[5] JOSEPH,[4] JOHN,[3] JOHN,[2] ROBERT,[1]) third son of JOSEPH and MINDWELL (KING) PEASE, was born at Suffield, July 27, 1760; married Cynthia Smith, daughter of Seth Smith, June 3, 1795; died 1843, aged 83 years. He was a worthy physician of Suffield for more than forty years; town clerk for twenty years or more; a justice of the peace, and for a long time judge of probate for Suffield district.

His child was:

643.   1. EMILY L., b. at Suffield, March 5, 1796.   m.   Clark.

214.

ROYAL PEASE,⁶ (Joseph,⁵ Joseph,⁴ John,³ John,² Robert,¹) fourth son of Joseph and Mindwell (King) Pease, was born at Suffield, April 15, 1762; married Deborah Meacham, December 10, 1798. He removed to Poultney, Vt., where he died, 1830, aged 68 years.

His children were:

644. 1. Delia, b. at   , April 27, 1799.
645. 2. Albert, b. at   , September 18, 1800.
646. 3. Eliza, b. at   . m. Elisha Ward, a counselor, May 28, 1833, and settled at Silver Creek, Chautauque County, N. Y. [New England Genealogical and Historical Register, and History of the Ward Family.]

215.

SETH PEASE,⁶ (Joseph,⁵ Joseph,⁴ John,³ John,² Robert,¹) son of Joseph and Mindwell (King) Pease, was born at Suffield, January 9, 1764; married Bathsheba Kent, December 21, 1785, and died in Philadelphia, September 1, 1819. He was " a man of sterling work, accurate and scientific. He was surveyor-general of the United States for a series of years, and afterwards assistant postmaster-general under Gideon Granger, when he was postmaster-general, during the administration of Jefferson and Madison."

His children were:

647. 1. Betsey, b. at   , April 4, 1786. m. Noah Fletcher, and resides at Washington, D. C., (1868.)
648. 2. James, b. at   , April 10, 1788. d. 1812, unmarried.
649. 3. Gamaliel, b. at Suffield, January 26, 1790.
650. 4. Alfred, b. at   , May 28, 1793.

217.

JOSEPH PEASE,⁶ (Joseph,⁵ Joseph,⁴ John,³ John,² Robert,¹) brother of the preceding, was born at Suffield, September 11, 1766; married Elizabeth Pierce of Suffield, August 18, 1790, and first settled in Suffield, where his wife died, 1829. He died at Carrolton, O., June 1, 1842.

His children were:

651. 1. HORACE, b. at Suffield, February 14, 1791.
652. 2. EDWARD, b. at Suffield, November 3, 1792.
653. 3. PERRY, b. at Suffield, January 23, 1797.
654. 4. GEORGE, b. at Suffield, November 25, 1798.
655. 5. MINDWELL, b. at Suffield, February 10, 1801. She married Daniel W. Norton, Esq., of Suffield, November 28, 1822, and died March 17, 1857. Her children were:
    1. ELIZABETH P., b. February 17, 1826, who m. Calvin Phileo, Esq., November 7, 1840.
    2. LUCY K., b. June 18, 1830.
    3. MARY E., b. June 6, 1836; m. George W. Loomis, June 4, 1860.
    4. JOHN H., b. March 26, 1839.
    5. EMILY L., b. January 19, 1841.
656. 6. ALBERT, b. at Suffield, March 26, 1803. d. in Ohio, unmarried.
657. 7. ELIZABETH, b. at Suffield, April 18, 1805; m. John Hughs; resides at Hagerstown, Ind.
658. 8. MARY, b. at Suffield, October 14, 1806; m. William Machir; resides at Dayton, Ohio.
659. 9. BATHSHEBA, b. at Suffield, January 18, 1810. Never married.
660. 10. ———— a daughter, b. at April, 1812. d. in infancy.
661. 11. JOSEPH, b. at Suffield, July 14, 1818. d. at Carrolton, September 8, 1838, unmarried.

220.

WILLIAM PEASE,[6] (JOSEPH,[5] JOSEPH,[4] JOHN,[3] JOHN,[2] ROBERT,[1]) son of JOSEPH and MINDWELL (KING) PEASE, was born at Suffield, Ct., June 22, 1722; married Zilpha Spencer of Suffield, October 10, 1792; died at Suffield, 1846, aged 78 years.

His children were:

662. 1. LUCY, b. at Suffield, February 10, 1795.
663. 2. DON, b. at Suffield, May 10, 1797.

Calvin Pease

221.

Hon. CALVIN PEASE,⁶ (Joseph,⁵ Joseph,⁴ John,³ John,² Robert,¹) brother of the preceding, was born at Suffield, Ct., September 9, 1776; married Laura G. Risley, daughter of Benjamin Risley, June 22, 1804. Soon after his admission to the bar in his native State, he emigrated to Ohio, then a territory, where he sustained the hardships and privations incident to a pioneer life, and rose to distinction among his fellow-citizens. He was appointed prothonotary of the Court of Common Pleas and quarterly sessions for the county of Trumbull, under the territorial government in the year 1800, which office he held for two or three years; and on the admission of the State of Ohio into the Union, in 1803, he was appointed president judge of the circuit, which at that time embraced a large section of the eastern portion of the State. In 1810, he resigned this office, and continued in the practice of the law till the year 1816. During this interval, in the Fall of 1812 he was elected a senator to the State Legislature. In 1816 he was elected judge of the Supreme Court, and having been re-elected in 1823, continued in this office till 1830, being a period of fourteen years; during a part of which time he was chief judge of the Supreme Court. After leaving the bench, he resumed the practice of the law. For a few of the last years of his life he felt admonished, by increasing infirmities of age, to retire from active business to the enjoyment of private life. He died at his residence, Warren, O., September 17, 1839.

His children were:

664.   1. Calvin, b. at   ; June 4, 1805. Resides in Warren, unmarried, (1865.)
665.   2. Laura M., b. at   , February 28, 1807; married, first, George W. Tallmadge of Tallmadge, Ohio, September 13, 1824, who died September 8, 1835; married, second,

Hon. Van R. Humphrey of Hudson, Ohio, August 27, 1839. Her children by her first marriage were:

1. LAURA P., b. September 3, 1825; d. March 26, 1832.
2. HENRY AUGUSTUS, b. December 12, 1830. He entered the Ninth Ohio Battery in the late war as private, and was promoted to first lieutenant.

Her children by her second marriage were:

1. CALVIN P., b. June 21, 1840; m. Delphina C. Wheeler, September 20, 1864.
2. Clarence, b. August 27, 1846.

666. 3. BENJAMIN R., b. at   , February 22, 1809. d. August 3, 1815.
667. 4. CHARLES, b. at   , Februray 7, 1811.
668. 5. LAWRENCE, b. at   , May 15, 1814. d. July 9, 1815.
669. 6. NANCY, b. at   , June 29, 1816. m. John Ewen of Cleveland, Ohio, June 27, 1836. Her children were:

1. CALVIN P., b. May 17, 1837; d. December 26, 1854.
2. CORNELIA P., b. August 9, 1839; m. Dr. William H. Beaumont of Cleveland, March 24, 1862.
3. LAURA G., b. September 10, 1841; m. Charles E. Pease of Memphis, Tenn., October 3, 1865.
4. LILLY, b. August 26, 1843.
5. ARTHUR, b. October 10, 1845.
6. FLORENCE, b. November 17, 1847.
7. MARY, b. January 29, 1850.
8. KATE G., b. April 9, 1852.
9. GRACE, b. August 24, 1854. d. December 24, 1854.
10. LAWRENCE, b. April 26, 1817.

670. 7. CORNELIA G., b. at   , May 11, 1820; m. Frederick Kinsman of Warren, O., March 25, 1840. Her children were:

1. FREDERICK, b. August 26, 1841.
2. JOHN, b. April 2, 1843.
3. THOMAS, b. March 4, 1846.
4. CHARLES, b. December 7, 1847.
5. HENRY P., b. October 25, 1850.

———o———

222.

PETER PEASE,[6] (STEPHEN,[5] JOSEPH,[4] JOHN,[3] JOHN,[2] ROBERT,[1]) son of STEPHEN and ELIZABETH (   ) PEASE of Somers, last of Springfield, Mass., (Sixteen Acres) and was a first cousin of the preceding. He was born at Somers, February 23, 1760; married Desire Munsell, March 15, 1783. He was by occupation a carpenter, and first settled in East Windsor, Ct., but removed to Hadley, Mass., about 1806, where he died July 4, 1838, aged 77 years. He appears to have enlisted in the continental army, and was in the battle at Germantown, 1777, at the age of 17 years. He was a Revolutionary pensioner.

His children were:

671.   1. Alvin, b. at East Windsor, February 20, 1784.
672.   2. Eliphalet, b. at East Windsor, November 14, 1785.
673.   3. Orrin, b. at East Windsor, January 28, 1788.
674.   4. Peter, b. at East Windsor, January 7, 1790.
675.   5. Lemuel, b. at East Windsor, January 20, 1792.
676.   6. Lucina, b. at East Windsor, May 8, 1794.   m. Henry F. Stanley of Amherst, Mass.
677.   7. Willis, b. at East Windsor, April 16, 1798.
678.   8. Hannah, b. at East Windsor, April 25, 1800.   d. in infancy.
679.   9. Lorin, b. at East Windsor, April 30, 1802.
680. 10. Anna, b. at East Windsor, August 5, 1804.   m. Frederick H. Rhodes, and lives at North Amherst.

226.

AMOS PEASE,⁶ (Stephen,⁵ Joseph,⁴ John,³ John,² Robert,¹) a brother of the preceding, was born at Somers, January 1, 1770; married Polly (Mary) Pease, about 1800.

His children were:

681.   1. Reuben, b. at Enfield, 1802.
682.   2. Harvey, b. at Enfield, March 5, 1805.
683.   3. Phineas, b. at East Windsor, 1806.

230.

DAVID PEASE,⁶ (Jonathan,⁵ Joseph,⁴ John,³ John,² Robert,¹) son of Jonathan and   Pease of Ellington, Ct., and first cousin of the preceding, was born at   1772; married Hannah Post. He removed from Massa-

chusetts and settled at Portland, Me., where he died,
September, 1857, aged 85 years. He was a grocer and
successful business man, and for many years teller in a
bank. Was noted for his upright and systematic discharge of business transactions.

His children were:

684.	1. Lewis, b. at	
685.	2. Mary, b. at	, 1799. m. Amos P.
	Knox of Portland, Me.	
686.	3. Harriett, b. at	. d. young
687.	4. Adaline L., b. at	. m. Hon. Moody
	F. Walker.	
688.	5. Sophia, b. at	m. Alvin Sweetzer.
689.	6. Levi, b. at	. Never married.
690.	7. David, b. at	
691.	8. Jane Maria, b. at	. d. young lady,
	unmarried.	

231.

RUSSELL PEASE,[6] (Jonathan,[5] Joseph,[4] John,[3] John,[2]
Robert,[1]) brother of the preceding, was born at
November 30, 1789; married Margaret Carpenter, and
first settled in Turin, N. Y., subsequently removed to
Middlefield, Mass., where he died, 1864.

His children were:

692.	1. Sarah, b. at Turin, N. Y., February 1, 1823. m. and settled in Hinsdale, Mass.	
693.	2. James, b. at Turin, N. Y., October 22, 1825.	
694.	3. Joel, b. at Turin, N. Y., 1827.	
695.	4. George, b. at Turin, N. Y., April 28, 1829.	
696.	5. Jane, b. at Turin, N. Y., April 24, 1832.	
697.	6. Esther, b. at Turin, N. Y., December 10, 1835. d. unmarried.	
698.	7. Hiram, b. at Turin, N. Y., April 15, 1837. d. unmarried.	
699.	8. Orrin, b. at Turin, N. Y., June 14, 1839.	
700.	9. Lucy, b. at Turin, N. Y., February 19, 1842.	

———o0o———

DESCENT OF ROBERT.³

FAMILY OF ROBERT.⁴

232.

ROBERT PEASE,⁶ (ROBERT,⁵ ROBERT,⁴ ROBERT,³ JOHN,² ROBERT,¹) eldest son of ROBERT and HANNAH (SEXTON) PEASE of Somers, Ct., and third cousin of the preceding, was born at Somers, September 3, 1749; married Ruby Cooley of Springfield, Mass., March 6, 1776; married second, Ann Sexton, March 25, 1779, and settled in the south part of Somers, where he died.

His children were:

701. 1. RUBY, b. at Somers, December 30, 1776.

BY SECOND WIFE:

702. 2. ANN, b. at Somers, June 2, 1779. m. Rev. Luke Wood.
703. 3. DOROTHY, b. at Somers, July 20, 1780.
704. 4. OLIVER, b. at Somers, July 16, 1783.
705. 5. EUNICE, b. at Somers, August 20, 1785. m.   Risley.
706. 6. ROBERT, b. at Somers, December 3, 1790. d. young.
707. 7. ROXANA, b. at   m. John Strong of Salsbury.

235.

STEPHEN PEASE,⁶ (ROBERT,⁵ ROBERT,⁴ ROBERT,³ JOHN,² ROBERT,¹) brother of the preceding, was born at Somers July 4, 1755; married Mary Wood, November 7, 1774; married second, Sarah Morris, November 25, 1782; married third, Roxana Snow. He settled in Somers, was a tanner and shoemaker; died at Somers, June 23, 1838. Was a soldier in the Revolutionary War, and was engaged in the battle of Stillwater at the taking of Burgoyne.

His children were:

708. 1. STEPHEN, b. at Somers, February 25, 1775.
709. 2. MARY, b. at Somers, September 7, 1777. m. Samuel Chapin, 1804, and first settled in Somers; subsequently lived in

9

Springfield, Mass.   M. & E. S. Chapin, proprietors of the
Massasoit House, were their sons.   She died at the Massasoit
House, 1857.   Her children were :

1. MARVIN, b. at Somers.   He married Harriet Stowe of
Westfield, Mass.

2. ETHAN S., b. at Somers, and m.   Burns.

3. ALBERT P., b. at Somers, November 12, 1816 ; m. Olive
Bolton, July 28, and resides in Granby, Mass.

4. HORACE J., b. at Somers, and lives in Springfield, Mass.,
on the Massasoit farm.

710.   3. LOIS, b. at Somers ; m. Oliver F. Pinney of Somers ; d. in
Amherst, Mass., April, 1865.   She had a daughter, Mary,
who married Oliver Pease of Amherst ; also, Caroline, b.
February, 1814 ; m. Henry Burt and resides in Amherst.

711.   4. ABIEL, b. at Somers, February 11, 1780.

BY SECOND WIFE :

712.   5. SARAH, b. at Somers, 1786.   d. July 10, 1820.

BY THIRD WIFE :

713.   6. ERASTUS, b. at Somers, August 30, 1789.
714.   7. AZEL, b. at Somers, February 15, 1795.
715.   8. ENOS, b. at Somers, September 19, 1804.
716.   9. ROXANA, b. at Somers, December 25, 1808 ; m. Lyman Kingsbury, April, 1835, and settled in Amherst ; subsequently
removed to Danville, Ill., and died there.

236.

CAPT. ABNER PEASE,[6] (ROBERT,[5] ROBERT,[4] ROBERT,[3]
JOHN,[2] ROBERT,[1]) third son of ROBERT and HANNAH (SEXTON)
PEASE, was born at Somers, November 9, 1757 ; married
Chloe Viets of Becket, Mass., May 25, 1785.   He removed
to Blandford at the age of 25 years, where he died.

His children were :

717.   1. LEVI, b. at   , May 29, 1787.   d. a member of
College.

718.   2. RUTH, b. at   , September 22, 1789.   m. Orrin Sage,
Esq., now of Ware, Mass., 1817.

719.   3. ELI, b. at Somers, January 23, 1793.
720.   4. CHLOE, b. at   , November 30, 1796.   d. September
17, 1802.

237.

ERASTUS PEASE,⁶ (ROBERT,⁵ ROBERT,⁴ ROBERT,³ JOHN,² ROBERT,¹) fourth son of ROBERT and HANNAH (SEXTON) PEASE, was born at Somers, 1759; married and settled at Newport, R. I. He was, by occupation, a shoemaker, and set up his business in that city about the close of the Revolutionary War, where he died. He had only one child.

721. 1. ANN, b. at Newport. m.   Coe.

238.

MAJOR ALPHEUS PEASE,⁶ (ROBERT,⁵ ROBERT,⁴ ROBERT,³ JOHN,² ROBERT,¹) fifth son of ROBERT and HANNAH (SEXTON) PEASE, was born at Somers, April 16, 1762; married Olive Anderson, 1787, who died, 1799; married, second, Dorothy Spencer, daughter of Jonathan Spencer of Somers, April, 1801. He first settled at Somers. His farm was in the south part of the town. He removed from Somers to Leyden, Lewis County, N. Y., 1803, where he died, 1816, aged 54 years. He served in the Revolutionary War; was taken prisoner by the British, and confined in the prison-ship near New York city, where he suffered greatly from starvation and sickness. He attributed the salvation of his life, under God, to the humanity and kind attentions of the cook, a negro, who, at great risk, so ministered to his wants as to save his life. Prior to his leaving Somers, he was, for some time, employed in business for John Brown of Providence, R. I., which resulted in his removal to what was then called the Black River country, where he settled when it was quite new, and where most of his children now reside. His widow died at West Leyden.

His children were:

722. 1. LUCY, b. at   , 1787. m. Jabez Hartson, and settled at German Flats.

723.　2. Jabez, b. at Somers, June 17, 1788.

724.　3. Olive, b. at Somers, November 6, 1791.　m. Luke Harger, and settled at Boonville, N. Y.

725.　4. Lyman, b. at Somers, July 20, 1793.

726.　5. Hannah, b. at Somers, June 29, 1796.　m. Peter Hartwell, and settled at Clarkson, N. Y.

BY SECOND WIFE:

727.　6. Alpheus, b. at West Leyden, September 11, 1803.

728.　7. Charles, b. at West Leyden, June 11, 1804.

729.　8. Jonathan A. S., b. at West Leyden, March 10, 1810.

239.

CHARLES PEASE,[6] (Robert,[5] Robert,[4] Robert,[3] John,[2] Robert,[1]) sixth and youngest son of Robert and Hannah (Sexton) Pease, was born at Somers, 1764; married Elizabeth Spencer, second daughter of Jonathan Spencer of Somers, 1789. He settled and died at Somers. He entered the army in the Revolution, at the age of 11 years, as a drummer, and, before he was 16, was selected, for his stature and manly form, to carry his musket in a select corps for La Fayette. He was a carpenter and joiner, which he took up of his own teaching, being a natural mechanic, and had only to see a thing in that line to do it, whether a house or a mill. He was an upright man and an exemplary Christian. He died at Somers, 1839, aged 75 years. His widow died, 1853.

His children were:

730.　1. Elizabeth, b. at Somers, September 23, 1790.

731.　2. Panthea, b. at Somers, September 30, 1792.　m. Dea. Asa B. Woods of Windsor Locks, Ct.; died.　She was the mother of Dr. William B. Woods of Somers.

732.　3. Charles, b. at Somers, November 30, 1796.

733.　4. Laurana, b. at Somers, December 3, 1801.

243.

DAVID PEASE,[6] (Emery,[5] Robert,[4] Robert,[3] John,[2] Robert,[1]) eldest son of Emery and Mary (Horton)

PEASE of Somers, Ct., and first cousin to the preceding. He was born at Somers, August 24, 1755; married Jerusha Bellows, November 16, 1779. First settled in Somers, occupying in part the old homestead; but removed from thence.

His children were:

734. 1. DAVID H., b. at Somers, April 17, 1783.
735. 2. ELIAS, b. at Somers, April 28, 1786. d. a child.
736. 3. CYRUS, b. at Somers, February 15, 1804.

244.

EMERY PEASE,⁶ (EMERY,⁵ ROBERT,⁴ ROBERT,³ JOHN,² ROBERT,¹) brother of the preceding, was born at Somers, August 26, 1757; married Sybil Pease, daughter of Isaac Pease of Enfield, Ct., 1783, and lived and died upon the homestead at Somers.

His children were:

737. 1. JABEZ, b. at Somers, January 24, 1784. d. young.
738. 2. EMERY, b. at Somers, April 12, 1789.
739. 3. LUMAN, b. at Somers, July   , 1791.
740. 4. SYBIL, b. at Somers, November 6, 1786. m. Rodolphus Kibbe, son of Capt. Amariah Kibbe of Somers; married, second, Calvin Lancton, and settled in Somers.
741. 5. MARCIA, b. at Somers, October 30, 1794. m. Martin Eno, and settled in Somers.
742. 6. MARY, b. at Somers, September 19, 1802. m. Sumner Root, March 1, 1826, and settled in Somers. She died May 19, 1841. She had a daughter, Mary E., b. June 14, 1830. m. William S. Arms, March 17, 1851, and resides in Springfield, Mass.

245.

DEA. AUGUSTUS PEASE,⁶ (EMERY,⁵ ROBERT,⁴ ROBERT,³ JOHN,² ROBERT,¹) third son of EMERY and MARY (HORTON) PEASE, was born at Somers, July 19, 1759; married Tirzah Hall of Somers, about 1782. She died January 21, 1813. Married second, Rebecca Davis, 1814. His family were by his first marriage. He removed from Somers to Weston, Vt., soon after his first marriage, where he lived, and died of a cancer on his face, November 15, 1851, aged 72 years. He was a deacon in the Congregational Church at Weston, a justice of the peace, and familiarly known as "Capt. Pease," having in his younger days been captain of a militia company. [William Warren, Esq., Weston.] Mr. Pease did military service in the Revolution under his father, who commanded a company, and was at New York, 1776, then 17 years old, highly esteemed and beloved by his associates in arms.

His children were:

743. 1. Lucina, b. at Weston, 1783.   m. Samuel Peabody of Weston, July, 1802.
744. 2. Asenath, b. at Weston, February 24, 1785.   m. James Foster, and settled in Weston.
745. 3. Augustus, b. at Weston, December 15, 1786.
746. 4. Elizabeth, b. at Weston, October 31, 1788.   m. Henry Lovejoy.
747. 5. Abiel, b. at Weston, September 3, 1790.
748. 6. Calvin, b. at Weston, February 25, 1792.
749. 7. Polly, (Mary,) b. at Weston, January 28, 1795.   m. Holt, and lived in Keene, N. H.
750. 8. Ethan H., b. at Weston, September 2, 1796.
751. 9. David, b. at Weston, July 26, 1798.
752. 10. Alpheus, b. at Weston, September 25, 1800.

246.

SYLVANUS PEASE,[6] (Emery,[5] Robert,[4] Robert,[3] John,[2] Robert,[1]) fourth son of Emery and Mary (Horton) Pease, was born at Somers, October 3, 1761; married Asenath Root. He married at somewhat of an advanced age; lived in Somers, where he died without posterity.

249.

GAIUS PEASE,[6] (Emery,[5] Robert,[4] Robert,[3] John,[2] Robert,[1]) fifth and youngest son of Emery and Mary (Horton) Pease, was born at Somers, December 1, 1768; married Wealthy Wolcott. He lived in Somers, was a carpenter and house-joiner, and died at Somers, 1846, aged 78 years.

His children were:

753.   1. Wolcott, b. at   . Was drowned when a child.

754.   2. Augustus Emery, b. at Somers, 1837.   He was in the War of the Rebellion, and connected with the Thirty-seventh Regiment of Massachusetts Volunteers, and was killed in the battle of Winchester, September 19, 1864.

755.   3. Margaret, b. at Somers,   . m. Ralph McClester, and resides at Springfield, Mass.

756.   4. Maria, b. at Somers,   . m. Hiram Davenport, and resides at Springfield, Mass.

---o---

254.

GILES PEASE, Esq.,[6] (Noah,[5] Robert,[4] Robert,[3] John,[2] Robert,[1]) son of Noah and Mary (Ward) Pease of Somers, Ct., and cousin to the preceding, was born at Somers, April 13, 1763; married Jerusha, daughter of Thomas Pitkin, Esq., of Somers, September 26, 1786. He was a successful merchant in Somers, justice of the peace, and a useful and worthy citizen of his day; died at Somers, September 26, 1823.

His children were:

757.   1. Theodore, b. at Somers, January 30, 1789.

758.   2. Noah, b. at Somers, July 1, 1792.

759.   3. Augustus, b. at Somers, October 3, 1793.

760.   4. Jerusha, b. at Somers, July 20, 1796. m. Israel Kellogg of Somers.

761.   5. Rebecca, b. at Somers, January 27, 1798. m. Cyrus Russell, and removed to Missouri, 1838.

762.   6. Henry, b. at Somers, April 12, 1800.

763.   7. Martin, b. at Somers, June 1, 1802.

764.   8. Giles, b. at Somers, December 28, 1804.

765.   9. Giles,[2] b. at Somers, December 2, 1805.

766.   10. Mary, b. at Somers, April 5, 1808. m. Edwin W. Collins, and removed to Rochester, N. Y.

767.   11. Sanford, b. at Somers, June 10, 1810.

---oo---

FAMILY OF SAMUEL.[4]
259.

ELI PEASE,[6] (SAMUEL,[5] SAMUEL,[4] ROBERT,[3] JOHN,[2] ROBERT,[1]) eldest son of SAMUEL and ZERUIAH (CHAPIN) PEASE of Enfield, Ct., and second cousin to the preceding, was born at Enfield, November 12, 1749; married Eunice Bugbee, August 30, 1770; married second, Huldah Kellogg of Westfield, Mass., 1781. He settled in Enfield, and ultimately united with the Shakers.

His children were:

768. 1. JOANNA, b. at Enfield, March 31, 1771.
769. 2. ELI, b. at Enfield, October 17, 1772.
770. 3. JONATHAN, b. at Enfield, January 22, 1778.
771. 4. SAMUEL, b. at Enfield.
772. 5. ANTHONY, b. at Enfield.

261.

ELIAS PEASE,[6] (SAMUEL,[5] SAMUEL,[4] ROBERT,[3] JOHN,[2] ROBERT,[1]) second son of SAMUEL and ZERUIAH (CHAPIN) PEASE, born at Enfield, September 28, 1754; married Mary Parsons, February 15, 1776. He joined the Shakers.

His children were:

773. 1. ELIAS, b. at Enfield,   . d. young.
774. 2. DANIEL.
775. 3. EZRA.
776. 4. RHODA.

265.

EDWARD PEASE,[6] (SAMUEL,[5] SAMUEL,[4] ROBERT,[3] JOHN,[2] ROBERT,[1]) brother of the preceding, was born at Enfield, February 22, 1763; married, first, Hannah Rogers; married, second   . He first settled in Enfield, but subsequently removed to Brookfield, Vt., where he died, July 21, 1840, aged 77 years.

His children were:

777. 1. ELIHU, b. at Enfield, June 24, 1781.
778. 2. ALVIN, b. at Enfield, November 8, 1785.
779. 3. WALTER, b. at Enfield, August 18, 1787.
780. 4. HANNAH, b. at Enfield, September 4, 1789. d. unmarried.
781. 5. SAMUEL, b. at Enfield, August 5, 1791. d. a child.
782. 6. SAMUEL,² b. at Enfield, March 1, 1793. d. a child.
783. 7. EDWARD, b. at Enfield, December 20, 1794; went to Arkansas; no further history known of him.
784. 8. ERASTUS, b. at Enfield, November 12, 1796.
785. 9. ASENATH, b. at Enfield, November 18, 1799. m. Daniel H. Wilson, and lived at Montpelier, Vt.
786. 10. PERSIS, b. at Brookfield, April 24, 1802. d. July 29, 1804.

———o———

275.

AARON PEASE,⁶ (AARON,⁵ SAMUEL,⁴ ROBERT,³ JOHN,² ROBERT,¹) eldest son of AARON and ANN (GEER) PEASE of Enfield, Ct., and cousin to the preceding, was born at Enfield, June 3, 1752; married Huldah Spencer, daughter of Jonathan Spencer, Sen., of Somers, Ct.; lived and died in Enfield.

His children were:

787. 1. HANNAH, b. at Enfield,   . m., first,
        m., second,   Benjamin. She was his widow in 1849.
788. 2. HULDAH, b. at Enfield,   . m. Pliny Cadwell of Wilbraham.
789. 3. TABITHA, b. at Enfield,   . m. Dudley Summers of Chatham, Ct.
790. 4. AURELIA, b. at Enfield,   . m.   Gilbert of Tolland, Ct.
791. 5. RUTH, b. at Enfield,   . d. a young lady, unmarried.
792. 6. JERUSHA, b. at Enfield,   . m. Joseph Sheldon of Hartford, Ct.
793. 7. AARON, b. at Enfield, September 9, 1777.
794. 8. AGIFT, b. at Enfield, September, 1779.
795. 9. LEVI, b. at Enfield.
796. 10. SPENCER, b. at Enfield.
797. 11. RANDOLPH, b. at Enfield, 1788.

276.

LEVI PEASE,[6] (AARON,[5] SAMUEL,[4] ROBERT,[3] JOHN,[2] ROBERT,[1]) brother of the preceding, was born at Enfield, June 22, 1754; married Abiah Pease, a daughter of Robert Pease of .Somers, January 10, 1775, and settled at Somers; married, second, Roxa.

His children were:

798.   1. ABIAH, b. at Somers, October 17, 1775.
799.   2. SARAH, b. at Somers, May 17, 1780.

BY SECOND WIFE:

800.   3. ROXA, b. at Somers, August 20, 1793.

278.

STONE PEASE,[6] (AARON,[5] SAMUEL,[4] ROBERT,[3] JOHN,[2] ROBERT,[1]) brother of the preceding, was born at Enfield, June 11, 1759; married Asenath Pease, daughter of Israel Pease, September 15, 1780. He lived at Enfield.

His children were:

801.   1. STONE, b. at Enfield, July 9, 1781.
802.   2. HORACE, b. at Enfield, July 7, 1783.
803.   3. CHAUNCEY, b. at Enfield, May 4, 1786.
804.   4. ASENATH, b. at Enfield, August 13, 1787.   m. John Hawkins, and settled in Ohio.
805.   5. MARY, b. at Enfield, June 1, 1789.   m. Henry Barber, and settled in East Windsor.
806.   6. CHAUNCEY,[2] b. at Enfield, August 19, 1792.
807.   7. NANCY, b. at Enfield, August   , 1796.   m. Moses Pease, and settled at Enfield.
808.   8. TUDOR, b. at Enfield, February 3, 1799.   d. April, 1843, unmarried.
809.   9. AGNES, b. at Enfield, January 10, 1801.   m. William Loomis, and settled at East Windsor.
810.   10. GEER C., b. at Enfield, December 18, 1804.

280.

EPHRAIM PEASE,[6] (AARON,[5] SAMUEL,[4] ROBERT,[3] JOHN,[2] ROBERT,[1]) brother of the preceding, was born at Enfield, Ct., 1763; married Jemima Phelps, November 24, 1785, and first settled at Enfield; but subsequently removed thence to Lee, N. Y., 1804, where he died.

His children were:

811. ' 1. ARVIN B., b. at Enfield, July 6, 1787.
812.   2. ORRIN, b. at Enfield, December 19, 1788.
813.   3. WILLIS F., b. at Enfield, September 4, 1792. d. young.

283.

ELAM PEASE,[6] (AARON,[5] SAMUEL,[4] ROBERT,[3] JOHN,[2] ROBERT,[1]) son of AARON and his second wife, MARY (TERRY) PEASE of Enfield, Ct., and half brother to the preceding, was born at Enfield, August 26, 1770; married Jemima Bush, 1792; married second, widow Olive (Prentice) Clark. He first settled at Enfield, but removed to Charlton, N. Y., 1798; from thence to Litchfield, Herkimer County, N. Y., and thence to Lee, Oneida County, N. Y., 1800; from Lee he removed to Denmark, Lawrence County, N. Y., in 1822; thence to Copenhagen, a village in Denmark, where he died, January 31, 1853, aged 82 years. He was by occupation a farmer.

His children were:

814. 1. PERSIS, b. at Enfield, December 14, 1792. m. Caleb Ufford of Daytonville, N. Y., in 1822, and died May 22, 1839, aged 47 years.
815. 2. LUCINA B., b. at Enfield, December 26, 1794.' Settled in the City of Rome, N. Y.
816. 3. JEMIMA, b. at Enfield, January 26, 1797. m. A. Frink at Rome, 1818, and died at Vienna, N. Y., in 1828.
817. 4. MARY ANN, b. at Litchfield, March 6, 1799. m. Lathrop Frink, 1821, died in Indiana, in 1837.

818.   5. Louisa, b. at Lee, February 16, 1801. m. A. T. Smith in
            1843, and in 1862 was living a widow in the City of Rome,
            N. Y.

819.   6. Almira, b. at Lee, June 1, 1803. m. John P. Smith, 1829,
            and lived at Norwich, N. Y., 1861.

820.   7. Augustus E., b. at Lee, September 9, 1805. d. 1820.

821.   8. Agnes Eliza, b. at Lee, November 17, 1807. m. Elam Brown,
            April 30, 1861, and lives at Champion, N. Y.

822.   9. Clarissa, b. at Lee, December 26, 1812. Lived at Rome,
            1861.

823. 10. Henry F., b. at Lee, May 23, 1815. d. March   , 1823.

BY SECOND WIFE:

824. 11. Elam C., b. at Denmark, N. Y., April 23, 1835.

———o———

285.

PHINEAS PEASE,[6] (Nathaniel,[5] Samuel,[4] Robert,[3]
John,[2] Robert,[1]) eldest son of Nathaniel and Eunice
(Allen) Pease, first, of Enfield, Ct., last, of Norfolk, Ct.,
and cousin to the preceding, was born at Enfield, January
9, 1755; married Betsey Lawrence of Canaan, Ct., daughter of Nehemiah Lawrence of that place, November 25,
1779; died at Stockbridge, Mass., the place of his residence, July 11, 1836, aged 82 years. His wife died April
10, 1837, aged 74 years. He was a tanner and shoemaker; served as a musician in the Revolutionary War.
—[New England Historical and Genealogical Register.]
There is a story related by a respectable man who served
his apprenticeship with him, in testimony of his reputation as an honest and upright man. He says that Mr.
Pease purchased a tract of land of an Indian, among the
remaining natives of that place. A part of the price
was paid down, the remainder, to a large amount, was put
in a note to be paid at a stipulated time or times. The
Indian one day came to Mr. Pease, saying he was going
off to a distance, hunting, and expected to be gone a long
time, and did not know what might happen, and desiring

the note to be in safe keeping, wished he would "take him, and keep him, until he returned." Mr. Pease told him that was not the way of doing business; possibly he might not be honest and give up the note on his return, and so cheat him out of his money. "No," said the Indian, "Mr. Pease be good man;—he be honest;—he no cheat poor Indian;" and so it proved, for Mr. Pease took the note, and after many months the Indian returned, and the note was restored, and in due time cancelled. [As given in the New England Historical and Genealogical Register.]

His children were:

825. 1. FLAVIUS, b. at   , November 23, 1780.

826. 2. SARAH B., b. at   , January 30, 1783. m. Minorias Day, August 21, 1804.

827. 3. PELERA, b. at   , February 6, 1785. m. Asahel Byington, September 10, 1807. d. at Carlton, N. Y., September 4, 1828.

828. 4. MARTHA A., b. at   , December 19, 1786. d. September 29, 1847, aged 61 years.

829. 5. ELIZABETH L., b. at   , October 16, 1788. m. Alfred Avery, October 15, 1816.

830. 6. ELECTA, b. at   , February 22, 1791. m. Henry Lincoln, November 10, 1815.

831. 7. PHINEAS, b. at   , December 19, 1792. d. at Rochester, N. Y., September 3, 1818, aged 26 years.

832. 8. PETER P., b. at   , April 12, 1795.

833. 9. HIRAM A., b. at   , April 19, 1797.

834. 10. ALONZO, b. at   , August 4, 1799. Was drowned 1802, aged about 3 years.

835. 11. AURELIA, b. at   , August 7, 1801. m. Daniel F. Milliken, January 6, 1820.

836. 12. AMANDA, S., b. at   , April 18, 1804. m. Ira Patterson, August 28, 1837.

286.

CALVIN PEASE,⁶ (NATHANIEL,⁵ SAMUEL,⁴ ROBERT,³ JOHN,² ROBERT,¹) brother of the preceding, was born at Enfield, September 14, 1757; married Sally, daughter of

Titus Ives—the mother of all his children. Married second, Susan, widow of Joseph Benjamin, of Sheffield, or Egremont, Mass. He was a farmer, and for many years an innkeeper in Canaan, Ct., where he died. He was in the Revolutionary War as a drummer.

His children were :

837. 1. SALMON, b. at   , June 14, 1783.
838. 2. NEHEMIAH P., b. at   , May 1, 1789.
839. 3. SALLY, b. at   , May 1, 1792. d. young.
[Enfield Town Records, and New England Historical and Genealogical Register.]

288.

ALLEN PEASE,[6] (NATHANIEL,[5] SAMUEL,[4] ROBERT,[3] JOHN,[2] ROBERT,[1]) third son of NATHANIEL and EUNICE (ALLEN) PEASE, was born at   October 12, 1762; married Rachael Tibballs of Norfolk, Ct.; married second, Tamsin Sears of Sharon, Ct. He was a clothier; died in Sheffield, Mass., April 8, 1843, aged 81 years.

His children were :

840. 1. ARTEMESIA, b. at   , October 11, 1787. d. January 21, 1789.
841. 2. ELECTA, b. at   , September 6, 1792. m. James Collar.
842. 3. URI, b. at   , February 20, 1794. d. October 11, 1798.
843. 4. SARAH, b. at   , September 15, 1795. m. Henry Sardam.
844. 5. HARLOW, b. at   , April 17, 1798.
845. 6. EUNICE, b. at   , March 13, 1806. m. Philo C. Howland.
846. 7. JOHN S., b. at   , July 17, 1807.

289.

NATHANIEL PEASE,[6] (NATHANIEL,[5] SAMUEL,[4] ROBERT,[3] JOHN,[2] ROBERT,[1]) fourth son of NATHANIEL and EUNICE (ALLEN) PEASE, was born at Goshen, Ct., October

22, 1764; married Jerusha, daughter of Dea.
Hall of Norfolk, Ct.; died at Poughkeepsie, N. Y., November 6, 1815, aged 51 years. He was a blacksmith.

His children were:

847. 1. DUDLEY S., b. at   , March 5, 1785.
848. 2. GROVE A., b. at Norfolk, August 4, 1789.
849. 3. ALMIRA, b. at   ,   , 1792. m. Oliver Dubois, 1817, and removed to New Orleans, La.
850. 4. ELIZABETH, b. at   , 1795. m.   Anthony of Zanesville, Ohio.

290.

OBADIAH PEASE,⁶ (NATHANIEL,⁵ SAMUEL,⁴ ROBERT,³ JOHN,² ROBERT,¹) fifth son of NATHANIEL and EUNICE (ALLEN) PEASE, was born at Goshen, Ct., November 21, 1766; married Daziah Pettibone of Norfolk; was a tanner and shoemaker. Died at Norfolk, February 10, 1809, aged 43 years.

His children were:

851. 1. DAZIAH, b. at   , October 10, 1789. m. Abel Camp of Litchfield, Ct., February 22, 1808.
852. 2. AUGUSTUS P., b. at   , June 8, 1792.
853. 3. HENRIETTA, b. at   , February 6, 1795. m. Jedadiah Phelps of Norfolk, April 6, 1818.
854. 4. OBADIAH, b. at Norfolk, Ct., December 1, 1798.
855. 5. AGNES, b. at   , July, 1800. d. an infant.
856. 6. EMILY A., b. at   , November 20, 1804. m. Marshall H. Weed of Litchfield, Ct., April 2, 1834.

296.

EARL P. PEASE,⁶ (NATHANIEL,⁵ SAMUEL,⁴ ROBERT,³ JOHN,² ROBERT,¹) youngest son of NATHANIEL and EUNICE (ALLEN) PEASE, was born at Norfolk, Ct., July 30, 1778; married Mary Ives, daughter of Joseph Ives, of New Haven, April 8, 1802. He learned the trade of a clothier with his brother Allen, in Sharon, Ct. He established the first factory for woolen cloths in his native town. He was active and foremost in many enterprises of his times. About the year 1825, Mr. Pease removed to Hartford, Ct., and in 1829, to Albany, N. Y., where he remained several years. He subsequently removed to Brooklyn, N. Y., and died there, February 11, 1864. His last wish, almost his last words, were "Lay me beside my mother—Bury me beside my mother." His dying request was gratified. The following affecting lines composed by his eldest son were most feelingly read by the officiating clergyman as he was lowered to his final resting-place:

I.

"Lay me beside my mother!" such the word
    The pale lips of the dying grandsire said;
The listening ear a feebler echo heard—
    "Bury me by my mother, when I'm dead."

II.

For fourscore years, the wintry storms of life,
    Drifted their snows upon his heart and head;
The spring-time comes at last, with gladness rife,
    And all is sunshine now where all was shade.

III.

Through the last dreary hours of woe and pain,
    Sweet dreams of boyhood days around him played;
The long lost home scenes came to him again;
    Beside the babbling brook again he strayed.

IV.

Forgotten all the long and dreary years;
    The tumult and the toil, for fame or bread;
New lands he sees, new music now he hears,
    O'er the green pastures—by the still waters led.

V.

A loving nature! oft and sorely tried;
    With scars unseen, and wounds that inly bled;
Piercing life's shams, what wonder that he cried,
    "Lay me beside my mother, when I'm dead!"

VI.

And now he sleeps beside that faithful breast,
   Prone on the native hills he loved to tread,
"After life's fitful fever" calm he'll rest,
   Till earth and sea give up their countless dead.

VII.

Oh! mother, Love! that throbs through all disguise,
   The first, last pillow of man's aching head;
God grant this prayer, written with streaming eyes,
   Bury me by my mother, when I'm dead.

His children were:

857. 1. MARY E., b. at Canaan, Ct., March 19, 1803. m. Enoch Noyes at East Hartford, Ct., March 18, 1828. d. at Albany, November 21, 1829.
858. 2. JOSEPH I., b. at Norfolk, August 9, 1809.
859. 3. RICHARD H., b. at Norfolk, February 12, 1813.
860. 4. ROGER M. S., b. at Norfolk, January 13, 1822.

——∞——

FAMILY OF DANIEL.⁴

299.

WILLIAM PEASE,⁶ (DANIEL,⁵ DANIEL,⁴ ROBERT,³ JOHN,² ROBERT,¹) eldest son of DANIEL and HANNAH (JONES) PEASE, first of Somers and last of Canaan, N. Y., and second cousin to the preceding, was born at Somers, October 29, 1752; married   and settled at Canaan, N. Y.

His children were:

861. 1. ALANSON, b. at Canaan, 1779.
862. 2. WILLIAM, b. at Canaan, March 4, 1781.
863. 3. WALTER, b. at Canaan, May 24, 1785.
864. 4. WARREN, b. at Canaan, January, 1789.
865. 5. DORUS, b. at Canaan.
866. 6. RHODA, b. at Canaan.
867. 7. LAURA, b. at Canaan, 1793. d. aged 14 years.
    [Furnished by William Pease of Pompey.]

11

/ **300.**

DANIEL PEASE,[6] (DANIEL,[5] DANIEL,[4] ROBERT,[3] JOHN,[2] ROBERT,[1]) brother of the preceding, was born at Somers, February 11, 1754. [Somers Town Records.] Married Keziah Dean. He removed from Somers to Canaan, Columbia County, N. Y., with his father when five years old, where he died, February 4, 1798, aged 44 years. His widow died October 11, 1806.

His children were :

868.   1. RACHAEL, b. at Canaan, September 9, 1780. m. Amos Stone.
869.   2. DANIEL, b. at Canaan, May 7, 1782.
870.   3. SYLVIA, b. at Canaan, August 17, 1784. m. Joseph Norton of Fabius, N. Y.; m., second, Capt. Jona. Farnam of Cazenovia.
871.   4. LEWIS, b. at Canaan, August 7, 1786.
872.   5. PHILO, b. at Canaan, February 21, 1788.
873.   6. CHLOE, b. at Canaan, May 18, 1791. m. Rev. Phineas Cook of the Methodist Episcopal Church.
874.   7. LOVISA, b. at Canaan, April 18, 1793. m. Charles Law.
875.   8. JOHN B., b. at Canaan, July 9, 1795.
876.   9. ELIZABETH, b. at Canaan, October 27, 1797. m. Matthew Brogue.
877.   10. WILLIAM S., b. at Canaan, April 18, 1800.
878.   11. ELECTA, b. at Canaan, July 28, 1802. m. Almon Ticknor.
[Family Records by Mrs. Sylvia Farnam.]

305.

EPHRAIM PEASE,[6] (DANIEL,[5] DANIEL,[4] ROBERT,[3] JOHN,[2] ROBERT,[1]) brother of the preceding, was born at Somers, June, 1764; married Sarah Wright, 1790, and first settled in Canaan, N. Y. In 1821 he removed to Lisle, Broome County, N. Y., where he died September 12, 1846. He was a farmer.

His children were :

879.   1. WILLIAM R., b. at Canaan, January 13, 1791.
880.   2. SARAH D., b. at Canaan, September 25, 1794. m. John Kendall, May 27, 1822, and resides in Richford, Tioga County, N. Y.

881. 3. HANNAH G., b. at Canaan, May 25, 1797. m. Demas Orton, January 20, 1817. d. in Lisle, January 27, 1854, leaving three children; two sons, Henry and James, served in the Twenty-first Regiment New York Cavalry under Gen. Sheridan.

882. 4. NANCY D., b. at Canaan, July 14, 1799. m. E. P. Higbee, Esq., and resides in Newark, N. Y.

883. 5. POLLY, b. at Canaan, April 19, 1802. m. Dan Culver, 1820, and lived in Lisle. d. 1832.

884. 6. EPHRAIM B., b. at Canaan, September 21, 1806.

885. 7. LUCINA A., b. at Canaan, August 5, 1810. m. Henry Folk, September 9, 1832; removed to Ohio, and died at Marion, February 21, 1841. One of her sons, Richard E., was in the Red River expedition, and died there. Another, William H., is supposed to have died in a rebel prison.

886. 8. ELIZABETH E., b. at Canaan, January 22, 1815. m. Samuel Granger. d. at Richford, N. Y., April 12, 1858.

887. 9. HENRY F., b. at Canaan, April 5, 1817.

————o o————

FAMILY OF EBENEZER.⁴

307.

EBENEZER PEASE,⁶ (EBENEZER,⁵ EBENEZER,⁴ ROBERT,³ JOHN,² ROBERT,¹) eldest son of EBENEZER and MARY (TERRY) PEASE of Enfield, Ct., and second cousin of the preceding, was born at Enfield, October 16, 1742; married Huldah Pease, daughter of Nathaniel and Miriam Pease, July 5, 1771, and first settled in Enfield, Ct.

His children were:

888. 1. HULDAH, b. at Enfield, January 9, 1772. m. Charles Terry of Enfield.

889. 2. JOHN B., b. at Enfield, September 9, 1774.

890. 3. GEORGE, b. at Enfield.

891. 4. EBENEZER, b. at

892. 5. NATHANIEL, b. at

893. 6. LUCRETIA, b. at   m. Truman Barnard of Whitestown, N. Y.

894. 7. ANN, b. at   m. Shelburn Ives of Litchfield, Ct.

895. 8. HEPZIBAH, b. at
896. 9. MARTHA, b. at
    [Enfield Town Records and New England Historical and
      Genealogical Register.]

311.

JAMES PEASE,[6] (EBENEZER,[5] EBENEZER,[4] ROBERT,[3]
JOHN,[2] ROBERT,[1]) brother of the preceding, was born at
Enfield, December 14, 1754; married Lucy Meacham,
December 30, 1778, and settled soon after his marriage
in East Windsor, Ct. He removed from there in 1796 to
the old town of Partridgefield, (now Peru,) and in that
part which is now Hinsdale, Berkshire County, Mass. In
1817 he removed to Auburn, N. Y., where he died August
, 1844.

His children were:

897. 1. JAMES, b. at   about 1781.
898. 2. JABEZ, b. at East Windsor, March 30, 1783.
899. 3. ERASTUS, b. at East Windsor, May 30, 1785.
900. 4. LUCY, b. at East Windsor, November 22, 1788. m. David
       Buck, and settled in Auburn, N. Y.
901. 5. RUFUS, b. at East Windsor, June 1, 1790. d. 1800.
902. 6. NANCY, b. at East Windsor, October 2, 1792. m. Alpheus
       Paine and resided at Batavia, N. Y.
903. 7. AURELIA, b. at   . m.   Williams

312.

PETER PEASE,[6] (EBENEZER,[5] EBENEZER,[4] ROBERT,[3]
JOHN,[2] ROBERT,[1]) brother of the preceding, was born at
Enfield, October 14, 1763; married Huldah Stebbins of
Springfield, Mass., November 25, 1785, and settled at En-
field, where he died June 25, 1822, aged 60 years.

His children were:

904. 1. FRANCIS, b. at Enfield, July 8, 1787.
905. 2. WILLIAM, b. at Enfield, April 21, 1790.
906. 3. MARGARET, b. at Enfield, July 16, 1792. m. Horace Hawkins.
907. 4. PETER P., b. at Enfield, May 3, 1797. d. in South Carolina.

908. 5. HULDAH, b. at Enfield, July 18, 1799. m. Solomon Silsbee of
Reading, Steuben County, N. Y.
909. 6. MARY, b. at Enfield, February 7, 1804. m. C. Allen of Enfield.
910. 7. HORATIO N., b. at Enfield, April 29, 1806.
[Enfield Town Records, and New England Historical and'
Genealogical Register.]

———○○○———

DESCENT OF JONATHAN.³

FAMILY OF JOSIAH.⁴

315.

AARON PEASE,⁶ (JOSIAH,⁵ JOSIAH,⁴ JONATHAN,³ JOHN,²
ROBERT,¹) eldest son of JOSIAH and LYDIA (   )
PEASE of Upton, Mass., and third cousin of the preceding,
was born at Upton, November 25, 1770; married
               and settled in Upton. From thence he re-
moved to Dover, Vt., and subsequently to St. Albans, Vt.

His children were :

911. 1. AARON, b. at
912. 2. CHARLES A., b. at

316.

JOSIAH PEASE,⁶ (JOSIAH,⁵ JOSIAH,⁴ JONATHAN,³ JOHN,²
ROBERT,¹) brother of the preceding, was born at Upton,
May 25, 1774; married Polly Beals, and lived at Upton
until 1821, when he removed to Middlebury, Vt. In
1822 he removed to Norfolk, St. Lawrence County, N. Y.,
where he was killed by the fall of a tree in 1830.

His children were:

913. 1. MARY, b. at Upton, September 28, 1801. m. Amos Stearns,
and settled at Upton, where she d. July 7, 1850.
914. 2. BETSY, b. at Upton, June 24, 1803. m. Sumner S. White, and
settled in Upton, where she d. November 30, 1825.
915. 3. ORTON, b. at Upton, March 30, 1806.
916. 4. LYDIA, b. at Upton,   , 1808. m. John E. Chard,
February, 1845, and resides in New Haven, Ct.

917. 5. ANN J., b. at Upton, September 26, 1810. m. John J. McLoy, December 25, 1835, and resides at Valleyfield, Beauharnois County, Canada East.
918. 6. LUCY, b. at Upton, August 21, 1812. m. John Madden, and d. in Canada, June, 1849.
919. 7. LOUISA, b. at Upton, September 10, 1814. m. Oliver S. Kent, November 27, 1844, and resides in Upton, Mass.
920. 8. DANIEL B., b. at Upton, June 9, 1819.

———oo———

FAMILY OF PELATIAH.[4]

318.

PELATIAH PEASE,[6] (PELATIAH,[5] PELATIAH,[4] JONA-THAN,[3] JOHN,[2] ROBERT,[1]) son of PELATIAH and PEASE of   , and second cousin of the preceding.

319.

JONATHAN PEASE,[6] (PELATIAH,[5] PELATIAH,[4] JONA-THAN,[3] JOHN,[2] ROBERT,[1]) son of PELATIAH and PEASE of

320.

NOADIAH PEASE,[6] (PELATIAH,[5] PELATIAH,[4] JONA-THAN,[3] JOHN,[2] ROBERT,[1]) son of PELATIAH and PEASE of

321.

OLIVER PEASE,[6] (PELATIAH,[5] PELATIAH,[4] JONATHAN,[3] JOHN,[2] ROBERT,[1]) son of PELATIAH and   PEASE of

———o———

322.

SAMUEL PEASE,[6] (SAMUEL,[5] PELATIAH,[4] JONATHAN,[3] JOHN,[2] ROBERT,[1]) was the eldest son of SAMUEL and HAN-NAH (BOOTH) PEASE of Enfield, Ct., and first cousin of the preceding, was born at Enfield, September 6, 1770; married widow Gibbs. He was a farmer and common school teacher, and known as Capt. Samuel Pease; died in Enfield, aged 82 years. He had no issue.

325.

DEACON JONATHAN PEASE,⁶ (SAMUEL,⁵ PELATIAH,⁴ JONATHAN,³ JOHN,² ROBERT,¹) brother to the preceding, was born at Enfield, January 22, 1778; married Eleanor Gleason, October 6, 1800, and settled at Enfield. He was for many years a Deacon in the First Congregational Church in that town. He is, by occupation, a farmer, and lives in the south-east part of the town. (1868.)

His children were:

921.   1. JONATHAN, b. at Enfield, September 5, 1801.
922.   2. OSEE, b. at Enfield, August 30, 1803.
   923.   3. HANNAH B., b. at Enfield, November 3, 1807.
924.   4. LATHROP, b. at Enfield, October 26, 1809.
   925.   5. NANCY G., b. at Enfield, July 5, 1813.
   926.   6. LUCINDA and ⎫
   927.   7. SOPHRONIA,   ⎬ b. at Enfield, July 3, 1816.
928.   8. SAMUEL R., b. at Enfield, July 25, 1820.
929.   9. SOLOMON G., b. at Enfield, September 24, 1822.

330.

JOHN PEASE,⁶ (JOHN,⁵ PELATIAH,⁴ JONATHAN,³ JOHN,² ROBERT,¹) eldest son of JOHN and BEULAH (BOOTH) PEASE of Enfield, Ct., and cousin to the preceding, was born at Enfield, August 23, 1777; married Patty Allen, April 25, 1799. He removed to Conway, Mass., May 2, 1800. There he continued until February, 1811, when he removed to Ashfield, Mass., where he died. He was a farmer, and in early life, a common school and sacred music teacher.

His children were:

930. 1. MARTHA, b. at Enfield, March 19, 1800.   m. Sumner Graves.
931. 2. JOHN, b. at Conway, November, 1801.
932. 3. MIRIAM, b. at Conway, March 14, 1804.   m. Lovell H. Oakes,
           lived in Ellington, Ct., and d. in 1864.
933. 4. DAVID A., b. at Conway, December 9, 1805.
934. 5. LUMAN, b. at Conway, August 26, 1808.
935. 6. DIANTHA, b. at Conway, February 11, 1810.   m. Daniel Clark,
           settled in Conway, and d. December, 1864.
936. 7. HART F., b. at Conway, December 27, 1811.
937. 8. MARONETT, b. at Ashfield, November 21, 1813.   m. James
           Childs, and settled in South Deerfield.
938. 9. REUEL, b. at Ashfield, October 6, 1815.
939. 10. GEORGE, b. at Ashfield, March 20, 1817.
940. 11. LIBERTY, b. at Ashfield, December 19, 1822.

331.

ASHER PEASE,[6] (JOHN,[5] PELATIAH,[4] JONATHAN,[3] JOHN,[2] ROBERT,[1]) second son of JOHN and BEULAH (BOOTH) PEASE of Enfield, Ct., brother of the preceding, was born at Enfield, September 21, 1780; married Elizabeth Chaffee. He settled at Conway, Mass.

His children were:

941. 1. NEWTON, b. at Conway.
942. 2. FRANKLIN, b. at Conway.
943. 3. LORIN, b. at Conway.
944. 4. ELIZA, b. at Conway.
945. 5. MARIA, b. at Conway.
946. 6. BEULAH, b. at Conway.
947. 7. HARRIET, b. at Conway.
948. 8. CAROLINE, b. at Conway.

332.

LYMAN PEASE,[6] (JOHN,[5] PELATIAH,[4] JONATHAN,[3] JOHN,[2] ROBERT,[1]) brother of the preceding, was born at Enfield, May 26, 1784; married Fanny Chaffee. He removed from Enfield, soon after his marriage, to Southampton, Mass., also resided some time at Easthampton, likewise at Springfield, Mass.; finally emigrated to Michigan, and was living at Jackson City, in that State, 1858.

His children were:

949. 1. WILLIAM, b. at Enfield, June 30, 1805.
950. 2. MARY A., b. at Southampton,   . m. Stephen
        Field, 1834. d. 1848.
951. 3. LYMAN, b. at Southampton,   , 1808.
952. 4. FANNY, b. at Southampton,   , 1811. m. Alfred Driggs, and settled at St. Joseph, Mich.
953. 5. LORENZO, b. at Easthampton,   , 1813.
954. 6. ADALINE, b. at Easthampton,   , 1815. m. Sumner Wing, 1834. d. 1856, at Jackson, Mich., aged 41 years.
955. 7. DOROTHY, b. at Easthampton,   , 1817. m. William Morey of Vermont, and d. 1839.
956. 8. PHILANDER, b. at Easthampton, December   , 1820.
957. 9. HENRY, b. at Springfield,   , 1827.
        [Furnished by Lyman Pease, Jackson City, Michigan, 1858.]

———ooo———

DESCENT OF JAMES.³

FAMILY OF JOSEPH⁴ (OF JAMES.³)

333.

CAPT. JUSTUS PEASE,⁶ (WAREHAM,⁵ JOSEPH,⁴ JAMES,³ JOHN,² ROBERT,¹) eldest son of WAREHAM and JERUSHA (KENT) PEASE, of Suffield, Ct., and third cousin to the preceding, was born at Suffield; married Esther Warner, and lived and died in Suffield.

His children were:

958. 1. ESTHER, b. at Suffield, October   , 1784. m. Samuel Griffin, and lived at Suffield, 1860.
959. 2. JUSTUS, b. at Suffield, November 12, 1786.
960. 3. BEULAH, b. at Suffield, September   , 1789. d. at Suffield, 1841; it appears unmarried; aged 52 years.
        12

961. 4. Lovisa, b. at Suffield,   , 1791. m. Lewis
        Langdon, and lived in Indiana, 1860.
962. 5. Delight, b. at Suffield, March 18, 1794. m. Ebenezer K.
        Mason of Southwick, Mass. d. 1843, aged 49 years.
963. 6. Anna, b. at Suffield. July 28, 1796.
964. 7. Jerusha, b. at Suffield, June   , 1798. m. Jonathan R. Pomeroy.
965. 8. Lester J., b. at Suffield, October 5, 1800.
966. 9. Betsey, b. at Suffield, April   , 1802. m. Amos Webb of
        Southwick, and was living there, 1860.
967. 10. Mary, b. at Suffield, May 17, 1804. m. Sidney Moore of
        Granby, Ct.
968. 11. Philo P., b. at Suffield, January 13, 1806.
969. 12. Sybil, b. at Suffield April 26, 1808. m. Newton Day of
        Granby, Ct., 1834.

334.

SILAS PEASE,[6] (Wareham,[5] Joseph,[4] James,[3] John,[2] Robert,[1]) brother to the preceding, was born at Suffield, probably, somewhere about 1760, and died in the State of New York, about 1834, over 70 years old. He married at Neversink, N. Y. He served in the Revolutionary Army, and was one of the "*during the war*" soldiers, and a pensioner of that class, and was thought to have lost much of his money by unfair dealing on the part of those who aided him in procuring it, which made him unhappy in his last years. The history of him is, as yet, quite imperfect. He is said to have lived some time at Skaneateles, N. Y.; had four children,— two sons and two daughters.

His children were:

970. 1.
971. 2.
972. 3.
973. 4.

335.

TITUS PEASE,[6] (Wareham,[5] Joseph,[4] James,[3] John,[2] Robert,[1]) brother of the preceding, was born at   married Mary Bagg, and lived and died at Westfield, Mass.

His children were:

974. 1. MARY, b. at   m. Franklin Arthur
          of Westfield.
975. 2. ISABEL, b. at   ·   d. unmarried.
976. 3. TITUS, b. at
977. 4. ELIZA, b. at   m. Daniel Bush.
978. 5. FREDERICK G., b. at Westfield, September 8, 1808.
979. 6. CLARISSA, b. at   m. Daniel Bush.
980. 7. MARIETTA, b. at   m. Daniel Stocking.

336.

GROVE PEASE,⁶ (WAREHAM,⁵ JOSEPH,⁴ JAMES,³ JOHN,²
ROBERT,¹) fourth son of WAREHAM and JERUSHA (KENT)
PEASE, was born at Suffield, December 12, 1780; married
Fannie Noble, 1803. He lived at Westfield and died
there, in 1820, aged 40 years.

His children were:

981. 1. MARIA, b. at Westfield,   ; 1804. d. an infant.
982. 2. MARIA,² b. at Westfield,   , 1805.
983. 3. ORSON, b. at Westfield, March 28, 1807. d. a child.
984. 4. NANCY, b. at Westfield, July 10, 1810. m. Ephraim Crary,
          1850.
985. 5. LOTON, b. at Westfield, July 29, 1813. d. a child.
986. 6. JANE, b. at Westfield, September 5, 1818. d. a child. .

340.

WAREHAM PEASE,⁶ (WAREHAM,⁵ JOSEPH,⁴ JAMES,³
JOHN,² ROBERT,¹) youngest son of WAREHAM and JERU-
SHA (KENT) PEASE, was born at Suffield, about 1784;
married Lucy Wright and settled at Westfield, Mass.;
was, by occupation, a hatter; died at Westfield, 1858,
aged 74 years.

His children were:

987. 1. BENJAMIN F., b at
988. 2. MARY, b. at Westfield. d. a young lady.

———o———

344.

JOSIAH PEASE,[6] (JAMES,[5] JOSEPH,[4] JAMES,[3] JOHN,[2] ROBERT,[1]) only son of JAMES and SARAH (COLTON) PEASE of Somers, Ct., and cousin to the preceding, was born at Somers, September 9, 1783; married Relief Wakefield, and settled in Somers; died, 1860, aged 77 years.

His children were:

989. 1. MARY, b. at Somers, April 10, 1814.
990. 2. WILLIAM, b. at Somers, September 21, 1816.
991. 3. LUCINDA, b. at Somers, August 29, 1817. m. W. Parsons
         Simons of Enfield.
992. 4. CHESTER, b. at Somers, May 3, 1819.
993. 5. FIDELIA, b. at Somers, January 8, 1821.
994. 6. JAMES, b. at Somers, December 14, 1823.

———o———

348.

JAMES PEASE,[6] (EBENEZER,[5] JOSEPH,[4] JAMES,[3] JOHN,[2] ROBERT,[1]) son of EBENEZER and SARAH (ROOT) PEASE of Canaan, N. Y., and first cousin to the preceding, was born at Canaan, N. Y., probably, in 1793; married Phebe Cogswell of Richmond, Mass., and lived in Pittsfield, Mass.; was by occupation, a tanner and currier. He was accidentally drowned at, or near Northampton, June 22, 1820.

His children were:

995. 1. HENRIETTA E., b. at Pittsfield,   , 1814. m. Henry
         B. Burt of Pittsfield, and removed to Buffalo, N. Y., where
         she died, 1858.
996. 2. JAMES R., b. at Pittsfield, May 7, 1817.
997. 3. RALPH P., b. at Pittsfield, November 17, 1820.

349.

GIDEON PEASE,[6] (EBENEZER,[5] JOSEPH,[4] JAMES,[3] JOHN,[2] ROBERT,[1]) son of EBENEZER and SARAH (ROOT) PEASE of Canaan, N. Y., and brother of the preceding, was born at
; married

351.

NOBLE PEASE,⁶ (EBENEZER,⁵ JOSEPH,⁴ JAMES,³ JOHN,²
ROBERT,¹) son of EBENEZER and SARAH (ROOT) PEASE of
Canaan, N. Y., and brother of the preceding.

———ooo———

DESCENT OF ISAAC.³

FAMILY OF ISAAC.⁴

355.

JEHIEL PEASE,⁶ (ISAAC,⁵ ISAAC,⁴ ISAAC,³ JOHN,² ROB-
ERT,¹) eldest son of ISAAC and RACHEL (HALL) PEASE of
Enfield, Ct., and third cousin of the preceding, was born
at Enfield, May 3, 1750; married Hepsah Dodge. He
left Enfield and settled in Sandisfield, Mass., where he had
a family; but all left Sandisfield.

His children were:

998. 1. ELAM, b. at Sandisfield.
999. 2. FRANCIS, b. at
1000. 3. ELIJAH and ⎫
1001. 4. ELISHA,   ⎬ twins, b. at
1002. 5. ISAAC, b. at

356.

SOLOMON PEASE,⁶ (ISAAC,⁵ ISAAC,⁴ ISAAC,³ JOHN,²
ROBERT,¹) brother of the preceding, was born at Enfield,
September 14, 1751; married Keziah Hall of Somers.
He removed from Enfield to Hatfield, Mass., where he re-
sided for some time. From thence he removed to Heath,
Mass., and afterwards (about 1811) to Winhall, Vt. He
was a farmer and hay-rake manufacturer.

His children were:

1003. 1. ROSWELL, b. at
1004. 2. CYNTHIA, b. at

1005. 3. Solomon, b. at
1006. 4. Hannah, b. at
1007. 5. Keziah, b. at
1008. 6. Levi, b. at

357.

ISAAC PEASE,[6] (Isaac,[5] Isaac,[4] Isaac,[3] John,[2] Robert,[1]) brother of the preceding, was born at Enfield, June 14, 1753; married Dorcas Pease, daughter of Timothy Pease of Enfield, October 16, 1778. He first settled in Enfield, subsequently removed to Ohio and settled at Bondstown.

His children were:

1009. 1. Chandler, b. at Enfield, August 24, 1779.
1010. 2. Abigail, b. at Enfield, April 22, 1781. m. Noah Ashley of Springfield, Mass.
1011. 3. Dorcas, b. at Enfield, August 8, 1783. m. Henry Brown, August 4, 1816. d. January 2, 1837.
1012. 4. Anson, b. at Enfield, January 18, 1787.
1013. 5. Merrick, b. at Enfield, January 17, 1789.
1014. 6. Tabitha, b. at Enfield, January 21, 1791.

359.

RUFUS PEASE,[6] (Isaac,[5] Isaac,[4] Isaac,[3] John,[2] Robert,[1]) fourth son of Isaac and Rachel (Hall) Pease of Enfield, Ct., was born at Enfield, May 17, 1757; married Ruth Cooley, 1782, and settled in Enfield, where he died, 1801, aged 44 years.

His children were:

1015. 1. Rufus, b. at Enfield,   , 1783.
1016. 2. Alpheus, b. at Enfield, January 25, 1785.
1017. 3. Enos, b. at Enfield, August 9, 1786.
1018. 4. Ruth, b. at Enfield, January 15, 1789.
1019. 5. Dorothy, b. at Enfield, October 23, 1790. m. William Hills, March 3, 1838, and died at Enfield, May 14, 1848.
1020. • 6. Cooley, b. at Enfield, June 12, 1792.
1021. 7. Augustus, b. at Enfield, August   , 1794.

362.

GEORGE PEASE,[6] (Isaac,[5] Isaac,[4] Isaac,[3] John,[2] Robert,[1]) fifth and youngest son of Isaac and Rachel (Hall) Pease of Enfield, Ct., was born at Enfield, October 13, 1766; married Esther Sexton, January 4, 1787.

——o——

364.

JACOB PEASE,[6] (Jacob,[5] Isaac,[4] Isaac,[3] John,[2] Robert,[1]) eldest surviving son of Jacob and Mary Pease of Enfield, Ct., and cousin to the preceding, was born at Enfield, March 7, 1759. [Enfield Town Records.] He appears to have removed with his father when young to Vermont.

368.

ELISHA PEASE,[6] (Jacob,[5] Isaac,[4] Isaac,[3] John,[2] Robert,[1]) son of Jacob and Mary   Pease, was born at Enfield, April 11, 1767, and probably removed when young to Vermont.

369.

ELIPHALET PEASE,[6] (Jacob,[5] Isaac,[4] Isaac,[3] John,[2] Robert,[1]) brother of the preceding, was born at Enfield, November 1, 1769.

370.

GAIUS PEASE,[6] (Jacob,[5] Isaac,[4] Isaac,[3] John,[2] Robert,[1]) brother of the preceding, was born at Enfield, October 21, 1771, and removed with his father when a child to Vermont. He married Abigail Baird in Rockingham, Vt. Soon after his marriage he removed to the town of Jericho, Vt., where he lived. He died about 1855, aged 83 years.

His children were:

1022. 1. Horace, b. at Jericho, January 15, 1799. m. Polly Prouty, 1824. d. September 12, 1862.

1023. 2. Simeon, b. at Jericho, May 5, 1800. m. Annie Prouty.

1024. 3. Abigail, b. at Jericho, December 15, 1801; living 1866, unmarried.

1025. 4. Alvah, b. at Jericho, December 28, 1803. d. 1804.

1026. 5. Alvah,[2] b. at Jericho, December 14, 1805.

1027. 6. Leonard, b. at Jericho, April 10, 1808. Resides in Jericho, unmarried.

1028. 7. Amy, b. at Jericho March 20, 1810. m. Joshua Martin, residence, Jericho. d. 1836.

1029. 8. Hannah, b. at Jericho, May 12, 1812. m. Benjamin Joy. d. 1855.

1030. 9. Sally, b. at Jericho, May 18, 1814. d. March, 1857.

371.

CHESTER PEASE,[6] (Jacob,[5] Isaac,[4] Isaac,[3] John,[2] Robert,[1]) brother of the preceding, was born at

———o———

372.

ABNER PEASE,[6] (Abner,[5] Isaac,[4] Isaac,[3] John,[2] Robert,[1]) eldest son of Abner and Elizabeth (Farrington) Pease, first of Somers, Ct., last of Stephentown, N. Y., and cousin of the preceding, was born at Somers, 1763; married Polly Blackburn, daughter of Maj. Blackburn of Middletown, Ct., at Chester, Mass., December 25, 1790. He first settled in Chester, next in Worcester, Otsego County, N. Y.; subsequently, in 1808, he removed to Aurora, Portage County, Ohio, where he died, June 26, 1836.

His children were:

1031. 1. James, b. at Chester, January 5, 1794.

1032. 2. Betsey, b. at Chester, September 11, 1796. m. James Darrow, 1815, and d. 1825.

1033. 3. Sally, b. at Worcester, N. Y., July 13, 1798. m. Samuel Norton, and resides in Solon, Ohio.

1034.   4. Polly, b. at Worcester, June 22, 1800. m. twice. d. 1855.
1035.   5. Samuel, b. at Worcester, September 4, 1802.
1036.   6. Fannie, (a twin,) b. at Worcester, September 4, 1802. m.
       Warren Warner. d. November 14, 1851.
1037.   7. John, b. at Worcester, December 25, 1804.
1038.   8. Alden M., b. at Worcester, July 19, 1807.
1039.   9. Melinda, b. at Aurora, March 24, 1811.

373.

JAMES PEASE,⁶ (Abner,⁵ Isaac,⁴ Isaac,³ John,² Robert,¹) brother of the preceding, was born at Canaan, N. Y., October 14, 1771; married Lucy Day of Chester, Mass., January 28, 1795. He first settled at Chester, but soon after his marriage removed to Worcester, Otsego County, N. Y., where he died, May 25, 1813, aged 42 years.

His children were:

1040.   1. Dexter, b. at Chester, January 24, 1796.
1041.   2. Lucy, b. at Chester, October 21, 1798. m. George Wilson
       of Westford, N. Y. d. at Newbury, Ohio.
1042.   3. Chauncey D., b. at Chester, September 17, 1800.
1043.   4. Erastus, b. at Worcester, N. Y., March 9, 1802.
1044.   5. Sybil, b. at Worcester, July 17, 1804. d. unmarried, November 25, 1825, aged 21 years.
1045.   6. John F., b. at Worcester, April 21, 1806.
1046.   7. Joshua I., b. at Worcester, July 18, 1808.
1047.   8. Clarissa A., b. at Worcester, May 10, 1810. m. John Wright.
1048.   9. Ira, b. at Worcester, May 21, 1812. d. an infant.
1049.   10. James, b. at Worcester, August 28, 1813. He lived in Chester, Mass., unmarried, (1866).

375.

JOHN PEASE,⁶ (Abner,⁵ Isaac,⁴ Isaac,³ John,² Robert,¹) brother of the preceding, was born at
married Belinda Hayes of Brattleboro', Vt., and died 1804.

His child was:

1050.   1. John R., b. at

376.

SAMUEL PEASE,[6] (ABNER,[5] ISAAC,[4] ISAAC,[3] JOHN,[2] ROBERT,[1]) brother of the preceding, was born at married Clarissa Horton of Vermont.

His children were:

1051.	1. HENRY G., b. at	.	d. unmarried.
1052.	2. JOHN, b. at	.	d. young.

380.

NOADIAH PEASE,[6] (NOADIAH,[5] ISAAC,[4] ISAAC,[3] JOHN,[2] ROBERT,[1]) eldest son of NOADIAH and TIRZAH (SMITH) PEASE, first of Enfield, Ct., last of Sandisfield, Mass., and cousin to the preceding, was born at Enfield, Ct., September 6, 1765; married widow Abigail Breck of Northampton, where he settled; died at Northampton.

His children were:

1053.	1. FANNIE B., b. at	. m.	Eastman.
1054.	2. ABBIE, b. at	.	d. unmarried.

385.

WALTER PEASE,[6] (NOADIAH,[5] ISAAC,[4] ISAAC,[3] JOHN,[2] ROBERT,[1]) brother of the preceding, was born at Enfield, Ct., December 23, 1774; married Naomi Clark of Northampton, Mass., where he settled in business as a carriage-maker; died at Northampton, February 17, 1820, aged 46 years.

His child was:

1055. 1. WILLIAM W., b. at Northampton, September 19, 1818; was unmarried in 1868.

386.

ASAPH PEASE,[6] (NOADIAH,[5] ISAAC,[4] ISAAC,[3] JOHN,[2] ROBERT,[1]) brother of the preceding, was born at Enfield, Ct., October 16, 1776; married Clotilda Hoyt of Guilford,

Ct., February, 1805. He settled first at Colebrook, Ct., subsequently, at East Guilford, Ct., (now Madison), next at Winsted, Ct., and last at New Britain, Ct., where he died, December 12, 1856, aged 80 years; was a tanner and currier.

His children were:

1056.   1. LUMAS, b. at Colebrook, Ct., May 9, 1806; drowned, August 23, 1808.
1057.   2. MARY C., b. at Colebrook, Ct., November   , 1808; unmarried, (1865.)
1058.   3. LUMAS H., b. at Colebrook, June 20, 1811. He graduated at Williams College at Williamstown, Mass., 1835, and at East Windsor, Ct., Theological Seminary, 1838; studied some time at Andover and New York, and spent several years travelling in Europe and Asia; was ordained by the Albany Presbytery in 1845. He was Chaplain of the Forty-fourth Regiment New York State Volunteers (the Ellsworth's) in ~ the late Rebellion. Afterwards labored a year as delegate of the U. S. Christian Commission. In the Fall of 1865 he received an appointment as Seamen's Chaplain at Savannah, Ga.
1059. 4. JULIUS W., b. at Colebrook, May 19, 1814.
1060.   5. LUCY J., b. at East Guilford, Ct., April 10, 1817; lives in Springfield, Mass., unmarried, (1865.)
1061.   6. LAURA P., b. at Winsted, Ct., April 22, 1824. m. Everett C. Holmes, and resides in Winsted, Ct.

390.

ALVAH PEASE,⁶ (NOADIAH,⁵ ISAAC,⁴ ISAAC,³ JOHN,² ROBERT,¹) brother of the preceding, was born at Sandisfield, December 7, 1786; married Abigail Severance of Hartford, Ct. He settled at Colebrook, Ct., where he lived until after the death of his first wife, when he removed to Worcester County, Mass. He married second, He ultimately returned to Sandisfield, where he died.

His children were:

1062.   1. CAROLINE M., b. at Colebrook,   m. Levi Pease of Sandisfield.

1063. 2. Erastus C., b. at Colebrook,   1813.
1064. 3. Richard S., b. at Colebrook.
1065. 4. Warren W., b. at Colebrook,   1826.   d.
               1851, aged 25 years, unmarried.

391.

SIMEON PEASE,[6] (Noadiah,[5] Isaac,[4] Isaac,[3] John,[2] Robert,[1]) youngest son of Noadiah and Sarah (Crouch) Pease, and half brother of the preceding, was born at Sandisfield, Mass., December 3, 1792; married Elizabeth Arnold. He first settled at Sandisfield, subsequently removed to Canandaigua, N. Y., where he died, August 6, 1856, aged 64 years.

His children were:

1066. 1. Sarah M., b. at Sandisfield, October 24, 1814. m. William K. Gray of Salisbury, Ct.
1067. 2. Philena S., b. at Sandisfield, March 22, 1816. m. Elisha Smith of Howell, Mich., and d. about 1848.
1068. 3. Emeline E., b. at Sandisfield, December 9, 1818. m. Morgan Abbot, and lives in Fleming, Mich.
1069. 4. Jarvis B., b. at Sandisfield.
1070. 5. Noadiah S., b. at Sandisfield, March 5, 1820.
1071. 6. Orlo A., b. at Sandisfield, June 4, 1825.
1072. 7. Ann E., b. at Sandisfield, August 22, 1827. m. Henry Frazier.
1073. 8. Clarissa E., b. at Sandisfield, January 24, 1831. m. Andrew Hall of Flint, Mich.
1074. 9. Orville W., b. at Sandisfield, October 9, 1833.
1075. 10. Sidney F., b. at Canandaigua, N. Y., February 17, 1836.
1076. 11. Mary A., b. at Canandaigua, September 5, 1838.
1077. 12. Allen D., b. at Canandaigua, June 3, 1840.

———o○———

FAMILY OF ABRAHAM.[4]

392.

JOHN PEASE,[6] (John,[5] Abraham,[4] Isaac,[3] John,[2] Robert,[1]) eldest son of John and   (Wright) Pease of Suffield, Ct., was born at Suffield, was second cousin of the preceding. He left Suffield; married and is said to have had a family.

393.

LEVI PEASE,⁶ (JOHN,⁵ ABRAHAM,⁴ ISAAC,³ JOHN,² ROBERT,¹) son of JOHN and   (WRIGHT) PEASE of Suffield, Ct., brother of the preceding, was born at Suffield; married   Gibbs; married second, widow Chloe (Burbank) King; died at Suffield.

His children were:

1078. 1. LUTHER, b. at Suffield.
1079. 2. JULIUS, b. at Suffield,   d. unmarried.
1080. 3. ALANSON, b. at Suffield,   d. aged 37 years, unmarried.

BY SECOND WIFE:

1081. 4. EBENEZER B., b. at Suffield, October   , 1812; was unmarried in 1865.
1082. 5. EUNICE K., b. at Suffield, January 27, 1815. m. John R. Ball.

———o———

397.

MOSES PEASE,⁶ (MOSES,⁵ ABRAHAM,⁴ ISAAC,³ JOHN,² ROBERT,¹) eldest son of MOSES and JEMIMA (BOOTH) PEASE of Enfield, Ct., and cousin of the preceding, was born at Enfield, October 27, 1758; married Lovisa Markham, 1786; lived in Enfield, where he died, October 4, 1835, aged 77 years.

His children were:

1083. 1. JEDIDIAH, b. at Enfield, March 21, 1788. d. a child, aged 3 years.
1084. 2. CYRUS, b. at Enfield, October 30, 1789.
1085. 3. MOSES, b. at Enfield, July 14, 1791.
1086. 4. BARNABAS, b. at Enfield, August 8, 1795.
1087. 5. JULIUS, b. at Enfield, September 30, 1798.
1088. 6. FREDERICK, b. at Enfield, October 2, 1801.

400.

LEMUEL PEASE,[6] (Moses,[5] Abraham,[4] Isaac,[3] John,[2] Robert,[1]) brother of the preceding, was born at Enfield, December 6, 1763; married   He lived in Enfield; by occupation a farmer; died October, 1836, aged 74 years.

His children were:

1089.   1. Mary, b. at Enfield,   , 1789.   m. Francis Pease.
1090.   2. Lemuel, b. at Enfield,   , 1791.
1091.   3. Phila, b. at Enfield,   , 1793.   m. Joshua Abbe,
              and settled in Enfield.
1092.   4. Walter, b. at Enfield, June 21, 1795.
1093.   5. Achsah, b. at Enfield   , 1799.   m. Daniel Baker,
              and settled in Enfield.
1094.   6. Erastus, b. at Enfield, October   , 1804.

405.

BENJAMIN PEASE,[6] (Moses,[5] Abraham,[4] Isaac,[3] John,[2] Robert,[1]) brother of the preceding; was born at Enfield, March 13, 1776; married Clorinda Richardson, December 23, 1799, and settled in Enfield.

His children were:

1095.   1. Benjamin, b. at Enfield, August 25, 1800.
1096.   2. Henry, b. at Enfield, December 17, 1802.
1097.   3. Alfred, b. at Enfield, September 17, 1804.
1098.   4. Clarissa, b. at Enfield, September 26, 1806.   m. Osse Phelps,
              and settled in Enfield.
1099.   5. Harvey, b. at Enfield, April 15, 1807.
1100.   6. Lewis, b. at Enfield, June 13, 1808.
1101.   7. Caroline, b. at Enfield, January 16, 1813.   m. Gilbert Ware.

———o———

407.

ABIEL PEASE,[6] (Samuel,[5] Abraham,[4] Isaac,[3] John,[2] Robert,[1]) eldest son of Samuel and Tryphena (Bancroft) Pease of Enfield, Ct., and first cousin of the pre-

ceding; was born at Enfield, May 27, 1761; married
Lovina Fowler, June 30, 1785, and settled at Enfield,
where he died, March 5, 1828, nearly 67 years old. He
was a natural mechanic, could make anything he saw and
do it well; but did the most at clock-making, on a small
and large scale, both common, town or church clocks.
His first clock was made when a lad, with his jack-knife.
From that he continued until he set in motion the clock-
making business of Connecticut, which now furnishes a
large portion of the world with that kind of time-measurer.

His children were:

1102. 1. Roxana, b. at Enfield, February 19, 1786. m. George
Warren.
1103. 2. Lovina, b. at Enfield, February 8, 1788. m. David Gates.
1104. 3. Marcia, b. at Enfield, March 18, 1792. m. William Hunt.
1105. 4. Tryphena, b. at Enfield, November 10, 1793. m. Joel Prior,
and settled in East Windsor, Ct.
1106. 5. Maria, b. at Enfield,   , 1795. m. Barnabas
Pease, and settled in Enfield.
1107. 6. Abiel, b. at Enfield, March 17, 1797.

408.

CHESTER PEASE,[6] (Samuel,[5] Abraham,[4] Isaac,[3] John,[2]
Robert,[1]) brother of the preceding, was born at Enfield,
            ; married Eunice Church, somewhat
advanced in life, and settled at East Longmeadow, Mass.,
where he died without posterity. He was a hatter by
trade, and for some time lived at Somers.

409.

AUGUSTUS PEASE,[6] (Samuel,[5] Abraham,[4] Isaac,[3]
John,[2] Robert,[1]) brother of the preceding, was born at
Enfield,   ; married Etha Warner; mar-
ried, second, widow Loomis. He settled at Southwick,
Mass., where he died.

His children were:

1108. 1. SAMUEL, b. at Southwick.
1109. 2. CHESTER, b. at Southwick.
1110. 3. SIDNEY, b. at Southwick.
1111. 4. ETHA M., b. at Southwick.
1112. 5. GRANT, b. at Southwick.

———o———

411.

JOEL PEASE,[6] (JOEL,[5] ABRAHAM,[4] ISAAC,[3] JOHN,[2] ROBERT,[1]) son of JOEL and LOIS (WARNER) PEASE of East Windsor, Ct., and cousin of the preceding, was born at East Windsor, November 6, 1764; married and settled in the State of New York.

His children were:

1113. 1.
1114. 2.
1115. 3.
1116. 4.
1117. 5.
1118. 6.
1119. 7.

415.

ENOCH PEASE,[6] (JOEL,[5] ABRAHAM,[4] ISAAC,[3] JOHN,[2] ROBERT,[1]) brother of the preceding, was born at East Windsor, August 9, 1771; married and removed to the State of Vermont. He had one son and one daughter.

His children were:

1120. 1.
1121. 2.

416.

ELAM PEASE,[6] (JOEL,[5] ABRAHAM,[4] ISAAC,[3] JOHN,[2] ROBERT,[1]) brother of the preceding, was born at East Windsor, August 13, 1776; married Abigail Allen, and settled in East Windsor. In 1836 he removed from East Windsor to Farmington, Ill., where he died, July , 1842.

His children were:

1122. 1. PAMELIA, b. at   d. in infancy.
1123. 2. GROVE B., b. at   d. aged 18 years.
1124. 3. ELAM A., b. at East Windsor, February 11, 1804.

———o———

419. •

DEA. NATHAN PEASE,⁶ (NATHAN,⁵ ABRAHAM,⁴ ISAAC,³ JOHN,² ROBERT,¹) eldest son of NATHAN and HANNAH (PATTON) PEASE, first of Enfield, Ct., last of Wilbraham, Mass., and cousin of the preceding, was born at Enfield, June 5, 1765; married Sylvia Sisson. He lived at Wilbraham; was a farmer, and deacon of the Baptist Church, South Wilbraham; died

His children were:

1125. 1. SABRA, b. at Wilbraham.
1126. 2. MARIA, b. at Wilbraham.
1127. 3. JUSTUS, b. at Wilbraham, October 17, 1799.
1128. 4. SYLVIA, b. at Wilbraham.

424.

AMOS PEASE,⁶ (NATHAN,⁵ ABRAHAM,⁴ ISAAC,³ JOHN,² ROBERT,¹) brother of the preceding, was born at Enfield, February 16, 1776; married Tabitha Firman, December 13, 1798, and settled a farmer in Monson, Mass. The following facts we take from the Springfield Republican of December, 1865:

"Mr. Amos Pease of Monson has just passed his ninetieth summer. He stood as a minute man in the war of 1812, and sold the first lot of coal to the United States, used at the Springfield Armory, and his strict honesty enabled him to sell the government many loads of coal with only his word for the weight.

"The present season he has picked two bushels of chestnuts, a part of them from trees one hundred feet
14

high and standing on the same ground where he cut rye when he was 18 years old."

The writer saw Mr. Pease, October, 1868, and found him in good strength of body and mind. He has worked with considerable regularity the past summer in the corn and hay-fields. At the time of our interview he was in doors repairing farming utensils, because the stormy day would not allow him to be out harvesting.

His children were:

1129. 1. TABITHA, b. at Monson, November 13, 1799. m. Rev. Dexter Munger, a Baptist clergyman. d. October 26, 1856.

1130. 2. AMOS, b. at Monson, October 20, 1801. d. aged 21 years.

1131. 3. ORRIN, b. at Monson, November 9, 1803.

1132. 4. LUCY F., b. at Monson, November 30, 1806. m. Jenks W. Leonard, and resides in Stafford, Ct. She had a son, Elbridge K. Leonard, b. December 13, 1833. m. Marietta P. Anderson, June 26, 1857, and resides at Broad Brook, a practicing physician.

1133. 5. DAVID F., b. at Monson, July 4, 1809.

1134. 6. ESTHER, b. at Monson, November 11, 1811. m. Jacob L. Broadley and settled in Monson.

1135. 7. RUFUS M., b. at Monson, October 29, 1813.

1136. 8. MARY, b. at Monson, January 19, 1816. m. Hubbard Wood, and first settled in Monson.

425.

DEA. NATHANIEL PEASE,[6] (NATHAN,[5] ABRAHAM,[4] ISAAC,[3] JOHN,[2] ROBERT,[1]) brother of the preceding, was born at Enfield, June 5, 1777; married Nancy Stanton and settled at Wilbraham, Mass., where he was deacon in the Baptist Church. He afterwards removed to West Springfield, where he died, 1844.

His children were:

1137. 1. LYMAN, b. at Wilbraham, , 1808.

1138. 2. LOUISA, b. at Wilbraham, , 1809.

1139. 3. WILLIAM A., b. at Wilbraham, December 29, 1811.

1140. 4. CAROLINE, b. at Wilbraham, , 1814. m. James Webb.

1141. 5. PAMELIA, b. at Wilbraham,   , 1816. m.
            Strong West.
1142. 6. LUCRETIA, b. at Wilbraham,   , 1818. m.
            Horace Coombs. Married, second, Walter Bodurtha of Iowa.

———o———

426.

GIDEON PEASE,[6] (GIDEON,[5] ABRAHAM,[4] ISAAC,[3] JOHN,[2] ROBERT,[1]) eldest son of GIDEON and SYBIL (MARKHAM) PEASE, first of Enfield, Ct., last of Monson, Mass., and cousin to the preceding, was born at Enfield, May 20, 1765; married Hannah Rood, and settled in the State of New York.

His children were:

1143. 1. CANDACE, b. at Monson,   m. Benjamin Stowel.
1144. 2. PERSIS, b. at Monson.

429.

DAN PEASE,[6] (GIDEON,[5] ABRAHAM,[4] ISAAC,[3] JOHN,[2] ROBERT,[1]) brother of the preceding, was born at Enfield, December 11, 1771; married Abigail Johnson at Willington, Ct., about 1795, where he first settled, from which place he appears to have removed to Plainfield, N. Y., and died with his son Dan, at Floyd, N. Y., July 18, 1856, aged 85 years.

His children were:

1145. 1. DAN, b. at Willington, November 24, 1796.
1146. 2. TRUMAN, b. at Willington, September 28, 1798.
1147. 3. JAMES J., b. at Willington, March 13, 1803.
1148. 4. ABIGAIL, b. at Plainfield, May 30, 1806. m. David Gilbert,
            1831. Lives at Cleveland, N. Y.
1149. 5. SABRA, b. at Plainfield, October 7, 1808. m. John J. Bur-
            lington, May 6, 1832, and lived at Vienna, Oneida County,
            N. Y., in 1857.

431.

URBANE PEASE,[6] (GIDEON,[5] ABRAHAM,[4] ISAAC,[3] JOHN,[2] ROBERT,[1]) brother of the preceding, was born at Enfield,

June 8, 1778;, married Judith Piper of Acton, Vt., February 5, 1803.   He was for some time a resident of New York, from which State he subsequently removed to Webster, Mich., where he died, October 6, 1842.   His widow was living in Webster, at the advanced age of 90 years, (February, 1866.)

His children were:

1150. 1. Moses, b. at Plainfield, N. Y., August 31, 1804.

1151. 2. Sybil, b. at Cincinnatus, N. Y., February 14, 1807.   m. James Wells, November 26, 1837.

1152. 3. Gideon, b. at Cincinnatus, January 19, 1809.

1153. 4. Esther, b. at Cincinnatus, December 11, 1810.   m. Francis Tuthill, and resided in Jackson, Mich.   d. 1855.

1154. 5. Polly, b. at Solon, N. Y., February 3, 1813.   m. Amos Ball, July 19, 1835, and lives in Webster.

1155. 6. Betsey, b. at Homer, N. Y., October 1, 1815.   m. Henry Dwight, and resides in Delhi, Mich.

1156. 7. Francis, b. at Homer, November 2, 1817.

1157. 8. Sarah E., b. at Sempronius, N. Y., December 3, 1818.   m. Truman Hart, June 22, 1845, and lives in Kingsville, Ohio.

1158. 9. Lucy, b. at Sempronius, May 9, 1822.   m. James Craine, and resided at North Lake, Mich.   d. July 12, 1825.

1159. 10. Minerva, b. at Sempronius, August 28, 1824.   d. February 26, 1825.

1160. 11. Laura E., b. at Sempronius, November 17, 1826.   m. Aaron Lyon, Esq.; resides in Staunton, Montcalm County, Mich.

1161. 12. Jerusha, b. at Sempronius, September 14, 1827.   m. James Bignell, and resides in Melhorton, Mich.

1162. 13. John D., b. at Sempronius, July 3, 1830.

433.

IRA PEASE,[6] (Gideon,[5] Abraham,[4] Isaac,[3] John,[2] Robert,[1]) son of Gideon and Deborah (Meacham) Pease, half-brother to the preceding, was born at
married Sally Tupper of Monson.

His children were:

1163. 1. Dwight, b. at

1164. 2. Marcus J., b. at

1165. 3. MARY, b. at   m.   Sykes of
          Ludlow, Mass.
1166. 4. DEBORAH, b. at   m. Nehemiah Under-
          wood, and settled in Holland, Mass.

434.

ABRAHAM PEASE,⁶ (GIDEON,⁵ ABRAHAM,⁴ ISAAC,³ JOHN,² ROBERT,¹) brother of the preceding, was born at   ; married Mary Davis, and settled and died in Monson.

His children were:

1167. 1. HARRIET, b. at Monson,   m. Marcus
          Works of Monson.
1168. 2. MARIA, b. at Monson,   d. young.
1169. 3. ORSON, b. at Monson.
1170. 4. PERSIS, b. at Monson,   m. John L.
          Chaffee.
1171. 5. HIRAM, b. at Monson,   , 1811.
1172. 6. FREDERICK, b. at Monson.
1173. 7. ROXANA, b. at Monson,   m.
          Durgee of Somers.
1174. 8. DAVIS, b. at Monson,   , 1815.
1175. 9. BILLINGS, b. at Monson.
1176. 10. JOHN, b. at Monson,   d. aged 19 years.
1177. 11. JARVIS, b. at Monson.

435.

SALMON PEASE,⁶ (GIDEON,⁵ ABRAHAM,⁴ ISAAC,³ JOHN,² ROBERT,¹) brother of the preceding, was born at Monson, 1788; married Roxana Hoar, and lived in Monson, where he died, July 9, 1839.

His children were:

1178. 1. HORACE, b. at Monson, July 3, 1812.
1179. 2. CHESTER M., b. at Monson, November 1, 1813.
1180. 3. JONATHAN H., b. at Monson, October 6, 1816.
1181. 4. HARRISON S., b. at Monson, August 11, 1819. d. a young
          man, unmarried.
1182. 5. CALVIN S., b. at Monson, July 25, 1824.
1183. 6. LUCY ANN, b. at Monson, October 4, 1828.   m. Warren
          Stebbins.

436.

SAMUEL PEASE,[6] (GIDEON,[5] ABRAHAM,[4] ISAAC,[3] JOHN,[2] ROBERT,[1]) youngest son of GIDEON and DEBORAH (MEACHAM) PEASE, last of Monson, was born at Monson, Mass.; married Catharine Underwood, March, 1816, and settled in Monson; died April, 1848.

His children were:

1184. 1. SYLVANUS, b. at Monson, November   , 1816.
1185. 2. LAURA, b. at Monson, March   , 1818. m. Jonathan H. Pease, son of Salmon Pease. d. 1851.
1186. 3. ROSWELL, b. at Monson, January, 1824.
1187. 4. IRA, b. at Monson, February   , 1827.
1188. 5. SAMUEL, b. at Monson,   1830.
1189. 6. LUCINDA, b. at Monson,   1834.
1190. 7. LOVINA, b. at Monson, October   , 1837.

———o———

441.

WILLIAM PEASE,[6] (WILLIAM,[5] ABRAHAM,[4] ISAAC,[3] JOHN,[2] ROBERT,[1]) eldest son of WILLIAM and MARTHA (WEBSTER) PEASE of Enfield, Ct., and cousin to the preceding, was born at Enfield, January, 1780; married Elizabeth Green, 1804, and settled in Enfield.

His children were:

1191. 1. ELIZABETH, b. at Enfield,   , 1805. m. Asa M. Hunn, and settled in Edinton, Me.
1192. 2. HARRIET, b. at Enfield,   , 1808.
1193. 3. WEBSTER, b. at Enfield, April   , 1811.
1194. 4. ABNER, b. at Enfield, January, 1813.
1195. 5. SARAH, b. at Enfield,   1815. m. John Butler, lives at Blandford, Mass.
1196. 6. NORMAND, b. at Enfield, September   , 1817.
1197. 7. MARY, b. at Enfield, May   , 1820. d. June 11, 1834, aged 14 years.
1198. 8. ALVIN, b. at Enfield, November   , 1823.

1199.   9. EMELINE, b. at Enfield July 4, 1825.

1200. 10. EDMUND, b. at Enfield, September 5, 1828.

1201. 11. DELIA A., b. at Enfield, March 9, 1831.   m. Charles Shadrick.

1202. 12. LUCINDA, b. at Enfield, September 20, 1833.

443.

WARREN PEASE,[6] (WILLIAM,[5] ABRAHAM,[4] ISAAC,[3] JOHN,[2] ROBERT,[1]) brother of the preceding, was born at Enfield; married   and removed to Rome, N. Y.

His child was:

1203. 1. CARLOS W., b. at   , February 5, 1815.

449.

ZEBULON PEASE,[6] (ZEBULON,[5] ABRAHAM,[4] ISAAC,[3] JOHN,[2] ROBERT,[1]) eldest son of ZEBULON and HANNAH (RUGG) PEASE of Enfield, Ct., cousin to the preceding, was born at Enfield, 1780; married Sybil Chandler of Enfield, June 2, 1805, and settled in Enfield, where he died soon after his marriage, leaving one child, a daughter.

His child was:

1204.   1. JANE, b. at Enfield, June 5, 1807.   m. Kellogg Pease.

452.

JABEZ PEASE,[6] (ZEBULON,[5] ABRAHAM,[4] ISAAC,[3] JOHN,[2] ROBERT,[1]) brother to the preceding, was born at Enfield, August 6, 1784; married Philena Green, 1810, and settled at Enfield.   He was a joiner and cabinet-maker by trade; died at Enfield.

His children were:

1205.   1. ALBERT M., b. at Enfield, September   , 1811.

1206.   2. GEORGE, b. at Enfield, August   , 1813.

1207. 3. JARED, b. at Enfield, December 9, 1815.

1208. 4. NANCY, b. at Enfield, March 1, 1818.
1209. 5. MARY, b. at Enfield, May 4, 1821.
1210. 6. JAMES, b. at Enfield, July 7, 1823.
1211. 7. LOUISA N., b. at Enfield, March 6, 1826.

453.

SAMUEL PEASE,[6] (ZEBULON,[5] ABRAHAM,[4] ISAAC,[3] JOHN,[2] ROBERT,[1]) brother to the preceding, was born at Enfield, July 29, 1787; married Abi Collins, daughter of John Collins of Somers, Ct. He removed to Ohio, where he died without issue.

456.

HARVEY B. PEASE,[6] (ZEBULON,[5] ABRAHAM,[4] ISAAC,[3] JOHN,[2] ROBERT,[1]) brother to the preceding, was born at Enfield, February 4, 1798; married Maria Chapin. He resided for some time in Enfield, afterwards went to Wilbraham.

His children were :

1212. 1. CAROLINE, b. at   d. in childhood.
1213. 2. THEORISSA, b. at
1214. 3. MARY, b. at   m.
1215. 4. MORRIS C., b. at
1216. 5. CHARLES, b. at   d. infant.

————oo————

FAMILY OF ISRAEL.[4]

458.

SIMEON PEASE,[6] (ISRAEL,[5] ISRAEL,[4] ISAAC,[3] JOHN,[2] ROBERT,[1]) eldest son of ISRAEL and ANN (   ) PEASE of Enfield, Ct., and second cousin of the preceding, was born at Enfield, February 7, 1758; married Mabel Allen, May 21, 1786, who died at the age of 36 years, being the mother of twelve children. He married, second, the widow Sybil (Terry) Billings. He was a farmer, and lived in Enfield, Ct., where he died, 1847, aged 89 years.

His children were :

1217. 1. MABEL, b. at Enfield, January 3, 1787. m. Simeon Prior, and lived in Somers.

1218. 2. DOROTHY, b. at Enfield, September 19, 1788. m. Calvin Pease of Longmeadow, 1839.

1219. 3. SIMEON, b. at Enfield, May 29, 1790.

1220. 4. ALLEN, b. at Enfield, June 18, 1792.

1221. 5. ANNA, b. at Enfield, June 18, 1794. m. David Bolyn, and settled in Newbury, N. Y.

1222. 6. ALVA, b. at Enfield, October 19, 1795.

1223. 7. SALLY, b. at Enfield, August 25, 1797. m. Henry Griswold of Enfield, and there settled.

1224. 8. RHEUMA, b. at Enfield, February 17, 1799. m. Solomon Allen of East Windsor, Ct.

1225. 9. WELLS, b. at Enfield, March 17, 1801.

1226. 10. ARVIN and ⎫
1227. 11. LORIN, ⎬ b. at Enfield, October 30, 1802.

1228. 12. EARL, b. at Enfield, October 26, 1804. d. September 19, 1805.

BY SECOND WIFE :

1229. 13. SYBIL, b. at Enfield, March 31, 1811.

1230. 14. KELLOGG, b. at Enfield, December 1, 1813.

1231. 15. RHODA, b. at Enfield, August 26, 1815. m. Chauncey Sexton, and settled at Somers.

461.

ISRAEL PEASE,⁶ (ISRAEL,⁵ ISRAEL,⁴ ISAAC,³ JOHN,² ROBERT,¹) brother of the preceding, was born at Enfield, February 27, 1766 ; married Mary Pease, daughter of Dea. Jonathan Pease of Ellington, Ct., January 10, 1789. He settled in Middlefield, Mass., and was by occupation a farmer.   He died at Middlefield, September 25, 1842, aged 76 years.

His children were :

1232. 1. MARY, b. at Middlefield, January 10, 1790. m. Chauncey Coats, and removed to Oswego, N. Y.

1233. 2. ISRAEL, b. at Middlefield, September 28, 1791.

1234. 3. DANIEL, b. at Middlefield, April 19, 1793.

1235. 4. HARVEY, b. at Middlefield, October 29, 1794.

15

1236. 5. NANCY, b. at Middlefield, May 28, 1796. m., first, Alvah
          Benjamin; m., second, Salmon Loomis of Hinsdale, Mass.,
          where she d. October 24, 1864.

1237. 6. HORACE, b. at Middlefield, March 2, 1798.

1238. 7. NIAL, b. at Middlefield, July 6, 1801; was unmarried, 1868.

1239. 8. OLIVER, b. at Middlefield, December 29, 1802.

1240. 9. AUSTIN, b. at Middlefield, April 23, 1806.

1241. 10. ABIEL, b. at Middlefield, February 28, 1808. d. September
          18, 1816.

463.

GAD PEASE,[6] (ISRAEL,[5] ISRAEL,[4] ISAAC,[3] JOHN,[2] ROB-
ERT,[1]) brother of the preceding, was born at Enfield, January 10, 1771; married   and removed
to Meredith, Delaware County, N. Y.

His children were:

1242. 1. MARY, b. at
1243. 2. ABIGAIL, b. at
1244. 3. AGNES, b. at   m.   Smith.
1245. 4. LOVISA, b. at   m. Elias Ballou of
          Becket, Mass.
1245[1]. 5. GAD, b. at

464.

DAN PEASE,[6] (ISRAEL,[5] ISRAEL,[4] ISRAEL,[3] JOHN,[2] ROB-
ERT,[1]) youngest son of ISRAEL and ANN   PEASE,
first of Enfield, last of Middlefield, Mass. He was born
at Enfield, Ct., April 25, 1773; married Sally Wright of
Middlefield, 1799, and settled in that town, where he died
1853 or '4.

His children were:

1246. 1. DAN, b. at Middlefield, October 21, 1802.

1247. 2. SALLY, b. at Middlefield, December 10, 1803. m. Harvey
          Root, January 24, 1822, and settled in Middlefield. Her
          children were:
              1. FRANKLIN H., b. November 5, 1822. d. April 19,
                 1843.
              2. SOLOMON, b. November 6, 1824. d. September 9,
                 1828.

        3. Sarah A. and Mary A., twins. b. April 5, 1827.
          Mary A. d. February 29, 1852, and Sarah A. d.
          March 5, 1852.
        4. Lester, b. September 15, 1829.
        5. Corinth, b. February 13, 1832. d. December 9,
          1839.
        6. Amanda, b. September 19, 1834. d. March 10, 1843.
        7. George, b. February 26, 1837. d. March 19, 1843.
        8. Harriet N., b. May 27, 1839. d. March 9, 1843.
        9. Judson, b. April 9, 1842. d. March 16, 1843.
      10. Laura, b. January 15, 1844.

1248. 3. Mary, b. at Middlefield, November 19, 1805. d. 1837, aged
      32 years.

1249. 4. Walter, b. at Middlefield, September 12, 1807.

1250. 5. Sybil, b. at Middlefield, January 27, 1810. m. Ebenezer
      Smith, November 4, 1829, and resided in Middlefield. d.
      July 20, 1855. Her children were:
        1. Morgan, b. February 14, 1831. d. at Elgin, Ill.,
          December 11, 1860.
        2. Albert, b. September 30, 1832, and resides at Elgin,
          Ill.
        3. William, b. November 24, 1834. d. September 19,
          1853.
        4. Martha, b. January 2, 1837. d. May 18, 1856.
        5. Howard, b. November 4, 1839.
        6. Rosina, b. May 30, 1842. d. August 30, 1855.

1251. 6. Eldridge, b. at Middlefield, March 14, 1812.

1252. 7. Morgan, b, at Middlefield, September 25, 1814.

1253. 8. Amanda, b. at Middlefield, February 12, 1817. m. George
      Crane of Washington, Mass. d. September 11, 1852.
      Her children were:
        1. George, b.   d. young.
        2. Charles, b.
        3. Amos, b.
        4. George W., b.
        5. Myron, b.

1254. 9. Arnold, b. at Middlefield, April 19, 1819.

1255. 10. Harriet, b. at Middlefield, March 6, 1822. m. Hezekiah
      Taylor, October 26, 1846, and resides at Westfield, Mass.
      Her children are:
        1. Henry, b. August 13, 1848.
        2. Harriet A., b. August 9, 1854.
        3. Edward H., b. June 10, 1861.

1256. 11. LAURA A., b. at Middlefield, April 4, 1824. m. William
Stevens of Chester, Mass., June 15, 1848. d. June 23,
1863. Her children were:
1. WILLIS F., b. May 30, 1849.
2. LAURA, b. March 5, 1851.
3. CHARLES, b. June 28, 1853.
4. CLARENCE and CLARA, twins, b. May 30, 1855. Clarence, d. August 8, 1863.
5. NELLIE, b. July 23, 1857.

———o———

468.

DAVID PEASE,[6] (DAVID,[5] ISRAEL,[4] ISAAC,[3] JOHN,[2] ROBERT,[1]) eldest son of DAVID and OLIVE (PRIOR) PEASE of Enfield, Ct., and cousin of the preceding, was born at Enfield, March 24, 1767; married Hannah Butler; married, second, Mary A. Butler. He appears to have first settled at East Windsor, subsequently lived at Springfield, Mass., also at Suffield, Ct.; died at Enfield, April 16, 1843.

His children were:

1257.   1. HIBBARD, b. at East Windsor, August   , 1804.
1258.   2. MARY, b. at East Windsor, June 30, 1806.   m. William Beebe of Suffield.
1259.   3. WILLIAM, b. at Springfield,   1809.
1260.   4. HANNAH, b. at Springfield, November   , 1813.   m. Addison Griswold, 1836.

BY SECOND WIFE:
1261.   5. MARY A., b. at Suffield,   1830.

471.

LEVI PEASE,[6] (DAVID,[5] ISRAEL,[4] ISAAC,[3] JOHN,[2] ROBERT,[1]) brother of the preceding, was born at Enfield; married Experience Hemmingway, February 16, 1808. Lived at Suffield, Ct., where he died July 4, 1840.

His children were:

1262.   1. MARY H., b. at Suffield, February 26, 1810.   m. John Murray.
1263.   2. EXPERIENCE, b. at Suffield, February 8, 1812.   d. March   , 1812.

1264. 3. Maria, b. at Suffield, August 19, 1813. m. John Ives, and settled in Suffield.

1265. 4. Lovina, b. at Suffield, August 17, 1815. m. first, Bishop Stowel; m. second, Hibbard Pease, and lives at Suffield.

1266. 5. David B., b. at Suffield, February 1, 1819.

1267. 6. Olive, b. at Suffield, March 1, 1823. m. James Hunn of Springfield.

1268. 7. Caroline, b. at Suffield, December 13, 1825. d January , 1826.

1269. 8. Samuel, b. at Suffield, February 15, 1828.

———o———

479.

LEMUEL PEASE,⁶ (Hezekiah,⁵ Israel,⁴ Isaac,³ John,² Robert,¹) son of Hezekiah and Hannah (Meacham) Pease of Enfield, Ct., and cousin of the preceding, was born at Enfield, January 7, 1772; married Esther Butler, 1793; died without issue.

481.

SETH PEASE,⁶ (Hezekiah,⁵ Israel,⁴ Isaac,³ John,² Robert,¹) brother of the preceding, was born at Enfield, June 4, 1779; married Patty Chapin, 1804. He joined the Shakers after the birth of his children.

His children were:

1270. 1. Patty, (Martha,) b. at Enfield, May 23, 1805.

1271. 2. Hezekiah, b. at Enfield, March 26, 1807.

1272. 3. Alanson, b. at Enfield, February 12, 1809.

1273. 4. Seth, b. at Enfield, 1811.

1274. 5. Homer, b. at Enfield, 1813. Remains among the Shakers.

———o———

483.

JESSE PEASE,⁶ (Jesse,⁵ Israel,⁴ Isaac,³ John,² Robert,¹) only son of Jesse and Martha Pease of Enfield, Ct., cousin of the preceding, was born at Enfield,

December 28, 1789; married Abigail   He removed from Enfield to Ashfield, Mass., and thence to the State of New York.

His children were:

1275. 1. ABIGAIL M., b. at Enfield,   1806.
1276. 2. MARTHA M., b. at Enfield, August   , 1807.
1277. 3.
1278. 4.
1279. 5.

————o————

485.

NATHAN PEASE,[6] (NATHAN,[5] ISRAEL,[4] ISAAC,[3] JOHN,[2] ROBERT,[1]) son of NATHAN and   (ROOT) PEASE of Enfield, Ct., and cousin of the preceding, was born at Enfield, April 1, 1782; married Polly Collins; died at Enfield, March 18, 1857.

His children were:

1280. 1. ORLANDO, b. at Enfield, September 2, 1803.
1281. 2. ALVAH, b. at Enfield, August 31, 1805. d. August 5, 1808.
1282. 3. ACHSAH, b. at Enfield, June 10, 1807. m. Almon Lazelle, and settled at Groveland, N. Y.
1283. 4. ALVAH,[2] b. at Enfield, June 21, 1809. d. June 8, 1842; never married.
1284. 5. ELIPHALET C., b. at Enfield, June 17, 1811.
1285. 6. SIMEON, b. at Enfield, June 4, 1813.
1286. 7. MARY, b. at Enfield, September 17, 1815. m. Daniel Vaughan, July 3, 1844.
1287. 8. NATHAN S., b. at Enfield, September 26, 1818. d. January 12, 1821.

————oo————

FAMILY OF BENJAMIN.[4]

489.

SHARON PEASE,[6] (SHARON,[5] BENJAMIN,[4] ISAAC,[3] JOHN,[2] ROBERT,[1]) eldest son of SHARON and MARY (PRIOR) PEASE of Enfield, Ct., and second cousin of the preceding, was born at Enfield, October 3, 1772; married Mary Brooks, and first settled in Enfield, but subsequently removed to Shutesbury, Mass. He died at Enfield.

His children were:

1288. 1. BENJAMIN, b. at Enfield, August 28, 1798.
1289. 2. DANIEL, b. at Enfield, 1799.
1290. 3. HOSEA, b. at Enfield, April, 1800.
1291. 4. GEORGE B., b. at Enfield, August 4, 1805.
1292. 5. MARY, b. at Enfield, d. young.
1293. 6. MARY,² b. at Enfield, m. Caleb W. Newhall.
1294. 7. LOIS, b. at Enfield, m. John Hopkins; m., second, William H. Ensign, and lived at Amherst, Mass.
1295. 8. LORIN, b. at Shutesbury, d. young.
1296. 9. ALBERT, b. at Shutesbury.
1297. 10. CLARISSA C., b. at Shutesbury, m. James Hastings, April 7, 1841, and lived at Amherst, Mass.

———oo———

FAMILY OF EZEKIEL.⁴
491.

EZEKIEL PEASE,⁶ (EZEKIEL,⁵ EZEKIEL,⁴ ISAAC,³ JOHN,² ROBERT,¹) eldest son of EZEKIEL and JEMIMA (MARKHAM) PEASE, first of Enfield, Ct., last of Weston, Vt., and second cousin to the preceding, was born at Enfield, March 22, 1756; married Lydia Pease, daughter of Timothy Pease, Sen., of Enfield, May 8, 1782. He first settled at Enfield, but subsequently removed to Weston, Vt.; died at Starksboro, Vt., February 8, 1838.

His children were:

1298. 1. EZEKIEL, b. at Enfield, November 19, 1783. d. in Illinois, September 13, 1839, aged about 55 years.
1299. 2. AMOS, b. at Enfield, March 18, 1785. d. unmarried.
1300. 3. LYDIA, b. at Enfield, July 9, 1787. d. May 12, 1795, aged 8 years.
1301. 4. OBED, b. at Weston, April 20, 1789.
1302. 5. BEULAH, b. at Weston, July 6, 1792. m. Milo Stow, February 8, 1822, and settled in Weybridge, Vt. d. suddenly.

494.

OBADIAH PEASE,[6] (Ezekiel,[5] Ezekiel,[4] Isaac,[3] John,[2] Robert,[1]) brother of the preceding, was born at Enfield, Ct., September 8, 1766; married Achsah Bement, of Chicopee, Mass. He settled in the town of Landgrove, Vt. He had twelve children, but six of whom lived to grow to maturity.

His children were:

1303.   1. Achsah, b. at Landgrove, April   , 1794.   m. Prescott
Lawrence of Pepperill, Mass.

1304.   2. Obadiah, b. at Landgrove.
1305.   3. Clarissa, b. at Landgrove, March   , 1798.   d. unmarried.

1306.   4. Ambrose, b. at Landgrove.
1307.   5. Elihu, b. at Landgrove,   1803.
1308.   6. Amos, b. at Landgrove.

495.

ELIJAH PEASE,[6] (Ezekiel,[5] Ezekiel,[4] Isaac,[3] John,[2] Robert,[1]) son of Ezekiel and Jemima (Markham) Pease, was born at Enfield, July 13, 1770; married Polly Allen, March 21, 1796, by whom he had his children; married second, Polly Foster; died at Weston, February 1, 1856, aged 86 years.

His children were:

1309.   1. Elijah, b. at Weston, December 8, 1796.
1310.   2. Mary. b. at Weston, August 29, 1798.   m. J. T. McLaughlin, September 8, 1823, and settled at Troy, N. Y.
1311.   3. Melinda, b. at Weston, June 5, 1800.   m. Albert Dale, and settled at LaGrange, Ohio.
1312.   4. Anson, b. at Weston, February 15, 1802.
1313.   5. Lucy, b. at Weston, June 18, 1804.   m. Addison Foster, and settled at LaGrange, Ohio.
1314.   6. Albert, b. at Weston, March 22, 1806.
1315.   7. Enoch, b. at Weston, January 13, 1809.
1316.   8. Ira, b. at Weston, September 10, 1812.   d. 1826, aged 14 years.
1317.   9. Harmon, b. at Weston, June 24, 1816.
1318.   10. Samuel M., b. at Weston, December 19, 1819.

496.

AMBROSE PEASE,⁶ (EZEKIEL,⁵ EZEKIEL,⁴ ISAAC,³ JOHN,²
ROBERT,¹) son of EZEKIEL and JEMIMA (MARKHAM) PEASE,
was born at   ; married   He
was for a time a resident at Sackett's Harbor, N. Y., which
place he left with his family, which consisted of three
daughters, as nearly as can now be ascertained.   It is supposed he removed to Canada.

His children were:

1319. 1.
1320. 2.
1321. 3.

———o———

502.

HENRY PEASE,⁶ (HENRY C.,⁵ EZEKIEL,⁴ ISAAC,³ JOHN,²
ROBERT,¹) son of HENRY C. and RUTH (CHAPIN) PEASE,
first of Enfield and last of Sandisfield, Mass., and first
cousin of the preceding, was born at Sandisfield, 1771;
married Huldah Tilden, 1793, and removed to Livonia,
Livingston County, N. Y., September, 1805, where he
died, January 8, 1827.   His widow married Silas Whitney
of Geneva.

His children were:

1322. 1. HENRY, b. at Sandisfield, March   , 1794.
1323. 2. WILLIAM C., b. at Sandisfield, August 18, 1795.
1324. 3. HULDAH, b. at Sandisfield, October 24, 1796. m. Turner
              Chappell of Avon, N. Y.   d. 1826.
1325. 4. THOMAS, b. at Sandisfield, August 13, 1798.
1326. 5. ELIZABETH, b. at Sandisfield, January 13, 1800.   m. Dr.
              Justin Gates of Mendon, N. Y., July 20, 1819.
1327. 6. ROBERT, b. at Sandisfield, October 23, 1801.   d. 1802.
1328. 7. HANNAH, b. at Sandisfield, May 22, 1803.   m. Giles B. Bliss,
              1825.   d. 1841.
1329. 8. BELINDA, b. at Livonia, December 3, 1806.   d. 1808.
1330. 9. HARVEY, b. at Livonia, March 17, 1808.
1331. 10. AUSTIN, b. at Livonia, November 22, 1809.
1332. 11. CHANDLER, b. at Livonia, November 25, 1811.

16

1333. 12. JANE, b. at Livonia, March 31, 1814. m. Almon M. Chapin of Livonia, July 16, 1835, and now resides at Eden, Mich.

1334. 13. JAMES H., b. at Livonia, January 11, 1817.

1335. 14. EMERY T. and } twins, b. at Livonia, September 20, 1820.
1336. 15. EMILY,   }   Emily d. 1822.

503.

OLIVER PEASE,[6] (HENRY C.,[5] EZEKIEL,[4] ISAAC,[3] JOHN,[2] ROBERT,[1]) brother of the preceding, was born at Sandisfield, 1777; married Ruth Hubbard; married second, Esther Elmore. He first settled in Sandisfield, and removed from thence to Cambria, Niagara County, N. Y., May, 1828; from thence to Blissfield, Lenawee County, Michigan.

His children were:

1337. 1. ALICE, b. at Sandisfield, August 22, 1801. m. Jedidiah White.

1338. 2. OLIVER C., b. at Sandisfield, May 30, 1803.

1339. 3. PERSIS, b. at Sandisfield, December 3, 1804. m. Ami Richards.

1340. 4. LEVI, b. at Sandisfield, August 25, 1806.

1341. 5. HENRY C., b. at Sandisfield, July 5, 1808.

1342. 6. ELIZA, b. at Sandisfield, September 2, 1810. m. John Kimball, and settled in Michigan.

1343. 7. ERASTUS, b. at Sandisfield, July 16, 1812.

1344. 8. ORIS, b. at Sandisfield, May 20, 1815. d. a child.

1345. 9. RUTH, b. at Sandisfield, December 2, 1817. m. Nelson Goodrich, and lives in Blissfield.

BY SECOND WIFE:

1346. 10. MARY J., b. at Blissfield, January 15, 1826.

504.

OLIVER PEASE,[6] (ISAAC,[5] EZEKIEL,[4] ISAAC,[3] JOHN,[2] ROBERT,[1]) eldest son of ISAAC and SUBMIT (SPENCER) PEASE of Enfield, Ct., and cousin of the preceding, was born at Enfield, 1777; married Catherine Chappell, September, 1804, and settled in Washington, Mass., where he died, April 13, 1850, aged 73 years. He was a farmer.

His children were:

1347.   1. EZEKIEL, b. at Washington, July 2, 1805. d. February , 1806.

1348.   2. SARAH, b. at Washington, May 29, 1807. m. Samuel C. Barnum, April 6, 1831, and settled at Washington.

1349.   3. SPENCER, b. at Washington, February 20, 1809.

1350.   4. LUCINDA, b. at Washington, February 3, 1811.

1351.   5. OLIVER, b. at Washington, December 1, 1812.

1352.   6. NANCY, b. at Washington, October 21, 1814. m. Allen C. French, 1840, and settled at Washington.

1353.   7. ANNA, b. at Washington, May 14, 1818. d. June 22, 1829.

1354.   8. MARTHA, b. at Washington, February 22, 1820. m. Ira Higgings of Washington.

1355.   9. SUSAN, b. at Washington, June 2, 1822. m.

1356.   10. ISAAC, b. at Washington, February 4, 1825.

505.

ISAAC PEASE,⁶ (ISAAC,⁵ EZEKIEL,⁴ ISAAC,³ JOHN,² ROBERT,¹) brother of the preceding, was born at Enfield, March 27, 1779; married Elizabeth Terry, daughter of Col. Asaph Terry of Enfield. He first settled at East Longmeadow, Mass., and was a clothier by trade. He returned to Enfield, where he died, November 1, 1836, aged 58 years.

His children were:

1357.   1. SUBMIT, b. at Longmeadow, February 14, 1803. d. an infant.

1358.   2. ELIZABETH, b. at Longmeadow, June 17, 1804. m. Wells Pease, son of Simeon Pease, 1830, and settled at Enfield.

1359.   3. SOLOMON, b. at Longmeadow, September 9, 1806. d. December 19, 1826, aged 21 years.

1360.   4. ISAAC T., b. at Longmeadow, April 11, 1809.

1361.   5. HENRY S., b. at Longmeadow, April 14, 1812.

1362.   6. THEODORE, b. at Longmeadow, January 22, 1815.

1363.   7. SAMANTHA, b. at Longmeadow, June 6, 1817. d. March , 1829, aged 12 years.

1364.   8. LOVISA, b. at Longmeadow, March 24, 1821. m. Henry J. Wright of Granville, Mass.

507.

DANIEL PEASE,[6] (Isaac,[5] Ezekiel,[4] Isaac,[3] John,[2] Robert,[1]) third son of Isaac and Submit (Spencer) Pease of Enfield, Ct., was born at Enfield, October 3, 1780; married Lois Henry, 1807, by whom he had one child; married second, Margaret Allen of East Windsor, Ct., October 18, 1809. He settled in the east part of Springfield, Mass. He was a farmer; died by a fall from the great beam of his barn, July 10, 1838.

His children were:

1365.   1. Lois, b. at Springfield, November 10, 1807.   m. Solomon Hill of East Longmeadow.

1366.   2. Daniel, b. at Springfield, August 10, 1810.   d. February 5, 1852, unmarried.

1367.   3. Margaret, b. at Springfield, November 27, 1811.   m. Marvin Dart of Enfield.

1368.   4. Agnes, b. at Springfield, March 4, 1813.   d. young.

1369.   5. Hiram, b. at Springfield, April 18, 1814.

1370.   6. Emily, b. at Springfield, December 10, 1815.   m. Newton Loomer of Richmond, Iowa.

1371.   7. Harriet, b. at Springfield, September, 4, 1818.   m. James Osborn.

1372.   8. Luke A., b. at Springfield, October 3, 1821.

1373.   9. Delina, b. at Springfield, August 28, 1823.   d. September 25, 1838.

1374.   10. Albert, b. at Springfield, May 30, 1824.

1375.   11. Miriam, b. at Springfield, December 29, 1826.   m. Horace Pease, son of Horace Pease of Springfield, Mass., and settled in Somers, Ct.

508.

REUBEN PEASE,[6] (Isaac,[5] Ezekiel,[4] Isaac,[3] John,[2] Robert,[1]) fourth son of Isaac and Submit (Spencer) Pease of Enfield, Ct., was born at Enfield, December 28, 1781; married Abi Gowdy, daughter of Alexander Gowdy of Enfield, December 7, 1807, and settled, a farmer, in Enfield, where he died, October 16, 1826, aged 45 years.

His children were :

1376.   1. ALMITTEE, b. at Enfield, September 2, 1808.   m. Lorin Pease, son of Simeon Pease of Enfield, December 27, 1827, and lives at Longmeadow, Mass.

1377.   2. LORINDA, b. at Enfield, April 1, 1810.   m. Arnold Olmstead of Enfield, January 5, 1831, and first settled in Enfield, where her children were born; she afterwards resided in Manchester, Ct., but now resides in Springfield, Mass.   Her children were :

    1. LAURINDA, b. February 15, 1832. d. October 18, 1840.

    2. LAURANA, (twin sister,) d. March 18, 1843.

    3. OLIVIA L., b. January 7, 1834.   m. Rev. George W. Mansfield of the New England Conference of the Methodist Episcopal Church, August 6, 1858.

1378.   3 ABI SELINA, b. at Enfield, February 20, 1812.   d. September 25, 1826.

1379.   4. REUBEN A., b. at Enfield, July 28, 1814.

1380.   5. LINUS, b. at Enfield, December 25, 1816. d. September 5, 1826.

1381.   6. AUSTIN S., b. at Enfield, May 9, 1820.

1382.   7. ALEXANDER G., b. at Enfield, September 5, 1822.

510.

CALVIN PEASE,⁶ (ISAAC,⁵ EZEKIEL,⁴ ISAAC,³ JOHN,² ROBERT,¹) fifth son of ISAAC and SUBMIT (SPENCER) PEASE of Enfield, Ct., was born at Enfield, April 13, 1785; married Mary Hale, March 7, 1808; married second, Dorothy Pease, 1839. His children were by his first wife. He was a farmer, and first settled in Enfield; subsequently removed to Longmeadow, Mass., where he died, November 18, 1847, aged 63 years.

His children were :

1383.   1. CALVIN, b. at Enfield, November 15, 1809.

1384.   2. ABIEL, b. at Enfield, December 10, 1811; was unmarried, 1868; resides in East Longmeadow.

1385.   3. ALONZO, b. at Enfield, January 12, 1814.

1386.   4. HENRY, b. at Longmeadow, August 10, 1816. d. March 8, 1837, aged 21 years.

1387.   5. MERVIN H., b. at Longmeadow, February 20, 1819.

1388.   6. MARY, b. at Longmeadow, May 4, 1821.   m. Sylvester Kibbe, and settled at Longmeadow.

511.

ABEL PEASE,[6] (Isaac,[5] Ezekiel,[4] Isaac,[3] John,[2] Robert,[1]) sixth and youngest son of Isaac and Submit (Spencer) Pease of Enfield, Ct., was born at Enfield, May 16, 1787; married Hannah McGregory of East Longmeadow, Mass., in which place he settled. He was a farmer by occupation; died 1854, aged about 67 years.

His children were:

1389. 1. Lucy M., b. at East Longmeadow, August 28, 1809. m. Luther Hills, January 28, 1831, and lives in Longmeadow.
1390. 2. Mary A., b. at East Longmeadow, March 29, 1811. m. Warren Frost, November   , 1835, and settled in Longmeadow.
1391. 3. Orville, b. at East Longmeadow, January 25, 1813.
1392. 4. Abel, b. at East Longmeadow,   , 1815.
1393. 5. Warren, b. at East Longmeadow,   , 1818.
1394. 6. William, b. at East Longmeadow,   , 1820. d. an infant.
1395. 7. Hancy, b. at East Longmeadow,   , 1822. m. Sidney Kibbe, and settled at East Longmeadow.
1396. 8. Selina, b. at East Longmeadow,   , 1826. m. Samuel Hubbard, and resides in Hartford, Ct.
1397. 9. Francis A., b. at East Longmeadow,   , 1829. m. Samuel Indicot, Jr., and settled in South Wilbraham, Mass.
1398. 10. Elizabeth S., b. at East Longmeadow,   , 1830. d. aged 13 years.

———oo———

FAMILY OF TIMOTHY.[4]

513.

Dea. ABIEL PEASE,[6] (Timothy,[5] Timothy,[4] Isaac,[3] John,[2] Robert,[1]) second son of Timothy and Ruth (Hale) Pease of Enfield, Ct., and second cousin of the preceding, was born at Enfield, November 13, 1764; married Rachel

Hale, November 6, 1787, and settled in Longmeadow, Mass.
He was for many years a deacon in the Baptist Church in
East Longmeadow, he having filled that office from the
time of its first gathering; died without issue, November,
1845, aged 81 years.

517.

JONATHAN PEASE,⁶ (Timothy,⁵ Timothy,⁴ Isaac,³
John,² Robert,¹) brother of the preceding, was born at
Enfield, Ct., August 23, 1774; married Lurana Sweatland
of East Longmeadow in 1812. She died, 1834; married
second, Ruth Holloway, October 7, 1834. He was for
some time connected with the Shaker Society, with his
parents, brothers and a sister; but the Shakers say:—
"Jonathan took his own head, and followed the example
of his eldest brother, Abiel." He died September 20,
1841, aged 67 years.

His children were:

1399. 1. Ruth, b. at Longmeadow,   , 1812. m. William
        Heath in 1837.
1400. 2. Rhoda R., b. at Springfield, February   , 1815. m. Orlando
        Kibbe, 1839, and settled in East Longmeadow.
1401. 3. Luana, b. at Springfield, April 24, 1816. m. Marcus W.
        Fay, 1847.
1402. 4. Jonathan B., b. at Springfield, May 7, 1829.
1403. 5. Amelia, b. at Springfield, October 14, 1833. d. 1850, aged
        17 years.

519.

TIMOTHY PEASE,⁶ (Edward,⁵ Timothy,⁴ Isaac,³
John,² Robert,¹) eldest son of Edward and Abigail
(Hale) Pease of Enfield, and cousin of the preceding,
was born at Enfield, October 25, 1784; married Chloe
Hale, 1809, and settled in Enfield, where he died.

His children were:

1404. 1. CHLOE A., b. at Enfield, November 11, 1809. d. March 8. 1810.
1405. 2. TIMOTHY W., b. at Enfield, April 30, 1811.
1406. 3. AMANDA M., b. at Enfield, November 5, 1816. m. Theodore Terry, 1840, and settled in Enfield; m. second, J. Hubbard.
1407. 4. NAOMI D., b. at Enfield, December 14, 1822.

521.

HEBER PEASE,[6] (EDWARD,[5] TIMOTHY,[4] ISAAC,[3] JOHN,[2] ROBERT,[1]) brother of the preceding, was born at Enfield, June 17, 1798; married Miriam Allen, January 11, 1821, and settled in Enfield, a farmer. He died, November 12, 1866.

His children were:

1408. 1. FRANCIS L., b. at Enfield, May 15, 1822.
1409. 2. MARY A., b. at Enfield, January 22, 1824. m. James R. Hodge, November   , 1848, and resides in Springfield, Mass.
1410. 3. SIMEON H., b. at Enfield, May 31, 1826.
1411. 4. JULIA A., b. at Enfield, December 9, 1827.
1412. 5. CECILIA M., b. at Enfield, May 8, 1830. m. Wolcott King, and resides in Enfield.
1413. 6. CARLOS A., b. at Enfield, April 29, 1832. d. August 18, 1843.
1414. 7. AMELIA W., b. at Enfield, April 3, 1839. m. Mitchel Roddy, and resides in Boston, Mass.
1415. 8. LUTHER A., b. at Enfield, June 12, 1836.
1416. 9. FREDERICK A. B., b. at Enfield, March 9, 1840.
1417. 10. CHARLOTTE A., b. at Enfield, January 18, 1844.

527.

JAMES PEASE,[6] (JAMES,[5] TIMOTHY,[4] ISAAC,[3] JOHN,[2] ROBERT,[1]) eldest son of JAMES and MARY (LARKHAM) PEASE of Enfield, Ct., and cousin of the preceding, was born at Enfield, April 23, 1776; married Rhoda Parsons, January 19, 1803.

His children were :

1418. 1. HARRIET, b. at Enfield, October 17, 1804. m. James H. Twiss, and settled at Enfield.
1419. 2. RHODA, b. at Enfield, August 2, 1806. m.   Miller.
1420. 3. LOVISA, b. at Enfield, October 20, 1808. m. Ebenezer P. Terry, and settled at Enfield.
1421. 4. PERSIS, b. at Enfield,   d. unmarried, aged 19 years.
1422. 5. MARY, b. at Enfield,   m. Job B. Allen,
        1842, and settled at Enfield. [Martha Allen, Enfield.]

531.

LUTHER PEASE,[6] (JAMES,[5] TIMOTHY,[4] ISAAC,[3] JOHN,[2] ROBERT,[1]) brother of the preceding, was born at Enfield, February 28, 1788; married Nancy Pease, daughter of Cummings Pease, September 19, 1810, and settled at Springfield, Mass. He subsequently removed to Burton, Ohio, 1817, and in 1820 he again removed to Hampden, Ohio, where he died, October 22, 1826.

His children were :

1423. 1. NANCY L., b. at Springfield, Mass., July 24, 1811. m. Ransom Wilcox, and resides at Sycamore, Ohio.
1424. 2. LUTHER L., b. at Springfield, Mass., January 10, 1813.
1425. 3. JAMES C., b. at Enfield, Ct., January 9, 1815.
1426. 4. LORIN A., b. at Burton, Ohio, March 10, 1818.

532.

JACOB PEASE,[6] (JAMES,[5] TIMOTHY,[4] ISAAC,[3] JOHN,[2] ROBERT,[1]) youngest son of JAMES and MARY (LARKUM) PEASE, was born at Enfield, November 7, 1792. He left Enfield and removed to Ohio; married a Miss Warner, and died in the town of Mentor, Ohio, about 1821.

His children were :

1427. 1. SEYMORE, b. at   He was a machinist by trade, and in 1838 resided at Cleveland, Ohio.
1428. 2. CAROLINE, b. at
1429. 3. MARY A., b. at

FAMILY OF CUMMINGS.[4]

533.

ROSWELL PEASE,[6] (CUMMINGS,[5] CUMMINGS,[4] ISAAC,[3] JOHN,[2] ROBERT,[1]) eldest son of CUMMINGS and THANKFUL (CLELAND) PEASE, first of Enfield, Ct., subsequently of Wilbraham and Longmeadow, Mass., was born at Enfield, 1781, and second cousin of the preceding; married Ann Bliss, and settled at Chicopee, Mass.; was a farmer by occupation. He died March 23, 1866.

His children were:

1430.   1. MARY, b. at Chicopee, July 5, 1816.   m. Alonzo Blodgett of Belchertown, Mass., 1854.
1431.   2. ANN, b. at Chicopee, June 25, 1820.
1432.   3. JOHN Q. A., b. at Chicopee, April 24, 1826.

536.

DEACON WILDER C. PEASE,[6] (CUMMINGS,[5] CUMMINGS,[4] ISAAC,[3] JOHN,[2] ROBERT,[1]) second son of CUMMINGS and THANKFUL (CLELAND) PEASE, was born at Enfield, October 4, 1784; married Ruth Cadey, daughter of Cadey, Esq., of Stafford, Ct. He first settled at South Wilbraham, subsequently removed to Enfield, where he now resides, 1868. He has for many years held the office of Deacon in the Congregational Church, and is by occupation a farmer; has also been a teacher in the common schools. His present residence is about two miles east of Thompsonville.

His children were:

1433.   1. ELIZA C., b. at Wilbraham,   1813.   m. Dennis Pease of Enfield.
1434.   2. THEODORE W., b. at Wilbraham,   1816.
1435.   3. JOSEPH R., b. at Wilbraham,   1818.
1436.   4. HENRY A., b. at Wilbraham,   1821.
1437.   5. LEVI S., b. at Wilbraham,   1824.

539.

ABIONE PEASE,[6] (CUMMINGS,[5] CUMMINGS,[4] ISAAC,[3] JOHN,[2] ROBERT,[1]) third son of CUMMINGS and THANKFUL (CLELAND) PEASE, was born at Enfield, August 5, 1789; married Parthenia Lathrop, and appears to have removed to the State of Ohio, subsequently to Illinois, and settled in the town of Waverly, Morgan County, where he now lives, (1866), and is an extensive farmer.

His children were:

1438.   1. MARY ANN, b. at   January 3, 1821.
1439.   2. ELIZABETH, b. at   June 4, 1824. m. Peter W.
        Record of Woodstock, Ct., 1844, and lived in Cass County,
        Ill. d. October   , 1851.
1440.   3. LYDIA, b. at   August 4, 1826. d. March 11, 1866.
1441.   4. EPAPHROS L. P., b. at   June 20, 1828.
1442.   5. ELSEBA, b. at   August 13, 1830. d. July 2, 1831.
1443.   6. JAMES C., b. at Waverly, Ill., April 27, 1838. d. in the
        army, at Vicksburg, October 29, 1864.
1444.   7. HENRY L., b. at Waverly, October 29, 1840.

540.

JAMES C. PEASE,[6] (CUMMINGS,[5] CUMMINGS,[4] ISAAC,[3] JOHN,[2] ROBERT,[1]) fourth son of CUMMINGS and THANKFUL (CLELAND) PEASE, was born at Enfield, April 4, 1791; married Malinda Booth, November 25, 1812; married, second, Mary Terry, daughter of Rev. Ezekiel Terry. He settled at Wilbraham. His farm and residence was west from, and in view of, the village in which is located the Methodist Seminary; died October   1853.

His children were:

1445.   1. JAMES H., b. at Wilbraham, May 9, 1813.
1446.   2. LORIN C., b. at Wilbraham, July 15, 1815.
1447.   3. ALBERT A., b. at Wilbraham, December 9, 1817.
1448.   4. EMELINE M., b. at Wilbraham, October 17, 1819. m. Orrin
        Pease of Monson.

1449.　5. FIDELIA, b. at Wilbraham, February 28, 1822. m. Alanson
　　　　　Calkins, April 16, 1843, and lives at Wilbraham.
1450.　6. CAROLINE, b. at Wilbraham, October 25, 1825. m. John
　　　　　Abbe of Springfield, January　, 1846.
1451.　7. MARY, b. at Wilbraham, October 9, 1827. m. Cutler Cooley
　　　　　of Longmeadow.

BY SECOND WIFE:

1452.　8. JEROME, b. at Wilbraham, March 7, 1830.
1453.　9. MUNROE, b. at Wilbraham, March 28, 1832.
1454. 10. AMANDA, b. at Wilbraham, March 28, 1834. m. William
　　　　　Keyes of Springfield.
1455. 11. JANE E., b. at Wilbraham, June 11, 1836. d. November　,
　　　　　1838.
1456. 12. CHARLES H., b. at Wilbraham, November 9, 1838. d. aged
　　　　　16 years.
1457. 13. GEORGE F., b. at Wilbraham, November 23, 1842.
1458. 14. JANE E.,[2] b. at Wilbraham,　, 1844. m. Henry
　　　　　Clark, and lives in Wilbraham.
1459. 15. GILBERT H., b. at Wilbraham,　1847.
1460. 16. EMMA, b. at Wilbraham.

541.

SHUBAEL PEASE,[6] (CUMMINGS,[5] CUMMINGS,[4] ISAAC,[3]
JOHN,[2] ROBERT,[1]) youngest son of CUMMINGS and THANK-
FUL (CLELAND) PEASE, was born at Wilbraham,
1796; married Elizabeth Kibbe of Somers, 1821, and
lives at the north part of Somers, Ct.

His children were :

1461.　1. ANGELINE, b. at Longmeadow, December　, 1821.
1462.　2. CARLOS, b. at Springfield, May 16, 1825.
1463.　3. ERSKINE, b. at Springfield, May　, 1827.
1464.　4. LEANORA, b. at Wilbraham September 20, 1829. m. Carlos
　　　　　Hale.
1465.　5. JERUSHA, b. at Wilbraham, December 12, 1832. m. Harlow
　　　　　H. Hyde.

———o———

543.

EBENEZER PEASE,[6] (EBENEZER,[5] CUMMINGS,[4] ISAAC,[3]
JOHN,[2] ROBERT,[1]) eldest son of EBENEZER and REBECCA

(HILL) PEASE, first of Longmeadow, Mass., last of Georgia, Vt., was born at Longmeadow, August 20, 1773; cousin of the preceding; married Abigail Kibbe, September 1791, and lived last at Brasher, St. Lawrence County, N. Y.

His children were:

1466. 1. MERRIL, b. at Andover, Vt.
1467. 2. ALANSON, b. at Georgia, Vt.
1468. 3. EBENEZER, b. at Georgia,   , 1802.
1469. 4. BRADLEY, b. at Georgia.
1470. 5. NELSON, b. at Georgia.
1471. 6. MARGERY, b. at Andover.   d. in Indiana.
1472. 7. ABIGAIL, b. at Woodford, Vt.   m. William
        Hawkins, and lived at Brasher.
1473. 8. CELESTIA, b. at Georgia.

544.

ENOCH PEASE,⁶ (EBENEZER,⁵ CUMMINGS,⁴ ISAAC,³ JOHN,² ROBERT,¹) brother of the preceding, was born at November 15, 1775; married Betsey Houghton of Bakersfield, Vt., 1802, and settled at Enosburgh, Vt. He was a farmer. Died at Fairfield, Vt., October 4, 1845, aged 65 years.

His children were:

1474. 1. AMANDA, b. at Enosburgh, May 13, 1805. m. Daniel Story, 1828, and lived and died at Fairfield, July 19, 1835.
1475. 2. CYNTHIA M., b. at Enosburgh, March 18, 1806. m. Bartlett Williams of Enosburgh, 1834, and settled at New Ipswich, N. H., where she d. 1837.
1476. 3. ELIZABETH, b. at Enosburgh, December 25, 1808. m. Hiram Howard, 1830, and lived at Fairfax, Vt.
1477. 4. ELSIE, b. at Enosburgh, March 31, 1811. m. Roger H. Beemace, November 11, 1834, and settled at Bolton, Vt.
1478. 5. LEONARD, b. at Enosburgh, April   , 1813. d. unmarried.
1479. 6. SARAH, b. at Enosburgh, June 1, 1814. m. Barnabas H. Lewis of Fairfax, Vt., December 21, 1841, and settled at Rushford, Vt.
1480. 7. JOEL H., b. at Enosburgh, May 4, 1818.
1481. 8. FIDELIA, b. at Enosburgh, June 28, 1820. m. Daniel Story, March 4, 1843, and settled at Fairfield.
1482. 9. HUBBARD W., b. at Enosburgh, September 10, 1822.

1483. 10. Lucetta N., b. at Bakersfield, March 15, 1824.   d. 1854,
        aged 30 years.
1484. 11. Charlotte A., b. at Bakersfield, March 19, 1826.   d. 1844,
        aged 18 years.

545.

ENOS PEASE,[6] (Ebenezer,[5] Cummings,[4] Isaac,[3] John,[2] Robert,[1]) brother of the preceding, was born at
          ; married   ; died in the State of Indiana, 1842.

His children were:

1485. 1. Alvin, b. at
1486. 2. Asa, b. at
1487. 3. Enos, b. at
1488. 4. David, b. at
1489. 5. Buenos A., b. at
1490. 6. Susan, b. at   d. a child.
1491. 7. Rebecca, b. at.
1492. 8. Susan,[2] b. at

546.

ABEL PEASE,[6] (Ebenezer,[5] Cummings,[4] Isaac,[3] John,[2] Robert,[1]) brother of the preceding, was born at Longmeadow, June 26, 1784; married Lucy Laughlin, January 20, 1806.   In 1833 he removed to Lawrence, N. Y., where he resided in 1866.

His children were:

1493. 1. Cordon, b. at Georgia, Vt., October 4, 1807.
1494. 2. Samuel I., b. in Canada, July 4, 1809.
1495. 3. Lorania, b. in Canada, October 9, 1811.   m. James McCarthy, and lived at Lawrence, N. Y.
1496. 4. Horatio N., b. in Canada, October 14, 1813.
1497. 5. George W., b. in Canada, March 26, 1815.
1498. 6. Abel, b. at Georgia, April 4, 1817.
1499. 7. Martha, b. at Fairfax, Vt., December 3, 1821.   m. Robert McCarthy, and lived in Potsdam, N. Y.
1500. 8. Chauncey O., b. at Georgia, September 26, 1825.
1501. 9. Diana, b. at Georgia, May 16, 1827.
1502. 10. Achsah, b. at Georgia, July 10, 1829.   m. Sanford Blaisdell, and lived in Lawrence, N. Y.

550.

MAJOR ELAM PEASE,[6] (ASA,[5] CUMMINGS,[4] ISAAC,[3] JOHN,[2] ROBERT,[1]) eldest son of LIEUT. ASA and BATHSHEBA (MEACHAM) PEASE of Enfield, Ct., and cousin of the preceding, was born at Enfield, April 22, 1778; married Ann Terry, June 28, 1807; lived and died at Enfield, was by occupation a farmer and surveyor. He was a man esteemed for his integrity and faithful discharge of his official duties. He was noted for unusual physical strength.

His children were:

1503. 1. BATHUA A., b. at Enfield,   1809. m. Hosea Nichols.
1504. 2. ELAM L., b. at Enfield, October 21, 1814.
1505. 3. JAMES E., b. at Enfield, January 14, 1819. was unmarried in 1865.
1506. 4. CELECIA, b. at Enfield.
1507. 5. CAROLINE, b. at Enfield,   1823. m. Romain R. Gleason.
1508. 6. MARY T., b. at   1825.

552.

MAJOR GAIUS PEASE,[6] (ASA,[5] CUMMINGS,[4] ISAAC,[3] JOHN,[2] ROBERT,[1]) brother of the preceding, was born at Enfield, March   , 1780; married Philura Ames, 1814.

His children were:

1509. 1. JANE P., b. at Enfield, May 21, 1816. m. Charles Noble, 1835.
1510. 2. ANN E., b. at Painesville, Ohio, August 3, 1818. m. Orville Douglass, and lived at Suffield, Ct.
1511. 3. GAIUS, b. at Painesville,   , 1820. d. an infant.

553.

ALPHEUS PEASE,[6] (ASA,[5] CUMMINGS,[4] ISAAC,[3] JOHN,[2] ROBERT,[1]) brother of the preceding, was born at Enfield,   ; married Azubia Kingsbury. He removed from Enfield, after the birth of his children, to Pennsylvania.

His children were :

1512. 1. PAULINA, b. at Enfield,   , 1810. m.
            Drinkwater.
1513. 2. ALPHEUS O., b. at Enfield.
1514. 3. ELIZABETH K., b. at Enfield, May 25, 1814.
1515. 4. CALISTA M., b. at Enfield, June 23, 1816.
1516. 5. LEMUEL K., b. at Enfield, January 16, 1819.
1517. 6. JOSEPH, b. at Enfield, December 25, 1820.

---o---

555.

HEMAN PEASE,[6] (HEMAN,[5] CUMMINGS,[4] ISAAC,[3] JOHN,[2]
ROBERT,[1]) eldest son of HEMAN and HANNAH (WARD)
PEASE, first of Enfield, last of Longmeadow, and cousin
of the preceding, was born at Somers, Ct.; married Abigail Combs; died in

His children were :

1518. 1. JEROME, b. at Enfield, February 22, 1815.
1519. 2. SOPHRONIA, b. at Somers, May 15, 1819. m. Austin Lyman
            of Southampton, Mass.
1520. 3. NATHANIEL b. at Somers, September 30, 1824.

556.

PLINY PEASE,[6] (HEMAN,[5] CUMMINGS,[4] ISAAC,[3] JOHN,[2]
ROBERT,[1]) second son of HEMAN and HANNAH (WARD)
PEASE, was born at Enfield, October 20, 1787; married
Hannah Fox of Bristol, N. Y., January 1, 1824, and first
settled at Bristol, after which he removed and settled at
Cannon, Mich., where he died, January 8, 1862, aged 75
years, in the hope and joy of the religion of Jesus, which
he professed in the days of his youth in New England.

His children were :

1521. 1. ACHSAH S., b. at Bristol, October 24, 1824. m. William L.
            Smith, March 28, 1849.
1522. 2. HANNAH, b. at Wolcott, August 8, 1827. m. Joseph Pines,
            November 19, 1853.

1523. 3 ABIGAIL A., b. at Bristol, December 7, 1832.
1524. 4. LESTER H., b. at Bristol, February 1, 1836.
1525. 5. FRANCES D., b. at Canadice, March 14, 1845.

559.

CHAUNCEY PEASE,⁶ (HEMAN,⁵ CUMMINGS,⁴ ISAAC,³ JOHN,² ROBERT,¹) third son of HEMAN and HANNAH (WARD) PEASE, was born at Enfield, February 20, 1792; married Harriet Crocker of Madison, Madison County, N. Y., at Wolcott, N. Y., March 4, 1828, and lived at Cannon, Kent County, Mich.

His children were :

1526. 1. AMANDA H., b. at Bristol, N. Y., October 7, 1829. m. W. P. Meddler, November   , 1852.
1527. 2. CAROLINE O., b. at Bristol, January 21, 1832. m. John H. Slack, August   , 1852, and settled at Paris, Mich.
1528. 3. HARMON B., b. at Bristol, January 9, 1837.
1529. 4. CYNTHIA L., b. at Bristol, May 27, 1840.
1530. 5. CHAUNCEY J., b. at Bristol, May 5, 1843.
1531. 6. CHARLES D., b. at Putnam, Mich., March 3, 1845.
1532. 7. WILLIAM H., b. at Cannon, Mich., July 3, 1847.
1533. 8. HARRIET E., b. at Cannon, July 16, 1850.
1534. 9. CHARITY J., b. at Cannon, March 21, 1853.

560.

ASA PEASE,⁶ (HEMAN,⁵ CUMMINGS,⁴ ISAAC,³ JOHN,² ROBERT,¹) fourth and youngest son of HEMAN and HANNAH (WARD) PEASE, was born at   ʻ   , 1794; married Amanda Dunlap, and settled in Enfield.

His children were :

1535. 1. MARY ANN, b. at   m. Howard Carpenter.
1536. 2. ALONZO, b. at   , February 14, 1824.
1537. 3. SALINA, b. at   , 1830. m. Osee Pease.
1538. 4. LUCINDA, b. at   , November 12, 1848.
1539. 5. ALBERT, b. at   . d. young.

563.

DAVID PEASE,[6] (DAVID,[5] CUMMINGS,[4] ISAAC,[3] JOHN,[2] ROBERT,[1]) eldest son of DR. DAVID and JERUSHA (SPENCER) PEASE, first of East Windsor, Ct., last of New Shoreham, R. I., and cousin of the preceding, was born at East Windsor, November 9, 1783; married Dorcas Ayres of Granby, Mass., only daughter of Eleazer Ayres, December 31, 1812. She died at Cazenovia, N. Y., June 16, 1853; married, second, Sarah Taylor of Ashfield, Mass., January 16, 1855. He was ordained as pastor of the Baptist Church in Belchertown, Mass., June 20, 1810. In 1818 he removed to Conway, Mass., and in 1823 was called to the pastorate of the Baptist Church in Cazenovia Village, N. Y. In 1827 he was dismissed from his charge of that people, to answer the request of the Baptist Church and society in Conway, to return to them and again resume the pastoral relation. Up to the year 1854 his ministerial services had been about equally divided between the States of Massachusetts and New York, when he was for the third time called to the pastorate of the Church in Conway. In the spring of 1857 he removed to Sunderland, Mass., became pastor of the Baptist Church of Sunderland and Montague, and preached for them nine years. In 1866 he removed to Ashfield, Mass., his present residence, where soon afterwards he was requested to preach to the Baptist society and which he continued eighteen months. He now regularly supplies the Baptist pulpit at Savoy, Mass.

His children were:

1540. 1. WILLIAM C., b. at Belchertown, June 17, 1814. d. July 9, 1814.

1541. 2. DAVID, b. at Belchertown, September 24, 1815.

1542. 3. EUSEBIA, b. at Belchertown, August 29, 1817. d. at Geneva, N. Y., July 1, 1844. She was Principal some time in the female department of Fayetteville Academy, Fayetteville, N. Y.

1543. 4. JOSEPHINE, b. at Conway, Mass., May 5, 1819. m. Col. A.
W. Spencer of Cazenovia Village, October   , 1837. d.
July 2, 1841. She left a son, David J., who d., aged 15
years.

1543.[1] 5. ROGER W., b. at Dana, Mass., February 22, 1822. d. at
Cazenovia, August   , 1822.

1544. 6. SARAH E., b. at Cazenovia Village, September 12, 1823. m.
Langdon Ayres, May 11, 1853, and settled at South Hadley, Mass. Her children are:
1. FREDERIC L., b. April 16, 1854.
2. FRANK P., b. February 25, 1856.
3. JAMES C., b. July 6, 1857.
4. ARTHUR S., b. September 5,.1862.

1545. 7. SPENCER A., b. at Cazenovia Village, September 24, 1825.

1546. 8. ROGER W.,[2] b. at Conway, May 31, 1828.

567.

JONATHAN S. PEASE,[6] (DAVID,[5] CUMMINGS,[4] ISAAC,[3]
JOHN,[2] ROBERT,[1]) brother of the preceding, was born at
Washington, Mass., April 13, 1791; married Hannah
Wood, daughter of Capt. Asa Wood of Somers, Ct., 1810,
and settled in Somers. He was a boot and shoemaker
by trade. Died at Somers of consumption, March 28,
1832, aged 41 years, in the triumph of a consistent hope
of eternal life through Jesus Christ.

His children were:

1547. 1. ASA W., b. at Somers,   , 1810. d. unmarried,
November 21, 1833, aged 24 years.

1548. 2. JAMES S., b. at Somers, July 17, 1813. d. May 16, 1835,
aged 22 years.

1549. 3. DAVID E., b. at Somers, July 18, 1815. m. and d. in Georgia.

1550. 4. JOHN W., b. at Somers, June 14, 1818.

1551. 5. JERUSHA, b. at Somers, October 24, 1821. d. July 9, 1850,
unmarried.

1552. 6. HANNAH, b. at Somers, January 12, 1823. d. November 13,
1840, aged 17 years.

1553. 7. DOROTHY, b. at Somers, June 28, 1825. m. J. Colwell, and
d. in Somers, January 23, 1849, aged 25 years.

1554. 8. CHERRY A., b. at Somers, November 19, 1827. d. in Somers,
unmarried.

569.

ASA PEASE,[6] (DAVID,[5] CUMMINGS,[4] ISAAC,[3] JOHN,[2] ROBERT,[1]) youngest son of DR. DAVID and JERUSHA (SPENCER) PEASE, first of East Windsor, Ct., last of New Shoreham, R. I., was born at New Shoreham, March 22, 1796; married Lydia Sheldon of Ovid, N. Y., December 10, 1818, and settled in Parma, N. Y.

His children were:

1555.   1. JONATHAN S., b. at Ovid, N. Y., March 11, 1820.

1556.   2. ELIZABETH, b. at Parma, June 16, 1822. d. 1824.

1557.   3. SARAH E., b. at Parma, November 1, 1824. m. William Coon, and settled in Albion, Mich.

1558.   4. ABIGAIL, b. at Parma, November 13, 1826. m. Daniel Knapp, and lives in Parma.

1559.   5. CORNELIA, b. at Parma, January 3, 1830. m. George Rogers, and lives in Parma.

1560.   6. ASA and } twins, b. at Parma, May 6, 1833. Asa d. infant.
         7. ASAHEL, }

1561.   8. ROSANNA, b. at Parma,   . m. Alonzo C. Bidwell of Albion, Mich., and removed to Sacramento, Cal.

L. T. Pease

SEVENTH GENERATION.

DESCENT OF JOHN.³

FAMILY OF JOHN.⁴

572.

Dr. JOHN C. PEASE,⁷ (John,⁶ John,⁵ John,⁴ John,³ John,² Robert,¹) eldest son of John and Charity (Thompson) Pease of Enfield, Ct., was born at Enfield, June 1, 1782; married Naomi G. Niles of Windsor, Ct. He entered Yale College about 1801, but at the end of the third year he gave up his college course and began the study of medicine. He entered upon his medical profession at Warehouse Point, Ct.; practiced next at Windsor and afterwards at Avon, Ct. In 1812 he removed his practice to Enfield. During his residence at Enfield he held the office of postmaster under the administration of President Madison.

In 1816 Dr. Pease gave up his medical profession, removed to Hartford, Ct., and in company with his brother-in-law, the Hon. John M. Niles, began the publication of the Hartford Times, a journal which did much in its discussions towards establishing religious freedom and political equality in the State prior to the adoption of the present State Constitution that superseded the old English Charter.

In 1821 he removed to Agawam, Mass., and resumed the practice of medicine. Remaining here two years, Dr. Pease again removed to Enfield, and continued his practice there until 1831, when he took up his residence at Hartford.

In 1849 he accepted an appointment in the Treasury Department at Washington. In consequence of feeble health, he held the appointment but a short time.

A paralytic affection terminated his life at Hartford, January 30, 1859 in the 77th year of his age.

Though Dr. Pease was much engaged in political affairs he was not an aspirant for office, but preferred to be an earnest advocate for liberty of conscience and equal rights. He was peculiar in his diet, and for more than thirty years abstained entirely from animal food and intoxicating drinks, because he thought it more conducive to his health and intellect. His memory was wonderfully retentive. He seemed able to recall every day of his life and the dates of events as they occurred. When connected with the Hartford Times, Dr. Pease wrote and published the Connecticut and Rhode Island Gazetteer. In 1842, in connection with his old college friend, the Hon. Royal Hinman, he wrote the "American Revolution," a work of much labor and research.

Among his unpublished works is the history of the town of Enfield, brought down to the period of the American Revolution. In that work we are greatly indebted to him for rescuing from oblivion the memory of many of the members of the Enfield Peases.

His children were:

1562. 1. JOHN R., b. at Windsor, Ct., April 13, 1808, and resides in Hartford, Ct., unmarried.
1563. 2. MARGARET A., b. at Farmington, Ct., March 12, 1810.
1564. 3. CALISTA N., b. at Enfield,   , 1812.   m. Rev. Theodore D. Cook, 1841, and resides in Utica, N. Y.
1565. 4. AUGUSTA D., b. at Enfield, 1815.   d. March 11, 1817.
1566. 5. ERASMUS D., b. at Enfield,   , 1824, and resides in Hartford, unmarried.

573.

WALTER PEASE,[7] (JOHN,[6] JOHN,[5] JOHN,[4] JOHN,[3] JOHN,[2] ROBERT,[1]) brother of the preceding, was born at Enfield,

March 29, 1784; married Rhoda Terry, December 31, 1807, with whom, and numerous friends, he celebrated his sixtieth anniversary wedding day.   He settled in Enfield, a farmer, where he still resides, (1868.)

His children were:

1567. 1. RHODA L., b. at Enfield, December 21, 1808. m. Wilder
          Parker, November 26, 1835, and settled in Enfield.
1568. 2. ORPHA D., b. at Enfield, August 14, 1810, and resides in
          Enfield, unmarried.
1569. 3. WALTER R., b. at Enfield, January 3, 1813. m. Sophia Bid-
          well, February 10, 1839, and lives in Manchester, Ct.
1570. 4. NANCY P., b. at Enfield, May 18, 1817, and resides in Enfield,
          unmarried.
1571. 5. CAROLINE A., b. at Enfield, January 23, 1824. m. Lyman
          Terry, April 20, 1851, and settled in Enfield.

574.

HON. LORRAIN T. PEASE,⁷ (JOHN,⁶ JOHN,⁵ JOHN,⁴ JOHN,³ JOHN,² ROBERT,¹) brother of the preceding, was born at Enfield, April 17, 1788; married Sarah Marshall of Windsor, Ct.,   , 1809.   Judge Pease was, by profession, a lawyer.   He first settled in his native town, where his children were born.   With the exception of three years at Green Bay, Wis., he spent the remainder of his life in Hartford, Ct.   He held many important public offices, the gifts of his native town, his state, and of the general government.   He has been a member of both branches of the State Legislature; for several years was Judge of Probate for the town of Enfield, and subsequently was Judge of the County Court.   He died at Hartford, 1848, aged 60 years.   His remains were buried in his native town, there to mingle with the dust of his ancestors.

His children were:

1572. 1. MARIA A. C., b. at Enfield, March 11, 1810. d. August 16,
          1822.
1573. 2. ELISHA M., b. at Enfield, January 5, 1812. m. Lucadia
          Niles, daughter of Col. Richard Niles of Windsor, Ct.,

August   , 1850, and resides at Austin, Texas. He is, by profession, a lawyer.

Mr. Pease went to Texas in 1834, and was among the first who met in council to consider the expediency of taking up arms against Mexico, and for a short time was in active military service in the war which Texas had with Mexico after the State had declared its independence.

In 1853, he was elected Governor of Texas, and held the office two terms.

At the time of the breaking out of the late Rebellion in the South, Gov. Pease was a true Union man, and he remained so through the war. Soon after Maj. Gen. Sheridan was appointed to the command of that department, Gov. Pease was appointed Military Governor of Texas, and he holds the position at the present time of writing. (April, 1868.)

1574. 3. SARAH A., b. at Enfield, January   , 1814. d. in infancy.
1575. 4. LORRAIN T., b. at Enfield, August 11, 1815. He went to Texas when quite a young man, was in military service in the war against Mexico, and with others was taken prisoner by the Mexicans. By means of a daring exploit on the way to his execution, he, with a few others, escaped the Fannin massacre. He sickened and died, August 31, 1836, in consequence of hunger, fatigue, and exposures which he suffered before he reached friendly lines after his escape.

1576. 5. JOHN J. R., b. at Enfield, June 25, 1817. m. Cornelia M. Ruger, July 14, 1851. He is, by profession, a lawyer, and resides at Janesville, Wis. He was Mayor of the city of Janesville in 1856.

1577. 6. SARAH M., b. at Enfield, September 10, 1822. m. Maj. Gen. John C. Robinson of the United States Army, who is now stationed at Detroit, Mich.

1578. 7. CAROLINE A., b. at Enfield, October 8, 1826. m. Hon. Hamilton Richardson, and resides at Janesville, Wis.

582.

THOMAS PEASE,[7] (THOMAS,[6] JOHN,[5] JOHN,[4] JOHN,[3] JOHN,[2] ROBERT,[1]) son of THOMAS and MERCY (HALL) PEASE, first of Enfield, Ct., subsequently of Ellington, Ct., and first cousin to the preceding, was born at Enfield,

1782; married Ruth Pease, daughter of Rufus Pease of Enfield, 1811, and settled in Ellington. He returned to Enfield in 1856, where he died.

His children were:

1579. 1. RUTH A., b. at Ellington, , 1812. m. Elijah P. Davis of Somers, 1847, and d. in Enfield, 1849.

1580. 2. CLARISSA, b. at Ellington, February 22, 1814. m. Charles Saunders of Enfield. d. in Enfield, April , 1845.

1581. 3. THOMAS C., b. at Ellington, July 12, 1815. m. Fidelia M. Reed, May 3, 1840, and lives in Enfield.

1582. 4. HARRIET, b. at Ellington, June 11, 1817. d. in Enfield, , 1847, aged 30 years, unmarried.

1583. 5. RHODA, b. at Ellington, , 1819. m. Joshua Crowell of Ware, Mass., February 28, 1848.

1584. 6. ROSETTA, b. at Ellington, May 11, 1821. m. Alden Markham of Enfield; m. second, Dr. Wallace, and resides in Detroit, Mich.

1585. 7. LAURA S., b. at Ellington, , 1824. m. Peter Moore of Ware, 1847. d. December , 1848.

583.

SALMON PEASE,⁷ (THOMAS,⁶ JOHN,⁵ JOHN,⁴ JOHN,³ JOHN,² ROBERT,¹) brother of the preceding, was born at Enfield, April 10, 1784; married Polly Parsons, 1816; married, second, Amanda Algies; married, third, Azuba Woodworth. He settled in Ellington, and died, 1855, aged 71 years. His children were all by his first wife.

His children were:

1586. 1. RODOLPHUS, b. at Ellington, , 1817. d. a child.

1587. 2. ERASTUS P., b. at Ellington, February 17, 1819.

1588. 3. CYRUS, b. at Ellington, December 3, 1821. m. Maria Loomis of Lebanon, Ct.

1589. 4. POLLY, b. at Ellington, February 3, 1824. m. Daniel Avery of Stafford, Ct., June 3, 1843.

1590. 5. SALMON, b. at Ellington, March 22, 1826. d. 1839, aged 13 years.

1591. 6. THEODORE, b. at Ellington, February 10, 1829. d. a child.

19

584.

CAPT. WILLIS PEASE,[7] (THOMAS,[6] JOHN,[5] JOHN,[4] JOHN,[3] JOHN,[2] ROBERT,[1]) brother of the preceding, was born at Ellington, February , 1786; married Hannah Bradley of Tolland, Ct., January 17, 1821, and died at Vernon, Ct., October 11, 1853, aged 67 years.

His children were:

1592. 1. ELIZABETH, b. at Ellington, September , 1821. m. Orville Dimmock of Stafford, Ct., 1840.

1593. 2. LAURA, b. at Ellington, November , 1822. m. Edward Low, and lived at Vernon, Ct.

1594. 3. CHESTER, b. at Ellington, February , 1824.

1595. 4. CHESTER,[2] b. at Tolland, April , 1826. m. Eliza Harrington, 1849.

1596. 5. PHILANDER, b. at Ellington, , 1834.

586.

CALVIN PEASE,[7] (THOMAS,[6] JOHN,[5] JOHN,[4] JOHN,[3] JOHN,[2] ROBERT,[1]) brother of the preceding, was born at Ellington, March 12, 1797; married Roxana Smith of Ellington, March 11, 1819, and lived in Ellington, 1856.

His children were:

1597. 1. CALVIN, b. at Ellington, September 13, 1820. m. Octa Strong. He practiced medicine for a time at Lebanon, Ct., went out as surgeon with a Connecticut Regiment of Volunteers in the late rebellion, and subsequently died South.

1598. 2. ROXANA, b. at Ellington, December 23, 1822. m. Col. Anson Fowler of Lebanon, Ct., January, 1850.

1599. 3. MARY ANN, b. at Ellington, April 19, 1825. d. December 23, 1843, aged 18 years; unmarried.

1600. 4. SOPHRONIA, b. at Ellington, March 29, 1827. m. Daniel Chaffee of Ashford, Ct., October 23, 1850.

1601. 5. JANE, b. at Ellington, October 8, 1829. d. an infant.

588.

HORACE PEASE,⁷ (GIDEON,⁶ JOHN,⁵ JOHN,⁴ JOHN,³ JOHN,² ROBERT,¹) eldest son of GIDEON and PRUDENCE (SEXTON) PEASE, first of Enfield, Ct., last of Weston, Vt., and cousin of the preceding, was born at Enfield, September 14, 1784; married Betsey Watts, October 27, 1805, and settled, first, at Manlius, Onondaga County, N. Y., next, at Spafford, of the same County, and subsequently at Salem, Wis. He died, April 12, 1863. He was a farmer.

His children were :

1602.   1. LUCIUS, b. at Manlius,   , 1807. d. June 24, 1816.
1603.   2. AARON A., b. at Manlius, February 25, 1811.   m. Julia Wetherby, and resides in Iowa.
1604.   3. MINERVA E., b. at Spafford, February 15, 1813.   m., first, George Codington ; m., second, James Marwick, September   , 1847, and resides at Adrian, Mich.
1605.   4. GALUSHA J., b. at Spafford, February 28, 1815.   m.   , and lives at Adrian, Mich.
1606.   5. SPENCER A., b. at Spafford, February 23, 1817.   m., first, Hannah Paddock,   , 1839 ; m., second, Julia A. Olden,   , 1851, and resides at Montillo, Marquette County, Wis.

Our kinsman began the profession of law but abandoned it for the study of medicine, and after graduating he commenced " a lively practice."

In 1858 Dr. Pease purchased a printing-office and became editor and proprietor of a journal called The Express. Within the past five years he has taken up the practice of law in connection with his other callings. During the past two terms (1867,) Dr. Pease has been a member of the Wisconsin Legislature.

1607.   6. CHARLOTTE A., b. at Spafford, March 30, 1819.   m. Edmund Whipple, and resides in Iowa.
1608.   7. ALMIRA S., b. at Spafford, April 29, 1821.   m. Henry Osborn, and resides at Auburn, N. Y.
1609.   8. ALLEN W., b. at Spafford, August 19, 1823.   m.   , and resides at Salem, Racine County, Wis.
1610.   9. MARY A., b. at Spafford, August 2, 1825.   m. Samuel Whipple, and resides in Indiana.

589.

MARTIN PEASE,[7] (GIDEON,[6] JOHN,[5] JOHN,[4] JOHN,[3] JOHN,[2] ROBERT,[1]) brother of the preceding, was born at Enfield, May 30, 1786 ; married   , and first settled at Marcellus, N. Y., and from thence went to Pennsylvania.

His children were:

1611. 1.
1612. 2.
1613. 3.
1614. 4.

594.

WARREN PEASE,[7] (GIDEON,[6] JOHN,[5] JOHN,[4] JOHN,[3] JOHN,[2] ROBERT,[1]) brother of the preceding, was born at Weston, February 25, 1799 ; married Fannie Field, March   , 1824, and settled in Weston, Vt., a shoemaker; died at Weston, May 6, 1862, aged 63 years. [Nelson Pease and Family Records.]

His children were:

1615. 1. MARION, b. at Weston.
1616. 2. LAURAETTA, b. at Weston.
1617. 3. LUTHER, b. at Weston.
1618. 4. CHARLES L., b. at Weston.
1619. 5. LUCINDA, b. at Weston.
1620. 6. MARTHA J., b. at Weston.
1621. 7. HULDAH, b. at Weston.

596.

NELSON PEASE,[7] (GIDEON,[6] JOHN,[5] JOHN,[4] JOHN,[3] JOHN,[2] ROBERT,[1]) brother of the preceding, was born at Weston,   ; married Anna Hamilton,   , 1830, and settled in Weston, Vt.

His children were:

1622. 1. ELIZA A., b. at Weston, June 30, 1831. m. Wilbur C. Tenny, March 12, 1850, and first settled at Nashua, N. H ; m., second, W. P. Tenny, 1861.

1623. 2. Rhoda A., b. at Weston, August 22, 1832. m. James Wright of Nashua, N. H., February 12, 1854, and d. there.

1624. 3. Betsey A., b. at Weston, June 21, 1833. m. Charles W. Turner, April 14, 1855, and lives in Weston.

1625. 4. Hiland N., b. at Weston, November 7, 1835. m. Lydia Chapin, February 13, 1858, and lived in Weston.

1626. 5. Mary M., b. at Weston, October 21, 1838. m. Harvy Willibe, April 5, 1856, and lives in Hollis, N. H.

1627. 6. Nancy J., b. at Weston, February 16, 1841. m. Isaac L. Smith, June 10, 1856, and lives in Weston.

1628. 7. Lorin H., b. at Weston, October 13, 1843. . He was in the army, Tenth Regiment of Vermont Volunteers, for the suppression of the late rebellion.

597.

ASAHEL PEASE,⁷ (Gideon,⁶ John,⁵ John,⁴ John,³ John,² Robert,¹) brother of the preceding, was born at Weston, May 6, 1808; married Sally Ray of Coxsackie, N. Y., November 20, 1836, and settled in Weston, Vt. [Family Records.)

His children were:

1629. 1. Edwin A., b. at Weston, July 29, 1838. He was connected with the Tenth Regiment of Vermont Volunteers, 1865.

1630. 2. William H., b. at Weston, April 23, 1840. d. September 13, 1862, in New Orleans, La. He was connected with the army, belonging to the Seventh Regiment of Vermont Volunteers.

1631. 3. Clark W., b. at Weston, December 6, 1841. He was a member of the Vermont Frontier Cavalry, 1865.

1632. 4. James R., b. at Weston, January 2, 1843. d. June 23, 1858.

1633. 5. John Q., b. at Weston, August 19, 1844.

599.

HARVEY PEASE,⁷ (Simeon,⁶ John,⁵ John,⁴ John,³ John,² Robert,¹) son of Simeon and Susan (McGregory) Pease of Enfield, Ct., last of Hartford, Ct., and cousin of the preceding, was born at Enfield, April 15, 1790; married Martha Pease, daughter of John Pease, April 4, 1819, and settled in Hartford, where he died, August 16, 1835, aged 45 years.

His children were:

1634. 1. Orrin, b. at Hartford, June 4, 1820. d. October 13, 1839, aged 19 years.

1635. 2. James H., b. at Hartford, November 4, 1821. d. August 22, 1822.

1636. 3. Edwin T., b. at Hartford, January 23, 1823. m. Frances Geer, October 29, 1845, and settled in Hartford, a bookseller. He d. January 27, 1856, leaving two children.

1637. 4. Ann A., b. at Hartford, March 7, 1825. d. November 9, 1826.

1638. 5. James M., b. at Hartford, December 12, 1826. d. September 12, 1828.

1639. 6. Martha A., b. at Hartford, January 21, 1829. d. February 12, 1855.

1640. 7. Adalaide A., b. at Hartford, February 12, 1831.

1641. 8. Jane M. A., b. at Hartford, April 18, 1832. d. June 5, 1852.

1642. 9. John A., b. at Hartford, September 27, 1835. He has been clerk in the post office at Hartford for several years past.

602.

THEODORE PEASE,[7] (Simeon,[6] John,[5] John,[4] John,[3] John,[2] Robert,[1]) brother of the preceding, was born at Enfield, March 15, 1797; married, first, married, second, ; d. at Hartford, Ct., October 26, 1844, aged 47 years.

His children were:

1643. 1. William and } b. at Hartford, Nov. 8, 1823. William d. infant.
1644. 2. Elizabeth, }

1645. 3. Frances A., b. at Hartford, January 8, 1826.

BY SECOND WIFE:

1646. 4. Eliza, b. at Hartford, December 28, 1836.

1647. 5. Norman b. at Hartford, February 20, 1842. d. February 20, 1847.

606.

SIMEON PEASE,⁷ (SIMEON,⁶ JOHN,⁵ JOHN,⁴ JOHN,³ JOHN,² ROBERT,¹) brother of the preceding, was born at Hartford, August 9, 1807 ; married   , and settled at Philadelphia, Pa., where he died.

His children were :

1648. 1. ELIZABETH, b. at
1649. 2. WILLIAM, b. at
1650. 3. SIMEON, b. at

———ooo———

FAMILY OF JAMES.⁴

607.

ELIJAH PEASE,⁷ (JOHN,⁶ JAMES,⁵ JAMES,⁴ JOHN,³ JOHN,² ROBERT,¹) eldest child of JOHN and ZEPARY (COY) PEASE of Somers, Ct., and third cousin of the preceding, was born at Somers, February 12, 1770 ; married   , and lived some time near Somers, Ct., and in Stafford, Ct., and finally removed to the State of New York, where he left a family.

His children were :

1651. 1. WILLIAM, b. at
1652. 2.

609.

AARON PEASE,⁷ (JOHN,⁶ JAMES,⁵ JAMES,⁴ JOHN,³ JOHN,² ROBERT,¹) brother of the preceding, was born at March   , 1786 ; married Tabitha Sargent of Spencer, Mass., June   , 1812, and settled in Marlboro, Vt., where he died, February 15, 1855.

His children were :

1653. 1. AARON, b. at Marlboro, May 15, 1813. m. Louisa S. May, December 5, 1838, and lives in Marlboro. He has eleven children.

1654. 2. ABRAHAM, b. at Marlboro, March 8, 1815. m.
, and first settled in Marlboro; was living in 1865 in Warren County, N. Y.

1655. 3. EDMUND N., b. at Marlboro, February 15, 1817. d. unmarried, May , 1855.

1656. 4. ISAAC, b. at Marlboro, February 25, 1819. d. 1836.

1657. 5. LOIS, b. at Marlboro, March 21, 1821.

1658. 6. SUSAN E., b. at Marlboro, February 1, 1823. m. John L. A. Winchester, January 9, 1815, and lives in Marlboro.

1659. 7. EUNICE, b. at Marlboro, October 10, 1825. d. February 2, 1831.

1660. 8. ZIPPORAH A., b. at Marlboro, June 10, 1827. d. February 9, 1831.

1661. 9. MIRIAM, b. at Marlboro, January 28, 1829. m. Horatio T. Bellows, October , 1849. d. February , 1857.

1662. 10. SARAH, b. at Marlboro, April 28, 1830. d. September, 1857.

1663. 11. MARY A., b. at Marlboro, May 17, 1832. d. August 26, 1836.

———o———

614.

JOEL PEASE,[7] (JOEL,[6] JAMES,[5] JAMES,[4] JOHN,[3] JOHN,[2] ROBERT,[1]) son of CAPT. JOEL and LOVISA (MEACHAM) PEASE, first of Somers, Ct., subsequently of Wilbraham, Mass., last of Vermont, and cousin of the preceding.

615.

JAMES PEASE,[7] (JOEL,[6] JAMES,[5] JAMES,[4] JOHN,[3] JOHN,[2] ROBERT,[1]) brother of the preceding, was born at ; moved to Vermont.

616.

FREDERICK M. PEASE,[7] (JOEL,[6] JAMES,[5] JAMES,[4] JOHN,[3] JOHN,[2] ROBERT,[1]) brother of the preceding, was born at

———oo———

621.

SETH PEASE,[7] (SAMUEL,[6] RICHARD,[5] JAMES,[4] JOHN,[3] JOHN,[2] ROBERT,[1]) second son of SAMUEL and SARAH (ROOT)

PEASE of Somers, and second cousin of the preceding, was born at Somers, August 7, 1796; married Ann Kibbe, daughter of Luke Kibbe of Somers, May 13, 1822, and settled in Somers, a farmer. He died, September 28, 1854.

His children were:

1664. 1. SETH P., b. at Somers, January 31, 1824. m., first, Pamelia
Pomeroy; m., second,   of Illinois.

1665. 2. LIDORA A., b. at Somers, June 24, 1825. d.,
aged 13 years.

1666. 3. LUKE K., b. at Somers, September 8, 1828. m. Louisa
Kibbe, May 15, 1851, and resides in Somers.

1667. 4. LEVERETT E., b. at Somers,   . m. Sarah J.
Brown, and resides in Hartford, Ct.

1668. 5. HORATIO E., b. at Somers,   . m. Carrie T.
Bradley.

1669. 6. JOSEPH A., b. at Somers   . m. Lidora Hunn,
and resides in Somers.

623.

SOLOMON PEASE,⁷ (SAMUEL,⁶ RICHARD,⁵ JAMES,⁴ JOHN,³ JOHN,² ROBERT,¹) brother of the preceding, was born at Somers, November 3, 1804; married Esther Shaw, and settled in Somers, but subsequently removed to Northampton, Mass. He had no children in 1868.

————o————

624.

RICHARD PEASE,⁷ (RICHARD,⁶ RICHARD,⁵ JAMES,⁴ JOHN,³ JOHN,² ROBERT,¹) eldest son of CAPT. RICHARD and SOVIER (PARSONS) PEASE of Somers, Ct., and cousin of the preceding, was born at Somers, September 3, 1789; married Philena Jones, daughter of Benjamin Jones of Somers, May 14, 1816, and settled, a farmer, in Somers.

His child was:

1670. 1. PHILENA, b. at Somers,   . m. John Russell, and lives upon her father's homestead.
20

626.

WALTER PEASE,[7] (RICHARD,[6] RICHARD,[5] JAMES,[4] JOHN,[3] JOHN,[2] ROBERT,[1]) brother of the preceding, was born at Somers, July 4, 1795; married Louisa Spencer, January 26, 1826, and settled in Somers, a farmer, where he died, November 8, 1864.

His children were:

1671. 1. LUKE H., b. at Somers, November 16, 1826. m., first, Louisa Hall, April 28, 1853; m., second, Charlotte Phelps, December 24, 1862, and resides in Springfield, Mass.

He came to Springfield in 1853, and was engaged two years in the manufacture of soap. He next purchased a livery stable and omnibus stage business which he continued in until his public official duties called for his undivided attention to them. In 1858 he was appointed Assistant City Marshal, and in 1862 he received the appointment of City Marshal, a position he has held since, except 1863. During the past five years he has been one of the Overseers of the Poor, and Almoner of that Board. In the administration of his official duties he has most signally gained the approval of the law-abiding citizens of all political parties.

He was among the earliest of our kinsmen to give cheering testimonials of approval for the labors in which the senior compiler of this work has been so long engaged, and a valuable counselor to the associate editor in the duties of his position.

1672. 2. MARY L., b. at Somers, February 4, 1828. m. Henry I. Fuller, May 5, 1852, and resides in Springfield.

1673. 3. NEWTON W., b. at Somers, November 12, 1830. m. Augusta M. Lull, December 9, 1855; m., second, Harriet E. Russell, October 26, 1863; resided several years in Springfield, Mass., and in 1865 removed to Granby, Mass.

1674. 4. EDWIN S., b. at Somers, November 2, 1832. d. August 5, 1854.

1675. 5. LUMAN S., b. at Somers, May 26, 1835. m. Agnes Gauley, May 10, 1866, and resides at San Francisco, Cal. He is general book-keeper in the Banking and Commercial House of John Parrot & Co.

1676. 6. SANFORD C., b. at Somers, October 5, 1841,

627.

ORRIN PEASE,⁷ (Richard,⁶ Richard,⁵ James,⁴ John,³ John,² Robert,¹) brother of the preceding, was born at Somers, June 10, 1797; married Delina Sexton, March 31, 1824, and settled in Somers, where he died, June 30, 1852, aged 55 years.

His child was:

1677.   1. Orrin E., b. at Somers, September 2, 1832.   m. Josephine Owen, May 11, 1861.   She d. August 11, 1865.   He resides in Springfield, Mass.

628.

ALPHEUS PEASE,⁷ (Richard,⁶ Richard,⁵ James,⁴ John,³ John,² Robert,¹) brother of the preceding, was born at Somers, Ct., July 18, 1799; married Clarissa Jones, daughter of Benjamin Jones of Somers, December 7, 1825, and settled in Somers, where he died, October 16, 1849, aged 51 years.

His children were:

1678.   1. Alpheus, b. at Somers, September 23, 1826.
1679.   2. Abiel J., b. at Somers, August 11, 1828.   d. March 13, 1829.
1680.   3. Richard F., b. at Somers, February 25, 1830.   m. Harriet M. Kenyon, and resides at Hartford, Ct., a merchant, 1868.
1681.   4. Benjamin J., b. at Somers, June 2, 1840.   d. January 1861 while a clerk in his brother's store.

630.

AUSTIN PEASE,⁷ (Richard,⁶ Richard,⁵ James,⁴ John,³ John,² Robert,¹) brother of the preceding, was born at Somers, March 8, 1804; married Olive Waters, August 23, 1825; married, second, Mary Russell; married, third, Sarah Silcox.   He lives in Somers, and is well known as a veterinary surgeon.

His children were :

BY FIRST WIFE:

1682. 1. OLIVE M., b. at Somers, January 10, 1831. m. Samuel Slater, and d at Enfield, December 30, 1865.

1683. 2. ABIGAIL S., b. at Somers,   , 1835.

1684. 3. AUSTIN C., b. at Somers May 16, 1838.

BY THIRD WIFE:

1685. 4.. WILLIAM C., b. at Somers, May 3, 1853.

631.

AZARIAH PEASE,[7] (RICHARD,[6] RICHARD,[5] JAMES,[4] JOHN,[3] JOHN,[2] ROBERT,[1]) brother of the preceding, was born at Somers, May 22, 1806; married Abigail Edson, , 1841; died, July 26, 1844.

His child was :

1686. 1. SARAH E., b. at   , February 4, 1843. d. an infant.

———ooo———

FAMILY OF JOSEPH.[4]

638.

HENRY PEASE,[7] (ZENO,[6] JOSEPH,[5] JOSEPH,[4] JOHN,[3] JOHN,[2] ROBERT,[1]) son of ZENO and HANNAH (LEAVITT) PEASE of Suffield, and third cousin of the preceding, was born at Norwich, Mass., January 14, 1787; married Sarah King,   . He settled in Suffield.

His children were :

1687. 1. HENRY, b. at Suffield, April 18, 1818. m., first, Laura M. Booth, January 16, 1845; m., second, Anne E. Church, May 22, 1856, and resides at Hartford, Ct.

1688. 2. CYNTHIA, b. at Suffield, July 18, 1821. m. Henry A. Loomis, August   , 1844, and settled in Suffield.

1689. 3. ZENO K., b. at Suffield, September 18, 1823. m., first, Harriet P. Loomis, October 13, 1847; m., second, Lydia L. Chapman, September 29, 1858, and resides at Hartford, Ct.

1690. 4. SARAH I., b. at Suffield, October 18, 1830. m. Alva Oatman.   , 1855, and resided in New York City.

1690.[2] 5. HELEN M., b. at Suffield, June 23, 1834.

641.

CHAUNCEY PEASE,⁷ (ZENO,⁶ JOSEPH,⁵ JOSEPH,⁴ JOHN,³ JOHN,² ROBERT,¹) brother of the preceding, was born at , February 1, 1793 ; married Julia Fowler, and settled in Westfield, Mass., a farmer, where he died, December 22, 1855.

His children were :

1691. 1. STEUBEN, b. at Westfield,   , 1819. m. Lucinda
Palmer, and lived in Westfield, where he d. 1866.

1692. 2. ADALINE, b. at Westfield, May 3, 1821. m. Milo Underhill,
March 16, 1850, and resides at East Granville, Mass.

1693. 3. HENRY, b. at Westfield, March 27, 1823. m. Fally Phelon,
April 12, 1849, and resides in Westfield.

1694. 4. HANNAH, b. at Westfield,   , 1825. d., aged 22
years, unmarried.

1695. 5. JULIA, b. at Westfield,   . m., first, Henry Carrier ;
m., second, Azariah Judson. d.   , 1863.

1696. 6. JAMES, b. at Westfield,   . m. Mariette Moody,
and resides in Westfield.

1697. 7. JOHN, b. at Westfield,   . d. young.

1698. 8. MARIAM, b. at Westfield,   . . d., aged 13 years.

1699. 9. MARTHA, b. at Westfield,   . d. young.

1700. 10. CHARLOTTE, b. at Westfield,   . m. Franklin
Terrett, June   , 1868.

————o————

649.

GAMALIEL PEASE,⁷ (SETH,⁶ JOSEPH,⁵ JOSEPH,⁴ JOHN,³ JOHN,² ROBERT,¹) second son of SETH and BATHSHEBA (KENT) PEASE, last of Philadelphia, and cousin of the preceding, was born at Suffield, June 26, 1790 ; married Frances F. Oliver, August 6, 1817, and resided sometime at Washington, Miss., where he died, September 12, 1823. He was a mail contractor and land agent.

His children were :

1700.³ 1. JAMES O., b. at Washington, June 1, 1818. m. Mary D. Rath-
bone, October 30, 1850, and resides at Germantown, Pa.
He is a dry goods and commission merchant in Philadelphia.

1700.⁴ 2. FRANCES A., b. at Washington, October 8, 1819. m. John
              L. Erringer, November 22, 1849, and resides in Phila-
              delphia.
1700.⁵ 3. MARY L., b. at   , February 5, 1822. d. Sep-
              tember 16, 1823.
1700.⁶ 4., GAMALIEL, b. at   , January 30, 1824. d. Feb-
              ruary 3, 1831.

650.

ALFRED PEASE,⁷ (SETH,⁶ JOSEPH,⁵ JOSEPH,⁴ JOHN,³
JOHN,² ROBERT,¹) brother of the preceding, was born at
         , May 28, 1793; married Amelia Lowry.
From 1810 to 1831 he resided at Washington, D. C., since
then he has lived at Carrolton, Ohio.

His children were:

1700.⁷   1. LUCY, b. at   , October 14, 1820.
1700.⁸   2. HANNAH, b. at   , December 15, 1821.
1700.⁹   3. SETH, b. at   , February 23, 1824. m. Margaret,
              daughter of Thomas Dodds of Carrolton, Ohio.
1700.¹⁰ 4. JAMES A., b. at   ➤   , October 16, 1826. d. 1828.
1700.¹¹ 5. ALFRED, b. at   , October 22, 1829. d. August
              30, 1838.
1700.¹² 6. ELIZABETH, b. at   , June 8, 1832. m. John H.
              Lowry of Stafford County, Va., December 26, 1866.
1700.¹³ 7. Infant, d. young.

——o——

651.

HORACE PEASE,⁷ (JOSEPH,⁶ JOSEPH,⁵ JOSEPH,⁴ JOHN,³
JOHN,² ROBERT,¹) eldest son of JOSEPH and ELIZABETH
(PIERCE) PEASE, first of Suffield, Ct., and last of Carrolton,
Ohio, and cousin of the preceding, was born at Suffield, Ct.,
February 14, 1791; married, first, Ann Stilts, January   ,
1821; married, second, Sarah Bellville, February 7, 1832.
He lived in Cincinnati, Ohio, from 1818 to 1827; the next
four years at Hole's Creek, Montgomery, Ohio; from 1831
to 1839 at Carrolton, Ohio, and since then at Dayton, Ohio.

His children were:

1700.¹⁴ - 1. James, b. at   , October 28, 1821. d. in California, 1850.

1700.¹⁵ 2. Webster H., b. at   , January 29, 1823. m. Emma C. Smith, May 7, 1846, and resides at Fulton Rock, Wis.

1700.¹⁶ 3. Ellen M., b. at   , February 2, 1825.

1700.¹⁷ 4. William, b. at   , April 16, 1829. d. May 5, 1830.

BY SECOND WIFE:

1700.¹⁸ 5. Walter B., b. at   , December 14, 1832. He was among the first in Ohio to respond to President Lincoln's call for ninety days' men upon the breaking out of the Rebellion. He had under his command a Company of State Militia, called the "Dayton Light Guards." He was ordered to the defense of Washington, and served under Brig.-Gen. Robert C. Schenck. At the expiration of his term of service, he was commissioned as Captain in the Seventeenth Regiment of United States Infantry, and served as such through the whole of Gen. McClellan's campaigns. When under Gen. Grant, he was taken prisoner at Cold Harbor, Va., and first thrown into Libby Prison, next to one in Georgia, and last at Columbia, S. C., where he was paroled with greatly impaired health, only a short time before the surrender of the Southern Rebel Army to Gen. Sherman.

In 1867 Capt. Pease was ordered to Texas where he has served in various responsible military capacities to the present time, (November 20, 1868). He now holds the appointment of Lieutenant-Colonel by brevet.

1700.¹⁹ 6. Francis E., b. at   , March 12, 1835. d. August 18, 1835.

1700.²⁰ 7. Charles E., b. at   , August 20, 1836. m. Laura G. Ervin, granddaughter of the late Judge Calvin Pease of Warren, Ohio, October 3, 1865. He served as a volunteer in the defense of Cincinnati when threatened by the rebel Gen. Kirby Smith. He afterwards served as Quartermaster at Nashville, Tenn.

1700.²¹ 8. Mary J., b. at   , March 15, 1839. m. James Stockstell, February 5, 1861.

1700.²² 9. Infant, d. young.

1700.²³ 10. Harriet B., b. at   , September 11, 1844. m. Charles B. Clegg, October 31, 1865.

1700.²⁴ 11. Anna E., b. at   , June 1, 1848.

652.

EDWARD PEASE,[7] (Joseph,[6] Joseph,[5] Joseph,[4] John,[3] John,[2] Robert,[1]) brother of the preceding, was born at Suffield, Ct., November 3, 1792; married Martha Phifer, February 7, 1824, and first settled at Hole's Creek, Ohio; died at Dayton Ohio, October 15, 1850.

His children were:

1700.[25] 1. Oliver W., b. at   , November 4, 1824. m. Isabella Dodds of Carrollton, Ohio.

1700.[26] 2. Horace, b. at   , January 22, 1827.

1700.[27] 3. Henry, b. at   , May 2, 1830. d. August 31, 1851.

1700.[28] 4. Albert, b. at   , June 28, 1832. d. May 24, 1852.

1700.[29] 5. Perry, b. at   , March 1, 1835. m. Ann Remley.

1700.[30] 6. Joseph, b. at   , August 4, 1838. d. in the hospital at Murfreesboro, Tenn., June 17, 1863, while in his country's service. He was in the Ninety-Third Ohio Regiment of Volunteers, and once taken prisoner and held for a short time by Kirby Smith.

1700.[31] 7. Elizabeth, (twin,) b. at   , August 4, 1838. m. John L. Hole, and lived at Hole's Creek, Ohio, where she d., September 28, 1864.

1700.[32] 8. Mary E., b. at   , January 22, 1845.

653.

PERRY PEASE,[7] (Joseph,[6] Joseph,[5] Joseph,[4] John,[3] John,[2] Robert,[1]) brother of the preceding, was born at Suffield, January 29, 1797; married, first, Catharine E. Smith, December 3, 1822 who died October 4, 1851; married, second, Mrs. Caroline M. Vanburen, daughter of Peter Groat of Chatham, N. Y., October 17, 1856. He, resided at Carrolton, Ohio, where he died, September 8, 1863.

His children were:

1700.[33] 1. George M., b. at   , December 10, 1825. d. May 1, 1841.

1700.[34] 2. Caroline, b. at   , May 13, 1828. d. June 18, 1838.

1700.³⁵   3. WILLIAM, b. at   , August 1, 1830. m. Cornelia
J. Gray, August 14, 1851. Capt. Pease served during the
late war of the rebellion in the First Ohio Heavy Artillery.

1700.³⁶   4. JOSEPH, b. at   , November 10, 1832. m. Sarah
C. Cotterell, November 30, 1854. He d. May 14, 1861.

1700.³⁷   5. JULIA, b. at   ·   , March 2, 1835. m. Israel L.
Spencer, October 17, 1854, and resides at Suffield, Ct.

1700.³⁸   6. ELIZABETH, b. at   , July 24, 1837. m. John Zim-
merman, October 5, and resides at Carrolton, Ohio, (1858.)

1700.³⁹   7. GEORGE M., b. at   , February 25, 1841. d.
March 29, 1862.

1700.⁴⁰   8. BATHSHEBA, b. at   , May 12, 1843. m. Charles
F. Cox., December 5, 1865, and resides at Saratoga, N. Y.

BY SECOND WIFE :

1700.⁴¹   9. ALICE M., b. at   May 3, 1859.

654.

GEORGE PEASE,⁷ (JOSEPH,⁶ JOSEPH,⁵ JOSEPH,⁴ JOHN,³
JOHN,² ROBERT,¹) brother of the preceding, was born at
Suffield, Ct., November 25, 1798; married, first, Ellen
Wheatley, November 16, 1839; married, second, Mary A.
Lamme, April 6, 1841. He removed to Carrolton, Ohio,
1825, where it is supposed he still resides.

His children were :

1700.⁴²   1. MARY D., b. at   , June 9, 1832.
1700.⁴³   2. MINDWELL, b. at   , April 19, 1834.
1700.⁴⁴   3. GAMALIEL, b. at   , May 31, 1837. He served in
the Union Army during the late Rebellion; three years as
private in the Sixty-Ninth Ohio Regiment of Volunteers, and
was engaged in the battles of Stone River, Chicamauga,
Mission Ridge, and many other sharp skirmishes.

1700.⁴⁵   4. ELLEN, b. at   , November 5, 1839. m. Hezekiah
Ulm, March 15, 1866.

BY SECOND WIFE :

1700.⁴⁶   5. HORACE, b. at   , September 18, 1842. He served
in an Ohio Regiment of Volunteers for the defense of Cincinnati when threatened by the rebel Gen. Kirby Smith,
and afterwards in the One Hundred and Thirty-Second Ohio
21

Regiment of Volunteers of "one hundred days' men," and
was stationed at Bermuda Hundred, Va.

1700⁴⁷.   6. DAVID W., b. at   , September 22, 1846.

1700⁴⁸.   7. HARRIET, b. at   , July 12, 1851.*

———o———

663.

DON PEASE,⁷ (WILLIAM,⁶ JOSEPH,⁵ JOSEPH,⁴ JOHN,³
JOHN,² ROBERT,¹) only son of WILLIAM and ZILPHA
(SPENCER) PEASE of Suffield, Ct.; and cousin of the preceding, was born at Suffield, May 11, 1797; married
Sarah Alden, daughter of Dr. Alden of Suffield. He settled and lived in Suffield, and was, by occupation, a house
painter. He died, November 28, 1868.

His children were:

1701.   1. SARAH L., b. at Suffield,   , 1844.

1702.   2. LUCY G., b. at Suffield, March 12, 1847.

1703.   3. WILLIAM H., b. at Suffield, May 9, 1850.

———o———

667.

CHARLES PEASE,⁷ (CALVIN,⁶ JOSEPH,⁵ JOSEPH,⁴ JOHN,³
JOHN,² ROBERT,¹) third son of HON. CALVIN and LAURA
(RISLEY) PEASE of Warren, Ohio, and first cousin of the
preceding, was born at Warren, February 11, 1811; married Mary E., daughter of Israel P. Kirtland, July 24,
1832. For a time he was a resident of Warren, Ohio.
He now resides in Cleveland, Ohio, and is Secretary of
the Cleveland, Wooster and Zanesville Railroad Company.

---

* The history of the last five families was prepared and furnished for this work
by Mrs. Elizabeth P. Phileo, daughter of D. W. Norton, Esq., and his wife, Mindwell. (See No. 655.) She has our thanks. She gave us at the same time the history of Capt. James H. Hughes, son of John Hughes, Esq., and his wife, Elizabeth,
(See No. 657,) which came too late for insertion in its proper place. Capt. Hughes
served in the army, for the suppression of the Rebellion, in the Fifty-Ninth Regiment of Indiana Volunteers, Company H., first as Second, next as First Lieutenant,
and afterwards as Captain. His regiment was engaged in the siege at Vicksburgh,
afterwards in the battles at Chicamauga, Lookout Mountain, etc., and was with Gen.
Sherman in his famous march through Georgia to the sea-coast.

His children were:

1704. 1. JARED P. K., b. at   , July 18, 1833. d. December 17, 1836.

1705. 2. CHARLES, b. at   , August 17, 1835. m. Hester M., daughter of Orvis W. Hotchkiss of Rockport, Ohio, September 12, 1859. He served one year on the Mississippi River, during the late war, as fourth Master on the Gunboat Conestoga, and was honorably discharged on account of sickness contracted in the service. He was afterwards in the employ of the Collins Overland Telegraph Company in Russian America, and in command of the first steam-boat that ever navigated the Youcan River.

1706. 3. CAROLINE A., b. at   , September 23, 1838. m. William L. Cutter of Cleveland, Ohio., October 5, 1859.

1707. 4. FREDERICK K., b. at   , March 17, 1843. d. May 27, 1854.

————oo————

671.

ALVIN PEASE,⁷ (PETER,⁶ STEPHEN,⁵ JOSEPH,⁴ JOHN,³ JOHN,² ROBERT,¹) eldest son of PETER and DESIRE (MUNSEL) PEASE, first of East Windsor, Ct., last of Hadley, Mass., and second cousin to the preceding, was born at East Windsor, February 20, 1784; married, first, Mary Brown; married, second, Mary Beecher. He died at Windsor, N. Y.

His children were:

1708. 1. LUCINA, b. at
1709. 2. LORIN, b. at
1710. 3. JUSTUS B., b. at
1711. 4. HARRIET, b. at

BY SECOND WIFE:

1712. 5. SARAH, b. at
1713. 6. MARY, b. at
1714. 7. ALVIN, b. at
1715. 8. EDWARD and } b. at
1716. 9. EDWIN,

672.

ELIPHALET PEASE,[7] (PETER,[6] STEPHEN,[5] JOSEPH,[4] JOHN,[3] JOHN,[2] ROBERT,[1]) brother of the preceding, was born at East Windsor, November 14, 1785; married Elizabeth Lee. He settled in Coventry, N. Y.

His children were:

1717.	1. ELIPHALET L., b. at		
1718.	2. SAMANTHA S., b. at		
1719.	3. CHARLES P., b. at		d. young.
1720.	4. GEORGE, b. at		
1721.	5. CHARLES P.,[2] b. at		

673.

ORRIN PEASE,[7] (PETER,[6] STEPHEN,[5] JOSEPH,[4] JOHN,[3] JOHN,[2] ROBERT,[1]) brother of the preceding, was born at East Windsor, January 28, 1788; married Caroline Dummer, July 4, 1811. He lived in Ithica, N. Y., where he died, April 19, 1856, aged 68 years. He was a painter by trade.

His children were:

1722.	1. ANN MARIA, b. at	, March 19, 1817. m. Rev.
	Alpheus Hamilton, a Methodist minister, in Wisconsin.	
1723.	2. EDWARD W., b. at	, July 5, 1819.
1724.	3. LOUISA C., b. at	, April 7, 1821. m. Gilbert
	Travis of Freetown, N. Y.	
1725.	4. CHARLES F., b. at	, June 5, 1823.
1726.	5. ORRIN W., b. at	, October 17, 1825.
1727.	6. ADALINE S., b. at	, November 4, 1827. d.
	January 31, 1831.	
1728.	7. LUCIUS F., b. at	, November 24, 1829.
1729.	8. HARMON D., b. at	, November 24, 1832.
1730.	9. MARY ANN, b. at	, December 3, 1834.

674.

PETER PEASE,[7] (PETER,[6] STEPHEN,[5] JOSEPH,[4] JOHN,[3] JOHN,[2] ROBERT,[1]) brother of the preceding, was born at

East Windsor, January 7, 1790; married Martha Chapin, January 18, 1824. He lived in Wilbraham, Mass., where he died, November   , 1838, aged 48 years.

His children were:

1731. 1. MARGARET, b. at
1732. 2. HARTWELL, b. at
1733. 3. FRANCIS, b. at

675.

LEMUEL PEASE,⁷ (PETER,⁶ STEPHEN,⁵ JOSEPH,⁴ JOHN,³ JOHN,² ROBERT,¹) brother of the preceding, was born at East Windsor, January 20, 1792; married   , and settled at East Windsor, but subsequently removed to Hadley, where he died, March 17, 1835, aged 44 years.

His children were:

1734. 1. MARTHA, b. at East Windsor,   . m. Levi
           Chapin, and settled in Chicopee.
1735. 2. CAROLINE, b. at East Windsor.
1736. 3. JOHN, b. at East Windsor, January 17, 1827. m. Elizabeth
           A. Rhodes and lives in Springfield, Mass.

677.

WILLIS PEASE,⁷ (PETER,⁶ STEPHEN,⁵ JOSEPH,⁴ JOHN,³ JOHN,² ROBERT,¹) brother of the preceding, was born at East Windsor, April 16, 1798; married Lucy Weeks, September 10, 1834, and first settled in Hadley, Mass., removed thence and settled in Northampton, his present residence. He is, by occupation, a house painter.

His children were:

1737. 1. LUCY ELLEN, b. at Hadley, July 8, 1835. m. Edwin Pelton,
           June 2, 1855, and lives in Northampton.
1738. 2. ISADORE, b. at Hadley, August 9, 1836.
1739. 3. ADELIA D., b. at Hadley, October 31, 1837.
1740. 4. AMANDA M., b. at Northampton, December 27, 1838. d.
           November 4, 1839.

1741.   5. EMERSON F., b. at Northampton, March 21, 1840.   d. March 2, 1844.
1742.   6. EDWARD W., b. at Northampton, December 2, 1841.
1743.   7. EMERSON F.,[2] b. at Northampton, March 24, 1843.
1744.   8. LORENZO M., b. at Northampton, July 13, 1845.
1745.   9. GEORGE A., b. at Northampton, February 26, 1847.
1746. 10. AMANDA M.,[2] b. at Northampton, July 4, 1848.
1747. 11. MARTHA ANN, b. at Northampton, August 3, 1850.
1748. 12. ALICE LILLY, b. at Northampton, February 3, 1853.

679.

LORIN PEASE,[7] (PETER,[6] STEPHEN,[5] JOSEPH,[4] JOHN,[3] JOHN,[2] ROBERT,[1]) brother of the preceding, was born at East Windsor, April 30, 1802; married, first, Chloe Stark; married, second, Lucinda Griswold, December   , 1841, and lives in Hadley, near the foot of Mount Holyoke.

His children were:

1749.   1. LUCINA, b. at Hadley, April 1, 1832.   m. John Barton, 1851.
1750.   2. LORISSA, b. at Hadley, December 24, 1834.   m. Hiram Shumway, 1853.
1751.   3. ALVA, b. at Hadley, February 28 1836.   m. and lives in Hadley.

BY SECOND WIFE:

1752.   4. LUCIUS M., b. at Hadley, January 7, 1842.
1753.   5. MARIA L., b. at Hadley, December 8, 1844.   d. September , 1864.

681.

REUBEN PEASE,[7] (AMOS,[6] STEPHEN,[5] JOSEPH,[4] JOHN,[3] JOHN,[2] ROBERT,[1]) eldest son of AMOS and POLLY, or MARY (PEASE) PEASE, first of Enfield, Ct., last of Lenoxville, Pa., and first cousin of the preceding, was born at Enfield, December 3, 1802; married Hannah Crane, October 12, 1829, and settled in Wilbraham, near the Seminary in that place, and is, by occupation, a boot and shoemaker.

His children were:

1754. 1. WILLIAM GEORGE, b. at Wilbraham, July 13, 1833.
1755. 2. REUBEN R., b. at Wilbraham,   , 1836. d. September 26, 1853, aged 17 years.

—————oo—————

684.

LEWIS PEASE,[7] (DAVID,[6] JONATHAN,[5] JOSEPH,[4] JOHN,[3] JOHN,[2] ROBERT,[1]) second son of DAVID and HANNAH (POST) PEASE, last of Portland, Me., and second cousin of the preceding, was born at   ; married Lydia C. Barker,   , 1826, lived at Portland, and was a successful merchant in that place, where he died.

His children were:

1756. 1. KATE B., b. at Portland,   . . m. Henry Fuller, Esq. of Westfield, Mass.
1757. 2. LEWIS, b. at Portland,   . d. an infant.

690.

DAVID PEASE,[7] (DAVID,[6] JONATHAN,[5] JONATHAN,[4] JOHN,[3] JOHN,[2] ROBERT,[1]) youngest brother of the preceding, was born at   ; married Elizabeth A. Vandyke, and lives at Philadelphia, Pa.

His children were:

1758. 1. FREDERICK, b. at
1759. 2. ADALINE W., b. at

—————o—————

693.

JAMES PEASE,[7] (RUSSELL,[6] JONATHAN,[5] JOSEPH,[4] JOHN,[3] JOHN,[2] ROBERT,[1]) eldest son of RUSSELL and MARGARET (CARPENTER) PEASE, last of Middlefield, Mass., and first cousin to the preceding, was born at Turin, N. Y.. 1825; married Martha Baldwin, April 27, 1857, and lived at Dalton, 1865, afterwards at Hinsdale, Mass., and is, by occupation, a farmer.

His children were:

1760.   1. MARGARET, b. at Windsor, Mass., January 14, 1859.   d. an
   infant.
1761.   2. CLARENCE B., b. at Windsor, April 10, 1860.
1762.   3. HANCIE E., b. at Hinsdale, June 18, 1862.

694.

JOEL PEASE,[7] (RUSSELL,[6] JONATHAN,[5] JOSEPH,[4] JOHN,[3]
JOHN,[2] ROBERT,[1]) second son of RUSSELL and MARGARET
(CARPENTER) PEASE, was born at Turin, Lewis County,
N. Y., 1827; married Sarah Barnes, of Becket, Mass.,
November 22, 1858, and lives in Becket; is a farmer.

His child was:

1763.   1. JENNIE, b. at   , January 8, 1862.

———oooo———

DESCENT OF ROBERT.[3]

FAMILY OF ROBERT.[4]

704.

OLIVER PEASE,[7] (ROBERT,[6] ROBERT,[5] ROBERT,[4] ROB-
ERT,[3] JOHN,[2] ROBERT,[1]) eldest son of ROBERT and ANN
(SEXTON) PEASE of Somers, Ct., and fourth cousin of the
preceding, was born at Somers, July 16, 1783; married
Nancy Cone, May 14, 1803, and settled upon the home-
stead of his father, a farmer, where he died, 1864.

His children were:

1764.   1. DANIEL C., b. at Somers, February 25, 1806. m. Matilda
   Collins, and settled in Somers. He has a son, William C.,
   who m. Cornelia Coomes, and resides in Longmeadow, Mass.
1765.   2. ROBERT, b. at Somers, March 28, 1808. m., first, Amersha
   Arnold, April 7, 1831; m., second, Mrs. Eliza B. (Hall)
   Terry, February 15, 1852; is, by occupation, a farmer, and
   lives in Somers. He has a son, Loren H., b. at Somers,
   July 14, 1835, who was surgeon in the Tenth Regiment of
   Connecticut Volunteers in the late war of the rebellion.
   He was on duty in the field at Hilton Head and Morris

Island, S. C., and for a time was surgeon in charge of the Portsmouth, N. C., general hospital. He is a druggist and physician in Thompsonville, (Enfield,) Ct. He m. Marcia A. Pease, daughter of R. Ashmun Pease of Enfield, July 21, 1859.

1766. 3. OLIVER, b. at Somers, January 9, 1810. m. Mary Pinney, 1837; m. second, Mrs. Elizabeth Hill, and resides in Amherst, Mass.

1767. 4. NANCY, b. at Somers, September 23, 1817. m. George Baker of Amherst, Mass., May 28, 1840.

1768. 5. AMOS S., b. at Somers, March 16, 1824. d. 1827.

1769. 6. AMOS, b. at Somers, April 16, 1828. m. Marietta Moore, May 24, 1848, and settled in Somers. He has for several years held the office of sheriff of Tolland County, (1868.)

708.

STEPHEN PEASE,⁷ (STEPHEN,⁶ ROBERT,⁵ ROBERT,⁴ ROBERT,³ JOHN,² ROBERT,¹) eldest son of STEPHEN and MARY (WOOD) PEASE of Somers, Ct., and first cousin of the preceding, was born at Somers, February 25, 1775; married Abigail Hall of Somers, 1797, and settled in the north part of Somers, where he died.

His children were:

1770. 1. ABIGAIL, b. at Somers,   , 1798. m. Col. Gaius Wood of Somers, and settled there.

1771. 2. HORACE, b. at Somers, July 6, 1799. m. Ann Wallace, December 17, 1820, and first settled in Somers, but subsequently removed to that part of Springfield known as "Sixteen Acres;" is, by occupation, a farmer.

1772. 3. ARETHUSA, b. at Somers, October 5, 1801. m. Dr. Orson Wood of Somers, and resides there.

1773. 4. CHAUNCEY, b. at Somers,   . m.

1774. 5. SAMANTHA, b. at Somers, December 15, 1810. m. Archelaus Sweatland, and resides in Somers.

1775. 6. SELONA, b. at Somers, July 10, 1813. m. Portus Ives; m., second, John Garland.

1776. 7. MARY H., b. at Somers,   , 1816. m. Asa Shelden of Somers, now lives in Springfield.

1777. 8. FLORA E., b. at Somers, August 15, 1820. m. John C. Burns, and settled in Somers.

22

711.

ABIEL PEASE,[7] (STEPHEN,[6] ROBERT,[5] ROBERT,[4] ROBERT,[3] JOHN,[2] ROBERT,[1]) brother of the preceding, was born at Somers, February 11, 1780; married Polly Filly, January 29, 1803; married, second, Ruby Cooley, February 26, 1821. He first settled in Simsbury, Ct., and subsequently returned to Somers, where he died, January 28, 1856.

His children were:

1778.   1. URSULA S., b. at Simsbury, Ct., October 27, 1803. d. January 23, 1817.

1779.   2. POLLY, b. at Simsbury, December 15, 1805. d. January 23, 1806. .

1780.   3. JOHN W., b. at Simsbury, December 5, 1806. m. Salome A. Kibbe, and resides in Hartford, Ct. He is a merchant. One of his sons, Henry K., b. August 15, 1830, m. Frances A. Glazier, March 18, 1850. He resides in Hartford, a merchant.

1781.   4. ABIEL H., b. at Simsbury, July 13, 1809. m. Celestia Moses of Simsbury, November 25, 1831, and resides in Lee, Mass. He has for several years held the office of deputy sheriff in Berkshire County. He has two sons living in Lee, viz.: Moses H., b. February 22, 1835; m. Adelaide M. Griswold. Frank M., b. May 22, 1839; m. Agnes A. Griswold.

1782.   5. POLLY A., b. at Simsbury, February 16, 1812. m. Butler Andrus, a farmer, and resides in Simsbury, Ct.

1783.   6. ELANORA, b. at Simsbury, September 18, 1813; resides in Wilbraham, Mass.

1784.   7. LUCINA, b. at Simsbury, October 12, 1815. m. Bissell, and resides in Covington, Ky.

1785.   8. URSULA S., b. at Simsbury, November 14, 1817. m. Lyman M. Kellogg, and settled in Wilbraham. d. 1864.

1786.   9. SARAH S. F., b. at Simsbury, December 24, 1819. m. Hutchinson, and resided in Cleveland, Ohio. d. October 9, 1844.

1787. 10. CYNTHIA A., b. at Somers, November 22, 1821. m. Henry A. Babcock, May 10, 1848, and resides at Mount Pleasant, Iowa.

1788. 11. HORACE C., b. at Somers, January 15, 1823. d. March 28, 1824.

1789. 12. HORACE G., b. at Somers, February 10, 1825. m. Miranda J. Helyer, Nevember 28, 1848, and resides in Des Moines, Iôwa. Is a railroad superintendent.

1790. 13. PHINEAS, b. at Somers, April 16, 1826. m. Elizabeth M. Edson, June 3, 1849. He resided several years in Columbus, Ohio, subsequently he removed to Centralia, Ill., where he now resides He entered the volunteer service of the United States, September 27, 1861, as Lieut.-Col. of the Forty-Ninth Regiment of Illinois Infantry, and was engaged in the battles of Fort Donelson, Tenn., Shiloh, (Pittsburgh Landing,) where he was wounded. Also, in Corinth, Miss., Little Rock, Ark., Meridian, Miss., Fort de Russey, La., Pleasant Hill, La., Bayou de Glaize, La., Chicat Lake, Ark., Tupelo, Miss., Tallahatchie, Miss., Franklin, Mo., and Nashville, Tenn. Was promoted to Colonel, December 13, 1862, and honorably discharged, January 9, 1865, at the expiration of his term of service.

1791. 14. OLIVE Z., b. at Somers, February 7, 1828. m. Gideon P. Butterfield, October 28, 1855, and resides in California.

1792. 15. HORATIO C., b. at Somers, February 3, 1830. He is a railroad engineer, and lives in Centralia, Ill.

1793. 16. WILLIAM S., b. at Somers, January 6, 1832. m. Margaret A. Billings, July 4, 1859, and removed to Chinese Camp, Cal. He entered the volunteer service of the U. S. Navy, October 1, 1862, as Ensign of the U. S. iron-clad "Indianola" of the Mississippi squadron, which ran the batteries at Vicksburg, Miss., February 11, 1863. She was attacked by the Rebel fleet near Carthage, La., February 24. The "Indianola" was sunk, and her officers and crew were taken prisoners. Ensign Pease was exchanged, June 6, 1863, and ordered to the U. S. Monitor ship, "Osage" of the Mississippi squadron, July 9. He was engaged with the Rebel steamers "Robert Fulton" and "Argus," October 7, 1863, which resulted in their capture. Was promoted to Master, January 5, 1864, and resigned, January 17, 1865.

1794. 17. CHARLES O., b. at Somers, November 14, 1833. m. Sarah M. Bond, May 28, 1855, and resided in Cincinnati, Ohio, a railroad conductor. Now, (1866) a hardware merchant in Centralia, Ill.

713.

ERASTUS PEASE,⁷ (STEPHEN,⁶ ROBERT,⁵ ROBERT,⁴ ROBERT,³ JOHN,² ROBERT,¹) son of STEPHEN and ROXANA

(Snow) Pease, and half brother of the preceding, was born at Somers, August 30, 1789; married Clarissa Hume of Windsor, Mass., December 6, 1816, with whom he passed his fiftieth anniversary wedding day.   He first settled in Somers, Ct., a farmer; in 1846 he removed to Wayne, Mich.; in 1864, to Xenia, Ohio, where he now resides, (1867.)

His children were :

1795.   1. Frances W., b. at Somers, Ct., January 23, 1818.   m. John Krider, a farmer, April 7, 1850, and settled in Wayne, Mich.

1796.   2. Theodore O., b. at Somers, August 26, 1819.   m. Lydia J. Russell of Ellington, Ct., April 26, 1846.   First settled in Wayne, Mich., and subsequently removed to Excelsior, Minn., where he d. August 28, 1855.   He was a farmer.

1797.   3. Morris H., b. at Somers, January 4, 1821.   m. Mary E. Jones of Excelsior, Minn., October 10, 1858.   He first settled in Excelsior, but subsequently removed to Xenia, Ohio, where he is clerk in a railroad office.

1798.   4. Lorenzo E., b. at Somers, September 5, 1824.   d. October 6, 1843.

1799.   5. David H., b. at Somers, November 9, 1826.   m., first, Anne M. Lewis of Sharpsburgh, Pa., May 6, 1852, who d. August 11, 1856; m., second, Sarah A. Burton of Cleveland, Ohio, September 1, 1857, and resides at Norwalk, Huron County, Ohio.   He is a merchant, and has been Treasurer of the County of Huron.

    We have found him a valuable Western correspondent, and he has furnished us an amount of information concerning the Pease families in Ohio and other Western States that has added much interest to this work.

1800.   6. Oscar S., b. at Somers, January 23, 1829.   m. Frances J. Goss of Berea, Ohio, February 14, 1856, and settled in Xenia, Ohio.   He is assistant superintendent of the L. M. and C. and X. R. R. (1867.)

1801.   7. Milo S., b. at Somers, April 27, 1831.   d. at Wayne, Mich., January 30, 1854.

1802.   8. Theodore C, b. at Somers, April 19, 1834, and resides in Xenia.

1803.   9. Charlotte C., b. at Somers, October 7, 1837, and resides in Xenia.

714.

AZEL PEASE,⁷ (Stephen,⁶ Robert,⁵ Robert,⁴ Robert,³ John,² Robert,¹) brother of the preceding, was born at Somers, 1795; married Bathsheba W. Hume of Windsor, Mass., 1819; married, second, Hannah Ashley, 1826. He settled in Somers.

His children were:

BY SECOND WIFE:

1804. 1. BATHSHEBA H., b. at Somers, January   , 1828. m. Royal G. N. Tyler.

1805. 2. HANNAH C., b. at Somers, March 7, 1830. m. Josiah White of Hadley, Mass., and lives on her father's homestead in Somers.

1806. 3. ALMIRA S., b. at Somers, November 16, 1832. d. a child.

1807. 4. WILLIAM A., b. at Somers, February 14, 1834. d. an infant.

1808. 5. WILLIAM A.,² b. at Somers, May 13, 1836. m. Jennie L. Kingsley, June 15, 1852, and settled in Springfield, Mass.

715.

ENOS PEASE,⁷ (Stephen,⁶ Robert,⁵ Robert,⁴ Robert,³ John,² Robert,¹) brother of the preceding, was born at Somers, September 19, 1804; married Mary Van Meter of Salem, N. J.; married, second, Sarah McMillin of the same place, who died in Cleveland, Ohio, August   , 1857. He first settled in Somers, and removed to Pittsburg, Pa., in 1842. In 1854 he removed to Cleveland, Ohio. Was teacher of music, and author of " PEASE'S NUMERAL METHOD OF MUSICAL NOTATION." In 1861 he volunteered as musician, and was two years in the war with the Forty-First Ohio Volunteers, first under Gen. Rosecrans, and subsequently under Gen. Sherman. In 1863 he received an honorable discharge by surgeon's certificate. He lives (1868) in Springfield, Mass.

His children were:

1809. 1. ROBERT A., b. at Salem, N. J., March 25, 1843. d. at Pittsburg, Pa., August 25, 1850.

1810. 2. ARTHUR Y., b. at Somers, October 12, 1838.   d. at Pittsburg,
            Pa., October 6, 1851.

1811. 3. ELLA, b. at Pittsburg, May 24, 1843.

1812. 4. JAMES, b. at Pittsburg, March 25, 1845. He was a volunteer
            in the late war, and mustered in with the Forty-First Ohio
            Volunteers at Cleveland, September 18, 1861 ; was severely
            wounded at Missionary Ridge, Ga., November   , 1843,
            but recovered so far as to join his regiment again, and was
            with Gen. Sherman through the siege and capture of Atlanta,
            Ga.   He received an honorable discharge in December,
            1864, and was subsequently engineer on the Ohio and Mis-
            sissippi Railroad.   He died of congestive fever after five
            days' sickness in Seymour, Ind., September 25, 1866, and
            was buried in Mount Auburn Cemetery, Alleghany City, Pa.

1813. 5. MARY, b. at Pittsburg, February 8, 1848.

1814. 6. FRANK, b. at Pittsburg, February 16, 1852.

——o——

719.

DEACON ELI PEASE,[7] (ABNER,[6] ROBERT,[5] ROBERT,[4]
ROBERT,[3] JOHN,[2] ROBERT,[1]) youngest son of ABNER and
CHLOE (VIETS) PEASE of Blandford, Mass., and first cousin
of the preceding, was born at Blandford, January 23,
1793; married Cynthia White of Longmeadow, Mass.,
December 3, 1819, and settled on the homestead in Blandford.   He removed to Independence, Iowa, in 1861, where
he died, December 31, 1863, in the full assurance of a
blessed immortality through the merits of Jesus Christ.

His children were:

1815. 1. FRANKLIN W., b. at Blandford, Mass., March 9, 1822. m. Alice
            B. Dewey, July 29, 1845. He was Captain of Company
            B., Thirty Seventh Massachusetts Regiment of Volunteers.
            d. May 12, 1864, from wounds received in the battle of the
            Wilderness ; was a brave soldier and consistent Christian.
            He lived some time in Pittsfield, Mass.

1816. 2. MARY, b. at Blandford,   ; lives in Inde-
            pendence, Iowa.

1817. 3. DELIA, b. at Blandford,   . m. Mr. Wood-
            ruff, and lives in Independence, Iowa.

1818. 4. WILLIAM E., b. at Blandford,   . He was
        Orderly Sergeant in Company B., Thirty-Seventh Massa-
        chusetts Volunteers. d. of fever at Gettysburg, Pa., July
        4, 1863, unmarried.
1819. 5. MARIA, b. at Blandford,   .. m. Mr. Wright,
        and lives in Iowa.

——o——

723.

JABEZ PEASE,⁷ (ALPHEUS,⁶ ROBERT,⁵ ROBERT,⁴ ROB-
ERT,³ JOHN,² ROBERT,¹) eldest son of MAJ. ALPHEUS and
OLIVE (ANDERSON) PEASE, first of Somers, Ct., last of
West Leyden, N. Y., and first cousin of the preceding,
was born at Somers, June 17, 1788; married Fanny
Dewey, October 19, 1809; married, second, Almira Spin-
ing, January 29, 1829. He lives in Martinsburgh, N. Y.,
a farmer.

His children are :

1820. 1. JABEZ L., b. at   , November 1, 1812. m. Har-
        riet Tinker, and lives in Constableville, N. Y.
1821. 2. DIODATE B., b. at   , February 7, 1815. m.
        Amanda M. Pitcher, and lives in Martinsburgh, N. Y.
1822. 3. ALPHEUS D., b. at   , August 20, 1817. m.
        Nancy Miller.
1823. 4. ABRAHAM D., b, at   , June 19, 1819. m.
        Alzina Hartwell, and lives in Utica, N. Y.
1824. 5. FANNY M., b. at   , June 10, 1821. m. Leonard
        Pitcher of Martinsburgh.
1825. 6. LYDIA D., b. at   , March 19, 1825. m. Ebenezer
        Rice of Martinsburgh.

BY SECOND WIFE:

1826. 7. WILLIAM C., b. at

725.

LYMAN PEASE,⁷ (ALPHEUS,⁶ ROBERT,⁵ ROBERT,⁴ ROB-
ERT,³ JOHN,² ROBERT,¹) brother of the preceding, was born
at Somers, July 20, 1793; married Pamelia Barnes, and
removed from New York to Hudson, Mich.

His children were:

1827.	1.	CLINTON, b. at
1828.	2.	MARY A., b. at
1829.	3.	GEORGE, b. at
1830.	4.	EMELINE, b. at
1831.	5.	CHARLES, b. at
1832.	6.	WILLIAM, b. at

727.

ALPHEUS PEASE,[7] (ALPHEUS,[6] ROBERT,[5] ROBERT,[4] ROBERT,[3] JOHN,[2] ROBERT,[1]) son of MAJ. ALPHEUS, and DOROTHY (SPENCER) PEASE, first of Somers, Ct., last of West Leyden, N. Y., and half brother of the preceding, was born at West Leyden, September 11, 1803; married Persis M. Hunt, March 7, 1833, and lives in West Leyden, a farmer and cattle dealer.

His children are:

1833. 1. AMELIA R., b. at West Leyden, November 23, 1834.
1834. 2. JAY, b. at West Leyden, January 1, 1838.

728.

CHARLES PEASE,[7] (ALPHEUS,[6] ROBERT,[5] ROBERT,[4] ROBERT,[3] JOHN,[2] ROBERT,[1]) brother of the preceding, was born at West Leyden, N. Y.,   , 1804; married Julia Fowler,   , 1828, who died,   , 1829; married, second, Julia Preston,   , 1831; married, third, Maria Kent   , 1845, and lives in West Leyden, a farmer.

His children are:

1835. 1. CHARLES L., b. at West Leyden, May 16, 1829.

BY SECOND WIFE:

1836. 2. ADDISON, b. at West Leyden, August 16, 1834. m. Catharine Burk,   , 1853.
1837. 3. JULIA, b. at West Leyden, March 23, 1838.
1838. 4. JAMES, b. at West Leyden, June 30, 1840.

BY THIRD WIFE:

1839. 5. JOHN M., b. at West Leyden, May 28, 1847.
1840. 6. LAURANIA, b. at West Leyden, August 4, 1850.
1841. 7. ALPHEUS, b. at West Leyden, June 17, 1853.

729.

JONATHAN A. S. PEASE,⁷ (ALPHEUS,⁶ ROBERT,⁵ ROB-
ERT,⁴ ROBERT,³ JOHN,² ROBERT,¹) brother of the preceding, was born at West Leyden, N. Y., March 18, 1810;
married Emily Terry. He settled in West Leyden, and is
a house joiner.

His child was:

1842. 1.

---o---

732.

CHARLES PEASE,⁷ (CHARLES,⁶ ROBERT,⁵ ROBERT,⁴
ROBERT,³ JOHN,² ROBERT,¹) only son of CHARLES and
ELIZABETH (SPENCER) PEASE of Somers, Ct., and first
cousin of the preceding, was born at Somers, September
30, 1796; married Mary Wood, daughter of Dr. John
Wood of Somers, and lives in Somers.

His child was:

1843. 1. MARY P., b. at Somers,   , 1825. d. August 23,
         1841, aged 16 years.

---oo---

734.

DAVID H. PEASE,⁷ (DAVID,⁶ EMERY,⁵ ROBERT,⁴ ROB-
ERT,³ JOHN,² ROBERT,¹) eldest son of DAVID and JERUSHA
(BELLOWS) PEASE, first of Somers, last of New York
State, and second cousin of the preceding, was born at
Somers, April 17, 1783; married Martha Coats; removed
from Somers to Johnstown, N. Y., where he died and left
a family, whose record we have failed to obtain with the
exception of the eldest child.

23

His child was:

1844.   1. Sylvanus H., b. at Somers, August 17, 1806. m. Emeline
          Roberts, July   , 1832, and lived in Winsted, Ct.
          This kinsman has six sons all of whom in some capacity
          participated in direct aid for the suppression of the late Re-
          bellion. The compiler having failed to receive answers to
          his interrogatories is unable to give the names of all of these
          sons, or the part they acted in the war. One of them,
          Henry R. Pease, entered the service with musket in hand,
          and was in active service through the siege of Port Hudson.
          He afterwards arose to positions of honor and trust, and he
          has filled the offices of Assistant Provost Marshal and Assist-
          ant Judge Advocate General. In November, 1865, he held
          the office of General Superintendent of Education for refu-
          gees and freedmen in the State of Louisiana with the rank
          of Captain. His office was one of large responsibility, as
          he had nearly twenty thousand children who were receiving
          rudimental instruction in schools of his establishing.
          Byron W. Pease, M. D., was an Assistant Surgeon dur-
          ing the Rebellion. In November, 1865, he was a civilian
          employe in the Bureau of Refugees, Freedmen and Aban-
          doned Lands as assistant in charge.
          Franklin Pease served all through the Virginia campaigns
          under Generals McClellan, Burnside, Mead, Butler and
          Grant.
          Robert Pease served in a military capacity.
          Horton Pease, another participant in the war, was, in
          November 1865, a clerk in the office of General Superin-
          tendent of Education of Refugees and Freedmen at New
          Orleans, La.; "making in the aggregate fourteen years of
          service this family has given the government, and, strange
          to say, they have all escaped disease and the deadly bullet,
          and come out with comparatively few scars."

736.

CYRUS PEASE,[7] (David,[6] Emery,[5] Robert,[4] Robert,[3]
John,[2] Robert,[1]) brother of the preceding, was born at
Somers,   , 1804; he married in the State of
New York, where he died and left a family of children.

Leverett E. Pease

738.

EMERY PEASE,⁷ (Emery,⁶ Emery,⁵ Robert,⁴ Robert,³ John,² Robert,¹) son of Emery and Sybil (Pease) Pease of Somers, Ct., and first cousin of the preceding, was born at Somers, April 12, 1789; married Harriet Kibbe, daughter of Capt. Amariah Kibbe of Somers. He settled in Somers, a merchant, where he died.

His child was:

1852. 1. Leverett E., b. at Somers, February 14, 1818. m. Julia Hyde, daughter of Dr. Hyde, and settled in Somers, a merchant. In 1866 he was elected Secretary of State, and re-elected in 1867 and '68. He has held the office of postmaster since 1860.

739.

LUMAN PEASE,⁷ (Emery,⁶ Emery,⁵ Robert,⁴ Robert,³ John,² Robert,¹) brother of the preceding, was born at Somers, July 6, 1791; married Mary Ford, daughter of Capt. John Ford of Somers. He was a wealthy and successful merchant in South Deerfield, Mass., and died in the city of New York, suddenly, while on business. He had no children.

———o———

745.

AUGUSTUS PEASE,⁷ (Augustus,⁶ Emery,⁵ Robert,⁴ Robert,³ John,² Robert,¹) eldest son of Augustus and Tirzah (Hall) Pease of Weston, Vt., and first cousin of the preceding, was born at Weston, December 15, 1786; married Patty Allen, and first settled in Weston. He was a deacon in the Baptist Church in that place. He removed from Vermont to Ohio, and was living in the vicinity of Cleveland, 1854. He had no children.

747.

ABIEL PEASE,[7] (Augustus,[6] Emery,[5] Robert,[4] Robert,[3] John,[2] Robert,[1]) second son of Augustus and Tirzah (Hall) Pease of Weston, Vt., was born at Weston, September 3, 1790; married Sarah Lampson, and settled in Sterling, Cayuga County, N. Y., and died there soon after his settlement in that place. He had but one son and one daughter, both supposed to be dead, leaving no issue.

His children were:

1853. 1.
1854. 2.

748.

CALVIN PEASE,[7] (Augustus,[6] Emery,[5] Robert,[4] Robert,[3] John,[2] Robert,[1]) brother of the preceding, was born at Weston, Vt., February 25, 1792; married Mary Wilson, October 28, 1819; married, second, Widow Sally Swift, May 11, 1843. He first settled in Troy, N. Y. In 1842 he removed to Dresden, N. Y., his present residence, and is, by occupation, a shoemaker.

His children are:

1855. 1. Mary E., b. at Troy, N. Y., November 20, 1820. m. William Peabody, April 19, 1848, and resides in Putnam, N. Y.

BY SECOND WIFE:

1856. 2. Sarah A., b. at Dresden, September 6, 1847. m. Nathaniel King, January 28, 1863, and resides in Dresden.

750.

ETHAN H. PEASE,[7] (Augustus,[6] Emery,[5] Robert,[4] Robert,[3] John,[2] Robert,[1]) brother of the preceding, was born at Weston, September 2, 1796; married Sophia M. Taylor, September 14, 1826; married, second,
                , 1839, and resides in Parishville, N. Y. He has one child by his first wife.

His child is:

BY FIRST WIFE:

1857.   1. Sophia C., b. at Parishville, February 18, 1838. m. John
W. Parker, January 1, 1862, and resides in Parishville.

751.

Dr. DAVID PEASE,⁷ (Augustus,⁶ Emery,⁵ Robert,⁴
Robert,³ John,² Robert,¹) fifth son of Augustus and
Tirzah (Hall) Pease, was born at Weston, July 26, 1798;
married Hannah Holt. He lived some time in Keene,
subsequently in Chesterfield, N. Y., from thence he removed to Brooklyn, N. Y., where he died with the cholera
while practicing medicine in that city, July 29, 1849.

His children were:

1858.   1. Caroline J., b. at Keene, N. Y., February 7, 1830. m. A.
H. Stevens, February 20, 1850, and resides in Weston, Vt.
1859.   2. Henry T., b. at Chesterfield, October 14, 1834. d. June 10,
1842.
1860.   3. Timothy W., b. at Chesterfield, February 6, 1837. d. January 1, 1858.
1861.   4. Maria L., b. at Chesterfield, November 10, 1839.
1862.   5. James F., b. at Chesterfield, September 24, 1843. He served
two years in the late war in a Vermont Regiment of Volunteers.
1863.   6. Francis, b. at   , December 14, 1845.

752.

ALPHEUS PEASE,⁷ (Augustus,⁶ Emery,⁵ Robert,⁴
Robert,³ John,² Robert,¹) youngest son of Augustus
and Tirzah (Hall) Pease, was born at Weston, September 25, 1800; married Lucy Foster, December 27, 1821,
and settled at Weston, a farmer.

His children are:

1864.   1. William A., b. at Weston, November 23, 1822. m. Harriet
Wheeler, February   , 1853, and resides at Chatfield,
Minn.
1865.   2. Lucy L., b. at Weston, December 25, 1825. m. Artemas
Whiting, November 11, 1847, and resides at Sudbury, Mass.

1866.   3. AUGUSTA H., b. at Weston, August 31, 1828. m. Benjamin
           Smith, February 28, 1849, and resides at Stowe, Mass.
1867.   4. CELESTIA W., b. at Weston, January 31, 1831. m. Clark A. Rich-
           ardson, December 16, 1852, and resides at Somerville, Mass.
1868.   5. CHARLES P., b. at Weston, May 31, 1837. He was a member
           of the First Michigan Regiment in aiding to suppress the
           late rebellion ; was wounded at the second Bull Run fight
           and honorably discharged.
1869.   6. MARY R., b. at Weston, March 29, 1841. m. Daniel L. Han-
           num, March 10, 1859, and resides at Weston.

—————oo—————

757.

THEODORE PEASE,[7] (GILES,[6] NOAH,[5] ROBERT,[4] ROB-
ERT,[3] JOHN,[2] ROBERT,[1]) eldest son of GILES and JERUSHA
(PITKIN) PEASE of Somers, Ct., and second cousin of the
preceding, was born at Somers, January 30, 1789; married Sarah Russell, daughter of John Russell of Somers.
He settled in Hartford, Ct., where he died, July 26, 1819,
aged 30 years.   He was a merchant.

His children were:

1870.   1. HENRIETTA M., b. at   , December 17, 1810. m.
           Jabez Collins of Somers. d.   , 1837, aged 27 years.
1871.   2. THEODORE P., b. at Hartford, February 11, 1813. m. Augusta
           I. Powell, July 7, 1847.
1872.   3. CLAUDIUS B., b. at Somers, April 22, 1815. m. Elmira A.
           Smith, September 16, 1846, who d. 1855. m., second,
           Harriet R. Park, October 28, 1857, who d. 1864. m.,
           third, Mary W. Chapin, who was for several years Principal
           of the Mount Holyoke Female Seminary. He resides at
           Somers.
1873.   4. SARAH ANN R., b. at Somers, January 18, 1818. m. John
           Smith, October   , 1845, and lived in Somers.

758.

DEACON NOAH PEASE,[7] (GILES,[6] NOAH,[5] ROBERT,[4]
ROBERT,[3] JOHN,[2] ROBERT,[1]) brother of the preceding, was
born at Somers, July 1, 1792; married Lucinda, daughter
of John Russell of Somers.

His children were:

1874. 1. LUCINDA, b. at   , March 6, 1814.
1875. 2. WILLIAM R., b. at Somers, September 23, 1816. m. Esther
        Lyman.
1876. 3. NOAH EDWARD, b. at Somers,   , 1818. m. Jane
        E. Topliff.
1877. 4. PHILANDER P., b. at Somers, February 18, 1821. m. Emma
        Powell.
1878. 5. CALVIN P., b. at Somers, August 19, 1823. m. Sarah E.
        Chapin, October 10, 1859, and resided for a time in Fulton,
        Whitesides County, Ill., a merchant.
1879. 6. ORPHA H., b. at Somers, February 4, 1827.
1880. 7. THEODORE A., b. at Somers, October 10, 1829. d. October
        8, 1856.
1881. 8. HENRY M., b. at Somers,   , 1832. d. October
        , 1854.

759.

AUGUSTUS PEASE,⁷ (GILES,⁶ NOAH,⁵ ROBERT,⁴ ROB-
ERT,³ JOHN,² ROBERT,¹) third son of GILES and JERUSHA
(PITKIN) PEASE, was born at Somers, October 3, 1793;
married Elizabeth McKinstry of Ellington, Ct.,   ;
married, second, Miss Van Doren of Arcadia, Mo., June
12, 1839. He was a merchant, and did business some
time in Colchester, Ct. After the death of his brother,
Theodore, he removed to Hartford, Ct.; about 1830 to
Utica, N. Y., afterwards to Watertown, N. Y., again back
to Hartford, and subsequently to Arcadia, Mo., where he
died, January 5, 1843.

His children were:

1882. 1. JULIUS A., b. at Somers, November 28, 1817. m. Miss Teets
        of Philadelphia, May 3, 1844, and resides in Brooklyn,
        N. Y.
1883. 2. JERUSHA E., b. at Hartford, July 8, 1820. d. September 11,
        1821.
1884. 3. CORNELIUS, b. at Hartford, December 1, 1822. d. March 10,
        1853.
1885. 4. ELIZABETH, b. at Hartford, September 9, 1824. m. George
        Dutton, Jr., of Utica, N. Y.

1886. 5. CLAUDIUS A., b. at Hartford, July 9, 1826. m. Miss Van
Doren at Morrisania, July 11, 1854 ; is a dealer in coal
and iron, and resides in New York.

1887. 6. CHARLES S., b. at Watertown, N. Y., November 9, 1832. d.
August 4, 1833.

BY SECOND WIFE :

1888. 7. MARY P., b. at Arcadia, March 12, 1840.

762.

HENRY PEASE,[7] (GILES,[6] NOAH,[5] ROBERT,[4] ROBERT,[3]
JOHN,[2] ROBERT,[1]) brother of the preceding, was born at
Somers, April 12, 1800 ; married Mary Warburton,
, 1823. He first settled in Hartford, Ct.. In 1827
he removed to Washington County, Mo., but now resides
at Albany, Whitesides County, Ill., having been in the
mercantile business thirty-five years, (1866.)

His children are :

1889. 1. SARAH P., b. in Missouri, September   , 1829. m. Ezekiel
Old, December 29, 1852, and resides in Albany, Ill.

1890. 2. HENRIETTA, b. in Missouri, September   , 1833. m. Edward W. Durant, December 29, 1853, and resides at Stillwater, Minn.

1891. 3. GILES W., b. in Missouri, October   , 1835.

1892. 4. EDWIN H., b. in Missouri, August 18, 1838. He enlisted in
August, 1862, to aid in crushing the rebellion, and was Sergeant in Company F of the Ninety-Third Illinois Infantry.
Soon after the fall of Vicksburg, he was detailed to serve in
the Adjutant-General's department, and subsequently in the
Division Quartermaster's department, thence to the Head-
quarters of the Fifteenth Corps, where he remained to the
end of the war. He now resides (1866) at Pittsburg, Pa.,
general agent of the Ætna Life Insurance Company of Hartford, Ct.

1893. 5. MARY E., b. at   , April 8, 1840.

1894. 6. FRANCES A., b. at   , June 20, 1845.

1895. 7. CELIA M., b. at   , May 1, 1849.

763.

MARTIN PEASE,[7] (GILES,[6] NOAH,[5] ROBERT,[4] ROBERT,[3]
JOHN,[2] ROBERT,[1]) brother of the preceding, was born at

Somers, June 1, 1802; married Flavia Billings, daughter of Dea. Solomon Billings of Somers. He removed to Hartford, Ct., about 1825. He also lived in Ohio, and about 1839 removed to Missouri. He was a merchant, and died at Arcadia, Mo., September 15, 1846, aged about 44 years.

His children were:

1896. 1. MARTIN F., b. at Somers, February 16, 1823. He served as a volunteer in the First Iowa Cavalry about three years, and subsequently re-enlisted as First Lieutenant in the Third Arkansas Volunteers where he remained until the war closed.

1897. 2. FLAVIA F., b. at Hartford, Ct., May 18, 1824. m. at Arcadia, Mo., March 24, 1842.

1898. 3. MARLOW F., b. at Hartford, February 7, 1826; is by trade, a printer.

1899. 4. MELISSA F., b. at Hartford, April 8, 1827. m. at Arcadia June 6, 1848.

1900. 5. HELEN M., b. at Somers, Ct., April 29, 1829. m. at Arcadia, May 18, 1848.

1901. 6. SANFORD O., b. at Cherry Valley, Ohio, April 25, 1831; is by trade, a blacksmith. He served in the Seventh California Volunteers as musician in the late war.

1902. 7. JANE E., b. in Ohio, May 9, 1833. d. at Andover, Ohio, September 2, 1835.

1903. 8. CLARISSA E., b. at Andover, March 24, 1835. d. at Arcadia, August 7, 1840.

1904. 9. ANN E., b. at Andover, June 20, 1837. m. at Arcadia, August 6, 1857.

1905. 10. HORACE E., b. at Andover, November 26, 1839. m. at Arcadia, June 6, 1862.

1906. 11. CAROLINE E., b. at Arcadia, November 23, 1841. m. at Arcadia, December 17, 1857.

1907. 12. HENRY B., b. at Arcadia, June 28, 1843; is by trade a printer.

1908. 13. JAMES M., b. at Arcadia, July 15, 1846. d. at Arcadia April 12, 1864.

765.

DR. GILES PEASE,⁷ (GILES,⁶ NOAH,⁵ ROBERT,⁴ ROBERT,³ JOHN,² ROBERT,¹) brother of the preceding, was born at Somers, December 2, 1805; married Mabel R. Mosely, daughter of William Mosely of South Wilbraham. He was a graduate of Yale College, and ordained as an evangelist, and labored several years as such in Connecticut, Massachusetts and Rhode Island. In 1833 he was installed over an Orthodox Congregational Church in Lowell, Mass., and in 1835, on account of ill ·health, received a dismission. In 1842 he settled in Sandwich, Mass., as pastor, but on account of continued ill health he left his pastoral duties and turned his attention to the profession of medicine, and is now a practicing physician in Boston, (1868.)

His children were :

1909.   1. GILES M., b. at Boston, May 3, 1839. He received his diploma of M. D., from the Harvard Medical College, and entered the U. S. Navy as Assistant Surgeon in December, 1861; continued there about one year, but resigned on account of ill health, having been stationed with the fleet in the Gulf of Mexico. He received a commission as Assistant Surgeon in the Fifty-Fourth Regiment of Massachusetts Volunteers in July, 1863, and continued in the service about one year; was stationed with the above regiment several months on Morris Island, S. C., during the siege of Charleston; also at Hilton Head, and in Florida, participating in the battle of Olustee. He has since been in medical practice in Boston.

1910.   2. EMMA H., b. at Cambridge, Mass., May 24, 1841.

1911.   3. EDWARD C., b. at Boston, Mass., June 18, 1845.   d. March 7, 1860, of injuries received by an accident in gymnastic exercises, aged 15 years.

1912.   4. JENNETTE M. S., b. at Sandwich, May 6, 1852.

767.

SANFORD PEASE,[7] (GILES,[6] NOAH,[5] ROBERT,[4] ROBERT,[3] JOHN,[2] ROBERT,[1]) brother of the preceding, was born at Somers, June 10, 1810; married Elizabeth Hitchcock, November   , 1834, who died soon after; married, second, Charlotte Gillett, September, 1836. He died at Greenville, Bond County, Ill., while on his way to Missouri, February 23, 1837, leaving no issue.

———ooo———

FAMILY OF SAMUEL.⁴

769.

ELI PEASE,⁷ (Eli,⁶ Samuel,⁵ Samuel,⁴ Robert,³ John,² Robert,¹) eldest son of Eli and Eunice (Bugbee) Pease of Enfield, Ct., and third cousin of the preceding, was born at Enfield, October 17, 1772; married Cynthia Terry, , 1796, and lived in Enfield, where he died, September 2, 1845, aged nearly 73 years.

His children were:

1913. 1. Cynthia, b. at Enfield, May 27, 1799. m. Jonathan Bugbee, and settled at Hartford, Vt.

1914. 2. Eli, b. at Enfield, January 13, 1801. m. Lydia P. King, and settled in Enfield.

1915. 3. Emily, b. at Enfield, October 10, 1804. m. Jeremiah Allen of Enfield.

1916. 4. Gaius, b. at Enfield, August 26, 1806. m. Eliza Barber, May 19, 1831, and resides in Springfield, Mass. He is a machinist. His children were:

> 1. Eliza B., b. July 9, 1839. m. John A. Bolen, a die sinker, June 19, 1856, and resides in Springfield.
> 2. Julia M., b. July 14, 1836.
> 3. Mary J., b. October 2, 1838.

1917. 5. Amelia, b. at Enfield, January 16, 1809. m. Nehemiah Holcomb.

1918. 6. Dennis, b. at Enfield, January 15, 1814. m. Eliza C. Pease, daughter of Dea. Wilder C. Pease of Enfield, November 23, 1837, and resides in Enfield, a farmer. He has one son Theodore D. m. Julia Allen, and lives at Springfield, Mass.

1919. 7. Lucinda, b. at Enfield, February 14, 1816. d. May 16, 1834.

770.

JONATHAN PEASE,⁷ (Eli,⁶ Samuel,⁵ Samuel,⁴ Robert,³ John,² Robert,¹) brother of the preceding, was born at Enfield, January 22, 1778; married Hannah Collins, August 28, 1800, and settled in Springfield, Mass., where he died, April 4, 1839.

His children were:

1920. 1. MARY, b. at Springfield, September 20, 1801. d. October 7, 1802.

1921. 2. JONATHAN, b. at Springfield, March 30, 1803; was lost at sea, 1820.

1922. 3. MARY S., b. at Springfield, August 19, 1804. m. Allen Macomber, and resides at Freetown, Mass.

1923. 4. HENRY, b. at Springfield, December 27, 1805. m. Cynthia Waterman, and lived for some time in Troy, N. Y., but has since removed West.

1924. 5. GEORGE, b. at Springfield, October 30, 1807. m. Ann Lancton, May 10, 1831, and resided sometime in Troy, N. Y., but now lives in Springfield.

1925. 6. HANNAH, b. at Springfield, October 22, 1809. m. J. Hubbard Clark, and resides in Springfield.

1926. 7. WILLIAM, b. at Springfield, April 19, 1812. d. an infant.

1927. 8. BETSEY C., b. at Springfield, July 29, 1813. m. Charles Blake, and settled in Springfield, where she d. November 20, 1846.

1928. 9. WILLIAM,[2] b. at Springfield, October 10, 1815. m. Julia Hale, and lived some time in Troy, N. Y.

1929. 10. ARIEL C., b. at Springfield, March 9, 1818. m. Harriet Clapp, and died at Hartford, Ct., October 13, 1843.

1930. 11. GILES, b. at Springfield, March 7, 1820. m., first, Nancy Dunlap. m., second, Matilda Dunlap, and resides at Springfield, a farmer.

771.

SAMUEL PEASE,[7] (ELI,[6] SAMUEL,[5] SAMUEL,[4] ROBERT,[3] JOHN,[2] ROBERT,[1]) third son of ELI and EUNICE (BUGBEE) PEASE, was born at Enfield,   ; married   , and removed to Canada East, and settled in the town of Ascott, where he died and left a family.

His children were:

1931. 1. IRA, b. at

1932. 2. SYLVESTER, b. at

1933. 3. CHAUNCEY, b. at

1934. 4. SILAS, b. at

1935. 5. ELI, b. at

772.

ANTHONY PEASE,⁷ (ELI,⁶ SAMUEL,⁵ SAMUEL,⁴ ROBERT,³ JOHN,² ROBERT,¹) youngest son of ELI and EUNICE (BUGBEE) PEASE, was born at Enfield ; married , and removed to Canada East, and settled at Ascott, where he died, leaving a family.

His children were:

1936. 1. THEOPHILUS, b. at
1937. 2.

774.

DANIEL PEASE,⁷ (ELIAS,⁶ SAMUEL,⁵ SAMUEL,⁴ ROBERT,³ JOHN,² ROBERT,¹) second son of ELIAS and MARY (PARSONS) PEASE, and cousin of the preceding, was born at . He lived with the Shakers until somewhat advanced in life, then left them; married Cynthia Parsons, and lived in Enfield, where he died without issue.

777.

ELIHU PEASE,⁷ (EDWARD,⁶ SAMUEL,⁵ SAMUEL,⁴ ROBERT,³ JOHN,² ROBERT,¹) eldest son of EDWARD and HANNAH (ROGERS) PEASE, last of Brookfield, Vt., and cousin of the preceding, was born at, Enfield, June 24, 1781; married Catharine Cummer, 1819. He resided at Buffalo, N. Y., two or three years after his marriage but soon returned to York, near Toronto, C. W., where he had some time lived before his marriage, and where he died, September 4, 1854. He was a leather manufacturer.

His children were:

1938. 1. ELIZABETH, b. at Buffalo, June 6, 1822. m. Andrew Davis, August 1, 1848, and resides at Watertown, C. W.
1939. 2. EDWARD, b. at , September 15, 1824. m. Sarah Castle, September 15, 1866, and resides at King, C. W. He is a tanner and currier, (1866).

1940.   3. HANNAH, b. at   , February 5, 1832.   m. Joseph
        Marsh, July 5, 1860, and resides at Thornburgh, C. W.
1941.   4. ASENATH, b. at   , June 1, 1834.   m. Christo-
        pher Harrison, December 12, 1853, and resides at York,
        C. W.

778.

ALVIN PEASE,[7] (EDWARD,[6] SAMUEL,[5] SAMUEL,[4] ROB-
ERT,[3] JOHN,[2] ROBERT,[1]) second son of EDWARD and HAN-
NAH (ROGERS) PEASE, was born at Enfield, November 8,
1785; married, first, Harriet Holt; married, second, Phebe
Salsbury, June   , 1832.   He resided for some time after
his first marriage at Auburn, N. Y., next at Buffalo, subsequently at Aurora, now at Holland, N. Y., and is, by
trade, a blacksmith.

His children were:

1942.   1. HORACE, b. at Auburn, January   , 1814.   d. at the age of
        18 years.
1943.   2. HENRY B., b. at Auburn, September   , 1816.   m. Sarah
        A. Stafford ; is by trade, a blacksmith.
1944.   3. RACHEL, b. at   , 1820.   m. Henry Van
        Vleet. d. 1847.
1945.   4. WARREN, b. at   , 1832.   m.
        in Canada.
1946.   5. ORSON, b. at   , October   , 1834.   m. Maria
        Van Vleet. He is a blacksmith, and lives in Illinois.

779.

WALTER PEASE,[7] (EDWARD,[6] SAMUEL,[5] SAMUEL,[4] ROB-
ERT,[3] JOHN,[2] ROBERT,[1]) son of EDWARD and HANNAH (ROG-
ERS) PEASE, was born at Enfield, August 18, 1787; mar-
ried Eunice Durkee, January   , 1810, and settled in
Hartford, Vt.

His children were:

1947.   1. HORACE, b. at   , October   , 1810.   m. Eunice
        Tufts of New Orleans, 1842. He commanded a steamer on
        the Mississippi River, on which he was killed by the explo-
        sion of her boiler, in 1848.

1948. 2. SAMUEL, b. at   , August 8, 1812. d. an infant.
1949. 3. SAMUEL,² b. at   , July 24, 1813. d. an infant.
1950. 4. LUTHER, b. at   , November 14, 1814. m. Harriet Cone, March 1, 1843, and settled in Hartford, Vt. He has a son, Allen L. Pease, living in Hartford, Vt.
1951. 5. PERSIS, b. at   , September 8, 1816. m. Samuel Pratt, 1841, and settled in Woodstock. d. 1843.
1952. 6. EDWARD P., b. at   , December 8, 1818. m. at Paducah, Ky.
1953. 7. WILLIAM H., b. at   , June 16, 1821. m. and settled in Illinois.
1954. 8. LEVI P., b. at   , January 1, 1823. m. and lives in Paducah, Ky.
1955. 9. JOHN D., b. at   , February 25, 1826. m. Caroline Paddleford, February 25, 1851, and settled at Hartford, Vt.
1956. 10. GEORGE W., b. at   , October 20, 1828. m. Arabella Moon, October   , 1850, and settled at Hartford, Vt.
1957. 11. CHARLES A., b. at   , March 7, 1831. m. and lives in Lawrence, Kansas.

784.

ERASTUS PEASE,⁷ (EDWARD,⁶ SAMUEL,⁵ SAMUEL,⁴ ROBERT,³ JOHN,² ROBERT,¹) youngest son of EDWARD and HANNAH (ROGERS) PEASE, was born at Enfield, November 12, 1796; married Mary Downing, September   , 1833, and settled in East Brookfield, Vt.

His children are:

1958. 1. RUFUS, b. at   , March 20, 1835.
1959. 2. MARTHA, b. at   , November 19, 1836.
1960. 3. ERASTUS, b. at   , July 11, 1841.

——oo——

793.

AARON PEASE,⁷ (AARON,⁶ AARON,⁵ SAMUEL,⁴ ROBERT,³ JOHN,² ROBERT,¹) eldest son of AARON and HULDAH (SPENCER) PEASE of Enfield, Ct., and second cousin of the pre-

ceding, was born at Enfield, September 9, 1777; married
Nancy Griswold, February 27, 1812, and settled in Middletown, Ct., where he died.

His children were:

1961.   1. MARY M., b. at Middletown, February 3, 1813. m. Arel
Utley; m., second, Homer Franklin.
1962.   2. NANCY A., b. at Middletown, December 26, 1814. m. Ezra
White.
1963.   3. AARON G., b. at Middletown, January 7, 1817.
1964.   4. ROBERT A., b. at Middletown, August 30, 1819. m. Sarah
A. Jones; m., second, Hannah A. Spencer.
1965.   5. RANDOLPH, b. at Middletown, September 20, 1824.
1966.   6. FRANCES L., b. at Middletown,   , 1826.

794.

AGIFT PEASE,[7] (AARON,[6] AARON,[5] SAMUEL,[4] ROBERT,[3]
JOHN,[2] ROBERT,[1]) second son of AARON and HULDAH
(SPENCER) PEASE, was born at Enfield,   1779;
married Betsey Ranney, and resided near Middletown, Ct.

His children were:

1967.   1. FRANKLIN, b. at   . m. Deborah Kelsey.
1968.   2. SPENCER, b. at
1969.   3. AARON, b. at   . m. Lovinia Johnson.
1970.   4. HENRY, b. at   . m. Caroline Post.
1971.   5. AGIFT, b. at   . m. Betsey Smith.
1972.   6. RUTH, b. at   . m. Philip Smith.
1973.   7. CYNTHIA, b. at   . m. Enos Bell.
1974.   8. SUSAN, b. at   . m. Griswold Beebe.
1975.   9. ELIZA, b. at   d. young, unmarried.
1976.   10. EDWARD, b. at   . m. Lovinia Chapman.

795.

LEVI PEASE,[7] (AARON,[6] AARON,[5] SAMUEL,[4] ROBERT,[3]
JOHN,[2] ROBERT,[1]) third son of AARON and HULDAH (SPEN-
CER) PEASE, was born at Enfield,   ; married
Almira Banks,   , 1811.

His children were:

1977. 1. Catharine, b. at
1978. 2. Charles, b. at

796.

SPENCER PEASE,⁷ (Aaron,⁶ Aaron,⁵ Samuel,⁴ Robert,³ John,² Robert,¹) fourth son of Aaron and Huldah (Spencer) Pease, was born at Enfield,   ;
married   , and settled at Providence, R. I., where he died. He had no children.

797.

RANDOLPH PEASE,⁷ (Aaron,⁶ Aaron,⁵ Samuel,⁴ Robert,³ John,² Robert,¹) youngest son of Aaron and Huldah (Spencer) Pease, was born at Enfield, about 1788; married Susan Paddock,   , 1807, and settled in Middletown, Ct., where he died, May 1, 1860, aged 72 years.

His children were:

1979. 1. Randolph and ⎫ b. at Middletown,   , 1807. d. infants.
1980. 2. Samuel,   ⎬
1981. 3. Susan, b. at Middletown,   , 1808.
1982. 4. Aurelia, b. at Middletown, June   , 1811. m. Patrick Saygon.
1983. 5. Susan,² b. at Middletown, September 12, 1820. m. Christopher Collins, 1839, and settled in Middletown.
1984. 6. Lucy A., b. at Middletown, May 26, 1826.

---o---

801.

STONE PEASE,⁷ (Stone,⁶ Aaron,⁵ Samuel,⁴ Robert,³ John,² Robert,¹) eldest son of Stone and Asenath (Pease) Pease of Enfield, Ct., and first cousin of the preceding, was born at Enfield, July 2, 1781; married   , October 20, 1807, and settled in Enfield; died March 9, 1825, aged 45 years.

25

His children were:

1985. 1. Horace B., b. at Enfield, April 19, 1810. d. December 7, 1830, aged 20 years.
1986. 2. Joseph S., b. at Enfield, January 7, 1815. d. February 28, 1847.
1987. 3. Elizabeth S., b. at Enfield, September 12, 1817.

802.

HORACE PEASE,[7] (Stone,[6] Aaron,[5] Samuel,[4] Robert,[3] John,[2] Robert,[1]) second son of Stone and Asenath (Pease) Pease, was born at Enfield, July 7, 1783; married Mrs. Rebecca (Parsons) Carrier, November 2, 1815, and lived in Enfield; was a plough manufacturer; died at Enfield, December 3, 1828, aged 46 years.

His children were:

1988. 1. Sophronia R., b. at Enfield, September 14, 1816. m. Roderick Allen, October 13, 1835, and settled in Enfield.
1989. 2. Amelia P., b. at Enfield, June 12, 1822. m. Edward Ingraham, January 15, 1844, and settled in Saybrook, Ct.
1990. 3. Harriet P., b. at Enfield, September 26, 1826.

806.

CHAUNCEY PEASE,[7] (Stone,[6] Aaron,[5] Samuel,[4] Robert,[3] John,[2] Robert,[1]) son of Stone and Asenath (Pease) Pease, was born at Enfield, August 19, 1792; married Elizabeth Holcomb, October 7, 1821, and resided last at Hartford, Ct.; was by occupation a blacksmith. He had but one child.

His child was:

1991. 1. Milton L., b. at Springfield, February 17, 1823. m. Dorothy A. Cadwell, May   , 1845, and resided first in Springfield, but now in Hartford, Ct. He is a blacksmith.

810.

GEER C. PEASE,[7] (Stone,[6] Aaron,[5] Samuel,[4] Robert,[3] John,[2] Robert,[1]) youngest son of Stone and Ase-

NATH (PEASE) PEASE, was born at Enfield, December 18, 1804; married Almira Chapin, August 31, 1831, and settled in Enfield, where he died, May 10, 1837, aged 34 years.

His children were:

1992. 1. HENRY B., b. at Enfield, June 24, 1832. d. January 23, 1838.

* 1993. 2. MARY M., b. at Enfield, October 20, 1833. d. May 27, 1836.

1994. 3. AGNES A., b. at Enfield, November 21, 1834.

1995. 4. EDWIN G., b. at Enfield, August 31, 1836.

----o----

811.

ARVIN B. PEASE,⁷ (EPHRAIM,⁶ AARON,⁵ SAMUEL,⁴ ROBERT,³ JOHN,² ROBERT,¹) son of EPHRAIM and JEMIMA (PHELPS) PEASE, first of Enfield, Ct., last of Lee, N. Y., and first cousin of the preceding, was born at Enfield, July 6, 1787; married Sedate Yeomans, November 17, 1808, and settled in Lee, N. Y.

His children were:

1996. 1. ABBY, b. at Lee, September 22, 1810. m. Lorenzo Baker, 1831.

1997. 2. JEMIMA, b. at Lee, January 7, 1812. m. Samuel Underhill, March 6, 1832.

1998. 3. ELIZA, b. at Lee, May 7, 1815. m. Charles C. Hovey, July 6, 1834.

1999. 4. HENRY G., b. at Lee, December 5, 1818. m. Harriet Twitchell, November 8, 1826.

2000. 5. MORRIS A., b. at Lee, June 8, 1821. d. in London, England, November 11, 1842.

2001. 6. ZENANA, b. at Lee, May 5, 1824. m. Joseph DeCory, April 4, 1844.

812.

ORRIN PEASE,⁷ (EPHRAIM,⁶ AARON,⁵ SAMUEL,⁴ ROBERT,³ JOHN,² ROBERT,¹) brother of the preceding, was born at Enfield, December 19, 1788; married and removed to Wisconsin, and settled in Watertown.

His children were:

2002. 1.
2003. 2.
2004. 3.
2005. 4.
2006. 5.

———o———

824.

ELAM C. PEASE,[7] (ELAM,[6] AARON,[5] SAMUEL,[4] ROBERT,[3] JOHN,[2] ROBERT,[1]) only surviving son of ELAM and OLIVE (PRENTICE CLARK) PEASE of Enfield, Ct., last of Copenhagen, N. Y., and first cousin of the preceding, was born at Denmark, N. Y., April 23, 1835; married   , and removed from New York State to Michigan, and settled at Evansville.

His children were:

2007. 1.
2008. 2.
2009. 3.
2010. 4.

———oo———

825.

FLAVIUS PEASE,[7] (PHINEAS,[6] NATHANIEL,[5] SAMUEL,[4] ROBERT,[3] JOHN,[2] ROBERT,[1]) eldest son of PHINEAS and BETSEY (LAWRENCE) PEASE of Stockbridge, Mass., and second cousin of the preceding, was born at Stockbridge, November 23, 1780; married Eleanor Day, September 23, 1804; died March 6, 1845, and his widow died February 2, 1847, leaving no children.

832.

PETER P. PEASE,[7] (PHINEAS,[6] NATHANIEL,[5] SAMUEL,[4] ROBERT,[3] JOHN,[2] ROBERT,[1]) brother of the preceding, was born at Stockbridge, April 12, 1795; married Ruth H. Crocker, July 12, 1821, and first settled at Brownhelm,

Ohio. He gives the following account of his experience in pioneer life:

"In the fall of 1816, at the age of 21½ years, I left Stockbridge, my native place, to seek my fortune in the West, and settled in what is now called Brownhelm, then an entire wilderness, and known as town No. 6, in the nineteenth range of the Connecticut Western Reserve. Three young men of us built the first house in town, and wintered there in the employ of Col. Henry Brown of Stockbridge, Mass. From whence a colony was formed of about twenty families, who settled the town, enjoying the pleasures and suffering the privations of a pioneer life, common to all new settlements. I, with my family of five children, left Brownhelm in April, 1833, for the express purpose of commencing the Oberlin enterprise, and we were the first family that penetrated this, then dense forest, and thus took a second trial of pioneering, which was much shorter than the first, and I have been an eye-witness to what God hath wrought in and for this place, and for this great valley of the Mississippi, and do praise and magnify his name!" He died October 22, 1861.

His children were:

2011.   1. AMANDA R., b. at Brownhelm, November 3, 1822. m. Rev. R. J. Williams, August 9, 1857, and settled in Dexter, Mich.

2012.   2. FLAVIUS E., b. at Brownhelm, April 17, 1825. m. Mary A. Drake, February 16, 1848, and settled in Wisconsin.

2013.   3. ELIZA C., b. at Brownhelm, February 10, 1827. m. J. H. Livingston, October 30, 1844, and settled in Oberlin.

2014.   4. SAMANTHA C., b. at Brownhelm, January 3, 1830. m. Henry F. Shepard, August 16, 1848, and settled in Wisconsin.

2015.   5. MARGARET J., b. at Brownhelm, October 27, 1832. m. David S. Hull, November 1, 1850, and settled in Oberlin.

2016.   6. WALTER C., b. at Oberlin, June 17, 1837.

2017.   7. FREDERICK H., b. at Oberlin, August 24, 1839. m. Josephine A. Dolsen, November 7, 1859, and settled in Michigan.

2018.   8. FRANKLIN E., b. at Oberlin, May 8, 1841.

2019.   9. HERBERT A., b. at Oberlin, April 4, 1843. d. October 27, 1849.

2020. 10. Lucius F., b. at Oberlin, February 20, 1845. d. July 9, 1845.
2021. 11. Phineas L., b. at Oberlin, December 27, 1846.

833.

HIRAM A. PEASE,⁷ (Phineas,⁶ Nathaniel,⁵ Samuel,⁴ Robert,³ John,² Robert,¹) son of Phineas and Betsey (Lawrence) Pease of Stockbridge, Mass., was born at Stockbridge, April 19, 1797; married Lydia Remile, May 3, 1818. He first settled in Berkshire County, but removed to Ohio, about 1828, and finally settled at Oberlin, where he now resides, (1866.) He is, by occupation, a farmer.

His children were:

2022. 1. Phineas B., b. at Lee, Mass., June 6, 1819. m. Cornelia Reed, November 14, 1840. He prepared and entered the Oberlin College, Ohio, but never graduated. He is a minister of the Gospel, and is connected with the Wisconsin Conference of the Methodist Episcopal Church. He was ordained elder, in 1852, and is in the itinerant work. Of the seven Methodist preachers bearing our name, who are descendants of our common ancestor, Rev. Phineas B. is the fifth one who is of the descent of Robert.³ He is the father of eight children, the second of whom, Marcus A., b. September 24, 1843, was in the army for the suppression of the rebellion, a member of Company F of the First Wisconsin Cavalry. He died near Helena, Ark., August 24, 1862. His father writes "he served faithfully one year, died a Christian and sleeps in a soldier's unmarked grave."
2023. 2. Hiram A., b. at Stockbridge, Mass., December 23, 1820. m. Delana Parsons, May 10, 1844. He is an artist,—a portrait painter.
2024. 3. Louisa L., b. at Stockbridge, March 26, 1822. m. Rev. John L. Johnson, August 22, 1842. d. at Oberlin, May 20, 1853.
2025. 4. Electa S., b. at Stockbridge, September 4, 1823. m. H. R. Granis,   , 1844.
2026. 5. Martin L., b. at Stockbridge, January 13, 1825. d. in Kansas, October 2, 1857. He was a musician.
2027. 6. Harlow T., b. at Stockbridge, October 23, 1828. m. Susie Hutley.

2028. 7. EMILY C., b. at Brownhelm, Ohio, July 12, 1831. m. Urial
Vantyne, January 20, 1854.

2029. 8. THEODORE, b. at Brownhelm, April 12, 1833. d. September
11, 1834.

2030. 9. THEODORE W., b. at Oberlin, April 4, 1836. He graduated
with high honors at Oberlin College, and d. at Spencertown,
N. Y., January 25, 1863.

2031. 10. LUCY ELLEN, b. at Berea, Ohio, September 7, 1838.

——o——

837.

SALMON PEASE,⁷ (CALVIN,⁶ NATHANIEL,⁵ SAMUEL,⁴
ROBERT,³ JOHN,² ROBERT,¹) eldest son of CALVIN and
SALLY (IVES) PEASE of Canaan, Ct., and first cousin of
the preceding, was born at Norfolk, Ct., June 14, 1783;
married Matilda Huntington, daughter of Dr. Thomas
Huntington of Canaan, Ct., June 14, 1803. He resided
at Canaan until the fall of 1826, when he removed to
Charlotte, Vt. He was, by occupation, a farmer, and for
several years he held a commission of Justice of Peace.
He died at Charlotte, July 23, 1857. His widow is still
living on the old homestead at Charlotte, "at the age of
88 years, in good health and sound mind, the pride and
joy of her children." (January, 1869.)

His children were:

2032. 1. FREDERICK S., b. at Canaan, May 21, 1804. m. Julia Lawrence, September 18, 1832, and resided in Albany, N. Y.,
where he d. of consumption, March 22, 1867. He was, by
occupation, an accountant, and for about thirty years was
book-keeper in the Commercial Bank of Albany.

Mr. Pease had no other advantages in early life for an
educational training than those afforded him by the Common
Schools of his native town in Connecticut, and his own exer-
tions by the fireside. His productions in after years show
plainly that his youthful hours were not misspent, or that he
had only fitted himself for the position of a banker's accountant.

He was the compiler of the work called "Pease Family" that was published in the New England Historical and Genealogical Register, 1849, Vol. iii. ; a periodical published under the patronage of the New England Historic-Genealogical Society, of which he was a corresponding member. The work, though compiled largely from manuscript already prepared by the late Dr. John C. Pease, was prefaced with considerable information concerning the Peases in England, the early settlement of the Peases in this country, and it had a large amount of valuable genealogical and historical matter added to it which he acquired by a large correspondence. The work awakened a deep interest in the minds of the Enfield Peases, into whose hands it chanced to fall, and to whom it principally related. Its circulation ought to have been much more extensive among them. It was only three years after Mr. Pease became interested in his work, that it was published; a period far too short considering the magnitude of the field his work embraced.

He has since prepared and published, through the same medium, other papers which showed a reflective mind, and subsequent discoveries have not only proved the correctness of his conclusions, but greatly enhanced the value of his productions. We refer particularly to his article in the New England Historical and Genealogical Register, Vol. x., and which is republished in the "Early History of the Pease Families in America," Chapter iv.

2033. 2. CALVIN, b. at Canaan, August 20, 1806. d. young.

2034. 3. ERASTUS H., b. at Canaan, September 10, 1807. m. Lydia B. Fry of Albany, N. Y., April 15, 1835, and resides at Albany. He is a bookseller and stationer.

2035. 4. AARON G., b. at Canaan, February 22, 1811. m. Anne Page, sister of Governor Page of Vermont, October 18, 1842. He graduated from the Vermont University in the class of 1837, studied theology and became pastor of a church, first at Pittsford, Vt., next at Waterbury, and last at Norwich. He is now superintendent of the Vermont State Reform School at Waterbury, where he resides.

Mr. Pease represented the town of Norwich in the State Legislature in 1864 and '65, and was made chairman of a committee to report a bill for the establishment of a State Reform School. The bill passed and he was appointed first commissioner to locate the school and set it in operation. He was afterwards appointed superintendent of the school.

2036.   5. CALVIN,[2] b. at Canaan, August 12, 1813.   m. Martha Howse of Montpelier, Vt., May 17, 1843.

The following tribute to his memory we take from the Annual American Cyclopedia for 1863:

" Calvin Pease, D. D., an American clergyman, was born at Canaan, Litchfield County, Ct., August 12, 1813; died at Burlington, Vt., September 17, 1863. His parents were both of Puritan stock, and his early training was judicious and eminently calculated to lay the foundation of the purity of character which marked his maturer years. In November, 1826, his family removed to Charlotte, Vt., where he was occupied upon his father's farm until 1832, when he entered Hinesburgh Academy to fit for college, and at the expiration of a year, entered the university of Vermont, at Burlington. Here he at once took a high position, which he maintained to the end of his college course. He graduated in 1838, and from that time until 1842, was employed as principal in the academy at Montpelier. In 1841, he delivered the master's oration at Burlington, and received the degree of A. M. In 1842, he delivered the annual address before the associate literary societies of the university, and the same year was elected to the professorship of the Greek and Latin languages in that institution. He continued in this position until December, 1855, when he was elected to succeed Dr. Worthington Smith, as president. Late in the period of his professorship he was licensed to preach the Gospel by the Winooski Association. Though he had not made theology a systematic study, yet he was urged to this step by his friends who knew his rare ability as a writer and speaker, and his eminent qualifications, spiritual and intellectual for usefulness in the pulpit. At the commencement, in 1856, he was inaugurated as president of the university, and a few weeks later received the degree of Doctor of Divinity from Middlebury College, Vt. During his presidency he received various marks of appreciation and regard, among which were his appointment as a member of the Vermont Board of Education, at its organization in 1856, and his election to the presidency of the Vermont Teachers' Association the same year, both of which offices he held until he left the State, and by his activity and usefulness in these positions had a leading part in shaping the present highly successful educational policy of the State. In November, 1861, he received a call to the ·

26

pastorate of the First Presbyterian Church in Rochester, N., Y., which, in consideration of the demands of his health, and the claims of his family, he deemed it his duty to accept. He entered upon his ministry in Rochester, in January, 1862, and in May, was installed as pastor of the church. The period of his ministry here, though short, was eminently successful and happy, embracing the most interesting portion of his life; within these few months he did his greatest and best work, for which all his previous life, labor and experience were but the preparation, and it was their fitting crown and reward. During the last year of his life, he was elected a member of the American Philosophical Society of Philadelphia.

"Dr. Pease left many valuable manuscripts and sermons, but published only a few. His earliest published work was a 'Discourse on the Import and Value of the Popular Lecturing of the Day,' delivered before the literary societies of the university of Vermont, (1842.) Subsequently he published in the Bibliotheca Sacra, 'Classical Studies,' (July, 1852); the 'Distinctive Idea of Preaching,' (1853); 'Characteristics of the Eloquence of the Pulpit,' delivered as an address before the Rhetorical Society of Auburn Theological Seminary, (1858); 'The Idea of the New England College and its Power of Culture,' delivered at his inauguration as President of the University, (1856); 'Address before the Medical Department of the University,' (1856); 'Baccalaureate Sermons,' (1856, 1857, 1859, 1860), and a number of occasional sermons."

The following extract describing Dr. Pease as a preacher of the Gospel we copy from the Rochester "American and Democrat" of September 22, 1863:

. . . . "None of his hearers will soon forget the blended modesty and authority of his presence in the sacred desk,—that voice, usually low, like distant music, but occasionally loud, like a rising storm; the eye kindling in appeal; the right arm launched forth in demonstration. Sin his soul hated. In whatever refuge it lurked, he dragged it forth; in whatever citadel it flaunted defiance, he challenged and assailed it; in whatsoever worldly allurements it smiled, it was to him 'an evil and bitter thing.' Priest craft, State craft, and Mammon craft he could scourge with a whip of scorpions. On the other hand, truth, right and duty, as they relate to God and His Word, man and his

destiny,—truth as it is expressed in Christian doctrine, and
illustrated in Christian character,—the truth as it is in Jesus,
—were to him most dear and supreme, the sweetest of all
the influences of heaven, and the most majestic of all the
forces of earth, 'fair as the moon, clear as the sun, and ter-
rible as an army with banners.'"

Dr. Pease sickened while away from his home and pastoral duties, spending his summer vacation, and died with
dysentery at the residence of his brother-in-law, George
Francis, Esq.

2037. 6. THOMAS H., b. at Canaan, October 24, 1815. m., first,
Catharine N. Coon of Brooklyn, N. Y., April 16, 1838;
m., second, Elizabeth Graham of New Haven, Ct., April
17, 1848; m., third, Eliza Morris of Bethel, Vt., June 2,
1852, and resides in New Haven, Ct. For the past thirty
years he has been a book dealer, first in New York City, and
since 1842 in the city of New Haven. He has two sons
and two daughters.

One of his sons, William B. Pease, was born at New
Haven, January 30, 1844. He enlisted as private in the
Fifteenth Infantry Regiment of Connecticut Volunteers, for
the suppression of the late rebellion, August 11, 1862.
He left the regiment a few days before the disastrous bat-
tles of Fredericksburg, and afterwards received a commis-
sion as Lieutenant in the Eighth Regiment of United States
Colored Troops. He was engaged in the bloody battle of
Olustee, Fla., at which time his regiment suffered severely.
It was afterwards ordered to Virginia, did good service in
the trenches before Petersburg, and was one of the first
regiments of the Union Army to enter that city. After the
surrender of Lee and his army he went with his regiment to
Brownsville, Texas, to assist in restoring order in that State.

Resigning his commission in his regiment, he returned
home. On the 7th of March, 1867, he received a commission as First Lieutenant in the Eleventh Regiment of the
Regular Army. For several months past he has been doing
duty as Commissioner of the Twelfth and Thirteenth Dis-
tricts of Virginia, embracing eight counties.

2038. 7. PETER E., b. at Canaan, May 11, 1818. m. Cordelia Rich
of Charlotte, Vt., January 14, 1841, and resides at Charlotte, a farmer.

2039. 8. MARY M., b. at Canaan, August 20, 1820. m. George Francis, September 21, 1841, and resides at Burlington, Vt.

2040.   9. Reuben O., b. at Canaan, August 23, 1823. d. unmarried,
aged 24 years.

2041. 10. Roscius M., b. at Canaan, March 7, 1825. d. October 12, 1844.

838.

NEHEMIAH P. PEASE,[7] (Calvin,[6] Nathaniel,[5] Samuel,[4] Robert,[3] John,[2] Robert,[1]) brother of the preceding, was born at Canaan, Ct., May 1, 1798; married Lucy
Williams of Canaan, March 5, 1816, and resided in Canaan,
where he died, December 2, 1838.

His children were:

2042.   1. Sally I., b. at Canaan, January 18, 1818. d. 1848, unmarried.

2043.   2. Seth, b. at Canaan, May 20, 1820. m. Eunice M. Sheldon
of New Marlboro, Mass., May 20, 1846. He graduated
from the Medical College at New Haven, Ct., in 1846, and
settled at New Marlboro, Berkshire County, Mass., a physician.

———o———

844.

Deacon HARLOW PEASE,[7] (Allen,[6] Nathaniel,[5]
Samuel,[4] Robert,[3] John,[2] Robert,[1]) son of Allen and
Rachael (Tibballs) Pease of Sheffield, Mass., and first
cousin of the preceding, was born at Sheffield, April 17,
1798; married Ann Jane Clark of Sheffield, January 30,
1826. He first settled in Sheffield, and was a clothier,
wool-carder and silk-dyer. About 1839 he removed to
the town of Alford, Mass., and engaged in farming, having a farm, grist-mill, and saw-mill. He has been a man
of active business habits, though now suffering from feeble
health from paralysis. He appears to have had the confidence of the community in which he has lived, having
filled for many years, with acceptance, the office of deacon of the Congregational Church, and being appointed a
justice of the peace.

His children were :

2044. 1.   d. in early infancy.
2045. 2.   d. in early infancy.
2046. 3. CLARK A., b. at Sheffield, July 23, 1829.   d. February 26,
           1831, aged 1 year, 7 months.
2047. 4. HENRY, b. at Sheffield, December 17, 1831.   m. Emily Marion
           Higgins of Spencertown, N. Y., April 20, 1859, and set-
           tled in Alford, Mass., a merchant.
2048. 5. ANN JANE, b. at Sheffield, September 26, 1834.   d. October
           26, 1841.
2049. 6. SARAH LODEMA, b. at Sheffield, March 5, 1837.   m. John
           Callender of Cambridge, Mass., February 20, 1856, and
           resides at Alford.

846.

JOHN S. PEASE,[7] (ALLEN,[6] NATHANIEL,[5] SAMUEL,[4] ROB-
ERT,[3] JOHN,[2] ROBERT,[1]) youngest son of ALLEN and TAM-
SIN (SEARS) PEASE of Sheffield, Mass., and half-brother
of the preceding, was born at Ashley Falls, Mass., July
17, 1807; married Emily Ingraham, of Ashley Falls, November 26, 1829. He is, by occupation, a farmer, and
lives at Ashley Falls.

His children were :

2050. 1. EUNICE, b. at Ashley Falls, October 30, 1830.   m. William
           Ives of Ashley Falls, May 11, 1852, and d. at West Stock-
           bridge, Mass, July 16, 1856.
2051. 2. JOHN A., b. at Ashley Falls, November 2, 1832.   m. Sarah
           E. Austin of Sheffield, August 31, 1856.   He is a black-
           smith and lives at Ashley Falls.
2052. 3. GEORGE, b. at Ashley Falls, November 8, 1834.   He did
           service in Grant's army during the rebellion.
2053. 4. JOSEPH, b. at Ashley Falls, January 2, 1840.   m. Harriet
           Elizabeth Scoville, daughter of Dr. John Scoville of Ashley
           Falls; lives in Lee, and is a photographer.
2054. 5. EMMA, b. at Ashley Falls, May 24, 1842.   d. September 24,
           1843.
2055. 6. ELIZABETH J., b. at Ashley Falls, May 30, 1849.

847.

DUDLEY S. PEASE,[7] (NATHANIEL,[6] NATHANIEL,[5] SAM-
UEL,[4] ROBERT,[3] JOHN,[2] ROBERT,[1]) eldest son of NATHANIEL
and JERUSHA (HALL) PEASE of Poughkeepsie, N. Y., and
first cousin of the preceding, was born at Norwalk, Ct.,
March 5, 1785; married, first, Leurilly Loomis, November
14, 1805; married, second, Maria Sears, November , 1810;
married, third, Sarah Rilley, , 1814. He lived
in Poughkeepsie, where he died, March 17, 1855.

His children were:

2056.   1. CHARLES L., b. at Poughkeepsie, N. Y., , 1806.
m. Ann Booth of Poughkeepsie. d. August 12, 1836.

2057.   2. SYLVIA, b. at Poughkeepsie, . m. Clark
Mills of Cleveland, Ohio. She d. about 1850.

BY SECOND WIFE:

2058.   3. MARIA L., b. at Poughkeepsie, . m. in 1833
Anthony McClary, and lives in Kingston, N. Y.

2059.   4. A boy who d. in infancy.

BY THIRD WIFE:

2060.   5. RICHARD P., b. at Poughkeepsie, February 13, 1816. m.
Hannah Otis of Brooklyn, N. Y., April 23, 1838, and
lives in Brooklyn, and is a turner and stair-builder.

2061.   6. MARGARET R., b. at Poughkeepsie, April 24, 1818. m. Henry
Sitzer of Poughkeepsie.

2062.   7. EDWIN R., b. at Poughkeepsie, June 21, 1820. m. Cornelia
Stanton of Poughkeepsie, and lives in that place. He is a
boot and shoe-dealer.

2063.   8. BENJAMIN F., b. at Poughkeepsie, November 17, 1822. He
has for the past fifteen years been a resident of Lima, Peru,
South America, where he married a native of the country, of
Spanish descent, by whom he has several children. He is an
artist.

2064.   9. CATHARINE J., b. at Poughkeepsie, June 5, 1824. m. George
E. Ranoas of New York City, December 10, 1846, where
she now resides.

2065.   10. ALBERT S., b. at Poughkeepsie, September 27, 1828. m.
Sarah E. Denton, June 25, 1851, and resides at Buskirk's
Bridge, Rensselaer County, N. Y., (1867.)

Mr. Pease served an apprenticeship with Mr. E. B. Rilley of the Poughkeepsie Telegraph as a printer. At the expiration of his term of service, he became a partner with Mr. Rilley in the printing business. In consequence of the death of his partner, at the end of one year he assumed the entire control of the business. During the administration of President Pierce, he was postmaster of the city of Poughkeepsie. Mr. Pease subsequently sold his interest in the printing business, studied law, and was admitted to the practice at the bar of all the Courts in the State,—a profession he never followed. In 1858 he purchased the Poughkeepsie Daily Press establishment, and again became editor and proprietor of a newspaper.

To answer the call of his country during the late rebellion, Mr. Pease sold his interest in the printing business, and in 1861 went as first Lieutenant of Company E, Twentieth Regiment of New York State Militia, Col. George W. Pratt commanding. On his return from the war, he repurchased the Daily Press office, and in 1863 moved the material of the office as well as the name to Troy, N. Y., where he conducted the Daily and Weekly Press until the fall of 1867, when he sold out his interest in the paper.

2066. 11. WALTER S., b. at Poughkeepsie, July 3, 1832. d. at Lima, Peru, March 11, 1854, unmarried.

2067. 12. EGBERT R., b. at Poughkeepsie, January 21, 1835. d. March , 1842.

848.

GROVE A. PEASE,⁷ (NATHANIEL,⁶ NATHANIEL,⁵ SAMUEL,⁴ ROBERT,³ JOHN,² ROBERT,¹) brother of the preceding, was born at Norfolk, Ct., August 4, 1789; married Harriet S. Jewett, daughter of the late Joshua R. Jewett of Granby, Ct., May 2, 1814. He settled in Granby, where he is at present (1868) living, after having spent some thirty years at the South.

His children were:

2068. 1. ALBERT J., b. at Poughkeepsie, January 26, 1815. m. Sarah J. Stevens of Claremont, N. H., August 23, 1843, and lived in Boston several years as clerk at the Revere House. He is now in New York, (1868.)

2069.   2. Edward R., b. at Poughkeepsie, April 3, 1819. m. Martha
E. Curd of Macon, Ga., June 8, 1843. Residence, Macon,
but during the rebellion temporarily resided in Granby.

2070.   3. Mary Ann, b. at Webbville, Fla., December 3, 1829. m.
John C. Welborn of Eufaula, Ala., April 29, 1847 ; m.,
second, Dr. John LeHarris of Talladega, Ala., where she
d. April 12, 1861.

2071.   4. George A., b. at St. Joseph, Fla., April 28, 1839. He lives
at Macon, Ga., and has no family, (1865.)

————o————

852.

AUGUSTUS P. PEASE,[7] (Obadiah,[6] Nathaniel,[5] Samuel,[4] Robert,[3] John,[2] Robert,[1]) eldest son of Obadiah
and Daziah (Pettibone) Pease of Norfolk, Ct., and first
cousin of the preceding, was born at Norfolk, June 8, 1792;
married Almira Holt, daughter of Stephen Holt of Norfolk, January 1, 1818. He lived in Norfolk, where he
died, July 11, 1848, aged about 56 years. He was, by
occupation, a farmer.

His children were:

2072.   1. William A., b. at   , November , 1818.   He
is a dental surgeon, and lives in Dayton, Ohio, (1865.)

2073.   2. Elizabeth, b. at   , September 6, 1821. m. Frederick Lawrence of Canaan, Ct.

2074.   3. Edward H., b. at   , October 24, 1823.

2075.   4. Mary H., b. at   , December 13, 1826. m. Frederick Lawrence.

2076.   5. Stephen H., b. at   , September 9, 1829. He is
in the mining regions West, (1865.)

2077.   6. Hattie A., b. at   , August 20, 1835. m. A.
P. Lawrence of Norfolk.

2078.   7. George E. H., b. at   , August 31, 1837. m.
. He is a lawyer, and lives in Cairo,
Ill., (1865.)

854.

OBADIAH PEASE,[7] (Obadiah,[6] Nathaniel,[5] Samuel,[4]
Robert,[3] John,[2] Robert,[1]) second and youngest son of
Obadiah and Daziah (Pettibone) Pease, was born at

, December 1, 1798; married Mary E. Brewster, eldest daughter of James Brewster of New Haven, Ct., April 28, 1830. He is now (1865) living in New Haven, a banker and broker.

His children were:

2079. 1. MARY B., b. at   , May 12, 1831. m. George E. Hubbel, a lawyer, of Davenport, Iowa.
2080. 2. JOSEPHINE A., b. at   , July 16, 1833.

---o---

858.

JOSEPH IVES PEASE,⁷ (EARL P.,⁶ NATHANIEL,⁵ SAMUEL,⁴ ROBERT,³ JOHN,² ROBERT,¹) eldest son of EARL P. and MARY (IVES) PEASE, some time of Norfolk, Ct., and first cousin of the preceding, was born at Norfolk, August 9, 1809; married Mary Spencer of Baltimore, Md., December 8, 1841, who died 1851.

Mr. Pease is an engraver in the portrait, historical and landscape style, and in the line manner; also by aquatint process. When a boy he showed an unusually well-developed inventive and constructive faculty. He amused his young schoolmates with a variety of fancy articles which he made with a turning-lathe of his own construction. Before he supposed it had been thought of he built a power-loom which wove a strip of cloth six inches wide by simply turning a crank. "While yet a boy he got up a propeller on the identical model of those in present use, and fitted it into a boat of one squirrel power," which caused the astonishment of old and young in his native village at seeing the little craft "go ahead" without visible sail or wheel. This in itself may appear like a simple thing, but it involved a principle which was not brought to public notice until several years afterwards; and which, since its adoption, has produced an entire change in the mode of building ships for naval

27

warfare or for fast sailing freighting vessels.* Notwith-standing he showed at this early age an uncommon me-chanical genius, his father placed him as a clerk in a store at Hartford, Ct. The son managed to extricate himself from a business not congenial to his tastes, and began a pursuit more in harmony with his feelings, and which he has since followed.

The smaller productions of his burin may be found in many of the gift books and magazines of the past thirty years. Some of his larger works are "Old '76 and young '48" engraved for the old New York Art Union; a copy of Raphael Morghen's "Last Supper," published by Led-yard Bill of New York, and a view of Haines' Falls, Cats-kill Mountains, in a work published by William Pate of New York.

He was, for a number of years, connected with the American Bank Note Company. Many of their most fin-ished vignettes, portraits and fancy heads for bank notes were his work. The "battle of Lexington" on the twenty dollar bill, national currency, is one of them, though by no means his best.

Aside from his regular pursuit, Mr. Pease has contrib-uted several poems which need no other recommendation than to say they were published in the early volumes of Godey's and Graham's Magazines, and in Harper's Weekly and Monthly periodicals. He has spent the greater portion of his business life in the cities of Boston, Albany, Philadelphia and New York. He now resides at Stockbridge, Mass.

His children are:

2081.   1. Fanny I., b. at Albany, N. Y., September 17, 1842.
2082.   2. Ernest S., b. at Philadelphia, November 20, 1846.
2083.   3. Willard P., b. at Cooperstown, N. Y., July 7, 1848.

---

* It was not until sometime after 1833, that Ericsson attempted to call the British government to the principle of propelling boats by a force acting entirely under water. Failing there, he came to the United States, where he met with more en-couragement, and applied the propeller with success to the steamship, "Princeton," in 1841. [Appleton's American Cyclopedia.]

I am, as of Old,

Yours truly —

Joseph Ives Pease

859.

RICHARD H. PEASE,⁷ (EARL P.,⁶ NATHANIEL,⁵ SAMUEL,⁴ ROBERT,³ JOHN,² ROBERT,¹) brother of the preceding, was born at Norfolk, Ct., February 19, 1813; married Mary E. Dawes of Philadelphia, Pa., January 10, 1835, and resided for some time at Albany, N. Y. He now resides in New York City; is, by occupation, an engraver on wood. He was largely engaged at one time in furnishing engraved illustrations for works published by authority of the State of New York. He has been a publisher of toy books and other illustrated works for children, as Grandpapa Pease's works.

His children were :

2084.	1. CLARA I., b. at W. Eggleston.	m. William
2085.	2. HENRY E., b. at	m. Sarah L. Gay.
2086.	3. CHARLES E., b. at , about 1841. He was in military service in the late rebellion, held the rank of Major, and was Assistant Adjutant General in the Army of the Potomac.	
2087.	4. MARY E., b. at	m. George Wm. Warren.
2088.	5. FRANCIS I., b. at	d. young.
2089.	6. MARTHA H., b. at	
2090.	7. ELLA L., b. at	m. Theodore Sill.
2091.	8. RICHARD, b. at	d. an infant.
2092.	9. RICHARD H., b. at , about 1848.	
2093.	10. GEORGE W., b. at , about 1853.	

860.

ROGER M. S. PEASE,⁷ (EARL P.,⁶ NATHANIEL,⁵ SAMUEL,⁴ ROBERT,³ JOHN,² ROBERT,¹) youngest son of EARL P. and MARY (IVES) PEASE, was born at Norfolk, Ct., January 13, 1822; married, first, Abby E. Slack of Albany, N. Y., January 26, 1841; married, second, Mary A. Russell of North-East New York, May 8, 1854, and resides at St. Paul, Minn., (1866.) He is a minister of the Gospel in connection with the Baptist denomination.

His children were:

BY FIRST WIFE:

2094. 1. ABBY L., b. at Albany, N. Y., October 24, 1841. d. August
            3, 1846.
2095. 2. MINOT H., b. at Albany, August 19, 1843. He enlisted in
            Company D, of the Second Minnesota Volunteers, Septem-
            ber 23, 1861, at Fort Snelling. d. of chronic dysentery at
            St. Paul, September 23, 1862.
2096. 3. GRANVILLE B., b. at Albany, September 15, 1845.
2097. 4. MAY L., b. at Albany, April 18, 1847. m. Henry E. Seelye
            of St. Francis, Minn., August 27, 1865.
2098. 5. ROGER S., b. at Newtonville, N. Y., December 19, 1849.
2099. 6. ANNIE S., b. at Brooklyn, N. Y., June 6, 1852.
2100. 7. CARRIE R., b. at Brooklyn, July 11, 1853.

BY SECOND WIFE:

2101. 8. CHARLES H., b. at St. Paul, April 29, 1857. d. September
            20, 1857.
2102. 9. NELLIE R., b. at St. Paul, December 24, 1863.

———o○o———

FAMILY OF DANIEL.[4]

861.

ALANSON PEASE,[7] (WILLIAM,[6] DANIEL,[5] DANIEL,[4]
ROBERT,[3] JOHN,[2] ROBERT,[1]) eldest son of WILLIAM and
(   ) PEASE of Canaan, N. Y., and third
cousin of the preceding, was born at Canaan,   ,
1779; married Betsey Lee.

862.

WILLIAM PEASE,[7] (WILLIAM,[6] DANIEL,[5] DANIEL,[4]
ROBERT,[3] JOHN,[2] ROBERT,[1]) brother of the preceding, was
born at Canaan, March 4, 1781; married Obedience Stone.
He settled, a farmer, among the early settlers in the town
of Pompey, N. Y.

His children were:

2103. 1. AMANDA, b. at Pompey, N. Y.,   , 1810.
2104. 2. WILLIAM G., b. at Pompey,   , 1812. m. Electa Col-
            burn; m., second, Margaret Butler; m., third, Sylvia Butler.

2105.   3. EMILY, b. at Pompey. April 2, 1814.
2106.   4. MAHALA E., b. at Pompey, June 22, 1816.   m. Joseph
        Hanchett,   , 1836.
2107.   5. LUCY ANN, b. at Pompey,   , 1818.
2108.   6. MARIA C., b. at Pompey, December 20, 1820.
2109.   7. JULIETTE, b. at Pompey, May 30, 1823.
2110.   8. SYLVIA, b. at Pompey, December 11, 1825.   m. George W.
        Humphrey.

863.

WALTER PEASE,⁷ (WILLIAM,⁶ DANIEL,⁵ DANIEL,⁴ ROB-
ERT,³ JOHN,² ROBERT,¹) third son of WILLIAM and
(   ) PEASE of Canaan, N. Y., was born at Canaan,
May 14, 1785; married   ; had no children.

864.

WARREN PEASE,⁷ (WILLIAM,⁶ DANIEL,⁵ DANIEL,⁴ ROB-
ERT,³ JOHN,² ROBERT,¹) brother of the preceding, was born
at Canaan, January   , 1789; married Chloe Sutton, and
removed to Indiana, and settled in the town of Lafayette.

His children were:

. 2111.   1.
  2112.   2.

865.

DORAS PEASE,⁷ (WILLIAM,⁶ DANIEL,⁵ DANIEL,⁴ ROB-
ERT,³ JOHN,² ROBERT,¹) son of WILLIAM and
(   ) PEASE of Canaan, N. Y., and brother of the
preceding, was born at Canaan.

———o———

869.

DANIEL PEASE,⁷ (DANIEL,⁶ DANIEL,⁵ DANIEL,⁴ ROB-
ERT,³ JOHN,² ROBERT,¹) eldest son of DANIEL and KEZIAH
(DEAN) PEASE of Canaan, N. Y., and first cousin of the
preceding, was born at Canaan, May 7, 1782; married
Betsey Williams, and settled, a farmer, in Canaan.

His children were:

2113. 1. Daniel W., b. at Canaan,   , 1817. m. Susan
S. Sedgwick of Lee, Mass., March 1, 1846, and resides in
Canaan, a farmer.

2114. 2. George L., b. at Canaan, 1819. m. Rachel Smith,
, 1852. d.   , 1862.

2115. 3. William H., b. at Canaan,   , and resides at
Canaan.

2116. 4. Catharine, b. at Canaan.

2117. 5. Sylvia J., b. at Canaan.

871.

Rev. LEWIS PEASE,[7] (Daniel,[6] Daniel,[5] Daniel,[4]
Robert,[3] John,[2] Robert,[1]) brother of the preceding, was
born at Canaan, N. Y., August 7, 1786; married, first,
Pamelia Norton of Goshen, Ct., March 29, 1808; married, second, Ann E. Wheeler, December 2, 1835. He
was an itinerant minister of the Gospel. In 1807, at the
early age of 21 years, he was "received on trial" by the
New York Conference of the Methodist Episcopal Church.
At the end of his probation, (1811) he was ordained elder
by the same conference.

When he entered the ministry the New York Conference embraced a portion of New Jersey, the eastern part
of New York State, the west half of Connecticut, Berkshire County in Massachusetts, and the western portion
of Vermont. Over this extensive territory the preachers
of that body during his early ministry were liable to be
stationed from year to year.

While in the active ministry, Mr. Pease was appointed
to the most responsible positions within the bounds of his
conference; Troy and Albany, N. Y., New York City, and
Hartford, Ct., were among his appointments. He was
once transferred, and preached two years at Philadelphia,
Pa. He was an ardent, eloquent and successful laborer
in his Master's vineyard. It is said by those who have
heard him he possessed the faculty of holding the atten-

tion of his audience, rarely excelled by any public speaker of his times. For many years before his decease, his ministrations were greatly retarded by feeble health. At length, borne down by a peculiar chronic disease, he died at Richmond, Mass., September 25, 1843, aged 57 years. His remains were buried in his native town.

His children were:

BY SECOND WIFE:

2118.   1. PAMELIA A., b. at New York City, February 15, 1837.   m. Rev. Mr. Steel.

2119.   2. LEWIS Y., b. at Richmond, Mass., December 2, 1839.   d. July 4, 1849.

2120.   3. WILLIAM E., b. at Richmond, February 18, 1841.

872.

PHILO PEASE,⁷ (DANIEL,⁶ DANIEL,⁵ DANIEL,⁴ ROBERT,³ JOHN,² ROBERT,¹) third son of DANIEL and KEZIAH (DEAN) PEASE, was born at Canaan, September 21, 1788; married Polly Orton about 1810, and first settled at Canaan, but subsequently removed to Lisle, N. Y., where he died, April 10, 1837.

His children were:

2121.   1. JOHN M., b. at Canaan, September 25, 1811.   m. Artemisia White, daughter of Rev. Nicholas White, May 29, 1826.

Mr. Pease entered the ministry of the Gospel and joined the New York Conference of the Methodist Episcopal Church in 1834. He was ordained elder in 1838, and continued in the itinerancy of the church until the fall of 1853, when he went to Philadelphia as secretary of the Pennsylvania State Colonization Society. He dissolved his relation with this society in the spring of 1855, and soon after became engaged in organizing an "African Exploration Society." He was appointed traveling agent for the purpose of obtaining funds to help carry out the object of the society with the expectation of embarking for the coast of Africa as soon as the necessary funds were obtained. He left his home in

Brooklyn, N. Y., in August, 1856, on a tour through the
State, was taken suddenly ill at Rochester, and returned to
some friends at Auburn, where he died, September 29, 1856.

2122.   2. MARIETTE L., b. at Canaan, March 7, 1814.   m. Linus Dickinson, and d. at Lisle, September 4, 1839.

2123.   3. CAROLINE P., b. at Canaan, May 8, 1816.   m. Edson
A. Blair, and resides at Castle Creek, Broome County,
N. Y.

2124.   4. LEWIS M., b. at Lisle, August 25, 1818.   m. Ann E. Pinney.
Mr. Lewis M. Pease also joined the New York Confer-
ence of the Methodist Episcopal Church, and was ordained
elder in 1845.   Before the meeting of the annual conference in 1850, the ladies of the Home Missionary Society of
the Methodist Episcopal Church of New York City, asked
the bishop for a missionary to be appointed from the conference to labor as such at the Five Points Mission, a field
which the above society had for sometime occupied.   Mr.
Pease was selected as the man for the place.   At the end of
one year he was removed by the conference and another
appointed.

Mr. Pease had labored long enough here to become satisfied that the demand for missionary operations in the vicinity
of Five Points was of sufficient magnitude to justify the
continuance of his labors under an independent organization.   Accordingly he withdrew from the Methodist Conference and organized the Five Points House of Industry.
In 1854 it became an incorporated institution, governed by
a board of trustees elected annually by the incorporators,
of which incorporate body Mr. Pease was a member.   He
held the position of superintendent of the institution for
some eight years.   He afterwards retired to a farm owned
by the institution at Westchester, N. Y., where boys were
sent from the Mission to receive instruction in farming.

2125.   5. HARRIET E., b. at Lisle, July 7, 1822.   m. Charles Abbott,
d. May 23, 1845.

2126.   6. JOSEPH N., b. at Lisle, December 1, 1824.   m. Jane Marsh,
and resides at Virgil Corners, N. Y. ; is a farmer.

2127.   7. WILLIAM S., b. at Lisle, April 11, 1827.   d. at Triangle,
N. Y., November 30, 1846.

2128.   8. ANN E., b. at Lisle, September 16, 1829.   d. at Rio Janeiro,
South America, February 22, 1850.

2129.   9. PHILO C., b. at Lisle, October 31, 1835.   He is a physician,
and resided at West Farms, N. Y.

875.

JOHN B. PEASE,⁷ (Daniel,⁶ Daniel,⁵ Daniel,⁴ Robert,³ John,² Robert,¹) fourth son of Daniel and Keziah
(Dean) Pease, was born at Canaan, July 9, 1795; married, first, Abigail Hunt, November 4, 1818; married,
second, Mary Bushnel, February 6, 1854. He removed
from Canaan, soon after his first marriage. For a time
he resided at Nassau, Rensselaer County, N. Y., thence at
De Ruyter, Madison County, next at Manlius, and subsequently at the village of Lake Port, town of Sullivan,
where he now resides, (1866.) He is, by occupation, a
farmer.

His children were:

2130. 1. Mary A., b. at New Lebanon, N. Y., April 5, 1820. m.
Charles Smith, September 12, 1842, and resides at Pitcher,
Chenango County, N. Y.

2131. 2. Sylvia N., b. at Nassau, August 27, 1821. m. Almon Perkins of Cazenovia, July 1, 1844.

2132. 3. Harvey C., b. at Nassau, April 30, 1823. m. Sarah Earl,
July 11, 1847, and resides at Manlius. He is, by occupation, a farmer.

2133. 4. William H., b. at Nassau, September 15, 1825. m. Susan
Wyman, October 28, 1847, and resides at De Witt. He
is, by occupation, a cooper.

2134. 5. Pamelia, b. at Nassau, October 22, 1827. m. Rufus Cornell,
September 19, 1857, and resides at Sullivan.

2135. 6. John F., b. at De Ruyter, December 15, 1829. m. Catharine Derrick, November 3, 1850, and resides at Syracuse,
N. Y. He is, by occupation, a coppersmith.

877.

Rev. WILLIAM S. PEASE,⁷ (Daniel,⁶ Daniel,⁵ Daniel,⁴ Robert,³ John,² Robert,¹) fifth and youngest son of
Daniel and Keziah (Dean) Pease, was born at Canaan,
April 5, 1800; married Jane Edwards,   He
died February 22, 1826, leaving no children. We take
the following from the Methodist Magazine of 1826:—

"At the age of 8 years he was made partaker of pardoning mercy, and in 1821, he entered the traveling ministry, in which he continued until his death. The disease with which he died caused him many painful hours; but he bore them with patience and resignation, often expressing his confidence in God and his prospects of future felicity. When death approached him he said, 'Can this be dying? I never was so happy. I am free from pain, both of body and mind.' In this happy frame of mind he sank peacefully into the arms of death. In his death the church has lost a 'young minister of much promise, as he gave every presage of future usefulness to his fellow-men.''

---o---

879.

WILLIAM R. PEASE,[7] (EPHRAIM,[6] DANIEL,[5] DANIEL,[4] ROBERT,[3] JOHN,[2] ROBERT,[1]) eldest son of EPHRAIM and SARAH (WRIGHT) PEASE, first of Canaan, N. Y., last of Lisle, N. Y., and first cousin of the preceding, was born at Canaan, January 3, 1791; married Susannah Baker, October 25, 1818. He died at Lisle, October 2, 1856. He was, by occupation, a farmer.

His children were:

2136.   1. CHARLES W., b. at Canaan, September 7, 1819. m. Mary A. Hulse, and resides at Green Point, L. I. He is, by occupation, a ship builder, and is a foreman in the employ of the U. S. Government.

2137.   2. HENRY F., b. at Canaan, April 12, 1824. m. Sarah Frazier, and resides at Westfield, N. J. He is, by occupation, a farmer.

2138.   3. EPHRAIM H., b. at Canaan, May 20, 1827. m. Sarepta Hulse,.and resides at Green Point, L. I. He is, by occupation, a ship carpenter.

2139.   4. SUSAN D., b. at Canaan,   . m.   Graves.

884.

EPHRAIM B. PEASE,[7] (EPHRAIM,[6] DANIEL,[5] DANIEL,[4] ROBERT,[3] JOHN,[2] ROBERT,[1]) brother of the preceding, was born at Canaan, N. Y., September 21, 1806; married Caroline Barnes, February 17, 1833. He now (1866) resides at Walnut Grove, Knox County, Ill. He is, by occupation, a farmer.

His children are:

2140.   1. WALTER D., b. at Preble, November 22, 1834.
2141.   2. VIRGIA, b. at
2142.   3. ELIZA, b. at

887.

HENRY F. PEASE,⁷ (EPHRAIM,⁶ DANIEL,⁵ DANIEL,⁴ ROBERT,³ JOHN,² ROBERT,¹) brother of the preceding, was born at Canaan, N. Y., April 5, 1817; married Clarinda Pellett, November 12, 1840. He resides at Lisle, and is, by occupation, a carpenter.

His children are:

2143.   1. SUSAN D., b. at Lisle, August 31, 1844.
2144.   2. FRANCIS H., b. at Lisle, June 18, 1848.
2145.   3. JOHN M., b. at Lisle, September 30, 1852.
2146.   4. GEORGE W., b. at Lisle, October 9, 1856.

——ooo——

FAMILY OF EBENEZER.⁴

889.

JOHN B. PEASE,⁷ (EBENEZER,⁶ EBENEZER,⁵ EBENEZER,⁴ ROBERT,³ JOHN,² ROBERT,¹) eldest son of EBENEZER and HULDAH (PEASE) PEASE of Enfield, Ct., and third cousin of the preceding, was born at Enfield, September 9, 1774; married Freelove Frink of Preston, Ct.,   , 1799, and settled in Whitesboro, N. Y.

His children were:

2147.   1. HARMON, b. at   , 1800. m. Hannah
        S. Moyston of Schenectady, N. Y. m., second,
                , and settled at Rome, N. Y.

2148. 2. HENRY H., b. at   , July 25, 1804. m. Lydia
Harris of Rhode Island, and removed to Mississippi in
1836. His wife died there. He was thrown from his carriage and killed there in 1840.

2149.   3. LEWIS S., b. at   , October 13, 1806, and removed to Mississippi in 1835. d. of fever, April   , 1837.

2150. 4. JOHN. b. at   , January 28, 1809. m. Elizabeth Debrill of Nashville, Tenn., and removed to Nashville.
d. of fever, August   , 1842.

2151. 5. JAMES M., b. at   , September 14, 1811. m.
Louisa Van Antwerp of Brooklyn, N. Y., and removed to
Mississippi. He was shot and killed by an enemy on his
plantation, October 24, 1842.

2152.   6. WILLIAM I., b. at   , September 5, 1813, and
removed to Mississippi. d. of fever, April 21, 1837.

2153.   7. CHARLES E., b. at   , February 2, 1816, and removed to Mississippi in the fall of 1842. d. there March
      , 1843.

890.

GEORGE PEASE,[7] (EBENEZER,[6] EBENEZER,[5] EBENEZER,[4]
ROBERT,[3] JOHN,[2] ROBERT,[1]) brother of the preceding, was
born at Enfield,   ; married Esther Thompson of Goshen, Ct., and removed to Ohio.

891.

EBENEZER PEASE,[7] (EBENEZER,[6] EBENEZER,[5] EBEN-
EZER,[4] ROBERT,[3] JOHN,[2] ROBERT,[1]) brother of the preceding, was born at Enfield,   , and removed to
Ohio, where he married,   ; died,
1813. [New England Historical and Genealogical Register.]

892.

NATHANIEL PEASE,[7] (EBENEZER,[6] EBENEZER,[5] EBEN-
EZER,[4] ROBERT,[3] JOHN,[2] ROBERT,[1]) brother of the preced-
ing, was born at Enfield,   ; married
Buell of Galway, N. Y. [New England Historical and
Genealogical Register.]

Mary Eugenia Chapman

897.

JAMES PEASE,⁷ (JAMES,⁶ EBENEZER,⁵ EBENEZER,⁴ ROB-
ERT,³ JOHN,² ROBERT,¹) eldest son of JAMES and LUCY
(MEACHAM) PEASE, some time of Hinsdale, Mass., and
last of Auburn, N. Y., and cousin of the preceding, was
born at   about 1781; married Olive Thompson of
Berkshire County, Mass.,   , 1806, and probably
first settled at Hinsdale, Mass. In 1813 and '14, he resided at Albany, N. Y., and was in company with his
brother Jabez in the leather business. [F. S. Pease.] He
was also in company with his brother Erastus at Auburn,
not far from the last date. He subsequently removed to
Syracuse, N. Y., (or vicinity) then to the State of Ohio,
residing near Cleveland. He finally removed to Portage
City, Wis., where he died, December 9, 1855.

His children were:

2154.   1. JAMES T., b. at   , May 15, 1808.   d. January
      24, 1824.

2155.   2. MARY E., b. at   , December 27, 1811. m. Prof.
      Chandler B. Chapman, A. M., M. D., June 1, 1837, and
      resides at Madison, Wis. She has a son, Chandler Pease
      Chapman, a real estate broker, and resides at Madison, Wis.

2156.   3. OLIVE M., b. at   , May 31, 1816. m. William
      Crane, M. D., July 25, 1842, and resides at Cottage Grove,
      Wis.

2157.   4. RUFUS De G., b. at   , August 8, 1820, and
      resides at Chicago, Ill., unmarried, (1868.)

898.

JABEZ PEASE,⁷ (JAMES,⁶ EBENEZER,⁵ EBENEZER,⁴ ROB-
ERT,³ JOHN,² ROBERT,¹) brother of the preceding, was born
at East Windsor, Ct., March 5, 1783; married Sybil San-
derson of Ashfield, Mass.,   , 1810. He seems
to have first settled at Geneva, N. Y., where he lived
most of the time until about 1822, when he removed to

Auburn, N. Y. Here he was in copartnership with his brother Erastus that closed about 1835. He finally removed to South Deerfield, Mass., where he died.

His children were:

2158. 1. ELIZA ANN, b. at Geneva, N. Y., December 31, 1811. m. Dr. A. D. Wood, and settled at Geneva, N. Y.

2159. 2. JOHN H. S., b. at Geneva,   , 1814.

2160. 3. SARAH A., b. at Geneva, October 13, 1817.

2161. 4. ROBERT M., b. at Geneva, June 6, 1820. m. Elizabeth Schemerhorn of Schodack, N. Y., May   , 1853. He resided for sometime at South Deerfield, Mass., but at present resides in New York City.

2162. 5. HELEN M., b. at Auburn, August 18, 1823.

2163. 6. CHARLES J., b. at Auburn, May 3, 1825. d., aged 16 years.

<hr>

899.

ERASTUS PEASE,[7] (JAMES,[6] EBENEZER,[5] EBENEZER,[4] ROBERT,[3] JOHN,[2] ROBERT,[1]) brother of the preceding, was born at East Windsor, Ct., May 30, 1785; married Persis Chapin of West Springfield, Mass., January 10, 1808. After a short residence at Hinsdale, Mass., he removed to Auburn, N. Y., where he was engaged in active business until near the close of life. He died, August 24, 1857, at the Insane Asylum, Ithica, N. Y.

His children were:

2164. 1. LORENZO W., b. at Hinsdale, May 20, 1809. He graduated at Hamilton College, Clinton, N. Y., 1828, and at the Auburn Theological Seminary, 1833. m. Lucinda Leonard, June 25, 1833, and the August following went under care of the A. B. C. F. M. as missionary to Larnica, Island of Cyprus, where he d., August 21, 1839.

2165. 2. HENRY C., b. at Hinsdale, August 23, 1810. m. Amy Daily, 1830, and resides at La Porte, Ind.

2166. 3. PERSIS C., b. at Auburn, March 23, 1813. m. James Y. Brown of Windsor, Broome County, N. Y., October 8, 1844.

2167. 4. HARRIET M., b. at Auburn, May 23, 1815. d. August 27, 1857.

2168.   5. LAURA A., b. at Auburn, August 3, 1817. · m. Rev. Addison Muzzy, August 22, 1843. He was a graduate of Hamilton College and Auburn Theological Seminary and resides at Chenoa, Ill.

2169.   6. CATHARINE E., b. at Auburn, March 29, 1819. m. Rev. H. W. Gilbert, June 1, 1841, late of Binghamton, N. Y., but now, (1868) pastor of the Congregational Church at Long Ridge, Fairfield County, Ct.

2170.   7. CHARLOTTE C., b. at Auburn, August 19, 1821. m. Rev. William B. Worden, October 8, 1839. d. at Auburn, August 7, 1848.

2171.   8. THEODORE D., b. at Auburn, March 21, 1829. d. March 10, 1830.

———o———

904.

FRANCIS PEASE,⁷ (PETER,⁶ EBENEZER,⁵ EBENEZER,⁴ ROBERT,³ JOHN,² ROBERT,¹) eldest son of PETER and HULDAH (STEBBINS) PEASE of Enfield, Ct., and cousin of the preceding,· was born at Enfield, July 8, 1787;. married Mary Pease, daughter of Lemuel Pease. He died in Enfield without issue.

905.

WILLIAM PEASE,⁷ (PETER,⁶ EBENEZER,⁵ EBENEZER,⁴ ROBERT,³ JOHN,² ROBERT,¹) brother of the preceding, was born at Enfield, April 21, 1790; married Electa Crittenden of Seneca, N. Y., December 29, 1814. He was largely engaged for some time in the hardware business at Rochester, N. Y. In 1834 he removed to Buffalo, N. Y., and continued in the same business until within a few years of his death. He was in the war of 1812, and was at Buffalo at the attacking of Fort Erie. He died at Geneva, N. Y., March 29, 1850.

His children were:

2172.   1. WILLIAM H., b. at Reading, N. Y., March 4, 1820. m. Jane E. Thompson. He is a merchant, and resides at Buffalo, N. Y.

2173. 2. Francis S., b. at Rochester, December 29, 1822. m. Lucretia A. Goodale, July 6, 1840, and resides at Buffalo, N. Y. He is a manufacturer and extensive dealer in oils.

2174. 3. Mary C., b. at Rochester, May , 1825. m. Ashley H. Ball of Rochester.

2175. 4. Henry P., b. at Rochester,   . m. Josephine Hiccox. He was engaged in the late war of the rebellion.

2176. 5. Harriet M., b. at   . d. in infancy.

910.

HORATIO N. PEASE,[7] (Peter,[6] Ebenezer,[5] Ebenezer,[4] Robert,[3] John,[2] Robert,[1]) youngest son of Peter and Huldah (Stebbins) Pease of Enfield, Ct., was born at Enfield, April 29, 1806; married   Chapin of Mackinaw. He died in Michigan, and it is supposed he left no children.

——oooo——

DESCENT OF JONATHAN.[3]

FAMILY OF JOSIAH.[4]

911.

AARON PEASE,[7] (Aaron,[6] Josiah,[5] Josiah,[4] Jonathan,[3] John,[2] Robert,[1]) first son of Aaron and (   ) Pease, first of Upton, Mass., and subsequently of St. Albans, Vt., was born at   ; married   (history unknown.)

912.

CHARLES A. PEASE,[7] (Aaron,[6] Josiah,[5] Josiah,[4] Jonathan,[3] John,[2] Robert,[1]) second son of Aaron and (   ) Pease, first of Upton, Mass., and subsequently of St. Albans, Vt., was born at   ; married

His child was :

2177.   1. CHANDLER C., b. at   , and resides at
Malone, Franklin County, N. Y.

———o———

915.

ORTON PEASE,⁷ (JOSIAH,⁶ JOSIAH,⁵ JOSIAH,⁴ JONA-
THAN,³ JOHN,² ROBERT,¹) eldest son of JOSIAH and POLLY
(BEALS) PEASE, first of Upton, Mass., and last of Norfolk,
St. Lawrence County, N. Y., and first cousin of the preceding, was born at Upton, Mass., March 30, 1806; married Mary Hare, February 16, 1830. In 1823 he took up
his residence in Coteau Landing, Canada East, where he
yet resides. He is, by occupation, a merchant, (1866.)

His children were :

2178.   1. ASAEL, b. at Coteau Landing, December 25, 1830. d. February 25, 1831.
2179.   2. ANNA M., b. at Coteau Landing, January 26, 1832. m.
Charles McLean, and d. January 18, 1857.
2180.   3. MARY E., b. at Coteau Landing, January 11, 1834. m. Benjamin W. Bridges, July 2, 1855.
2181.   4. CHARLES O., b. at Coteau Landing, December 11, 1835. m.
Georgiana Perry, February 18, 1863, and resides at Coteau
Landing, a merchant.
2182.   5. LUCY A., b. at Coteau Landing, November 7, 1837. m. William Perry, May 2, 1859. d. April 30, 1864.
2183.   6. GEORGE A., b. at Coteau Landing, May 29, 1842. He
graduated at McGill College, and has since received the
degree of A. M. He resides in New York City,
(1866.)
2184.   7. JANE E., b. at Coteau Landing, October 29, 1844.
2185.   8. LYDIA A., b. at Coteau Landing, November 26, 1846.
2186.   9. DANIEL A., b. at Coteau Landing, March 12, 1849. d. October 14, 1852.
2187. 10. EDMUND C., b. at Coteau Landing, October 15, 1851.
2188. 11. ELIZA J., b. at Coteau Landing, July 6, 1854.
2189. 12. EDSON L., b. at Coteau Landing, September 2, 1856.
2190. 13. ORVAL W., b. at Coteau Landing, January 10, 1860.
29

920.

DANIEL B. PEASE,[7] (Josiah,[6] Josiah,[5] Josiah,[4] Jonathan,[3] John,[2] Robert,[1]) brother of the preceding, was born at Upton, Mass., June 9, 1819; married Selina Kennedy, January 30, 1845. He removed from Norfolk, N. Y., to Canada, in 1832, and resides at Valleyfield, Beauharnais County, Canada East, (1866.)

His children are:

2191.	1. Octavia S., b. at	October 5, 1845.
2192.	2. Daniel O., b. at	October 30, 1850.

——oo——

FAMILY OF PELATIAH.[4]

921.

JONATHAN PEASE,[7] (Jonathan,[6] Samuel,[5] Pelatiah,[4] Jonathan,[3] John,[2] Robert,[1]) eldest son of Dea. Jonathan and Eleanor (Gleason) Pease of Enfield, Ct., and second cousin of the preceding, was born at Enfield, September 5, 1801; married Emeline King, October 10, 1827, and settled in Chicopee, Mass., where his family were born; died   , 1849, aged 48 years.

His children were:

2193.   1. Samuel K., b. at Chicopee, August 10, 1828.   d. at Enfield, May 27, 1848.

2194.   2. Jonathan H., b. at Chicopee, May 1, 1832. He is dead.

2195.   3. Emeline L., b. at Chicopee, December 17, 1833.

2196.   4. Caroline S., b. at Chicopee, November 20, 1836.

2197.   5. James L., b. at Chicopee, October 31, 1842, and resides at Chicopee. He is clerk in the counting-room of the Gaylord Manufacturing Company.

922.

OSEE PEASE,[7] (Jonathan,[6] Samuel,[5] Pelatiah,[4] Jonathan,[3] John,[2] Robert,[1]) brother of the preceding, was

born at Enfield, August 30, 1803; married, first,
; married, second, Selina Pease, daughter of
Asa Pease of Enfield, Ct., and widow of Nelson McClester.
He resides in Springfield. He has no children.

924.

LATHROP PEASE,[7] (JONATHAN,[6] SAMUEL,[5] PELATIAH,[4]
JONATHAN,[3] JOHN,[2] ROBERT,[1]) third son of DEA. JONA-
THAN and ELEANOR (GLEASON) PEASE, was born at Enfield,
October 26, 1809; married Sarah Goodwell, April , 1841,
and settled in Vernon, Ct., subsequently in Enfield, but
now resides in Ellington, Ct.

His children are:

2198. 1. EDWIN L., b at Vernon, Ct., January   , 1842.
2199. 2. CHARLES W., b. at Vernon, September 15, 1843.
2200. 3. SARAH E., b. at Vernon, May 31, 1845.
2201. 4. ARTHUR G., b. at Vernon, April 2, 1847.
2202. 5. SARAH M., b. at Vernon, December 23, 1848.
2203. 6. EMMA R., b. at Vernon, September 29, 1850.
2204. 7. ADELBERT T., b. at Vernon, May 29, 1853.
2205. 8. EDGAR G., b. at Hartleton, Pa., May   , 1856.
2206. 9. ALICE, b. at Hartleton, March 23, 1858.

928.

SAMUEL R. PEASE,[7] (JONATHAN,[6] SAMUEL,[5] PELATIAH,[4]
JONATHAN,[3] JOHN,[2] ROBERT,[1]) fourth son of DEA. JONA-
THAN and ELEANOR (GLEASON) PEASE, was born at Enfield, July 25, 1820; married Lavinia E. Boyington, February 16, 1854, and settled in Enfield.

His children are:

2207. 1. EMERETTE L., b. at Enfield, December 31, 1854.
2208. 2. ESTHER S., b. at Enfield, November 27, 1856.
2208.[68] 3. MARY E., b. at Enfield, February 24, 1858.
2208.[69] 4. EDITH M., b. at Enfield, January 10, 1860.
2208.[70] 5. FRANKLIN J., b. at Enfield, October 3, 1862.
2208.[71] 6. SAMUEL D., b. at Enfield, January 1, 1865.
2208.[72] 7. RUTH A., b. at Enfield, January 13, 1868.

929.

SOLOMON G. PEASE, (JONATHAN,[6] SAMUEL,[5] PELA-TIAH,[4] JONATHAN,[3] JOHN,[2] ROBERT,[1]) fifth and youngest son of DEA. JONATHAN and ELEANOR (GLEASON) PEASE, was born at Enfield, September 24, 1822. He went to Ohio, where he married, and died about 1853, leaving one child. ·

His child was:

2209.   1.

———oo———

931.

JOHN PEASE,[7] (JOHN,[6] JOHN,[5] PELATIAH,[4] JONATHAN,[3] JOHN,[2] ROBERT,[1]) eldest son of JOHN and PATTY (ALLEN) PEASE, last of Ashfield, Mass., and second cousin of the preceding, was born at Conway, Mass., November 24, 1801; married Louisa Bartlett, and settled in Utica, N. Y., 1825, in the mercantile business, where his wife died, 1840.

His children were:

2210.   1. MIRANDA, b. at Ashfield, Mass., November 27, 1824. d. at Utica, July 16, 1841.

2211.   2. LUCINDA, b. at Utica, February 19, 1826. m. Edward Francis of Clinton, N. Y., 1862, a farmer.

2212.   3. CAROLINE, b. at Utica, January 28, 1828. m. Peter Germond, 1854, a farmer, and lives in New Hartford, N. Y.

2213.   4. HENRY C., b. at Utica, November 6, 1829. He went to California in 1853, and was engaged in mining until 1861, when he enlisted as a volunteer in the army to serve against the rebellion; was honorably discharged after three years' service in 1864; returned to Utica, and re-enlisted in Hancock's Corps of Veterans, March, 1865, for one year, and was discharged March, 1866.

2214.   5. WILLIAM R., b. at Utica, July 8, 1831. He entered the United States Military Academy at West Point, June 1, 1850; graduated as Brevet Second Lieutenant, July 1, 1855. He is the first of the name among the graduates of the United States Military Academy. He was assigned to duty with the Tenth Regiment of United States Infantry; promoted to Second Lieutenant, October 18, 1855, and ordered to duty with the Seventh Regiment of United States Infantry, serving in the Cherokee and Choctaw Indian country. In January, 1857, he was ordered on duty as recruiting officer at Rochester, N. Y. In February, 1858, he was ordered from Rochester to join the Seventh Regiment of Infantry at Jefferson Barracks, Mo., to prepare for the campaign against the Mormons in Utah Territory; served in that campaign until September, 1859, when from ill health was permitted to return to the States; March, 1861, was promoted First Lieutenant, and in June, 1861, was promoted to Captain, and engaged in mustering into service the Ohio three years' Volunteers; August, 1861, was appointed mustering and disbursing officer for Central New York, with station at Utica; August, 1862, was raised to Colonel and led to the field the One Hundred and Seventeenth Regiment of New York Volunteers; participated in the defense of the National Capital in the engagement between General Pope and Stonewall Jackson, commanding a brigade; April, 1863, was ordered with his regiment to Suffolk, Va., and participated in the defense of that place during its siege by the rebel General Longstreet, commanding the Third Brigade of the First Division of the Ninth Army Corps. In June, 1863, after the siege of Suffolk, he was compelled to resign his commission as Colonel of Volunteers. August, 1863, he was placed on the relief list on account of disability incurred in the line of duty; assigned to duty in the Provost Marshal General's office at Washington, D. C; April 30, 1864, was ordered to Hartford, Ct., as mustering and disbursing officer for Connecticut and Rhode Island; continued in this duty until January, 1866, when he was appointed Assistant Provost Marshal General, and chief mustering officer for Connecticut and Rhode Island, and appointed Brevet Major of the United States Army for faithful and meritorious service during the war. He has recently (1868) been appointed Brevet Brigadier General of the United States Army.

General Pease married Rowena C., daughter of Rev. Hart F. Pease of Brooklyn, N. Y.

2215. 6. HELEN, b. at Utica, September , 1833. m. Oliver Carpenter, a farmer, September 11, 1854, and resides in Paris, N. Y.

2216. 7. FRANCIS, b. at Utica,   , 1835. d. 1836.

2217.   8. HARRISON, b. at Utica, March 15, 1840.   He enlisted as a
private in the Twenty-Sixth Regiment of New York Volunteers, April, 1861, and served as such until September
5, 1862.   During this time he was in the battles of Cedar
Mountain, Brandy Station, Thoroughfare Gap, Second Bull
Run, and Chancellorsville, Va.; September 5, 1862, was
appointed First Lieutenant in the One Hundred and Seventeenth Regiment of New York Volunteers, and participated
with that regiment in the defense of Suffolk, Va., in April
and May, 1863, and the raid on Richmond under General
Dix in June and July, 1863, also in the siege of Charlestown, S. C., from August, 1863, to April, 1864; was in
the siege of Petersburg, Va., from April, 1864, until February, 1865; was severely wounded, May 16, 1864, at the
battle of Drury's Bluff, Va.; was promoted Captain for
gallant conduct in battle, June 19, 1864; rendered in one
of Sherman's columns in North Carolina, from March 15,
1865, to June 8, 1865; was mustered out and honorably
discharged with the regiment, June 8, 1865.

933.

DR. DAVID A. PEASE, (JOHN,[6] JOHN,[5] PELATIAH,[4]
JONATHAN,[3] JOHN,[2] ROBERT,[1]) brother of the preceding,
was born at Conway, December 9, 1805; married Sophia
Wilcox of Utica, N. Y.,   , 1826. For a time he
resided in Utica, after which he appears to have been a
resident of Rochester, N. Y., and subsequently of Cincinnati, Ohio; in 1865 was living in Detroit, Mich. He is,
by profession, a physician.

His children were:

2218.   1. HENRY A., b. at Utica, N. Y., December 2, 1827.   d June 3,
1829.
2219.   2. MARY A., b. at Rochester, September 22, 1830.   m. at Cincinnati, Ohio, William A. Trowbridge, September 20, 1848,
and resides at Seven Miles, Butler County, Ohio.
2220.   3. DAVID A., b. at Rochester, June 10, 1833.   d. June 10,
1834.
2221.   4 JANETTE M., b. at Utica, May 10, 1835.
2222.   5. DAVID A., b. at Pittsburg, Pa., February 21, 1838.   m.
Louisa A. J. Smith, January 21, 1860 and removed to

Bridgeport, Ill. He joined a company which was forming for the First Regiment of Western Sharp-shooters, afterwards called the Sixty-sixth Illinois Volunteers, and held the office of Orderly Sergeant; was engaged in the battles at Fort Donelson, Pittsburg Landing, and Corinth. He was promoted to a First Lieutenancy in the First Alabama Cavalry, which position he held until the fall of 1864, when he resigned and received an honorable discharge. He now (1865) resides at Detroit, Mich.

2223.   6. HENRY F., b. at Putnam, Ohio, November 4, 1840. d. March 22, 1851.

2224.   7. SOPHIA, b. at Putnam, May 2, 1843.

934.

LUMAN PEASE,⁷ (JOHN,⁶ JOHN,⁵ PELATIAH,⁴ JONATHAN,³ JOHN,² ROBERT¹). brother of the preceding, was born at Conway, April 26, 1808; married Gratia Hawks, 1832. He settled near Shelby, Richland County, Ohio, a farmer.

His children were:

2225.   1. ALONZO, b. at

2226.   2. TIRZAH A., b. at

2227.   3. GEORGE, b. at

936.

REV. HART F. PEASE,⁷ (JOHN,⁶ JOHN,⁵ PELATIAH,⁴ JONATHAN,³ JOHN,² ROBERT,¹) fourth son of JOHN and PATTY (ALLEN) PEASE, was born at Conway, December 27, 1811; married Louisa S. Ives of Cheshire, Ct., , 1836. He entered the ministry of the Methodist Episcopal Church, and joined the New York Conference in 1834, and was ordained elder in 1838. He is a member of the New York East Conference, a presiding elder of New York district, and resides at Brooklyn, N. Y.

His children were:

2228.   1. MARONETT AUGUSTA, b. at   August 22, 1838.
            m. William Brown of Brooklyn, N. Y., 1867.

2229.   2. ROWENA CYTHERA, b. at   , July 4, 1840.   m.
            Gen. W. R. Pease, United States Army.

2230. 3. FRANCES J., b. at   , September 19, 1842.
2231. 4. MARY L., b. at   , October 29, 1845. d. young.
2232. 5. JOHN S., b. at   , August 16, 1848.
2233. 6. EMMA L., b. at   , July 9, 1852.
2233.[73] 7. HART E., b. at   , July 21, 1857.

938.

REUEL PEASE,[7] (JOHN,[6] JOHN,[5] PELATIAH,[4] JONATHAN,[3] JOHN,[2] ROBERT,[1]) fifth son of JOHN and PATTY (ALLEN) PEASE, was born at Ashfield, October 6, 1815; married Sarah Macomber, and now occupies his father's homestead in Ashfield, Mass.

His children are:

2234. 1. WILLIAM H., b. at Ashfield, March 10, 1840.
2235. 2. SOLOMON A., b. at Ashfield, April 20, 1841.
2236. 3. GEORGE, b. at Ashfield, February 6, 1843.
2237. 4. ANGELIA MARIA, b. at Ashfield, January 1, 1845.
2238. 5. DARWIN E., b. at Ashfield, May 1, 1847.
2239. 6. FRANCES JANE, b. at Ashfield, February 6, 1849.
2240. 7. MARTHA ALLEN, b. at Conway, November 12, 1852.

939.

GEORGE PEASE,[7] (JOHN,[6] JOHN,[5] PELATIAH,[4] JONATHAN,[3] JOHN,[2] ROBERT,[1]) sixth son of JOHN and PATTY (ALLEN) PEASE, was born at Ashfield, March 20, 1817; married Almira Griffin. He was a physician, and settled in his profession in Kinderhook, N. Y., where he died, 1848, aged 31 years.

His children were:

2241. 1. Infant, d. young.
2242. 2. Infant, d. young.
2243. 3. GEORGE G., b. at Kinderhook.

940.

LIBERTY PEASE,[7] (JOHN,[6] JOHN,[5] PELATIAH,[4] JONATHAN,[3] JOHN,[2] ROBERT,[1]) seventh and youngest son of JOHN and PATTY (ALLEN) PEASE, was born at Ashfield, December 19, 1822; married, first, Emeline C. Payne,

January 30, 1844; married, second, Philenia Field, October 3, 1850. He appears to have resided for a time at Conneaut, Ohio, next at Ashfield, Mass., and subsequently at Kewanee, Ill., his present residence.

His children were:

2244. 1. George H., b. at Conneaut, Ohio, January 4, 1845. d. January 20, 1845.
2245. 2. Mary L., b. at Ashfield, Mass., October 12, 1851.
2246. 3. George H.,² b. at Ashfield, February 14, 1854.
2247. 4. Martha A., b. at Ashfield, November 22, 1855.
2248. 5. Philenia E., b. at Kewanee, Ill., March 17, 1858.
2249. 6. John E., b. at Kewanee, September 5, 1860.
2250. 7. Jessie M., b. at Kewanee, August 20, 1862.
2251. 8. Kittie M., b. at Kewanee, February 20, 1865.

941.

NEWTON PEASE,⁷ (Asher,⁶ John,⁵ Pelatiah,⁴ Jonathan,³ John,² Robert,¹) eldest son of Asher and Elizabeth (Chaffee) Pease of Conway, Mass., and first cousin of the preceding, was born at Conway,   ; married Sarah Dwight, and settled in Conway, a farmer and cattle-dealer.

His children were:

2252. 1. Sarah Caroline, b. at Conway,   , 1834.
2253. 2. Edward F., b. at Conway, October   , 1837. d. in childhood.
2254. 3. Ellen Maria, b. at Conway, January   , 1840.
2255. 4. Harris Dwight, b. at Conway, April   , 1842.
2256. 5. Jane Eliza, b. at Conway, March   , 1844.
2257. 6. Henry Edward, b. at Conway, May   , 1846. d. an infant.
2258. 7. Harriet A., b. at Conway, January   , 1849.

942.

FRANKLIN PEASE,⁷ (Asher,⁶ John,⁵ Pelatiah,⁴ Jonathan,³ John,² Robert,¹) brother of the preceding, was born at Conway,   ; married Minerva Nims, and lives in Conway. Has no children.

949.

WILLIAM PEASE,[7] (LYMAN,[6] JOHN,[5] PELATIAH,[4] JONATHAN,[3] JOHN,[2] ROBERT,[1]) eldest son of LYMAN and FANNIE (CHAFFEE) PEASE, some time of Southampton, Mass., last of Jackson City, Mich., and first cousin of the preceding, was born at Enfield, June 30, 1805; married Sarah Wilcox,   , 1834.   He removed to California, and is an Attorney at Law in that State.

His children were:

2259.	1. AMELIA, b. at	. m.	Pierce.
2260.	2. CAROLINE, b. at	. m.	Houston.
2261.	3. SARAH, b. at		

951.

LYMAN PEASE,[7] (LYMAN,[6] JOHN,[5] PELATIAH,[4] JONATHAN,[3] JOHN,[2] ROBERT,[1]) brother of the preceding, was born at Southampton,   , 1808; married Lowell, and removed to Texas, and is supposed to be dead, as there is no further history of him, whether he left posterity or not.   It appears he did not live long after his removal to Texas.

956.

PHILANDER PEASE,[7] (LYMAN,[6] JOHN,[5] PELATIAH,[4] JONATHAN,[3] JOHN,[2] ROBERT,[1]) fourth son of LYMAN and FANNIE (CHAFFEE) PEASE, was born at Southampton, December   , 1820; married   1848. He lives in Jackson, Mich.

His children were:

2262.	1. HENRY, b. at	
2263.	2. HELEN, b. at	

957.

HENRY PEASE,[7] (LYMAN,[6] JOHN,[5] PELATIAH,[4] JONATHAN,[3] JOHN,[2] ROBERT,[1]) youngest son of LYMAN and

Fannie (Chaffee) Pease, was born at Springfield, Mass.,
, 1827; married   , 1853;
died   , 1854, aged 27 years.   He was a carpenter by trade.

————o○○○+———

DESCENT OF JAMES.³

FAMILY OF JOSEPH,⁴ (OF JAMES.³)

959.

JUSTUS PEASE,⁷ (Justus,⁶ Wareham,⁵ Joseph,⁴
James,³ John,² Robert,¹) eldest son of Capt. Justus and
Esther (Warner) Pease of Suffield, Ct., and fourth
cousin of the preceding, was born at Suffield, November
12, 1786; married Electa Johnson, December   , 1813,
and settled in the west part of Suffield.   He is, by occupation, a farmer.

His children were:

2264.   1. Electa A., b. at Suffield, April 27, 1815.   d. December 31,
        1837, unmarried.
2265.   2. Justus M., b. at Suffield, February 18, 1817, and resides in
        Suffield, unmarried.
2266.   3. Catherine, b. at Suffield, October 4, 1823.   d. November 19,
        1833.
2267.   4. Samantha, b. at Suffield, April 24, 1825.   m. Andrew D.
        Harmond, and resides in Southwick.

965.

LESTER J. PEASE,⁷ (Justus,⁶ Wareham,⁵ Joseph,⁴
James,³ John,² Robert,¹) brother of the preceding, was
born at Suffield, October 5, 1801; married Orena Phelps,
November   , 1823; died 1845.

His children were:

2268.   1. Candace O., b. at   , 1824.   m. Alvin
        Miller, and resides in Suffield, Ct.
2269.   2. Corintha D., b. at   , May 2, 1831.   m. Ben-
        jamin F. Copley, and lives in Suffield.

2270. 3. KETURAH A., b. at   , April 9, 1833. m.
    Hastings.

2271. 4. HARRISON L., b. at   , December 31, 1838. m.
    Phelps, and resides in Southwick, Mass.

968.

PHILO P. PEASE,[7] (JUSTUS,[6] WAREHAM,[5] JOSEPH,[4] JAMES,[3] JOHN,[2] ROBERT,[1]) brother of the preceding, was born at Suffield, January 13, 1806. He went West, and married Polly Kesmer. He lives in Grass Valley, Harrison County, Iowa.

His children were:

2272. 1. LESTER J., b. at
2273. 2. PHILO, b. at
2274. 3. LOVISA, b. at
2275. 4. JUSTUS, b. at
2276. 5. LEWIS, b. at
2277. 6. STEPHEN, b. at
2278. 7. WASHINGTON B., b. at
2279. 8. MARY, b. at
2280. 9. RACHEL A., b. at
2281. 10. COMMODORE PERRY, b. at

976.

TITUS PEASE,[7] (TITUS,[6] WAREHAM,[5] JOSEPH,[4] JAMES,[3] JOHN,[2] ROBERT,[1]) eldest son of TITUS and MARY (BAGG) PEASE of Westfield, Mass., and first cousin of the preceding, was born at   ; married Harriet Pomeroy, and lived some time in Westfield, Mass. It is said he had a family of children.

978.

MAJ. FREDERICK G. PEASE,[7] (TITUS,[6] WAREHAM,[5] JOSEPH,[4] JAMES,[3] JOHN,[2] ROBERT,[1]) brother of the preceding, was born at   , September 7, 1808; married Mary M. Arthur, , 1825, and settled in Westfield. He is, by occupation, a whip-maker.

His children were:

2282. 1. WILLIAM C., b. at   , September 7, 1826. d. 1850.
2283. 2. MILTON A., b. at   , April 28, 1828. d. 1853, at
       New Orleans.
2284. 3. ALEXIS, b. at   , December 13, 1830. m. Eliza-
       beth Bates, July 10, 1852, and resides at Springfield, Mass.
2285. 4. CLARA F., b. at   , February 20, 1832. m. S. B.
       Woolworth, 1862.
2286. 5. CORNELIA H., b. at   , March 12, 1833. m. Henry
       M. Adams,   , 1860, and lives in Wilbraham.
2287. 6. FREDERICK G., b. at   , February 12, 1835. d. 1837.
2288. 7. AMOS M., b. at   , July 14, 1837. d. 1855.
2289. 8. MARCUS M., b. at   , January 12, 1840.
2290. 9. ISABEL E., b. at   , January 12, 1845.

———o———

987.

BENJAMIN F. PEASE,⁷ (WAREHAM,⁶ WAREHAM,⁵ JO-
SEPH,⁴ JAMES,³ JOHN,² ROBERT,¹) son of WAREHAM and
(   ) PEASE of Westfield, Mass., and first
cousin of the preceding, was born at   ;
married   . He served in the army
for the suppression of the late rebellion. He now (1866)
resides in the city of New York.

His children are:

2291. 1.
2292. 2.

———oo———

990.

WILLIAM PEASE,⁷ (JOSIAH,⁶ JAMES,⁵ JOSEPH,⁴ JAMES,³
JOHN,² ROBERT,¹) eldest son of JOSIAH and RELIEF (WAKE-
FIELD) PEASE of Somers, Ct., and second cousin of the
preceding, was born at Somers, September 21, 1816; married Julia Kibbe, February 28, 1848, and lived some time
in Somers, but now resides in Norwich, Ct. He is a carpenter and joiner.

His child was:

2293. 1. JULIA, b. at

992.

CHESTER PEASE,[7] (JOSIAH,[6] JAMES,[5] JOSEPH,[4] JAMES,[3] JOHN,[2] ROBERT,[1]) brother of the preceding, was born at Somers, Ct., May 3, 1819; married Hancie Hall, October 17, 1844, and settled in Somers.

His children were:

2294. 1. HARRIET E., b. at Somers, May   , 1846.
2295. 2. RANDOLPH O., b. at Somers, April 16, 1848.
2296. 3. ALBERT, b. at Somers, March 10, 1854.

————oo————

996.

JAMES R. PEASE,[7] (JAMES,[6] EBENEZER,[5] JOSEPH,[4] JAMES,[3] JOHN,[2] ROBERT,[1]) son of JAMES and PHEBE (COGGSWELL) PEASE of Pittsfield, Mass., and second cousin of the preceding, was born at Pittsfield, May 7, 1817; married Sarah Hoadly of Utica, N. Y., October 27, 1840, and died at Covington, K. Y., May 21, 1848.

His children were:

2297. 1. MARY ELIZA, b. at Buffalo, N. Y., October 8, 1841.
2298. 2. LESTER J., b. at Williamsville, N. Y., July 15, 1843, and lives in Worcester, Mass.
2299. 3. HENRY C., b. at Williamsville, July 15, 1844. He was First Lieutenant in the army, and was some time Lieutenant-Colonel in a colored regiment.
2300. 4. GEORGE H., b. at Buffalo, January 31, 1847. d. 1849.

997.

RALPH P. PEASE,[7] (JAMES,[6] EBENEZER,[5] JOSEPH,[4] JAMES,[3] JOHN,[2] ROBERT,[1]) brother of the preceding, was born at Pittsfield, November 17, 1820; married Rebecca S. Galusha, March 22, 1848, and lives in Williamstown, Mass. He is, by occupation, a farmer.

His children were:

2301. 1. PHEBE C., b. at   , February 17, 1845. d. October 29, 1849.

2302. 2. HENRY J., b. at   , March 2, 1849.

2303. 3. HENRIETTA C., b. at   , August 28, 1852.

2304. 4. ARTHUR C., b. at   , December 21, 1854. d. February 16, 1855.

2305. 5. IDA R., b. at   , June 23, 1859.

2306. 6. WILLIE B., b. at   , November 3, 1862. d. an infant.

———oooo———

DESCENT OF ISAAC.³

FAMILY OF ISAAC.⁴

998.

ELAM PEASE,⁷ (JEHIEL,⁶ ISAAC,⁵ ISAAC,⁴ ISAAC,³ JOHN,² ROBERT,¹) son of JEHIEL and HEPSAH (DODGE) PEASE of Sandisfield, Mass., and fourth cousin of the preceding, was born at   ; married Sally Clark of Sandisfield, and settled at Sandisfield, but subsequently removed from that town, with his family, to Genesee County, N. Y.

His children were:

2307. 1. CLARK, b. at

2308. 2. ALVIN, b. at

2309. 3. LUCY, b. at

2310. 4. EUNICE, b. at

2311. 5. JULIA, b. at

2312. 6. SARAH, b. at

2313. 7. ELMIRA, b. at

2314. 8. ESTHER, b. at

1000.

ELIJAH PEASE,⁷ (JEHIEL,⁶ ISAAC,⁵ ISAAC,⁴ ISAAC,³ JOHN,² ROBERT,¹) brother of the preceding, was born at   ; married Anna Gilbert, and removed from Sandisfield, to the State of New York, and settled between Seneca and Cayuga Lakes.

His children were:

2315.   1. Austin, b. at
2316.   2. Anson, b. at
2317.   3. George, b. at
2318.   4. Dolly, b. at

1001.

ELISHA PEASE,[7] (Jehiel,[6] Isaac,[5] Isaac,[4] Isaac,[3] John,[2] Robert,[1]) brother of the preceding, was born at   ; married Ruth Rice, and removed from Sandisfield to the Black River country (so-called.)

1002.

ISAAC PEASE,[7] (Jehiel,[6] Isaac,[5] Isaac,[4] Isaac,[3] John,[2] Robert,[1]) brother of the preceding, was born at   ; married Hannah Hall of New Marlboro, Mass.,   , 1803. He first settled in Sandisfield, subsequently removed to Windsor, Broome County, N. Y.,   , 1826, and died the same year. He was, by occupation, a farmer.

His children were:

2319.   1. Lewis, b. at Sandisfield, Mass., May 22, 1804. m. Hannah Clark, and removed to   , Ill., where he d. January   , 1836. He was a farmer.

2320.   2. Noel, b. at Sandisfield, May 28, 1806. m. Betsey Lewis, and resides at Barker, Broome County, N. Y. He is a farmer.

2321.   3. Emily, b. at Sandisfield, May 9, 1810. m. Austin Blatchley. d. December 24, 1830.

2322.   4. William, b. at Sandisfield, January 28, 1815. m. Eliza Wait, and resides at Barker. He is a farmer.

2323.   5. Edward, b. at Sandisfield, August 29, 1819. m. Catharine Chase, and resides at Windsor N. Y. He is a farmer.

———o———

1003.

ROSWELL PEASE,[7] (Solomon,[6] Isaac,[5] Isaac,[4] Isaac,[3] John,[2] Robert,[1]) eldest son of Solomon and Keziah

(HALL) PEASE, first of Enfield, next of Hatfield, Mass., subsequently of Heath, Mass., and last of Winhall, Vt., and first cousin of the preceding, was born at   ; married   , and settled in the north part of Hatfield, Mass.

His children were:

2324. 1.   a son, b. at   d. a lad, with his grandfather, at Heath.
2325. 2. HIRAM, b. at Hatfield, March 7, 1807. He was Captain of a military company in Hatfield at one time, and removed out of the State about 1835.
2326. 3. ROXY, b. at
2327. 4. OLIVE, b. at

1005.

SOLOMON PEASE,[7] (SOLOMON,[6] ISAAC,[5] ISAAC,[4] ISAAC,[3] JOHN,[2] ROBERT,[1]) brother of the preceding, was born at   ; married Mary Wilson, daughter of James Wilson of Shelburne, Mass. He first lived in Heath, next at Deerfield, afterwards at Shelburne; about 1823 he removed to the vicinity of Dayton, N. Y.

His children were: *

2327.[49] 1. JANE M., b. at Heath, Mass., January 7, 1809. d. March 19, 1809.
2328. 2. JAMES W., b. at Heath, April 25, 1810.
2329. 3. MARY, b. at Heath, September 21, 1811.
2330. 4. CAROLINE J., b. at Deerfield, May 8, 1813. m. Charles J. Redfield, January 31, 1823.
2331. 5. DAVID M., b. at Deerfield, June 22, 1815.
2331.[50] 6. LAVINIA A., b. at Deerfield, June 25, 1817. d. June 3, 1818.
2332. 7. THOMAS W., b. at Shelburne, April 8, 1819.
2332.[51] 8. NANCY, b. at Shelburne, September 11, 1821. d. September 27, 1821.
2333. 9. HANNAH F., b. at Shelburne, December 2, 1822.

---

* Shelburne Town Records.

1008.

LEVI PEASE,[7] (Solomon,[6] Isaac,[5] Isaac,[4] Isaac,[3] John,[2] Robert,[1]) brother of the preceding, was born at ; married and removed to Winhall, Vt.

———oo———

1009.

CHANDLER PEASE,[7] (Isaac,[6] Isaac,[5] Isaac,[4] Isaac,[3] John,[2] Robert,[1]) eldest son of Isaac and Dorcas (Pease) Pease, first of Enfield, Ct., last of Ohio, and second cousin of the preceding, was born at Enfield, Ct., August 24, 1779; married Beulah Kibbe of Somers, Ct., December 9, 1804, and first settled in Enfield; from that town he removed to the Western Reserve, Ohio, in the summer of 1811,—then a wilderness, suffering not only the hardships and privations incident to the settlement of new countries, but upon the surrender of General Hull's army in the war of 1812, exposed to all the horrors of savage warfare. His father and two brothers with their families appear to have emigrated to Ohio at the same time, and first settled in the town of Hampden. He died September 22, 1837.

His children were:

2334.   1. Julia E., b. at Enfield, Ct., January 20, 1807. m. Charles Stebbins, April 13, 1828, and resides at Pecatonica, Ill.

2335.   2. Albert, b. at Enfield, March 16, 1809. m. Mariette Congden, January 24, 1848, and lives at Ogden City, Utah Territory,

2336.   3. Luke, b. at Hampden, Ohio, December 12, 1811. m. Amanda M. Call, October 16, 1834, and resides at Bellville, Wis.

2337.   4. Hannah, b. at Hampden, March 23, 1814. m. Levi Loveland, February 1, 1836, and resides in Bellville, Wis.

2338.   5. Henry, b. at Hampden, July 1, 1816. m. Sarah A. Johnson, November 1, 1843, and resides in Newark, Wis.

2339.   6. Elam, b. at Hampden, June 8, 1818. m. Mercy Woodworth, September 13, 1844, and resides at Ossian, Iowa.

1012.

ANSON PEASE,⁷ (ISAAC,⁶ ISAAC,⁵ ISAAC,⁴ ISAAC,³ JOHN,² ROBERT,¹) brother of the preceding, was born at Enfield, January 18, 1787; married Anna Pomeroy, April 15, 1811, and removed to Ohio, and settled on the reservation the same year with his father and brothers. He died March 10, 1828.

His children were:

2340. 1. ROYAL A., b. at   , July 24, 1812. m. Sally I.
Allen, March   , 1830, and had three sons, Erskine, Harrison and Tyler. Erskine served in the Union army against the rebellion, and was killed in a fight in or near Boonville, Mo., July 16, 1861. Harrison served through the war and was honorably discharged.

2341. 2. ORRIN, b. at   , 1814.

1013.

MERRICK PEASE,⁷ (ISAAC,⁶ ISAAC,⁵ ISAAC,⁴ ISAAC,³ JOHN,² ROBERT,¹) youngest son of ISAAC and DORCAS (PEASE) PEASE, was born at Enfield, January 17, 1789; married Sally Allen, December 3, 1813.

His children were:

2342. 1. PHILO, b. at Chardon, Ohio, September 18, 1814. m. Lucy Adams, July 7, 1836, and resides in Chardon. He had a son, Benjamin F., b. July 23, 1840, who served two years in the army against the rebellion, and was honorably discharged. He m. Martha Eldridge, December 4, 1865.

2343. 2. AMANDA, b. at Chardon,   m. Asahel Henderson in 1831. d. in Michigan, 1837.

2344. 3. LORENZO D., b. at Chardon, August 14, 1819. m. Mary Adams, March 24, 1842. He has a son, Erwin M., b. 1842, who enlisted and served one year in the late war, and was honorably discharged.

2345. 4. ALONZO, b. at Chardon, December 7, 1821. m. Amerila Root, April 10, 1845.

2346. 5. PERMELIA b. at Chardon, March 18, 1825. m. James W. McBride, August 27, 1844.

2347. 6. SHERMAN, b. at Chardon, March 25, 1827. m. Elizabeth Warner, October 10, 1847. He enlisted in the army in 1862, and served to the end of the war in putting down the rebellion; was connected with the One Hundred and Fifth Regiment of Ohio Volunteer Infantry; was with General Sherman in his march through Georgia and South Carolina; was in the battle of Perryville, the two days' fight at Chicamauga, and Missionary Ridge.

----o.----

1015.

RUFUS PEASE,[7] (RUFUS,[6] ISAAC,[5] ISAAC,[4] ISAAC,[3] JOHN,[2] ROBERT,[1]) eldest son of RUFUS and RUTH (COOLEY) PEASE of Enfield, Ct., and first cousin of the preceding, was born at Enfield, November 14, 1783; married Bathsheba Pease, daughter of Thomas Pease of Ellington, Ct., October 28, 1813. He first settled in Enfield, and after 1825 removed to Ellington. He died at Tolland, Ct., January 7, 1854, aged 71 years. [James C. Pease.]

His children were:

2348. 1. BATHSHEBA R., b. at Enfield, August 13, 1814. m. John Kingsbury of Tolland, September , 1843.

2349. 2. RUFUS H., b. at Enfield, January 20, 1817. d. 1833, aged 16 years.

2350. 3. CALVIN O., b. at Enfield, December 29, 1818.

2351. 4 LORENZO, b. at Enfield, November 27, 1820. d. at Somers, March 5, 1828.

2352. 5. LAURETTA, b. at Enfield, February 6, 1823. m. Charles Sparrow of Tolland, September , 1844.

2353. 6. SARAH M., b. at Enfield, March 10, 1825. d. at Somers, February , 1826.

2354. 7. JAMES S., b. at Somers, June 7, 1827. d. 1849, unmarried.

2355. 8. CALISTA, b. at Ellington, June 30, 1829. d. 1845, aged 16 years.

2356. 9. CYNTHIA M., b. at Tolland, July 14, 1834. m. William Richardson of Tolland, July , 1853.

1016.

ALPHEUS PEASE,[7] (RUFUS,[6] ISAAC,[5] ISAAC,[4] ISAAC,[3] JOHN,[2] ROBERT,[1]) brother of the preceding, was born at

Enfield, January 25, 1785; married Lois Dwight of Somers, Ct., January 29, 1812, and settled in Enfield.

His children were:

2357. 1. Lois, b. at Enfield, July 16, 1813. d. 1814.

2358. 2. Alpheus D., b. at Enfield, December 16, 1814. m. Phebe Hills, September 27, 1840, and settled in Enfield.

2359. 3. Cordelia L., b. at Enfield, September 25, 1816. d. 1823.

2360. 4. Henry, b. at Enfield, July 18, 1818. d. young.

2361. 5. Miranda, b. at Enfield, December 20, 1821. m. Luther Stearns, December 12, 1848.

2362. 6. Esther C., b. at Enfield, January 27, 1826. m. Charles G. Tiffany of Somers, April 25, 1849.

1017.

ENOS PEASE,[7] (Rufus,[6] Isaac,[5] Isaac,[4] Isaac,[3] John,[2] Robert,[1]) brother of the preceding, was born at Enfield, August 9, 1786; married Lucy Adams of Stafford, Ct., November 21, 1816, and first settled in Enfield, but removed to Somers.

His children were:

2363. 1. Lucy V., b. at Enfield, February 8, 1818. m. Daniel W. Fraganzie, April 2, 1837, and resides at Springfield, Mass.

2364. 2. Lyman L., b. at Enfield, July 12, 1820. m. Mary A. Kibbe of Somers, November 17, 1844, and for some time resided at Somers.

2365. 3. Lucinda, b. at Enfield,   , 1822.

2366. 4. Enos D., b. at Enfield, February 26, 1825. m. Mary A. Cook of Longmeadow, June 14, 1847.

2367. 5. Ellen, b. at Enfield, March 27, 1830. d. in Somers in her eighteenth year.

2368. 6. Lorin, b. at Enfield, July 21, 1833. m. Cordelia Sparks of Springfield, August 25, 1855. d. 1866. [James C. Pease.]

1020.

COOLEY PEASE, (Rufus,[6] Isaac,[5] Isaac,[4] Isaac,[3] John,[2] Robert,[1]) brother of the preceding, was born at Enfield, June 12, 1792; married Sarah Pease, daughter of Thomas Pease of Ellington, June 27, 1820. He settled in Enfield, but appears to have gone to Somers after the birth of his children. He died March 2, 1853, aged 61 years.

His children were:

2369. 1. JAMES C., b. at Enfield, November 22, 1820, and resides in Somers, unmarried, (1868.)

2370. 2. SALMON F., b. at Enfield, November 8, 1822, and resides in Somers, unmarried, (1868.)

2371. 3. SIMEON A., b. at Enfield, December 23, 1825. d. in infancy.

2372. 4. SARAH E., b. at Enfield, August 28, 1827.

1021.

AUGUSTUS PEASE,[7] (RUFUS,[6] ISAAC,[5] ISAAC,[4] ISAAC,[3] JOHN,[2] ROBERT,[1]) brother of the preceding, was born at Enfield, August, 1794; married Maria Knight, , 1821, and settled in Enfield.

His children were:

2373. 1. EMERY and
2374. 2. EMILY, } b. at Enfield, , 1826.

2375. 3. THOMAS J. and
2376. 4. ANDREW J., } b. at Enfield, , 1830. d. young.

———oo———

1022.

HORACE PEASE,[7] (GAIUS,[6] JACOB,[5] ISAAC,[4] ISAAC,[3] JOHN,[2] ROBERT,[1]) eldest son of GAIUS and ABIGAIL (BAIRD) PEASE of Jericho, Vt., and second cousin of the preceding, was born at Jericho, January 15, 1799; married Polly Prouty, , 1825, and settled in Jericho, where he died September 12, 1862.

His children were:

2380. 1. LYDIA, b. at Jericho, Vt., , 1825. m. George Downing.

2381. 2. GAIUS, b. at Jericho, , 1827, m. Achsah Hale, 1856.

2382.   3. EDWIN H., b. at Jericho,   , 1829.   m. Lucy
Hinkson, 1848. He has removed to Lowell, Dodge County,
Wis.

2383.   4. HOBERT, b. at Jericho,   , 1831.

2384.   5. WILLIAM H., b. at Jericho, 1835. m. Dora E. Colgrove,
1862, and lives at Jericho.

2385.   6. CHESTER, b. at Jericho,   , 1838. m. Belinda
Hall, 1863, and resides at West Bolton, Vt.

2386.   7. GEORGE A., b. at Jericho,   , 1845.

1023.

SIMEON PEASE,⁷ (GAIUS,⁶ JACOB,⁵ ISAAC,⁴ ISAAC,³
JOHN,² ROBERT,¹) brother of the preceding, was born at
Jericho, May 5, 1800; married Annie Prouty, and resides
in Jericho.

His children were:

2387.   1. SARAH S., b. at Jericho.   d.

2388.   2. SMITH, b. at

2389.   3. EVELINA, b. at   m. John Whittier.

2390.   4. ROLLIN, b. at   . He served in the
Thirteenth Regiment of Vermont Volunteers, returned, and
was discharged with the regiment.

2391.   5. JOSEPHINE, b. at   . d.

1026.

ALVAH PEASE,⁷ (GAIUS,⁶ JACOB,⁵ ISAAC,⁴ ISAAC,³
JOHN,² ROBERT,¹) brother of the preceding, was born at
Jericho, May 14, 1805; married Balona A. Benham,
     , 1831. She died August 24, 1853. He mar-
ried second, Helen -E. Foster, July 9, 1856, and resides
in Jericho. Post-office, West Bolton.

His children were:-

2392.   1. SUSAN F., b. at Jericho, May 20, 1821. m. N. Prouty, December 17, 1857.

2393.   2. FRANK W., b. at Jericho, August 28, 1845.

BY SECOND WIFE:

2394.   3. ELIZABETH H., b. at Jericho, May 3, 1860. d. an infant.

——oo——

1031.

JAMES PEASE,⁷ (ABNER,⁶ ABNER,⁵ ISAAC,⁴ ISAAC,³ JOHN,² ROBERT,¹) eldest son of ABNER and POLLY (BLACK-BURN) PEASE, some time of Chester, Mass., and last of Aurora, Portage County, Ohio., and second cousin of the preceding, was born at Chester, January 5, 1794; married, first, Amanda Parrish, October   , 1818; married, second, Achah Parker,   , 1829. He appears to have resided first at Aurora, subsequently at Mantua. He now resides at Newbury, Ohio. He is, by occupation, a farmer.

His children were:

2395. 1. ANSON, b. at Aurora, Ohio, November 28, 1819. m. Eliza Per Lee, April 6, 1844, and resides at Masillon, Ohio. He is, by profession, a lawyer.

2396. 2. FITCH, b. at Mantua, Ohio, September 15, 1821. m.   , and resides at Burton, Geauga County, Ohio. He is a farmer.

2397. 3. CLARA, b. at Mantua, June 12, 1825. m. Dr. Case, and removed to Tennessee, where she died some years ago.

2398. 4. AMANDA, b. at Mantua, December 28, 1827. She has m. twice, and is now widow Babcock, and resides at St. Paul, Minn.

BY SECOND WIFE:

2399. 5. MINERVA, b. at Mantua, May 24, 1831. d. 1833.

2400. 6. CELIA, b. at Mantua, May 27, 1833.

2401. 7. MELINDA, b. at Mantua, October 29, 1836.

2402. 8. SYLVIA, b. at Mantua, February 22, 1838.

2403. 9. BYRON, b. at Mantua, May 7, 1841. He was a private in an Ohio regiment during the late war of the rebellion, " and was killed in one of the battles before Atlanta," August 4, 1864.

2404. 10. HELEN, b. at Mantua, May 22, 1843.

2405. 11. ABNER, b. at Mantua, April 21, 1845. He was in the army for the suppression of the rebellion.

2406. 12. SAMUEL, b. at Mantua, April 21, 1845. He was in the army for the suppression of the rebellion.

2407. 13. FRANK, b. at Mantua, January 28, 1850.

1035.

SAMUEL PEASE,[7] (ABNER,[6] ABNER,[5] ISAAC,[4] ISAAC,[3] JOHN,[2] ROBERT,[1]) brother of the preceding, was born at Worcester, Otsego County, N. Y., September 4, 1802; married Ann Louisa Shepherdson, May 14, 1835, at Massillon, Stark County, Ohio, where he now resides, (1866.) He is, by profession, a lawyer.

His children were:

2408. 1. FRANCES, b. at Masillon, Ohio, February 11, 1836. m. John N. Church, December 10, 1856, and resides at Canton, Ohio.
2409. 2. HIRAM S., b. at Masillon, September 20, 1838. d. April 7, 1839.
2410. 3. ELIZA, b. at Masillon, December 10, 1840.
2411. 4. T. PERCY, b. at Masillon, May 30, 1845. He was among the one hundred days' men in the war of the late rebellion.

1037.

JOHN PEASE,[7] (ABNER,[6] ABNER,[5] ISAAC,[4] ISAAC,[3] JOHN,[2] ROBERT,[1]) brother of the preceding, was born at Worcester, N. Y., December 25, 1804; married, first, Frances Plumer, May 23, 1835; married, second, Sophia Olin; married, third, Nancy J. Green, September 10, 1851. He settled at Streetsborough, Portage County, Ohio, but now (1866) resides near Jefferson, Ashtabula County, Ohio. He is, by occupation, a farmer.

His children were:

2412. 1. MARIAH, b. at Streetsborough, Ohio, July 25, 1826. d. November 10, 1855.
2413. 2. SAMUEL H., b. at Streetsborough, March 15, 1828. m. Lydia S. Doyl, March 9, 1848, and lives at Streetsborough. He is a farmer. He was in the late war.
2414. 3. LORENZO D., b. at Streetsborough, January 14, 1830. m. Emily L. Olin, December 28, 1851.

BY SECOND WIFE:

2415. 4. EMILY B., b. at Streetsborough, April 23, 1843.

32

2416. 5. Polly M., b. at Streetsborough, October 17, 1845.   m. Nathan
H. Ward, December 20, 1865.

2417. 6. George W., b. at Streetsborough, February 20, 1851.

BY THIRD WIFE:

2418. 7. Charles N., b. at Streetsborough, September 15, 1852.

2419. 8. Albert C., b. at Streetsborough, April 2, 1853.   d. June 4,
1860.

2420. 9. James N., b. at Streetsborough, June 15, 1855.

1038.

ALDEN M. PEASE,[7] (Abner,[6] Abner,[5] Isaac,[4] Isaac,[3]
John,[2] Robert,[1]) brother of the preceding, was born at
Worcester, N. Y., July 19, 1807; married Charlotte Gran-
ger, and settled at Streetsborough, Portage County, Ohio.
He is, by occupation, a farmer.

His child was:

2421. 1. Corwin A., b. at Streetsborough, November 9, 1841.   m.
H. C. Brown, September 9, 1861.   He was in the United
States army in 1865.

------o------

1040.

DEXTER PEASE,[7] (James,[6] Abner,[5] Isaac,[4] Isaac,[3]
John,[2] Robert,[1]) eldest son of James and Lucy (Day)
Pease, first of Chester, Mass., last of Worcester, N. Y.,
and first cousin of the preceding, was born at Chester,
January 24, 1796; married, first, Anna Seward; married,
second,   ; married third, Esther Pad-
dock, April 10, 1859.   He left Massachusetts for the New
Connecticut, Ohio, when a young man, with nothing but
his knapsack and ax, but is now a wealthy farmer in
Bainbridge, Ohio.   He had no children, (1859.)

1042.

CHAUNCEY D. PEASE,[7] (James,[6] Abner,[5] Isaac,[4]
Isaac,[3] John,[2] Robert,[1]) brother of the preceding, was

born at Chester, September 17, 1800; married Melinda Flint of Worcester, N. Y., October , 1824, and lives in Hudson, Columbia County, N. Y. He is, by occupation, a piano-forte maker.

His child was:

2422. 1. MARY A., b. at Cooperstown, N. Y., July 22, 1825. m. Thomas U. Faulden, , 1842. He d. at New York City, , 1864.

1043.

ERASTUS PEASE,⁷ (JAMES,⁶ ABNER,⁵ ISAAC,⁴ ISAAC,³ JOHN,² ROBERT,¹) brother of the preceding, was born at Worcester, N. Y., March 19, 1802; married Sally Converse of Worthington, Mass., March 28, 1827, and settled in Chester, a farmer. He died October , 1860.

His children were:

2423. 1. SARAH A., b. at Chester, November 1, 1828. m. Charles Nooney, April , 1847, and settled in Chester.

2424. • 2. ERASTUS F., b. at Chester, October 27, 1830. m. Catherine Dietz, November 25, 1852.

2425. 3. LUCY A., b. at Chester, October 27, 1832. m. Alvin D. Ormsby, , 1853, and settled in Chester.

2426. 4. SUSAN M., b. at Chester, March 15, 1835. m. Chauncey Stratton, July 4, 1864, and resides at Suffield, Ct.

2427. 5. JOHN C., b. at Chester, March 28, 1837. m. Cordelia Markham, _, 1860, and resides at East Longmeadow.

2428. 6. JAMES M., b. at Chester, May 15, 1839. m. Mary B. Cole, and resides at East Longmeadow.

2429. 7. ELISHA C., b. at Chester, April 5, 1841.

2430. 8. ELIZABETH Y., b. at Chester, September 3, 1848. d. 1849.

1045.

JOHN F. PEASE,⁷ (JAMES,⁶ ABNER,⁵ ISAAC,⁴ ISAAC,³ JOHN,² ROBERT,¹) brother of the preceding, was born at Worcester, N. Y., April 21, 1806; married Betsey Converse of Worthington, Mass. He lives in Worthington, a farmer.

His children were:

2431. 1. CHAUNCEY D., b. at Worthington, November 3, 1836. m. first, Jennie Frasoni, April 2, 1859. m. second, Mary C. Johnson, 1864. He is a piano-forte maker, and resides in New York City.

2432. 2. AMANDA E., b. at Worthington, September 23, 1838.

2433. 3. SAMUEL C., b. at Worthington, August 21, 1842.

2434. 4. JOHN D., b. at Worthington, July 4, 1844. m. Mary L. Hollis, November 24, 1864, and resides at Worthington. He was a member of the Forty-ninth Regiment of Massachusetts Volunteers in the late war.

2435. 5. MARTHA F., b. at Worthington, October 15, 1846.

2436. 6. GEORGE W., b. at Worthington, May 31, 1849.

2437. 7. CHARLES B., b. at Worthington, December 26, 1856.

1046.

JOSHUA I. PEASE,[7] (JAMES,[6] ABNER,[5] ISAAC,[4] ISAAC,[3] JOHN,[2] ROBERT,[1]) brother of the preceding, was born at Worcester, N. Y., July 18, 1808; married
He removed to Michigan, and settled in Richland, where he is living with his second wife. (1866).

His child was:

2438. 1. EDWARD, b. at

1050.

JOHN R. PEASE,[7] (JOHN,[6] ABNER,[5] ISAAC,[4] ISAAC,[3] JOHN,[2] ROBERT,[1]) son of JOHN and BELINDA (HAYS) PEASE of   , and first cousin of the preceding; was born at   ; married   , and resided at Fremont, Ohio. He was a merchant and accumulated a large fortune.

His child was:

2439. 1. A daughter, b. at

1059.

JULIUS W. PEASE,[7] (Asaph,[6] Noadiah,[5] Isaac,[4] Isaac,[3] John,[2] Robert,[1]) youngest son of Asaph and Clotilda (Hoyt) Pease, first of Colebrook, Ct., last of New Britain, Ct., and first cousin of the preceding, was born at Colebrook, May 19, 1814; married Mary Hotchkiss of Burlington, Ct., June 1, 1844. He first settled at Winsted, Ct., subsequently at New Britain, Ct., where he resided, 1868.

His children were :

2440.   1. Lumas H., b. at Winsted, Ct., January 20, 1845.
2441.   2. Martha F., b. at Winsted, November 28, 1846.
2442.   3. Julius W., b. at Winsted, July 7, 1847. d. September 13, 1847.
2443.   4. Julius H., b. at New Britain, Ct., November 22, 1848.
2444.   5. William W., b. at New Britain, November 2, 1850.
2445.   6. Mary E., b. at New Britain, February 18, 1853.
2446.   7. Edward C., b. at New Britain, December 2, 1854. d. August 18, 1855.
2447.   8. Clarence, b. at New Britain, February 14, 1857. d. January 11, 1858.
2448.   9. Charles W., b. at New Britain, June 13, 1859. d. September 24, 1859.

---o---

1063.

ERASTUS C. PEASE,[7] (Alvah,[6] Noadiah,[5] Isaac,[4] Isaac,[3] John,[2] Robert,[1]) eldest son of Alvah and Abigail (Severance) Pease, first of Colebrook, Ct., subsequently of Worcester, Mass., last of Sandisfield, Mass., and first cousin of the preceding, was born at Colebrook, April 11, 1813; married Lucy Rice of Southbridge, and settled in Providence, R. I., and from that city he removed to Athol, Mass., where he now lives, (1868), and is, by occupation, a jeweller. He was also a music teacher

His child was :

2449.   1. Erastus A., b. at

1064.

RICHARD S. PEASE,[7] (ALVAH,[6] NOADIAH,[5] ISAAC,[4] ISAAC,[3] JOHN,[2] ROBERT,[1]) brother of the preceding, was born at   ; married Eliza Nichols and settled in Providence, R. I.   He is a goldsmith by trade.

His children were:

2450.   1. EDWIN, b. at
2451.   2. ESTELLA, b. at

———o———

1069.

JARVIS B. PEASE,[7] (SIMEON,[6] NOADIAH,[5] ISAAC,[4] ISAAC,[3] JOHN,[2] ROBERT,[1]) eldest son of SIMEON and ELIZABETH (ARNOLD) PEASE, first of Sandisfield, Mass., last of Canandaigua, N. Y., and first cousin of the preceding, was born at Sandisfield, April 16, 1821; married Ann C. Hall, June 6, 1844, and resides at Canandaigua, N. Y.

His children were:

2452.   1. MARY C., b. at Canandaigua, N. Y., April 27, 1845.   m. Joshua
             K. Lincoln, March 13, 1861.
2453.   2. SUSAN E., b. at Canandaigua, September 6, 1847.   d. March
             13, 1851.
2454.   3. PHILENA S., b. at Canandaigua, February 16, 1849.
2455.   4. GEORGE W., b. at Canandaigua, June 27, 1851.   d. July 4,
             1853.
2456.   5. SIMEON H., b. at South Bristol, N. Y., January 5, 1855.
2457.   6. ELIZABETH S., b. at Starkey, N. Y., January 5, 1857.
2458.   7. WALTER G., b. at Starkey, April 24, 1859.   d. June 13, 1862.
2459.   8. DORA A., b. at Canandaigua, February 6, 1864.

1070.

NOADIAH S. PEASE,[7] (SIMEON,[6] NOADIAH,[5] ISAAC,[4] ISAAC,[3] JOHN,[2] ROBERT,[1]) brother of the preceding, was born at Sandisfield, Mass., March 5, 1823; married Agnes

Swetland of Hockton, Steuben County, N. Y., December
, 1843. He now, (1866,) lives in Norwalk, Ohio, and
is, by trade, a mason.

His children were:

2460.	1. MARY, b. at		, July 27, 1844.
2461.	2. FRANCIS, b. at		, September 27, 1845.
2462.	3. OSCAR, b. at		, June 29, 1848.
2463.	4. FRANCES, b. at		, December 20, 1851.
2464.	5. AGNES, b. at		, May 4, 1854.
2465.	6. GEORGE A., b. at		, May 13, 1856.

1071.

ORLO A. PEASE,⁷ (SIMEON,⁶ NOADIAH,⁵ ISAAC,⁴ ISAAC,³
JOHN,² ROBERT,¹) brother of the preceding, was born at
Sandisfield, June 4, 1825; married Cynthia E. Morris,
January 17, 1844, and resides at Owasso, Sheawassee
County, Mich., (1866.) He has two sons and two daugh-
ters.

His children were:

2466. 1. EDWARD, b. at   . He enlisted in
      the army for the suppression of the rebellion, December 24,
      1863, and continued through the war.
2467. 2. CHARLES, b. at   . He enlisted in
      the army, September 4, 1864, and served through the war.
2468. 3.
2469. 4.

1074.

ORVILLE W. PEASE,⁷ (SIMEON,⁶ NOADIAH,⁵ ISAAC,⁴
ISAAC,³ JOHN,² ROBERT,¹) brother of the preceding, was
born at Sandisfield, October 9, 1833; married Amanda
Vrodenburgh of Great Barrington, Mass. He removed
to Canandaigua, N. Y.

1075.

SIDNEY F. PEASE,⁷ (SIMEON,⁶ NOADIAH,⁵ ISAAC,⁴
ISAAC,³ JOHN,² ROBERT,¹) brother of the preceding, was
born at Canandaigua, N. Y., February 17, 1836; married

1077.

ALLEN D. PEASE,[7] (Simeon,[6] Noadiah,[5] Isaac,[4] Isaac,[3] John,[2] Robert,[1]) sixth and youngest son of Simeon and Elizabeth (Arnold) Pease, was born at Canandaigua, June 3, 1840; married   , and settled in Canandaigua.

———o o o———

FAMILY OF ABRAHAM.[4]

1078.

LUTHER PEASE,[7] (Levi,[6] John,[5] Abraham,[4] Isaac,[3] John,[2] Robert,[1]) eldest son of Levi and   (Gibbs) Pease of Suffield, Ct., and third cousin of the preceding, was born at Suffield,   ; married Jael Trumbull.

His children were:

2470. 1. Mary Jael, b. at Suffield.   d.
2471. 2. Caroline, b. at Suffield.   d.
2472. 3. Justus, b. at Suffield.   d.

———o o———

1084.

CYRUS PEASE,[7] (Moses,[6] Moses,[5] Abraham,[4] Isaac,[3] John,[2] Robert,[1]) second son of Moses and Lovisa (Markham) Pease of Enfield, Ct., and second cousin of the preceding, was born at Enfield, October 30, 1789; married Nancy Saulsbury, and lived in Enfield. He died January 12, 1841, aged 52 years.

His children were:

2473. 1. Ann L., b. at Enfield, Ct., January 2, 1817, m. Hiram Terry.
2474. 2. George, b. at Enfield, May 4, 1818. m. Elizabeth M. Hall, March 5, 1841.

2475. 3. MARCIA, b. at Enfield, July 11, 1819. d. October 21, 1838, aged 20 years.
2476. 4. MARTHA, b. at Enfield, August 8, 1820. d. February 28, 1848.
2477. 5. JANE, b. at Enfield, February 17, 1823. m. Lorenzo Dennison.

1085.

MOSES PEASE,⁷ (MOSES,⁶ MOSES,⁵ ABRAHAM,⁴ ISAAC,³ JOHN,² ROBERT,¹) brother of the preceding, was born at Enfield, July 14, 1791; married Nancy Pease, daughter of Stone Pease, March 27, 1815, and settled in Enfield.

His children were:

2478. 1. ROWENA S., b. at Enfield, July 20, 1817. m.   Hawley, and settled in Hadley, Mass.
2479. 2. MILTON, b. at Enfield, May 8, 1821. m.
and some time lived in Springfield, Mass., but now resides in New York City. He is a railroad conductor.
2480. 3. NEWTON, b. at Enfield, February 14, 1825. d. November 29, 1826.
2481. 4. CORDELIA, b. at Enfield, February 19, 1826.

1086.

BARNABAS PEASE,⁷ (MOSES,⁶ MOSES,⁵ ABRAHAM,⁴ ISAAC,³ JOHN,² ROBERT,¹) brother of the preceding, was born at Enfield, August 8, 1795; married Maria Pease, daughter of Abiel Pease of Enfield, January 30, 1823, and settled in Enfield.

His children were:

2482. 1. GUY B., b. at Enfield, January 30, 1824. m. Elizabeth Walker, and settled at Springfield, Ill.
2483. 2. EMILY, b. at Enfield, December 4, 1825.
2484. 3. JAMES, b. at Enfield, July 17, 1827.
2485. 4. MARIA, b. at Enfield, April 29, 1829. d.
2486. 5. LYMAN F., b. at Enfield, February 12, 1831.
2487. 6. JOHN C., b. at Enfield, June 15, 1833.

1087.

JULIUS PEASE,[7] (Moses,[6] Moses,[5] Abraham,[4] Isaac,[3] John,[2] Robert,[1]) brother of the preceding, was born at Enfield, September 30, 1798; married Mary Griffin, March 29, 1826, and settled at Warehouse Point, Ct.

His children were:

2488.   1. Mary, b. at Enfield, June 2, 1827.   m. Elam L. Pease of Enfield, 1850, and settled in Enfield.
2489.   2. Erskine, b. at Enfield, September 29, 1828.   d. January 10, 1840.
2490.   3. Zelotes M., b. at Enfield, June 20, 1830.   d. an infant.
2491.   4. Elizabeth, b. at Enfield, October 4, 1831.
2492.   5. Zelotes,[2] b. at Enfield, April 24, 1834.   d. an infant.
2493.   6. Adaline, b. at Enfield, March 5, 1836.
2494.   7. Ann R., b. at Enfield, February 22, 1844.   d. 1845.

1088.

FREDERICK PEASE,[7] (Moses,[6] Moses,[5] Abraham,[4] Isaac,[3] John,[2] Robert,[1]) brother of the preceding, was born at Enfield, October 2, 1801; married Huldah Lord, , 1824, and settled in East Windsor, Ct. He died March 5, 1852.

His children were:

2495.   1. Harris, b. at   , January 26, 1825.
2496.   2. Almira, b. at   , January 11, 1827.
2497.   3. Frederick N., b. at   , December 2, 1828.   m. Maria L. Shultus,   , 1854.
2497.[1]   4. Huldah A., b. at   , August 24, 1830.   d. young.
2498.   5. John M., b. at   , November 20, 1832.   m. Lucinda Phelps, and resides at East Windsor.
2499.   6. Edgar, b. at   , October 28, 1834.   d. October 4, 1856.
2500.   7. Ephraim, b. at   , February 2, 1837.
2501.   8. Belinda H., b. at   , October 16, 1841.

1092.

WALTER PEASE,⁷ (Lemuel,⁶ Moses,⁵ Abraham,⁴ Isaac,³ John,² Robert,¹) second son of Lemuel and (   ) Pease of Enfield, Ct., and first cousin of the preceding, was born at Enfield, June 21, 1795; married Eliza Filer, and settled in Enfield.

His children were:

2502. 1. Harlow W., b. at Enfield, April 3, 1822. m. Maria White, October 18, 1840.
2503. 2. Mary A., b. at Enfield, January 5, 1824. m.   Hart, and settled in New Haven, Ct.
2504. 3. Martha M., b. at Enfield, January 26, 1826. m. Charles Coon.
2505. 4. Lemuel F., b. at Enfield, June   , 1828. d. November 5, 1853.
2506. 5. Lorinda E., b. at Enfield, December 31, 1830. d. 1832, aged 2 years.

1094.

ERASTUS PEASE,⁷ (Lemuel,⁶ Moses,⁵ Abraham,⁴ Isaac,³ John,² Robert,¹) youngest son of Lemuel and (   ) Pease, was born at Enfield, October , 1804; married Harriet Bartlett.

His children were:

2507. 1. Russell B., b. at   , July 16, 1828. d. May 15, 1848.
2508. 2. Hollis P., b. at   , October 8, 1831. d. April 6, 1856.
2509. 3. Giles W., b. at   , February 11, 1834. d. January , 1854.
2510. 4. Marcia I., b. at   , February 7, 1838.

———o———

1095.

BENJAMIN PEASE,⁷ (Benjamin,⁶ Moses,⁵ Abraham,⁴ Isaac,³ John,² Robert,¹) eldest son of Benjamin and Clarinda (Richardson) Pease of Enfield, Ct., and first

cousin of the preceding, was born at Enfield, August 25,
1800; married, first, Laura Button; married, second,
Velona Jencks, October 3, 1866. He was for many years
an inn-keeper in the south part of Enfield. He now resides at Warehouse Point, Ct.

His child was:

2511.   1. CORNELIA L., b. at Enfield, December 6, 1832.   m. Julius
H. Baker, December 23, 1852, and lives at Warehouse
Point, Ct.

1096.

HENRY PEASE,[7] (BENJAMIN,[6] MOSES,[5] ABRAHAM,[4]
ISAAC,[3] JOHN,[2] ROBERT,[1]) brother of the preceding, was
born at Enfield, December 17, 1802; married
, and removed to the State of New York, and
now resides at Adams' Basin, Monroe County, N. Y.

His children were:

2512.   1. ADALINE, b. at
2513.   2. HENRY, b. at

1097.

ALFRED PEASE,[7] (BENJAMIN,[6] MOSES,[5] ABRAHAM,[4]
ISAAC,[3] JOHN,[2] ROBERT,[1]) brother of the preceding, was
born at Enfield, September 17, 1804; married Amanda
Combs, and settled in Enfield.

His children are:

2514.   1. ESTHER, b. at Enfield, September   , 1840.   m. Alanson
Abbe, January   , 1862, and resides at Enfield.
2515.   2. ALICE, b. at Enfield, September 27, 1842.   m. Dwight N.
Hathaway.

1099.

HARVEY PEASE,[7] (BENJAMIN,[6] MOSES,[5] ABRAHAM,[4]
ISAAC,[3] JOHN,[2] ROBERT,[1]) brother of the preceding, was
born at Enfield, April 15, 1807; married, first, Jenette

Jones,   , 1833; married, second, Lovisa Vining, , 1860, and resided at Warehouse Point, Ct. He enlisted in the Second Connecticut Heavy Artillery, Company H, January 15, 1864. He was shot near Peters-burg, June 21, 1864, and died the next day.

His children were:

2516. 1. WALLACE, b. at   , April 1, 1835. m. Frances
M. Crocker, February 18, 1864. He served in the Twenty-seventh Regiment of Massachusetts Volunteers of three years' men in the late war.

2517. 2. FRANCES, b. at   , March 10, 1837.

2518. 3. NEWTON, b. at   , December 21, 1840. m. Mary
L. Crocker, February 26, 1864. He was also a member of the Twenty-seventh Regiment of Massachusetts Volunteers.

2519. 4. MARIETTA, (twin) b. at   , December 21, 1840.
m. William Myers.

2520. 5. WILSON B., b. at   , October 12, 1842. d. 1844.

2521. 6. WILBUR F., b. at   , June 18, 1848. He was a
member of the Second Connecticut Light Artillery in the late war.

2522. 7. OPHELIA, b. at East Windsor, Ct., November 7, 1850.

2523. 8. LEANNA, b. at East Windsor, October 26, 1853.

1100.

LEWIS PEASE,⁷ (BENJAMIN,⁶ MOSES,⁵ ABRAHAM,⁴ ISAAC,³ JOHN,² ROBERT,¹) brother of the preceding, was born at Enfield, June 13, 1808; married Zilpha Baker, May 3, 1836. He appears to have resided some time in Tolland County, Ct., but subsequently removed to the State of Ohio, and now resides at Brownhelm, Lorain County, Ohio. He is a farmer and vintager.

His children were:

2524. 1. GEORGE W., b. at Ellington, Ct., February 26, 1838. He
was a sailor, and was drowned in Lake Erie, September 11, 1855.

2525. 2. CAROLINE, b. at Tolland, Ct., June 27, 1839. She was twice
married, and died February 7, 1863.

2526. 3. Rowena, b. at Tolland, January 11, 1841. m. Burton Farnsworth, November 4, 1855.

2527. 4. Benjamin, b. at Ellington, January 15, 1843. He served two years and two months in the Sixty-second Regiment of Ohio Volunteers, and then re-enlisted for three years more in another regiment. He was once wounded slightly on the neck, and suffered five months in a rebel prison.

2528. 5. Lauriett, b. at Ellington, February 3, 1845. m. Frank Oberlo, December 5, 1860.

2529. 6. Anson, b. at Henrietta, Ohio, May 8, 1847. He enlisted in 1862 to aid in crushing the rebellion; served two years in one regiment and then re-enlisted in the Fifty-fifth Regiment of Volunteers of Ohio Veterans. He had his canteen and knapsack shot off in the battle at Chancellorsville, Va., and was with General Sherman's army in their march from Atlanta to the Atlantic coast.

2530. 7. Mary J., b. at Henrietta, May 4, 1849. m. Laban D. Lowry, February 21, 1866.

2531. 8. Lewis, b. at Brownhelm, Ohio, December 26, 1851.

2532. 9. Louisa, b. at Brownhelm, March 6, 1854. d. April 7, 1855.

2533. 10. Zilpha S., b. at Brownhelm, February 17, 1857.

2534. 11. Margaret, b. at Brownhelm, October 13, 1859.

2535. 12. Lorenzo, b. at Brownhelm, April 4, 1863.

——o o——

1107.

ABIEL PEASE,[7] (Abiel,[6] Samuel,[5] Abraham,[4] Isaac,[3] John,[2] Robert,[1]) only son of Abiel and Lovina (Fowler) Pease of Enfield, Ct., and second cousin of the preceding, was born at Enfield, March 17, 1797; married, first, Sophronia Stebbins; married, second, Esther Stebbins,   , 1830, and settled in Enfield. He was a bell-founder, coppersmith, goldsmith, clock-maker, and any other "smith" or "maker" he wished to be. A true son of *Tubal Cain*,—best of all, a conscientious Christian. He died in 1864.

His children were :

2536. 1. Ralph, b. at Enfield, June 28, 1824. m. Susan Howe, June 16, 1857.

2537. 2. John R., b. at Enfield, June 27, 1826, and resides at Meriden, Ct.

2538.   3. JULIA P., b. at Enfield, August 29, 1827. d. September 29, 1851.

2539.   4. ALBERT R., b. at Enfield, November 11, 1831. m. Kingsbury. He is in business in New York City.

———o———

1108.

SAMUEL PEASE,⁷ (AUGUSTUS,⁶ SAMUEL,⁵ ABRAHAM,⁴ ISAAC,³ JOHN,² ROBERT,¹) eldest son of AUGUSTUS and ETHA (WARNER) PEASE of Southwick, Mass., and first cousin of the preceding, was born at Southwick,
     ; married   , and removed to Ohio.

———oo———

1124.

ELAM A. PEASE,⁷ (ELAM,⁶ JOEL,⁵ ABRAHAM,⁴ ISAAC,³ JOHN,² ROBERT,¹) second son of ELAM and ABIGAIL (ALLEN) PEASE, first of East Windsor, Ct., and last of Farmington, Ill., and second cousin of the preceding, was born at East Windsor, February 11, 1804; married Phila Wells, August 2, 1826. He appears first to have lived in Tolland County, Ct., but removed to Illinois in 1832, and resides at Victoria. He is, by occupation, a merchant.

His children were:

2540.   1. ALFRED W., b. at Tolland, Ct., June 9, 1828. d. February 15, 1829.

2541.   2. ALONZO T., b. at Vernon, Ct., April 21, 1830. m. Emily L. Strong, May 3, 1860. He is, by occupation, a harness maker.

2542.   3. AUSTIN, b. at Quincy, Ill., December 7, 1834. d. January 18, 1835.

2543.   4. HARRIET E., b. at Quincy, January 26, 1836. m. Thomas Whitney, September 22, 1857. He was killed at Chicamauga, 1863.

2544.   5. PHILINDA T., b. at St. Mary's, Ill., October 12, 1838. m. Milan Hammond, 1865.

2545.   6. NAOMI, b. at Farmington, Ill., August 9, 1840. d. February
3, 1841.

2546.   7. ALLEN G., b. at Farmington, October 2, 1843. He is, by
occupation, a wheelwright.

2547.   8. STILLMAN A., b. at Farmington, April 18, 1846.

————oo————

1127.

JUSTUS PEASE,[7] (NATHAN,[6] NATHAN,[5] ABRAHAM,[4]
ISAAC,[3] JOHN,[2] ROBERT,[1]) only son of NATHAN and SYL-
VIA (SISSON) PEASE of South Wilbraham, Mass., and
second cousin of the preceding, was born at South Wilbraham, October 17, 1799; married Chloe Mixter,
, 1827, and settled in South Wilbraham, a farmer.

His children were:

2548.   1. LOVINA E., b. at South Wilbraham, Mass.,   , 1831.
2549.   2. NATHAN W., b. at South Wilbraham, September   , 1833.
m. Sarah A. Howard of Rahway, N. J., December 25,
1851, and was Principal of Franklin High School of that
city in 1864.

————o————

1131.

ORRIN PEASE,[7] (AMOS,[6] NATHAN,[5] ABRAHAM,[4] ISAAC,[3]
JOHN,[2] ROBERT,[1]) son of AMOS and TABITHA (FIRMAN)
PEASE of Monson, Mass., and first cousin of the preceding, was born at Monson, November 9, 1803; married,
first, Caroline Colton,   ; married, second, Emeline
M. Pease,   ; daughter of James C. Pease of Wilbraham, Mass.,   , 1855, and settled in Monson,
a farmer.

His children were:

2550.   1. MARY JANE, b. at Monson, Mass.,   , 1835. She
was teacher of a High School in Cleveland, Ohio, in 1864,
and has since married Albert Beebe of South Wilbraham.

2551.   2. HERBERT O., b. at Monson, November 11, 1856.

2552.   3. CARRIE E., b. at Monson, April 12, 1858.

1133.

DAVID F. PEASE,⁷ (Amos,⁶ Nathan,⁵ Abraham,⁴ Isaac,³ John,² Robert,¹) brother of the preceding, was born at Monson, July 4, 1809; married Lucinda West, March 30, 1837. He settled in Monson, a farmer.

His children were:

2553. 1. Julia L., b. at Monson, Mass., March 25, 1838. m. Porter, and resides at Springfield, Mass.
2554. 2. Henry D., b. at Monson, June 3, 1839.
2555. 3. James W., b. at Monson, March 13, 1843.

1135.

RUFUS M. PEASE,⁷ (Amos,⁶ Nathan,⁵ Abraham,⁴ Isaac,³ John,² Robert,¹) brother of the preceding, was born at Monson, October 29, 1813; married Lucy Stacy, December 16, 1840, and settled in Monson upon the homestead. He is, by occupation, a farmer.

His children were:

2556. 1. Rufus C., b. at Monson, Mass., October 5, 1841.
2557. 2. Lucy A., b. at Monson, November 21, 1842. m. Alfred H. Day, September 20, 1865, and resides in Ohio.
2558. 3. Mary, b. at Monson, March 18, 1844.
2559. 4. Monroe, b. at Monson, September 1, 1845.
2560. 5. Edwin S., b. at Monson, April 13, 1846.
2561. 6. Jerome, b. at Monson, April 26, 1848.
2562. 7. Lewis, b. at Monson, December 6, 1850.
2562.⁵² 8. Clinton E., b. at Monson, September 10, 1858. d. August 18, 1859.

1137.

LYMAN PEASE,⁷ (Nathaniel,⁶ Nathan,⁵ Abraham,⁴ Isaac,³ John,² Robert,¹) eldest son of Dea. Nathaniel and Nancy (Stanton) Pease of Wilbraham, Mass., and first cousin of the preceding, was born at Wilbraham,

34

, 1808; married Louisa Couch, and settled, first, in Wilbraham, but subsequently removed to Michigan, where he resided in 1868.

His child was:

2563.   1. CAROLINE, b. at Wilbraham, Mass.,   m. Frank
         Goodman,   , 1866, and resides in Michigan.

1139.

REV. WILLIAM A. PEASE,[7] (NATHANIEL,[6] NATHAN,[5] ABRAHAM,[4] ISAAC,[3] JOHN,[2] ROBERT,[1]) brother of the preceding, was born at Wilbraham, Mass., December 29, 1811; married Nancy Porter of Agawam, Mass., November 26, 1846. He was a minister of the gospel in connection with the Baptist denomination. Mr. Pease was licensed to preach by the Baptist Church in Agawam, Mass., and entered the ministry, according to the usages of the Baptist denomination, as a licentiate, in 1844. He was ordained as pastor of the Baptist Church in Plainfield, Mass., 1846, where he preached three years; at the close of which, he preached with the Baptist Church in Deerfield one year and a half; was pastor of the Baptist Church in Shutesbury, Mass., three years and a half, and for two and a half years pastor of the Baptist Church in North Leverett. After spending some time as an evangelist, he settled, and labored as pastor of the Baptist Church in Haddam, Ct., for five years, and was for three years pastor of the Baptist Church in Willington, Ct., where he died in 1866. We take the following from the "Christian Watchman and Reflector" of Boston:—

"The usefulness of this brother as a minister is not to be estimated solely by the results of his labors among the churches he served as pastor, as his twenty years of ministerial service were mainly divided between five churches; he spent with each one sufficient time to make his mark, and leave precious memorials behind him. But at no time did he confine his labors to the church of which he was then pastor. He was always ready to 'go into the highways and hedges, and compel them to come in.' His labors were much blessed with revivals, and he was much sought during seasons of special religious interest in other places than those of his residence. His great effort was as a winner of souls to Jesus Christ wherever he could find them. This was the aim of his preaching. It was warm from the heart, earnest, scriptural and direct. It was largely reinforced by his prayers. No one who heard him preach and pray could doubt that he was a man of faith and prayer,—one who had power with God. He was a growing man up to the close of his life. This was quite apparent to those who knew him in the first half of his ministry, which he spent in Massachusetts, and in the last half, which has been in Connecticut. Probably he showed in the last year of his life greater elements of strength than in any preceding year. Undoubtedly he was never more esteemed and beloved than he was and is in the church and community generally in Willington. And probably no previous winter of his ministry was more faithfully filled up in the Master's service than was the last. At its beginning he assisted in a revival in West Woodstock, and for a longer period in a precious work in Mansfield,—this in addition to increased labor among his own people. And this he continued till the outbreak of fatal disease suddenly brought his work to an end. His last sickness was of seven weeks of great suffering which he bore with the greatest patience, never uttering a word of murmur or complaint. He felt in his soul the peaceful assurance that death would bring him to the rest that remaineth for the people of God and he longed to depart and be with Christ. At the same time that his sickness was one of suffering he had never before experienced, his joys were greater than he had ever before known. 'I am almost home,' he said to the writer, four days before he died. 'God is about to bestow a wonderful favor upon me, to take me from a world of sin to a world of holiness.' And thus trusting in Christ and triumphing in the hope of the gospel he passed away to the reward of the saints above.　J. F. S."

————oo————

1145.

DAN PEASE,[7] (DAN,[6] GIDEON,[5] ABRAHAM,[4] ISAAC,[3] JOHN,[2] ROBERT,[1]) eldest son of DAN and ABIGAIL (JOHNSON) PEASE, first of Willington, Ct., last of Floyd, N. Y., and second cousin of the preceding was born at Willington, November 24, 1796; married Harriet Bartlett of Winfield, N. Y., July 5, 1821. It appears he first settled in Winfield, but subsequently removed to Floyd. He was the inventor of a "smutting machine," and has obtained patents for several *other* useful inventions. He lives in Floyd, (1868,) and is a manufacturer of agricultural implements.

His children were:

2564. 1. HARRIET S., b. at Winfield, N. Y., December　, 1822.

2565. 2. REUBEN M., b. at Winfield, August　, 1824.　m. Catherine M. Ostrander of Marcy, N. Y.,　, 1846, and settled at Superior, Wis.

1146.

TRUMAN PEASE,[7] (DAN,[6] GIDEON,[5] ABRAHAM,[4] ISAAC,[3] JOHN,[2] ROBERT,[1]) brother of the preceding, was born at Willington, September 28, 1798; married Maria Hay, March　, 1825, and settled, first, in Brookfield, N. Y., but subsequently removed to Floyd, N. Y., where he resided in 1866.

His children were:

2566. 1. ANN MARIA, b. at Brookfield, N. Y., February 6, 1826.　m. Daniel Olmstead, of Floyd,　, 1847. d. at Davenport, Iowa,　, 1856.

2567.   2. TRUMAN H., b. at Floyd, N. Y., July 8, 1829.   m. Susan
Easterly of Floyd,   , 1856, and settled in Floyd.
He served nearly three years as a volunteer in the army for
the suppression of the rebellion, and is supposed to have
died in a rebel prison.   He left no children.

2568.   3. ELIZABETH H., b. at Floyd, September 22, 1833.   d. unmarried.

1147.

JAMES J. PEASE,⁷ (DAN,⁶ GIDEON,⁵ ABRAHAM,⁴ ISAAC,³
JOHN,² ROBERT,¹) brother of the preceding, was born at
Willington, March 13, 1803; married Rhoda Bartlett of
Winfield, N. Y., September 2, 1830; died November 17,
1837, aged 34 years.   He was a farmer and mechanic.⋅

His children were:

2569.   1. JULIA A., b. at Marcy, N. Y., July 15, 1831., She was a
teacher in Winfield.

2570.   2. JAMES J., b. at Marcy,.October 19, 1833.   m. Amelia Dumont of Davenport, Iowa,   , 1856.   In 1866
he was Principal of Gilbertsville Academy and Collegiate
Institute, located in Butternuts, Otsego County, N. Y.
During the war of the rebellion, he was some time engaged
in visiting our soldiers, as a member of the United States
Christian Commission.

———o———

1150.

MOSES PEASE,⁷ (URBAN,⁶ GIDEON,⁵ ABRAHAM,⁴ ISAAC,³
JOHN,² ROBERT,¹) eldest son of URBAN and JUDITH
(PIPER) PEASE, some time of the State of New York, and
last of Webster, Mich., and first cousin of the preceding,
was born at Plainfield, Otsego County, N. Y., August 31,
1804; married Ruth Pearsall, July 4, 1830, and settled in
Floyd, N. Y.   He subsequently removed to the State of
Ohio, and now resides at Kingsville, Ashtabula County,
Ohio.   He is, by trade, a mason.

His children were:

2571. 1. Samuel U., b. at Floyd, N. Y., February 24, 1831. m. Susie M. Green, April 26, 1857, and resides at Kingsville, Ohio. He is, by trade, a mason.

2572. 2. Sarah H., b. at Sheffield, Ohio, February 26, 1833. m. Thomas Richmond, August 3, 1853. d. November 2, 1865.

2573. 3. Clarinda M., b. at Sheffield, December 3, 1834. d. February 26, 1847.

2574. 4. Francis R., b. at Sheffield, December 28, 1836. m. Cynthia Richards, and resides at St. Johns, Mich. He is a mason.

2575. 5. Nellie M., b. at Kingsville, Ohio, June 10, 1840. m. George Thompson, May 5, 1861, and resides at Kingsville.

2576. 6. Henry H., b. at Kingsville, March 18, 1848.

1152.

GIDEON PEASE,[7] (Urban,[6] Gideon,[5] Abraham,[4] Isaac,[3] John,[2] Robert,[1]) brother of the preceding, was born at Cincinnatus, Cortland County, N. Y., January 19, 1809; married Lydia Crippin,   , and resides at Oxford Corners, Mich.

His children were:

2577. 1.
2578. 2.

1156.

FRANCIS PEASE,[7] (Urban,[6] Gideon,[5] Abraham,[4] Isaac,[3] John,[2] Robert,[1]) brother of the preceding, was born at Homer, N. Y., November 2, 1817; married Azuba Debarr,   ; died July 21, 1855.

His children were:

2579. 1.
2580. 2.
2581. 3.

1162.

JOHN D. PEASE,[7] (Urban,[6] Gideon,[5] Abraham,[4] Isaac,[3] John,[2] Robert,[1]) brother of the preceding, was born at Sempronius, Cayuga County, N. Y., July 3, 1830;

married Alice E. Parker, April 20, 1854, and resides at Kingsville, Ohio. He enlisted as a private in Company G., One Hundred and Fifth Ohio Volunteer Infantry, August , 1862, and was engaged in the battles at Perrysville, Chicamauga, Mission Ridge, Buzzard's Roost, and various other places. He was discharged from service in June, 1865. He is, by trade, a carpenter.

---o---

1163.

DWIGHT PEASE,[7] (IRA,[6] GIDEON,[5] ABRAHAM,[4] ISAAC,[3] JOHN,[2] ROBERT,[1]) eldest son of IRA and SALLY (TUPPER) PEASE of Monson, Mass., and first cousin of the preceding, was born at Monson,   ; married

His child was:

2582.   1.

1164.

MARCUS J. PEASE,[7] (IRA,[6] GIDEON,[5] ABRAHAM,[4] ISAAC,[3] JOHN,[2] ROBERT,[1]) brother of the preceding, was born at Monson,   ; married Sarah C. Aldridge,   , and settled at Collinsville, Ct.

His children were:

2583.   1. DWIGHT A., b. at   d. young.
2584.   2. MYRON M., b. at   , 1838.   d. 1853.
        aged 15 years.
2585.   3. ADDIE R., b. at Collinsville, Ct., March   , 1841.
2586.   4. MARY J., b. at Collinsville,   , 1843.   m. James Hamilton, and settled in Westfield, Mass.
2587.   5. SARAH L., b. at Collinsville, February   , 1846.
2588.   6. MARCUS J., b. at Collinsville, October   , 1848.
2589.   7. ORRIN A., b. at Collinsville, November   , 1851.
2590.   8. ZENEVA, b. at Collinsville, October   , 1855.

---o---

1169.

ORSON PEASE,[7] (ABRAHAM,[6] GIDEON,[5] ABRAHAM,[4] ISAAC,[3] JOHN,[2] ROBERT,[1]) eldest son of ABRAHAM and MARY (DAVIS) PEASE of Monson, Mass., and first cousin of the preceding; was born at Monson, November 6, 1806; married Sophia Royce, March 13, 1837, and resides at Stafford, Ct.

His children were:

2591. 1. EDWIN O., b. at , July 12, 1839. m. Elsie Lamberton, December 6, 1865.

2592. 2. ERASTUS B., b. at , June 3, 1841. He was a private in the Thirty-seventh Regiment of Massachusetts Volunteers, Company I. He possessed and showed a daring bravery peculiar to himself and which made him noted among the men of his company and regiment. He was shot in the head and killed while in an engagement with the army at Gaines' Mills, Va., June 3, 1864, after a service of two years.

2593. 3. JOHN A., b. at , March 30, 1843. He was a private in the Thirty-first Regiment of Massachusetts Volunteers, Company F, and was four years in the service.

2594. 4. MARTHA M., b. at Monson, November 15, 1844.

2595, 5. MARCIA S., (twin,) b. at Monson, November 15, 1844. d. November 15, 1847.

2596. 6. MARCIUS, b. at , January 24, 1847. d. September 23, 1847.

2597. 7. IDA A., b. at , March 12, 1849.

2598. 8. LUCY V., b. at , December 5, 1850.

2599. 9. MONROE L., b. at , September 8, 1854.

1171.

HIRAM PEASE,[7] (ABRAHAM,[6] GIDEON,[5] ABRAHAM,[4] ISAAC,[3] JOHN,[2] ROBERT,[1]) brother of the preceding, was born at Monson, March 29, 1811; married Sophia Works, November 23, 1834, and settled in Somers, Ct., a farmer.

His children were:

2600. 1. SOPHRONIA C., b. at Somers, Ct., September 5, 1835. m. Henry M. Wood, May 18, 1856, and resides at Springfield, Mass.

2601.   2. MARIA C., b. at Somers, October 28, 1836. m. James L.
Thompson, October   , 1865, and resides in New York City.

2602.   3. ELVIRA E., b. at Somers, November 9, 1839. m. Watson J.
Prentice, November 11, 1862, and resides at Somers.

2603.   4. HIRAM C., b. at Somers, March 4, 1841. d. December 7, 1861.

2604.   5. JANE E., b. at Somers, March 16, 1850.

2605.   6. FRANKLIN W., b. at Somers, October 9, 1852.

1172.

FREDERICK PEASE,⁷ (ABRAHAM,⁶ GIDEON,⁵ ABRAHAM,⁴
ISAAC,³ JOHN,² ROBERT,¹) brother of the preceding, was
born at Monson,   ; married Louisa Smith;
married second, Julia Brown. He died in Stafford, Ct.,
about 1853.

His children were:

2606.   1. JANE L., b. at   , February 25, 1844. m. Gilbert
Chapman, and resides at Stafford, Ct.

BY SECOND WIFE:

2607.   2. JEANETTE, b. at   d. in infancy.

2608.   3. MARY F., b. at   d. young.

2609.   4. MARCUS H., b. at   about 1852.

1174.

DAVIS PEASE,⁷ (ABRAHAM,⁶ GIDEON,⁵ ABRAHAM,⁴
ISAAC,³ JOHN,² ROBERT,¹) brother of the preceding, was
born at Monson,   1815; married Elmira Calkins,
and settled in Wilbraham, Mass.

His children were:

2610.   1. MARY A., b. at Wilbraham, June 7, 1839. d. February 11,
1856.

2611.   2. LUCIA D., b. at Monson, July 22, 1840.

2612.   3. JOHN A., b. at Wilbraham, December 22, 1843. d. August
13, 1856.

2613.   4. BIANCA V., b. at Wilbraham, August 23, 1847.

2614.   5. IRVIN D., b. at Wilbraham, February 22, 1849. d. May 13,
1855.

2615.   6. ELSIE, b. at Wilbraham, July 27, 1853.

2616.   7. LAURA A., b. at Wilbraham, August 22, 1856.

1175.

BILLINGS PEASE,[7] (ABRAHAM,[6] GIDEON,[5] ABRAHAM,[4] ISAAC,[3] JOHN,[2] ROBERT,[1]) brother of the preceding, was born at Monson,   ; married Almira Foskit, 1844, and settled in Wilbraham, Mass.

His children were:

2617. 1. FRANCIS, b. at Wilbraham,   , 1844.
2618. 2. EUGENE, b. at Wilbraham,   , 1846.
2619. 3. MARY, b. at
2620. 4.

1177.

JARVIS PEASE,[7] (ABRAHAM,[6] GIDEON,[5] ABRAHAM,[4] ISAAC,[3] JOHN,[2] ROBERT,[1]) seventh and youngest son of ABRAHAM and MARY (DAVIS) PEASE, was born at Monson,   ; married   Butler, March, 1854.

———o———

His child was:

2621. 1.   d. in childhood.

1178.

HORACE PEASE,[7] (SALMON,[6] GIDEON,[5] ABRAHAM,[4] ISAAC,[3] JOHN,[2] ROBERT,[1]) eldest son of SALMON and ROXA (HOAR) PEASE of Monson, Mass., and first cousin of the preceding, was born at Monson, July 3, 1812; married Almira Stebbins, and settled in Wilbraham, Mass.

His children were:

2622. 1. WALTER S., b. at   , September   , 1838. He served in the army against the rebellion, and was connected with the Second Massachusetts Heavy Artillery.
2623. 2. ORISSA A., b. at   , April   , 1844.

1179.

CHESTER M. PEASE,[7] (SALMON,[6] GIDEON,[5] ABRAHAM,[4] ISAAC,[3] JOHN,[2] ROBERT,[1]) brother of the preceding, was born at Monson, November 1, 1813; married Sarah Munger, November 6, 1837; married second, Mary A. Horton, August 29, 1866. He settled in Monson, and is engaged in the bonnet factory in that place.

1180.

JONATHAN H. PEASE,⁷ (Salmon,⁶ Gideon,⁵ Abraham,⁴ Isaac,³ John,² Robert,¹) brother of the preceding, was born at Monson, October 6, 1816; married Laura Pease, daughter of Samuel Pease, 1849. He died, 1851.

His child was:

2624. 1. Laurin H., b. at   , December 12, 1850.

1182.

CALVIN S. PEASE,⁷ (Salmon,⁶ Gideon,⁵ Abraham,⁴ Isaac,³ John,² Robert,¹) the fifth and youngest son of Salmon and Roxa (Hoar) Pease, was born at Monson, July 25, 1824; married Julia M. White, April 27, 1851, and resides at Monson. He is a farmer.

His children were:

2625. 1. Myron H., b. at Monson, May 5, 1855. d. in childhood.
2626. 2. Jesse O., b. at Monson, August 31, 1856. d. a child.
2626.⁵³ 3. Alice E., b. at Monson, May 13, 1866.

---o---

1184.

SYLVANUS PEASE,⁷ (Samuel,⁶ Gideon,⁵ Abraham,⁴ Isaac,³ John,² Robert,¹) eldest son of Samuel and Catharine (Underwood) Pease, of Monson, Mass., and first cousin of the preceding, was born at Monson, November, 1816; married first, Delia Ann Smith,   1842; she died, 1847; married second, Lavinia Leonard, 1851, and settled in Monson.

His child was:

2627. 1. Ellen E., b. at Monson,   , 1843

1186.

ROSWELL PEASE,[7] (SAMUEL,[6] GIDEON,[5] ABRAHAM,[4] ISAAC,[3] JOHN,[2] ROBERT,[1]) brother of the preceding, was born at Monson, January, 1824; married Catharine Gale, 1846, and resides at Monson.

His children were:

2628.	1. GEORGE B., b. at		, 1847.
2629.	2. LAURA, b. at		, 1848.
2630.	3. JOHN, b. at		, 1850.
2631.	4. ELLA, b. at		, 1854.

1187.

IRA PEASE,[7] (SAMUEL,[6] GIDEON,[5] ABRAHAM,[4] ISAAC,[3] JOHN,[2] ROBERT,[1]) third son of SAMUEL and CATHARINE (UNDERWOOD) PEASE, was born at Monson, February, 1827; married Griswold. He settled in Wilbraham.

His children were:

2632. 1. ELLA, b. at Wilbraham.
2633. 2. DELBERT, b. at Wilbraham, , 1862.

1188.

SAMUEL PEASE,[7] (SAMUEL,[6] GIDEON,[5] ABRAHAM,[4] ISAAC,[3] JOHN,[2] ROBERT,[1]) brother of the preceding, was born at Monson, , 1830; married Butler; married second, widow Jarvis Pease. Had but one child, a daughter, which was by his first marriage. He lived in Monson.

His child was:

2634. 1.

———oo———

1193.

WEBSTER PEASE,[7] (WILLIAM,[6] WILLIAM,[5] ABRAHAM,[4] ISAAC,[3] JOHN,[2] ROBERT,[1]) eldest son of WILLIAM and ELIZABETH (GREENE) PEASE, of Enfield, Ct., and second cousin

of the preceding, was born at Enfield, April 10, 1811;
married first, Lucinda Robinson; married second, Lucy
Elmore. He removed to Wisconsin.

His children were:

2635.   1. EMELINE, b at
2636.   2. GEORGE M., b. at
2637.   3. ADALINE, b. at

1194.

ABNER PEASE,⁷ (WILLIAM,⁶ WILLIAM,⁵ ABRAHAM,⁴
ISAAC,³ JOHN,² ROBERT,¹) brother of the preceding, was
born at Enfield, January 23, 1813; married Hannah Moore.
He removed to Wisconsin, and settled in Sharon.

His child was:

2638.   1. MARIA, b. at   1849.

1196.

NORMAND PEASE,⁷ (WILLIAM,⁶ WILLIAM,⁵ ABRAHAM,⁴
ISAAC,³ JOHN,² ROBERT,¹) brother of the preceding, was
born at Enfield, September 25, 1817; married
                                  He died at Rome, N. Y.

His child was:

2639.   1.   d. young.

1198.

ALVIN PEASE,⁷ (WILLIAM,⁶ WILLIAM,⁵ ABRAHAM,⁴
ISAAC,³ JOHN,² ROBERT,¹) brother of the preceding, was
born at Enfield, November   , 1823; married Julia Bancroft, September 14, 1856, and settled in Enfield.

His children were:

2640.   1.
2641.   2.
2642.   3.
2643.   4.

1203.

CARLOS W. PEASE,[7] (WARREN,[6] WILLIAM,[5] ABRAHAM,[4] ISAAC,[3] JOHN,[2] ROBERT,[1]) son of WARREN and PEASE, and first cousin of the preceding, was born at East Windsor, Ct., February 5, 1815; married Olive J. Stilkey. First settled in Augusta, Me., subsequently removed thence to Springfield, Mass., where he now resides (1869).

His children were:

2644. 1. HARRIET E., b. at   , February 19, 1844. d. young.
2645. 2. LUCY C., b. at   , November 7, 1846. m. Charles W. Mutell, December 20, 1867, and resides in Springfield.
2646. 3. CHARLES C., b. at   , August 12, 1848.
2647. 4. SYLVIA G., b. at   , July 21, 1855. d. July , 1857.

———oo———

1207.

JARED PEASE,[7] (JABEZ,[6] ZEBULON,[5] ABRAHAM,[4] ISAAC,[3] JOHN,[2] ROBERT,[1]) third son of JABEZ and PHILENA (GREENE) PEASE, of Enfield, Ct., and second cousin of the preceding, was born at Enfield, Ct., December 9, 1815; married Honora O'Neil,   , 1858, and lives in Enfield.

His children are:

2648. 1. FRANCIS J., b. at Enfield, August 7, 1859.
2649. 2. ANN M., b. at Enfield, November 27, 1860.
2650. 3. JOHN T., b. at Enfield, September 6, 1862.
2651. 4. CATHARINE E., b. at

1210.

JAMES PEASE,[7] (JABEZ,[6] ZEBULON,[5] ABRAHAM,[4] ISAAC,[3] JOHN,[2] ROBERT,[1]) brother of the preceding, was born at Enfield, July 7, 1823; married Catharine E. Murthy,   , 1855, and lives in Enfield.

Engraved by J. van Drew

Simeon Pease,

The Superior wisdom of their

Benj'F. Pease

His children are:

2652.   1. JAMES R., b. at Enfield, April 25, 1856.
2653.   2. FREDERICK, b. at Enfield, November 21, 1857.
2654.   3. GEORGE, b. at Enfield, May 23, 1859.
2655.   4. PHILENA, b. at Enfield, January   , 1861.
2656.   5. LOUIS, b. at Enfield, January 3, 1864.

1215.

MORRIS C. PEASE,[7] (HARVEY B.,[6] ZEBULON,[5] ABRA-
HAM,[4] ISAAC,[3] JOHN,[2] ROBERT,[1]) eldest son of HARVEY B.
and MARIA (CHAPIN) PEASE, and first cousin of the pre-
ceding, was born at   ; married
Charlotte Harwood, May 19, 1852, and settled in South
Wilbraham.

His children are:

2657.   1. CLIFTON, b. at Somers, Ct., March 21, 1854.
2658.   2. WILLIE M., b. at Wilbraham, Mass., April 24, 1858.

FAMILY OF ISRAEL.⁴

1219.

SIMEON PEASE,[7] (SIMEON,[6] ISRAEL,[5] ISRAEL,[4] ISAAC,[3]
JOHN,[2] ROBERT,[1]) eldest son of SIMEON and MABEL (AL-
LEN) PEASE, of Enfield, Ct., and third cousin to the preceding, was born at Enfield, May 29, 1790; married
Cynthia Markham, January 8, 1815, and settled in the
town of Ulysses, Tompkins County, N. Y., (now Trumansburgh Village,) where he commenced clearing up a farm
of fifty acres, which he afterwards increased to two hundred; and died there in 1866.

His children were:

2659.   1. AUGUSTINE H., b. at Ulysses, N. Y., November 19, 1817.   m
         Ann Hopkins, April 8, 1846. At twenty years of age he
         commenced preparing for college, and graduated at Union
         College, July, 1843. In 1858 he received the degree of

A. M. For the most part of his life since he left college, he has been a successful educator of youth, and was at one time Principal of Trumansburgh Academy. He has recently resumed the quiet life of a farmer and lives in the town of Ulysses, near Trumansburgh.

2660. 2. Cynthia, b. at Ulysses, March 5, 1819. m. George Robinson, February 3, 1841.

2661. 3. Dorothy S., b. at Ulysses, March 12, 1821. m. first, John S. Hopkins, December 2, 1840; m. second, Orange S. Graves, October , 1843.

2662. 4. Simeon, b. at Ulysses, March 28, 1824. d. June 20, 1843.

2663. 5. Harriet, b. at Ulysses, March 1, 1826. m. Wakeman M. Osborn, November 2, 1849.

2664. 6. Annis, b. at Ulysses, April 21, 1828. m. Rev. David Osborn, a Baptist clergyman, April 1, 1846.

2665. 7. Minerva, b. at Ulysses, March 29, 1830. m. Abel D. Woodworth, June 2, 1857.

2666. 8. Antoinette, b. at Ulysses, November 1, 1832. m. Garrett Van Sickle, May 15, 1855. d. May 8, 1864.

2667. 9. Emily M., b. at Ulysses, January 9, 1837. m. David S. Pratt, April 9, 1860.

2668. 10. Benjamin F., b. at Ulysses, April 10, 1839. m. Augusta A. Pratt, August 10, 1860, and resides in Ulysses.

1220.

ALLEN PEASE,[7] (Simeon,[6] Israel,[5] Israel,[4] Isaac,[3] John,[2] Robert,[1]) brother of the preceding, was born at Enfield, Ct., June 18, 1792; married Grace Bolyen, January 10, 1814, and settled in Ulysses, Tompkins County, N. Y., (now Trumansburgh Village.) He is a farmer.

His children were :

2669. 1. Bartlett, b. at , July 1, 1815. m. Sarah Wheeler, September 22, 1838. d. September 21, 1859.

2670. 2. Earl A., b. at , September 24, 1816. m. Catharine Creque, March 7, 1839, and lives in Trumansburgh.

2671. 3. Mabel, b. at , July 26, 1819. m. Herman Creque, November 22, 1838.

2672. 4. Dana, b. at , January 28, 1821. d. August 9, 1836.

2673. 5. Loton H., b. at , August 6, 1823. d. August 18, 1844.

2674. 6. EMELINE G., b. at   , June 11, 1825. m. Joseph Gould, December 14, 1847.

2675. 7. CLARISSA G., b. at   , May 20, 1827. m. Reuben S. Smith, June 4, 1845.

2676. 8. ANDREW J., b. at   , November 30, 1828. m. Eliza A. Smith, January 4, 1854.

1222.

ALVA PEASE,⁷ (SIMEON,⁶ ISRAEL,⁵ ISRAEL,⁴ ISAAC,³ JOHN,² ROBERT,¹) brother of the preceding, was born at Enfield, October 19, 1795; married Clarissa Gowdy, and settled in Ulysses (now Trumansburgh Village,) N. Y., where he died, 1852.

His children were:

2677. 1. SUSAN, b. at   , July 20, 1818. m. Ornan Osborn, January 25, 1837.

2678. 2. ALVIN, b. at   , August 10, 1820. m. Rachel Woodruff, September   , 1841.

2679. 3. ROXANNA, b. at   , March 8, 1822. m. Alex. Race, September 2, 1841. d. March 18, 1846.

1225.

WELLS PEASE,⁷ (SIMEON,⁶ ISRAEL,⁵ ISRAEL,⁴ ISAAC,³ JOHN,² ROBERT,¹) brother of the preceding, was born at Enfield, Ct., March 17, 1801; married Elizabeth Pease, daughter of Isaac Pease,   , 1830. For some time resided at Enfield, but now lives in Windsor, Ct. He is, by occupation, a farmer.

His children were:

2680. 1. ELIZA A. L., b. at Enfield, November 4, 1832.

2681. 2. SAMANTHA, b. at Enfield, July 12, 1834.

2682. 3. SIMEON E., b. at Enfield, May   , 1836. d. December 21, 1836.

2683. 4. NILES, b. at Enfield, October 13, 1838. m. Cornelia Gleason, March 25, 1860, and lives in Thompsonville, Ct. He is a stove and tin-ware dealer.

2684. 5. MYRON, b. at Enfield, Ct., February 1, 1840. m. Sarah Moritter, and resides at Enfield, a farmer.

2685. 6. ALVAH, b. at Enfield, March 19, 1842. m. Mary J. Young, April 28, 1869, and resides at Thompsonville.

36

2686.   7. ALLEN, b. at Enfield, March 22, 1846,
2687.   8. LEONORA B., b. at Enfield, November 21, 1848.   m. William
          Bailey, November 29, 1866, and resides at Windsor, Ct.
2688.   9. KNEELAND W., b. at Enfield, August 3, 1851.

1226.

ARVIN PEASE,[7] (SIMEON,[6] ISRAEL,[5] ISRAEL,[4] ISAAC,[3] JOHN,[2] ROBERT,[1]) brother of the preceding, was born at Enfield, October 30, 1802; married Polly Gowdy, , 1822, and settled in Enfield.   He died, , 1846.

His children were:

2689.   1. MARSHALL, b. at Enfield, October 28, 1825.   m. Eliza Eaton, and lived some time in Bridgeport, Ct., next in Springfield, Mass., (1868.)   In 1869 he again removed to Bridgeport.

2690.   2. LUMAN, b. at Enfield, October 23, 1828.   m. Clarissa Buck, October 16, 1852.   d. in Enfield, , 1864.

2691.   3. DOROTHY, b. at Enfield, June 13, 1832.   m. Theodore Spencer, and settled in Somers, where she now resides.

2692.   4. ARVIN, b. at Enfield, January 7, 1834.   m. Mrs. Mary A. (McKendlees) Alcock, and resides at Enfield.

2693.   5. MARTIN V., b. at Enfield, January 4, 1840.   m. Elizabeth Miller, January , 1864.   d. in Andersonville rebel prison, Ga., August 29, 1864.*   He was a member of Company C, Harris' Light Cavalry of New York State, and taken prisoner when in General Kilpatrick's division.

1227.

LORIN PEASE,[7] (SIMEON,[6] ISRAEL,[5] ISRAEL,[4] ISAAC,[3] JOHN,[2] ROBERT,[1]) twin brother of the preceding, was born at Enfield, October 30, 1802; married Almitte Pease, daughter of Reuben Pease, of Enfield, December 27, 1827, and first settled in Longmeadow, Mass., subsequently lived sometime in Enfield, and thence back to Longmeadow, his present residence.   He is a farmer.

---

* We understand the monument erected to his memory at Hazardville, Ct., bears another date.   His brother Marshall thinks the above the correct one, as it was communicated to him by his brother's comrade who knew him well, was with him in his dying hours, and received messages from him for his friends at home.

His children were : *

2694.　1. SABRINA, b. at Longmeadow, Mass., September 4, 1828.　m.
Francis Chapin, March 18, 1846, and resides in Enfield.

2695.　2. SALINA, b. at Enfield, April 14, 1830.　d. September 19,
1836.

2696.　3. CALISTA, b. at Enfield, January 14, 1834.　m. George W.
Allen, February 8, 1853, and resides at East Windsor, Ct.

2697.　4. CATHARINE A., b. at Enfield, February 15, 1837.　d. 1837.

2698.　5. ELIZA B., b. at Enfield, November 13, 1839.　d. March 12,
1844.

2699.　6. DALLAS M., b. at Enfield, November 23, 1845.　m. Ann
Eliza Coombs, April 24, 1867.　He was a member of the
Forty-sixth Massachusetts Regiment of Volunteers, nine
months' men, and subsequently a member of the Second
Massachusetts Heavy Artillery, in which he served to the
end of the war.

2700.　7. SEWALL L., b. at Enfield, March 30, 1847.　m. Jennie E.
Pope, December 24, 1868, and resides in Longmeadow,
Mass.

2701.　8. RANSOM R., b. at Enfield, May 23, 1849.

1230.

KELLOGG PEASE,⁷ (SIMEON,⁶ ISRAEL,⁵ ISRAEL,⁴ ISAAC,³
JOHN,² ROBERT,¹) youngest son of SIMEON and SYBIL
(TERRY) [BILLINGS] PEASE, his second wife, of Enfield,
Ct., and half-brother of the preceding, was born at Enfield,
December 1, 1813; married Jane Pease, daughter of Zeb-
ulon Pease, of Enfield; married second, Ann Parsons.
He lives in Enfield, and has no children living.

————o————

1233.

ISRAEL PEASE,⁷ (ISRAEL,⁶ ISRAEL,⁵ ISRAEL,⁴ ISAAC,³
JOHN,² ROBERT,¹) eldest son of ISRAEL and MARY (PEASE)

---

* The mother of the children in this family is third cousin to her husband's
brother, Mr. Wells Pease. She is second cousin to his wife on their maternal side,
and first cousin to her on their paternal side. Consequently, the children of one
family are first, second, third and fourth cousins to those of the other.

PEASE of Middlefield, Mass., and first cousin of the preceding, was born at Middlefield, September 28, 1791; married first, Nancy Gillett, May 6, 1817, who died December 18, 1824; married second, Charity Perdenn, March 21, 1825. He removed to Hector (Reynoldsville,) Tompkins County, N. Y., about 1818 or 1819, and died there September 28, 1847.

His children were:

2702. 1. LAURA, b. at   , January 18, 1818. m. Joel Reynolds, October 27, 1840, and lives at Reynoldsville, N. Y., a farmer.

2703. 2. WILLIAM, b. at Hector, N. Y., June 2, 1822. m. Mary E. Coats, March 25, 1849, and at the time of his death his family resided at Leoni, Jackson County, Mich. Mr. Pease was, by occupation, an instructor of youth, a profession he followed more than twenty years. He had been early taught to hate the slave oligarchy by a father who was an earnest and early worker in the anti-slavery cause. Hence, after Congress had repealed the Missouri Compromise, he felt it his duty as did thousands of others at the North to remove to Kansas, that he might by his influence and vote help keep a territory free which had once been dedicated to freedom. He settled six miles east of Lawrence where he and his family suffered much from border ruffians. When the same oligarchy had lifted its hand to destroy our Union he was teaching in Illinois.

Though possessing a feeble constitution, he felt it his duty to fight in defense of the Union. He accordingly enlisted in the Thirty-third Illinois Regiment of Volunteers, Colonel Hovey commanding, Company G. While his regiment was doing service in Arkansas he fell a victim to disease and death after eleven months' service. He was buried by his comrades near Clarendon, Ark., under an oak tree.

> "They dug his grave deep,
> And there let him sleep
> In the shade of the old oak tree,
> He's no stone for his head
> And he's alone in his bed;
> But the patriot's name
> On the page of fame
> It never forgotten shall be."

2704. 3. NORMAN, b. at Hector, March 15, 1824. m. Lydia A. Davis, January 7, 1849, and resides in Reynoldsville, a farmer.

BY SECOND WIFE:

2705. 4. ISRAEL, b. at Hector, May 3, 1826, and lives in Reynoldsville, a farmer.

2706. 5. DAVID P., b. at Hector, March 27, 1830. m. Fanny Rusco, , and resides at Sparta Center, Kent County, Mich., a farmer.

2707. 6. NANCY, b. at Hector, December 9, 1833. m. Oliver E. Granger, October 20, 1859, and resides at Lodi Center, Seneca County, N. Y., a farmer.

2708. 7. Mary A., b. at Hector, June 23, 1836. m. Charles W. Davis, October 20, 1859, and resides at Reynoldsville, a farmer.

1234.

DANIEL PEASE,⁷ (ISRAEL,⁶ ISRAEL,⁵ ISRAEL,⁴ ISAAC,³ JOHN,² ROBERT,¹) brother of the preceding, was born at Middlefield, Mass., April 19, 1793; married Miriam Rice, , 1816, and removed to Oswego, N. Y., where he died, December 26, 1847.

His children were:

2709. 1. LEVI, b. at Oswego, N. Y., November 23, 1816. m. Mary B. Rhodes, November 23, 1848, and settled at Oswego, a farmer.

2710. 2. LAURA, b. at Oswego, February 26, 1818. d. February 10, 1841.

2711. 3. CHARLOTTE, b. at Oswego, November 14, 1819. d. October 7, 1846.

2712. 4. NANCY, b. at Oswego, July 15, 1822. m. Dr. S. H. Plumb, July 25, 1848, and resides at Victoria, N. Y. Dr. Plumb was a surgeon in a New York Regiment of Volunteers.

2713. 5. WILLIAM, b. at Oswego, September 11, 1823. m. first, Emily Fowler, October 8, 1850; m. second, Marcia H. Place, September 25, 1862. d. March 30, 1865.

2714. 6. ALFRED, b. at Oswego, November 7, 1825. m. Mary Gorsline, October 27, 1848, and settled in Oswego, a farmer.

2715. 7. AMOS, b. at Oswego, May 26, 1827. m. Julia E. Bishop March 1, 1863, and settled in Oswego, a farmer.

1235.

HARVEY PEASE,[7] (ISRAEL,[6] ISRAEL,[5] ISRAEL,[4] ISAAC,[3] JOHN,[2] ROBERT,[1]) brother of the preceding, was born at Middlefield, Mass., October 29, 1794; married   . He lives at Walnut Grove, Scott County, Iowa. He had four daughters.

His children were:

2716. 1.
2717. 2.
2718. 3.
2719. 4.

1237.

HORACE PEASE,[7] (ISRAEL,[6] ISRAEL,[5] ISRAEL,[4] ISAAC,[3] JOHN,[2] ROBERT,[1]) brother of the preceding, was born at Middlefield, Mass., March 2, 1798; married Ann Vining of East Windsor,   , 1829, and appears to have settled first in Middlefield, subsequently removed to Somers, Ct., and next at Meadville, Pa. In 1869 he removed to East Hartford, Ct. He is a farmer.

His children were:

2720. 1. HORACE A., b. at Middlefield,   , 1830. m.   , and settled in the vicinity of Winchester, Va., before the rebellion.
2721. 2. ABIAL, b. at Middlefield, Mass., November 13, 1833, and resides at East Hartford, Ct.
2722. 3. JULIA A., b. at Middlefield, August 12, 1834.
2723. 4. HARRIET M., b. at Middlefield,   , 1837. d., aged seven years.

1239.

OLIVER PEASE,[7] (ISRAEL,[6] ISRAEL,[5] ISRAEL,[4] ISAAC,[3] JOHN,[2] ROBERT,[1]) brother of the preceding, was born at Middlefield, Mass., December 29, 1802; married Delia Jones, and resides at Bloomington, McLean County, Ill. He has no children.

1240.

AUSTIN PEASE,⁷ (ISRAEL,⁶ ISRAEL,⁵ ISRAEL,⁴ ISAAC,³ JOHN,² ROBERT,¹) brother of the preceding, was born at Middlefield, Mass., April 23, 1806; married first, Emily Fisk of Chesterfield, Mass., October 15, 1829; married second, Martha A. Barry,   . He first settled at Chesterfield, next at Hawley, and subsequently at Charlemont, Mass., where he died, April 20, 1857. He was a leather manufacturer.

His children were:

2724. 1. LUMAN, b. at Chesterfield, Mass., November 12, 1830. m. Adelaide Smith, and resides at Bloomington, Ill.

2725. 2. RUSSELL, b. at Hawley, Mass., August   , 1833. m. Cornelia A. Hawkes, daughter of Edward D. Hawkes of Charlemont, Mass., September 18, 1860, and resides at Charlemont, a farmer.

2726. 3. LORINTHA, b. at Hawley, October 10, 1841.

———o———

1246.

DAN PEASE,⁷ (DAN,⁶ ISRAEL,⁵ ISRAEL,⁴ ISAAC,³ JOHN,² ROBERT,¹) eldest son of DAN and SALLY (WRIGHT) PEASE of Middlefield, Mass., and first cousin of the preceding, was born at Middlefield, October 21, 1802; married Mary Root, March 16, 1825, and first settled in Middlefield, where he remained until the year 1855; he then removed to Worthington, Mass. He is a farmer.

His children were:

2727. 1. DAN F., b. at Middlefield, Mass., December 30, 1826. m. Rachael Russell, August 7, 1860, and removed to Illinois.

2728. 2. MARY CAROLINE, b. at Middlefield, December 17, 1827. m. Daniel Corey, and settled in Illinois.

2729. 3. JULIA, b. at Middlefield, March 28, 1830. m. E. J. Ingham, and settled in Middlefield.

2730. 4. ASHER, b. at Middlefield, July 10, 1831. m. Cynthia Stanton, May 14, 1856, and settled in Middlefield.

2731. 5. MARIA, b. at Middlefield, September 4, 1834. m. Charles
F. Cole, and removed to Illinois.

2732. 6. HENRY, b. at Middlefield, June 9, 1836. m. Lydia B. Stanton
of Huntington, Mass., November , 1856, where he settled.

2733. 7. JAMES B., b. at Middlefield, August 7, 1839. m. Eliza Cole
of Chesterfield, Mass., and lives in Worthington, Mass.

1249.

WALTER PEASE,[7] (DAN,[6] ISRAEL,[5] ISRAEL,[4] ISAAC,[3]
JOHN,[2] ROBERT,[1]) brother of the preceding, was born at
Middlefield, Mass., September 12, 1807; married Mary
Ingham, February 23, 1831, and first settled in Middle-
field, but removed to Stephentown, N. Y., in 1855, where
he now lives. He is, by occupation, a farmer.

His children were:

2734. 1. WALTER LESTER, b. at Middlefield, Mass., January 14, 1833,
m. Mary A. Barnes of Becket, April 3, 1856, and lives in
Stephentown, N. Y.

2735. 2. CHARLES, b. at Middlefield, June 22, 1835. d. April 9, 1839.

2736. 3. MARY, b. at Middlefield, November 26, 1837.

2737. 4. MARIA, b. at Middlefield, October 30, 1840. m. Joseph Ely,
November 11, 1863, and lives in Westfield, Mass.

2738. 5. HENRY, b. at Middlefield, March 7, 1843. d. April 9, 1843.

2739. 6. MYRON, b. at Middlefield, March 15, 1845. d. March , 1845.

2740. 7. EMMA J., b. at Middlefield, February 1, 1856.

2741. 8. EUGENE M., b. at Middlefield, February 15, 1858.

1251.

ELDRIDGE PEASE,[7] (DAN,[6] ISRAEL,[5] ISRAEL,[4] ISAAC,[3]
JOHN,[2] ROBERT,[1]) brother of the preceding, was born at
Middlefield, Mass., March 14, 1812; married Persis Ballou
of Peru, Mass., May 7, 1834, and settled in Middlefield,
where he died, January 23, 1861. He was, by occupation,
a farmer.

His children were:

2742. 1. MARTIN, b. at Middlefield, Mass., April 19, 1837. m. Mary
J. Cross, December 31, 1864.

2743.   2. EDWARD, b. at Middlefield, September 13, 1838. He was in the army for the suppression of the late rebellion, having enlisted April 1, 1862, at New Haven, Ct., as private in the First Regiment of Connecticut Heavy Artillery, Company K. He was soon after appointed Corporal. His regiment was with General McClellan at the siege of Yorktown, Va., and was in the several engagements which soon followed on the peninsula.

September 1, 1863, Corporal Pease received permission and went before the Examining Board at Washington. His examination resulted in his appointment as First Lieutenant in the Second United States Colored Infantry. In July, 1864, he was appointed as Captain. His regiment was stationed for some time at Key West, at which post Captain Pease was detailed to act as Acting Inspector General, Brigadier-General John Newton commanding. He held this position until after the surrender of the Confederate army, when he returned to his regiment, and it was ordered to Tallahassee, Fla., where it remained until January 2, 1866, when by order of the Secretary of War the regiment was ordered to Washington and there discharged. Captain Pease is now, (1868,) a merchant in Huntington, Mass.

2744.   3. SARAH A., b. at Middlefield, September 22, 1840. m. George Alderman, April 19, 1860.

2745.   4. ALBERT, b. at Middlefield, August 20, 1843. m. Maria S. Hawes of Middlefield. d. May   , 1866.

2746.   5. MARIETTA, b. at Middlefield, May 21, 1848. m. Asahel Raymond, May 2, 1866, and resides at Dalton, Mass.

2747.   6. GEORGE, b. at Middlefield, August 9, 1849.

2748.   7. ELMER, b. at Middlefield, January 27, 1856.

1252.

MORGAN PEASE,⁷ (DAN,⁶ ISRAEL,⁵ ISRAEL,⁴ ISAAC,³ JOHN,² ROBERT,¹) brother of the preceding, was born at Middlefield, Mass., September 25, 1814; married first, Harriet Metcalf, April 15, 1839, by whom he had no children; married second, Rowena Fay, May 18, 1852, and lives in Middlefield, a farmer.

His children were:

2749.   1. EDSON M., b. at Middlefield, Mass., June 3, 1853.

2750.   2. HARRIET R., b. at Middlefield, November 19, 1855.

37

2751.   3. Charles E., b. at Middlefield, November 5, 1857.   d. February 18, 1858.
2752.   4. Frank W., b. at Middlefield, April 15, 1859.   d. June 23, 1859.
2753.   5. Lizzie Bell, b. at Middlefield, August 22, 1860.
2754.   6 Charles S., b. at Middlefield, October 29, 1862.

1254.

ARNOLD PEASE,[7] (Dan,[6] Israel,[5] Israel,[4] Isaac,[3] John,[2] Robert,[1]) brother of the preceding, was born at Middlefield, Mass., April 19, 1819; married Charlotte B. Stevens of Chester, Mass., June 15, 1848, and settled in Middlefield, a model farmer and stock raiser.

His children were:

2755.   1. Idella A., b. at Middlefield, March 30, 1849.   d. November 14, 1867.
2756.   2. Wallace A., b. at Middlefield, January 18, 1851.
2757.   3. Alice N., b. at Middlefield, June 29, 1857.
2758.   4. Arthur D., b. at Middlefield, October 17, 1862.

1257.

HIBBARD PEASE,[7] (David,[6] David,[5] Israel,[4] Isaac,[3] John,[2] Robert,[1]) eldest son of David and Hannah (Butler) Pease, first of East Windsor, Ct., subsequently of Springfield, Mass., and Suffield, Ct., and second cousin of the preceding, was born at East Windsor, August 18, 1804; married Lovina Pease, May 15, 1855, and settled in Suffield, Ct.

1259.

WILLIAM PEASE,[7] (David,[6] David,[5] Israel,[4] Isaac,[3] John,[2] Robert,[1]) brother of the preceding, was born at Springfield, Mass.,   , 1809; married Hannah Beebe, January   , 1834, who died two years after their marriage. He has since remained unmarried, and resides in Suffield, a farmer.

His child is:

2759. 1. WATSON W., b. at Suffield,   , 1834.   m. Adelaide
A. Griswold, October   , 1864, and resides at Suffield.
He is proprietor of the steam ferry at Thompsonville.

———o———

1266.

DAVID B. PEASE,⁷ (LEVI,⁶ DAVID,⁵ ISRAEL,⁴ ISAAC,³
JOHN,² ROBERT,¹) eldest son of LEVI and EXPERIENCE
(HEMINWAY) PEASE of Suffield, Ct., and first cousin of
the preceding, was born at Suffield, February 1, 1819;
married Elizabeth Cook, and died at   , May 31,
1843, aged 24 years. He left no issue.

1269.

SAMUEL PEASE,⁷ (LEVI,⁶ DAVID,⁵ ISRAEL,⁴ ISAAC,³
JOHN,² ROBERT,¹) brother of the preceding, was born at
Suffield, Ct., February 15, 1828; married Jerusha Fuller,
August 9, 1849, and settled in Springfield, Mass. He is
now proprietor of the Sulphur Springs Hotel, Indian
Orchard.

His children are:

2760. 1. GEORGE S., b. at   , September 29, 1851.
2761. 2. CHARLES H., b. at   , March 19, 1853.
2762. 3. ADELAIDE R., b. at   , March 13, 1855.

———o o———

1271.

HEZEKIAH PEASE,⁷ (SETH,⁶ HEZEKIAH,⁵ ISRAEL,⁴
ISAAC,³ JOHN,² ROBERT,¹) eldest son of SETH and PATTY
(CHAPIN) PEASE of Enfield, Ct., and second cousin of the
preceding, was born at Enfield, March 26, 1807; married
Elvira Sessions, February 22, 1838, and settled in Long-
meadow, Mass., a farmer.

His children were:

2763. 1. LOVISA, b. at   , July 27, 1841.
2764. 2. HOMER C., b. at   , January 1, 1845.

* **1272.**

ALANSON PEASE,[7] (SETH,[6] HEZEKIAH,[5] ISRAEL,[4] ISAAC,[3] JOHN,[2] ROBERT,[1]) brother of the preceding, was born at Enfield, Ct., February 12, 1809; married Tirzah Fosket, April 12, 1838, and settled in Monson, Mass.

His children are:

2765.   1. OMAR, b. at Monson, March 3, 1840.
2766.   2. MARTHA, b. at Monson, May 27, 1842.
2767.   3. LUCY A., b. at Monson, June 3, 1843.
2768.   4. TIRZAH J., b. at Monson, September 27, 1845.
2769.   5. RHODA F., b. at Monson, September 27, 1847.
2770.   6. ANN F., b. at Monson, November 2, 1848.
2771.   7. MARY E., b. at Monson, September 5, 1850.
2772.   8. LYDIA F., b. at Monson, October 1, 1853.

1273.

SETH PEASE,[7] (SETH,[6] HEZEKIAH,[5] ISRAEL,[4] ISAAC,[3] JOHN,[2] ROBERT,[1]) brother of the preceding, was born at Enfield, Ct.,   , 1811; married first, Dorothy Kibbe,   ; married second, Achsah Combs, November 16, 1850, and settled in East Longmeadow, Mass.

He went with his father when a child, to live with the Shakers in Enfield. When about fourteen years old, he lost by accident his right arm, and had nothing left after amputation of the limb, but a short stump. At the age of eighteen years, he left the Shakers and home to make his way, as best he could, through the world, and by his own efforts,—without any other means or aid than the left hand,—he has acquired, by manual labor, a good and comfortable home, with a farm of some fifty acres of good land. An example for neatness and improvement. He performs most of the labor on his farm with his own left hand. During the winter of 1852 he chopped down in the woods, cut, split and put up for market, one hundred cords of wood, with *his one hand*, going one and a half miles to his work, and taking care of his stock, etc.!

His children are:

2773. 1. OLIVER, b. at East Longmeadow, Mass.
2774. 2. FLAVIA, b. at East Longmeadow,   , 1840. m. Syl-
            vester Rockwell of Warehouse Point, Ct.
2775. 3. EMILY, b. at East Longmeadow,   , 1842.
2776. 4. AMELIA, b. at East Longmeadow, 1844. m. Edwin O. Truesdell,
            May 19, 1866, and resides in West Stafford, Ct.

BY SECOND WIFE:

2777. 5. ARTHUR, b. at East Longmeadow,   , 1851.
2778. 6. SETH, b. at East Longmeadow,   , 1853.

———oo———

1280.

ORLANDO PEASE,⁷ (NATHAN,⁶ NATHAN,⁵ ISRAEL,⁴ ISAAC,³ JOHN,² ROBERT,¹) eldest son of NATHAN and POLLY (COLLINS) PEASE of Enfield, Ct., and second cousin of the preceding, was born at Enfield, September 2, 1803; married Asenath Goddard,   , and lives in Winsted, Ct. He is, by trade, a mason.

His children were:

2779. 1. JANE, b. at Granby, Ct.,   d. a child.
2780. 2. JAMES A., b. at Winsted, Ct., January , 1840. He was in the
            army in 1862, and belonged to the Seventh Connecticut
            Volunteers.
2781. 3. GEORGE L., b. at Winsted, October , 1842.

1284.

ELIPHALET C. PEASE,⁷ (NATHAN,⁶ NATHAN,⁵ ISRAEL,⁴ ISAAC,³ JOHN,² ROBERT,¹) brother of the preceding, was born at Enfield, Ct., June 17, 1811; married Mary Maxson, March 11, 1841, and settled at Dansville, N. Y; died , 1862, without children, at the age of 51 years.

1285.

SIMEON PEASE,⁷ (NATHAN,⁶ NATHAN,⁵ ISRAEL,⁴ ISAAC,³ JOHN,² ROBERT,¹) brother of the preceding, was born at

Enfield, Ct., June 4, 1813; married first, Selina Chalker, , 1837; married second, Mary S. Hatch, , 1853, and removed to Dansville, N. Y., where he now lives, (1863.)

His children were:

2782.	1. CHARLES N., b. at Easthampton, Mass.,	, 1838.
2783.	2. NELSON, b. at Collinsville, Ct.,	, 1840. d. a child.
2784.	3. NELSON S., b. at Berlin, Ct.,	, 1843. d. a child.
2785.	4. MARY A., (twin,) b. at Berlin,	, 1843.
2786.	5. ALVA W., b. at Southington, Ct.,	, 1847. d. a child.

BY SECOND WIFE:

2787. 6. ALVA W.,[2] b. at Dansville, N. Y.

———ooo———

FAMILY OF BENJAMIN.[4]

1288.

BENJAMIN PEASE,[7] (SHARON,[6] SHARON,[5] BENJAMIN,[4] ISAAC,[3] JOHN,[2] ROBERT,[1]) eldest son of SHARON and MARY (BROOKS) PEASE, first of Enfield, Ct., subsequently of Shutesbury, Mass., and third cousin of the preceding, was born at Enfield, August 28, 1798; married Matilda Stewart, who was born July 9, 1803, and settled in Watertown, N. Y.

His children are:

2788.	1. LORIN S., b. at	, March 26, 1823.
2789.	2. ALBERT, b. at	, July 26, 1825.
2790.	3. LUCY, b. at	, November 29, 1827.
2791.	4. CAROLINE, b. at	, April 27, 1836.
2792.	5. MARY, b. at	, April 23, 1841.
2793.	6. MARTHA, b. at	, March 1, 1844.

1289.

DANIEL PEASE,[7] (SHARON,[6] SHARON,[5] BENJAMIN,[4] ISAAC,[3] JOHN,[2] ROBERT,[1]) brother of the preceding, was born at Enfield, August 17, 1799; married first, Sarah

Cobb, by whom he had his children; married second, Mary J. Catlin, and removed to Michigan, and died at Orion, June 28, 1850. He was a lawyer.

His children were:

2794.   1. DANIEL, b. at   . d. young.
2795.   2. HANNAH, b. at   , April 2, 1830. m.
         Graham,   . d.   , 1863.
2796.   3. GEORGE B., b. at   , August   , 1832. d. July   ,
         1843.
2797. 4. DANIEL C., b. at   , February 4, 1834. m.
                  , and resides at Grand Rapids, Mich.
2798.   5. MARTIN, b. at   , August 14, 1836. He served in
         the army through the late war and resides at Órion, Mich.
2799.   6. ELIZABETH, b. at   , 1838. d.   ,
         1843.
2800.   7. ALBERT, b. at   , 1840. d.   , 1842.
2801.   8. CHARLES L , b. at   , August 3, 1843.

1290.

HOSEA PEASE,⁷ (SHARON,⁶ SHARON,⁵ BENJAMIN,⁴ ISAAC,³ JOHN,² ROBERT,¹) brother of the preceding, was born at Enfield, Ct., April   , 1800; married Susanna Shubrook of Belchertown, Mass., December 31, 1832. He resided a few years at West Brookfield, Mass., next at Prospect, Me., and subsequently at Whately, Mass., where he has resided most of the time for the past twenty years.

His children were:

2802.   1. GEORGE B., b. at West Brookfield, Mass.,   , 1833.
         He is supposed to have died at sea.
2803. 2. HENRY C., b. at West Brookfield, September 16, 1835. m.
         Mrs. Louisa (Smith) Rockwell, June 4, 1861, and resides
         at Whately, a farmer,
2804.   3. SUSAN A., b. at Prospect, Me., February 2, 1837. m. Luther
         Clark, and resides at Northampton, Mass.
2805. 4. CHARLES F., b. at Prospect, January 14, 1838. m. Julia M.
         Perkins, June 8, 1862, and resides at Whately, a farmer.
2806.   5. JOHN F., b. at Prospect, June 15, 1841. m. Celestia Witter,
         December 31, 1868, and resides at Northampton, Mass.

He was a private in the Thirty-seventh Regiment of Massachusetts Volunteers in the late war.

2807.   6. Freeman S., b. at Whately,   , 1843. d. in infancy.

2808.   7. James H., b at Whately, February 25, 1848.

1291.

GEORGE B. PEASE,[7] (Sharon,[6] Sharon,[5] Benjamin,[4] Isaac,[3] John,[2] Robert,[1]) brother of the preceding, was born at Enfield, August 4, 1805; married first, Mary Priest at Parishville, N. Y., October   , 1834; married second, Caroline A. Jones of Detroit, August 10, 1844; married third, Caroline M. Butler at Cleveland, Ohio, August 4, 1856. Immediately after his first marriage he removed to Painsville, Ohio, and from thence he removed to Detroit, where he now lives. He is a dealer in paper stock, paper, and printer's material; in partnership with his eldest son.

His children were:

2809.   1. George L., b. at Painsville, Ohio, June 10, 1835. m. J. Frances Gregory, February 6, 1866, and resides at Detroit, a merchant.

2810.   2. Mary, b. at Painsville, August 20, 1836. m. Caleb B. Burnap of Parishville, N. Y., September   , 1860. d. 1863.

BY SECOND WIFE:

2811.   3. Clara A., b. at Detroit, July 12, 1847. m. Fred. S. Lawrence, August 28, 1866.

2812.   4. Elisha B., b. at Detroit, December 23, 1848.

2813.   5. Kate M., b. at Detroit, February 12, 1854.

BY THIRD WIFE:

2814.   6. Millie S., b. at Detroit, September 12, 1857.

2815.   7. Robert H., b. at Detroit, February 8, 1859.

2816.   8. Charles G., b. at Detroit, June 11, 1864.

1296.

ALBERT PEASE,[7] (Sharon,[6] Sharon,[5] Benjamin,[4] Isaac,[3] John,[2] Robert,[1]) brother of the preceding, was born at Shutesbury,   ; married Susan Darrow, February 5, 1835, and lives at Northampton, Mass.

His children were:

2817. 1. ALBERT M., b. at Amherst, Mass.,   , 1836. d.
                    , 1840.
2818. 2. HENRY C., b. at Amherst, February 22, 1838. d.   , 1849.
2819. 3. EDWIN S., b. at Greenwich, Mass., July 1, 1840. He was a
              member of the Tenth Regiment of Massachusetts Volun-
              teers in the Army of the Potomac, and died of disease con-
              tracted in the service.
2820. 4. FRANKLIN C., b. at Hatfield, March 14, 1843. He was in
              the army in 1863.
2821. 5. MONROE E., b. at Hatfield, September 23, 1850.

———○○○———

FAMILY OF EZEKIEL.[4]

1301.

OBED PEASE,[7] (EZEKIEL,[6] EZEKIEL,[5] EZEKIEL,[4] ISAAC,[3]
JOHN,[2] ROBERT,[1]) third son of EZEKIEL and LYDIA (PEASE)
PEASE, first of Enfield, Ct., subsequently of Starksboro,
Vt., and third cousin to the preceding, was born at
        , April 10, 1789; married Lydia Lamas, April 11,
1811. He removed from Vermont in 1839 to Farming-
ton, Ill.

His children were:

2822.   1. AMANDA, b. at   . m. Enoch
                Varney, and settled in Bristol, Vt.
2823.   2. MARVIN K., b. at   , August 12, 1814. m. Lucinda
                Atwood. He is blind, and has lectured on temperance in
                several Western States. He resided at Farmington, Ill.,
                in 1857.
2824.   3. SYLVIA, b. at   , February 1, 1816.
2825.   4. MELISSA, b. at   , May 19, 1818. d. December   , 1838.
2826.   5. LUCINDA, b. at   , May 19, 1820. d. September 27, 1842.
2827.   6. LYDIA, b. at   , March 17, 1822.
2828.   7. JOHN, b. at   , September 26, 1824. m. Miss
                Foster, and resided at Farmington, Ill., in 1857.
2829.   8. PAULINA, b. at   , February 19, 1828.
2830.   9. LOUISA, b. at   , September 9, 1834.
2831. 10. CORDELIA, b. at   , August 6, 1837.

———○———

1304.

OBADIAH PEASE,[7] (OBADIAH,[6] EZEKIEL,[5] EZEKIEL,[4] ISAAC,[3] JOHN,[2] ROBERT,[1]) eldest son of OBADIAH and ACHSAH (BEMENT) PEASE of Landgrove, Vt., and first cousin of the preceding, was born at   ; married Isabella Houghton, and settled in Glen Falls, N. Y.

His children were:

2832.   1. SILAS H., b. at
2833.   2. HANNAH L., b. at
2834.   3. AMBROSE, b. at
2835.   4. SOLOMON, b. at
2836.   5. CLARISSA, b. at
2837.   6. MARY, b. at
2838.   7. OBADIAH, b. at

1306.

AMBROSE PEASE,[7] (OBADIAH,[6] EZEKIEL,[5] EZEKIEL,[4] ISAAC,[3] JOHN,[2] ROBERT,[1]) brother of the preceding, was born at   ; married Lucy P. Lawrence of Weston, Vt.

His children were:

2839.   1. SYLVANUS A., b. at   . d.
2840.   2. LUCY L., b. at   , and lives in Delphi, Ia.
2841.   3. ANGELINE L., b. at   . m. David O. Gale, and settled in Londonderry, Vt.
2842.   4. ANDREW J., b. at   . m. Lucy Cragin, and settled in Dubuque, Ia.
2843.   5. PLINY M., b. at   , and settled in Delphi, Ia.
2844.   6. ALONA A., b. at   . d. young.
2845.   7. LAWRENCE P., b. at   , and settled in Logansport, Ia.

1307.

ELIHU PEASE,[7] (OBADIAH,[6] EZEKIEL,[5] EZEKIEL,[4] ISAAC,[3] JOHN,[2] ROBERT,[1]) brother of the preceding, was born at Landgrove, Vt., April 16, 1803; married Lucinda Glasier of Manchester, Vt., and settled in Landgrove.

His children were:

2846. 1. DEXTER E., b. at Landgrove, Vt.,   , and
settled in Rockbridge, Wis.
2847. 2. CLARISSA, b. at Landgrove,   , and settled in Rockbridge, Wis.
2848. 3. ELVIRA L., b. at Landgrove.
2849. 4. MYRON C., b. at Landgrove.

1308.

AMOS PEASE,[7] (OBADIAH,[6] EZEKIEL,[5] EZEKIEL,[4] ISAAC,[3] JOHN,[2] ROBERT,[1]) brother of the preceding, was born at Landgrove, Vt., March 3, 1805; married Mary Marston of Salem, Mass., and settled in Boston, Mass.

His children are:

2850. 1. WILLIAM, b. at
2851. 2. SUSAN, b. at

——o——

1309.

ELIJAH PEASE,[7] (ELIJAH,[6] EZEKIEL,[5] EZEKIEL,[4] ISAAC,[3] JOHN,[2] ROBERT,[1]) eldest son of ELIJAH, and POLLY (ALLEN) PEASE of Weston, Vt., and first cousin of the preceding, was born at Weston,   , 1796; married Roby Arnold, October 5, 1823, and settled in Weston. He died March 24, 1867. He was a farmer.

His children were:

2852. 1. MARY ANN, b. at Weston, Vt., September 6, 1824.
2853. 2. PLATT TITUS, b. at Weston, May 22, 1826. m. Sarah J. Rock, January 1, 1852, and settled in Troy, N. Y. He was in the late war for suppressing the rebellion.
2854. 3. SUSAN MARIA, b. at Weston, September 26, 1827.
2855. 4. GEORGE A., b. at Weston, April 9, 1829. m. Electa Smith December 5, 1855, and settled in Landgrove, Vt.
2856. 5. LUCY A., b. at Weston, October 18, 1831.
2857. 6. ELVIRA NANCY, b. at Weston, March 3, 1833.
2858. 7. ANNA DELIA, b. at Weston, October 23, 1834.
2859. 8. HARRIET, b. at Weston, May 2, 1837.

born at Weston, Vt., December 19, 1819; married Abby
C. Sawyer, May 2, 1850; and settled in Weston, a farmer.

His children are:

2881.   1. ABBY J., b. at Weston, Vt., March   , 1851.
2882.   2. HANNAH E., b. at Weston, April 15, 1852.
2883.   3. MILO M., b. àt Weston, September 4, 1853.
2884.   4. IRA A., b. at Weston, May 7, 1856.

————oo————

1322.

HENRY PEASE,[7] (HENRY,[6] HENRY C.,[5] EZEKIEL,[4]
ISAAC,[3] JOHN,[2] ROBERT,[1]) eldest son of HENRY and
HULDAH (TILDEN) PEASE of Sandisfield, Mass., subsequently of Livonia, N. Y., and second cousin of the
preceding, was born at Sandisfield, March   , 1794;
married first, Polly Gould, March 19, 1817; married
second, Rowena Spafford, January 16, 1838, and resides
at Livonia. He has had eight children, three of whom
died young. He is a farmer.

His children are:

2885.   1. LOUISA, b. at   . m. Elam Bene-
              dict, and resides at Livonia, N. Y.
2886.   2. JONATHAN, b. at   . m. Martha
              Decker, and resides at South Lima, N. Y.
2887.   3. HENRY C., b. at   . m. Hannah
              Hoag, and resides at Livonia.
2888.   4. MARY JANE, b. at   . m.
              Case and resides at South Lima.
2889.   5. MARTHA, b. at

1323.

WILLIAM C. PEASE,[7] (HENRY,[6] HENRY C.,[5] EZEKIEL,[4]
ISAAC,[3] JOHN,[2] ROBERT,[1]) brother of the preceding, was
born at Sandisfield, Mass., August 18, 1795; married Mrs.
Hannah Lee of Livonia, N. Y., March 10, 1825, and resides at Lakeville, Livingston County, N. Y., a farmer.

His children are:

2890. 1. WILLIAM W., b. at   . m.
                        , and resides at Groveland, N. Y.
2891. 2. EMERSON, b. at   . m. Henrietta
          Pierson, and resides at Lakeville, N. Y.
2892.   3. SARAH JANE, b. at

1325.

THOMAS PEASE,⁷ (HENRY,⁶ HENRY C.,⁵ EZEKIEL,⁴
ISAAC,³ JOHN,² ROBERT,¹) brother of the preceding, was
born at Sandisfield, Mass., July 13, 1798; married first,
Rebecca Rull of Lima, N. Y., September 19, 1824; married second, Jane Trimble of Phelps, N. Y., May 10, 1832,
and settled at Rochester, N. Y., where he died July ,
1859. He had eight children, three of whom died young.
He was a forwarding and commission merchant.

His children were:

2893. 1. MYRON H., b. at Rochester, N. Y.   . m. Anna
          MacNamara,   . They are both dead.
2894.   2. NELSON L., b. at Rochester,   . m.   ,
          and resides at San Francisco, Cal.

BY SECOND WIFE:

2895.   3. REBECCA, b. at Rochester,   . d. unmarried, 1863.
2896.   4. CAROLINE A., b. at Rochester, September 27, 1837. m. Erastus
          Burnham, May 12, 1859, and resides at Cincinnati, Ohio.
2897.   5. HATTIE A., b. at Rochester, January 8, 1843.˙

1330.

HARVEY PEASE,⁷ (HENRY,⁶ HENRY C.,⁵ EZEKIEL,⁴
ISAAC,³ JOHN,² ROBERT,¹) brother of the preceding, was
born at Livonia, N. Y., March 17, 1808; married Mary
Hicks of Avon, N. Y., March 6, 1834, and settled at Livonia, N. Y., where he died September 17, 1863. He was
a farmer.

His children were:

2898.   1. ELIZABETH, b. at   . m. Augustus Annis, and
          resides at Livonia, N. Y.

2899. 2. MINNIE, b. at   . m.   Gillet,
                                    , d.   , 1865.
2900. 3. ETTA, b. at   . m.   Gillet, and
          resides at Livonia.

1331.

AUSTIN PEASE,[7] (HENRY,[6] HENRY C.,[5] EZEKIEL,[4] ISAAC,[3] JOHN,[2] ROBERT,[1]) brother of the preceding, was born at Livonia, N. Y., November 22, 1809; married Martha Osborne of Rochester, N. Y., December 24, 1834. He removed from New York State to Michigan in 1850, and died there in September of the same year. He was a farmer. He had eight children, three of whom died young.

His children were:

2901. 1. AUSTIN S., b. at   , and resides at
          San Francisco, Cal.
2902. 2. TURNER, b. at   d.   , 1856,
          unmarried.
2903. 3. CHARLES H., b. at   . m.
                              , and resides at Tekousha, Mich.
2904. 4. WILLIAM S., b. at
2905. 5. JULIETTE, b. at
2906. 6. GEORGE, b. at

1332.

CHANDLER PEASE,[7] (HENRY,[6] HENRY C.,[5] EZEKIEL,[4] ISAAC,[3] JOHN,[2] ROBERT,[1]) brother of the preceding, was born at Livonia, N. Y., November 25, 1811; married first, Laurena Gale, of Rochester, N. Y., December 24, 1835; married second, Mary Patrick of Palmyra, N. Y., June 15,   , and settled at Rochester, where he died April 1, 1865.

His child was:

2907. 1. EMERY T., b. at   , and resides at
          Rochester, N. Y.

1334.

JAMES H. PEASE,⁷ (HENRY,⁶ HENRY C.,⁵ EZEKIEL,⁴
ISAAC,³ JOHN,² ROBERT,¹) brother of the preceding, was
born at Livonia, N. Y., January 11, 1817. He for some·
time resided at Albany, N. Y.; married ,
, 1857, and removed to San Francisco, Cal. He
next returned to Livonia, where he died September 17,
1863, leaving no issue. He was a commission merchant.

1335.

EMERY T. PEASE,⁷ (HENRY,⁶ HENRY C.,⁵ EZEKIEL,⁴
ISAAC,³ JOHN,² ROBERT,¹) brother of the preceding, was
born at Livonia, N. Y., September 20, 1820; married Mary
R. Whaley, February 8, 1848. He removed to New York
City, and was a commission merchant. He now resides
at San Francisco, Cal., a banker. He has no children,
(1867).

———o———

1338.

OLIVER C. PEASE,⁷ (OLIVER,⁶ HENRY C.,⁵ EZEKIEL,⁴
ISAAC,³ JOHN,² ROBERT,¹) eldest son of OLIVER and RUTH
(HUBBARD) PEASE, first of Sandisfield, Mass., subsequently
of Cambria, N. Y., and last of Blissfield, Mich., and first
cousin of the preceding, was born at Sandisfield, May 30,
1803; married first, Maria Depue, May 9, 1827; married
second, widow Lucy Palmer of Palmyra, Mich., March 17,
1851. He removed from Cambria to Blissfield in June,
1836, and from thence to Palmyra, Mich., in 1865. He is,
by occupation, a farmer.

His children were:

2908. 1. SARAH, b. at Cambria, N. Y., May 13, 1830. m. Milo
Stearns, March 11, 1852. d. February 11, 1856, leaving
two children.

2909. 2. SETH H., b. at Cambria, May 29, 1832. m. Esther Storer,
December 15, 1860, and lives in Blissfield, a merchant.

39

2910. 3. RICHARD D., b. at Cambria, June 28, 1835, and lives in California.

2911. 4. JOHN, b. at Blissfield, Mich., January 7, 1839. m. Martha Spencer, , 1863.

2912. 5. RUTH, (twin,) b. at Blissfield, January 7, 1839. m. William Roe of Comstock, Mich., April , 1861, and removed to California.

BY SECOND WIFE:

2913. 6. ELZORA A., b. at Blissfield, May 13, 1852.

1340.

LEVI PEASE,[7] (OLIVER,[6] HENRY C.,[5] EZEKIEL,[4] ISAAC,[3] JOHN,[2] ROBERT,[1]) brother of the preceding, was born at Sandisfield, Mass., August 25, 1806; married Caroline M. Pease, daughter of Alvah Pease, , 1831, and settled in Sandisfield, a blacksmith.

His children were :

2914. 1. HELEN K., b. at Sandisfield, Mass., May 19, 1833. m. Crossman Olds, September 26, 1854.

2915. 2. LUCY M., b. at Sandisfield, July 9, 1837.

2916. 3. EUNICE E., b. at Sandisfield, August 3, 1847.

1341.

HENRY C. PEASE,[7] (OLIVER,[6] HENRY C.,[5] EZEKIEL,[4] ISAAC,[3] JOHN,[2] ROBERT,[1]) brother of the preceding, was born at Sandisfield, Mass., July 5, 1808; married Louisa Turner, March 23, 1840, and lived for a time in Blissfield, Mich., but now lives in Urbanna, Benton County, Iowa. He is, by occupation, a farmer.

His children were :

2917. 1. REBECCA R. S., b. at , February 22, 1841.

2918. 2. ZIBA W., b. at , November 11, 1842.

2919. 3. HENRY E., b. at , October 29, 1845.

2920. 4. OLIVER C., b. at , October 4, 1847.

2921. 5. HAMPTON A., b. at , February 1, 1849.

2922. 6. ALFRED L., b. at , November 22, 1850.

2923. 7. LOVISA R., b. at , April 27, 1853.

2924. 8. VIANA A., b. at , January 19, 1855.

2925. 9. ELLA W., b. at , November 12, 1860.

1343.

ERASTUS PEASE,⁷ (OLIVER,⁶ HENRY C.,⁵ EZEKIEL,⁴ ISAAC,³ JOHN,² ROBERT,¹) brother of the preceding, was born at Sandisfield, Mass., July 16, 1812; married Charlotte Wolcott,   , and settled in Kalamazoo, Mich., next in Climax, Mich. He died October 9, 1863.

His children were:

2926. 1. MARTHA, b. at   . m.
                    . d. January 4, 1864, leaving two children.
2927. 2. SARAH, b. at   . m. .
2928. 3. RUTH, b. at
2929. 4. DELIA, b. at
2930. 5. AUSTIN, b. at

———oo———

1349.

SPENCER PEASE,⁷ (OLIVER,⁶ ISAAC,⁵ EZEKIEL,⁴ ISAAC,³ JOHN,² ROBERT,¹) second son of OLIVER and CATHERINE (CHAPPELL) PEASE, of Washington, Mass., and second cousin of the preceding, was born at Washington, February 20, 1809; married Lepha French, January 18, 1841, and settled in Washington.

His children were:

2931. 1. ANNA, b. at Washington, Mass., December 19, 1842. m. Porter Jenks, and resides at South Adams, Mass.
2932. 2. CHLOE, b. at Washington, March 31, 1845. d. January , 1847.
2933. 3. WILLIAM, b. at Washington, April 13, 1848.

1351.

OLIVER PEASE,⁷ (OLIVER,⁶ ISAAC,⁵ EZEKIEL,⁴ ISAAC,³ JOHN,² ROBERT,¹) brother of the preceding, was born at Washington, Mass., December 1, 1812; married Mercy D. Clapp, January 18, 1838, and lived some time in Washington. He now resides at East Longmeadow, Mass., a farmer.

His children were:

2934. 1. MARY J., b. at Washington, January 29, 1839.
2935. 2. MERCY D., b. at Washington, March 23, 1841. m. Mathias
           Udell, November   , 1867, and resides at St. Louis, Mo.
2936. 3. GEORGE R., b. at Washington, March 12, 1843.
2937. 4. ALBERT L., b. at Washington, December 19, 1845. m. Mary
           Hough, November   , 1868, and resides at Meriden, Ct.
2938. 5. ASAHEL, b. at Washington, August 8, 1846. m. Emma
           Chapin, November   , 1867, and resides at Springfield,
           Mass.
2939. 6. CHARLES D., b. at Washington, October 2, 1847.
2940. 7. RANSOM O., b. at Washington, September 6, 1851.
2941. 8. OLIVER A., b. at Washington, May 8, 1853.
2942. 9. ISAAC M., b. at Washington, May 27, 1856.
2942.⁵⁵ 10. FRANK E., b. at Washington, August   , 1859.

1356.

ISAAC PEASE,[7] (OLIVER,[6] ISAAC,[5] EZEKIEL,[4] ISAAC,[3] JOHN,[2] ROBERT,[1]) brother of the preceding, was born at Washington, Mass., February 4, 1825; married Maria Perry of Lenox, Mass., October 9, 1863, and resides at Lenox.

———o———

1360.

ISAAC T. PEASE,[7] (ISAAC,[6] ISAAC,[5] EZEKIEL,[4] ISAAC,[3] JOHN,[2] ROBERT,[1]) second son of ISAAC and ELIZABETH (TERRY) PEASE, some time of East Longmeadow, Mass., and last of Enfield, Ct., and first cousin of the preceding, was born at East Longmeadow, April 11, 1809; married first, Margaret Terry,   ; married second, Mrs. Margaret (Collins) Kingsbury, April 10, 1858, and resides at Enfield. He is an ingenious mechanic, and is the inventor of a fire and burglar alarm which promises to be of considerable importance.

His children were:

2943. 1. MARGARET E., b. at Enfield, April 19, 1836. m. Ruggles
           Gleason,   . d. at Enfield, April 29, 1864.

2944. 2. James, b. at Enfield, February 3, 1838. m. Chloe Hayden, and resides at Hartford, Ct.

2945. 3. Catharine, b. at Enfield, June 21, 1841. m. Abraham Cope, a tinner, March 10, 1869, and resides in Thompsonville, Ct.

1361.

HENRY S. PEASE,[7] (Isaac,[6] Isaac,[5] Ezekiel,[4] Isaac,[3] John,[2] Robert,[1]) brother of the preceding, was born at East Longmeadow, April 14, 1812; married Mabel Squire, April 19, 1836. He was a carriage maker, and lived some time in Somers, Ct. He died in Enfield, February 7, 1847.

His child was:

2946. 1. Mandana S., b. at   , June 12, 1837. d. December 20, 1864, unmarried.

1362.

THEODORE PEASE,[7] (Isaac,[6] Isaac,[5] Ezekiel,[4] Isaac,[3] John,[2] Robert,[1]) brother of the preceding, was born at East Longmeadow, Mass., January 22, 1815; married first, Evelina Killam, November 15, 1838; married second, Julia E. Steele, September 10, 1867, and resides at Enfield. He was for a time a tin-ware manufacturer, but is now a farmer and dealer in lumber.

His children were:

2947. 1. Julia A., b. at Enfield, Ct., July 23, 1840. d. May , 1843.

2948. 2. Harriet E., b. at Enfield, September 21, 1843. m. Albert Terry, a farmer, January 1, 1869, and resides at Enfield.

2949. 3. Theodore I., b. at Enfield, September 18, 1844. m. Jane E. Ellis, January 1, 1868, and resides at Enfield. He is Town Clerk and Treasurer.

2950. 4. Julia A., b. at Enfield, January 21, 1846.

2951. 5. Henry S., b. at Enfield, November 27, 1847.

2952. 6. Leora R., b. at Enfield, June 10, 1854.

1369.

HIRAM PEASE,[7] (DANIEL,[6] ISAAC,[5] EZEKIEL,[4] ISAAC,[3] JOHN,[2] ROBERT,[1]) second son of DANIEL and MARGARET (ALLEN) PEASE of Springfield, Mass., and first cousin of the preceding, was born at Springfield, April 18, 1814; married Agnes Allen,   , 1839. He lived in the east part of Springfield, and died suddenly, December 30, 1853, while eating at the table.

His children were:

2953. 1. ELIZA ANN, b. at Springfield, Mass.,   , 1840.
2954. 2. JEROME H., b. at Springfield, February 21, 1841. He was drowned in 1845.
2955. 3. LAURETTA A., b. at Springfield, April 16, 1844.
2956. 4. ALBERT A., b. at Springfield, October 22, 1850.

1372.

LUKE A. PEASE,[7] (DANIEL,[6] ISAAC,[5] EZEKIEL,[4] ISAAC,[3] JOHN,[2] ROBERT,[1]) brother of the preceding, was born at Springfield, Mass., October 3, 1821; married Mary G. Ufford of Springfield, December 2, 1847, and settled in South Wilbraham, Mass.

His children were:

2957. 1. NELLIE M., b. at East Longmeadow, Mass., November 14, 1848.
2958. 2. EDWARD L., b. at East Longmeadow, January 17, 1850. d. of diphtheria, December 5, 1864, aged 15 years.
2959. 3. FRANK G., b. at South Hadley, Mass., October 13, 1855.
2960. 4. ROLLO C., b. at South Wilbraham, Mass., July 10, 1858. d. of diphtheria, December 5, 1864, aged 7 years. Edward and Rollo died the same day:—Thus faded the beautiful flowers and cherished hopes of this afflicted family, in one sorrowful day. Lovely in life and undivided in death!

1374.

ALBERT PEASE,[7] (DANIEL,[6] ISAAC,[5] EZEKIEL,[4] ISAAC,[3] JOHN,[2] ROBERT,[1]) brother of the preceding, was born at

Springfield, Mass., May 30, 1824; married Emily M. Poole of Springfield, January 16, 1853. He was for several years a pilot on the steamer "Granite State" between Hartford and New York. He died at Nicaragua, December 9, 1856.

His child was:

2961. 1. WILLIS A., b. at Springfield, June   , 1854.

———o———

1379.

REUBEN A. PEASE,[7] (REUBEN,[6] ISAAC,[5] EZEKIEL,[4] ISAAC,[3] JOHN,[2] ROBERT,[1]) eldest son of REUBEN and ABI (GOWDY) PEASE of Enfield, Ct., known from a child as "Ashmun Pease," and first cousin of the preceding, was born at Enfield, July 28, 1814; married first, Hancy A. Hall of Somers, Ct., October 17, 1837; married second, Jane S. Cooley of Somers, March 7, 1850, and settled a farmer upon the "old homestead" in Enfield, in the village of Scitico. He died July 24, 1867, leaving a cherished memory as an esteemed citizen and devoted Christian. He had been honored many times with responsible public offices of trust, the gifts of his townsmen. For nearly thirty-seven years he had led a life of daily prayer, and been an exemplary member of a branch of the Christian church. When he had departed, members of his church and members of the community exclaimed, "whom have we to make his place good?"

Mr. Pease took a deep interest in the proposed publication of this work, and rode over his native and adjoining towns, calling upon his kinsmen and obtained the first list of subscribers for the work, that gave prestige of its final success.

His children were:

2962. 1. MARCIA M., b. at Enfield, Ct., July 31, 1839. m. Loren H.
      Pease, M. D., July 21, 1859, and resides at Thompsonville, Ct.
2963. 2. LAURINDA O., b. at Enfield, August 24, 1841. d. May 17,
      1847.

2964.   3. Denslow A., b. at Enfield, January 20, 1845.   m. Delia M.
        Merrill, March 11, 1868, and resides at Ashland, Mass., a
        merchant.
2965.   4. Orlando T., b. at Enfield, September 16, 1847.   d. September 16, 1849.

BY SECOND WIFE:

2966.   5. Harriet E., b. at Enfield, May 12, 1852.
2967.   6. Hancie J., b. at Enfield, July 23, 1857.
2968.   7. A son, b. at Enfield, January 18, 1860.   d. an infant.

1381.

AUSTIN S. PEASE,[7] (Reuben,[6] Isaac,[5] Ezekiel,[4]
Isaac,[3] John,[2] Robert,[1]) brother of the preceding, was
born at Enfield, May 9, 1820; married Sarah W., daughter of William Richardson of Hadley, Mass., April 18,
1849, and first settled in Springfield.   In 1857 he removed
to Dalton, Mass.; to Boston in 1866, and again to Springfield in 1868.

Mr. Pease began his academic education at the Wes-
leyan Academy, Wilbraham, Mass., and completed it at
the South New Market (N. H.) Seminary.   He learned
the trade of a mason and alternated this trade and that
of school teaching as an occupation for some twelve
years of his life.   For the past twenty years he has been
engaged chiefly in mercantile pursuits.   During the past
thirteen years· he has largely employed his leisure hours
as an assistant in collecting material for an extended
genealogy of the Enfield (Ct.) Peases.   When residing
at Boston, he conceived the plan of preparing an early
history of the Pease families in America.   With a taste
for genealogical pursuits which he possessed, his two
years' residence at Boston afforded him rare facilities for
his work.

His children are:

2969.   1. Artie A., b. at Springfield, Mass., April 10, 1850.
2970.   2. Louis A., b. at Springfield, July 6, 1852.
2971.   3. Clara A., b. at Springfield, April 19, 1856.
2972.   4. Sarah L., b. at Dalton, Mass., January 1, 1862.

1382.

ALEXANDER G. PEASE,[7] (Reuben,[6] Isaac,[5] Ezekiel,[4] Isaac,[3] John,[2] Robert,[1]) brother of the preceding, was born at Enfield, Ct., September 5, 1822; married Amanda H. Stevens, November 1, 1849; died at Springfield, Mass., November 27, 1861, aged 39 years. He had no children.

———o———

1383.

CALVIN PEASE,[7] (Calvin,[6] Isaac,[5] Ezekiel,[4] Isaac,[3] John,[2] Robert,[1]) eldest son of Calvin and Mary (Hale) Pease, first of Enfield, Ct., last of Longmeadow, Mass., and first cousin of the preceding, was born at Enfield, November 25, 1809; married Mary Scott, April 11, 1839, and settled in East Longmeadow, a farmer, and died there.

His children were:

2973.   1. Mary A., b. at Longmeadow, Mass.,   , 1841.
          m. Billings Cooley of Longmeadow, April 30, 1862.   d. August 18, 1867.
2974.   2. Harriet L., b. at Longmeadow, October 9, 1846.
2975.   3. Henry C., b. at Longmeadow, August 1, 1848.

1385.

ALONZO PEASE,[7] (Calvin,[6] Isaac,[5] Ezekiel,[4] Isaac,[3] John,[2] Robert,[1]) brother of the preceding, was born at Enfield, Ct., January 12, 1814; married Marcia Nead, May 11, 1855, and resides at East Longmeadow, Mass., a farmer. He has no children.

1387.

MERVIN H. PEASE,[7] (Calvin,[6] Isaac,[5] Ezekiel,[4] Isaac,[3] John,[2] Robert,[1]) brother of the preceding, was

born at Longmeadow, Mass., February 20, 1819; married
Mrs. Ruby S. (Brace) Hale, January 22, 1851, and resides
at East Longmeadow, a farmer.

His children were:

2976.   1. REBECCA A., b. at Longmeadow, Mass., December 10. 1853.
2976.⁵⁶   2. MERVIN H., b. at Longmeadow, January 22, 1860.

---o---

1391.

ORVILLE PEASE,⁷ (ABEL,⁶ ISAAC,⁵ EZEKIEL,⁴ ISAAC,³
JOHN,² ROBERT,¹) eldest son of ABEL and HANNAH (MC-
GREGORY) PEASE of East Longmeadow, Mass., and first
cousin of the preceding, was born at East Longmeadow,
June 25, 1813; married Julia Indicott, January 13, 1836,
and resided some time at East Longmeadow, but now
resides at South Wilbraham, Mass. He is a farmer and
manufacturer.

His children are:

2977.   1. MORTIMER, b. at East Longmeadow, December 27, 1837. m.
          Ellen Cunningham, March 29, 1864, and resides at South
          Wilbraham, Mass., a farmer. He was in the late war for the
          suppression of the rebellion, in the Forty-sixth Regiment of
          Massachusetts Volunteers, Company I. He was taken
          prisoner and confined in Libby prison, Richmond, Va.,
          but soon afterwards liberated on parole and allowed to go
          home.
2978.   2. JULIA O., b. at East Longmeadow, March 26, 1850. m.
          J. Marshall Burt, November 20, 1867, and resides at East
          Longmeadow.

1392.

ABEL PEASE,⁷ (ABEL,⁶ ISAAC,⁵ EZEKIEL,⁴ ISAAC,³
JOHN,² ROBERT,¹) brother of the preceding, was born
at East Longmeadow, Mass.,   , 1815; married
Louisa Ainsworth of East Longmeadow,   , 1838,
and settled in East Longmeadow, a farmer.

His children are:

2979.   1. Foster A., b. at East Longmeadow, Mass.,   , 1839.
         m. Francina McGregory, May 31, 1860, and resides at
         Longmeadow.
2980.   2. Frank, b. at East Longmeadow, July 30, 1842.
2981.   3. Ella L., b. at East Longmeadow, June 25, 1849.
2981.⁷⁷   4. Lilla, b. at East Longmeadow, March 3, 1858.

1393.

DEA. WARREN PEASE,⁷ (ABEL,⁶ ISAAC,⁵ EZEKIEL,⁴ ISAAC,³ JOHN,² ROBERT,¹) brother of the preceding, was born at East Longmeadow, Mass., September 25, 1818; married Lois Ainsworth, December 30, 1841, and settled a farmer in East Longmeadow, but now resides at Springfield, Mass.

His children are:

2982.   1. Landemer, b. at East Longmeadow,   - , 1844.
2983.   2. Edward W., b. at East Longmeadow, January   , 1850.
2984.   3. Clarence A., b. at East Longmeadow, May   , 1853.
2985.   4. Ellen L., b. at East Longmeadow, November 11, 1858.

——ooo——

FAMILY OF TIMOTHY.⁴

1402.

JONATHAN B. PEASE,⁷ (JONATHAN,⁶ TIMOTHY,⁵ TIMOTHY,⁴ ISAAC,³ JOHN,² ROBERT,¹) only son of JONATHAN aud LURANA (SWEATLAND) PEASE, first of Longmeadow, Mass., last of Springfield, Mass., and third cousin of the preceding, was born at Springfield, May 7, 1829; married Elizabeth Putnam, October   , 1861. He left Springfield and settled in Painsville, Minn., and is a Justice of the Peace in that place.

His children are:

2986.   1. John, b. at
2987.   2.

——oo——

1405.

TIMOTHY W. PEASE,[7] (TIMOTHY,[6] EDWARD,[5] TIM-OTHY,[4] ISAAC,[3] JOHN,[2] ROBERT,[1]) only son of TIMOTHY and ABIGAIL (HALE) PEASE of Enfield, Ct., and second cousin of the preceding, was born at Enfield, April 30, 1811; married   , and settled in (Hazard-ville) Enfield.

———o———

1408.

FRANCIS L. PEASE,[7] (HEBER,[6] EDWARD,[5] TIMOTHY,[4] ISAAC,[3] JOHN,[2] ROBERT,[1]) eldest son of HEBER and MI-NERVA (ALLEN) PEASE of Enfield, Ct., and first cousin of the preceding, was born at Enfield, May 15, 1822; mar-ried Julia Parker, December 25, 1843, and settled in Springfield, Mass., where he now resides.

His child is:

2988.   1. SANFORD D., b. at Springfield, Mass., 1844.   m. Katharine
Field, December 6, 1867, and resides at Springfield.

1410.

SIMEON H. PEASE,[7] (HEBER,[6] EDWARD,[5] TIMOTHY,[4] ISAAC,[3] JOHN,[2] ROBERT,[1]) brother of the preceding, was born at Enfield, Ct., May 31, 1826; married Mary J. Parsons, May 1, 1856, and resides at Milford, Mass.

His child is:

2989.   1. CHARLES H., b. at   , 1851.

1415.

LUTHER A. PEASE,[7] (HEBER,[6] EDWARD,[5] TIMOTHY,[4] ISAAC,[3] JOHN,[2] ROBERT,[1]) brother of the preceding, was born at Enfield, June 12, 1836; married Catherine Wolfe, September 27, 1856, and lives in New York City.

His children are:

2989.⁵⁸ 1. GEORGE, b. at

2989.⁵⁹ 2. KATHARINE, b. at

2989.⁶⁰ 3. FRANCES, b. at

2989.⁶¹ 4. CHARLES, b. at

———oo———

1424.

DR. LUTHER L. PEASE,⁷ (LUTHER,⁶ JAMES,⁵ TIMOTHY,⁴ ISAAC,³ JOHN,² ROBERT,¹) eldest son of LUTHER and NANCY (PEASE) PEASE of   , and second cousin of the preceding, was born at Springfield, Mass., January 10, 1813; married Miss   Baker, May , 1861. He is, by profession, a physician, and resides at Mount Vernon, Iowa. He was a surgeon in the army during the late war.

His children are:

2990. 1. LUTHER, b. at Fort Dodge, Iowa,   , 1862.

2991. 2. ELIZABETH, b. at Fort Dodge,   , 1864.

1425.

JAMES C. PEASE,⁷ (LUTHER,⁶ JAMES,⁵ TIMOTHY,⁴ ISAAC,³ JOHN,² ROBERT,¹) brother of the preceding, was born at Enfield, Ct., January 9, 1815; married Eliza Hall of Concord, Ohio, October 24, 1839, and resides at Sycamore, Wyandott County, Ohio, a farmer.

His children were:

2992. 1. MARTHA M., b. at Sycamore, Ohio, June 29, 1839. d. April 16, 1866.

2993. 2. JAMES V., b. at Sycamore, February 28, 1842.

2994. 3. JOSEPHINE E., b. at Sycamore, January 28, 1844.

2995. 4. MYRON E., b. at Sycamore, January 9, 1848.

2996. 5. LUTHER D., b. at Sycamore, November 18, 1856.

1426.

LORIN A. PEASE,⁷ (LUTHER,⁶ JAMES,⁵ TIMOTHY,⁴ ISAAC,³ JOHN,² ROBERT,¹) brother of the preceding, was born at Burton, Ohio, March 10, 1818; married first Elizabeth Vaughn, November 30, 1837; married second, Nancy A. Parsons, September 16, 1843, and resides at Sycamore, Ohio. He is, by occupation, a farmer.

His children were:

2997. 1. EUGENE C., b. at Sycamore, Ohio, June 29, 1839. m. Amanda C. Lee, April 2, 1862.

2998. 2. VICTOR C., b. at Sycamore, November 29, 1841.

BY SECOND WIFE:

2999. 3. FRANCINA L., b. at Sycamore, July 8, 1846. d. December 14, 1846.

———o———

1427.

SEYMORE PEASE,[7] (JACOB,[6] JAMES,[5] TIMOTHY,[4] ISAAC,[3] JOHN,[2] ROBERT,[1]) son of JACOB and (WARNER) PEASE, last of Mentor, Ohio, and first cousin of the preceding, was born at   , Ohio,   . He ,was, by trade, a machinist, and in 1838 resided in Cleveland, Ohio.

———ooo———

FAMILY OF CUMMINGS.[4]

1432.

JOHN Q. A. PEASE,[7] (ROSWELL,[6] CUMMINGS,[5] CUMMINGS,[4] ISAAC,[3] JOHN,[2] ROBERT,[1]) only son of ROSWELL and AVON (BLISS) PEASE of Chicopee, Mass., and third cousin of the preceding, was born at Chicopee, April 14, 1826; married first, Mariette Eaton, January 10, 1856; married second, S. Sophia Allen, November 4, 1858, and settled in Chicopee, a farmer.

His children are:

3000. 1. GEORGE H., b. at Chicopee, Mass., February 8, 1860.

3001. 2. CLARENCE E., b. at Chicopee, December 3, 1861.

3002. 3. JOHN A., b. at Chicopee, July 10, 1864.

3002.[62] 4. ETHWALD C., b. at Chicopee, January 13, 1869.

———o———

1434.

THEODORE W. PEASE,⁷ (WILDER C.,⁶ CUMMINGS,⁵ CUMMINGS,⁴ ISAAC,³ JOHN,² ROBERT,¹) eldest son of DEA. WILDER C., and RUTH (CADY) PEASE, first of Wilbraham, Mass., subsequently of Enfield, Ct., and first cousin of the preceding, was born at Wilbraham, October 15, 1816; married Catharine Chapin, April 26, 1847, and resided for some time at Thompsonville, Ct. He now resides at Cohoes, N. Y., (1868,) and is superintendent of a stockinet manufactory.

His children are:

3003.   1. NORMAN T., b. at Enfield, Ct., August 14, 1850.
3004.   2. MARY H., b. at Enfield, January 19, 1853.
3005.   3. CHARLES S., b. at Enfield, December 10, 1865.

1435.

JOSEPH R. PEASE,⁷ (WILDER C.,⁶ CUMMINGS,⁵ CUMMINGS,⁴ ISAAC,³ JOHN,² ROBERT,¹) brother of the preceding, was born at Wilbraham, Mass.,   , 1818; married first, Lucinda Bush,   ; married second, Mary Lawler,   , 1852, and settled in Enfield.

His children were:

3006.   1. JOHN R., b. at Enfield, Ct.

BY SECOND WIFE:

3007.   2. ROBERT R., b. at Enfield.
3008.   3. EMMA L., b. at Enfield.
3009.   4. WILLIAM, b. at Enfield, September   , 1860.

1436.

HENRY A. PEASE,⁷ (WILDER C.,⁶ CUMMINGS,⁵ CUMMINGS,⁴ ISAAC,³ JOHN,² ROBERT,¹) brother of the preceding, was born at Wilbraham, Mass.,   , 1821; married first, Harriet Chapin; married second, Alice Albro,   , 1855, and resides at Hartford, Ct.

His child was:

3010.   1. HARRIET E., b. at

1437.

DR. LEVI S. PEASE,[7] (WILDER C.,[6] CUMMINGS,[5] CUM-MINGS,[4] ISAAC,[3] JOHN,[2] ROBERT,[1]) brother of the preceding, was born at Wilbraham, Mass.,   , 1824; married Susan Stebbins, and settled at Thompsonville, (Enfield,) Ct., a physician.   He went out as assistant surgeon in the Eighth Connecticut Regiment of Volunteers, in 1862, and acted as surgeon in that regiment and others, and hospital service over three years.

His children are:

3011.   1. NOEL M., b. at   , August 9, 1851.
3012.   2. WILDER C., b. at   , February   , 1856,

1445.

JAMES H. PEASE,[7] (JAMES C.,[6] CUMMINGS,[5] CUM-MINGS,[4] ISAAC,[3] JOHN,[2] ROBERT,[1]) eldest son of JAMES C., and MALINDA (BOOTH) PEASE of Wilbraham, Mass., and first cousin of the preceding, was born at Wilbraham, May 9, 1813; married Jennette Giddings,   , 1858, and settled in Springfield.   He is, by occupation, a stone dealer and farmer.

His child is:

3013.   1. CLIFFORD E., b. at Springfield, April 1, 1862.

1446.

LORIN C. PEASE,[7] (JAMES C.,[6] CUMMINGS,[5] CUM-MINGS,[4] ISAAC,[3] JOHN,[2] ROBERT,[1]) brother of the preceding, was born at Wilbraham, Mass., July 15, 1815; married Sarah Turner, April 11, 1848, and settled in Wilbraham.

His children were:

3014. 1. George L., b. at Wilbraham, Mass., January 31, 1849.
3015. 2. John M., b. at Wilbraham, March 1, 1851.
3016. 3. Lillie E., b. at Wilbraham, July 23, 1858. d. November 18, 1862.
3017. 4. Frederick C., b. at Wilbraham, February 18, 1865.

1447.

ALBERT A. PEASE,[7] (James C.,[6] Cummings,[5] Cummings,[4] Isaac,[3] John,[2] Robert,[1]) brother of the preceding, was born at Wilbraham, Mass., December 9, 1817; married Mary Hill, December 16, 1840; died 1859.

His child was:

3018. 1. Albert K., b. at

1452.

JEROME PEASE,[7] (James C.,[6] Cummings,[5] Cummings,[4] Isaac,[3] John,[2] Robert,[1]) son of James C. and Mary (Terry) Pease, and half-brother of the preceding, was born at Wilbraham, Mass., March 7, 1830; married Lucinda Burr,   , and settled in Wilbraham.

His children were:

3019. 1. Martha A., b. at Wilbraham, Mass.,   , 1856.
3020. 2. Lizzie M., b. at Wilbraham, October   , 1857.
3021. 3. Ida L., b. at   , 1862.
3022. 4. Willie J., b. at   , 1864.   d. an infant.
3023. 5. Minnie E., (twin) b. at   , 1864.

1453.

MONROE PEASE,[7] (James C.,[6] Cummings,[5] Cummings,[4] Isaac,[3] John,[2] Robert,[1]) brother of the preceding, was born at Wilbraham, Mass., March 28, 1832; married Harriet Foster, May 17, 1855, and settled in Wilbraham.

41

His children were :

3024. 1. CHARLES M., b. at Wilbraham, Mass.,   , 1856.
3025. 2. ADELBERT F., b. at Wilbraham, August 4, 1860. d. January 13, 1862.
3026. 3. HATTIE E., b. at Wilbraham, July 5, 1862. d. an infant.
3027. 4. CORA MAY, b. at Wilbraham, May 29, 1864.
3028. 5. ALBERT H., b. at Wilbraham, January 6, 1866.

1462.

CARLOS PEASE,[7] (SHUBAEL,[6] CUMMINGS,[5] CUMMINGS,[4] ISAAC,[3] JOHN,[2] ROBERT,[1]) eldest son of SHUBAEL and ELIZABETH (KIBBE) PEASE, first of Longmeadow, Mass., subsequently of Wilbraham, Mass., and now (1865) of Somers, Ct., and first cousin of the preceding, was born at Springfield, Mass., May 16, 1825; married Ruby A. Myers of North Adams, Mass., May 7, 1855, and lives at Springfield, (Indian Orchard.)

His children were :

3028.[63] 1. GILBERT C., b. at Springfield, Mass., February 4, 1857.
3028.[64] 2. CLARENCE, b. at Springfield, October 3, 1859. d. January 11, 1860.
3028.[65] 3. FREDDIE L., b. at Springfield, March 4, 1862. d. June 16, 1864.

1463.

ERSKINE PEASE,[7] (SHUBAEL,[6] CUMMINGS,[5] CUMMINGS,[4] ISAAC,[3] JOHN,[2] ROBERT,[1]) brother of the preceding, was born at   , May   , 1827; married Mary A. Gould,   , 1860, and settled in Springfield, Mass., (Indian Orchard.)

His children were :

3029. 1. MARY J., b. at Springfield, Mass., July , 1863.
3030. 2. MINERVA, b. at Springfield, February , 1865.

1466.

MERRIL PEASE,[7] (EBENEZER,[6] EBENEZER,[5] CUMMINGS,[4] ISAAC,[3] JOHN,[2] ROBERT,[1]) eldest son of EBENEZER and

ABIGAIL (KIBBE) PEASE, first of Andover, Vt., subsequently of Brasher, N. Y., and second cousin of the preceding, was born at Andover, Vt.,   ; married Charlotte Lowns, and settled in Rose, Wayne County, N. Y., where he was living in 1860 without children.

1467.

ALANSON PEASE,⁷ (EBENEZER,⁶ EBENEZER,⁵ CUMMINGS,⁴ ISAAC,³ JOHN,² ROBERT,¹) brother of the preceding, was born at Georgia, Vt.,   ; married Nancy Jeffry,   , and directly upon the conclusion of the war of 1812, removed to Rose, Wayne County, N. Y., where he died,   , 1847.

His child was:

3031. 1. JOHN N., b. at

1468.

REV. EBENEZER PEASE,⁷ (EBENEZER,⁶ EBENEZER,⁵ CUMMINGS,⁴ ISAAC,³ JOHN,² ROBERT,¹) brother of the preceding, was born at Georgia, Vt.,   , 1802; married first, Catherine McCoy, December 21, 1826, who died January 27, 1829; married second,   ; married third, Nancy Healy, October 11, 1847. He had no children by his first two wives. He was licensed as an exhorter in the Methodist connection at South Hero, Vt., August 10, 1823, and as a local preacher by the district conference at Middlebury, Vt., and ordained as an elder in the Methodist Episcopal Church at Potsdam, N. Y. He has been a member and traveled in the Black River Conference ten years. His present home is at Brasher, N. Y.

His children are:

3032. 1. CATHARINE S., b. at Massena, N. Y., September   , 1848.
3033. 2. MARY G., b. at Lisbon, January 2, 1850.
3034. 3. NANCY MOTT, b. at Bangor, September 9, 1852.

1469.

BRADLEY PEASE,[7] (EBENEZER,[6] EBENEZER,[5] CUM-
MINGS,[4] ISAAC,[3] JOHN,[2] ROBERT,[1]) brother of the preceding, was born at Georgia, Vt.,   ; married
                    , and died in the State of Louisiana.

His child was:

3035. 1.   d. young.

1470.

NELSON PEASE,[7] (EBENEZER,[6] EBENEZER,[5] CUMMINGS,[4]
ISAAC,[3] JOHN,[2] ROBERT,[1]) brother of the preceding, was
born at Georgia, Vt.,   ; married Martha
Hawkins,   . He had seven children who
are all dead but one, and appear to have died unmarried.

His children were:

3036. 1. HANNAH, b. at
3037. 2.
3038. 3.
3039. 4.
3040. 5.
3041. 6.
3042. 7.

———o———

1480.

JOEL H. PEASE,[7] (ENOCH,[6] EBENEZER,[5] CUMMINGS,[4]
ISAAC,[3] JOHN,[2] ROBERT,[1]) second son of ENOCH and BET-
SEY (HOUGHTON) PEASE, first of Enosburgh, Vt., last of
Fairfield, Vt., and first cousin of the preceding, was born
at Enosburgh, May 4, 1818; married Lucinda W. Murphy,
January 19, 1842, and settled in Fairfax, Vt., a dealer in
produce.

His children were:

3043. 1. JOEL E., b. at Fairfax, Vt., December 4, 1843. d. December
          12, 1846.
3044. 2. CHARLOTTE A., b. at Fairfax, May 16, 1845. m. C. DeForest
          Currier of Troy, N. Y., October 27, 1865.

3045.   3. Joel E.,² b. at Fairfax, November 8, 1846.
3046.   4. Sarah L., b. at Fairfax, November 27, 1848.
3047.   5. James E., b. at Fairfax, December 22, 1849.
3048.   6. Cynthia A., b. at Fairfax, February 4, 1854.

1482.

HUBBARD W. PEASE,⁷ (Enoch,⁶ Ebenezer,⁵ Cummings,⁴ Isaac,³ John,² Robert,¹) brother of the preceding, was born at Enosburgh, Vt., September 10, 1822; married Maria Murphy of Swanton, Vt., October 9, 1843, and settled in Fairfax, a farmer.

His children were:

3049.   1. Julia A., b. at Fairfax, Vt., November 16, 1844.
3050.   2. Charles L., b. at Fairfax, February 11, 1846. d.   1848.
3051.   3. Charles E., b. at Richford, Vt., October 15, 1849.
3052.   4. Herbert L., b. at Richford, February 24, 1854.

———o———

1493.

CORDON PEASE,⁷ (Abel,⁶ Ebenezer,⁵ Cummings,⁴ Isaac,³ John,² Robert,¹) eldest son of Abel and Lucy (Laughlin) Pease, first of Georgia, Vt., last of Brasher, N. Y., and first cousin of the preceding, was born at Georgia,   , 1807; married Amy Wilson,   and removed to Chicago, Ill.

His children were:

3053.   1. Joel, b. at
3054.   2. Bradley, b. at
3055.   3. Aminia, b. at
3056.   4. Fanny, b. at
3057.   5. Ira, b. at

1494.

SAMUEL I. PEASE,⁷ (Abel,⁶ Ebenezer,⁵ Cummings,⁴ Isaac,³ John,² Robert,¹) brother of the preceding, was born in Canada, July 4, 1809; married Irena Hamlin, July 18, 1837, and settled in Lawrence, N. Y.

His children were:

3058. 1. JAMES A., b. at Brasher, N. Y., May 12, 1838. m. Melissa Shelten, July 4, 1858.

3059. 2. SYDNEY B., b. at Lawrence, N. Y., June 9, 1839.

3060. 3. CYRUS M., b. at Lawrence, October 14, 1841. m. Irene Rice, March 23, 1866, and lives in Illinois.

3061. 4. NELSON H., b. at Lawrence, December 8, 1844. m. Irene Riggs, March 23, 1866, and resides in Illinois.

3062. 5. MILO L., b. at Lawrence, January 5, 1847.

3063. 6. HIRAM A., b. at Lawrence, April 6, 1850.

3064. 7. JULIA E., b. at Lawrence, May 4, 1855.

1496.

HORATIO N. PEASE,[7] (ABEL,[6] EBENEZER,[5] CUMMINGS,[4] ISAAC,[3] JOHN,[2] ROBERT,[1]) brother of the preceding, was born in Canada, October 14, 1813; married Minerva Austin,   , 1855, and removed to Chicago, Ill., and since then to California. He has five children, two sons and three daughters.

His children were:

3065. 1.

3066. 2.

3067. 3.

3068. 4.

3069. 5.

1497.

GEORGE W. PEASE,[7] (ABEL,[6] EBENEZER,[5] CUMMINGS,[4] ISAAC,[3] JOHN,[2] ROBERT,[1]) brother of the preceding, was born in Canada, March 26, 1815; married Phebe Clark, , 1840, and settled in Lawrence, N. Y.

His children were:

3070. 1. AFFINIA, b. at   , 1841.

3071. 2. SARAH E., b. at   , 1843.

3072. 3. AMINIA, b. at

1498.

ABEL PEASE,[7] (ABEL,[6] EBENEZER,[5] CUMMINGS,[4] ISAAC,[3] JOHN,[2] ROBERT,[1]) brother of the preceding, was born at Georgia, Vt., April 4, 1817; married Sallie Clark, January 26, 1842, and resides at North Lawrence, N. Y.

His children were:

3073.   1. TRUMAN A., b. at Brasher, N. Y., November 27, 1842. He
served as assistant surgeon in the United States hospital at
Cumberland, Md., during the late rebellion.
3074.   2. BENJAMIN U., b. at Brasher, November 31, 1844. d. January
27, 1854.
3075.   3. LEWIS L., b. at Lawrence, N. Y., December 3, 1845. He
served in the late war.
3076.   4. CALVIN H., b. at Lawrence, April 1, 1848.
3077.   5. WILLIAM H., b. at Lawrence, November 29, 1849.
3078.   6. DAVID C., b. at Lawrence, April 5, 1852. d. July 1, 1863.

1500.

CHAUNCEY O. PEASE,⁷ (ABEL,⁶ EBENEZER,⁵ CUM-
MINGS,⁴ ISAAC,³ JOHN,² ROBERT,¹) brother of the preced-
ing, was born at   ; married Arvilla
Adams,   , 1849, and settled in Lawrence, N. Y.

His children were:

3079.   1. NELSON O., b. at Lawrence, N. Y., January 14, 1850.
3080.   2. ALMIRA E., b. at Lawrence, December 14, 1856.
3081.   3. GEORGE A. L., b. at Brasher, N. Y., October 13, 1860.

———OO———

1504.

ELAM L. PEASE,⁷ (ELAM,⁶ ASA,⁵ CUMMINGS,⁴ ISAAC,³
JOHN,² ROBERT,¹) eldest son of ELAM and ANN (TERRY)
PEASE of Enfield, Ct., and second cousin of the preceding,
was born at Enfield, October 21, 1814; married Mary
Pease, daughter of Julius Pease of Warehouse Point, Ct.,
        , 1850, and settled in Enfield, a farmer.

His children were:

3082.   1. MARIA E., b. at Enfield, Ct., April   , 1852.
3083.   2. ELAM H., b. at Enfield, January   , 1855.

———O———

1517.

JOSEPH PEASE,[7] (ALPHEUS,[6] ASA,[5] CUMMINGS,[4] ISAAC,[3] JOHN,[2] ROBERT,[1]) third and youngest son of ALPHEUS and AZUBA (KINGSBURY) PEASE of Pennsylvania, and first cousin of the preceding, was born at Enfield, Ct., December 25, 1820; married   , 1862, and lives in Warren, Bradford County, Pa.

———oo———

1518.

JEROME PEASE,[7] (HEMAN,[6] HEMAN,[5] CUMMINGS,[4] ISAAC,[3] JOHN,[2] ROBERT,[1]) eldest son of HEMAN and ABIGAIL (COMBS) PEASE, last of Somers, Ct., and second cousin of the preceding, was born at Enfield, Ct., February 22, 1815; married Deborah Demorest,   , 1843, and settled in Otisco, Ionia County, Mich.

His children were:

3084.	1.		d. in infancy.
3085.	2. CHARLOTTE, b. at	, 1846.	m. Chauncey
	I. Pease,	, 1860.	
3086.	3. JEROME, b. at		, 1848.
3087.	4. SOPHRONIA, b. at		, 1850.
3088.	5. DEBORAH A., b. at		, 1853.

1520.

NATHANIEL PEASE,[7] (HEMAN,[6] HEMAN,[5] CUMMINGS,[4] ISAAC,[3] JOHN,[2] ROBERT,[1]) brother of the preceding, was born at Somers, Ct., September 30, 1824; married   ; his wife died about 1863. He is a second advent preacher, and makes his home in the State of Michigan.

His children were:

3089. 1.
3090. 2.

———o———

1524.

LESTER H. PEASE,⁷ (Pliny,⁶ Heman,⁵ Cummings,⁴ Isaac,³ John,² Robert,¹) only son of Pliny and Hannah (Fox) Pease, first of Bristol, N. Y., last of Grattan, Mich., and first cousin of the preceding, was born at Bristol, February 1, 1836; married Melinda A. Fox, October 29, 1861, and settled in Michigan.

His children were:
3091. 1.
3092. 2.

———o———

1530.

CHAUNCEY I. PEASE,⁷ (Chauncey,⁶ Heman,⁵ Cummings,⁴ Isaac,³ John,² Robert,¹) second son of Chauncey and Harriet (Crocker) Pease of Cannon, Kent County, Mich., and first cousin of the preceding, was born at Bristol, N. Y., May 5, 1843; married Charlotte Pease, , 1860.

His children were:
3093. 1.
3094. 2.

———o———

1536.

ALONZO PEASE,⁷ (Asa,⁶ Heman,⁵ Cummings,⁴ Isaac,³ John,² Robert,¹) eldest son of Asa and Amanda (Dunlap) Pease of Enfield, Ct., and first cousin of the preceding, was born at , February 14, 1824; married Sarah Hughton, , and resides at Chicopee Falls, Mass.

His children were:
3095. 1. Infant, b. at   . d. in infancy.
3096. 2. Elbert A., b. at   , January 7, 1850.

———oo———

1541.

Rev. DAVID PEASE, D. D.,⁷ (David,⁶ David,⁵ Cummings,⁴ Isaac,³ John,² Robert,¹) son of Rev. David and

42

DORCAS (AYRES) PEASE, first of Belchertown, Mass., subsequently of Conway, Mass., Cazenovia, N. Y., and now of
Ashfield, Mass., and second cousin of the preceding, was
born at Belchertown, September 24, 1815; married Amelia S. Allison of New York City, June 24, 1846. He
graduated at Williams College, Mass., in 1838. His divinity course was pursued under the direction of Bishop
De Lancey of the Protestant Episcopal Church of Western New York, and he subsequently entered the ministry
of that denomination. The degree of Doctor of Divinity
was conferred on him in 1856 by the Board of Trustees
of Stewart College, Tenn. Dr. Pease's first parochial
cure was in Christ Church, Manlius, Onondaga County,
N. Y.; his next in Trinity Church, Fayetteville, N. Y.;
his third in Trinity Church, Clarksville, Montgomery
County, Tenn.; his fourth at St. Peter's Church, Columbia,
Tenn. He was rector at the latter place some thirteen
years, and he has recently closed it (March, 1868,) and accepted a rectorate at New Albany, Ind. Besides his duties
as rector at Columbia, he was professor of Belle Lettres
and Mental and Moral Science in the Columbia Female
College.

His children were:

3097.　1. FREDERIC D., b. at Manlius March 27, 1847. d. at Clarks-
　　　　　ville, February 16, 1851.
3098.　2. WILLIAM T., b. at Fayetteville, July 19, 1850.
3099.　3. JOSEPHINE A., b. at Clarksville, September 3, 1852.
3100.　4. FRANCIS A., b. at Columbia, June 23, 1856. d. at Columbia,
　　　　　October 20, 1861.
3101.　5. CHARLES T. A., b. at Columbia, October 25, 1857.
3102.　6. ELIZABETH R., b. at Columbia, October 24, 1859.

1545.

SPENCER A. PEASE,[7] (DAVID,[6] DAVID,[5] CUMMINGS,[4]
ISAAC,[3] JOHN,[2] ROBERT,[1]) brother of the preceding, was
born at Cazenovia Village, N. Y., September 8, 1825;
married Elizabeth Duguid, only daughter of Russell Du-

guid of Pompey, N. Y., and first settled in Fayetteville, N. Y., subsequently at Pompey Center, and ultimately at Pavilion, N. Y., and was, by occupation, a saddle and harness-maker. He volunteered, with a number of his fellow-townsmen in the service of his country for the suppression of the rebellion, January, 1864, and was a member of the Eighth New York Heavy Artillery, Company I. He was instantly killed while charging the enemy's works at Cold Harbor, Va., June 3, 1864, and buried by his fellow-soldiers on the spot where he fell, in the 39th year of his age, leaving a widow and two children. He sustained the character of a consistent Christian before and after he entered the service.

In a letter from his commanding officer to his brother, he says: "He was a noble soldier, steady, brave, and a man of good habits. In fighting, he did credit to his country, his company, and himself, and by his death we have lost a noble and brave soldier."

This is here recorded for the benefit of tender minds, now too young to know the loss they sustain in common with thousands of others whose father's have been laid in unknown graves by the late rebellion; and that they might preserve as sacred in their memory, a life and death worthy their veneration.

His children were:

3103.   1. ADELAIDE E., b. at Fayetteville, N. Y., April 9, 1850. d. August , 1862.
3104.   2. FREDERICK S., b. at Pavilion, January 11, 1856.
3105.   3. NETTIE C., b. at Pompey, N. Y.,   , 1864.

1546.

BREVET LIEUTENANT COLONEL ROGER W. PEASE, M. D.,⁷ (DAVID,⁶ DAVID,⁵ CUMMINGS,⁴ ISAAC,³ JOHN,² ROBERT,¹) brother of the preceding, was born at Conway, Mass., May 31, 1828; married Hannah Fuller, daughter of James C. Fuller of Skaneateles, N. Y., January 26, 1858. He graduated at the College of Medicine and Surgery at Geneva, N. Y., January 25, 1848, and soon after commenced the practice of a physician and surgeon at Syracuse, N. Y.

Dr. Pease was among the first to respond to the call of his State and his country during the late war for the suppression of the rebellion. He left a large and successful practice which his skill and industry had gained him at Syracuse, and joined the Twelfth Regiment of New York Volunteer Infantry, as surgeon. This regiment was connected with what was afterwards called the ·Army of the Potomac. It was in the Fourth Brigade of the First Division of McDowell's Corps, and was in the advance at the commencement of the first campaign of the Army of the Potomac, and participated in the first day's fight with the enemy at Blackburn's Ford, July 18, 1861, three days before the disastrous fight at Bull Run. The contest was a sanguinary one, and it is claimed for our kinsman that he had the honor of dressing the first wound caused by the enemy in that army, though the wounded soldier was not a member of the Twelfth New York Regiment.

It appears that the division was checked in its advance on that day by the fire of the enemy's batteries. To silence them, General David Tyler, commander of the division, ordered forward the Fourth Brigade, including Captain Bracket's squadron of the Second United States Cavalry, and two twelve-pounder howitzers commanded by Captain Ayres. The first shot from the enemy's guns struck Sergeant Rowhan of Captain Bracket's squadron. As it was surgeon Pease's fortune to be standing near the wounded soldier at the time, he had the satisfaction of dressing his wound, and probably the first made on that day. Soon after this the skirmishing became general.

Immediately after dressing Sergeant Rowhan's wound, Surgeon Pease established a field hospital in a ravine directly under the fire of the enemy. At this place he dressed the wound of the heroic Lieutenant Lorain of Sherman's battery. The Twelfth New York Regiment was not engaged with the enemy on the 21st, yet there was abundant work found for its surgeon on that memorable day. Owing to the severe labors of this short campaign and the poisonous atmosphere of the Potomac marshes, Surgeon Pease was obliged to resign his position August 30, following, and return home.

After a few months of rest his health became restored and he returned to the army, November 19, 1861, as surgeon of the Tenth New York Cavalry. He spent the following winter at Gettysburg, Pa. He was detached from his regiment, April 19, 1862, and ordered to report to Major-General Dix at Baltimore, Md. Here he was assigned to the Patterson Park United States Hospital which he organized with twelve hundred beds. In November following he again returned to the field and participated in the battle at Fredericksburg, December 13, under Major-General Burnside.

February 25, 1863, Surgeon Pease was made Medical Inspector of the cavalry corps then being organized by General Stoneman, and was placed on his staff. When General Stoneman was relieved from command by General Pleasanton, he was retained in the same position by the latter. During the celebrated Stoneman raid and Major-General Hooker's campaign, Surgeon Pease was ordered to organize a Cavalry Corps Hospital at Aquia Creek. This was maintained as a field hospital during the entire existence of the cavalry corps, and as such it maintained a high reputation.

The performance of this last order did not prevent Surgeon Pease from being present and participating in the engagement at Chancellorsville. He was with his corps in the battles at Gettysburg, July 1st, 2d and 3d, and joined in the pursuit of the enemy at Boonsboro,

Md. At this place he was ordered by Surgeon Pancoast, Medical Director of the cavalry corps, to take charge of the field hospitals and to concentrate them at Boonsboro. When this was done he joined the army at Salem and participated in the engagements which drove the enemy across the Rapidan.

After this Surgeon Pease was transferred to the corps of surgeons of volunteers, and was ordered to report to the General commanding the Middle Department at Baltimore. December 2, 1863, he was ordered to relieve Surgeon Pancoast and he again returned to the field as Medical Director of the corps which he had so long served as Medical Inspector. During the winter of 1863 and '64, the cavalry corps was reorganized and General Philip H. Sheridan was placed in command, without any change in its Medical Director.

Our space will not allow us to mention the many bold and daring adventures and hard fought battles of the cavalry corps under its new commander during the successful campaign of 1864, and while our kinsman was connected with it. The whole responsibility of the medical and surgical department rested on the Medical Director. He must provide medical stores, hospitals and means of transportation for the sick and wounded. Surrounded on every side by the enemy in an enemy's country, as the cavalry corps often found themselves, this latter responsibility was the most difficult. In the expedition of General Sheridan towards the Virginia Central Railroad, and after the engagement with the enemy, June 12, and 13, at Trevillion Station, Surgeon Pease had four hundred wounded soldiers to transport to the White House, a distance of nearly two hundred miles and he had only twelve ambulances to do it with. But by scouring the enemy's country and seizing every available vehicle that could be found, and with the aid of thirty baggage-wagons all were conducted safely beyond the reach of the enemy and the consequent sufferings of those who had the misfortune to become prisoners of war to the enemy.

During the early part of the campaign against Richmond in 1864, Surgeon Pease at one time became so disabled as to be unfitted for riding in the saddle, and he was obliged to ask to be temporarily relieved and to be put on other duty. He was accordingly given in charge one of the first trains of wounded soldiers (three thousand five hundred in number) which were taken from the battle-fields of the Wilderness and removed to Fredericksburg. He remained at Fredericksburg for a short time as Inspector of Hospitals, but again returned to his corps in time to participate in the battles of Old Tavern and Cold Harbor.

In consequence of exposures in the field for nearly two years and a half, Surgeon Pease's health became so much impaired that he was compelled to ask to be permanently relieved from his position. His request was granted, and on the 8th of August he was ordered to Baltimore again and was placed in charge of the Newton United States General Hospital. About one year from that time he was ordered to Charlestown, West Virginia, to close the hospital in that place and dispose of the property. This being done, Dr. Pease again returned to Baltimore and was mustered out of service, October 1, 1865, with the rank of Brevet Lieutenant Colonel from the United States Government.

Since Dr. Pease's return to his practice in Syracuse, N. Y., he has received a commission from the Governor of his State with the rank of Brevet Lieutenant Colonel, bearing date September 6, 1866. The commission states that it is "for faithful and meritorious services in the late war, and as a testimonial for zeal, fidelity and courage, with which you have maintained the honor of the State of New York in her efforts to enforce the Laws of the United States."

His children were:

3106.   1. FRANK W., b. at Syracuse, N. Y., January 21, 1859. d. August 13, 1859.
3107.   2. HENRY H., b. at Syracuse, April 26, 1860.
3108.   3. AMELIA F., b. at Syracuse, December 17, 1861.
3109.   4. MARY E., b. at Baltimore, Md., November 20, 1864.

——o——

1549.

DAVID E. PEASE,[7] (JONATHAN S.,[6] DAVID,[5] CUMMINGS,[4] ISAAC,[3] JOHN,[2] ROBERT,[1]) third son of JONATHAN S. and HANNAH (WOOD) PEASE of Somers, Ct., and first cousin of the preceding, was born at Somers, July 18, 1815; married Caroline W. Herst of Georgia, Vt., April 16, 1838, and settled in Georgia, a merchant. He died March 27, 1846, aged 31 years.

His children were :

3110.   1. AMELIA H., b. at   , January 3, 1839.
3111.   2. SPENCER, b. at   ,   , April 4, 1840. d. an infant.
3112.   3. MARIETTE A., b. at   June 14, 1842.
3113.   4. DAVID E., b. at   , June 12, 1843.
3114.   5. OLIVIA, b. at   , 1845. d.   , 1846.

1550.

JOHN W. PEASE,[7] (JONATHAN S.,[6] DAVID,[5] CUMMINGS,[4] ISAAC,[3] JOHN,[2] ROBERT,[1]) brother of the preceding, was born at Somers, Ct., June 18, 1818; married Jane Ann Norman of Columbus, Ga., January   , 1848, and settled in Columbus. He is a wholesale and retail book merchant, and resided in Savannah, Ga., in 1868.

His children were:

3115.   1. JOHN W., b. at Columbus, October 4, 1848. d. in infancy.
3116.   2. DORA A., b. at Columbus, August 7, 1849.
3117.   3. JOHN E., b. at Columbus, August 4, 1852. d.   , 1853.
3118.   4. MARY A., b. at Columbus, August 15, 1853. d. 1855.

——o——

1555.

JONATHAN S. PEASE,[7] (Asa,[6] David,[5] Cummings,[4] Isaac,[3] John,[2] Robert,[1]) eldest son of Asa and Lydia (Sheldon) Pease of Parma, N. Y., and first cousin of the preceding, was born at Ovid, N. Y., March 11, 1820; married Maria A. Medbury of New Berlin, N. Y., March 13, 1848, and settled in West Greece, N. Y. He is, by occupation, a mechanic and common school teacher.

His children are:

3119. 1. Amelia E., b. at West Greece, N. Y., February 12, 1849.
3120. 2. Anna A., b. at West Greece,   , 1856.
3121. 3. Julius, b. at West Greece,   , 1859.

1560.

ASAHEL PEASE,[7] (Asa,[6] David,[5] Cummings,[4] Isaac,[3] John,[2] Robert,[1]) brother of the preceding, was born at Parma, N. Y., May 6, 1833; married Emily Janes, and settled in Albion, Mich.

His children are:

3122. 1. John R., b. at Albion, Mich.,   , 1858.
3123. 2. Asa, b. at Albion,   , 1860.
3124. 3. Kate, b. at Albion,   , 1862.

43

ADDENDA.

(Page 20.)

168. Since preparing the history of OLIVER PEASE, we have found the following on the Town Records at Enfield:—"Oliver Pease, son of Ezekiel Pease, died at Greenwich, November 2, 1776, being in the army for the defense of his country." Greenwich is in Hampshire County, Mass. He was probably on his way home from the army. Not having seen the account book referred to, we are unable to account for the discrepancy in the dates.

(Page 24.)

205. It is probable that JOSEPH PEASE died while connected with the revolutionary army, as a memorandum prepared by Joseph Pease, Esq., of names of persons who went into that army from Suffield, and who died in it or from disease contracted in the service, contains the name of " Joseph Pease, 2d."

(Page 26.)

208. KETURAH PEASE, m. Azariah Hall, and removed to Halifax, Vt.

65. JONATHAN PEASE, born in Enfield in 1732, and removed to Glastenbury, Ct., about 1762; m. Mary Bidwell of Glastenbury in 1765. His children were:

    1. JONATHAN, b. at Glastenbury, 1766. m., and resided for some time in New England, and then removed to the State of New York in the vicinity of the "Holland Purchase."

    2. MARY, b. at Glastenbury, 1769.

    3. DAVID, b. at Glastenbury, 1771.

    4. DARIUS, b. at Glastenbury, 1773. m. and went West.

    5. HANNAH, b. at Glastenbury, 1776. m. Sylvester Emmons of Chester, Mass., and died there.

    6. GEORGE, b. at Ellington, Ct., 1782. m. and went to the State of New York with his brother Jonathan.

    7. SARAH, b. at Ellington, 1785. m. James Dickson of Middlefield, Mass., where she died in 1846.

8. JOSEPH, b. at Ellington, 1787. History unknown.
9. LEVI, b. at Ellington, 1789. He went West and married.
10. RUSSELL, b. at Ellington, 1792.

[Records from Mr. David Pease, No. **690**, other information from Mr. Horace Pease, No. **1237.**]

(Page 27.)

248. ELIZABETH, m.   Goodwin. and settled in New Hartford, Ct.
250. MARGARET, d. unmarried.
251. MATILDA, m. Dea. Elijah Goodwin, and settled in New Hartford, Ct.

(Page 29.)

271. SYBIL, as widow of Rev. Elam Potter, m. Rev. Nehemiah Prudden by whom she had issue.

(Page 30.)

86. AARON had a daughter, Mary, by his second wife, b. January 1, 1774, who m. Daniel Gowdy, Sen., and lived in Enfield.
277. SARAH, m. Daniel Abbe, Sen., and lived and died in Enfield.

(Page 32.)

308. AZUBAH,[2] m. Eliphalet Chapin, and lived in Enfield.

(Page 34.)

323. HANNAH, m. William Dimmock, and removed to Bridgewater, Vt.
324. SABRA, m. Joseph Dimmock, and removed to Vermont.
327. ELIZABETH, m. Stone Pease, page 193.
328. PERSIS, m. Dea. Ira Wells, and settled in East Windsor, Ct.

(Page 37.)

122. ABNER had another daughter, Elizabeth, who m. Alden Markham, and d. at Worcester, N. Y.

(Page 40.)

411. LOIS, m. Elisha Sperry of East Windsor, Ct.

(Page 43.)

140. ISRAEL PEASE, m. Ann Bartlett of Stafford, Ct., March 15, 1753.

(Page 44.)

144. HEZEKIAH PEASE had a daughter, Flavia, by his second wife, who
  •   m.   Jones, and died in Middletown, Ct.
472. MARY, m. Jehiel Griswold, and lived in Enfield.
478. HANNAH, m. Solomon Terry, and lived in Enfield.
480. ELECTA, m. Elijah Bullen, and died at Northampton.

(Page 48.)

526. MARY, m. Jonathan Allen, and removed to Ohio.
528. MARTHA, m.   .   Caswell, and settled in Springfield, Mass.

529. CLARISSA, m. Benjamin Wardwell, and died at Pittsfield, Mass.
530. RHODA, m. William Miller, and lived and died in Springfield, Mass.

(Page 60.)

662. LUCY, m. Apollos K. Gay, and settled in East Granby, Ct.

(Page 62.)

699. Mrs. NANCY ERWIN, d. April 10, 1869.

(Page 65.)

701. RUBY, m. Luke Hall of Somers, and removed to Chenango County, N. Y.
703. DOROTHY, m. Josiah Wales, and removed to Chenango County, N. Y.
705. EUNICE, m. George Risley, and died in Somers.

(Page 87.)

325. DEA. JONATHAN PEASE, and wife, ELEANOR, were living, in March, 1869. His wife was able to administer to all his comforts. It is a rare instance that a man and his wife should live together more than 68 years.
923. HANNAH B., m. John Chapin, and settled in New Philadelphia, Ohio.
926. NANCY G., m. Alonzo Bailey, and lives in Rockville, Ct.
927. SOPHRONIA, m. Sumner Root of Somers; was his second wife.

(Page 92.)

989. MARY, m. Owen Hunn, and settled in Somers.
993. FIDELIA, m. James S. Mallet, August 18, 1846, and resides in Somers.

(Page 117.)

470. LEMUEL PEASE removed to New York State where he died. His children were:
  1. HANNAH, m. Jedidiah Dudley, and died in New York State.
  2. ALMIRA, m.   Burnham of Springfield, Mass., and died in Middletown, Ct. Also other children.
[Information by Martha Pease, No. 1270.]
480. SETH PEASE had a daughter, Clarissa, who resides among the Shakers. She belongs to the ministry.
1270. MARTHA resides at the north family of Shakers at Enfield, and holds the office of Trustee.
1274. OMAR is also a Trustee at the north family of Shakers at Enfield.

(Page 167.)

690. DAVID PEASE was born at Portland, 1821. His children were:
  1. FREDERICK A., b. at Philadelphia, 1850.
  2. ADALINE E., b. at Philadelphia, 1851. d. 1853.

3. HENRY V., b. at Philadelphia, 1854. d. 1858.
4. ELIZABETH V., b. at Philadelphia, 1859.
5. AUGUSTA A., b. at Philadelphia, 1861.

(Page 188.)

1876. NOAH E., m. second, Amorett G. Edgerton, April 26, 1857, and resides at Somers.

1879. ORPHA H., m. Elisha Smith, and lives at Ellington, Ct.

(Page 193.)

801. STONE PEASE, m. Elizabeth Pease. No. 327.

(Page 194.)

1018. RUTH, m. Thomas Pease, No. **582.**

INDEX TO GIVEN NAMES.

[EXPLANATIONS.—The figures at the left of the name give the date of birth of the person named, and those at the right indicate the marginal or consecutive numbers which stand against the same name in the columns of figures that are found on the left margin of most of the preceding pages.

In indexing the given names, those of children known to have died young, the names of the children of the daughters who belong to the seventh generation and the sons belonging to the eighth, which have been inserted occasionally, are omitted here. The names of the infants omitted may be found by turning to the index or family number of the parent, and the others by turning to the consecutive number of the parent.

For explanations relative to the full-faced or large figures, see explanatory remarks found in the first part of the work.]

A.

Children of the Second and Third Generations.

BORN A. D.		Marginal No.	BORN A. D.		Marginal No.
1675.	Abigail, - - - -	• 8	1662.	Abraham, - - - -	4
1682.	Abigail, - - - -	19	1695.	Abraham, - - - -	44
1708.	Abigail, - - - -	39	1685.	Ann, - - - - -	13
1699.	Abigail, - - - -	46	1705.	Ann, - - - - -	48

Children of the Fourth Generation.

BORN		No.	BORN		No.
1726.	Aaron, - - - - -	86	1733.	Abner, - - - - -	122
1736.	Abiah, - - - - -	160	1729.	Abraham, - - - -	129
1736.	Abiel, - - - - -	77	1731.	Alexander, - - - -	106
1722.	Abigail, - - - - -	70	1736.	Alice, - - - - -	145
1727.	Abigail, - - - - -	98	1730.	Ann, - - - - -	74
1738.	Abigail, - - - - -	110	1735.	Ann, - - - - -	123
1739.	Abigail, - - - - -	150		Asa, - - - - -	90
1749.	Abigail, - - - - -	166	1750.	Asa, - - - - -	187
1747.	Abigail, - - - - -	175			

Children of the Fifth Generation.

BORN		No.	BORN		No.
1752.	Aaron, - - - - -	275	1784.	Abel, - - - - -	546
1770.	Aaron, - - - - -	315	1761.	Abiel, - - - - -	407
1753.	Abiah, - - - - -	234	1764.	Abiel, - - - - -	513
1787.	Abel, - - - - -	511	1744.	Abigail, - - - - -	201

Born A. D.		Marginal No.	Born A. D.		Marginal No.
1759.	Abigail,	313	1762.	Alpheus,	238
1760.	Abigail,	360		Alpheus,	553
1764.	Abigail,	401	1786.	Alvah,	390
1768.	Abigail,	462		Ambrose,	496
1762.	Abigail,	466	1770.	Amos,	226
1768.	Abigail,	488	1776.	Amos,	424
1763.	Abigail,	498	1765.	Amy,	367
1789.	Abigail,	522	1767.	Ann,	282
1789.	Abione,	539	1760.	Anna,	274
1757.	Abner,	236		Asa,	551
1763.	Abner,	372	1794.	Asa,	560
	Abraham,	434	1796.	Asa,	569
1778.	Achsah,	387	1763.	Asaph,	224
	Achsah,	484	1776.	Asaph,	386
	Achsah,	548	1761.	Asenath,	459
	Achsah,	561	1780.	Asher,	331
	Adah,	438	1757.	Augustine,	211
1760.	Agnes,	273	1759.	Augustus,	245
1781.	Agnes,	450		Augustus,	409
1764.	Alice,	476	1744.	Azuba,	308
1762.	Allen,	288			

Children of the Sixth Generation.

Born A. D.		Marginal No.	Born A. D.		Marginal No.
1786.	Aaron,	609	1801.	Adaline,	642
1777	Aaron,	793	1815.	Adaline,	954
	Aaron,	911		Adaline L.,	687
	Abbie,	1054	1779.	Agift,	794
1815.	Abel,	1392	1801.	Agnes,	809
1817.	Abel,	1498	1800.	Agnes,	855
1812.	Abi S.,	1378		Agnes,	1244
1775.	Abiah,	798	1813.	Agnes,	1368
1780.	Abiel,	711	1807.	Agnes E.,	821
1790.	Abiel,	747	1779.	Alanson,	861
1797.	Abiel,	1107		Alanson,	1080
1808.	Abiel,	1241	1809.	Alanson,	1272
1811.	Abiel,	1384		Alanson,	1467
1808.	Abigail,	632	1800.	Albert,	645
1781.	Abigail,	1010	1803.	Albert,	656
1801.	Abigail,	1024		Albert,	1296
1806.	Abigail,	1148	1806.	Albert,	1314
	Abigail,	1243	1824.	Albert,	1374
	Abigail,	1472	1817.	Albert, A.,	1447
1826.	Abigail,	1558	1811.	Albert, M.,	1205
1832.	Abigail A.,	1523	1807.	Alden, M.,	1038
1806.	Abigail M.,	1275	1822.	Alexander G.,	1382
1813.	Abner,	1194	1793.	Alfred,	650
1799.	Achsah,	1093	1804.	Alfred,	1097
1807.	Achsah,	1282	1801.	Alice,	1337
1794.	Achsah,	1303	1792.	Allen,	1220
1829.	Achsah,	1502	1840.	Allen D.,	1077
1824.	Achsah, S.,	1521	1803.	Almira,	819

BORN A. D.		Marginal No.	BORN A. D.		Marginal No.
1792.	Almira, - - - -	849	1820.	Ann, - - - - -	1431
1808.	Almitte, - - - -	1376	1827.	Ann E., - - - -	1072
1799.	Alonzo, - - - -	834	1818.	Ann E., - - - -	1510
1814.	Alonzo, - - - - -	**1385**	1810.	Ann J., - - - -	917
1824.	Alonzo, - - - -	**1536**	1804.	Anna, - - - -	680
1799.	Alpheus, - - - -	**628**	1796.	Anna, - - - -	963
1803.	Alpheus, - - - -	**727**	1794.	Anna, - - - -	1221
1800.	Alpheus, - - - -	**752**	1818.	Anna, - - - -	1353
1785.	Alpheus, - - - -	**1016**	1787.	Anson, - - - -	**1012**
	Alpheus O., - - -	1513	1802.	Anson, - - - -	**1312**
1795.	Alva, - - - - -	**1222**		Anthony, - - -	**772**
1805.	Alvah, - - - -	**1026**	1819.	Arnold, - - -	**1254**
1805.	Alvah, - - - -	**1281**	1787.	Artemesia, - - -	840
1809.	Alvah, - - - -	1283	1802.	Arvin, - - - -	**1226**
1784.	Alvin, - - - -	**671**	1787.	Arvin B., - - -	**811**
1785.	Alvin, - - - -	**778**		Asa, - - - - -	1486
1823.	Alvin, - - - -	**1198**	1810.	Asa W., - - - -	1547
	Alvin, - - - -	1485	1808.	Asahel, - - - -	**597**
1802.	Amanda, - - - -	604	1833.	Asahel, - - - -	**1560**
1817.	Amanda, - - - -	1253	1785.	Asenath, - - - -	744
1834.	Amanda, - - - -	1454	1799.	Asenath, - - - -	785
1805.	Amanda, - - - -	1474	1787.	Asenath, - - - -	804
1829.	Amanda H., - - -	1526	1786.	Augustus, - - -	**745**
1816.	Amanda M., - - -	1406	1793.	Augustus, - - -	**759**
1804.	Amanda S., - - -	836	1794.	Augustus, - - -	**1021**
	Ambrose, - - - -	**1306**	1837.	Augustus E., - -	754
1833.	Amelia, - - - -	1403	1805.	Augustus E., - -	820
1839.	Amelia W., - - -	1414	1792.	Augustus P., - -	**852**
1801.	Amos, - - - -	1130		Aurelia, - - - -	790
1785.	Amos, - - - -	1299	1801.	Aurelia, - - - -	903
	Amos, - - - -	**1308**	1804.	Austin, - - - -	**630**
1810.	Amy, - - - - -	1028	1806.	Austin, - - - -	**1240**
1821.	Angeline, - - -	1461	1809.	Austin, - - - -	**1331**
1779.	Ann, - - - - -	702	1820.	Austin S., - - -	**1381**
	Ann, - - - - -	721	1806.	Azariah, - - - -	**631**
	Ann, - - - - -	894	1795.	Azel, - - - - -	**714**

Children of the Seventh Generation.

BORN A. D.		Marginal No.	BORN A. D.		Marginal No.
1813.	Aaron, - - - -	**1653**	1845.	Abner, - - - -	2405
	Aaron, - - - -	**1969**	1815.	Abraham, - - -	**1654**
1811.	Aaron A., - - -	**1603**	1819.	Abraham D., - -	**1823**
1817.	Aaron G., - - -	1963	1821.	Adaline, - - - -	1692
1811.	Aaron G., - - -	**2035**	1836.	Adaline, - - - -	2493
1810.	Abby, - - - -	1996		Adaline, - - - -	2512
1851.	Abby J., - - - -	2881		Adaline, - - - -	2637
1841.	Abby L., - - - -	2094	1842.	Adaline M., - - -	2862
1833.	Abiel, - - - -	2721	1827.	Adaline S., - - -	1727
1809.	Abiel H., - - -	**1781**		Adaline W., - - -	1759
1829.	Abiel J., - - - -	1679	1841.	Addie R., - - -	2585
1798.	Abigail, - - - -	1770	1834.	Addison, - - - -	**1836**
1835.	Abigail S., - - -	1683	1831.	Adelaide A., - -	1640

Born A. D.		Marginal No.	Born A. D.		Marginal No.
1850.	Adelaide E., - - -	3103		Alva W., - - -	2787
1860.	Adelbert F., - - -	3025	1842.	Alvah, - - - -	2685
1853.	Adelbert T., - - -	2204		Alvin, - - - -	1714
1837.	Adelia D., - - -	1739		Alvin, - - - -	2308
1841.	Affinia, - - - -	3070	1820.	Alvin, - - - -	**2678**
	Agift, - - - -	**1971**	1810.	Amanda, - - - -	2103
1854.	Agnes, - - - -	2464		Amanda, - - - -	2343
1834.	Agnes A., - - -	1994	1827.	Amanda, - - - -	2398
1852.	Albert, - - - -	1700²⁸		Amanda, - - - -	2822
1854.	Albert, - - - -	2296	1838.	Amanda E., - - -	2432
1809.	Albert, - - - -	**2335**	1842.	Amanda L., - - -	2876
1843.	Albert, - - - -	**2745**	1848.	Amanda M., - - -	1746
1825.	Albert, - - - -	2789	1822.	Amanda R., - - -	2011
1840.	Albert, - - - -	2800		Ambrose, - - -	2834
1850.	Albert N., - - -	2956	1809.	Amelia, - - -	1917
1853.	Albert C., - - -	2419	1844.	Amelia, - - - -	2776
1840.	Albert E., - - -	2861		Amelia, - - - -	2259
1866.	Albert H., - - -	3028	1849.	Amelia E., - - -	3119
1815.	Albert J., - - -	**2068**	1861.	Amelia F., - - -	3108
	Albert K., - - -	3018	1839.	Amelia H., - - -	3110
1845.	Albert L., - - -	**2937**	1822.	Amelia P., - - -	1989
1836.	Albert M., - - -	2817	1834.	Amelia R., - - -	1833
1831.	Albert R., - - -	2539		Aminia, - - - -	3055
1828.	Albert S., - - -	**2065**		Aminia, - - - -	3072
1830.	Alexis, - - -	**2284**	1828.	Amos, - - - -	**1769**
1829.	Alfred, - - - -	1700¹¹	1827.	Amos, - - - -	**2715**
1825.	Alfred, - - - -	**2714**	1837.	Amos M., - - -	2288
1850.	Alfred L., - - -	2922	1824.	Amos S., - - -	1768
1828.	Alfred W., - - -	2540	1830.	Andrew J., - - -	**2376**
1858.	Alice, - - - -	2206	1828.	Andrew J., - - -	2676
1842.	Alice, - - - -	2515		Andrew J., - - -	**2842**
1866.	Alice E., - - - -	2626⁵³	1845.	Angelia M., - - -	2237
1853.	Alice L., - - - -	1748		Angeline L., - -	2841
1857.	Alice N., - - - -	2757	1825.	Ann A., - - - -	1637
1850.	Alice M., - - - -	1700⁴¹	1837.	Ann E., - - - -	1904
1846.	Allen, - - - -	2686	1829.	Ann E., - - - -	2128
1843.	Allen G., - - -	2546	1848.	Ann F., - - - -	2770
1823.	Allen W., - - -	**1609**	1834.	Ann J., - - - -	2048
1827.	Almira, - - - -	2496	1817.	Ann L., - - - -	2473
1856.	Almira E., - - -	3080	1836.	Ann L., - - - -	2868
1821.	Almira S., - - -	1608	1817.	Ann M., - - - -	1722
1832.	Almira S., - - -	1806	1826.	Ann M., - - -	2566
	Alona A., - - -	2844	1860.	Ann M., - - - -	2649
	Alonzo, - - - -	2225	1844.	Ann M., - - - -	2877
1821.	Alonzo, - - - -	**2345**	1844.	Ann R., - - - -	2494
1830.	Alonzo T., - - -	**2541**	1842.	Anna, - - - -	2931
1826.	Alpheus, - - - -	1678	1856.	Anna A., - - -	3120
1853.	Alpheus, - - - -	1841	1834.	Anna D., - - -	2858
1817.	Alpheus D., - - -	**1822**	1848.	Anna E., - - -	1700²⁴
1814.	.Alpheus D., - - -	**2358**	1832.	Anna M., - - -	2179
1836.	Alva, - - - -	1751	1852.	Annie S., - - -	2099

44

B.

Child of the Third Generation.

Children of the Fourth Generation.

Children of the Fifth Generation.

Children of the Sixth Generation.

Children of the Seventh Generation.

C.

Child of the Third Generation.

Born A. D.		Marginal No.	Born A. D.		Marginal No.
1715.	Cummings, - - -	52			

Children of the Fourth Generation.

1729.	Catharine, - - -	99	1744.	Cummings, - - -	184

Children of the Fifth Generation.

1768.	Calvin, - - - -	218	1792.	Chauncey, - - -	559
1776.	Calvin, - - - -	221		Chester, - - -	371
1757.	Calvin, - - - -	286		Chester, - - - -	408
1785.	Calvin, - - - -	510	1763.	Chloe, - - - -	304
1764.	Charles, - - - -	239	1802.	Cidnie, - - - -	457
	Charles, - - - -	451		Clarissa, - - - -	529
	Charlotte, - - -	448			

Children of the Sixth Generation.

1816.	Calista M., - - -	1515	1784.	Charlotte, - - -	636
1797.	Calvin, - - - -	586	1844.	Charlotte A., - -	1417
1805.	Calvin, - - - -	664	1826.	Charlotte A., - -	1484
1792.	Calvin, - - - -	748	1793.	Chauncey, - - -	641
1809.	Calvin, - - - -	1383	1792.	Chauncey, - - -	806
1824.	Calvin S., - - - -	1182	1800.	Chauncey D., - -	1042
	Candace, - - - -	1143	1843.	Chauncey J., - -	1530
1825.	Carlos, - - - -	1462	1825.	Chauncey O., - -	1500
1832.	Carlos A., - - -	1413	1827.	Cherry A., - - -	1554
1815.	Carlos W., - - -	1203	1819.	Chester, - - - -	992
	Caroline, - - - -	948		Chester, - - - -	1109
1813.	Caroline, - - - -	1101	1813.	Chester M., - - -	1179
1814.	Caroline, - - - -	1140	1796.	Chloe, - - - -	720
	Caroline, - - - -	1212	1819.	Chloe, - - - -	873
1825.	Caroline, - - - -	1268	1812.	Clarissa, - - - -	822
	Caroline, - - - -	1428		Clarissa, - - - -	979
1825.	Caroline, - - - -	1450	1806.	Clarissa, - - - -	1098
1823.	Caroline, - - - -	1507	1798.	Clarissa, - - - -	1305
	Caroline M., - - -	1062	1810.	Clarissa A., - - -	1041
1832.	Caroline O., - - -	1527		Clarissa C., - - -	1297
1830.	Cecilia M., - - -	1412	1831.	Clarissa E., - - -	1073
	Celecia, - - - -	1506	1792.	Cooley, - - - -	1020
	Celestia, - - - -	1473	1807.	Cordon, - - - -	1493
1779.	Chandler, - - -	1009	1830.	Cornelia, - - - -	1559
1811.	Chandler, - - - -	1332	1820.	Cornelia G., - - -	670
1797.	Charity, - - - -	578	1788.	Cynthia, - - - -	618
1853.	Charity J., - - -	1534	1790.	Cynthia, - - - -	640
1811.	Charles, - - - -	667		Cynthia, - - - -	1004
1804.	Charles, - - - -	728	1840.	Cynthia L., - - -	1529
1796.	Charles, - - - -	732	1806.	Cynthia M., - - -	1475
	Charles N., - - -	912	1804.	Cyrus, - - - -	736
1845.	Charles D., - - -	1531	1789.	Cyrus, - - - -	1084
1838.	Charles H., - - -	1456			

Children of the Seventh Generation.

Born A. D.		Marginal No.	Born A. D.		Marginal No.
1829.	Calista, - - - -	2335	1847.	Charles D., - - -	2939
1834.	Calista, - - - -	2696	1836.	Charles E., - - -	**-1700**[20]
1812.	Calista N., - - -	1564	1841.	Charles E., - - -	2086
1820.	Calvin, - - - -	**1597**	1816.	Charles E., - - -	2153
1813.	Calvin, - - - -	**-2036**	1849.	Charles E., - - -	2863
1848.	Calvin H., - - -	3076	1849.	Charles E., - - -	3051
1818.	Calvin O., - - -	2350	1823.	Charles F., - - -	1725
1823.	Calvin P., - - -	**1878**	1838.	Charles F., - - -	**-2805**
1824.	Candace O., - - -	2268	1864.	Charles G., - - -	2816
1828.	Caroline, - - -	**1700**[34]	1857.	Charles H., - - -	2101
	Caroline, - - -	1735	1853.	Charles H., - - -	2761
1828.	Caroline, - - -	2212		Charles H., - - -	**2903**
	Caroline, - - -	2260	1851.	Charles H., - - -	2989
	Caroline, - - -	2471	1825.	Charles J., - - -	2163
1839.	Caroline, - - -	2525		Charles L., - - -	1618
	Caroline, - - -	2563	1829.	Charles L., - - -	**1835**
1836.	Caroline, - - -	2791	1806.	Charles L., - - -	**-2056**
	Caroline, - - -	2896	1843.	Charles L., - - -	2801
1824.	Caroline A., - - -	1571	1856.	Charles M., - - -	3024
1826.	Caroline A., - - -	1578	1852.	Charles N., - - -	2418
1838.	Caroline A., - - -	1706	1838.	Charles N., - - -	2782
1841.	Caroline E., - - -	1906	1833.	Charles O., - - -	**1794**
1830.	Caroline J., - - -	1858	1835.	Charles O., - - -	**2181**
1813.	Caroline J., - - -	2330		Charles P., - - -	1721
1816.	Caroline P., - - -	2123	1837.	Charles P., - - -	1868
1836.	Caroline S., - - -	2196	1832.	Charles S., - - -	1887
1858.	Carrie E., - - -	2552	1865.	Charles S., - - -	3005
1853.	Carrie R., - - -	2100	1857.	Charles T. A., - - -	3101
	Catharine, - - -	1977	1819.	Charles W., - - -	**2136**
	Catharine, - - -	2116	1843.	Charles W., - - -	2199
1823.	Catharine, - - -	2266	1819.	Charlotte, - - -	2711
1841.	Catharine, - - -	2945		Charlotte, - - -	1700
1837.	Catharine A., - - -	2697	1846.	Charlotte, - - -	3085
1819.	Catharine E., - - -	2169	1819.	Charlotte A., - - -	1607
	Catharine E., - - -	2651	1845.	Charlotte A., - - -	3044
1824.	Catharine J., - - -	2064	1837.	Charlotte C., - - -	1803
1848.	Catharine S., - - -	3032	1821.	Charlotte C., - - -	2170
1831.	Celestia W., - - -	1867	1855.	Charlotte M., - - -	2880
1833.	Celia, - - - - -	2400		Chauncey, - - -	**1773**
1849.	Celia M., - - -	1895		Chauncey, - - -	1933
	Chandler C., - - -	2177	1836.	Chauncey D., - - -	**2431**
1835.	Charles, - - - -	**1705**	1826.	Chester, - - - -	**1595**
	Charles, - - - -	1831	1838.	Chester, - - - -	**-2385**
	Charles, - - - -	1978	1845.	Chloe, - - - -	2932
	Charles, - - - -	2467	1825.	Clara, - - - -	2397
1835.	Charles, - - - -	2735	1847.	Clara A., - - -	2811
1831.	Charles A., - - -	**1957**	1856.	Clara A., - - -	2971
1856.	Charles B., - - -	2437	1832.	Clara F., - - -	2285
1848.	Charles C., - - -	2646		Clara I., - - - -	2084

Born A. D.		Marginal No.	Born A. D.		Marginal No.
1857.	Clarence, - - - -	2447	1864.	Cora M., - - - -	3027
1853.	Clarence A., - -	2984	1826.	Cordelia, - - - -	2481
1860.	Clarence B., - -	1761	1837.	Cordelia, - - - -	2831
1861.	Clarence E., - - -	3001	1816.	Cordelia L., - - -	2359
1834.	Clarinda M., - - -	2573	1833.	Cornelia H., - - -	2286
1814.	Clarissa, - - - -	1580	1832.	Cornelia L., - - -	2511
	Clarissa, - - - -	2836	1822.	Cornelius, - - -	1884
	Clarissa, - - - -	2847	1831.	Corintha D., - - -	2269
1835.	Clarissa E., - - -	1903	1841.	Corwin A., - - - **2421**
1827.	Clarissa G., - - -	2675	1821.	Cynthia, - - - -	1688
	Clark, - - - -	2307	1799.	Cynthia, - - - -	1913
1829.	Clark A., - - -	2046		Cynthia, - - - -	1973
1841.	Clark W., - - -	1631	1819.	Cynthia, - - - -	2660
1826.	Claudius A., - - **1886**	1821.	Cynthia A., - - -	1787
1815.	Claudius B., - - **1872**	1854.	Cynthia A., - - -	3048
1854.	Clifton, - - - -	2657	1834.	Cynthia M., - - -	2356
1862.	Clifford E., - - -	3013	1821.	Cyrus, - - - - **1588**
	Clinton, - - - -	1827	1841.	Cyrus M., - - - **3060**
	Commodore P., - -	2281			

D.

Children of the Third Generation.

1692.	Daniel, - - - -	23	1698.	David, - - - -	29

Children of the Fourth Generation.

1753.	Damaris, - - - -	157	1742.	Deborah, - - - -	172
1718.	Daniel, - - - -	88	1741.	Desire, - - - -	135
1727.	David, - - - -	141	1751.	Dorcas, - - - -	177
1760.	David, - - - -	190			

Children of the Fifth Generation.

1771.	Dan, - - - - -	429	1783.	David, - - - -	563
1773.	Dan, - - - - -	464		Deborah, - - - -	437
1754.	Daniel, - - - -	300	1793.	Deborah, - - - -	524
	Daniel, - - - -	374		Deliverance, - - -	549
1780.	Daniel, - - - -	507		Desire, - - - -	395
1772.	David, - - - -	230	1765.	Diadama, - - - -	467
1755.	David, - - - -	243	1802.	Dorothy, - - - -	571
	David, - - - -	442	1768.	Dudley, - - - -	291
1767.	David, - - - -	468			

Children of the Sixth Generation.

1796.	Dan, - - - - -	1145	1799.	Daniel, - - - - **1289**
1802.	Dan, - - - - -	1246	1810.	Daniel, - - - -	1366
	Daniel, - - - -	774	1819.	Daniel B., - - -	920
1782.	Daniel, - - - -	869	1821.	David, - - - -	690
1793.	Daniel, - - - -	1234	1798.	David, - - - -	751

Children of the Fifth Generation.

Born A. D.		Marginal No.	Born A. D.		Marginal No.
1778.	Earl P., - - - -	**296**	1750.	Elizabeth, - - -	298
1747.	Ebenezer, - - -	**309**	1787.	Elizabeth, - - -	327
	Ebenezer, - - -	347		Elizabeth, - - -	339
1773.	Ebenezer, - - -	**543**		Elizabeth, - - -	445
	Edna, - - - -	542	1759.	Elizabeth, - - -	474
1763.	Edward, - - - -	**265**	1782.	Elizabeth, - - -	534
1786.	Edward, - - - -	520	1788.	Elizabeth, - - -	566
1770.	Elam, - - - -	**283**	1786.	Elseba, - - - -	537
1776.	Elam, - - - -	**416**	1757.	Emery, - - - -	**244**
1778.	Elam, - - - -	**550**	1773.	Enoch, - - - -	**415**
1760.	Eleanor, - - - -	303	1775.	Enoch, - - - -	**544**
1772.	Electa, - - - -	293		Enos, - - - - -	**545**
1772.	Electa, - - - -	403	1741.	Ephraim, - - - -	267
1774.	Electa, - - - -	480	1763.	Ephraim, - - - -	**280**
1749.	Eli, - - - - -	**259**	1764.	Ephraim, - - - -	**305**
1754.	Elias, - - - -	**261**	1759.	Erastus, - - - -	**237**
1770.	Elijah, - - - -	**495**	1783.	Erastus, - - - -	389
1762.	Eliphalet, - - -	223	1758.	Esther, - - - -	253
1769.	Eliphalet, - - -	369	1769.	Esther, - - - -	421
1767.	Elisha, - - - -	368	1770.	Eunice, - - - -	292
1767.	Elisha, - - - -	381	1769.	Eunice, - - - -	414
	Eliza, - - - -	499		Eunice, - - - -	440
1756.	Elizabeth, - - -	193	1774.	Experience, - - -	430
1738.	Elizabeth, - - -	198	1756.	Ezekiel, - - - -	**491**
1766.	Elizabeth, - - -	248			

Children of the Sixth Generation.

Born A. D.		Marginal No.	Born A. D.		Marginal No.
	Ebenezer, - - -	**891**	1811.	Eliphalet C., - -	**1284**
1802.	Ebenezer, - - -	**1468**		Elisha, - - - -	**1001**
1812.	Ebenezer B., - -	1081		Eliza, - - - -	646
1828.	Edmund, - - -	1200		Eliza, - - - -	944
1792.	Edward, - - - -	**652**		Eliza, - - - -	977
1794.	Edward, - - - -	783	1810.	Eliza, - - - -	1342
	Elam, - - - -	**998**	1813.	Eliza C., - - -	1433
1804.	Elam A., - - -	**1124**	1805.	Elizabeth, - - -	657
1835.	Elam C., - - -	**824**	1790.	Elizabeth, - - -	730
1814.	Elam L., - - -	**1504**	1795.	Elizabeth, - - -	850
1812.	Eldridge, - - -	**1251**	1797.	Elizabeth, - - -	876
1791.	Electa, - - - -	830	1805.	Elizabeth, - - -	1191
1792.	Electa, - - - -	841	1800.	Elizabeth, - - -	1326
1802.	Electa, - - - -	878	1804.	Elizabeth, - - -	1358
1793.	Eli, - - - - -	**719**	1824.	Elizabeth, - - -	1439
1772.	Eli, - - - - -	**769**	1808.	Elizabeth, - - -	1476
1781.	Elihu, - - - -	**777**	1822.	Elizabeth, - - -	1556
1803.	Elihu, - - - -	**1307**	1815.	Elizabeth E., - -	886
1770.	Elijah, - - - -	**607**	1814.	Elizabeth K., - -	1514
	Elijah, - - - -	1000	1788.	Elizabeth L., - -	829
1796.	Elijah, - - - -	**1309**	1830.	Elizabeth S., - -	1398
1785.	Eliphalet, - - -	**672**	1811.	Elsie, - - - -	1477

Born A. D.		Marginal No.	Born A. D.		Marginal No.
1825.	Emeline, - - - -	1199	1802.	Erastus, - - - -	**1043**
1818.	Emeline E., - - -	1068	1804.	Erastus, - - - -	**1094**
1819.	Emeline M., - - -	1448	1812.	Erastus, - - - -	**1343**
1789.	Emery, - - - -	**738**	1813.	Erastus C., - - -	**1063**
1820.	Emery T., - - -	**1335**	1827.	Erskine, - - - -	**1463**
1820.	Emily, - - - -	1336	1835.	Esther, - - - -	697
1815.	Emily, - - - -	1370	1784.	Esther, - - - -	958
1804.	Emily A., - - -	856	1811.	Esther, - - - -	1134
1796.	Emily L., - - -	643	1810.	Esther, - - - -	1153
	Emma, - - - -	1460		Etha M., - - - -	1111
1809.	Enoch, - - - -	**1315**	1796.	Ethan H., - - - -	**750**
1804.	Enos, - - - - -	**715**	1785.	Eunice, - - - -	705
1786.	Enos, - - - - -	1017	1806.	Eunice, - - - -	845
	Enos, - - - - -	1487	1815.	Eunice K., - - -	1082
1828.	Epaphros L. P., -	1441	1817.	Eusebia, - - - -	1542
1806.	Ephraim B., - - -	**884**	1812.	Experience, - - -	1263
1789.	Erastus, - - - -	**713**	1783.	Ezekiel, - - - -	1298
1796.	Erastus, - - - -	**784**		Ezra, - - - - -	775
1785.	Erastus, - - - -	**899**			

Children of the Seventh Generation.

Born A. D.		Marginal No.	Born A. D.		Marginal No.
1816.	Earl A., - - - -	**2670**	1838.	Edwin H., - - -	1892
1834.	Edgar, - - - - -	2499	1829.	Edwin H., - - -	**2382**
1856.	Edgar G., - - -	2205	1842.	Edwin L., - - -	2198
1860.	Edith M., - - -	2208	1839.	Edwin O., - - -	2591
1851.	Edmund C., - - -	2187	1820.	Edwin R., - - -	**2062**
1817.	Edmund N., - - -	1655	1832.	Edwin S., - - - -	1674
1856.	Edson L., - - -	2189	1846.	Edwin S., - - -	2560
1853.	Edson M., - - -	2749	1840.	Edwin S., - - -	2819
	Edward, - - - -	1715	1823.	Edwin T , - - -	**1636**
1824.	Edward, - - - -	**1939**	1835.	Egbert R., - - -	2067
	Edward, - - - -	**1976**	1818.	Elam, - - - - -	**2339**
1819.	Edward, - - - -	**2323**	1855.	Elam H., - - - -	3083
	Edward, - - - -	2438	1813.	Elanora, - - - -	1783
	Edward, - - - -	2466	1850.	Elbert A., - - -	3096
1838.	Edward, - - - -	2743	1815.	Electa A., - - -	2264
1845.	Edward C., - - -	1911	1823.	Electa S., - - -	2025
1854.	Edward C., - - -	2446	1801.	Eli, - - - - -	**1914**
	Edward E., - - -	2874[54]		Eli, - - - - -	1935
1823.	Edward H., - - -	2074		Eliphalet L., - - -	1717
1855.	Edward H., - - -	2874	1848.	Elisha B., - - -	2812
1850.	Edward L., - - -	2958	1841.	Elisha C., - - -	2429
1818.	Edward P., - - -	**1952**	1812.	Elisha M., - - -	**1573**
1819.	Edward R., - - -	**2069**	1836.	Eliza, - - - -	1646
1819.	Edward W., - - -	1723		Eliza, - - - -	1975
1841.	Edward W., - - -	1742	1815.	Eliza, - - - -	1998
1850.	Edward W., - - -	2983		Eliza, - - - -	2143
	Edwin, - - - -	1716		Eliza, - - - -	2410
	Edwin, - - - -	2450	1831.	Eliza A., - - - -	1622
1838.	Edwin A., - - -	1629	1811.	Eliza A., - - - -	2158
1836.	Edwin G., - - -	1995	1840.	Eliza A., - - - -	2953

Born A. D.		Marginal N	Born A. D.		Marginal No.
1832.	Eliza A. L., - - -	2680		Emerson, - - -	**2891**
1839.	Eliza B., - - - -	2698	1843.	Emerson F., - - -	1743
1827.	Eliza C., - - -	2013	1826.	Emery, - - - -	2373
1854.	Eliza J., - - -	2188		Emery F., - - -	2907
1821.	Elizabeth, - - -	1592	1804.	Emily, - - - -	1915
1823.	Elizabeth, - - -	1644	1814.	Emily, - - - -	2105
	Elizabeth, - - -	1648	1810.	Emily, - - - -	2321
1832.	Elizabeth, - - -	1700^{12}	1826.	Emily, - - - -	2374
1838.	Elizabeth, - - -	1700^{21}	1825.	Emily, - - - -	2483
1837.	Elizabeth, - - -	1700^{38}	1842.	Emily, - - - -	2775
1824.	Elizabeth, - - -	1885	1843.	Emily B., - - -	2415
1822.	Elizabeth, - - -	1938	1831.	Emily C., - - -	2028
1821.	Elizabeth, - - -	2073	1837.	Emily M., - - -	2667
1831.	Elizabeth, - - -	2491	1842.	Emma, - - - -	2054
1838.	Elizabeth, - - -	2799	1841.	Emma H., - - -	1910
	Elizabeth, - - -	2898	1856.	Emma J., - - -	2740
1864.	Elizabeth, - - -	2991	1852.	Emma L., - - -	2233
1833.	Elizabeth H., - -	2568		Emma L., - - -	3008
1849.	Elizabeth J., - -	2055	1850.	Emma R., - - -	2203
1859.	Elizabeth R., - -	3102	1825.	Enos D., - - - -	**2366**
1817.	Elizabeth S., - -	1987	1837.	Ephraim, - - - -	2500
1857.	Elizabeth S., - -	2457	1826.	Ephraim H., - - -	**2138**
1848.	Elizabeth Y., - -	2430	1825.	Erasmus D., - - -	1566
1843.	Ella, - - - - -	1811	1841.	Erastus, - - - -	1960
1854.	Ella, - - - - -	2631		Erastus A., - - -	2449
	Ella, - - - - -	2632	1841.	Erastus B., - - -	2592
	Ella L., - - - -	2090	1830.	Erastus F., - - -	**2424**
1849.	Ella L., - - - -	2981	1807.	Erastus H., - - -	2034
1860.	Ella W., - - - -	2925	1819.	Erastus P., - - -	1587
1839.	Ellen, - - - -	1700^{45}	1846.	Ernest S., - - -	2082
1830.	Ellen, - - - -	2367	1828.	Erskine, - - - -	2489
1843.	Ellen E., - - - -	2627		Estella, - - - -	2451
1858.	Ellen L., - - - -	2985		Esther, - - - -	2314
1825.	Ellen M., - - -	1700^{16}	1840.	Esther, - - - -	2514
1840.	Ellen M., - - -	2254	1856.	Esther S., - - -	2208
1856.	Elmer, - - - -	2748	1826.	Esther C., - - -	2362
	Elmira, - - - -	2313	1869.	Ethwald C., - - -	3002^{62}
1853.	Elsie, - - - -	2615		Etta, - - - -	2900
1839.	Elvira E., - - -	2602	1846.	Eugene, - - - -	2618
	Elvira L., - - -	2848	1839.	Eugene C., - - -	2997
1833.	Elvira N., - - -	2857	1852.	Eugene E., - - -	2873
1852.	Elzora A., - - -	2913	1858.	Eugene M., - - -	2741
	Emeline, - - - -	1830	1830.	Eunice, - - - -	2050
	Emeline, - - - -	2635		Eunice, - - - -	2310
1825.	Emeline G., - - -	2674	1825.	Eunice, - - - -	1659
1833.	Emeline L., - - -	2195	1847.	Eunice E., - - -	2916
1854.	Emerette, - - -	2207		Evelina, - - - -	2389

F.

Child of the Fifth Generation.

1776.	Flavius, - - - -	295

45

Children of the Sixth Generation.

Born A. D.		Marginal No.	Born A. D.		Marginal No.
1802.	Fannie, - - - -	1036		Francis, - - - -	**999**
	Fannie B., - - -	1053	1817.	Francis, - - - -	**1156**
1811.	Fanny, - - - -	952	1822.	Francis L., - - -	**1408**
1821.	Fidelia, - - - -	993		Franklin, - - -	**942**
1822.	Fidelia, - - - -	1449	1801.	Frederick, - - -	**1088**
1820.	Fidelia, - - - -	1481		Frederick, - - -	**1172**
1780.	Flavius, - - - -	**825**	1340.	Frederick A. B., -	1416
1829.	Frances A., - - -	1397	1308.	Frederick G., - -	**978**
1845.	Frances D., - - -	1525		Frederick M., - -	**616**
1787.	Francis, - - - -	**904**			

Children of the Seventh Generation.

	Fanny, - - - -	3056	1859.	Francis J., - - -	2648
1842.	Fanny I., - - -	2081	1836.	Francis R., - - -	**2574**
1821.	Fanny M., - - -	1824	1822.	Francis S., - - -	2173
1821.	Fitch, - - - -	**2396**	1852.	Frank, - - - -	1814
1840.	Flavia, - - - -	2774	1850.	Frank, - - - -	2407
1824.	Flavia F., - - -	1897	1842.	Frank, - - - -	2980
1825.	Flavius E., - - -	**2012**	1859.	Frank E., - - -	2942⁵⁵
1820.	Flora, - - - -	1777	1855.	Frank G., - - -	2959
1839.	Foster A., - - -	2979	1845.	Frank W., - - -	2393
1836.	Frances, - - -	2408	1859.	Frank W., - - -	2752
1851.	Frances, - - -	2463	1859.	Frank W., - - -	3106
1837.	Frances, - - -	2517		Franklin, - - -	**1967**
	Frances, - - -	2989⁶⁰	1843.	Franklin C., - -	2820
1826.	Frances A., - - -	1645	1841.	Franklin E., - -	2018
1819.	Frances A., - - -	1700⁴	1862.	Franklin J., - -	2208⁷⁰
1845.	Frances A., - - -	1894	1822.	Franklin W., - -	**1815**
1842.	Frances J., - - -	2230	1852.	Franklin W., - -	2605
1849.	Frances J., - - -	2239		Frederick, - - -	1758
1826.	Frances L., - - -	1966	1857.	Frederick, - - -	2653
1818.	Frances W., - - -	1795	1865.	Frederick C., - -	3017
1846.	Francina L., - -	2999	1847.	Frederick D., - -	3097
	Francis, - - -	1733	1835.	Frederick G., - -	2287
1845.	Francis, - - -	1863	1839.	Frederick H., - -	**2017**
1845.	Francis, - - -	2461	1843.	Frederick K., - -	1707
1844.	Francis, - - -	2617	1828.	Frederick N., - -	2497
1856.	Francis A., - - -	3100	1804.	Frederick S., - -	**2032**
1848.	Francis H., - - -	2144	1856.	Frederick S., - -	3104
	Francis I., - - -	2088	1843.	Freeman S., - - -	2807

G.

Children of the Fourth Generation.

1753.	Gideon, - - - -	**115**	1744.	Gideon, - - - -	**136**

Children of the Fifth Generation.

1771.	Gad, - - - -	**463**	1771.	Gaius, - - - -	**370**
1768.	Gaius, - - - -	**249**	1780.	Gaius, - - - -	552

BORN A. D.		Marginal No.	BORN A. D.		Marginal No.
1776.	George, - - -	362	1765.	Gideon, - - - -	426
1757.	Gideon, - - - -	194	1763.	Giles, - - - -	254
	Gideon, - - - -	349	1780.	Grove, - - - -	336

Children of the Sixth Generation.

BORN A. D.		Marginal No.	BORN A. D.		Marginal No.
	Gad, - - - - -	1245[1]	1842.	George F., - - -	1457
1790.	Gamaliel, - - - -	649	1815.	George W., - - -	1497
1804.	Geer C., - - - -	810	1809.	Gideon, - - - -	1152
1798.	George, - - - -	654	1847.	Gilbert H., - - -	1459
1829.	George, - - - -	695	1805.	Giles, - - - -	765
	George, - - - -	890		Grant, - - - -	1112
1817.	George, - - - -	939	1789.	Grove A., - - -	848
1813.	George, - - - -	1206		Grove B., - - -	1123
1805.	George B., - - -	1291			

Children of the Seventh Generation.

BORN A. D.		Marginal No.	BORN A. D.		Marginal No.
1806.	Gaius, - - - -	1916		George G., - - -	2243
1827.	Gaius, - - - -	2381	1854.	George H., - - -	2246
1815.	Galusha J., - - -	1605	1847.	George H., - - -	2300
1837.	Gamaliel, - - - -	1700[44]	1860.	George H., - - -	3000
	George, - - - -	1720	1819.	George L., - - -	2114
	George, - - - -	1829	1842.	George L., - - -	2781
1807.	George, - - - -	1924	1835.	George L., - - -	2809
1834.	George, - - - -	2052	1849.	George L., - - -	3014
	George, - - - -	2227	1825.	George M., - - -	1700[33]
1843.	George, - - - -	2236	1841.	George M., - - -	1700[39]
	George, - - - -	2386		George M., - - -	2636
1818.	George, - - - -	2474	1843.	George R., - - -	2936
1859.	George, - - - -	2654	1851.	George S., - - -	2760
1849.	George, - - - -	2747	1828.	George W., - - -	1956
	George, - - - -	2906	1853.	George W., - - -	2093
	George, - - - -	2989[58]	1856.	George W., - - -	2146
1847.	George A., - - -	1745	1851.	George W., - - -	2417
1839.	George A., - - -	2071	1849.	George W., - - -	2436
1842.	George A., - - -	2183	1851.	George W., - - -	2455
1845.	George A., - - -	2386	1838.	George W., - - -	2524
1856.	George A., - - -	2465	1857.	Gilbert C., - - -	3028[63]
1829.	George A., - - -	2855	1820.	Giles, - - - -	1930
1860.	George A. L., - -	3081	1839.	Giles M., - - -	1909
1847.	George B., - - -	2628	1835.	Giles W., - - -	1891
1832.	George B., - - -	2796	1834.	Giles W., - - -	2509
1833.	George B., - - -	2802	1845.	Granville S., - -	2095
1837.	George E. H., - -	2078	1824.	Guy B., - - - -	2482

H.

Children of the Third Generation.

BORN A. D.		Marginal No.	BORN A. D.		Marginal No.
1694.	Hannah, - - - -	24	1699.	Hannah, - - - -	36

Children of the Fourth Generation.

Children of the Fifth Generation.

Children of the Sixth Generation.

Born A. D.		Marginal No.	Born A. D.		Marginal No.
1798.	Horace, - - -	**1237**		Huldah, - - - -	788
1806.	Horatio N., - - -	**910**	1772.	Huldah, - - - -	888
1813.	Horatio N., - - -	**1496**	1799.	Huldah, - - - -	908
1800.	Hosea, - - -	**1290**	1796.	Huldah, - - - -	1324
1822.	Hubbard W., - -	**1482**			

Children of the Seventh Generation.

Born A. D.		Marginal No.	Born A. D.		Marginal No.
1849.	Hampton A., - -	2921	1857.	Hart E., - - - -	2233[73]
1862.	Hancie E., - - -	1762		Hartwell, - - -	1732
1857.	Hancie J., - - -	2967	1823.	Harvey C., - - -	**2132**
1825.	Hannah, - - - -	1694	1835.	Hattie A., - - -	2077
1821.	Hannah, - - - -	1700[8]	1843.	Hattie A., - - -	2897
1809.	Hannah, - - - -	1925	1862.	Hattie E., - - -	3026
1832.	Hannah, - - - -	1940	1833.	Helen, - - - -	2215
1814.	Hannah, - - - -	2337		Helen, - - - -	2263
1830.	Hannah, - - - -	2795	1843.	Helen, - - - -	2404
	Hannah, - - - -	3036	1833.	Helen K., - - -	2914
1830.	Hannah C., - - -	1805	1834.	Helen M., - - -	1690[2]
1836.	Hannah E., - - -	2867	1829.	Helen M., - - -	1900
1852.	Hannah E., - - -	2882	1823.	Helen M., - - -	2162
1822.	Hannah F., - - -	2333	1833.	Henrietta, - - -	1890
	Hannah I., - - -	2833	1852.	Henrietta C., - -	2303
1828.	Harlow T., - - -	**2027**	1810.	Henrietta M., - -	1870
1822.	Harlow W., - - -	**2502**	1818.	Henry, - - - -	**1687**
1800.	Harmon, - - -	**2147**	1830.	Henry, - - - -	**1700**[27]
1832.	Harmon D., - - -	1729	1823.	Henry, - - - -	**1693**
1817.	Harriet, - - - -	1582	1805.	Henry, - - - -	**1923**
1857.	Harriet, - - - -	1700[48]		Henry, - - - -	**1970**
	Harriet, - - - -	1711	1831.	Henry, - - - -	**2047**
1826.	Harriet, - - - -	2663		Henry, - - - -	2262
1837.	Harriet, - - - -	2859	1816.	Henry, - - - -	**2338**
1849.	Harriet A., - - -	2258	1818.	Henry, - - - -	2360
1844.	Harriet B., - - -	1700[23]		Henry, - - - -	2513
1822.	Harriet E., - - -	2125	1836.	Henry, - - - -	**2732**
1846.	Harriet E., - - -	2294	1843.	Henry B., - - -	1907
1836.	Harriet E., - - -	2543	1816.	Henry B., - - -	**1943**
1844.	Harriet E., - - -	2644	1832.	Henry B., - - -	1992
1843.	Harriet E., - - -	2948	1810.	Henry C., - - -	**2165**
1852.	Harriet E., - - -	2966	1829.	Henry C., - - -	2213
	Harriet E., - - -	3010	1844.	Henry C., - - -	2299
1846.	Harriet L., - - -	2974	1835.	Henry C., - - -	**2803**
1837.	Harriet M., - - -	2723	1838.	Henry C., - - -	2818
1815.	Harriet M., - - -	2167	1843.	Henry C., - - -	2870
	Harriet M., - - -	2176		Henry C., - - -	**2887**
1826.	Harriet P., - - -	1990	1848.	Henry C., - - -	2975
1855.	Harriet R., - - -	2750	1839.	Henry D., - - -	2554
1822.	Harriet S., - - -	2564		Henry E., - - -	**2085**
1825.	Harris, - - - -	2495	1845.	Henry E., - - -	2919
1842.	Harris D., - - -	2255	1824.	Henry F., - - -	**2137**
1840.	Harrison, - - -	2217	1840.	Henry F., - - -	2223
1838.	Harrison L., - - -	2271	1818.	Henry G., - - -	**1999**

46'

I.

Children of the Second and Third Generations.

Children of the Fourth Generation.

Children of the Fifth Generation.

Children of the Sixth Generation.

Children of the Seventh Generation.

J.

Children of the Second and Third Generations.

Born A. D.		Marginal No.	Born A. D.		Marginal No.
1670.	James,	6	1669.	Jonathan,	5
1679.	James,	10	1687.	Jonathan,	12
1697.	James,	35	1696.	Jonathan,	28
1716.	Jemima,	42	1692.	Joseph,	16
1654.	John,	1	1713.	Joseph,	41
1678.	John,	9	1706.	Josiah,	32
1702.	John,	31			

Children of the Fourth Generation.

Born A. D.		Marginal No.	Born A. D.		Marginal No.
1731.	Jacob,	121	1722.	Joannah,	84
1713.	James,	57	1726.	John,	55
1724.	James,	97	1725.	John,	61
1749.	James,	113	1748.	John,	105
1746.	James,	174	1725.	John,	128
1729.	Jane,	73	1740.	Jonathan,	65
1743.	Jane,	163	1741.	Jonathan,	103
1712.	Jemima,	67	1728.	Joseph,	62
1740.	Jemima,	102	1751.	Joseph,	114
1738.	Jesse,	146	1737.	Josiah,	100
1738.	Joel,	133			

Children of the Fifth Generation.

Born A. D.		Marginal No.	Born A. D.		Marginal No.
1784.	Jabez,	452	1760.	Joel,	207
1759.	Jacob,	364	1764.	Joel,	412
1792.	Jacob,	532	1753.	John,	191
1739.	James,	199	1742.	John,	200
1754.	James,	311	1777.	John,	330
1779.	James,	343		John,	375
	James,	348		John,	392
1771.	James,	373		Jonathan,	319
1776.	James,	527	1778.	Jonathan,	325
1791.	James C.,	540	1774.	Jonathan,	517
1774.	Jedidiah,	404	1791.	Jonathan,	567
1750.	Jehiel,	355	1755.	Joseph,	205
	Jemima,	394	1766.	Joseph,	217
1762.	Jemima,	399	1774.	Josiah,	316
	Jerusha,	337	1783.	Josiah,	344
	Jerusha,	432		Josiah,	410
1788.	Jerusha,	565	1780.	Justin,	518
	Jesse,	346		Justus,	333
1789.	Jesse,	483	1766.	Justus,	420
1766.	Joanna,	413			

Children of the Sixth Generation.

Born A. D.		Marginal No.	Born A. D.		Marginal No.
1788.	Jabez,	723	1783.	Jabez,	898
1784.	Jabez,	737		James,	615

360 PART I.—INDEX TO GIVEN NAMES.

Born A. D.	Name	Marginal No.
1788.	James,	648
1825.	James,	**693**
1781.	James,	**897**
1823.	James,	994
1794.	James,	**1031**
1813.	James,	1049
1823.	James,	**1210**
1815.	James C.,	1425
1835.	James C.,	1443
1819.	James E.,	1505
1817.	James H.,	**1334**
1813.	James H.,	**1445**
1803.	James J.,	**1147**
1817.	James R.,	**996**
1813.	James S.,	1548
1832.	Jane,	696
1818.	Jane,	986
1807.	Jane,	1204
1814.	Jane,	1333
1844.	Jane E.,	1458
	Jane M.,	691
1816.	Jane P.,	1509
1815.	Jared,	**1207**
	Jarvis,	**1177**
1821.	Jarvis B.,	**1069**
1788.	Jedidiah,	1083
1797.	Jemima,	816
1830.	Jerome,	**1452**
1815.	Jerome,	**1518**
1796.	Jerusha,	760
	Jerusha,	792
1798.	Jerusha,	964
1827.	Jerusha,	1161
1832.	Jerusha,	1465
1821.	Jerusha,	1551
1771.	Joanna,	768

Born A. D.	Name	Marginal No.
	Joel,	**614**
1827.	Joel,	**694**
1818.	Joel H.,	**1480**
1780.	John,	**608**
1801.	John,	**931**
1804.	John,	**1037**
	John,	1052
	John,	1176
1795.	John B.,	**875**
1774.	John B.,	**889**
1782.	John C.,	**572**
1830.	John D.,	**1162**
1806.	John F.,	**1045**
1826.	John Q. A.,	**1432**
	John R.,	**1050**
1807.	John S.,	**846**
1818.	John W.,	**1550**
1778.	Jonathan,	**770**
1801.	Jonathan,	**921**
1810.	Jonathan A. S.,	**729**
1829.	Jonathan B.,	**1402**
1816.	Jonathan H.,	**1180**
1820.	Jonathan S.,	**1555**
1818.	Joseph,	661
1820.	Joseph,	**1517**
1809.	Joseph I.,	**858**
1818.	Joseph R.,	**1435**
1819.	Josephine,	1543
1808.	Joshua J.,*	**1046**
1827.	Julia A.,	1411
	Julius,	1079
1798.	Julius,	**1087**
1814.	Julius W.,	**1059**
1786.	Justus,	**959**
1799.	Justus,	**1127**

Children of the Seventh Generation.

Born	Name	No.
1812.	Jabez L.,	**1820**
	James,	**1696**
1821.	James,	**1700**[14]
1845.	James,	1812
1812.	James,	1820
1840.	James,	1838
1827.	James,	2484
1838.	James,	**2944**
1840.	James A.,	2780
1838.	James A.,	3058
1839.	James B.,	**2733**

Born	Name	No.
1820.	James C.,	2369
1849.	James E.,	3047
1843.	James F.,	1862
1848.	James H.,	2808
1833.	James J.,	**2570**
1842.	James L.,	2197
1826.	James M.,	1638
1846.	James M.,	1908
1811.	James M.,	**2151**
1839.	James M.,	**2428**
1855.	James N.,	2420

*Joshua Jackson.

Born A. D.		Marginal No.	Born A. D.		Marginal No.
1818.	James O., - - -	1700³	1814.	John H. S., - - -	2159
1843.	James R., - - -	1632	1817.	John J. R., - - -	**1576**
1856.	James R., - - -	2652	1847.	John M., - - - -	1839
1827.	James S., - - -	2354	1811.	John M., - - - -	**2121**
1808.	James T., - - -	2154	1852.	John M., - - - -	2145
1842.	James V., - - -	2993	1832.	John M., - - - -	2498
1810.	James W., - - -	2328	1851.	John M., - - - -	3015
1843.	James W., - - -	2555		John N., - - - -	3031
1823.	Jane, - - - -	2477	1844.	John Q., - - - -	1633
1833.	Jane E., - - -	1902	1808.	John R., - - - -	1562
1844.	Jane E., - - - -	2184	1826.	John R., - - - -	2537
1844.	Jane E., - - - -	2256		John R., - - - -	3006
1850.	Jane E., - - -	2604	1858.	John R., - - - -	3122
1844.	Jane L., - - -	2606	1848.	John S., - - - -	2232
1849.	Jane L., - - -	2872	1862.	John T., - - - -	2650
1835.	Jane M., - - -	2221	1806.	John W.,- - - -	**1780**
1809.	Jane M., - - -	2327⁴⁹	1846.	John W.,- - - -	2871
1832.	Jane M. A.,- - -	1641	1803.	Jonathan, - - -	1921
1833.	Jared P. K., - -	1704		Jonathan, - - -	**2886**
1838.	Jay, - - - - -	1834	1832.	Jonathan H., - -	2194
1812.	Jemima, - - - -	1997	1838.	Joseph, - - - -	1700³⁰
	Jeannette, - - -	2607	1832.	Joseph, - - -	**1700**³⁶
1852.	Jennette M. S.,-	1912	1840.	Joseph, - - - -	**2053**
1862.	Jennie, - - - -	1763		Joseph A., - - -	**1669**
1848.	Jerome, - - - -	2561	1824.	Joseph N., - - -	**2126**
1848.	Jerome, - - - -	3086	1815.	Joseph S., - - -	1985
1841.	Jerome H., -- - -	2954		Josephine, - - -	2391
1820.	Jerusha E., - - -	1883	1833.	Josephine A., - -	2080
1856.	Jessie O., - - -	2626	1852.	Josephine A., - -	3099
1862.	Jessie M., - - -	2250	1844.	Josephine E., - -	2994
	Joel, - - - -	3053		Julia, - - - -	1695
1843.	Joel E., - - - -	3043	1835.	Julia, - - - -	1700³⁷
1846.	Joel E., - - - -	3045	1838.	Julia, - - - -	1837
1827.	John, - - - -	**1736**		Julia, - - - -	2293
1809.	John, - - - -	**2150**		Julia, - - - -	2311
1850.	John, - - - -	2630	1830.	Julia, - - - -	2729
1824.	John, - - - -	**2828**	1831.	Julia A., - - -	2569
1839.	John, - - - -	**2911**	1834.	Julia A., - - -	2722
	John, - - - -	2985	1848.	Julia A., - - -	2879
1835.	John A., - - -	1642	1840.	Julia A., - - -	2947
1832.	John A., - - -	**2051**	1846.	Julia A., - - -	2950
1843.	John A., - - -	2593	1844.	Julia A., - - -	3049
1843.	John A., - - -	2612	1807.	Julia E., - - -	2334
1864.	John A., - - -	3002	1855.	Julia E., - - -	3064
1837.	John C., - - -	**2427**	1838.	Julia L., - - -	2553
1833.	John C., - - -	2487	1850.	Julia O., - - -	2978
1826.	John D., - - -	**1955**	1827.	Julia P., - - -	2538
1844.	John D., - - -	**2434**	1823.	Juliette, - - -	2109
1860.	John E., - - -	2249		Juliette, - - -	2905
1829.	John F., - - -	**2135**	1859.	Julius, - - - -	3121
1841.	John F., - - -	**2806**	1817.	Julius A., - - -	**1882**

K.

Children of the Fifth Generation.

Children of the Sixth Generation.

Children of the Seventh Generation.

L.

Children of the Fourth Generation.

Children of the Fifth Generation.

Children of the Sixth Generation.

Born A. D.		Marginal No.	Born A. D.		Marginal No.
	Levi, - - - - -	**1008**	1783.	Lucina, - - - -	743
1806.	Levi, - - - - -	**1340**	1810.	Lucina A., - - -	885
1824.	Levi S., - - - -	**1437**	1794.	Lucina B., - - -	815
	Lewis, - - - -	**684**	1816.	Lucinda, - - - -	926
1786.	Lewis, - - - -	**871**	1817.	Lucinda, - - - -	991
1808.	Lewis, - - - - -	**1100**	1834.	Lucinda, - - - -	1189
1822.	Liberty, - - - -	**940**	1833.	Lucinda, - - - -	1202
1816.	Linus, - - - -	1380	1811.	Lucinda, - - - -	1350
	Lois, - - - - -	611	1848.	Lucinda, - - - -	1538
	Lois, - - - - -	710		Lucretia, - - - -	893
	Lois, - - - - -	1294	1818.	Lucretia, - - - -	1142
1807.	Lois, - - - - -	1365	1786.	Lucy, - - - - -	613
1811.	Lorania, - - - -	1495	1795.	Lucy, - - - - -	662
1813.	Lorenzo, - - - -	953	1842.	Lucy, - - - - -	700
1802.	Lorin, - - - - -	**679**	1787.	Lucy, - - - - -	722
	Lorin, - - - - -	943	1788.	Lucy, - - - - -	900
1802.	Lorin, - - - - -	**1227**	1812.	Lucy, - - - - -	918
	Lorin, - - - - -	1295	1798.	Lucy, - - - - -	1041
1818.	Lorin A., - - - -	**1426**	1822.	Lucy, - - - - -	1158
1815.	Lorin C., - - - -	**1446**	1804.	Lucy, - - - - -	1313
1810.	Lorinda, - - - -	1377	1828.	Lucy A., - - - -	1183
1788.	Lorrain T., - - -	**574**	1806.	Lucy F., - - - -	1132
1813.	Loton, - - - -	985	1817.	Lucy J., - - - -	1060
1801.	Louisa, - - - -	818	1809.	Lucy M., - - - -	1389
1814.	Louisa, - - - -	919	1793.	Luke, - - - - -	625
1809.	Louisa, - - - -	1138	1821.	Luke A., - - - -	**1372**
1826.	Louisa N., - - - -	1211	1791.	Luman, - - - -	**739**
1788.	Lovina, - - - -	1103	1808.	Luman, - - - -	**934**
1837.	Lovina, - - - -	1190	1811.	Lumas H., - - -	1058
1815.	Lovina, - - - -	1265		Luther, - - - -	**1078**
1790.	Lovisa, - - - -	591	1836.	Luther A., - - -	**1415**
1793.	Lovisa, - - - -	874	1813.	Luther L., - - -	**1424**
1791.	Lovisa, - - - -	961	1789.	Lydia, - - - -	639
	Lovisa, - - - -	1245	1808.	Lydia, - - - -	916
1821.	Lovisa, - - - -	1364	1787.	Lydia, - - - -	1300
1808.	Lovisa, - - - -	1420	1826.	Lydia, - - - -	1440
1816.	Luana, - - - -	1401	1793.	Lyman, - - - -	**725**
1824.	Lucetta N., - - -	1483	1808.	Lyman, - - - -	**951**
1794.	Lucina, - - - -	676	1808.	Lyman, - - - -	**1137**

Children of the Seventh Generation.

Born A. D.		Marginal No.	Born A. D.		Marginal No.
1844.	Landemer, - - -	2982	1823.	Lauretta, - - -	2352
1822.	Laura, - - - -	1593	1844.	Lauretta A., - - -	2955
1848.	Laura, - - - -	2629	1845.	Lauriett, - - - -	2528
1818.	Laura, - - - -	2702	1850.	Laurin H., - - -	2624
1818.	Laura, - - - -	2710	1817.	Lavinia A., - - -	2331[50]
1817.	Laura A., - - -	2168	1841.	Laurinda O., - -	2963
1856.	Laura A., - - -	2616		Lawrence P., - - -	2845
1824.	Laura S., - - -	1585	1853.	Leanna, - - - -	2523
1850.	Laurania, - - -	1840	1828.	Lemuel F., - - -	2505
	Lauraetta - - -	1616	1848.	Leonora B., - - -	2687

Born A. D.		Marginal No.	Born A. D.		Marginal No.
1854.	Leora R., - - -	2952	1832.	Lucina, - - - -	1749
	Lester J., - - -	2272	1815.	Lucina, - - - -	1784
1843.	Lester J., - - -	2298		Lucinda, - - - -	1619
	Leverett E., - - -	**1667**	1814.	Lucinda, - - - -	1874
1818.	Leverett E., - - -	**1852**	1816.	Lucinda, - - - -	1919
1816.	Levi, - - - - -	**2709**	1826.	Lucinda, - - - -	2211
1823.	Levi P., - - - -	**1954**	1822.	Lucinda, - - - -	2365
	Lewis, - - - -	1757	1820.	Lucinda, - - - -	2826
	Lewis, - - - -	2276	1807.	Lucius, - - - -	1602
1804.	Lewis, - - - -	2319	1829.	Lucius F., - - -	1728
1851.	Lewis, - - - -	2531	1845.	Lucius F., - - -	2020
1850.	Lewis, - - - -	2562	1842.	Lucius M., - - -	1752
1845.	Lewis L., - - - -	3075	1820.	Lucy, - - - - -	1700[7]
1818.	Lewis M., - - -	**2124**		Lucy, - - - - -	2309
1806.	Lewis S., - - -	2149	1827.	Lucy, - - - - -	2790
1839.	Lewis Y., - - -	2119	1826.	Lucy A., - - -	1984
1857.	Libbie E., - - -	2874[53]	1818.	Lucy A., - - -	2107
1825.	Lindora A., - - -	1665	1837.	Lucy A., - - -	2182
1858.	Lilla, - - - - -	2981[57]	1832.	Lucy A., - - -	2425
1858.	Lillie E., - - - -	3016	1842.	Lucy A., - - -	2557
1860.	Lizzie B., - - -	2753	1843.	Lucy A., - - -	2767
1857.	Lizzie M., - - -	3020	1831.	Lucy A., - - -	2856
1821.	Lois, - - - - -	1657	1846.	Lucy C., - - - -	2645
1813.	Lois, - - - - -	2357	1833.	Lucy C., - - - -	2864
1820.	Lorenzo, - - - -	2351	1835.	Lucy E., - - -	1737
1863.	Lorenzo, - - - -	2535	1838.	Lucy E., - - - -	2031
1819.	Lorenzo D., - - -	**2344**	1847.	Lucy G., - - - -	1702
1830.	Lorenzo D., - - -	**2414**	1825.	Lucy L., - - - -	1865
1824.	Lorenzo E., - - -	1798		Lucy L., - - - -	2840
1845.	Lorenzo M., - - -	1744	1837.	Lucy M., - - - -	2915
1809.	Lorenzo W., - - -	**2164**	1818.	Lucy V., - - - -	2363
	Lorin, - - - - -	1709	1850.	Lucy V., - - - -	2598
1833.	Lorin, - - - - -	2368	1811.	Luke, - - - -	**2336**
1843.	Lorin H., - - -	1628	1826.	Luke H., - - - -	**1671**
1823.	Lorin S., - - - -	2788	1828.	Luke K., - - - -	**1666**
1841.	Lorinthia, - - -	2726	1828.	Luman, - - - -	**2690**
1834.	Lorissa, - - - -	1750	1830.	Luman, - - - -	**2724**
1815.	Lorrain T., - - -	1575	1835.	Luman S., - - -	**1675**
1823.	Loton H., - - -	2673	1845.	Lumas H., - - -	2440
1864.	Louis, - - - -	2656		Luther, - - - -	1617
1852.	Louis A., - - -	2970	1814.	Luther, - - - -	1950
1834.	Louisa, - - - -	2830	1862.	Luther, - - - -	2990
	Louisa, - - - -	2885	1856.	Luther D., - - -	2996
1821.	Louisa C., - - -	1724	1825.	Lydia, - - - -	2380
1822.	Louisa L., - - -	2024	1822.	Lydia, - - - -	2827
1831.	Lovina E., - - -	2548	1846.	Lydia A., - - - -	2185
	Lovisa, - - - -	2274	1825.	Lydia D., - - -	1825
1841.	Lovisa, - - - -	2763	1853.	Lydia F., - - -	2772
1853.	Lovisa R., - - -	2923	1831.	Lyman F., - - -	2486
1840.	Lucia D., - - -	2611	1820.	Lyman L., - - -	**2364**
	Lucina, - - - -	1708			

M.

Children of the Second and Third Generations.

Born A. D.		Marginal No.	Born A. D.		Marginal No.
1683.	Margaret,	11	1681.	Mary,	18
1695.	Margaret,	25	1706.	Mary,	38
1658.	Mary,	3	1697.	Mindwell,	45
1688.	Mary,	14			

Children of the Fourth Generation.

Born A. D.		Marginal No.	Born A. D.		Marginal No.
1715.	Margaret,	58	1712.	Mehitable,	79
1741.	Martha,	171	1745.	Mehitable,	164
1711.	Mary,	56	1722.	Mindwell,	96
1734.	Mary,	64		Mindwell,	148
1734.	Mary,	76	1753.	Mindwell,	178
1723.	Mary,	85	1711.	Miriam,	66
1722.	Mary,	127	1734.	Moses,	**130**
1739.	Mary,	170			

Children of the Fifth Generation.

Born A. D.		Marginal No.	Born A. D.		Marginal No.
1749.	Margaret,	202	1755.	Mary,	472
1772.	Margaret,	250	1767.	Mary,	487
1776.	Margaret,	342	1774.	Mary,	526
1775.	Martha,	284	1774.	Matilda,	251
1781.	Martha,	297	1776.	Mathew,	225
	Martha,	444	1760.	Mehitable,	264
	Martha,	528	1769.	Mehitable,	402
	Martha A.,	486	1770.	Mehitable,	469
1787.	Martha D.,	482		Mehitable,	501
1769.	Mary,	227	1770.	Mindwell,	219
1764.	Mary,	247	1771.	Miriam,	242
1749.	Mary,	310	1772.	Miriam,	470
1763.	Mary,	314	1789.	Morris,	454
	Mary,	446	1758.	Moses,	**397**

Children of the Sixth Generation.

Born A. D.		Marginal No.	Born A. D.		Marginal No.
1787.	Mabel,	1217	1813.	Maria,	1264
1794.	Marcia,	741		Marietta,	980
1792.	Marcia,	1104	1813.	Maronett,	937
	Marcus J.,	**1164**	1793.	Martha,	576
	Margaret,	755		Martha,	896
1792.	Margaret,	906	1800.	Martha,	930
1811.	Margaret,	1367	1805.	Martha,	1270
	Margery,	1471	1820.	Martha,	1354
	Maria,	756	1821.	Martha,	1499
	Maria,	945	1786.	Martha A.,	828
1805.	Maria,	982	1807.	Martha M.,	1276
1795.	Maria,	1106	1786.	Martin,	**589**
	Maria,	1126	1802.	Martin,	**763**
	Maria,	1168	1782.	Mary,	633

Children of the Seventh Generation.

Born A. D.		Marginal No.	Born A. D.		Marginal No.
1825.	Marshall, - - - -	**2689**	1830.	Mary A., - - - -	2219
	Martha, - - - -	1699	1825.	Mary A., - - - -	2422
	Martha, - - - -	1734	1824.	Mary A., - - - -	2503
1836.	Martha, - - -	1959	1839.	Mary A., - - - -	2610
1820.	Martha, - - - -	2476	1836.	Mary A., - - - -	2708
1842.	Martha, - - - -	2766	1843.	Mary A., - - - -	2785
1844.	Martha, - - - -	2793	1824.	Mary A., - - - -	2852
	Martha, - - - -	2889	1841.	Mary A., - - - -	2973
	Martha, - - - -	2926	1853.	Mary A., - - - -	3118
1829.	Martha A., - - -	1639	1831.	Mary B., - - - -	2079
1850.	Martha A., - - -	1747	1825.	Mary C., - - - -	2174
1852.	Martha A., - - -	2240	1845.	Mary C., - - - -	2452
1855.	Martha A., - - -	2247	1827.	Mary C., - - - -	2728
1856.	Martha A., - - -	3019	1832.	Mary D., - - - -	1700^{42}
1845.	Martha F., - - -	2435	1845.	Mary E., - - - -	1700^{32}
1846.	Martha F., - - -	2441	1820.	Mary E., - - - -	1855
	Martha H., - - -	2089	1840.	Mary E., - - -	1893
	Martha J., - - -	1620		Mary E., - - - -	2087
1846.	Martha J., - - -	2878	1811.	Mary E., - - - -	2155
1826.	Martha M., - - -	2504	1834.	Mary E., - - - -	2180
1844.	Martha M., - - -	2594	1858.	Mary E., - - - -	2208^{68}
1839.	Martha M., - - -	2860	1841.	Mary E., - - - -	2297
1839.	Martha M., - - -	2992	1853.	Mary E., - - - -	2445
1837.	Martin, - - - -	**2742**	1850.	Mary E., - - - -	2771
1836.	Martin, - - - -	2798	1840.	Mary E., - - - -	2869
1823.	Martin F., - - -	1896	1840.	Mary E., - - - -	2875
1825.	Martin L., - - -	2026	1864.	Mary E., - - - -	3109
1840.	Martin V., - - -	**2693**		Mary F., - - - -	2608
1814.	Marvin K., - - -	**2823**	1850.	Mary G., - - -	3033
	Mary, - - - - -	1713	1816.	Mary H., - - - -	1776
1848.	Mary, - - - - -	1813	1826.	Mary H., - - - -	2075
	Mary, - - - - -	1816	1853.	Mary H., - - - -	3004
1801.	Mary, - - - - -	1920	1847.	Mary I., - - - -	2097
	Mary, - - - - -	2279	1839.	Mary J., - - - -	1700^{21}
1811.	Mary, - - - - -	2329		Mary J., - - - -	2470
1844.	Mary, - - - - -	2460	1849.	Mary J., - - - -	2530
1827.	Mary, - - - - -	2488	1835.	Mary J., - - - -	2550
1844.	Mary, - - - - -	2460	1843.	Mary J., - - - -	2586
1844.	Mary, - - - - -	2558		Mary J., - - - -	2888
	Mary, - - - - -	2619	1839.	Mary J., - - - -	2934
1837.	Mary, - - - - -	2736	1863.	Mary J., - - - -	3029
1841.	Mary, - - - - -	2792	1828.	Mary L., - - - -	1672
1836.	Mary, - - - - -	2810	1845.	Mary L., - - - -	2231
	Mary, - - - - -	2837	1851.	Mary L., - - - -	2245
1825.	Mary A., - - - -	1598	1838.	Mary M., - - - -	1626
1825.	Mary A., - - - -	1610	1813.	Mary M., - - - -	1961
1832.	Mary A., - - - -	1663	1833.	Mary M., - - - -	1993
1834.	Mary A., - - - -	1730	1820.	Mary M., - - - -	2039
	Mary A., - - - -	1828	1825.	Mary P., - - - -	1843
1829.	Mary A., - - - -	2070	1840.	Mary P., - - - -	1888
1820.	Mary A., - - - -	2130	1841.	Mary R., - - - -	1869

N.

Children of the Fourth Generation.

Children of the Fifth Generation.

Children of the Sixth Generation.

Children of the Seventh Generation.

Born A. D.		Marginal No.	Born A. D.		Marginal No.
1817.	Nancy, - - - -	1767	1850.	Nelson O., - - -	3079
1833.	Nancy, - - - -	2707	1843.	Nelson S., - - -	2784
1822.	Nancy, - - - -	2712	1864.	Nettie C., - - -	3105
1814.	Nancy A., - - -	1962	1824.	Newton, - - - -	2480
1841.	Nancy J., - - -	1627	1840.	Newton, - - - -	2518
1852.	Nancy M., - - -	3034	1830.	Newton W., - - -	1673
1817.	Nancy P., - - -	1570	1838.	Niles, - - - - -	2683
1840.	Naomi, - - - -	2545	1818.	Noah E., - - - -	1876
1833.	Nathan W., - - -	2549	1806.	Noel, - - - - -	2320
1848.	Nellie M., - - -	2957	1851.	Noel M., - - -	3011
1863.	Nellie R., - - -	2102	1842.	Norman, - - - -	1647
1844.	Nelson H., - - -	3061	1824.	Norman, - - - -	2704
	Nelson L., - - -	2894	1850.	Norman F., - - -	3003

O.

Children of the Fourth Generation.

1736.	Olive, - - - -	92	1754.	Oliver, - - - -	168

Children of the Fifth Generation.

1746.	Obadiah, - - - -	269		Oliver, - - - -	321
1766.	Obadiah, - - - -	290	1777.	Oliver, - - - -	503
1766.	Obadiah, - - - -	494	1777.	Oliver, - - - -	504
1756.	Olive, - - - - -	465	1781.	Osee, - - - - -	326
1760.	Oliver, - - - -	213			

Children of the Sixth Generation.

1798.	Obadiah, - - - -	854	1788.	Orrin, - - - -	598
	Obadiah, - - - -	1304	1797.	Orrin, - - - -	627
1789.	Obed, - - - - -	1301	1788.	Orrin, - - - -	673
1791.	Olive, - - - -	724	1839.	Orrin, - - - -	699
1823.	Olive, - - - -	1267	1788.	Orrin, - - - -	812
1783.	Oliver, - - - -	704	1803.	Orrin, - - - -	1131
1802.	Oliver, - - - -	1239	1815.	Oris, - - - - -	1344
1812.	Oliver, - - - -	1351	1807.	Orson, - - - -	983
1803.	Oliver C., - - -	1338		Orson, - - - -	1169
1813.	Omar, - - - -	1274*	1806.	Orton, - - - -	915
1803.	Orlando, - - - -	1280	1813.	Orville, - - - -	1391
1825.	Orlo A., - - - -	1071	1833.	Osee, - - - - -	922

Children of the Seventh Generation.

	Obadiah, - - - -	2838	1816.	Olive M., - - -	2156
1845.	Octavia S., - - -	2191	1828.	Olive Z., - - -	1791
	Olive, - - - - -	2327	1810.	Oliver, - - - -	1766
1831.	Olive M., - - -	1682		Oliver, - - - -	2773

* See Errata.

48

Born A.D.		Marginal No.	Born A.D.		Marginal No.
1853.	Oliver A.,	2941	1814.	Orrin,	2341
1847.	Oliver C.,	2920	1851.	Orrin A.,	2589
1824.	Oliver W.,	1700[25]	1832.	Orrin E.,	**1677**
1845.	Olivia,	3114	1825.	Orrin W.,	1726
1840.	Omar,	2765	1844.	Orissa A.,	2623
1847.	Orlando T.,	2965	1834.	Orson,	**1946**
1850.	Ophelia,	2522	1860.	Orval W.,	2190
1810.	Orpha D.,	1568	1848.	Oscar,	2462
1827.	Orpha H.,	1879	1829.	Oscar S.,	**1800**
1820.	Orrin,	1634			

P.

Child of the Third Generation.

1709. Pelatiah, - - - - **33**

Children of the Fourth Generation.

1738.	Pelatiah,	**101**	1729.	Phebe,	120

Children of the Fifth Generation.

Born A.D.		Marginal No.	Born A.D.		Marginal No.
1799.	Pamelia,	570	1763.	Peter,	**312**
	Pelatiah,	318	1771.	Philena,	383
1762.	Penelope,	475	1756.	Phineas,	**285**
1789.	Persis,	328	1787.	Pliny,	**556**
1781.	Persis,	388	1774.	Prudence,	341
1760.	Peter,	**222**		Prudence,	428
1767.	Peter,	266		Prudence,	439
1743.	Peter,	268			

Children of the Sixth Generation.

Born A.D.		Marginal No.	Born A.D.		Marginal No.
1816.	Pamelia,	1141	1797.	Peter P.,	907
	Pamelia,	1120	1793.	Phila,	1091
1792.	Panthea,	731	1820.	Philanda,	**956**
1802.	Patience,	595	1816.	Philena S.,	1067
1810.	Paulina,	1512	1788.	Philo,	**872**
1785.	Pelera,	827	1806.	Philo P.,	**968**
1797.	Perry,	**653**	1806.	Phineas,	683
1802.	Persis,	786	1792.	Phineas,	831
1792.	Persis,	814	1795.	Polly,	577
	Persis,	1144		Polly,	610
	Persis,	1170	1795.	Polly,	749
1804.	Persis,	1339	1802.	Polly,	883
	Persis,	1421	1800.	Polly,	1034
1790.	Peter,	**674**	1813.	Polly,	1154
1795.	Peter P.,	**832**	1788.	Prudence,	590

Children of the Seventh Generation.

Born A.D.		Marginal No.	Born A.D.		Marginal No.
1827.	Pamelia,	2134	1825.	Permelia,	2346
1837.	Pamelia A.,	2118	1835.	Perry,	**1700**[29]
1828.	Paulina,	2829	1816.	Persis,	1951

Born A. D.		Marginal No.	Born A. D.		Marginal No.
1813.	Persis C.,- - - -	2166	1814.	Philo, - - - - -	2342
1818.	Peter E., - - - -	**2038**	1835.	Philo C., - - - -	2129
1845.	Phebe C., - - -	2301	1826.	Phineas, - - - -	**1790**
1834.	Philander, - - -	1596	1819.	Phineas B., - - -	2022
1821.	Philander P., - -	**1877**	1846.	Phineas L., - - -	2021
	Philena, - - - -	1670	1826.	Platt F., - - - -	**2853**
1861.	Philena, - - - -	2655		Pliny M., - - -	2843
1849.	Philena S., - - -	2454	1824.	Polly, - - - - -	1589
1858.	Philenia E., - - -	2248	1805.	Polly, - - - - -	1779
1838.	Philinda T., - - -	2544	1812.	Polly A., - - - -	1782
	Philo, - - - - -	2273	1845.	Polly M., - - -	2416

R.

[Children of the Second and Third Generations.

1656.	Robert, - - - -	**2**	1684.	Robert, - - - -	**20**
1694.	Rebecca, - - - -	27			

Children of the Fourth Generation.

	Rebecca, - - - -	91	1751.	Rosa, - - - - -	156
1717.	Richard, - - - -	**59**	1746.	Rose, - - - - -	155
1724.	Robert, - - - -	**71**	1753.	Ruth, - - - - -	188

Children of the Fifth Generation.

1755.	Rachel, - - - -	358	1781.	Roswell, - - - -	533
1795.	Rebecca, - - - -	525		Roxanna, - - - -	338
	Rebecca, - - - -	547	1764.	Roxanna, - - - -	379
1781.	Reuben, - - - -	**508**	1815.	Roxanna, - - - -	562
	Rhoda, - - - -	352	1762.	Royal, - - - -	**214**
1763.	Rhoda, - - - -	366	1757.	Rufus, - - - -	**359**
1764.	Rhoda, - - - -	493	1789.	Russell, - - - -	**231**
	Rhoda, - - - -	530	1761.	Ruth, - - - - -	497
1758.	Richard, - - - -	**210**	1768.	Ruth, - - - - -	515
1749.	Robert, - - - -	**232**			

Children of the Sixth Generation.

1780.	Rachel, - - - -	868	1815.	Rhoda R., - - -	1400
1820.	Ralph P., - - -	**997**	1789.	Richard, - - -	**624**
1788.	Randolph, - - -	**797**	1813.	Richard H., - - -	**859**
1798.	Rebecca, - - - -	761		Richard S., - - -	**1064**
	Rebecca, - - - -	1491	1790.	Robert, - - - -	706
1802.	Reuben, - - - -	**681**	1822.	Roger M. S., - -	**860**
1814.	Reuben A., - - -	**1379**	1828.	Roger W., - - -	**1546**
1815.	Reuel, - - - -	**938**		Rosanna, - - - -	1561
1799.	Rheuma, - - - -	1224		Roswell, - - - -	**1003**
1796.	Rhoda, - - - -	593	1824.	Roswell, - - - -	**1186**
	Rhoda, - - - -	776	1793.	Roxa, - - - - -	800
	Rhoda, - - - -	866		Roxana, - - - -	707
1815.	Rhoda, - - - -	1231	1808.	Roxana, - - - -	716
1806.	Rhoda, - - - -	1419	1786.	Roxana, - - - -	1102

BORN A. D.		Marginal No.	BORN A. D.		Marginal No.
	Roxana, - - - -	1173	1794.	Ruth, - - - - -	592
1794.	Ruby, - - - - -	620	1789.	Ruth, - - - - -	718
1776.	Ruby, - - - - -	701		Ruth, - - - - -	791
1790.	Rufus, - - - -	901	1817.	Ruth, - - - - -	1345
1783.	Rufus, - - - -	**1015**	1812.	Ruth, - - - - -	1399
1813.	Rufus M., - -	**1135**			

Children of the Seventh Generation.

BORN A. D.		Marginal No.	BORN A. D.		Marginal No.
1820.	Rachel, - - - -	1944	1820.	Robert M., - - -	**2161**
	Rachel A., - - -	2280		Robert R., - - -	3007
1824.	Ralph, - - - -	**2536**	1817.	Rodolphus, - - -	1586
1824.	Randolph, - - -	1965	1849.	Roger S., - - -	2098
1807.	Randolph, - - -	1979		Rollin, - - - -	2390
1848.	Randolph O., - -	2295	1858.	Rollo C., - - - -	2960
1851.	Ransom O., - - -	2940	1825.	Roscius M., - - -	2041
1849.	Ransom R., - - -	2701	1821.	Rosetta, - - - -	1584
	Rebecca, - - - -	2895	1841.	Rowena, - - - -	2526
1853.	Rebecca A., - - -	2976	1840.	Rowena C., - - -	2229
1841.	Rebecca R. S., - -	2917	1817.	Rowena S., - - -	2478
1824.	Reuben M., - -	**2565**	1822.	Roxanna, - - - -	1598
1823.	Reuben O., - - -	2040	1822.	Roxanna, - - - -	2679
1836.	Reuben R., - - -	1755		Roxy, - - - - -	2326
1819.	Rhoda, - - - -	1583	1812.	Royal A., - -	**2340**
1832.	Rhoda A., - - -	1623	1835.	Rufus, - - - -	1958
1847.	Rhoda F., - - -	2769	1841.	Rufus C., - - -	2556
1808.	Rhoda L., - - -	1567	1820.	Rufus D. G., - -	2157
1835.	Richard D., - - -	2910	1817.	Rufus H., - - -	2349
1830.	Richard F., - -	**1680**	1833.	Russell, - - - -	**2725**
	Richard H., - - -	2092	1828.	Russell B., - - -	2507
1816.	Richard P., - -	**2060**		Ruth, - - - - -	1972
1808.	Robert, - - - -	**1765**	1839.	Ruth, - - - - -	2912
1843.	Robert A., - - -	1809		Ruth, - - - - -	2928
1819.	Robert A., - -	**1964**	1812.	Ruth A., - - - -	1579
1859.	Robert H., - - -	2815	1868.	Ruth A., - - - -	2208[12]

S.

Children of the Third Generation.

BORN A. D.		Marginal No.	BORN A. D.		Marginal No.
1686.	Samuel, - - - -	21	1689.	Sarah, - - - -	15
1700.	Samuel, - - - -	30	1710.	Sarah, - - - -	40

Children of the Fourth Generation.

BORN A. D.		Marginal No.	BORN A. D.		Marginal No.
1718.	Samuel, - - - -	82	1729.	Sarah, - - - -	143
1746.	Samuel, - - - -	104	1747.	Sarah, - - - -	165
1736.	Samuel, - - - -	132	1746.	Sharon, - - - -	154
1724.	Sarah, - - - -	54	1730.	Stephen, - - - -	63
1742.	Sarah, - - - -	112			

Children of the Fifth Generation.

Born A. D.		Marginal No.	Born A. D.		Marginal No.
1776.	Sabra, - - - -	324	1772.	Sharon, - - - -	489
	Sally, - - - - -	377	1796.	Shubael, - - - -	541
1788.	Salmon, - - - -	435	1760.	Silas, - - - - -	334
1756.	Samuel, - - - -	209	1764.	Simeon, - - - -	197
1770.	Samuel, - - - -	322	1792.	Simeon, - - - -	391
	Samuel, - - - -	376	1758.	Simeon, - - - -	458
	Samuel, - - - -	436	1751.	Solomon, - - - -	356
1787.	Samuel, - - - -	453	1755.	Stephen, - - - -	235
1762.	Sarah, - - - -	196		Stephen, - - - -	350
1785.	Sarah, - - - -	229	1759.	Stone, - - - - -	278
1766.	Sarah, - - - -	240	1778.	Stowel, - - - -	317
1756.	Sarah, - - - -	277		Susannah, - - -	422
	Sarah, - - - -	447	1754.	Sybil, - - - - -	271
1756.	Sarah, - - - -	473	1763.	Sybil, - - - - -	361
1785.	Sarah, - - - -	564	1767.	Sybil, - - - - -	378
1764.	Seth, - - - - -	215	1767.	Sybil, - - - - -	427
1779.	Seth, - - - - -	481	1761.	Sylvanus, - - - -	246

Children of the Sixth Generation.

Born A. D.		Marginal No.	Born A. D.		Marginal No.
	Sabra, - - - -	1125	1814.	Sarah, - - - -	1479
1808.	Sabra, - - - -	1149	1783.	Sarah B., - - - -	826
1830.	Salina, - - - -	1537	1794.	Sarah D., - - - -	880
1792.	Sally, - - - - -	839	1818.	Sarah E., - - -	1157
1814.	Sally, - - - - -	1030	1823.	Sarah E., - - -	1544
1798.	Sally, - - - - -	1033	1824.	Sarah E., - - -	1557
1797.	Sally, - - - - -	1223	1814.	Sarah M., - - -	1066
1803.	Sally, - - - - -	1247	1826.	Selina, - - - -	1396
1784.	Salmon, - - - -	583	1796.	Seth, - - - - -	621
1783.	Salmon, - - - -	837	1811.	Seth, - - - - -	1273
1817.	Samantha, - - -	1363		Seymore, - - - -	1427
1801.	Samuel, - - - -	622		Sidney, - - - -	1110
	Samuel, - - - -	771	1836.	Sidney F., - - -	1075
1793.	Samuel, - - - -	782	1807.	Simeon, - - - -	606
1802.	Samuel, - - - -	1035	1800.	Simeon, - - - -	1023
	Samuel, - - - -	1108	1813.	Simeon, - - - -	1285
1830.	Samuel, - - - -	1188	1826.	Simeon H., - - -	1410
1828.	Samuel, - - - -	1269	1804.	Solomon, - - - -	623
1809.	Samuel I., - - -	1494		Solomon, - - - -	1005
1819.	Samuel M., - - -	1318	1806.	Solomon, - - - -	1359
1820.	Samuel R., - - -	928	1822.	Solomon G., - - -	929
1810.	Sanford, - - - -	767		Sophia, - - - -	688
1799.	Sarah, - - - -	587	1816.	Sophronia, - - -	927
1787.	Sarah, - - - -	617	1819.	Sophronia, - - -	1519
1823.	Sarah, - - - -	692	1801.	Sovier, - - - -	629
1786.	Sarah, - - - -	712		Spencer, - - - -	796
1780.	Sarah, - - - -	799	1809.	Spencer, - - - -	1449
1795.	Sarah, - - - -	843	1825.	Spencer A., - - -	1545
1815.	Sarah, - - - -	1195		Stephen, - - - -	708
1807.	Sarah, - - - -	1348	1781.	Stone, - - - - -	801

BORN A.D.		Marginal No.	BORN A.D.		Marginal No.
1795.	Susan, - - - -	601	1807.	Sybil, - - - - -	1151
1822.	Susan, - - - -	1355	1811.	Sybil, - - - - -	1229
	Susan, - - - -	1492	1810.	Sybil, - - - - -	1250
1786.	Sybil, - - - - -	740	1816.	Sylvanus, - - -	**1184**
1808.	Sybil, - - - - -	969	1784.	Sylvia, - - - -	870
1804.	Sybil, - - - - -	1044		Sylvia, - - - -	1128

Children of the Seventh Generation.

BORN A.D.		Marginal No.	BORN A.D.		Marginal No.
1828.	Sabrina, - - - -	2694	1822.	Sarah M., - - -	1577
1830.	Salina, - - - -	2695	1848.	Sarah M., - - -	2202
1818.	Sally I., - - - -	2042	1825.	Sarah M., - - -	2353
1826.	Salmon, - - - -	1590	1829.	Sarah P., - - -	1889
1822.	Salmon F., - - -	2370	1819.	Sarah S., - - -	1786
1810.	Samantha, - - -	1774		Sarah S., - - - -	2387
1825.	Samantha, - - -	2267	1813.	Selona, - - - -	1775
1834.	Samantha, - - -	2681	1824.	Seth, - - - - -	**1700**⁹
1830.	Samantha C., - -	2014	1820.	Seth, - - - - -	**2043**
	Samantha S., - -	1718	1853.	Seth, - - - - -	2778
1845.	Samuel, - - - -	2406	1832.	Seth H., - - - -	**2909**
1842.	Samuel C., - - -	2433	1824.	Seth P., - - - -	**1664**
1865.	Samuel D., - - -	2208⁷¹	1847.	Sewall L., - - -	**2700**
1828.	Samuel H., - - -	**2413**	1827.	Sherman, - - - -	2347
1828.	Samuel K., - - -	2193	1827.	Silas, - - - - -	1934
1831.	Samuel U., - - -	**2571**		Silas H., - - - -	2832
1841.	Sanford C., - - -	1676		Simeon, - - - -	1650
1844.	Sanford D., - - -	2988	1824.	Simeon, - - - -	2662
1831.	Sanford O., - - -	1901	1825.	Simeon A., - - -	2371
1830.	Sarah, - - - -	1662	1836.	Simeon E., - - -	2682
	Sarah, - - - -	1712	1855.	Simeon H., - - -	2456
	Sarah, - - - -	2261		Smith, - - - -	2388
	Sarah, - - - -	2312		Solomon, - - - -	2835
1830.	Sarah, - - - -	2908	1841.	Solomon A., - -	2235
	Sarah, - - - -	2927	1843.	Sophia, - - - -	2224
1847.	Sarah A., - - -	1856	1838.	Sophia C., - - -	1857
1817.	Sarah A., - - -	2160	1827.	Sophronia, - - -	1600
1828.	Sarah A., - - -	2423	1850.	Sophronia, - - -	3087
1840.	Sarah A., - - -	2744	1835.	Sophronia C., - -	2600
1818.	Sarah A. R., - -	1873	1816.	Sophronia R., - -	1988
1834.	Sarah C., - - -	2252		Spencer, - - - -	1968
1845.	Sarah E., - - -	2200	1840.	Spencer, - - - -	3111
1827.	Sarah E., - - -	2372	1817.	Spencer A., - - -	**1606**
1843.	Sarah E., - - -	3071		Stephen, - - - -	2277
1833.	Sarah H., - - -	2572	1829.	Stephen H., - - -	2076
1830.	Sarah I., - - -	1690	1819.	Steuben, - - - -	**1691**
	Sarah J., - - -	2892	1846.	Stillman A., - - -	2547
1844.	Sarah L., - - -	1701		Susan, - - - -	1974
1837.	Sarah L., - - -	2049	1808.	Susan, - - - -	1981
1846.	Sarah L., - - -	2587	1820.	Susan, - - - -	1983
1862.	Sarah L., - - -	2972	1818.	Susan, - - - -	2677
1848.	Sarah L., - - -	3046		Susan, - - - -	2851

Born A. D.		Marginal No.	Born A. D.		Marginal No.
1837.	Susan A., - - -	2804		Sylvanus A., - -	2839
	Susan D., - - -	2139	1806.	Sylvanus H., - - **1844**
1844.	Susan D., - - -	2143		Sylvester, - - -	1932
1823.	Susan E., - - -	1658		Sylvia, - - - -	2059
1847.	Susan E., - - -	2453	1825.	Sylvia, - - - -	2110
1821.	Susan F., - - -	2392	1838.	Sylvia, - - - -	2402
1837.	Susan J., - - -	2865	1816.	Sylvia, - - - -	2824
1835.	Susan M., - - -	2426	1855.	Sylvia G., - - -	2647
1827.	Susan M., - - -	2854		Sylvia J., - - -	2117
1839.	Sydney B., - - **3059**	1821.	Sylvia N., - - -	2131

T.

Child of the Third Generation.

| 1713. | Timothy, - - - - | 51 | |

Child of the Fourth Generation.

| 1738. | Timothy, - - - - | 169 | |

Children of the Fifth Generation.

1749.	Tabitha, - - - -	270	1766.	Timothy, - - - -	**514**
1769.	Tabitha, - - - -	382	1784.	Timothy, - - - -	**519**
	Tabitha, - - - -	500	1773.	Tirzah, - - - -	384
1754.	Thomas, - - - -	**192**		Titus, - - - - -	**335**
1751.	Tilton, - - - -	203	1758.	Tryphena, - - -	263

Children of the Sixth Generation.

	Tabitha, - - - -	789	1782.	Thomas, - - - -	**582**
1791.	Tabitha, - - - -	1014	1798.	Thomas, - - - - **1325**
1799.	Tabitha, - - - -	1129	1811.	Timothy W., - - **1405**
1797.	Theodore, - - -	602		Titus, - - - -	**976**
1789.	Theodore, - - -	**757**	1798.	Truman, - - - - **1146**
1815.	Theodore, - - - **1362**	1793.	Tryphena, - - -	1105
1816.	Theodore W., - - **1434**	1799.	Tudor, - - - -	808
	Theorissa, - - -	1213			

Children of the Seventh Generation.

1834.	Theodora C., - -	1802	1830.	Thomas J., - - -	2375
1829.	Theodore A., - -	1880	1819.	Thomas W., - - -	2330
1829.	Theodore D., - -	2171	1837.	Timothy W., - -	1860
1844.	Theodore I., - - **2949**		Tirzah A., - - -	2226
1819.	Theodore O., - - **1796**	1845.	Tirzah J., - - -	2768
1813.	Theodore P., - - **1871**	1842.	Truman A., - - -	3073
1836.	Theodore W., - -	2030	1829.	Truman H., - - - **2567**
	Theophilus, - - -	1936	1845.	T. Percy, - - -	2411
1815.	Thomas C., - - - **1581**	1856.	Turner, - - - -	2902
1815.	Thomas H., - - - **2037**				

U.

Child of the Fourth Generation.

Born A. D.		Marginal No.	Born A. D.		Marginal No.
1740.	Uriah, - - - - -	111			

Child of the Fifth Generation.

1778.	Urbane, - - - -	**431**

Child of the Sixth Generation.

1794.	Uri, - - - - - -	842

Children of the Seventh Generation.

1803.	Ursula S., - - -	1778	1817.	Ursula S., - - -	1785

V.

Children of the Seventh Generation.

1855.	Viana, - - - - -	2924		Virgia, - - - -	2141
1841.	Victor C., - - - -	2998			

W.

Child of the Third Generation.

1679.	William, - - - -	17

Children of the Fourth Generation.

1734.	Wareham, - - -	**108**	1746.	William, - - - -	**138**
	William, - - - -	89			

Children of the Fifth Generation.

1774.	Walter, - - - -	**385**	1772.	William, - - - -	**220**
1784.	Wareham, - - - -	**340**	1751.	William, - - - -	**299**
	Warren, - - - -	**443**	1780.	William, - - - -	**441**
1784.	Wilder C., - - -	**536**			

Children of the Sixth Generation.

1784.	Walter, - - - -	**573**	1801.	Wells, - - - - -	**1225**
1795.	Walter, - - - -	**626**	1781.	William, - - - -	**862**
1787.	Walter, - - - -	**779**	1790.	William, - - - -	**905**
1785.	Walter, - - - -	**863**	1805.	William, - - - -	**949**
1795.	Walter, - - - -	**1092**	1816.	William, - - - -	**990**
1807.	Walter, - - - -	**1249**	1809.	William, - - - -	**1259**
1799.	Warren, - - - -	**594**	1811.	William A., - - -	**1139**
1789.	Warren, - - - -	**864**	1795.	William C., - - -	**1323**
1818.	Warren, - - - -	**1393**	1847.	William H., - - -	**1532**
1826.	Warren W., - - -	**1065**	1791.	William R., - - -	**879**
1811.	Webster, - - - -	**1193**	1800.	William S., - - -	**877**

Born A. D.		Marginal No.	Born A. D.		Marginal No.
1818.	William W., - - -	1055	1792.	Willis F., - - - -	813
1786.	Willis, - - - - -	584		Wolcott, - - - -	753
1798.	Willis, - - - - -	677			

Children of the Seventh Generation.

Born A. D.		Marginal No.	Born A. D.		Marginal No.
1835.	Wallace, - - - -	2516	1818.	William A., - - -	2072
1850.	Wallace A., - - -	2756	1853.	William C., - - -	1685
1833.	Walter A., - - -	2866		William C., - - -	1826
1832.	Walter B., - - -	1700[18]	1826.	William C., - - -	2282
1837.	Walter C., - - -	2016		William E., - - -	1818
1834.	Walter D., - - -	2140	1841.	William E., - - -	2120
1859.	Walter G., - - -	2458	1833.	William G., - - -	1754
1833.	Walter L., - - -	2734	1812.	William G., - - -	2104
1813.	Walter R., - - -	1569	1840.	William H., - - -	1630
1832.	Walter S., - - -	2066	1850.	William H., - - -	1703
1838.	Walter S., - - -	2662	1821.	William H., - - -	1953
1832.	Warren, - - - -	1945		William H., - - -	2115
	Washington B., - -	2278	1825.	William H., - - -	2133
1834.	Watson W., - - -	2759	1820.	William H., - - -	2172
1823.	Webster, - - - -	1700[15]	1840.	William H., - - -	2234
1848.	Wilbur F., - - -	2521	1835.	William H., - - -	2384
1856.	Wilder C., - - -	3012	1849.	William H., - - -	3077
1848.	Willard P., - - -	2083	1813.	William I., - - -	2152
	William, - - - -	1649	1816.	William R., - - -	1875
	William, - - - -	1651	1831.	William R., - - -	2214
1830.	William, - - - -	1700[35]	1832.	William S., - - -	1793
	William, - - - -	1832	1827.	William S., - - -	2127
1812.	William, - - - -	1926		William S., - - -	2904
1815.	William, - - - -	1928	1850.	William T., - - -	3098
1815.	William, - - - -	2322	1850.	William W., - - -	2444
1822.	William, - - - -	2703		William W., - - -	2890
1823.	William, - - - -	2713	1862.	Willie B., - - -	2306
	William, - - - -	2850	1864.	Willie J., - - -	3022
1848.	William, - - - -	2933	1858.	Willie M., - - -	2658
1860.	William, - - - -	3009	1854.	Willis A., - - -	2961
1836.	William A., - - -	1808	1842.	Wilson B., - - -	2520
1822.	William A., - - -	1864			

Z.

Child of the Fourth Generation.

1749.	Zebulon, - - - -	139

Children of the Fifth Generation.]

1780.	Zebulon, - - - -	449	1745.	Zeruiah, - - - -	257
1759.	Zeno, - - - - -	212			

Children of the Seventh Generation.

1834.	Zelotus, - - - -	2492	1855.	Zeneva, - - - -	2590
1830.	Zelotus M., - - -	2490	1842.	Ziba W., - - - -	2918
1823.	Zeno K., - - - -	1689	1857.	Zilpha S., - - - -	2533
1824.	Zenana, - - - -	2001	1827.	Zipporah A., - - -	1660

49

INDEX OF SURNAMES

OF PERSONS MARRYING INTO THE FAMILY, WHO ARE NOT
OF THE MALE DESCENT OF JOHN PEASE, SEN.

A.

Abbe, 6, 11, 29, 102, 132, 260, 339.
Abbot, 100, 216.
Adams, 5, 46, 237, 243, 243, 245, 327.
Ainsworth, 41, 314, 315.
Akin, 31.
Albro, 319.*
Alcock, 282.
Alden, 162.
Alderman, 289.
Aldridge, 271.

Algies, 145.
Allen, 13, 30, 37, 40, 85, 87, 104, 112, 115, 120, 124, 128, 129, 179, 187, 187, 194, 243, 243, 283, 310, 318, 339.
Allison, 330.
Ames, 38, 185.
Anderson, 67, 106.
Andrus, 170.
Annis, 303.

Anthony, 79.
Arms, 69.
Arnold, 28, 100, 168, 299.
Arthur, 91, 236.
Ashley, 94, 173.
Atwater, 46.
Atwell, 31.
Atwood, 297.
Austin, 57, 205, 326.
Avery, 77, 145.
Ayers, 138, 139.

B.

Babcock, 170, 248.
Bagg, 90.
Bailey, 282, 340.
Baird, 95.
Baker, 46, 102, 169, 195, 218, 260, 261, 317.
Baldwin, 167.
Ball, 101, 108, 224.
Ballou, 114, 288.
Bancroft, 40, 271.
Barber, 74, 187.
Barker, 167.
Barnard, 83.
Barnes, 168, 175, 219, 288.
Barnum, 123.
Barry, 287.
Bartlett, 228, 259, 268, 269, 339.
Barton, 166.
Bates, 237.
Beals, 85.
Beaumont, 62.
Beebe, 116, 192, 264, 290.
Beecher, 163.
Beemace, 133.
Bell, 192.
Bellows, 69, 152.
Bellville, 158.
Bement, 120.

Benedict, 302.
Benham, 247.
Benjamin, 78, 114.
Bennett, 41.
Bidwell, 140, 143, 338.
Bignell, 108.
Billings, 112, 171, 185.
Bishop, 285.
Bissell, 170.
Blackburn, 96.
Blair, 216.
Blaisdell, 134.
Blake, 188.
Blatchley, 240.
Bliss, 42, 121, 130.
Blodgett, 130.
Bodurtha, 107.
Bolen, 187.
Boleyn, 280.
Bolton, 66.
Bolyn, 113.
Bond, 171.
Booth, 7, 16, 18, 19, 33, 34, 39, 40, 131, 156, 206.
Brace, 314.
Bradley, 146, 153.
Breck, 98.
Boyington, 227.
Brewster, 209.

Bridges, 225.
Broadley, 106.
Bronson, 49.
Brooks, 47, 52, 119.
Broque, 82.*
Brown, 76, 94, 153, 163, 222, 231, 250, 273.
Buck, 13, 84, 282.
Bugbee, 72, 187.
Bull, 15.
Bullen, 339.
Bumpstead, 48.
Burbank, 101.
Burk, 176.
Burlington, 107.
Burns, 66, 169.
Burnap, 296.
Burnham, 303, 340.
Burt, 66, 92, 314.
Burton, 172.
Burr, 321.
Bush, 75, 91, 319.
Bushnell, 217.
Butler, 110, 116, 116, 117, 212, 274, 276, 296.*
Butterfield, 171.
Button, 260.
Byington, 77.

* See Errata.

C.

Cadey, 130.
Cadwell, 73, 194.
Calkins, 131, 273.
Call, 242.
Callender, 205.
Camp, 79.
Carpenter, 64, 187, 229.
Carlton, 300.
Carrier, 157, 194.
Case, 248, 302.
Castle, 189,
Caswell, 339.
Catlin, 295.
Chaffee, 88, 88, 109, 146.
Chalker, 294.
Chandler, 20, 21, 111.
Chapin, 8, 28, 34, 38, 46, 65, 112, 117, 122, 149, 165, 182, 183, 195, 222, 224, 288, 308, 319, 319, 339, 340.
Chapman, 156, 192, 221, 273,
Chappell, 121, 123.
Chard, 85.
Chase, 240.
Childs, 86.
Church, 103, 156, 249.

Clapp, 188, 307.
Clark, 58, 75, 88, 98, 132, 188, 204, 239, 240, 295, 326, 326.
Clegg, 159.
Clelland, 50.
Coats, 113, 177, 284.
Cobb, 295.
Codington, 147.
Coe, 67.
Cogswell, 92.
Colburn, 212.
Cole, 251, 288, 288.
Colgrove, 247.
Collar, 78.
Collins, 9, 19, 71, 112, 118, 168, 182* 187, 193.
Colton, 6, 85.
Colwell, 139.
Combs, 51, 136, 260, 292.
Cone, 168, 191.
Congdon, 242.
Converse, 251, 251.
Cook, 54, 56, 82, 142, 245, 291.
Cooley, 28, 35, 65, 94, 131, 170, 311.

Coombs, 107, 168, 283.
Coon, 140, 203, 259.
Cope, 309.
Copley, 235.
Corey, 287.
Cornell, 217.
Cotterell, 161.
Couch, 38.
Cox, 161.
Coy, 55.
Craine, 108.
Cragin, 298.
Crandal, 45.
Crane, 115, 166, 221.
Crary, 91.
Creque, 280, 280.
Crittenden, 223.
Crocker, 187, 196, 261, 261.
Cross, 288.
Crowell, 145.
Culver, 88.
Cummer, 189.
Cummings, 8.
Cunningham, 314.
Cuppin, 270,*
Curd, 208.

D.

Dailey, 222.
Dale, 120.
Darrow, 96, 296.
Dart, 124.
Davenport, 71.
Davis, 26, 51, 69, 109, 145, 189, 285, 285.
Dawes, 211.
Day, 77, 90, 97, 196, 222, 265.
Dean, 31, 82.
Deane, 81.
Debarr, 270.
Debrill, 220.
Decker, 302.
De Cory, 195
De Forrest, 324.

Demorest, 328.
Dennison, 257.
Denton, 206.
Depue, 305.
Derrick, 217.
Dewey, 174, 175.
Dickinson, 216.
Dickson, 338.
Dietz, 251.
Diggings, 29.
Dimmock, 146, 339, 339.
Dodds, 158, 160.
Dodge, 93.
Dolsen, 197.
Douglass, 135.
Dowd, 47.
Downing, 191, 246.

Doyle, 249.
Drake, 197.
Driggs, 89.
Dubois, 79.
Ducet, 44.
Dudley, 340.
Duguid, 331.
Dummer, 164.
Dumont, 269.
Dunlap, 187, 188.
Durant, 184.
Durgee, 109.
Durkee, 190.
Durmont, 269.
Dutton, 133.
Dwight, 28, 43, 108, 233, 245.

E.

Earl, 52, 52, 217.
Easterly, 269.
Eastman, 58, 98.
Eaton, 282, 318.
Edgerton, 341.
Edson, 156, 171.

Edwards, 217.
Eggleston, 211.
Eldridge, 243.
Ellis, 309.
Elmore, 122, 277.
Ely, 288.

Emery, 12.
Emmons, 338.
Eno, 69.
Ensign, 119.
Erringer, 158.
Erwin, 62,* 159.*

*See Errata.

F.

G.

H.

*See Errata.

I.

Indicot, 126.
Ingham, 287, 288.

Ingraham, 194, 205.

Ives, 78, 79, 83, 117, 205, 231.

J.

Janes, 327.
Jeffrey, 323.
Jencks, 260, 307.
Jewett, 207.

Johnson, 43, 107, 192, 235, 242.
Jones, 14, 23, 30, 153, 155,

172, 192,* 261, 286, 296, 339.
Joy, 96.
Judson, 157.

K.

Kellogg, 71, 72, 170.
Kelsey, 192.
Kendall, 82.
Kennedy, 226.
Kent, 34, 59, 86, 176.
Kenyon, 155.
Kesmer, 236.
Keyes, 132.
Kibbe, 38, 69, 125, 126,

127, 132, 133, 153, 153, 170, 179, 237, 242, 245, 292.
Killam, 9, 48, 309.
Kimball, 122.
King, 21, 25, 101, 128, 156, 180, 187, 226.
Kingsbury, 19, 51, 66, 135, 244, 263, 308.

Kinsman, 62.
Kirtland, 162.*
Knapp, 140.
Knight, 43, 246.
Knox, 64.
Krider, 172.
Lamas, 297.
Lamberton, 272.

L.

Lamme, 161.
Lampheare, 41, 42.
Lampson, 180.
Lancton, 188.
Langdon, 69,* 90.
Larkham, 48.
Lathrop, 181.
Laughlin, 184.
Law, 82.
Lawler, 319.
Lawrence, 76, 120, 199,

208, 208, 296, 298.
Lazelle, 118.
Leavitt, 58.
Lee, 164, 212, 302, 318.
Leonard, 106, 222, 275.
Lewis, 133, 172, 240.
Lincoln, 77, 254.
Livingston, 197.
Loomer, 124.
Loomis, 60, 74, 114, 145, 156, 206.

Lord, 6, 18, 19, 29, 258.
Lovejoy, 70.
Loveland, 242.
Low, 146.
Lowell, 284.
Lowns, 323.
Lowry, 158, 158, 262.
Lull, 154.
Lyman, 136, 183.
Lyon, 54, 104.

M.

Machir, 60.
Mack, 27.
MacNamara, 303.
Macomber, 188, 232.
Madden, 86.
Mallet, 340.
Mansfield, 125.
Markham, 20, 41, 46, 101, 145, 251, 279, 339.
Marsh, 190, 216.
Marshall, 43, 143.
Marston, 299.
Martin, 96.
Mason, 90.
Maxson, 292.
May, 151.
McBride, 243.
McCarthy, 184.
McClary, 206.
McClester, 71, 227.

McCoy, 323.
McGregory, 23, 54, 126.
McIntire, 54.
McKendlees, 282.
McKinstry, 183.
McLaughlin, 120.
McLean, 225.
McLoy, 86.
McMillin, 173.
Meacham, 9, 41, 44, 50, 56, 59, 84.
Medbury, 327.
Meddler, 137.
Mentor, 7.
Merrill, 312.
Metcalf, 289.
Miller, 7, 175, 235, 282, 340.
Milliken, 77.
Mills, 49, 206.

Mixter, 264.
Montague, 57.
Moody, 157.
Moon, 191.
Mooney, 251.
Moore, 90, 145, 169, 277.
Morey, 89.
Morris, 65, 203, 255.
Morritter, 281.
Moseley, 185.
Moses, 170.
Moyston, 219.
Munger, 106, 275.
Munsell, 68.
Murphy, 325, 334.
Murthy, 278.
Murray, 116, 301.
Mutell, 278.
Muzzy, 223.
Myers, 261, 322.

*See Errata.

*See Errata

Schermerhorn, 222.
Scott, 313.
Scoville, 205.
Sears, 78, 206.
Sedgwick, 214.
Seelye, 212.
Sessions, 291.
Severance, 99.
Seward, 250.
Sexton, 7, 12, 14, 26, 33, 54, 64, 95, 118, 155.
Shaw, 153.
Shadrick, 111.
Shelden, 169.
Sheldon, 13, 140, 204.
Shelton, 326.
Shepard, 197.
Sheperdson, 249.
Shubrook, 295.
Shultus, 258.
Shumway, 166.
Silcox, 155.
Sill, 211.
Silsbee, 85.*
Simons, 92.

Sisson, 105.
Sitzer, 206.
Slack, 137, 166,* 211.
Slater, 156.
Smith, 39, 58, 76, 76, 100, 114, 115, 136, 146, 149, 159, 160, 182, 182, 182, 192, 214, 217, 230, 278, 275, 281, 287, 295, 299, 300, 341.
Snow, 65.
Spafford, 302.
Sparrow, 244.
Sparks, 245.
Spencer, 11, 12, 47, 52, 60, 67, 68, 72, 139, 151, 154, 161, 192, 209, 282, 306.
Sperry, 339.
Spining, 175.
Squire, 309.
Stacy, 265.
Stafford, 190.
Stanley, 63.
Stanton, 106, 206, 287, 288.
Stearns, 85, 245, 305.

Stebbins, 84, 109, 242, 262, 274, 320.
Steel, 215.
Steele, 309.
Stevens, 116, 181, 207, 290, 313.
Stewart, 294.
Stilkey, 278.
Stilts, 158.
Stocking, 91.
Stockstell, 159.
Stone, 82, 212.
Storer, 305.
Stowe, 66, 119.
Stowell, 107, 117.
Stratton, 53, 251.
Strong, 65, 146, 263.
Summers, 73.
Sutton, 213.
Sweatland, 52, 127, 169, 255.
Sweetzer, 64.
Swift, 180.
Sykes, 109.

T.

Talcott, 36.
Tallmadge, 61.
Taylor, 115, 138, 180.
Teets, 183.
Tenny, 148.
Terrett, 157.
Terry, 9, 9, 9, 19, 21, 30, 32, 35, 33, 112, 123, 128, 129, 131, 135, 143, 143, 168, 177, 187, 256, 308, 309, 339.

Thompson, 53, 220, 221, 222, 270, 273.
Tibballs, 78.
Ticknor, 82.
Tiffany, 245,
Tilden, 121.
Tinker, 175.
Traganza, 245.*
Topliff, 183.
Travis, 164.
Trimble, 303.

Trowbridge, 230.
Truesdell, 293.
Trumbull, 256.
Tufts, 52, 190.
Tupper, 108.
Tuthill, 108.
Turner, 149, 306, 320.
Twiss, 129.
Twitchell, 195.
Tyler, 173.

U.

Udell, 308.
Ufford, 76, 310.

Ulm 161.
Underhill, 157, 195.

Underwood, 109, 110.

V.

VanAntwerp, 220.
VanBuren, 160.
VanDoren, 183, 184.
Vandyke, 167.
VanMeter, 173.

VanSickle, 280.
Vantyne, 199.
Van Vleet, 190, 190.
Varney, 297.
Vaughan, 118.

Vaughn, 318.
Vietz, 66.
Vining, 43, 44, 261, 286.
Vrodenburgh, 255.

W.

Wait, 240.
Wakefield, 92.
Wales, 340.
Wallace, 145, 169.
Walker, 64, 257.
Walter, 300.

Warburton, 184.
Ward, 51, 59, 250.
Ware, 102.
Wardwell, 52, 340.
Warner, 13, 18, 40, 89, 97, 100, 244.

Warren, 103, 211.
Waterman, 188.
Waters, 155.
Watts, 147.
Webster, 42.
Weed, 79.

*See Errata.

APPENDIX.

PREPARED FOR THIS WORK BY AUSTIN S. PEASE.

A.

THE OLD AND NEW LEGAL YEARS.

THAT the readers of this work may know why some of its dates of events differ here from those given by other writers, and that the dates of some of the subsequent documents in this appendix may be more generally understood, we have prepared this article.

The several European nations formerly had different periods for beginning the Legal or Civil year. With the exception of Scotland, Great Britain and her dependencies, for several centuries prior to 1752, began the new year on Conception day or March 25th. In 1752 Parliament enacted that that year should terminate with December 31st, and the new year should begin with January 1st. Several of the European nations had fixed on this time for beginning their Civil year, nearly seventy years before Great Britain did.

There had been in Great Britain an Historical year which began with January 1st; and there had arisen the practice of double dating, if the event happened between December 31st, and March 25th, which indicated both the Historical and Civil years,—thus: March 2, 1725-6. The figures at the left of the hyphen indicate the Civil or Legal year, and substituting the figure at the right of the hyphen in place of the first one at the left of it, the Historical year would be indicated. Sometimes the unit figure indicating the Historical year would be placed under the one indicating the Legal year,—thus: $172\frac{5}{6}$, or $17\frac{80}{87}$.

Occasionally double dating would be omitted. In which case it is safe to presume the old Legal year was expressed or meant, and not the Historical year. So far as our observation has extended, we have found it so. If the omission of double dating was done from forgetfulness, it is reasonable to suppose the Historical year would be left off.

It is a common practice now when mentioning an event in our words, (if it occurred between December 31st, and March 25th) to give the Historical year; as it corresponds with our present Civil year; and by such expression it is easier to calculate time. When, therefore, we find on record that the double date is omitted, and there is no positive evidence showing that the Historical year is meant, we see no reason why we should not supply such omission. Or in other words add one year to such date. We have

50

accordingly done so in the History of the Pease Families and in the families of John[3] and Robert[3] of the Enfield Peases, unless we have placed the date in quotation marks. The records of births of the family of John Pease, Sen., last of Enfield furnish an illustration. His fourth son, Jonathan was " born the 2d day of January 1668." It seems clear to our minds that the old Legal year is meant, which did not terminate until March 25th. We have accordingly added one year to the date, which makes the date of his birth January 1669. For the same reason we changed the date of the death of the child's mother to 1669. We make this explanation because other writers using their own words have made their dates " 1668."

Again, it is obvious to all, that when the year began in March it was the first month in the year, and April the second, and so on. It was very common two centuries ago to express the months in numerals instead of their proper names. Persons examining records where the months are thus expressed are liable to mistake the month, unless they bear in mind that March, and not January, was the first month. The above named records again furnish an illustration. A portion of them read thus : " John Pease his son John, bo. by Mary his wife y[e] 30th 3[d] '54; their son Robert 14th 3[d] '56 ; dar. Mary bo. y[e] 8th October '58 ; their son Abra'm b. 5th 4th '62." Accordingly John and Robert were born in May and not in March as others have it; and Abraham was born in July.

B.

OLD STYLE AND NEW STYLE.

No changes in dates have been made in this work from Old to New Style, by the compilers. As some of our readers may be desirous of ascertaining the exact anniversary day of an event, we will give in this article a brief explanation of the differences between Old Style and New Style, as applied to time or the Julian Calendar and Gregorian Calendar, that will enable our readers to make their own calculations, if they desire to change the date of an event from O. S. to N. S.

The Julian Calendar, which was adopted by the Council of Nice, and used by the Christian nations of Europe until 1582, allowed the year to be just 365 days and six hours long, and made every fourth year Bissextile. It made the solar year nearly eleven minutes longer than it really was, and resulted in a loss of about three days for every 400 years. A change was made in the Calendar in 1582 by Pope Gregory XIII. and was soon introduced into most or all of the Catholic countries. When the change of Calendar was made there had arisen an error of about ten days. To overcome the error it was ordained that ten days should be struck out of October 1582; and the day following October 4th became October 15th. To obviate any further irregularity it was ordained that no centurial year should be Bissextile except every fourth. The centurial years ending with two zeros (00), when divisible by 400, were to be Bissextile years.

Great Britain did not adopt the Gregorian Calendar until 1752, when because it had made A. D. 1700 Bissextile, it became necessary to strike eleven days from the Calendar. In 1751 Parliament enacted "that the natural day next immediately following the said 2d day of September 1752 shall be called, reckoned and accounted to be the 14th day of September." The 3d day of September, of the Julian Calendar in 1752 became the 14th day of September, agreeable to the Gregorian Calendar. The former Calendar took the name of Old Style and the latter New Style.*

From the above we may deduce the following rule : To change the date of an event from Old Style to New Style, add ten days to the date, if the event occurred between February 28, A. D. 1500 and the time ending with February 28, 1700. And add eleven days, if the event occurred after February 28, and before the change of Calendar took effect.

Thus : J. P. was born May 3, 1654, O. S. Add ten days to May 3, and we find the true anniversary of his birth occurs May 13, N. S. Again : E. P. was born June 2, 1710, O. S. Add eleven days to this date, and we find he was born June 13, 1710, N. S.

If it is desired to change the date from O. S. to N. S. farther back than A. D. 1500 we have only to add one day less to the date, for every century except those whose centurial years are divisible by 400.

C.

PROBATE RECORDS—ESTATE OF ROBERT PEASE, Sen.

The following records relating to the settlement of the estate of Robert Pease, Sen., last of Salem, Mass., are copied for this work from probate papers on file in the Judicial Court at Salem. The first record found is "An Inventory of all the goods and chattels of Robert Pease, late deceased, of Salem, brought in Court 27th of 6 mo., '44:"

	£	s.	d.
Imprimis fyve ewe goats and three lambs praysed at	3	6	0
Item on iron and iron kettle and a pose... and two pewter dishes with other small things of pewter preased at	1	0	0
Itt. on Tonell and on tube and three trays and on paile praysed at	0	7	0
Itt. on flock bed a teik and on cow hide and a little ruge praysed at	1	10	0
Itt. on sheet and on pil ow beer,	0	3	4
Itt. on stone hammer two trowels on lathing hammer on axe praysed	0	6	0
It. on barrel and a pecke,	0	2	6
It. on chest and a little table board praysed	0	5	0
It. on acre of wheat on of barley and a acre of peas,	2	0	0
It. four acres of Indian Corne praysed at	10	0	0
It. on musket with bandileers and the sword praysed at	0	16	0
It. on howse and a barne and a frame and a 11 acres of ground praysed at	14	0	0
It. two shutes of aparell and a coat praysed	3	10	0
It. on hat on payre of stockins on payre of shoes two shirts, two bands praysed at	0	10	0

---

* Russia still adheres to the Julian Calendar, so that the dates of days of months are twelve days behind ours.

	£	s.	d.
It. a sack praysed at .	0	1	0
It. the swine praysed	1	6	0
Itt. a Cannow praysed	0	10	0
	39	12	6
It. he was indebted to several persons	5	0	0
	84	12	6

The praysers of the goods,

JOHN ALDERMAN,

MAYHILL SHAFLINGE.

" Marie Pease widow appointed administrator and hath brought in this inventory upon hir own oath this 3 of 11 mo. '44 amounting to the sum and value of £39 12s. 6d., out of which there is to be substracted in debts of estate £5.   Out of which the Court apoints to Robert Pease being the eldest son and John Pease being the second son of Robert Pease deceased £9. Court orders that the rest of the estate being £25 12s. 6 to Marie Pease widow for the maintainance of herself and the rest of the children.   The Courte further orders that John the second son shall have his three pounds in 3 months time and Robert the eldest sonn shall have it at 12 mos."

In another book in the Clerk of Court's office is found recorded, on page 171, the following :

" Salem 13 of 11 mo. 1644.   Robert Pease the son of Robert Pease deceased is committed by the Courte unto his mother Marie Pease until the Courte to be held in Salem in December next to be find him meat drink and aparell.   The said Marie being apointed administratrix £34 12s. 6d and the said Robert Pease deceased dying intestate Marie Pease widow is granted administratrix as before mentioned and brought in inventory upon her oath. And Robert is to have paid him by her in 12 mo. time £6 and John her second son is to have £3 in 3 mos. time—the rest to maintain her children."

From the same book as the last mentioned, page 189, is taken the following :

" At Salem Court held the 31st of 10 mo. 1646.   It is ordered by this present Court upon the motion and by the consent of Both parties that Robert Pease son of Robert Pease deceased to be bound unto Thomas Roots of Salem, Weaver as an aprentice for fyve years from this day ; then to be complete and ended.   And said Thomas Roots is to learn the said Robert in the trade of a Weaver of linen and woolen and to have 2 suites of aparrel and twenty shillings at the end of his time."

D.

THE WILL OF MARGARET PEASE.

From probate papers on file in the Judicial Court at Salem, book No. 1, is copied the following :

" The will of Margaret Pease the first day 7 month 1644.

" This is the last will of Margaret Pease that is her grand chile John Pease the son of Robert Pease shall with the rest of her goods be put over to Thomas Wadsson of Salem to be as her true feoffee off trust to dispose off her estate as she directeth at this time being in parfite memory. First as before that the said John Pease shall, be given frely to the said Thomas Wadsson, that he shall dispose of him as his own child and secondly that the house she liffs in with the ground belonging therto shall be given to the said John Pease, also halfe an acker of Indian Corne, alsoe that he is to have my heifer, allsoe that John shall have my bede and all that belongs to it also that her grandchildren the children of Robert Pease her sonne shall give to the rest of them the tow goattes and kid to be equally disposed among them and for all her mouffeable goods are to be at Thomas Wadsson's disposal for the good of John, alsoe, her grand childe Robert Pease shall have her lesser chist and that if that the said John die then his brother Robert Pease shall have the rest of the estate, and all, that her daughter Pease the wife of Robert Pease is to have my best cloth gowne, and all perticlers are not set down the same must Thomas Wadsson to dispose for the good of John her grand child." (Her mark.)

" In witness wherof we have set to our hands.

JOHN BARBER.
OBADIAH HULM."

" It is the request of Ann the wife of Robert Isbell having taken a great deal of pains with the widow Pease decesed from the first of her sickness to the last in tending of her desire to take it into consideration about the satisfying of her."

" The deposition of Ann Isbell is that Margaret Pease widow after she made a written will did give and bequeath unto Faith Barber her best red pettecoate being in perfect memorie and that is the substance of what I can depose."

From records in the office of the clerk of the courts we take the following :

" 1st of 7 mo. 1644. Thomas Watson made ffeofee in trust of Margaret Pease hir will, an inventory of her goods and estate brought in Courte sworn to by Obadiah Holm and John Barber and other deposition-de legacies, also upon An the wife of Robert Isbell request g'dwffe* Watson must allow her for her pains or the court will."

The inventory of the widow Pease's estate had no date and when we compare the date at the head of her will with this last transaction we might infer that her will must have been made prior to " 1st 7 mo. 1644."

The following is taken from the records in the office of the clerk of the Courts at Salem dated " 30 4 mo. 1652 :

" Robert Pease and John his brother both of Salem came before the Court and acknowledged a bill bearing date the 6th 11 mo. 1651. Subscribed with their hands wherein they bind themselves jointly in the sum of £40 unto Tho. Watson to save harmless the said Tho. Watson agnst all manner of persons in regard of the estate of their grand mother Margaret Pease of whom he the said Tho. Watson was a feofee in trust as by the said bill more at large doth appear."

---

*An abbreviation of " goodwife." It should have been " goodman."

E.

PARENTAGE OF MARY GOODELL.

Robert Goodell and his wife Catharine, the parents of the first wife of John Pease, Sen., with three children, of whom Mary was the eldest (the custom-house book says her age was four years), were passengers on the ship Elizabeth, which sailed from Ipswich, England, the last of April, 1634. His name appears among the inhabitants of Salem in 1635, though there is no record of land being granted him in Salem until 1637.

Abner C. Goodell, Esq., of Salem, Mass., Register of Probate and Insolvency for Essex County, is a descendant of this Robert Goodell. The writer is indebted to him for much valuable assistance during his visits at Salem, when in search of information relating the history of the Salem Peases.

F.

FATHER OF ANN CUMMINGS.

It is not known when Isaac Cummings, the father of the second wife of John Pease, Sen., came to this country. He was made freeman in 1642. He resided at Topsfield when he died. In his will, dated May 3, 1677, he says: " I give unto my son-in-law John Pease thirty pounds, to be pay out of the stock of cattell and house hold goods as much as may be at present, and the rest in two years."

F. F.

ANCESTRY OF MINDWELL OSBORN.

Mindwell Osborn, the wife of Dea. Isaac Pease (page 9 of Part 1), and maternal ancestor of more than one-half of the descendants of John Pease, Sen., was the second child of John and Abagail (Eggleston) Osborn, of East Windsor Ct. She was born January 2, 1673. Her father, born January 10, 1645, was the oldest son of John and Ann (Oldage) Osborn, who were in Windsor Ct., in 1644. Tradition says the Osborns were of Welch origin.

The mother of Mindwell Osborn, born June 12, 1648, was the daughter of Begat and Sarah (Talcott) Eggleston. Mr. Eggleston came from England in 1630, and first settled at Dorchester, Mass. He removed to Windsor, Ct., in 1635.*

---

* Facts from the Genealogy of Ancient Windsor by Henry R. Styles.

G.

ENFIELD WITHOUT A MINISTER.

When a settlement in the Province of Massachusetts Bay became incorporated into a town, it became necessary for the inhabitants to hold public meetings for the worship of God on the Sabbath within its limits. Hence, soon after the town of Enfield was set off from Springfield. the town took the necessary steps to have religious meetings on the Sabbath, as will be seen by the following, taken from Enfield town records:

"July 15, 1683, the Committee went to Enfeild* to settle some way for carrying on the worshipping of God on the Sabbath, and having a meeting of the inhabitants it was put to a vote and past, that they would assemble together on the Sabbath forenoon and afternoon, except such as might goe to Springfeild or Suffeild, and carry on the day by prair and singing and reading sum good orthodox book, till they might get a supply of minister; and the persons appointed thereunto by a full voat were John Pease, Sen., Israel Meecham and Thomas Bancroft, who are to agree amongst themselves how and who to manage prayer and reading, &c."

H.

AN AGREEMENT.

"Behold how good and how pleasant it is for brethren to dwell together in unity."

The following copy of an instrument showing the manner of dividing the estate, of John Pease, Sen., last of Enfield, deceased, is taken from probate records at Northampton, Mass.:

"Mar. 24, 16⅜⅞.—These presents witnesseth an agreement made between John Pease, Robert Pease, Abraham Pease, Jonathan Pease, James Pease, Isaac Pease, the sons of John Pease, Sen., lately deceased, it having pleased our great and most glorious sovereign in his all-wise providence suddenly to take away our Honored father by death not having the advantage or opportunitie of makeing a will for the disposal of his estate which God has graciously given him unto his children according to his own pleasure we therefore whose names are written above for the prevention of all future troubles and that we might live together in love and unitie as becomes bretheren have mutually agreed to each man his portion of that estate left us by our Honored father in manner as followeth viz. to John Pease £17 13s. beside what he had received by his father before tyme which he being freed from all debts and future troubles whatsoever, doth except of as his full compleat portion of the estate and doth hereby promise and ingage never

---

* They lived in Springfield.

to make any further claime to any part thereof. To Robert Pease six pounds besides what he has received in his fathers life tyme which he being free from all debts and future troubles whatsoever doth except of as his full and compleat portion of his estate and doth hereby promise and ingage never to make any further claime to any part thereof and to Abraham Pease twenty-five pounds the other three bretheren viz. Jonathan Pease James Pease and Isaac Pease the same portion of twenty-five pounds a peice these four bretheren taking upon them the sole care of receiving in and paying out all debts due to and from the estate, to their sister Mary sixteen pounds as her portion and that it may evidently appear to all concerned that we have freely and heartily agreed to make this division as above expressed we do all hereto subscribe with our hands.

Witnesseth	JOHN PEASE,	JONATHAN PEASE,
ANTHONY AUSTIN, JR.,	ROBERT PEASE,	JAMES PEASE,
ANTHONY AUSTIN.	ABRAHAM PEASE,	ISAAC PEASE.

I.

EXPLANATIONS.

It is perhaps due the reader that we give our reasons for differing with others in the given name of the father of John Pease, Sen., last of Enfield, and state why we have said nothing of his holding certain honorable public positions before he left Salem as mentioned by others.

It seems probable those persons writing about him never examined the evidences of his paternity which are found in the court records at Salem, growing out of the settlement of the estates of Robert Pease, Sen., and his mother, Widow Margaret Pease, including her will. (See Appendix C. and D.) The given name of his father appears to have been "assumed" rather than proved.

The late Frederick S. Pease, Esq., saw the error into which he had fallen in his "Pease Family" a few years after it was published, and from no other evidence, as it seems, than because it could not be found at Salem, that the brother of Robert Pease, Sen., had a family there.

Again: Mr. Joseph B. Felt says in his "Annals of Salem," under date of December, 1682, that "Capt. John Pease, aged 52 years, had lately removed from Salem to Enfield. He had been deputy to General Court." This edition was published in 1827. A later edition of his work, though much more voluminous than the first, makes no mention of the incident.

As we have failed to find the name of John Pease on the Salem town records as deputy to the General Court, or in the lists of deputies at the State House at Boston, we think Mr. Felt must have been mistaken in saying he had been one. The title of Captain appears to have been first given to him by Mr. Felt in the quotation above mentioned. Though his name is frequently mentioned on the records at Salem, Enfield and Northampton, we have never seen the title of Captain prefixed to it. Military titles were then considered highly honorable. If this ancestor had been a Captain of a military company, we sh$uld have found the title prefixing the name when written afterwards.

Mr. John Farmer, in his Genealogical Register of the first settlers of New England, that was published two years later than Mr. Felt's " Annals of Salem," says " he was a member, of the Artillery Company, 1661, a Captain, and probably removed to Enfield before 1684." There was an individual by the name of John Pease who joined the Ancient and Honorable Artillery Company in 1661. It is probable Mr. Farmer supposed there was no other John Pease living in New England at that time than the one who afterwards went to Enfield; so he gave him the title of Captain, and sent him to Enfield by authority of Felt.

A history of the above company edited by Mr. Z. G. Whitman, A. M., and published in 1842, places the title of Captain before the name of John Pease, and evidently copying from Farmer says "he removed to Enfield before 1684." The Hon. Francis Brinly, who has the papers belonging to the Ancient and Honorable Company, informs us that John Pease was not Captain of that company, nor does he know where Mr. Whitman obtained the authority for placing the title of Captain before the name.

The eldest son of John Pease, Sen., (born in 1654,) was Captain of the first military company formed in Enfield, and the title of Captain is prefixed to his name in public records. He was more active in effecting the settlement at Enfield and in public affairs afterwards than was his father. Hence, some confusion may have arisen afterwards in distinguishing the two men, and it may have helped settle the title of Captain on the father which belonged exclusively to the son.

J.

INDIAN DEEDS.

The title of the present territory of Enfield and Somers from the original owners of the soil, is copied below from Old Hampshire County records. The northern portion of the territory appears to have been bought in 1678, when the Indian chiefs confirmed a sale previously made of the central portion of Springfield, an extract from which reads as follows:

"I did sell unto Mr. Wm. Pynchon late of Springfield for the use and behoof of the said town of Springfield a good portion or tract of land lying on the east side of the River Quinecticut and by the said river that is to say by the river al along from the lower end of the meadow called by the Indians Massacksick and by the English called Longmedow up to Chickuppe River. . . . . . And the tract of land which the said Wequagan and Wawwapaw Do hereby Sel as aforesaid Lyeth partly adjoineth to the South end and east side of the tract of land above described which they acknowledge was sold to the said Mr. William Pynchon as above said. That is to say All the land

51

which lie within the bound hereafter mentioned. And wherefore the south bounds whereof is the River called by the Indians Ashuntuck and by the English Freshwater River or freshwater brook soe from the mouth of that river viz. from Connecticut or Quinecticut River the bound runs up the said River to the meadow thereupon and from thence up the said river the bound takes in all the meadow on both sides of Freshwater River or Brooks that run into it to the upland on the southerly side of such meadow at the place where Freshwater River or Brook turns Northerly, the south bound extends Eastward to the River called Scantuck ; viz. that place by the falls * where the path that leads to Pequit or Mohegit † goes over that river and from thence the said River Scantuck is the general bounds of land contained in this purchase viz. up to the place where the said River cr River Scantuck comes down from the mountain, the foot of the mountain. Yet al the meadows on both sides Scantuck River are likewise contained in this purchase."

Three years after the above, a deed was obtained embracing the other portion of the territory.

" *To al people to whom these presents shall come :* I Tawtaps alias Notattuck the right Indian owner of al the land on the east of Connecticut River from Asnuntuck alias Freshwater River down to Umsquattanuck at the foot of the falls being willing to accommodate the English, viz. Lieut. Thomas Stebbings, Jonathan Burt, Benjamin Parsons, John Pease, William Downton, Thomas Gold and others who are settling of a plantation about Freshwater River, Doe agree and fully consent to a sale and surrender of the greatest part of my land whereto the sd. English and such others as shall there plant and settle. And wherefore know ye That the said Tawtaps alias Notattuck for and in consideration of the sum of five and twentie pounds sterling to me in hand paid by Major Jno. Pynchon of Springfeild at and before the ensealing of these presents wherewith I acknowledge myself fully satisfied and contented have bargained and sold and by these presents Doe give grant bargain sel alien assign and enfeoffe and confirm unto the said Major Pynchon in behalf of Lieut. Thomas Stebbings Jonathan Burt Benjamin Parsons John Pease William Downton Thomas Gold their assigns and successors forever al that tract of land on east side of Conecticut River which is against the Fals from Asnuntuck alias Freshwater River on the north down southward along by Conecticut River about three or four miles viz. to the Brook below the heap of stones which Brook is called by ye Indians Pogotossur and by the English Salstonstal's Brooke ‡ and so from the mouth of said Salstonstal's Brooke alias Pogotossur to run from the great river Conecticut River directly East Eight ful and complete miles to the mountains and the whole tract of land to be complete eight miles from the great River both at the southerly

---

* These Falls could have been nothing more than rapids and are probably those near the Massachusetts and Connecticut line in Somers where there was formerly a saw-mill owned by the late Mr. Isaac Davis. It is an interesting point.

† Pequot and Mohegan.

‡ Now known as Bullens' Brook. It empties into the Connecticut River below the Connecticut River Rail Road Bridge and above Warehouse Point village.

end and at the north end also and run ful to the mountains on the east with the profits and advantages to the said tract of land belonging whether woods underwoods brooks waters stones minerals, pastures medows or marshes and al the appurtenances to the same belonging. To have and to hold the above granted tract of land with al liberties and privileges appertaining thereunto unto them the said Lieut. Tho. Stebbings Jonathan Burt Benjamin Parsons John Pease William Downton Thomas Gold their assigns and successors and to their only use and benefit and behoof forever. And I the said Tawtaps alias Notattuck for myself and my heirs Do hereby covenant promise and grant to and with the said Tho. Stebbin Jonathan Burt Benjamin Parsons John Pease William Downton Thomas Gold and their heirs and assigns that I the said Tawtaps alias Notattuck at the time of ensealing hereof was the true and sole lawful owner of ye afore bargained priveliges and every part thereof and had in myself ful power and good right and lawful authority to grant convey and assign the same as above said as a good and sure estate of inheritance forever without any condition reservation or limitation of use or uses whatsoever except that I reserve libertie to myself of hunting on the comon land in the woods and catching of fish in the River yet not so as to exclude the English right thereunto also. And with this only exception shal and wil warrant and defend the same unto the said Tho. Stebbin Jonathan Burt Benjamin Parsons John Pease William Downton Thomas Gold their heirs and assigns and successors against me my heirs or any Indians lawfully claiming the same or any part thereof and shal and wil at any time hereafter do any further act or acts for the more ful and complete and sure making of the above bargained premises unto them the said Tho. Stebbin Jonathan Burt Benjamin Parsons John Pease William Downton Thomas Gold their heirs and assigns according to the true intent thereof and the laws of Massachusetts Jurisdiction. In witness whereof I have hereunto put my hands and seal the 16th day of March in the two and thirtieth year of the reign of our sovereign lord Charles the 2d by the grace of God King of England & Anno Domini 16$\frac{80}{81}$

TAWTAPS (his mark) *alias* NOTATTUCK."

K.

HISTORY OF ENFIELD.*

ENFIELD, CT.—ITS LOCALITY—ITS FORMER RELATION TO MASSACHUSETTS PPOVINCE —ITS FIRST SETTLEMENT AND ITS PRESENT HISTORY.

The town of Enfield, which has been the birthplace of so many of our name, is bounded on the north by Longmeadow in Massachusetts, east by Somers (which, until 1736, formed a part of Enfield), south by East Windsor, and West by the Connecticut River, which separates it from Suffield. It is in the north-eastern part of Hartford County, and about six miles in length from north to south, and about five and one-half miles in breadth.

* Compiled from various sources.

It is sixteen miles from Hartford, Ct., on the south, and eight miles from Springfield, Mass., on the north. The river Scantic or Scantuck as called by the Indians is formed in South Wilbraham, Mass., runs south-westerly through Somers and Enfield, and finds its way into the Connecticut River at the extreme northerly boundary of South Windsor. Freshwater Brook, the Indian's Asnuntuck, is formed in the north-easterly part of the town, and runs westerly into the Connecticut River at Thompsonville.

As Enfield with its neighboring towns of Suffield and Somers once belonged to Massachusetts Province, we will briefly state how they happened to be a part of that Province and why they are now a part of the State of Connecticut. The southern boundary of the Colony of Massachusetts Bay according to its charter ran west from a point three miles south of the most southerly branch of the Charles River.

In 1642 and soon after the settlement of the Connecticut Colony, by order of the General Court, two men named Nathan Woodward and Solomon Saffery were commissioned to run the boundary line between the two Colonies. They pretended to ascertain the southern point on the branch of the Charles River, and then sailing round to the mouth and going up the Connecticut River they attempted to fix the line there on the same latitude as on the Charles River. This point, as they thought, struck the chimney of the house of one Bissel who kept the ferry. The house stood in the north part of the settlement at Windsor.

In 1648 the General Court "ordered" that "all the land on the east side of the Connetecott Ryver from the towne of Springfeild downe to the warehouse which they formerly built there shal belong to the towne of Springfeild for the present and during the pleasure of the Courte and twenty pole beyond the warehouse." *

The Connecticut Colony were never satisfied with the Woodward and Saffery line, but before the two Colonies could come to a settlement of the controversy, the towns of Suffield and Enfield were settled under authority from the Massachusetts Province. At length, after considerable controversy between the Provinces, Commissioners fully empowered were chosen by each Colony who came to an agreement July 13, 1713. "They were both careful to secure the property to the persons to whom they had made grants of land, and to maintain the jurisdiction over the townes which they had settled. It was, therefore, expressly stipulated as a preliminary that the towns should remain to the general government by which they had been settled, and the property of as many acres as should appear to be gained by one Colony from the other should be conveyed out of other unimproved land as a satisfaction or equivalent. With respect to about two miles claimed by Windsor upon the town of Suffield, concerning the validity of which there had been a long contest, it was agreed that if the tract fell within the limits it should belong to Connecticut.

"On running the line it was found at Connecticut River to run ninety rods north of the north-east bounds of Suffield; and it appeared that Massa-

---

* This boundary embraced nearly the whole site of the present village of Warehouse Point.

chusetts had encroached upon Connecticut 107,793 acres, running a due west line from Woodward and Saffery's station. Massachusetts made the grant of such quantity of land to Connecticut, and it was accepted as equivalent."*

It was found that not only Suffield and Enfield were within the patent of Connecticut, but the town of Woodstock also, which had been settled by Massachusetts. There appears to be different opinions among historians as to how well satisfied these towns were with the settlement of the controversy. They continued under the jurisdiction of Massachusetts some thirty-four years, without making any remonstrance. In 1747 they preferred a memorial to the General Assembly of Connecticut, stating they were within the bounds of the Royal Charter of Connecticut; that they had been placed within the jurisdiction of Massachusetts without their consent. They therefore claimed to be taken under the protection of Connecticut. The General Assembly at first hesitated to do so. But after waiting two years, and finding no amicable arrangement could be made with her sister Colony, the Assembly concluded that, as the agreement between the two Colonies in 1713 had never received the sanction of the Royal Government, therefore the agreement so far as jurisdiction, was void.

The Town of Enfield held its first town-meeting the "fifth day of December, 1749 for electing town officers, etc., agreeable to the laws of the Colony of Connecticut." Among the items of debts for which the town voted to raise money at that meeting was to pay the "charges of the agent, etc., for prosecuting the defence of our getting into Connecticut."

Massachusetts did not at once acquiesce in this procedure. She continued to levy taxes against the inhabitants for several years and sent sheriffs to collect them but the people stoutly resisted their authority, and the contest was finally abandoned by Massachusetts.

THE SETTLEMENT OF ENFIELD.

The year 1679 marks the time when the first movements appear to have been made towards effecting the settlement at Enfield. The following extracts we take from the records of Old Hampshire County Court of Sessions bearing date September 30, 1679:

"The Selectmen of the town of Springfeild signifying the towne's intent to settle a small village or town out of their lands at a place called Freshwater Brook, and moving this Court to appoint and impower a Comittee according to law to order after what manner or form the people shall settle and where, this Court, accordingly appoint and impower Major John Pynchon Esq Benjamin Cooley George Coalton Samuel Marshfeild or any three of them of whom Major John Pynchon being one of them a comittee" who were to examine the grounds and give directions in writing "in what form the town shal be settled and erected so as to live near together for security against enemies and other good ends and accord to the direction of said comittee the inhabitants are to build and settle and not otherwise."

The first settlers of this new village were made up largely of emigrants from the town of Salem, Mass.

---

* Trumbull's History of Connecticut.

"The planters came on with numbers and strength. They brought with them two young gentlemen one Mr. Whiteadon for a schoolmaster and Mr. Welch a candidate for the ministry and to be their preacher." *

This large emigration did not take place from Salem until 1681. Whether any families moved from Salem to this new plantation before that time I have been unable to ascertain. It is quite likely none did. It is said the two eldest sons of John Pease, Sen., went there in the fall of 1679 and spent the following winter there. Other heads of families may have gone with them for the purpose of making clearings and to prepare places for their families.

In the spring of 1683 the inhabitants of the new settlement and others petitioned the General Court to be set off from Springfield into a separate town. The petitioners stated that the town of Springfield "by a clear and full vote manifested their readiness thereunto." They expressed their intention to "maintain and uphold the worship of God and his ordinances and discharge all public dues which will occur when the place shall be settled." "Beseeching your Honors" continued the petition "for this end to consider the nature of the land which your Honors may have ful information concerning, from the Worshipful Major John Pynchon, and Springfeild Deputy, who knows it well that the best of the land is not a mile and half in breadth eastward from the great river is woody and swampy land and must by hard labor be won for improvement, and then at the end of that mile and half and in some places not half a mile wide, the rest for about five miles eastward from the great river is piney and barren land and capable of no improvement so that much of the land to be improved is six or seven miles eastward of the great river." † For these reasons the petitioners asked for a large area of land for their township.

The certificate of the Selectmen of Springfield accompanied the petition on the same sheet bearing date May 12, 1683, stating the town had voted for the new township. The petition was received at Boston, May 18th.

The following is a copy of the answer to the petition by the General Court:

"In answer to the petition from Springfeild and others craving a township a little below Springfeild at Freshwater Brook this Courte doth grant a township there to the subscribers and others as the committee this Courte appoints shall associate to them and that the bounds of said plantation be from the land Springfeild hath yeilded to them viz. at the mouth of Longmeadow Brook below Springfeild; from thence to run Southward by Connecticot sixe miles and the bound or lyne betweene Springfeild and this new township to runn off from Connecticot Ryver upon a due east line tenn miles from the mouth of said Longmeadow Brooke where it empties itselfe into the Great Ryver alias Connecticot Ryver; and that the towne be called Enfeild; and for the admittance of inhabitants granting allotments and ordering all prudentiall affairs of said township this Courte doth appoint Major John Pynchon Lieut. Tho. Stebbins Mr. Samuel Marshfeild Jonathan Burt and Deacon Benjamin Parsons or any three of them Major Pynchon being

---

* Trumbull's History of Connecticut.
† From papers on file in the office of Secretary of State.

one of them to be a committee who are fully impowered to manage all the affaires of said township till the Courte take further orders; and that the said towne be freed from county rates for five years from this time."

Trumbull says the town was named Enfield for a town of the same name in England. The town of Springfield derived its name from one in England it is said, but we do not think Enfield did. It will be noticed that the names of the towns of Westfield, Suffield and Enfield which once joined Springfield or formed a part of it have the same termination as Springfield. And it seems probable that Westfield and Enfield derived the first syllable of their names as did Suffield. The committee, of whom Major Pynchon was one, who laid out the town of Suffield, used the following language in their report to the General Court:—The said " Committee doth also humbly propose . . . . . that the name of the place may be called Suffeild (an abreviation of Southfeild) it being the southermost towne that either at present is or like to be in that country and neere adjoining the south of our patent in in those parts." The name Enfield was undoubtedly an abbreviation of Endfield as was Suffield from Southfield and the names of those towns are frequently found thus on the records of Old Hampshire County.

It appears the inhabitants of the new settlement were unfortunate with their " candidate for the ministry" who accompanied them from Salem.* From the records of a court held at Springfield, September 30, 1684 we copy the following:

" The town of Enfield was by the grand jury presented to this Court for that they are without a preaching minister; but it being alleged that the said Towne is under a committee and also that the inhabitants have been endeavoring the attainment of a meet person for that worke so said Towne were discharged." At the same Court an indictment was presented against another town and the town was fined for not sustaining a public school in the place.

Thus did our forefathers aim to have mental and religious instruction go hand in hand with progress and civilization.

The first settlements in the town of Enfield were made in the west part of the town and south of Freshwater Brook. As the inhabitants became more numerous they pushed their settlements easterly. Benjamin Jones first began the settlement in that part of the town which is now Somers. He went out from Enfield and spent the summers on his new settlement but returned again to the village in the fall. A permanent settlement was begun there in 1713 when James Pease, Timothy Root and John McGregory, with their families, joined Jones to remain there permanently. This new settlement formed a part of the same ecclesiastical society with Enfield until 1726,† when the General Court formed it into a separate precinct called East Enfield. In 1736 it became an incorporated town called Somers. It is

---

* He died before he had been with them very long. The first " ordained minister" that was "installed" over the church in Enfield, was Rev. Nathaniel Collins, in 1699.

† Trumbull. A historical sermon, prepared by the Rev. Dr. Baccus, states that the first church in Somers was organized March 15, 1727.

said to have been named after Lord Somers at the request of Gov. Belcher.*

The town of Enfield increased steadily in population, wealth and religious interest after its settlement notwithstanding it possessed "woody and swampy land" "hard to be won for cultivation," and "piney and barren land capable of no improvement." Forty-four years after its incorporation the town was able to part with a portion of its territory (which was afterwards Somers) for the formation of another ecclesiastical society.

Between 1745 and '50 a Baptist society was formed and a house of worship erected with Rev. Joseph Meacham as pastor in the north-easterly part of Enfield. It was located in the vicinity where Ann Lee was most successful in spreading her Shaker doctrines, and a large portion of its members with their pastor joined the Shakers and the Baptist society became extinct. In 1762 a serious schism occurred in the original church which resulted in the "Second Ecclesiastical Society of Enfield."† The new church was known as the "Separates" or "Separatists." It afterwards became a Baptist Church. A small society now exists as its legal successor, most of the members of which are Adventists.

The town of Enfield has a population of about seven thousand inhabitants and sustains some twelve religious societies. It has four post-offices. The Enfield post-office is located on the broad river road which leads from Springfield to Hartford and near where the First Congregational Church has always been located. The town-house and two Orthodox Congregational Churches are located in this vicinity. But little business is done in this part of the town compared with that which was formerly done there.

The post-office village of Thompsonville is located on the Connecticut River and at the mouth of Freshwater Brook. It was formerly known as "Head of the falls" and "Lovejoy's Ferry." It derived its present name from Orrin Thompson, Esq., who commenced the manufacture of woolen carpets there some forty years ago. Carpets are still made there by the Hartford Carpet Company to a very large extent. It also has an extensive stockinet manufactory owned by the Enfield Manufacturing Company. The village has two Presbyterian Churches, one Methodist Episcopal Church, one Protestant Episcopal Church, and one Roman Catholic Church.

Scitico, (Skitico) located in the eastern part of the town, is a post-office village. The village has a grist-mill, saw-mill, gin-distillery, a manufactory of plows for southern market and a powder manufactory. The forge, the

* It is said that Lord Somers sent the town a church bell because it was named for him, but for some cause, not satisfactorily explained, the bell never reached its destination, and the Somers church building was without a bell until nearly a century afterwards.

† The late Rev. Francis L. Robbins stated in a printed pamphlet some years since, that the Separatist church was formed in 1770. In this he must have been mistaken. Mrs. M. C. Stephens of Springfield, Mass., has in her possession the original records of the first meetings of the society. The first meeting to consider the expediency of forming the society was held April 13, and the last one when a church covenant was agreed upon and numerously signed occurred August 20, 1762. Mr. Nathaniel Collins, then of Westfield, Mass., a son of Rev. Nathaniel Collins, the first ordained minister in Enfield, was called to be their pastor.

carding-machine works and clothiers works formerly located there are among the things which were.

About midway between Scitico and the Enfield post-office village and in the vicinity of the east burying-ground is the post-office village of Hazardville. It was named for the late Col. A. G. Hazard who for many years was a large owner and principal manager of the Hazard Powder Company's works located in this vicinity.

About thirty-one years ago the large farm owned by the late David Allen on the Scantic River was bought by the Messrs. Loomis of Suffield who immediately began erecting powder-mills on it. The works afterwards passed into the hands of the present company who greatly added to the business by purchasing additional water-power upon the Scantic and in the use of steam power. It makes one of the largest powder manufactories in the United States. This village has Methodist Episcopal, Protestant Episcopal and Roman Catholic Churches. About midway between Hazardville and Scitico is a Second Advent Church. A society of Shakers occupy the north-east corner of the town. This sect began to disseminate its doctrines in Enfield about 1780. They own over one thousand acres of well cultivated land. They raise annually large quantities of garden seeds. The Shakers live in four different families and number about two hundred persons.

ERRATA.

PAGE 13, second line, for 1711 read 1718.

Page 22, No. 183, for *Hill* read *Hills.*

Page 29, No. 273, for *Prudder* read *Prudden.*

Page 31, No. 305, for 1796 read 1764.

Page 34, in the ancestry of John Pease,[5] for *John*[1] read *Robert.*[1]

Page 31, bottom line, for 91 years read 88 years.

Page 40, No. 403, for *Reuben Pease* read *Reuben Pasco.*

Page 44, in the ancestry of Hezekiah Pease,[5] for *John*[1] read *Robert.*[1]

Page 45, No. 149, for *married   Root* read *married Anna, daughter of Hezekiah Spencer.*

Page 47, No. 505, for March 27, 1778 read March 27, 1779.

Page 47, No. 506, erase the line as James did not belong to family 167.

Page 55, in the ancestry of John Pease,[6] read *Robert*[1] in place of *John.*[1]

Page 58, first line, for 37 years read 34 years.

Page 60, No. 220, for 1722 read 1772.

Page 62, No. 669, for *Ewen* read *Erwin.*

Page 69, No. 740, for *Lancton* read *Langdon.*

Page 82, No. 876, for *Brogue* read *Broque.*

Page 85, No. 908, for *Solomon* read *Peter.*

Page 94, No. 1019, for 1838, read 1808.

Page 117, No. 479, for *without* read *leaving.* (See Addenda.)

Page 117, No. 1274, for *Homer* read *Omar.*

Page 124, No. 1365, for *Hill* read *Hills.*

Page 126, No. 1397, for *Francis* read *Frances.*

Page 129, No. 1419, for *m.   Miller* read *d. young, unmarried.*

Page 133, No. 544, for 1845 read 1835.

Page 159, No. 1700,[20] for *Ervin* read *Erwin.*

Page 162, No. 662, for *Israel P.* read *Jared P.*

Page 166, No. 679, for *Stark* read *Slack.*

Page 173, No. 1799, for *Treasurer* read *Auditor.*

Page 177, No. 1802, for *Theodore* read *Theodora.*

Page 182, No. 1870, for *Jabez Collins* read *William O. Collins.*

Page 201, first line, for *Howse* read *Howes.*

Page 208, No. 2070, for *John Le Harris,* read *John L. Harris.*

Page 224, No. 2173, for 1840 read 1846.

Page 228, No. 2211, for *Francis* read *Grannis.*

Page 229, following the words *after the siege of Suffolk* below the middle of the page add *in consequence of ill-health.* At the end of the line in the next sentence, for *relief* read *retired.*

Page 245, No. 2363, for *Fraganzie* read *Traganza.*

Page 252, No. 2434, for *forty-ninth* read *forty-sixth.*

Page 270, No. 1152, for *Crippen* read *Cuppin.*

Page 296, No. 1291, for *Caroline M. Butler* read *Cornelia M. Butler.*

Page 296, No. 2810, for *Caleb B.* read *Newton B.*

Page 318, No. 1432, for *Avon* read *Ann.*

Page 336, No. 1540, for *Georgia, Vt.,* read *State of Georgia.*

PART II.

Austin S. Pease

THE EARLY HISTORY

OF THE

PEASE FAMILIES

IN AMERICA,

BY

AUSTIN SPENCER PEASE.

———•◦•———

SPRINGFIELD, MASS.:
SAMUEL BOWLES AND COMPANY, PRINTERS.
1869.

PREFACE.

So little has been known of the Peases who first emigrated to New England by persons of modern times, much confusion has prevailed as to their relationship to each other, and to the personal identity of some of them who bore the same given name.

Between the years of 1635 and 1672, there lived in New England no less that six John Peases, whose names have appeared in print within the past few years. The ancestor of the writer, John Pease, Sen., last of Enfield, being one of them, and the supposition at one time that his father was another, led him to make a thorough inquiry into the history of those of the name of Pease who were among the early inhabitants of New England. These investigations form the basis of the following pages.

The extracts relating to the history of the founders of New England, which have been taken from ancient records and published within a few years past by historical societies, have served a good purpose in calling the attention of the genealogical student to the names of persons and locality of place where information may be found; but were he to rely entirely upon such extracts he would be often led astray in his conclusions. Hence, while gladly availing myself of all such channels of information, I have not rested satisfied to go no farther, but have, so far as possible, followed the channels to their fountain heads, and examined the original records myself.

I have been much interested in the investigation, but cannot expect the general reader will be equally interested in the perusal. I hope, at least, however, some of the chapters will explain to the genealogical student what may heretofore have seemed mystified

to him.   It has been my aim to study into the history of all bearing the name of Pease, who figured in the history of the early
settlements of the country, or who stood at the heads of families.
With this in view, I could not pass any of them by, although another may have been contemplating their history.

There have been many persons waiting many years to learn any
facts which may have been collected by the Hon. Richard L.
Pease in relation to the early history of his ancestor, and of his
settlement at Martha's Vineyard.   And it was not until after I
had been assured by him that he knew of no records in Duke's
County which would throw light upon the subject, that I ventured
to begin the chapter of Martha's Vineyard Peases.

"The Early History of the Pease Families" will be circulated
largely among the descendants of John Pease, Sen., last of Enfield.*   It is perhaps due to them that an investigation into the
history of the settlement of the Martha's Vineyard Branch, should
have been made by one of their number; since many of the Peases
of the Martha's Vineyard Branch have not been disposed to favor
the common tradition which has existed among the Enfield Peases,
as to the relationship of the two men who stand at the head of the
Salem Peases and the Martha's Vineyard Peases.

It may be observed that I have given not only the early but
the late histories of some branches of the Peases. They seemed
to be in want of a historian, and as none among their number was
ready to be one, I was encouraged by many to continue my history to later generations.

When I began to study the early history of the New Hampshire Peases, I did it with the belief that they sprang from Nathaniel Pease, Sen., of Salem. Before my visit to the ancient
records at Exeter, I became satisfied he left no male issue.   After

---

* "The Early History of the Pease Families in America," is published in two
forms. One form is a book by itself, and styled "Pease Families." The other form
is as Part II. of the "Pease Record," being bound with the "Historical and Genealogical Record of the Descendants of John Pease, Sen., last of Enfield, Ct.," as
Part I.

my visit there, I was highly gratified to find evidences which to my own mind confirmed the statements I had had more than once made to me by the New Hampshire Peases, that they were of Martha's Vineyard origin.

I feel under many obligations to the Hon. Richard L. Pease of Edgartown, Mass., who has so cheerfully co-operated with me and given me facts which were in his possession that have very materially added interest and value to the work. To the Essex County Institute of Salem, whose publications from the ancient records in that city have aided me in getting at facts, also to the publications and collections of the Massachusetts Historical and New England Historic-Genealogical Societies, I am considerably indebted. References have been made in the work to other persons who have given me information and they have my thanks.

AUSTIN S. PEASE.

SPRINGFIELD, MASS., *August*, 1869.

CONTENTS.

Sic Itur ad Astra

Optime de Patria Meruit.

THIS COAT OF ARMS, A RELIC OF THE EARLY ANCESTORS OF THE PEASE FAMILY, WAS GRANTED ORIGINALLY UNDER THE REIGN OF OTHO II., EMPEROR OF GERMANY. IT HAS BEEN PRESERVED FOR MANY GENERATIONS IN THE BRANCH OF WHICH THE LATE JOSEPH ROBINSON PEASE, ESQ., OF HESSLEWOOD, NEAR HULL, ENGLAND, WAS A MEMBER, AND USED BY HIM. HE PRESENTED IT TO THE AMERICAN BRANCH THROUGH THE LATE FREDERICK SALMON PEASE, ESQ., OF ALBANY, N. Y.

A COPY OF IT HAS BEEN INSERTED IN THIS WORK, NOT FOR ITS INTRINSIC VALUE AS AN EMBLEM ARMORIAL TO BE BORNE BY ANY OF THE NAME IN AMERICA, BUT BECAUSE OF ITS IMPORTANCE AS A HISTORICAL ILLUSTRATION OF THE ORIGIN, ANTIQUITY, AND NAME, OF THE PEASE FAMILY, VIZ.:—

PER FESSE ARGENT AND GULES, AN EAGLE DISPLAYED COUNTERCHANGED.

CREST—AN EAGLE'S HEAD ERASED, THE BEAK HOLDING A STALK OF PEA-HAULM, ALL PROPER. SAID TO SIGNIFY THAT THE PERSON TO WHOM IT WAS GRANTED HAD BEEN A COMMANDER, BUT NOT IN CHIEF.

Fred. S. Pease.

EARLY HISTORY

OF THE

PEASE FAMILIES IN AMERICA.

CHAPTER I.

ORIGIN OF THE PEASE FAMILIES.

THE Peases emigrating first to America came from England. The name has been common there for the past three hundred years, or as far back as parish registers have been kept to show it. A work published in England as early as 1472, mentions the name of John Pease, LL.D. Persons of this name are found there in all ranks of society; from the most respectable yeomanry to ministers of the gospel, bankers, projectors of the first public railways, members of Parliament, etc.*

The English Peases are said to be of German origin and their emigration is placed at a much later period than when the Saxons made their conquest in England.

*The late Frederick S. Pease, Esq., in the New England Historical and Genealogical Register, Vol. III. Mr. Frederick S. Pease is a descendant of the Enfield, Ct., Peases, and of the eighth generation from Robert Pease, Sen., whose history is mentioned in Chap. IV. of this work. His ancestry runs thus: FREDERICK SALMON,[8] SALMON,[7] CALVIN,[6] NATHANIEL,[5] SAMUEL,[4] ROBERT,[3] JOHN,[2] ROBERT.[1] He was born in Canaan, Ct., May 21, 1804. For more than thirty years he was book-keeper in the Commercial Bank of Albany. To him belongs the honor of being the first of the name to prepare and publish papers relating to the family of Peases in this country. They have done much in cultivating a taste and desire among those of his name to know more of the history of Peases in America. He married Julia Lawrence, September 18, 1832, and died at Albany, N. Y., March 22, 1867. For a further history of him, his father's family (among whom were the late Rev. Calvin Pease, D. D., sometime President of the Burlington University, and Rev. Aaron G. Pease, Principal of the Vermont State Reform School at Waterbury,) and of his ancestry, see Part I. of the Pease Record.

1

We have been informed by one who has seen it that an English work giving a history of the Peases in England states that they came from Germany some four or five hundred years ago. It would seem by the coat of arms displayed on a preceding page that the English Peases were in Germany as late as A. D., 971, as Otho II. was Monarch of Germany from 972 to 981. The name is found in Germany now and persons bearing it have emigrated from that country directly to this. The name has a different orthography in Germany, (Pies or Pees,) but those coming to this country not unfrequently change the orthography of it to conform with the Anglo-Saxon mode.

Several persons have expressed the opinion that the Peases sprang from the Latins. Of this we have no opinion. The father of the late Dr. Charles Constantine Pise* of Brooklyn, N. Y., was an Italian. One individual of the Enfield branch of Peases, of highly respectable family relations, and a gentleman of thorough education, is of the opinion we are of Italian origin, and he has changed the orthography of his name to Pise because he believes it to be like the original orthography of it.

It has been suggested that the name Pease may have originated some way by its association with that esculent plant called peas. It is probable it might have; and the origin quite ancient. Coats of arms used in families often give a clue to the origin of the name. It will be observed by the coat of arms granted by Otho II. that its crest has an eagle's head erased, the beak holding a stalk of pea-haulm, which makes it appear that the Pease family was in some way associated with the pea-plant.

The late Frederick S. Pease suggested in his "Pease Family" that the name may have been "derived or formed a part of the name of Peabody." He has since stated that he had become convinced that "there was no ground for the assumption."†

---

* Pronounced Pees.   † See New England Historical and Genealogical Register, Vol. IX.

CHAPTER II.

BOSTON PEASES.

The honor of being the first pioneer to America of the name belongs to Henry Pease. He is supposed to have come from England about the time Governor Winthrop did, (1630,) and settled in Boston. His name is found occasionally upon the town records of that place.* He was made Freeman in 1634. He had two wives; first, Susan, died in August, 1645; second, Bridget. He died August 7, 1647. In mentioning his decease, Governor Winthrop called him "my old servant." This fact renders it probable he had been in the employ of Governor Winthrop for some time. He had three children, viz: John, Henry and Susan.

SECOND GENERATION.

JOHN PEASE,² (Henry,¹) son of Henry and Susan Pease, has a public history in Boston for a period of some thirty-six years; although he was not noticed by Farmer, Savage, and others in their histories of the early settlers of New England. His name is found frequently in the Suffolk County records, and among the papers on file in the office of Secretary of State. He was brought under censure by the General Court, May 31, 1670, for having accompanied his townsman, Hope Allen, his daughter and a Mr. Deacon to Lynn where the two latter were married without having been legally published. Anticipating the action of the Court, he presented a petition†

* See Drake's "History of Boston."
† His signature to this petition is a fac-simile to others found among petitioners to the General Court who are known to have been inhabitants of Boston.

to that body, dated May 15, 1670. His petition admits he had received "caution and warning" from the honored Major-General that same day he committed the offense. He urged he did not disobey because of "any disregard or wilful transgression or contempt of the laws or authority of the country;" but, continues the petition, "to my imbecility and folly, transported by a preposterous zeal to pleasure my friend (who had for a considerable time sojourned with me) in order to his dispatch to sea, the vessel wherein I am somewhat concerned staying on purpose."* His reasons were not satisfactory to the General Court, and he was fined forty shillings† for yielding to a "preposterous zeal." He was by occupation a tobacconist, besides being "somewhat concerned" in a vessel.

In 1648 he had a wife named Martha. It is probable he had no issue by her. He afterwards had a wife named Hannah, by whom he had a daughter, Elizabeth, born May 15, 1677. The child died young and seems to have been his only issue. His last will and testament, made February 20, 1683, was proved the following December. His "great bible," which had been his father's, he gave to his "loving brother Henry Pease." The balance of his property, whether derived from his "father, Henry Pease, deceased," or acquired himself, he gave to his wife, Hannah.‡

HENRY PEASE,[2] (HENRY,[1]) brother of the preceding, was probably the second son of HENRY and SUSAN PEASE of Boston. As early as 1649, he with his wife, Gertrude, lived at Marblehead. In 1656 they sold their house and

---

*From papers in the office of the Secretary of State.
†See printed records of the Colony of Massachusetts Bay.
‡John Pease was elected a member of the Ancient and Honorable Artillery Company of Boston in 1661, and in 1668 he was chosen Second Sergeant of the Company. He may never have accepted that office, however, as his name (says the Hon. Francis Brinley), does not appear among the officers after the date of election. In the absence of any evidence to the contrary, it seems probable that John Pease of Boston had the honor of being a member of that Company.

land at Marblehead and probably returned to Boston, where their daughter Martha died in 1659, and at a later period his name appears as a resident there. We have no means of knowing how long he survived his brother John. The "widow Garthwrite" Pease died at Boston, June 25, 1701.* We cannot learn as he had any sons to perpetuate his name. His history closes the history of the Boston Peases.

---

* Suffolk and Essex County and Boston Town Records.

CHAPTER III.

JOHN PEASE OF SALEM VILLAGE.

AN individual bearing the name of John Pease appears
in Salem history in 1635. His conduct gave him a "strikeing" notoriety and gained the attention of the General
Court. We were inclined first to think he may have been
the John Pease who came to this country in the ship
Francis, in 1634, whose history we shall hereafter mention; and later that he may have been the tobacconist of
Boston. But the development of additional facts in his
and others' histories renders it conclusive he was neither.

At the November session of the General Court in 1635,
it was "ordered that John Peas shall be whipped and
bound to his good behavior for strikeing his mother, Mrs.
Weston, and deriding of her and other evil carriages."
Mrs. Weston was the wife of Francis Weston one of the
early settlers of Salem and a resident of Salem Village,
so called, now Danvers. As Francis Weston never had
issue,* it is probable this John Pease was the son of Mrs.
Weston by a former husband, and at the time of this
difficulty he may have been a minor and lived in the
family of Francis Weston. He remained in the Colony
of Massachusetts Bay, after religious persecution in 1638
had driven his step-father first to Providence, R. I., and
afterwards to Shawomet (now Warwick, R. I.) In 1643
the Governor of Massachusetts Bay Colony, claiming
jurisdiction over Shawomet, and because of some alleged
grievances, sent Commissioners with a body of soldiers to
Shawomet to arrest and deal with the leading men of the

---

* James Savage.

new settlement. Pease hastened there to "declare unto his father, out of his tenderness toward him, of the nearness of the soldiers' approach and as near as he could the end of their coming, to persuade his said father to escape for his life."* He was the first to apprise the settlers of their danger; and he afterwards acted as a bearer of dispatches between the hostile parties. His efforts to avert the storm which hung over the handful of settlers were unavailing. Francis Weston and others, (among whom was Samuel Gorton, the acknowledged leader in Shawomet,) were taken and carried off to Boston where they were tried, adjudged guilty and received sentence for heresy. They were sentenced to hard labor and were scattered about in towns in the vicinity of Boston. They were liberated in the spring following and allowed to return to Shawomet. In June of the same year Francis Weston died of consumption.†

Soon after the death of his step-father, Pease sold his house and farm at Salem Village. It is probable that he left the Colony about the same time as no record of him can be found in the Colony later than this sale of land. It is said no mention is made of him in the records of Warwick (formerly Shawomet,) where his mother probably remained after the death of her husband, and where we should naturally suppose he would have gone.

"Luce Pease, the wife of   Pease,"‡ who was brought before the General Court in 1643, on a charge of having embraced the religious opinions of Samuel Gorton, but finally acquitted, is supposed to have been the wife of John Pease, the subject of this sketch.

---

* Samuel Gorton.

† The above facts relating to the difficulties between the inhabitants of Shawomet and the Governor of Massachusetts Bay, and the action of Pease were gathered from Gorton's "Simplicity's Defence" which has been reprinted by the Rhode Island Historical Society.

‡ See printed records of the Colony of Massachusetts Bay.

CHAPTER IV.

ORIGIN OF THE SALEM AND ENFIELD PEASES.

Much is due to the memory of the late Dr. John Chauncey Pease* for his manuscript history of the Enfield Peases. He gathered many facts relating to their history after their emigration to Enfield, which, had it not been for his efforts, would have been lost to posterity. He appears, however, to have possessed but little information concerning the history of the family prior to its removal to Enfield, and no knowledge of the father of the elder Enfield Pease or of his relation to others of the name living at Salem.

We are indebted to the late Frederick S. Pease, Esq., of Albany, N. Y., for giving Dr. Pease's information to the public through that valuable periodical, the New England Historical and Genealogical Register in 1849, and for other valuable information and suggestions relating to the history of the Peases which he had presented to us from time to time through the same organ. But the rich material stored in the archives at Salem he did not

---

*Dr. John C. Pease is a descendant of the Enfield Peases of the seventh generation from Robert Pease, Sen., of this chapter. His ancestry runs thus: John Chauncey,[7] John,[6] John,[5] John,[4] John,[3] John,[2] Robert.[1] He was born at Enfield, Ct., June 1, 1782, entered Yale College about 1801, next studied medicine and practiced several years in his native and other towns. In 1816 he ceased practicing medicine and with his brother-in-law, the Hon. John M. Niles, began the publication of the "Hartford Times." The paper took a bold stand in the favor of Jeffersonian Democracy, and wielded a strong influence for more extended ecclesiastical and political privileges which finally resulted in the establishment of the present State Constitution in the place of the old Royal Charter. Dr. Pease wrote and published several historical works of considerable research. He prepared a history of the town of Enfield which he brought down to the American Revolution, but it has never been published. His work embraced a partial history of the Enfield Peases. Dr. Pease married Naomi G. Niles of Windsor, Ct. He died at Hartford, Ct., January 30, 1859. For a further history of him, his family and ancestry, see Part I. of the Pease Record.

explore. Recently these records have been thoroughly examined, and information has been brought to light which apparently precludes any further doubt or speculation as to the origin of the Enfield Peases and their relation to the Salem Peases.

Among those who took passage from Ipswich, England, in the ship Francis, John Cutting, master, bound for New England, toward the last of April, 1634, as shown by the custom-house books, were ROBERT and JOHN PEASE. Their ages upon the books were twenty-seven years each. It has been supposed that Robert Pease was the elder, and it may be that the probable ages of passengers were set down by the custom-house officers without questioning. The vessel was reported back to Ipswich as having arrived at Boston, Mass., without the loss of a single passenger. Neither of the men had wives with them. They must have come in a later vessel of which no record is extant as is the case of hundreds of others among the early settlers.*

A boy aged three years, named Robert Pease, was among the list of passengers of the ship Francis. It had been supposed that the child belonged to John Pease because of the proximity of their names upon the custom-house book, but the development of additional facts show that he must have been the son of Robert Pease. For more than thirty years after this emigration, Salem, Mass., is the only place where the name of Robert Pease is found in history in this country.

In January, 1637, ROBERT and JOHN PEASE had land granted them at Salem. A transaction growing out of these grants shows that the men were brothers. It seems conclusive that the Peases of the ship Francis in 1634 are identical with those who had land granted them at Salem in 1637. To this ROBERT PEASE of Salem belongs the distinction of being the progenitor of the Salem and Enfield Peases.

---

*John may have not been married.

It is not known positively from what part of England these men originally came, yet evidence has been produced within a few years past which throws considerable light upon their history and seems to point us to the family and locality in England from which they sprang.

The late Mr. Frederick S. Pease prepared a paper which was published in the New England Historical and Genealogical Register for 1856, Vol. X., which is directly to the point. He says:

"In Vol. III., page 30, New England Historical and Genealogical Register, there is mention of John Pease, aged 27, and Robert Pease, aged 27, who came from Ipswich, England, to Boston on board the ship Francis, in April, 1634, and removed to Salem where they were known to have been in 1637. It was assumed that John was the ancester of the families embraced in the account which was published in that volume and his name accordingly placed at the head; but farther research and more reflection have served to transfer the honor to Robert.

"Mr. Somberby, to whom much is due for his researches in England, writes under date of June 6, 1854, that while making some genealogical investigations in Essex, he met with the will of Robert Pease of Great Baddow, and considering it worth the trouble he visited that place and made extracts from the parish register:

"'Robert Pease, Co. of Essex, Locksmith, Will, dated May 10th 1623, Mentions his wife Margaret, sons Robert and John, daughter Elizabeth, son-in-law Abraham Page and brother-in-law Francis King. Will proved June 12th 1623.'

"From a long list of baptisms, marriages and burials dating from 1540 to 1623, the following have been selected:

"'John, son of Robert Pease baptized May 24, 1593. John infant son of Robert Pease buried Jan. 10, 1599. John son of Robert Pease baptized Nov. 20, 1608.'

"There is no record of the birth of Robert, the other son mentioned in the will, and Mr. Somberby thinks he must have been baptized in some other parish.

"It would be imprudent to assert positively that John and Robert, whose names are mentioned in the will, are the same who came in the ship Francis, but it seems not improbable that Great Baddow is the locality and the family of Robert Pease, that to which the ancestry of the family may be traced.

"Great Baddow is in what is called the Hundred of Chelmsford, about thirty miles north-east from London on the thoroughfare to Ipswich; the most convenient place of embarkation from that neighborhood, and old Norfolk and Essex here were settled chiefly by people from counties of the same name in England."

Since Mr. Pease published the above article it has been shown what was before only supposed, that Robert and John Pease who had land granted them at Salem in 1637, were brothers, and that the given name of the mother of Robert was Margaret. She probably emigrated to this country with the family of her son, Robert Pease. She was undoubtedly the "widow Pease" who joined the First Church at Salem, in 1639. Her will, made during her last sickness, and the inventory of her estate, were presented to the Court at Salem, September 1, 1644.* We can find no history of these brothers from the time of their embarkation at Ipswich until January 2, 1637, when they had land granted them at Salem. At this time Robert Pease was granted ten acres and John Pease twenty acres. It need not be inferred necessarily that they did not dwell at Salem before the above date. The records of land grants made at Salem prior to January 19, 1635, are not extant. There were but few grants made, comparatively from January 19, 1635, to January 2, 1637.

---

* See Appendix D.

It is known that there were certain persons living at
Salem as early as 1635, and some earlier, but we can find
no evidence that land was granted them until 1637. Yet
the subsequent history of these men show that they must
have owned land there before 1637. These brothers sold
the precise amount which was granted them in 1637, and
there is no record that Robert Pease had land granted him
afterwards, although when he died he was in possession
of 11 acres. These facts show that the brothers may have
gone to Salem the year they landed in America.

There is a transaction recorded at Salem in the book
of land grants, bearing date February 13, 1652, which
furnishes us an important fact. A portion of the record
reads thus:

"Robert Goodell having forty acres of land granted
him long since by the town and he having bought land
of several other persons that had land granted them"
[then follow the names of the persons of whom he
bought and the amount he bought of each] "in the whole
480 acres, it is ordered that the said Goodell shall enjoy
the said 480 acres, &c."

The record mentions the names of fifteen different persons of whom he made the purchases. Thirteen of these
persons had precisely the amount granted them in 1637,
which the record says Goodell bought of them. The
names of the other two persons are found among the
grantees in 1637, though the amount of land specified in
the two transactions do not agree.

Among these persons of whom he made the purchases,
were (to use the language of the record,) "*Robert Pease
and brother*, 30 acres." This action of the authorities
occurred after the two oldest sons of Robert Pease, Sen.,
were old enough to transact business for themselves. But
the sons had not had land granted them before that time
as shown by the book of land grants. Besides, had they
made such sales after their majority, they would probably

have been found on record in the office of Registry of Deeds. No transfers of land prior to 1644 are found recorded in the Registry's office. Sales after that date seem generally to have been recorded there. It is probable that Goodell presented the subject before the authorities for the purpose of having his purchases of land, that were made many years before, and of which no record had been made, properly sanctioned and legalized. It seems conclusive, therefore, that the men who had land granted them in 1637, were involved in the transaction, and not the sons of one of them. If this point is made clear it is equally clear that Robort and John Pease, to whom land was granted in 1637, were brothers. This incident furnishes us with the only direct proof we have of their relationship, and establishes the fact that there were two John Peases living in Salem, cotemporaneously, for a time before 1644. The one the son of Mrs. Weston, the other the son of Widow Margaret Pease.*

The history of the brother of Robert is briefer in Salem than that of his cotemporary of the same name. In only two instances besides those before mentioned in this and the preceding chapter does the name of John Pease appear in Salem history referring to either.

In April, 1638, John Pease had five acres of land granted him. This grant was near where the first grist-mill was located, and in the vicinity of the grants made originally to "Robert Pease and brother." Undoubtedly the brother of Robert is meant in this transaction. The name is again found in the Court records bearing date June 25, 1639. A copy of the record reads thus:

"It is ordered whereas Mr. Garvis Garford had a cow of John Pease for a year, the tyme being expired and

---

* The son of Mrs. Weston as shown by the locality of his farm lived in Salem Village, (now Danvers,) and several miles from the locality of the farm of Robert Goodell, a part of which had formerly been granted to John and Robert Pease. It is not probable these brothers were very nearly related to the son of Mrs. Weston, nor is it known they were to the Boston Peases.

the said John Pease not returned whereupon the said Mr. Garford requested advice what to do with her Upon which the Court ordered him to keep the cow until the party shall return, upon the same terms he kept her before." We are unable to determine which of the John Peases is meant in this transaction.

There is no evidence to show that the son of Mrs. Weston left Salem until five years after this unless he went with his mother and step-father to Providence in 1638 and remained with them for a time. Nor is there any evidence to show that the brother of Robert was there later than this transaction. What became of him we have no direct proof. It was at one time supposed that he died before December 29, 1639, and that it was his widow who joined the church at Salem at that time. This supposition was entertained before it was known that the mother of Robert and John Pease lived at Salem. As the person referred to on the church books was designated simply as "Widow Pease," it is probable that only one widow lived at Salem at that period. There are reasons for supposing he may have gone to Martha's Vineyard and formed the settlement there. Of this more will be said in Chapter VII.

The history of ROBERT PEASE, Sen., in the "New World" is brief, as he lived here only a decade. On the first day of October, 1643, he joined the First Church at Salem. Two weeks later three of his children, viz: Nathaniel, Sarah and Mary were baptized. Less than one year from this he was dead. The inventory of his estate, signed by two appraisers but without date, was brought into court at Salem, August 27, 1644. His estate was a small one though valuable to his posterity. For the records made at its settlement compared with the last will and testament of his mother, throw light upon his family history and furnish us with unmistakable evidences that he was the father of JOHN PEASE, SEN., last of Enfield, Ct. Since these records have been carefully examined, the given name of the father of the latter need no longer be "assumed" or held in doubt.[*]

The given name of the wife of Robert Pease was Marie,[†] the French orthography for Mary. Her name furnishes presumptive•evidence that her parents may have been Protestant refugees from France. The time of her decease is not known, as no record of the settlement of her estate or division of her property can be found. Her name appears only in connection with the settlement of her husband's estate and in the inventory of his mother's. We are unable to ascertain the exact number of children there were in the family. Five are all we have any knowledge of.

His children were :

1. 1. ROBERT, b. at
2. 2. JOHN, b. at
3. 3. NATHANIEL, b. at
4. 4. SARAH, b. at   . m. John Sampson of Beverly, October 22, 1667, and died before 1677.
5. 5. MARY, b. at   , and probably m. Hugh Pasco [‡] as his second wife.

There are some reasons for supposing there may have been another child in the family.

A petition was gotten up in 1714 and signed by those "having cottages or dwelling-places before the year 1661" who it appears had rights in the common lands in Salem which others did not possess. Among those petitioners were Nathaniel and Isaac Pease. This is the only instance where the name of Isaac Pease occurs, except in reference to the grandchildren of Robert Pease, Sen., or their posterity. This Isaac Pease may have been a son of Robert Pease, Sen., born and baptized in England, who

---

[*] For a copy of these records see Appendix C. and D.

[†] Pronounced Mareé

[‡] Town Records: Hugh Pasco bought the "house, barn and out-buildings" of John Pease, Sen., when he removed to Enfield.

with his brother Nathaniel, shared an interest in the
common lands of Salem as an heir to his mother's small
estate. Quite likely he had no family and his brothers
named sons for him.

SECOND GENERATION.

1.

ROBERT PEASE,[2] (ROBERT,[1]) eldest son of ROBERT
and MARIE PEASE, first of England, last of Salem, was
born in England in 1628 or '29, came to this country
when a lad with his father, in 1634, and settled in Salem.
Bereft of a father at an early age, he was bound out by
the Court, December 31, 1645, "upon motion and consent
of both parties, to Thomas Root, to learn the trade of a
weaver of woolen and linen." He was sometimes made
keeper of the town herd, and he must have been employed as herdsman during his apprenticeship, or prior to
it, for in 1704 he testified in Court that he had been a
"keeper of several lots of creatures, as neat cattle, goats,
&c., on the lands belonging to the inhabitants of Salem
above 60 years agone."* In 1655 he "was employed to
keep one hundred cows, being a part of the town drove,
and to have help so that he may attend worship every
third Sabbath."† During an early period of his manhood
he lived at Martha's Vineyard. As an inducement to
keep him there, several of the citizens agreed to furnish
him annually with one hundred pounds of fish. The
agreement contains the following clause:

"If the said Robert Pease leave the island he will leave
the fish resigning up again to the owners. Also the said
Robert Pease doth engage to weave cloth of the town
for such pay as the town can raise among themselves
except wampum."*

---

*Land County Records.   †Felt's "Annals of Salem."
‡From Edgartown Records furnished by Hon. Richard L. Pease.

It is not known how long he remained at Martha's Vineyard. No mention is made of him at Salem after 1655 until 1667, except in the records of the birth of his children. Some of them may have been born at Edgartown, as the record of his first five children was made at one time on the Salem books. He was with a Salem company in the French and Indian war in 1676.* The given name of his wife was Sarah. Both suffered imprisonment in 1692 because suspected of witchcraft. His wife was living in 1704, and he in 1713, at which latter date he was dismissed from the First Church at Salem to aid in forming the First Church at the Middle Precinct, afterwards South Danvers, but now Peabody. He has the distinction of being the ancestor of the SALEM BRANCH of the SALEM PEASES.

His children were:

6. 1. BETHIA, b. June 11, 1660. d. November , 1667.

7. 2. ELIZABETH, b. August 20, 1662. m. Thomas Venney of Marblehead October 28, 1703.

8. 3. DELIVERANCE, b. August 10, 1664.

9. 4. MARY, b. February 12, 1667. m. Alexander Reynolds, July 6, 1686.

10. 5. ROBERT, b. March 25, 1669. No other history is found of him at Salem. There is a strong probability that he left Salem before he was of age and went to Enfield, Ct. The subject will be taken up in the next chapter.

11. 6. ISAAC, b. November 30, 1671.

12. 7. DELIVERANCE, b. December 6, 1673.

13. 8. BETHIA, b. June 18, 1675.

14. 9. NATHANIEL, b. February 28, 1678.

2.

JOHN PEASE,[2] (ROBERT,[1]) brother of the preceding, was born in England, about 1630, came to this country not far from 1634, and settled in Salem. His grandmother, Margaret Pease, who died soon after her son, his father, gave him in her will most of her property and put

---

*From MSS. in the New England Historic Genealogical Society's rooms in Boston.

the boy in the care of Thomas Watson of Salem to "dispose of him as his own child;" married first, Mary Goodell, daughter of Robert Goodell of Salem, who died January 5, 1669; married second, Ann Cummings, daughter of Isaac Cummings of Topsfield. He settled a yeoman in the "Northfields" at Salem where he remained until the fall of 1681, when he removed with his large family (the two eldest sons of which already had families) and numerous neighbors to that part of Springfield, Mass., which afterwards became Enfield, Ct. He died July 8, 1689. To him belongs the distinction of being the ancestor of the ENFIELD BRANCH of the SALEM PEASES. His posterity is supposed to be more numerous than that of any other person of this name in this country. Six generations of the male descent whose names have been obtained number over three thousand persons.

His children were:

15.   1. JOHN, b. May 30,* 1654.
16.   2. ROBERT, b. May 14,* 1656.
17.   3. MARY, b. October 8, 1658.
18.   4. ABRAHAM, b. June 5, 1662.
19.   5. JONATHAN, b. January 2, 1669.*

BY SECOND WIFE:

20.   6. JAMES, b. December 23, 1670.
21.   7. ISAAC, b. July 15, 1672.
22.   8. ABIGAIL, b. December 15, 1675.

For a full history of the male descendants of the above family, see "The Genealogical and Historical Record of the Descendants of John Pease, Sen., last of Enfield, Ct." Compiled by Rev. David Pease, assisted by the author of this work.†

---

* See Appendix A.

† Rev. David Pease is a descendant of the Enfield, Ct., Peases and of the sixth generation from Robert Pease, Sen., of this chapter. His ancestry runs thus: DAVID,[6] DAVID,[5] CUMMINGS,[4] ISAAC,[3] JOHN,[2] ROBERT.[1] He was born at East Windsor, Ct., November 9, 1783. He was ordained pastor of the Baptist Church at Belchertown, Mass., 1810. His next pastoral charge was at Conway, Mass. In 1823 he was called to the pastorate of the Baptist Church at Cazenovia, N. Y. He has been pastor of various Baptist Churches in New York State and Massachusetts.

3.

NATHANIEL PEASE,[2] (ROBERT,[1]) brother of the preceding, may have been born in England, but was baptized at Salem in 1643; married Mary Hobbs, March 15, 1668, and settled at Salem; but little is known of his history. His name appears only twice in the land records and then as a witness. He was in the French and Indian war in 1675, and was living in 1714. There is no record that he had issue. As his brother Robert named a son for him ten years after Nathaniel's marriage, it seems probable he had no son to bear his name. The Mary Pease who was implicated in the Salem witchcraft in 1692 was undoubtedly his wife.

THIRD GENERATION.

6.

ISAAC PEASE,[3] (ROBERT,[2] ROBERT,[1]) second son of ROBERT and SARAH PEASE of Salem, was born at Salem, November 30, 1671; married Elizabeth Thomas, April 20, 1697, and first settled within the present limits of Salem, but subsequently removed to that part which afterwards became Danvers, next South Danvers, and now Peabody. He was a "husbandman." His will was proved July 12, 1745; it mentions wife Elizabeth and children of whom two daughters were then widows. But as if indicative of the final obscurity of their history, neither the names or the number of his children are mentioned in it.

Vigorous in his old age he has preached to the Baptist Church at Savoy the past year. He began to collect material for a history of the Enfield Peases about twenty-five years ago, and before knowing anything had been done towards it by others. Providence has kindly lengthened out his days and permitted him to see his work of so many years labor in print. He married first Dorcas Ayres of Granby, December 31, 1812, by whom he had eight children; married second Sarah Taylor of Ashfield, January 16, 1855. For a farther history of himself, his children, grandchildren and ancestry, see Part I. of the Pease Record.

The writer's ancestry runs thus: AUSTIN SPENCER,[7] REUBEN,[6] ISAAC,[5] EZEKIEL,[4] ISAAC,[3] JOHN,[2] ROBERT.[1]

His children were: *

23. 1. ELIZABETH, b. at Salem, February 2, 1698. m. a Mr. Whitte-
      more.
24. 2. ISAAC, b. at Salem, July 2, 1699.
25. 3. MARY, b. at Salem.
26. 4. JOSEPH.
27. 5. JOHN.
28. 6. RUTH.

The following is all the history we can gather of the sons of Isaac Pease[3]:

Isaac, the eldest son of this family, lived in Danvers, but we could not learn that he had any family. In 1747 he sold his interest in his father's estate; was then called a husbandman. In 1767 he was a dependent upon the town of Danvers.†

Joseph Pease, his brother, lived some time in the town of Salem, and died there not far from 1777 leaving no issue to inherit his small share in the estate of his father.‡ Though a resident of Salem, he appears to have belonged to the town of Danvers in 1769, as his name at that date was associated with his brother Isaac's.

John has a history more obscure than that of his brothers. We found his name mentioned in only one document. It was dated October 3, 1677, and stated that he was a resident of Danvers, and brother of Joseph Pease then deceased, and a son of "Isaac Pease late of Salem," then of "Danvers, deceased." He and sister Elizabeth Whittemore sold a two-fifths interest of their brother Joseph's share in their late father's estate to a daughter of the sister Whittemore.§

9.

NATHANIEL PEASE,[3] (ROBERT,[2] ROBERT,[1]) brother of the preceding, was born at Salem, February 28, 1678;

---

* Town, County and Church Records.   † Danvers Town Records.
‡ County Land Records.   § County Land Records.

married Elizabeth Ashly, October 20, 1701, and settled at Salem a husbandman. His will was proved June, 1737. It mentions as

His children:

29.   1. BENJAMIN, b. at Salem, May 10, 1702. It is probable he never had a family. He was living in 1755.

30.   2. JOHN, b. at Salem, February 4, 1704.

31.   3. ELIZABETH, b. at Salem, May 15, 1706. m.   French.

32.   4. JONATHAN.

33.   5. NATHANIEL.

34.   6. LYDIA, m. Joseph Brown, a mariner.

FOURTH GENERATION.

30.

JOHN PEASE,[4] (NATHANIEL,[3] ROBERT,[2] ROBERT,[1]) second son of NATHANIEL and ELIZABETH (ASHLY) PEASE of Salem, was born at Salem, February 4, 1704; married Elizabeth Goodwin of Newbury, July 29, 1726, and settled in Salem. He was a cordwainer. He was living at Salem in 1756; could find no record of the time of his death. Elizabeth Pease, widow, made her will dated 1788. She was probably his relict. She gave her property principally to three daughters, viz.:

35.   1. MARTHA PEASE, who was made executrix.

36.   2. SUSANNAH.

37.   3. SARAH.

Small legacies were given to the following who may also have been her children:

38.   4. PHEBE BLAKE.

39.   5. JAMES PEASE.

40.   6. MARY PEASE.

Essex County and Salem Town Records are silent as to any further history of the above named family. Felt, in his Annals of Salem, mentions under date of February,

1797, the name of James Pease, who, among others, had recently returned from Algerine captivity, and states that he was apportioned his share in a benefit given to such sufferers by the Boston Theater. It is probable he belonged to this family.

32.

JONATHAN PEASE,[4] (NATHANIEL,[3] ROBERT,[2] ROBERT,[1]) brother of the preceding, settled at Salem, and was by occupation a "carter." He died 1777, and his wife Sarah died soon afterwards. His will mentions as

His children:

41.　1. JONATHAN.
42.　2. BENJAMIN, whose history is unknown.
43.　3. MARY, the "wife of William Munday."
44.　4. ELIZABETH, the "wife of Peter Warner."
45.　5. ROBERT.
46.　6. DANIEL, who d. before June 17, 1775.
47.　7. SARAH.
48.　8. HANNAH.
49.　9. EUNICE, who m. Solomon Wyman, January 10, 1765.*

The last three named were minors at the time of their father's decease.

33.

NATHANIEL PEASE,[4] (NATHANIEL,[3] ROBERT,[2] ROBERT,[1]) brother of the preceding, resided at Salem, and was by occupation a "carter." He died, 1773. His will mentions wife Jemima and his children.

His children were:

50.　1. NATHANIEL.
51.　2. EDMUND.
52.　3. AMOS, then under age.
53.　4. MARY.
54.　5. JEMIMA.

The Town or County Records give no additional information concerning the history of Edmund or Amos.

*Danvers Town Records.

FIFTH GENERATION.

41.

JONATHAN PEASE,[5] (JONATHAN,[4] NATHANIEL,[3] ROBERT,[2] ROBERT,[1]) eldest son of JONATHAN and SARAH PEASE; married Hannah Curtis, and settled at Salem. In legal transactions he was sometimes called Mariner and sometimes Fisherman. Letters of administration were granted on his estate December 6, 1785.

His children were:

55. 1. SAMUEL.
56. 2. JONATHAN.
57. 3. RICHARD.
58. 4. BENJAMIN, who d. under age.

45.

ROBERT PEASE,[5] (JONATHAN,[4] NATHANIEL,[3] ROBERT,[2] ROBERT,[1]) brother of the preceding; married Hannah Woodman, April 12, 1778. The Probate and Land Records give us no history of this individual. The Salem Town Records only give his marriage. There are persons residing at Salem whose father and grandfather were named Robert Pease. They are unable to give us such information as will identify them positively with this branch, but it is probable they are the grandchildren of this man.

50.

NATHANIEL PEASE,[5] (NATHANIEL,[4] NATHANIEL,[3] ROBERT,[2] ROBERT,[1]) son of NATHANIEL and JEMIMA PEASE of Salem, and first cousin of the preceding; married Love Mullin, April 22, 1784. Nothing further is known of his history.

SIXTH GENERATION.

55.

SAMUEL PEASE,[6] (JONATHAN,[5] JONATHAN,[4] NATHANIEL,[3] ROBERT,[2] ROBERT,[1]) eldest son of JONATHAN and HANNAH (CURTIS) PEASE of Salem; married Mary Lawrence and settled in Salem. He was a mariner. Letters of administration were granted on his estate April 16, 1805. Probate Records mentioned as

His children:

59. 1. SAMUEL, then ten years old. He was living in Boston in 1837. Was employed on the mill dam.
60. 2. MARY, then five years old. She married a Mr. Emerson and settled at Providence, R. I.

56.

JONATHAN PEASE,[6] (JONATHAN,[5] JONATHAN,[4] NATHANIEL,[3] ROBERT,[2] ROBERT,[1]) brother of the preceding, was born about 1773; married Mary Pecketh, and settled in Salem. He was a mariner and died in 1812.

His children were:

61. 1. JONATHAN, b. 1779. d. unmarried.
62. 2. BENJAMIN, b. April 17, 1814. m. Mary J. Aikin and resides at Salem, a shoemaker.

57.

RICHARD PEASE,[6] (JONATHAN,[5] JONATHAN,[4] NATHANIEL,[3] ROBERT,[2] ROBERT,[1]) brother of the preceding, was born March 30, 1777; married Mary Derby, September 21, 1801, and settled in Salem. He was a mariner.

His children were:

63. 1. MARY, b.   , 1803. m.
64. 2. RICHARD, b. April 19, 1807. m. Harriet N. Burnham, 1842, and resides in Salem, a baker.
65. 3. ELIZABETH, b.   , 1861. d. young.

NOTE.

The records of marriages and births in the town of Salem during the last century were almost wholly neglected. Hence our principal sources of information for a history of the Salem Peases have been the Probate and Land Records of Essex County. It is probable the posterity of the Salem Peases are not numerous. From all our inquiries either by letter or otherwise we have in only one instance found a person by the name of Pease outside of Salem who claimed that place as his origin. Mr. Joseph Pease of Richmond, Me., informs us his father was a native of Salem, Mass., but we have failed to learn from him to which family he belonged. It is not improbable that there may be other Peases in Maine who belong to the Salem Peases.

4

CHAPTER V.

FAMILY OF "LATTER" ROBERT PEASE OF ENFIELD, CT.

A FEW years after the families of John Pease, Sen., and his sons, John Pease, Jr., and Robert Pease had settled in Enfield, another individual named Robert Pease came into the settlement. The committee allotted him a portion of land, November 30, 1687, after having been admitted an inhabitant by a vote of the town. In his grant of land he is called "Robert Pease who had been admitted an inhabitant." His marriage is recorded as Robert Pease, Jr. In legal documents he was called Robert Pease, 2d. Among his townsmen he was generally designated as "latter" Robert. Dr. John C. Pease states in his manuscript history of Enfield, that "according to tradition he came directly from England to Enfield, and was a distant relative of the original Pease family in that town."* We have some time been of the opinion that he may have come directly from Salem instead of England.

Since finding that the brother of John Pease, Sen., had a son named Robert, whose farther history or death could not be found in Salem or vicinity, and that his brothers did not perpetuate his name in their families, we have become confirmed in the belief that this "latter" Robert did not come from England, but that he was the eldest son of Robert Pease of Salem, the weaver, and a nephew of John Pease, Sen., last of Enfield. So far as we can learn, the later generations of John Pease, Sen., were

---

* New England Historical and Genealogical Register, Vol. III.

ignorant of the fact that their ancestor left a brother at Salem who had a large family of children. Hence, there may have sprung up the tradition that this relative of their ancestor came from England. It will be observed that if he was the son of Robert Pease of Salem, weaver, that. he was not nineteen years old when he came to Enfield and had land granted to him. Granting a minor land at Enfield was. not an irregular procedure. Jonathan, the fourth son of John Pease, Sen., had land granted him in 1681 when he was twelve years old, and James, the fifth son, had land granted him at the age of nineteen.

To our mind there seems no better reason why neither Isaac or Nathaniel Pease, sons of Robert Pease of Salem weaver, named a son Robert for their brother, father and grandfather, than the supposition that the brother lived to have sons of his own to whom he might have given the name. And as the name can be found nowhere in New England to answer for that brother, except at Enfield, it seems conclusive to us that he was Robert Pease, Jr., of Salem. It is true he did not perpetuate his given name in his family. It was probably owing to the fact that two of the Enfield Peases already bore it when he came there. Therefore, to avoid a confusion which he may have seen and felt at Salem, he gave his eldest son the name of his uncle Nathaniel. Robert Pease, 2d, married Hannah Warriner, December, 1691, and settled upon his allotment on the Somers road east of Enfield street. He was living in 1744.*

His children were:

1. 1. HANNAH, b. March 15, 1693.
2. 2. NATHANIEL, b.
3. 3. JOSEPH, b.   , 1707. He was living in Enfield in 1729. Nothing farther is known of his history.
4. 4. BENJAMIN, b.   , 1718. History unknown.

---

*Old Hampshire County Records.

SECOND GENERATION.

2.

NATHANIEL PEASE,[2] (ROBERT,[1]) eldest son of ROB-
ERT, 2D, and HANNAH (WARRINER) PEASE, last of Enfield, was born at Enfield, Ct.; married Miriam Pease,*
daughter of Robert Pease, a grandson of John Pease,
Sen., December 24, 1730. He was by trade a weaver,†
and first settled in Enfield. About 1759 he removed to
Blandford, Mass.,‡ and for several years kept a public
house there. He served on the Board of Selectmen of
Blandford three years. In 1771 he sold his farm and
tavern stand to his son Levi,§ and it is said he removed
to Stephentown, N. Y., and died there.

His children were:

5.   1. NATHANIEL, b. at Enfield,   , 1731.
6.   2. MIRIAM, b. at Enfield,   , 1733.
7.   3. HANNAH, b. at Enfield,   , 1735. m.   Wheeler.
8.   4. JOEL, b. at Enfield,   , 1737. He was living in Bland-
         ford in 1765, but we can learn nothing of his history farther.
9.   5. LEVI, b. at Enfield,   , 1739.
10. 6. ABEL, b. at Enfield, September 19, 1741. History unknown;
         probably d. young.
11. 7. WILLIAM, b. at
12. 8. GEORGE, b. at
13. 9. ELEANOR.

THIRD GENERATION.

5.

NATHANIEL PEASE,[3] (NATHANIEL[2] ROBERT,[1]) eldest
son of NATHANIEL and MIRIAM (PEASE) PEASE, first of
Enfield, Ct., and some time of Blandford, Mass., was born

---

* No. 66 of the descendants of John Pease, Sen., last of Enfield. See Part I. of
the Pease Record.
  † Old Hampshire County Land Records.   ‡ Ibid.
  § Blandford Town and Hampshire County Records.

at Enfield, 1731; married Sophia   , and settled at Enfield. "He is said to have been a seafaring man
and to have died at sea."*

His children are:

14. 1. HULDAH, b. at Enfield, March 4, 1752. m. Ebenezer Pease,†
        July 5, 1771, and settled in Enfield.
15. 2. NATHANIEL, b. at Enfield, December 28, 1753. History unknown.
16. 3. MIRIAM, b. at Enfield, September 25, 1757.

9.

CAPT. LEVI PEASE,³ (NATHANIEL,² ROBERT,¹)·brother
of the preceding, was born at Enfield, Ct., 1739; married
Hannah Sexton, and probably first settled in Stephentown,
N. Y., from which place about 1770 he removed and settled in Blandford, Mass.,‡ and kept a public house there.
In 1776 he sold his farm in Blandford to Robert Pease§
of Somers, to which latter place he soon after removed
his family. In 1786, '88 and '89 he resided at Boston,
Mass., and kept the New York stage house.‖ He purchased a farm and tavern stand in Shrewsbury, Mass.,
and removed there from Somers in 1794, where he remained until his death.

Mr. Pease was by trade a blacksmith, but his mind was
too energetic ·and enterprising to be confined within the
walls of a common blacksmith shop. During the Revolutionary War he was variously employed in responsible
positions by officers of the army. He was with General
Thomas on the northern frontier at the time of his death
with the small-pox. He had been a bearer of many important dispatches for the General which required great
caution and skill to convey them to their places of destina-

*Dr. John C. Pease.
†No. 807 of the descendants of John Pease, Sen., of Enfield. See Part I. of the
Pease Record.
‡ Old Hampshire County Land Records.
§ No. 71, Part I. of Pease Record.
‖ Boston Directory in the rooms of New England Historic-Genealogical Society.

tion without detection. General Wadsworth of Hartford, Ct., Commissary General, afterwards employed him to purchase beeves for the army. "Wadsworth many times gave him large packages of Continental money wherewith to make purchases, informing him of the amount but which Pease never counted or receipted; such was Wadsworth's confidence and it was not misplaced or abused."* On the arrival of the French fleet and army at Newport, R. I., he was directed to purchase horses to drag their artillery to Yorktown, Va., and he afterwards foraged for the army on its way there.

Not far from the close of the Revolutionary War "he commenced running a stage or carriage for the accommodation of passengers between Somers and Hartford, about twenty miles, which was the incipient step to his more extensive operations in that line of business."† Soon after this he started a line of stages between Hartford and Boston. He had a partner named Sikes (some years his junior) who also was a blacksmith by trade. The enterprise was stoutly opposed by the father of young Sikes. He told Pease he had enticed his son "into a ruinous scheme that would make them both in a short time tenants of the jail."‡ Nothing daunted, they furnished themselves with convenient wagons, and "began business October 22, 1783. One started from the sign of the Lamb in Boston every Monday morning at six o'clock, and stopped for the night at Martin's at Northboro; on Tuesday going through Worcester it rested at Rice's at Brookfield; on Wednesday it advanced to Pease's at Somers, and on Thursday it reached Hartford. The other leaving Hartford the same time and stopping at the same places, reached Boston in four days. Fare four pence per mile."§ In 1784 they included Springfield in their route.

---

* Ward's History of Shrewsbury. † Rev. David Pease.
‡ Ward. § William Lincoln's History of Worcester.

"In January, 1786, the energetic founders had established a line of stages from Portsmouth to Savannah, transporting the several mails. From Boston to Hartford coaches left the inn of Levi Pease opposite the Mall every Monday and Thursday morning, and made the trip in three days."* They had then reduced their fare to three pence per mile, and allowed passengers fourteen pounds baggage.† "For a long time Pease was the only contractor in New England known at the department for carrying the mails through its various thoroughfares by stage and on horseback; much of which he underlet to others, the responsibility of which rested upon him."‡§

Captain Levi Pease‖ "procured the first charter for a 'turnpike' road that was granted in Massachusetts. The road ran through Palmer and Wilbraham to Springfield, which before, almost impassable with wheels, was greatly improved. He took a large portion of the stock, expended much time and money upon the road for many years, and at last, by a depreciation of its stock, lost all he put into the concern."

How changed the conveniences for traveling on that same thoroughfare over which Captain Pease ran his stages! His grandchildren now living in Boston may leave their homes in one of three daily trains, visit their distant cousins in the distant city of Hartford and return in time for rest and sleep within twenty-four hours of starting. Captain Pease having survived all his children, died at Shrewsbury, January 28, 1824. "He left a good name, numerous friends, and ever will live in stage history as

---

* William Lincoln's History of Worcester.　　†Ibid.　　‡Ward.

§ Mr. James Parker of Springfield, Mass., at one time a stage agent and many years afterwards a conductor over the Western and Boston and Albany Railroad, has among his fine collection of ancient books and papers several original mail contracts signed by Levi Pease and the government officials. He has also one number of the Worcester Magazine published in 1786 in which Pease advertised the line of stages connecting Portsmouth, N. H., with Savannah, Ga.

‖ He was generally called by this title. It is not known he was ever a captain of a military company.

the father of the stages."* "The aged people of Somers speak of him as a remarkable, majestic appearing man, dignified, pleasant, and agreeable in manners. But few indeed are left to tell their tales of Captain Levi Pease's fine appearance."†

His children were:

17. 1. HANNAH, b. at   . m. Thomas H. Kimball of Boston,   , 1796.
18. 2. LEVI, b. at   , 1768.
19. 3. LEMUEL, b. at Blandford, December 16, 1771. d. at Shrewsbury, ,1816, unmarried.
20. 4. LORY, b. at Blandford, October 4, 1774.
21. 5. MARY, b. at Somers, May 11, 1779. m. Perry Chapin of Worcester, Mass.,   , 1807, and died there.
22. 6. JEREMIAH, b. at Somers, January 12, 1781. History unknown; probably died young.

11.

WILLIAM PEASE,[3] (NATHANIEL,[2] ROBERT,[1]) brother of the preceding, was born at   ; married Viola Cadwell.‡ In 1770 he resided at Blandford, Mass., but subsequently settled in New Hartford, Ct. He was engaged as a teamster in the Revolutionary War under direction of Commissary General Wadsworth of Hartford.§

His children were:

23. 1. WILLIAM, b. at
24. 2. WALTER, b. at   about 1772.
25. 3. ELIJAH, b. at
26. 4. GEORGE, b. at

FOURTH GENERATION.

18.

LEVI PEASE,[4] (LEVI,[3] NATHANIEL,[2] ROBERT,[1]) eldest son of CAPTAIN LEVI and HANNAH (SEXTON) PEASE, last

---

* Ward.

† Rev. David Pease. Some facts in Captain Pease's stage history which are not given here, and some of the above not in quotation marks, may be found in Mr. Ward's and Mr. Lincoln's works.   ‡ Mr. Lester Pease, No. 50 of this chapter.   § Ibid.

of Shrewsbury, Mass., was born, 1768; married Mary Gill, and settled in Northboro, Mass., where he died June 20, 1808.

His children were :

27. 1. HANNAH, b. at Worcester, Mass., February 14, 1789.*
28. 2. THOMAS, b. at Somers, Ct., November 4, 1790.*   d. at Cambridge, Mass.,   , 1824, leaving no issue.†
29. 3. MARY, b. at
30. 4. LEVI, ‡ b. at
31. 5. JEREMIAH, b. at   . m. Olive   , and lived in Shrewsbury for a time after marriage, subsequently in Southboro.
32. 6. JOHN, b. at
33. 7. PAMELIA, b. at
34. 8. SUSAN, b. at
35. 9. REBECCA, b. at

20.

LORY PEASE,[4] (LEVI,[3] NATHANIEL,[2] ROBERT,[1]) brother of the preceding, was born at Blandford, Mass., October 4, 1774; married Rebecca Bruce, March, 1798; died at Shrewsbury in 1811.

His children were :

36. 1. REBECCA, b. at   , 1798.   m. John Downes. d. at Shrewsbury.
37. 2. HANNAH K., b. at   , July 8, 1800.   m. Dennis O'Brien, and resides at Boston, Mass.
38. 3. MARY, b. at   , April   , 1802, and resides at Albany, N. Y., unmarried.
39. 4. SALLY E., b. at   , January 13, 1803.   d. unmarried.
40. 5. ELIZA E., b. at   ; June 8, 1806, and resides in Boston, unmarried.
41. 6. HARRIET D., b. at   , December 15, 1810.   m. George L. Brown, Esq., the artist, now of Boston.   She died at New York 1854.

————o————

---

* Rev. David Pease.

† Middlesex County Probate Records.

‡ The names of the last six children were furnished by Mrs. O'Brien, No. 37 of this chapter.

23.

WILLIAM PEASE,[4] (WILLIAM,[3] NATHANIEL,[2] ROBERT,[1])
eldest son of WILLIAM and VIOLA (CADWELL) PEASE,
sometime of New Hartford, Ct., and first cousin of the
preceding, was born at   ; married Stala
Hickock of Lanesboro, Mass., where for a time he carried
on the trade of a blacksmith. He afterwards removed to
Charlotte, Addison County, Vt.

His children were:

42. 1. ANNA, b. at   . m. Lyman Wooster,
       and settled in Charlotte.
43. 2. LYMAN, b. at   . m. Anna Wooster. He
       was sometime inn-keeper at Ferrisburg, Vt. He afterwards
       resided at Bridport, Vt. He has several children, among
       whom is George B., who has kept a public house and been a
       merchant at Port Henry, Essex County, N. Y.*
44. 3. MARY,† b. at   . m. James Walling of Canaan, Ct.
45. 4. LORIN, b. at   . m.   , and
       settled in Charlotte, Vt.
46. 5. MINERVA,† b. at   . m. John Sherman, and
       settled in Charlotte.
47. 6. WILLIAM, b. at   . d. young.
48. 7. AMBROSE, b. at   . d. young.
49. 8. WILLIAM R., b. at   . m.
       and lived for a time in Charlotte, but subsequently removed
       to Poultney, Vt., where he died.

24.

WALTER PEASE,[4] (WILLIAM,[3] NATHANIEL,[2] ROBERT,[1])
brother of the preceding, was born about 1772; married
Ruby Bissel of East Windsor, Ct., where he resided a
short time. He afterwards removed to Windsor, Ct.,
where he lived until advanced in years and then removed
to Watertown, Wis. He was by trade a hatter.

---

*We are indebted to George L., a son of Mr. George B., for many names of the
descendants of William Pease, No. 11 of this chapter.

†The late F. S. Pease placed these two children in the family of their grandfather.
Mr. Lester Pease, No. 50 of this chapter, thinks he had no daughters.

His children were: •

50. 1. LESTER,* b. at East Windsor, Ct., April 19, 1794.   m. Abigail
Elsworth,   , 1812, and settled in Windsor, a farmer,
where he now resides, (1869). He has had several children,
among whom are:

    1. ABIGAIL E., m. Edmund Hurlbut, and resided some time
in Hartford, Ct., but now in Windsor.

    2. ANN.

    3. ELIZABETH, m. Joseph Ritter, and settled in Hartford.

    4. GEORGE L., m. and resides in New York City, a silver
plater.

51. 2. WALTER, b. at Windsor,   , 1799.   m. Olive Denslow
of Windsor; m. second, Nancy Fuller; m. third, Mrs. Minerva (Hillyer) Griswold. He resided some time at Hartford,
Ct., a hatter, but subsequently removed to Watertown, Wis.

52. 3. ELIZA, b. at Windsor, January   , 1801.   She is unmarried.

[53. 4. GEORGE, b. at   .   d. young.

54. 5. RUBY, b. at   .   d. young.

25.

ELIJAH PEASE,[4] (WILLIAM,[3] NATHANIEL,[2] ROBERT,[1])
brother of the preceding, was born at   ;
married Abi Baker. He resided some time in Charlotte,
Vt., but afterwards settled at Potsdam, N. Y. He was
by trade a blacksmith.

His children were:

55. 1. NORMAN, b. at   .   m., and settled in Potsdam.

56. 2. GEORGE, b. at   .   m., and settled in Charlotte.

57. 3. THIRZA, b. at   .   m.   .   d. in
Michigan.

58. 4. MARY, b. at

59. 5. ELIZABETH, b. at

60. 6. LESTER, b. at

61. 7. PHILO.

62. 8. WILLIAM, b. at

26.

GEORGE PEASE,[4] (WILLIAM,[3] NATHANIEL,[2] ROBERT,[1])
brother of the preceding, was born at   ;

---

* We are largely indebted to Mr. Lester Pease for names of persons marrying and
residences of the descendants of William Pease, No. 11.

married first, Sarah Sheldon; married second, Esther Sheldon, by whom he had all his children. He settled in Charlotte, Vt. He was by trade a blacksmith.

His children were:

63	1. CAROLINE, b. at		; probably d. young.
64.	2. CHARLES, b. at		; probably d. young.
65.	3. GEORGE R., b. at	. m.	Russel.
66.	4. CHAUNCY, b. at	; is unmarried.	
67.	5. ELIZA, b. at	; is married.	

CHAPTER VI.

NEW JERSEY PEASES.

THE ancestors of the Peases who originated from New Jersey, settled there some time before the Revolutionary War, and constitute two branches, yet somewhat related. We regret we have been unable to awaken sufficient interest in the minds of those with whom we have corresponded, as would have aided us in throwing more satisfactory light upon their origin and family history. One branch is traced back to two brothers, Cornelius and Adam. They had a brother Jonathan who was a captain in the Revolutionary War, and was in the battle at Monmouth. He died without issue. These brothers settled in Freetown, Monmouth County, and were farmers and extensive land-holders. Cornelius was born April 1, 1735; married Elizabeth Clark, July 11, 1758. He had six sons and three daughters. The sons' names were David, John C., William, Adam and Josiah.* Adam, the brother of Cornelius, had two sons and three daughters. The names of the sons were David † and John.

Our information of the other branch of the New Jersey Peases is very limited. The name of the ancestor was Samuel and is said to have been cousin of the ancestor of the other branch of New Jersey Peases. Messrs. John Pease and sons,‡ who some years ago were large confec-

---

* Captain John A. Pease of Brooklyn, N. Y., is a son of Josiah, and we are indebted to him for some of the important facts which furnish the basis of this chapter.

† Mr. John N. Pease, sometime of Somersett, Niagara County, N. Y., is a son of David.

‡ Mr. William J. Pease, now of New York City and a member of that firm, gave Captain John A. Pease the name of his ancestor and his relationship to the ancestor of the other branch of New Jersey Peases.

tionery manufacturers in New York City, belonged to this branch. There are several persons bearing the name of Pease in New York City who claim origin in New Jersey, but we have been unable to get them to answer our letters of inquiry.

We have for some time been inclined to the opinion that the new Jersey Peases came originally from Enfield, Ct. John R. Pease, Esq., of Hartford, Ct., has recently informed us that he remembers of hearing Mr. John Pease, the confectioner, inform his father, the late Dr. John C. Pease, that his ancestor came from Enfield, Ct. It seems probable to us that they belong to the descendants of Jonathan, the fourth son of John Pease, Sen., of Enfield. He had six sons, viz.: Jonathan, b. 1696, David, b. 1698, Samuel, b. 1700, John, b. 1702, Josiah, b. 1706, and Pelatiah, b. 1709. Until recently we have been unable to ascertain the history of any of these sons except Pelatiah, who married and had a family in Enfield. The names of Jonathan, Samuel and John were not mentioned at all in Dr. John C. Pease's manuscript history of Enfield. He recorded that David removed to the Southern States, and that Josiah went to Massachusetts. These facts he probably gathered from the aged people of his times, and a note made of it some time before his conversation with Mr. John Pease of New York City. It has been only recently ascertained where in Massachusetts Josiah Pease settled. It was found that he removed into the south-eastern part of Worcester County, and settled in Upton.

David, another brother, is not mentioned in old Hampshire County Records later than 1721, when he was appointed administrator of his father's estate. It seems probable he left Enfield not long after the death of his father. If he only removed to New Jersey it might have been said in those times that he went to the Southern States. The comparison of the names found in the families of the first named branch of New Jersey Peases, with his and those of his brothers, furnishes us with presumptive evidence that he may have been the ancestor of that branch of Peases.

Nothing can be ascertained respecting the history of the brother Samuel from the Enfield Town or Hampshire County Records except his birth. But we learn from the Worcester County Records there lived in the town of Mendon, Mass., in 1738, a Samuel Pease, blacksmith. As the town of Mendon joined Upton where the brother Josiah Pease lived, it seems somewhat probable that the Samuel Pease of Mendon may have been the brother in question. This Samuel Pease bought a piece of land in Mendon in 1738, but it was soon afterwards sold by the sheriff. As no farther trace can be found of him in Worcester County by its records or by the records of births, marriages or deaths from the town of Mendon,* he may have gone to New Jersey and been the father of Samuel Pease, the cousin of Cornelius and Adam Pease, and the ancestor of one of the branches of Peases in New Jersey.

We hope the above suggestions relative to the probable origin of the two families in New Jersey may lead to a farther investigation hereafter.

---

* We are so informed by Dr. John G. Metcalf of Mendon.

CHAPTER VII.

MARTHA'S VINEYARD PEASES.

THE islands on the southern coast of New England were not included within the grants made to any of the colonists who settled upon the main land.

In 1641 Thomas Mayhew, Sen., and his son, Rev. Thomas Mayhew, Jr., then of Watertown, Mass., purchased the island of Martha's Vineyard and some other islands adjacent, of the persons laying English claim to them, and the following year Rev. Thomas Mayhew, Jr., accompanied by several families from Watertown and vicinity, removed to Martha's Vineyard and formed a government independent of the Plymouth and Massachusetts Bay colonies. It is conceded by all, that Mayhew and company were not the first English settlers there. Among those who preceded them and probably the leading person of the pioneers was JOHN PEASE.

There are no known documents extant to show when Pease and his companions began their settlement, the place from whence they came or the number comprised in the company; though it is supposed the company was not a large one. The settlement must have been known to the Mayhews before their purchase, if, as is supposed, the junior Mayhew had preached to the settlers prior to the purchase, and formed a church there the year the purchase was made.*

The origin of the first settlement is differently accounted for. One tradition is, the party came from Eng-

---

* Felt's Ecclesiastical History of New England, and Massachusetts Historical Society's collections, Vol. III., 2d Series.

land in a vessel destined directly for the coast of Virginia, but which fell in with the shoals south of Cape Cod and came up into Martha's Vineyard Sound; and because either of a fatal distemper prevailing on board or from scarcity of provisions, Pease and his companions asked and obtained permission to be put on shore where they remained. It is said that the natives of the island were greatly alarmed at the first appearance of the whites, but Pease allayed their fears by presenting the Indian chief with a red coat. This tradition has some credence on the island, and has been in print several years.

Another tradition is, that the party came into the harbor in a vessel in winter, were frozen in and obliged to remain there until spring. In the mean time Pease gained the confidence of the Indians by presenting the chief with a red coat. The chief in return gave Pease a deed of that part of the island which is now Edgartown. As the story continues, Pease left the island in the spring, was gone for a time (to England as the narrator thought) and then returned with his family. After the Mayhew settlement, the "black book," as it was called, which contained Pease's Indian deed of land was lost, and with it Pease lost his claim or title to it.

This last tradition was obtained by the Rev. David Pease, some thirty years ago, when residing on the island of Martha's Vineyard at Tisbury, from widow Timothy Pease, who was then about sixty years old. She had the story from an old lady many years before, who resided on the island and belonged to the Martha's Vineyard Peases. In some respects the two traditions resemble each other. According to both, Pease and his companions made an unexpected permanent landing there, and they agree as to the mode friendship was made with the Indians. There is a common tradition that Pease did obtain an Indian deed of the town of Edgartown, and there are

6

some evidences extant showing that Mayhew's company made concessions to them in dividing the lands.*

Observation has taught us that but little reliance can be placed upon tradition unless facts are discovered to support it. It may be true, yet it looks hardly credible to suppose the vessel which conveyed Pease and his companions, if bound from England to the coast of Virginia, should so far wander out of its course in that period of navigation as to come into Martha's Vineyard Sound according to the first tradition. Or that a company so small as this was supposed to have been should have come from a place so far off as England, agreeable to the tradition related by Widow Timothy Pease.

While there are no evidences found which support the traditions that John Pease, Sen., came directly from England, there has existed a tradition that he only came from Salem. This tradition is in harmony with other traditions relating to this subject, and is supported by circumstantial evidences which make a plausible hypothesis, that he was that John Pease, who, with his brother Robert, had land granted him at Salem in 1637. It has been very generally supposed by the Enfield, Ct., Pease family, that the father of John Pease, Sen., last of Enfield and the ancestor of the Martha's Vineyard Peases, were brothers.

A correspondent† from McLain's Mills, Knox County, Me., who belongs to the Martha's Vineyard Pease family, informs us that he has made considerable inquiry among the older members of his family in that vicinity, and "the whole agree that the Peases sprang from two brothers." Others of the Martha's Vineyard family have supposed that two of the eldest brothers of John Pease, Sen., of Martha's Vineyard, went from that place to Salem, and were the ancestors of the Peases originating there.

History is entirely at variance with this latter mode of

---

*Massachusetts Historical Society's Collections, Vol. III., 2d Series.
†Mr. Harrison C. Pease.

explaining the relationship of the ancestors of the two families. Until recently it has been supposed by those who had paid some attention to the imperfect abstracts from the records at Salem, that John Pease, who came to America in 1634 in the ship Francis with his brother Robert, was the father of John Pease, Sen., last of Enfield, and that his widow joined the church in Salem in 1639. This supposition precluded the idea that he could have been the one who lived at Martha's Vineyard at a much later period, or that the ancestor of the. Martha's Vineyard family could have been brother of the father of John Pease, Sen., of Enfield, as both would be of the same name. Hence, the conclusion by some that the brother of Robert of the ship Francis in 1634 was "not one of the first four settlers of Martha's Vineyard as by doubtful tradition."*

Since it has been ascertained beyond a doubt that the given name of the father of John Pease, Sen., of Enfield, was Robert, and that it was not the widow of his brother who joined the church at Salem in 1639, but his widowed mother, this objection to the tradition that the brother of Robert Pease, Sen., went to Martha's Vineyard is removed.

Again, were it not for one fact, to which our attention has been recently called, it might be urged with some plausibility that if the ancestors of these two families had been brothers, the name of Robert would have appeared in the early generations of the Martha's Vineyard Peases, which, so far as we have observed, is not the case. The name appears, however, in later generations of the family. In one instance the reason assigned for the given name of the son is precisely the same as we should have expected had it been given to sons of earlier generations.

The late Mr. Nathan Pease of Appleton, Me., who was born 1772, and who removed from Martha's Vineyard to Maine with his father, James, and two brothers, Aaron

---

* Genealogical Dictionary of New England, by James Savage.

and James, in 1789,* has repeatedly told his nephews
that he named a son Robert for his great uncle who came
from England. The nephews supposed this great uncle,
Robert Pease, was a brother of their Martha's Vineyard
ancestor. As Mr. Nathan Pease belonged to the sixth
generation of the Martha's Vineyard Peases, the Robert
Pease for whom his son was named, must have been a
great uncle of his grandfather. It is probable Mr. Nathan
Pease did not know how many generations his ancestry
went back in this country. For this reason he could have
only called the brother of his first American ancestor a
great uncle.†

Admitting this hypothesis as true, that John Pease,
Sen., of Martha's Vineyard was first in Salem, we have it
explained where the brother of Robert Pease, Sen.,
went when he disappeared from Salem. Without it his
disappearance would remain a mystery. Granting that
he went from Salem, the circumstances of his first landing
on the island and afterwards going for his family, may
have been similar to those related by Widow Timothy
Pease. It is not improbable to suppose that the place for
a settlement may have been suggested to the party
through some accidental circumstance, as many of the
new localities in those days were.

Before taking leave of the subject, we desire to intro-
duce the opinion of the late Frederick S. Pease, than
whom none up to the date of his letter had given more
reflection on this question. The letter was addressed to
the Rev. David Pease, and bears date June 3, 1865:

. . . . . I desire to place among your papers and to have printed the
suggestion, that as there is no record of the marriage or decease at Salem of
John Pease who came there with Robert in 1637 that *he probably went to*

---

* Hon. Richard L. Pease.
† The letter from which the above information was obtained was written me some
twelve years ago, by Mr. George Pease of Appleton, Me., but I had not read the
letter until recently for several years past.

Martha's Vineyard; and that Robert instead of John as has been assumed was our progenitor.

I did not discover until after the publication of my account of the family in 1849 this error into which all appear to have fallen.

The correction will be better made in this connection than by a note published in the Register so long posterior to the original publication.

Yours truly,
FRED. S. PEASE.

No records are extant at Martha's Vineyard in which the name of John Pease appears earlier than 1646. He was then a grantor in a deed of land. From that date until his decease his name stands associated with the history of the islanders. He is also identified as one of the original proprietors of the town of Norwich, Ct., in 1659. It is not probable he was among the first settlers there though he may have contemplated it at one time. He was usually called captain, a title it is supposed he acquired by having command of some small sailing crafts. He had two wives; by the first wife, Elizabeth, he had two sons who survived their father, viz.: James, born 1637, and John, born about 1640; by second wife, Mary, he had children; Thomas, born about 1656, Jonathan, Samuel, David, Abigail, Mary, Rebecca and Sarah.

His last will and testament in which the above named children were mentioned, bore date "March 4, 1674."* He was then "stricken in years" and he probably died not far from that time. His posterity rank next in number to those of John Pease, Sen., last of Enfield. They contributed largely to the settlement of the State of Maine, and we occasionally hear from them in the Western States.

The Pease families originating in Glastenbury† and

---

*This date was in the old civil year when the year did not begin until March 25. See Appendix A.

†We are informed that the ancestor of the Glastenbury Peases was Peter Pease. He was was a sergeant in the Revolutionary Army. It was probably this "Sargt. Peter Peas" who was in the Northern army at Ticonderoga in 1777. See New England Historical and Genealogical Register, Vol. XV.

Windham, Ct., are descendants from John Pease, Sen., of Martha's Vineyard. It is not our intention to give a history of the Pease familes originating at Martha's Vineyard, except in two instances where they come. in proximity of residence to the Enfield Peases.

The Hon. Richard L. Pease* of Edgartown, Mass., has occupied his leisure hours for many years in collecting material for a history of Martha's Vineyard which embraces a history of the families originating there. He has large material for a genealogy of the descendants of John Pease, Sen., of Martha's Vineyard. We hope he will be encouraged by the intelligent members of this family and others who trace their origin there, to prepare his work for publication.

SECOND GENERATION.

JAMES PEASE,[2] (John,[1]) eldest son of John, Sen., and Elizabeth (   ) Pease, last of Martha's Vineyard, remained on the island; married, and was the father of five sons and three daughters. He is the grandfather of Christopher Pease. The latter joined the church at Edgartown in 1742, but he had removed to Lebanon, Ct., in 1746. He subsequently removed to Hartford, Vt. He had a son named Christopher who had several sons and daughters, viz.: Jesse, Ariel, Abel, Benjamin, Charles, Christopher, Lucy, Rebecca, Susannah and Lncinda.

JOHN PEASE,[2] (John,[1]) brother of the preceding, removed from Edgartown and settled at Norwich, Ct; probably occupying the land set off to his father. In her history of Norwich, Miss Caulkins very naturally supposed the original proprietor of that place was the John Pease who figured in its history years afterwards. An extract from

----

* We are indebted to Mr. Pease for all the facts found recorded at Martha's Vineyard relating to his family which are used in this chapter.

the will of his father corrects her mistake. It reads thus: "My second son John Pease I have already given unto and do hereby give unto him all was given me at Mohegin with that frame of a house I set up upon some part of that land I say I give it unto My son John Pease and his heirs forever."

Miss Caulkins informs us in a private note that Norwich, when first settled, was frequently called Mohegan, as it lay within the territory of a tribe of Indians by that name. He never married. His bachelor life and other neglects of duty caused the people of Norwich some anxiety and trouble. "The court record for 1672 has the following item relating to his misdemeanors:

"'John Pease complained of by the townsmen of Norwich for living alone, for idleness, and not duly attending the worship of God. The Court orders that townsmen do provide that Pease be entertained into some suitable family. He paying for his board and accommodation and he employ himself in some lawful calling. Which if he reject or refuse to do, the townsmen may put him out to service in some approved family except he dispose of his accommodations and remove out of town.'"*

In what manner the judgment of Court was carried out we have no means of knowing. He lived there in 1682, but was dead in 1711. His brother James as heir to his estate sold it August 18, 1711.† "The spot then so solitary is now jubilant with machinery, the seat of the manufacturing village of Bozrahville."‡

THOMAS PEASE,² (JOHN,¹) half-brother of the preceding; married and settled upon the island. He had four sons and six daughters. He is the ancestor of two brothers who were Baptist clergymen named Jesse and Bartlett. Their pedigree runs thus: JESSE⁵ and BART-

---

* From History of Norwich by Miss Frances M. Caulkins.
† Dukes County Land Records.
                                                    ‡ Miss Caulkins.

LETT,[5] (ZACHARIAH,[4] DAVID,[3] THOMAS,[2] JOHN.[1]) Rev.
Jesse Pease was born July 8, 1787; married, had a large
family of children, and died at Martha's Vineyard June
20, 1857. Rev. Bartlett Pease was born February 19,
1790; married and had a family of children. In 1867
he resided at Hudson, N. H.

JONATHAN PEASE,[2] (JOHN,[1]) brother of the preceding, married and settled upon Martha's Vineyard and
left posterity.

SAMUEL PEASE,[2] (JOHN,[1]) brother of the preceding, has no history on the island later than the date of
his father's will. It is probable he left the place when a
young man. Hon. Richard L. Pease suggests "he may
have been the Captain Samuel Pease who was mortally
wounded in 1689 when fighting with pirates in Martha's
Vineyard Sound." This suggestion might be better entertained were it not known there was another Samuel
Pease living in Exeter, N. H., not far from the above date,
concerning whom, evidences strongly show he must have
been of Martha's Vineyard origin.

DAVID PEASE,[2] (JOHN[1]) brother of the preceding;
married and lived some time on the island. The number
of his children is not known, nor is it known where he
died. He is the ancestor of our esteemed co-laborer,
Hon. Richard L. Pease. His ancestry runs thus: RICH-
ARD LUCE PEASE,[7] ISAIAH,[6] NOAH,[5] SETH,[4] BENJAMIN,[3]
DAVID,[2] JOHN.[1] He was the grandfather of Job Pease,
Sen., the ancestor of the Ludlow Peases mentioned in
the next chapter.

CHAPTER VIII.

LUDLOW (MASS.) PEASES.

THIS branch of the Martha's Vineyard Peases have long been designated as the Ludlow Peases to distinguish them from the Peases living in the neighboring towns who were descendants of the Enfield, Ct., Peases. The town of Ludlow from which they derived their name is in Hampden County, partially joining Springfield and north-east of it.

FOURTH GENERATION.

JOB PEASE,[4] (BENJAMIN,[3] DAVID,[2] JOHN,[1] of Martha's Vineyard,) son of BENJAMIN and   PEASE* of Martha's Vineyard, was born about 1718. It is said he spent a few of his early years before his final leave of Martha's Vineyard in whaling. In 1745 he had removed to Stafford, Ct.,† a town in Tolland County next east of Somers. He was living there in 1750 with his wife Eunice.‡ It is probable he left Stafford not long after this and removed to Norwich, Ct. In 1778 he was living in that part of Norwich called New Concord,§ and which is now in the town of Bozrah. Not far from this date he removed to Ludlow, Mass., and in 1783 he removed to that part of Springfield, Mass., which is the site of the village of Chicopee Falls where he died. His wife Eunice "died Feb. 7th 1791 in the 71st year of her age." ‖

---

* Hon. Richard L. Pease.   † Stafford Town Records.
‡ Stafford Town Records.   § Old Hampshire County Land Records.
‖ Tombstone in Springfield Cemetery.

7

He married second, Widow Abigail Cooley, 1782.* He "died Oct. 11 1793 in 75th year of his age."† His will mentions as

His children: ‡

1. 1. JOB, who was executor of the will.
2. 2. NOAH, who had an equal share with his brother.§
3. 3. ABIAH, the wife of Asa Church.
4. 4. EUNICE, the wife of Aaron Beebe.
5. 5. KEZIAH, the wife of Samuel Warner.

FIFTH GENERATION.

1.

JOB PEASE,[5] (JOB,[4] BENJAMIN,[3] DAVID,[2] JOHN,[1]) son of JOB and EUNICE (   ) PEASE, last of Springfield, married Deborah Haskell at Yarmouth, Nova Scotia, August 17, 1767, where he had removed. Remaining there but a short time he returned back to Norwich, Ct. In 1779 he removed to Ludlow, Mass., next to Springfield, and back again to Ludlow where he died, 1814. ‖

His children were: ¶

6. 1. WILLIAM, b. at Yarmouth, March 21, 1768.
7. 2. ASA, b. at Norwich, 1771.
8. 3. JOSEPH.
9. 4. BENJAMIN.
10. 5. LEVI.
11. 6. SIMEON, b. at Springfield, September 20, 1783.**
12. 7. MERCY, m. Joshua Fuller and first settled in Springfield, but some time after 1814 removed into the State of New York.
13. 8. SALLY, m. David Orcutt and settled in Springfield.
14. 9. MARY, m. Levi Jones, and first settled in Springfield but after 1814 removed to Amherst, Mass., where she died.

---

* Springfield Town Records.
† Tombstone in Springfield Cemetery.
‡ Old Hampshire County Records at Northampton.
§ No farther clue can be found of his history on Old Hampshire County or Springfield Town Records. It is probable he did not come into Massachusetts to live.
‖ Old Hampshire County Records at Springfield.
¶ Old Hampshire County Reeords at Springfield. ** Old Springfield Town Records.

SIXTH GENERATION.

6.

WILLIAM PEASE,[6] (Job,[5] Job,[4] Benjamin,[3] David,[2] John,[1]) eldest son of Job and Deborah (Haskell) Pease, last of Ludlow, Mass., was born at Yarmouth, Nova Scotia, March 21, 1768; married Martha Moody, 1792. Soon after his marriage he removed to Granby, Mass., where he remained until 1807, when he removed to Ludlow and there died, August 4, 1844. He was a farmer.

His children were : *

15. 1. Jerusha, b. at Springfield, July 14, 1793. m. Joel Clark, and settled in Ludlow.
16. 2. Walter, b. at Granby, October 21, 1795. m. Clarissa Chaffee, December 3, 1819, and first settled in Ludlow, a farmer, where all his children were born. He now resides at Springfield, Mass. His children are :
     1. Julia A., m. Moseley M. Bates, and resides at Southampton, Mass.
     2. Jane M., m. Horace Cadwell, and resides at West Haven, Ct.
     3. Clarissa, m. Levi Moody, and resides at Springfield, Mass.
     4. Simeon C., b. September 13, 1826. m. Jane West, and settled in Springfield, where he died in 1864.
     5. George W., b. November 26, 1833. m. Hannah Dillingham, and lived some time in Somers, Ct., but now lives in Lowell, Mass., a paper box manufacturer.
     6. Lucius W., b. April 24, 1842. m. Harriet Parsons, and resides at Springfield, a box manufacturer.
17. 3. William, b. at Granby, December 5, 1797. m. Mary Barton, and settled in Ludlow. He afterwards removed to Chicopee, where he died in 1828.
18. 4. Warren, b. at Granby, April 9, 1800. m.   Crafts, and removed to Michigan, where he died, January 6, 1854.
19. 5. Robert, b. at Granby, September 19, 1802. m. Jerusha Willey, and settled in Ludlow, where he died in 1840.
20. 6. Pliny, b. at Granby, May 31, 1805. m.   Boggs, and settled in Belchertown, Mass.
21. 7. Simeon, b. at Ludlow, May 15, 1807 ; was drowned, 1813.

* Family Records.

7.

DEACON ASA PEASE,[6] (JOB,[5] JOB,[4] BENJAMIN,[3] DAVID,[2] JOHN,[1]) brother of the preceding, was born at Norwich, Ct., 1771; married Rhoda Clark, and settled in Granby, Mass., where he died, 1853. He was a deacon of the Congregational Church.*

His children were :†

22. 1. SYLVESTER, d. unmarried.
23. 2. ASA, m. Abigail Smith, and resides at Granby.
24. 3. ELECTA, m. Asa Bartlett, and settled in Granby.
25. 4. SOPHIA, m.   Hill.
26. 5. HARRIET.
27. 6. CAROLINE, m. John Dewit.
28. 7. MARY A.
29. 8. SARAH.
30. 9. JANE E.
31. 10. FANNY W.

8.

JOSEPH PEASE,[6] (JOB,[5] JOB,[4] BENJAMIN,[3] DAVID,[2] JOHN,[1]) brother of the preceding, married Bethiah Chapin, and settled in that part of Springfield, Mass., which is now Chicopee, where he died. He held many prominent positions in public affairs. He served several years on the board of Selectmen for the town of Springfield, was a captain of a military company, deacon of the Orthodox Congregational Church, and for several years he held a commission as Justice of Peace. He was a farmer and merchant.

His children were :

32. 1. JOSEPH H., b. June 11, 1807. d. in Chicopee unmarried.
33. 2. CHRISTOPHER H., b. December 21, 1808. m. Olive Sherman, and settled in Chicopee, a farmer. His children are:
    1. BENJAMIN F.
    2. AELSIE.

---

* The important fact that the ancestor of the Ludlow Peases came from Martha's Vineyard, and some other items of historical interest relating to the father of Dea. Asa Pease, were communicated by the latter a short time before his death, to the Rev. David Pease.
† Rev. David Pease.

34. 3. James, b. May 11, 1811. m. Mahala Hamilton, and removed to Steelville, Mo., where he died.

35. 4. Phineas C., b. May 22, 1813, and resides at Red Oak Grove, Ia., unmarried.

36. 5. Margaret, m. Charles Webster, and resides at Hartford, Ct.

37. 6. Julia, unmarried.

38. 7. Marshall, m. Harriet Chapin, and resides at Chicopee, a farmer. His children are:
    1. Marshall C.
    2. Daniel P.

39. 8. Romeyn, m. and resides at Red Oak Grove, Ia.

40. 9. Charles M., b. July 7, 1827. m. Thirsa A. P. Loomis of Southwick, Mass., and resides at Chicopee, Mass., a farmer. His child is:
    1. Clifford B.

9.

BENJAMIN PEASE,[6] (Job,[5] Job,[4] Benjamin,[3] David,[2] John,[1]) brother of the preceding; married Dolly Goodell, and settled in Ludlow where he died. He was a machinist.*

His child was:

41. 1. Benjamin. He served in the late war for the suppression of the rebellion.

10.

LEVI PEASE,[6] (Job,[5] Job,[4] Benjamin,[3] David,[2] John,[1]) brother of the preceding; married Asenath Jennings, and settled in Ludlow, where he died. He was by trade a mason. He had three children who removed West after the death of their father.

His children were:

42. 1.
43. 2.
44. 3.

11.

SIMEON PEASE,[6] (Job,[5] Job,[4] Benjamin,[3] David,[2] John,[1]) brother of the preceding, was born at Springfield,

* Information furnished by Mr. Walter Pease, No. 16 of this chapter.

September 20, 1783; married first Sophia Ward; married second, Robina Ward, and settled upon the homestead of his father in Ludlow, where he died at an advanced age.

His children were:

45.   1. DAVID, m. Widow Savin, and resides at Buffalo, N. Y.
46.   2. ROBERT, d. at Key West, unmarried.
47.   3. MERRICK, resides at New York.
48.   4. MARIAN.
49.   5. WILLIAM H. H., d. in the army for the suppression of the rebellion.
50.   6. LYMAN.

CHAPTER IX.

NEW HAMPSHIRE PEASES.

A CONSIDERABLE family of Peases trace their ancestry to NATHANIEL PEASE who died in the town of New Market, Rockingham County, N. H., in 1748. We have been unable to learn from any of his posterity, the given name of his father, his final place of settlement and death, or the early history of the son, except the date of his birth

Mr. Mark Pease,* a grandson of Nathaniel Pease, now seventy-eight years of age, (1868,) possessing a clear mind and retentive memory, informs us his great-grandfather Pease came from Martha's Vineyard, and was killed by hostile Indians when at work in his corn-field. His statements are corroborated by other members of the family. Exeter, a shire town of Rockingham County was the home of Nathaniel Pease in his early manhood. Hence, it is natural to look for the home of his father in that vicinity.

From 1690 to 1710 the Indians were very hostile to the inhabitants of the new settlement of Exeter. They were obliged to confine themselves in garrisons by night, and cultivate their fields by day in continual fear of their savage foe. Many of the inhabitants were murdered by them during this period, all of whose names unfortunately have not been preserved. It is possible to suppose, then, that Exeter may have been the place where the father of Nathaniel Pease lived and met his death as described by Mr. Mark Pease. This seems more probable from the fact that there lived in Exeter within the above period

---

*No. 50 of this chapter.

an individual bearing the name of Samuel Pease. It is found on a list of sixteen jurors who had been summoned in Exeter, January 16, 1694, to attend a coroner's inquest. The following year his name was returned as one of the jurors to attend court at Portsmouth.* In 1698 he had fifty acres of land granted him by the town of Exeter.† We could not find him mentioned later than his grant of land. His name next appears in the family of Nathaniel Pease. His eldest son bore the name instead of the father's, as was quite common in those days; while the eldest daughter took the name of her maternal grandmother instead of the mother's.

The question occurs, where did this Samuel Pease, Sen., originate? It seems highly probable he came from Martha's Vineyard. John Pease, Sen., of that place mentioned in his will a son Samuel, of whom no farther trace is found at Martha's Vineyard afterwards.‡ The posterity of Nathaniel Pease, Sen., say the father of the latter came from Martha's Vineyard.

As the history of the other sons of John Pease, Sen., will not admit of such an inference, it seems safe to conclude that his son Samuel must have been the father of Nathaniel Pease; that he removed in early life from Martha's Vineyard to Exeter, N. H., and met the fate of being killed by hostile Indians.

FIRST GENERATION.

NATHANIEL PEASE,[1] the supposed son of SAMUEL PEASE, last of Exeter, N. H., and grandson of JOHN PEASE, SEN., of Martha's Vineyard, was born 1691;§ married

---

* Both facts are from papers on file in the office of Registry of Deeds at Exeter.

† "At a town meeting Exeter Feb. 23 169¾ then granted to Samuel Peas fifty acres of land where he can find it comon not prajudice any former grants or highways allowed." [From Book of Land Grants at Exeter.]

‡ Hon. Richard L. Pease.   § Mr. Mark Pease.

Phebe Sanborn, (born February 6, 1706,) daughter of John and Sarah (Philbrick) Sanborn,* November, 1725. In 1721 he resided at Exeter. He was then a carpenter and a purchaser of land.† He settled in the parish of New Market when a part of the town of Exeter, where he died October 20, 1748.

His children were: ‡

1. 1. SARAH, b. July 10, 1726.
2. 2. SAMUEL, b. December 14, 1727.
3. 3. ANN, b. November 17, 1729.
4. 4. ABIGAIL, b. January   , 1732.
5. 5. BATHSHEBA, b. March 16, 1734.
6. 6. PHEBE, b. December 21, 1735.
7. 7. NATHANIEL, b. February 21, 1737.
8. 8. JOHN, b. July 10, 1739.
9. 9. ZEBULON, b. July 21, 1741. He is said to have died in the Continental army at Cambridge.§
10. 10. BENJAMIN, b. August 2, 1743.
11. 11. ELEANOR, b. June 2, 1745.
12. 12. SIMEON, b. March 24, 1747. He resided at Poplin, N. H., in 1769, and at Sanbornton in 1772.‖ It is said he died in the army at Cambridge.
13. 13. ELIPHALET, b. May 13, 1749.

SECOND GENERATION.

FAMILY OF SAMUEL.[1]

2.

DEACON SAMUEL PEASE,[2] (NATHANIEL,[1]) eldest son of NATHANIEL, Sen., and PHEBE (SANBORN) PEASE, last of New Market, N. H., was born December 14, 1727; married Dolly   , and first settled in New Market. He subsequently removed to Parsonsfield, Me., where he died January 6, 1805.

---

* New England Historical and Genealogical Register, Vol. X.
† County Records.   ‡ Mark Pease and Exeter Town Records.
§ Mr. Mark Pease.   ‖ County Records.

His children were : *

14. 1. NATHANIEL, b. June 15, 1749. No other history learned of him
       Probably he never had a family.
15. 2. MARY, b. October 19, 1750. d. February   , 1828.
16. 3. ELIZABETH, b. May 16, 1752. d. December   , 1788.
17. 4. SAMUEL, b. March 10, 1754.
18. 5. JOSEPH, b. November 12, 1755.
19. 6. LUCY, b. October 24, 1757. d. March 23, 1827.
20. 7. DOROTHY, b. September 25, 1759.
21. 8. ASA b. June 15, 1762. d. an infant.

FAMILY OF NATHANIEL.[2]
7.

NATHANIEL PEASE,[2] (NATHANIEL,[1]) brother of the preceding, was born February 21, 1737; married Lucy Page and settled in New Market, N. H.

His children were : †

22. 1. ZEBULON.
23. 2. DAVID; went West when a young man and nothing later was
       heard of him.
24. 3. NATHANIEL.
25. 4. ASA, b. July 18, 1769.
26. 5. JOSIAH.
27. 6. JOSEPH.
28. 7. LYDIA, m. Mr. Moulton.
29. 8. HANNAH, d. unmarried.
30. 9. SALLY, m. John Stevens.
31. 10. LUCY, m. Mr. Drew.

FAMILY OF JOHN.[2]
8.

JOHN PEASE,[2] (NATHANIEL,[1]) brother of the preceding, was born July 10, 1739; married and settled in Epping, N. H.

His children were : ‡

32. 1. JOHN.
33. 2. WINTHROP. We could obtain no farther information concerning
       the history of these men.

---

*From Records in possession of Widow of John Pease, No. 58 of this chapter.
†Information by John U. Pease, Esq., No. 79 of this chapter. ‡Mr. Mark Pease.

FAMILY OF BENJAMIN.[2]

10.

BENJAMIN PEASE,[2] (NATHANIEL,[1]) brother of the preceding, was born August 2, 1743; married first, Anna Sanborn; married second, Rebecca Pike, April 25, 1793, and settled in Meredith, N. H.

His children were: *

'34. 1. JAMES, b. October 15, 1764.
35. 2. JOSEPH, b. October 25, 1766. d. about 1770.|
36. 3. DOLLY, b. May 2, 1770. m. Nathaniel Sinclair.

BY SECOND WIFE:

37. 4. JOSEPH, b. March 10, 1774.
38. 5. BENJAMIN, b. December 17, 1775.
39. 6. SIMEON, b. June 11, 1778.
40. 7. NANCY, b. October 20, 1779. m. Benjamin St. Clair, June 2, 1805, and settled in New Hampton, N. H.
41. 8. ROBERT, b. December 24, 1782.
42. 9. REBECCA, b. November 28, 1786. m. Thomas Perkins.
43. 10. NATHANIEL, b. April 9, 1789.
44. 11. MARY, b. January 6, 1791. m. Thomas Woodman, and settled in New Hampton.

FAMILY OF ELIPHALET.[2]

13.

ELIPHALET PEASE,[2] (NATHANIEL,[1]) youngest and thirteenth child of NATHANIEL, SEN., and PHEBE (SANBORN) PEASE, and brother of the preceding, was born May 13, 1749; married Mary Pike, 1774, and first settled in Epping, N. H. In 1802 he removed to Cornish, Me., where he died about 1811. He was by trade a blacksmith.

His children were:

45. 1. STEPHEN, b. November 9, 1775.
46. 2. SIMEON.
47. 3. MARY, m. Henry Hyde. d. September , 1867.
48. 4. NANCY, b. about 1781. m. John Clark.
49. 5. JOHN, b. November 17, 1788.
50. 6. MARK, b. 1790.

*From Family Record procured by Mrs. Mary P. Rogers, No. 121 of this chapter.

THIRD GENERATION.

FAMILY OF SAMUEL.[2]

17.

MAJOR SAMUEL PEASE,[3] (SAMUEL,[2] NATHANIEL,[1])
second son of DEACON SAMUEL and DOLLY ( )
PEASE, last of Parsonsfield, Me., was born March 10, 1754;·
married Comfort , and settled in Parsonsfield. He
was a Drum Major in the Revolutionary Army, and died
September 7, 1834.

His children were : *

51.   1. COMFORT, b. August 1, 1781.   d. August 22, 1840.
52.   2. NANCY, b. July 10, 1781.· d. February , 1840.
53.   3. JOHN, b. March 21, 1786.
54.   4. SALLY, b. June 21, 1788.   d. 1865.
55.   5. ASA, b. June 3, 1791.   d. February 10, 1806.
56.   6. PHILENIA, b. May 8, 1794.

18.

JOSEPH PEASE,[3] (SAMUEL,[2] NATHANIEL,[1]) brother of
the preceding, was born November 12, 1735; married
Dolly Clark, and settled first in Parsonsfield, Me. About
1801 he removed to the settlement at Exeter, Me. He
was a member of the first board of selectmen in 1811
after the place became an incorporated town. He died in
Exeter in 1826.

His children were : †

57.   1. JUDITH, m. Nathaniel Pease. ‡
58.   2. NANCY, m. Josiah Barker of Exeter, Me.
59.   3. POLLY, m. Mr. Seavy.
60.   4. JOSEPH, b. January 29, 1785.
61.   5. ALBANA, b. August 15, 1788.
62.   6. McKENZIE, (twin,) b. August 15, 1788.
63.   7. SARAH, m. Nathaniel Barker, and settled in Exeter, Me.
64.   8. SAMUEL.
65.   9. DOLLY, m. Nathaniel Pease.§
66.   10. CLARK.

---

* From Mrs. John Pease.   † Information by his grandchildren.
‡ No. 24 of this chapter.   § No. 24 of this chapter.

FAMILY OF NATHANIEL.[2]

22.

ZEBULON PEASE,[3] (NATHANIEL,[2] NATHANIEL,[1]) eldest son of NATHANIEL and LUCY (PAGE) PEASE of New Market, N. H., and first cousin of the preceding; married and settled in Parsonsfield, Me.

His children were : *

67. 1. NATHANIEL, b. November 26, 1786.
68. 2. ANDREW, b. May 13, 1788.
69. 3. ZEBULON, b. September 21, 1795.
70. 4. BETSEY, d. unmarried.
71. 5. MARTHA, m. Abraham Smith, and settled in Newfane, N. Y.

24.

NATHANIEL PEASE,[3] (NATHANIEL,[2] NATHANIEL,[1]) brother of the preceding; married first, Judith Pease;† married second, Dolly Pease.‡

His children were:

72. 1. SOPHIA, m. Mr. Heely.

BY SECOND WIFE:
73. 2. NATHANIEL.
74. 3. SABRINA, m. Joseph Gilman.
75. 4. DOLLY, m. Thomas Gilman.

25.

ASA PEASE,[3] (NATHANIEL,[2] NATHANIEL,[1]) brother of the preceding, was born July 18, 1769; married Sally Parsons, October 23, 1791, and settled in Parsonsfield, Me.

His children were: §

76. 1. JOSEPH, b. July 9, 1792.
77. 2. SALLY, b. February 3, 1794. m. Joseph Libby, March 3, 1814, and removed to Newfane, N. Y.

---

*John U. Pease, Esq.   †No. 57 of this chapter.
‡No. 65 of this chapter.   §John U. Pease, Esq., No. 79 of this chapter.

78. 3. ASA, b. May 3, 1795. d. about 1811.
79. 4. JOHN U., b. August 6, 1796.
80. 5. LYDIA, b. February 17, 1799. d. about 1819.
81. 6. NATHANIEL, b. August 31, 1801.
82. 7. LUCY B., b. April 4, 1803. m. Nathaniel Church of Newfane,
N. Y., May 24, 1829.
83. 8. THOMAS P., b. April 6, 1807. d. about 1827.
84. 9. NANCY P., b. May 30, 1810. m. Dexter Valentine, November
2, 1851.

26.

JOSIAH PEASE,[3] (NATHANIEL,[2] NATHANIEL,[1]) brother
of the preceding; married Nancy Parsons, and first settled in Parsonsfield, Me., but some time before 1812 he
removed to Newfane, N. Y.

His children were: *

85. 1. ENOCH.
86. 2. NANCY.
87. 3. BETSEY, d. unmarried.
88. 4. LUCINDA, m. Alexander Butterfield.
89. 5. NATHANIEL.
90. 6. LOVINA, m. Andrew Peabody.
91. 7. JUDITH, m. Nathan Townes.
92. 8. SAMUEL.

27.

JOSEPH PEASE,[3] (NATHANIEL,[2] NATHANIEL,[1]) brother
of the preceding; married and settled in New Market, N. H.

His children were:

93. 1. HENRY.
94. 2. JOSEPH.
95. 3. JOHN.
96. 4. HOLLIS.
97. 5. MARY J., married Zebulon Pease,† and settled in Freedom, N. H.,
where she d. June 16, 1868.
98. 6. HANNAH, d. unmarried.

---o---

---

* John U. Pease, Esq.   . † No. 69 of this chapter.

FAMILY OF BENJAMIN.[2]

34.

JAMES PEASE,[3] (BENJAMIN,[2] NATHANIEL,[1]) eldest son of BENJAMIN and ANNA (SANBORN) PEASE, last of Meredith, N. H., and first cousin of the preceding, was born October 15, 1764; married Susan Mead, and settled in Meredith, where he died.

His children were: *

99. 1. ANNA, b. September 13, 1790. m. Samuel Hart.
100. 2. MARY, b. 1793. m. William Pike, and settled at Meredith, N. H.
101. 3. SUSAN, b. about 1797. m. Mark Whiton, and resides at Campton, N. H.
102. 4. JOHN, b. about 1798.

37.

JOSEPH PEASE,[3] (BENJAMIN,[2] NATHANIEL,[1]) son of BENJAMIN and REBECCA (PIKE) PEASE and half-brother of the preceding, was born March 10, 1774; married Hannah Folsom, and settled in Meredith, N. H., where he died.

His children were:

103. 1. BENJAMIN, b. September 25, 1797. He left home young. History unknown.
104. 2. LUCINDA, b. June 15, 1789.
105. 3. JOHN S., b. March 6, 1801.
106. 4. Betsey, b. October 29, 1802. m. Levi Woodman, and resides at Manchester, N. H.
107. 5. REBECCA, b. May 11, 1805, d. unmarried.
108. 6. WILLIAM P., b. September 18, 1806. He is said to reside somewhere in Connecticut or Massachusetts, unmarried.
109. 7. JOSEPH F., b. October 6, 1808.
110. 8. NATHANIEL, b. November 6, 1811.
111. 9. SIMEON D., b. July 7, 1812.
112. 10. ROBERT, b. June 18, 1814.
113. 11. HANNAH, b. June 29, 1817. m. Dudley Bartlett, February 7, 1844.

---

* The Family Records of this and families Nos. 37, 39, 41 and 42, were obtained by Mrs. Mary P. Rogers, No. 121 of this chapter.

38.

BENJAMIN PEASE,[3] (BENJAMIN,[2] NATHANIEL,[1]) brother of the preceding, was born December 17, 1775; married Polly Cram, and settled in Meredith, N. H., a farmer, where he died April 3, 1831.

His child was : *

114. 1. NOAH, b. April 10, 1811.

39.

SIMEON PEASE,[3] (BENJAMIN,[2] NATHANIEL,[1]) brother of the preceding, was born June 11, 1778; married Mehitable Wedgwood, February 16, 1802, and settled in Meredith, N. H., a farmer.

His children were:

115. 1. JOHN, b. July 14, 1804.
116. 2. SALLY, b. November 5, 1806. m. Benjamin Ward, June 30, 1834.
117. 3. MARY A., b. June 1, 1809. d. young.
118. 4. NANCY B., b. June 10, 1814. m. Samuel Ward, June 16, 1844, and resides at New Hampton, N. H.
119. 5. MOSES C., b. August 10, 1817.

41.

ROBERT PEASE,[3] (BENJAMIN,[2] NATHANIEL,[1]) brother of the preceding, was born December 24, 1782; married Polly Smith. He died soon after marriage leaving no issue.

42.

NATHANIEL PEASE,[3] (BENJAMIN,[2] NATHANIEL,[1]) brother of the preceding, was born April 9, 1789; married Mary Perkins of Malden, Mass., and first settled in Brighton, Mass. In 1835 he removed to Quincy, Ill., where he died July 24, 1836.

* Family Records.

His children were : *

120. 1. Rebecca, b. May 7, 1817. m. John Wheeler, November 30, 1807, and resides at Quincy, Ill.
121. 2. Mary P., b. August 8, 1818. m. Hiram Rogers, December 21, 1836, and resides at Quincy, Ill., a widow.
122. 3. Alfred, b. November 12, 1820. d. December 21, 1824.
123. 4. Nathaniel, b. January 10, 1823.

———o———

FAMILY OF ELIPHALET.

45.

STEPHEN PEASE,[3] (Eliphalet,[2] Nathaniel,[1]) eldest son of Eliphalet and Mary (Pike) Pease last of Cornish, Me., and first cousin of the preceding, was born November 9, 1775; married first, Sarah Johnson, January 5, 1795; married second, Widow Lydia (Grant) Thompson, and settled in Cornish, Me., where he died September 2, 1852. His children were by first wife.

His children were :†

124. 1. Stephen, b. September 27, 1796.
125. 2. Mark, b. September 28, 1798.
126. 3. Sarah, b. September 5, 1800. m. Erving Foster, October 30, 1858, and resides at Cornish.
127. 4. Nancy, b. August 21, 1802. m. George Douglas, 1823.
128. 5. Eliphalet, b. November 12, 1810.
129. 6. Simeon, b. September 28, 1813.
130. 7. Infant, d. young.
131. 8. Infant, d. young.

46.

SIMEON PEASE,[3] (Eliphalet,[2] Nathaniel,[1]) brother of the preceding; married first, Mary Lord; married second   , and settled in Cornish, Me., where he died. He had one child by first wife.

His child was:

132. 1. Hannah, m. Mr. Small, and settled in Cornish.

---

* Family Records.   † Family Records by Mrs. Foster.

49.

JOHN PEASE,[3] (ELIPHALET,[2] NATHANIEL,[1]) brother of the preceding, was born November 17, 1788; married first, Mary Phenix, February 22, 1805; married second, Mrs. Mary F. Snow, December, 1859, and settled in Cornish, Me., where he died April 19, 1865.

His children were: *

133. 1. WILLIAM, b. May 21, 1806.
134. 2. NATHANIEL, b. November 25, 1808.
135. 3. MARY A., b. March 24, 1811. m. Henry Lord. d. March 12, 1835.
136. 4. MERCY, b. August 7, 1813. m. Hooper Chase, and resides at Bangor, Me.
137. 5. NANCY C., b. April 23, 1816. m. James L. Small, February 15, 1840, and resides at Cornish.
138. 6. CAROLINE, b. January 8, 1819. m. Virgil Griswold, August, 1858, and resided at St. Louis, Mo. d. October 8, 1867.
139. 7. JOHN, b. July 20, 1821. d. February 28, 1838.
140. 8. BENJAMIN F., b. November 17, 1823.
141. 9. MELVILLE, b. February 1, 1827. d. January 15, 1860.

50.

MARK PEASE,[3] (ELIPHALET,[2] NATHANIEL,[1]) brother of the preceding, was born June 19, 1790; married first, Nancy Barker, July 14, 1817; married second, her sister, Sarah Barker; married third, Mrs. Rhoda (Allen) Sawtell, October 13, 1829, and settled in Cornish, Me., where he now resides, a farmer. He is supposed to be the only grandchild of Nathaniel Pease, Sen., now living. Happily for the genealogical student his clear testimony as to the origin of his ancestry has been obtained that it might be put in print and handed down to posterity as a boon.

His children were:

{142. 1. MARY J., d. in infancy.
143. 2. Infant.

---

*Family Records by B. F. Pease, No. 140 of this chapter.

BY SECOND WIFE:

144. 3. NANCY J., b. March 16, 1824. m. Gustavus D. Rundell of Laselle, Ill., October 18, 1867.
145. 4. WILLIAM B., b. June 29, 1827.

BY THIRD WIFE:

146. 5. CHARLES H., b. December 23, 1830.
147. 6. JOHN M., b. September 6, 1833.
148. 7. NATHAN W., b. June 4, 1836.

FOURTH GENERATION.

FAMILY OF SAMUEL.[2]

52.

DEACON JOHN PEASE,[4] (SAMUEL,[3] SAMUEL,[2] NATHANIEL,[1]) eldest son of MAJOR SAMUEL and COMFORT ( ) PEASE, last of Parsonsfield, Me., was born March 21, 1786; married first Sally Wiggin, January, 1811; married second, Hannah Mason, September 5, 1827, and settled in Parsonsfield, Me., where he died March 13, 1853.

His children were: *

149. 1. MARY A., b. October 4, 1811. m. John Hasty, May, 1831.
150. 2. SALLY, b. July 31, 1813. m. Samuel Burbank, 1831.
151. 3. OLIVE, b. April 16, 1816. m. Otis G. Smith, 1840. d. 1864.
152. 4. LOVINA, b. June 16, 1818. d. July 27, 1833.
153. 5. ALMIRA, b. November 27, 1820. m. Harrison Chapman.
154. 6. JOHN M., b. March 28, 1823. d. November 20, 1844.

60.

JOSEPH PEASE,[4] (JOSEPH,[3] SAMUEL,[2] NATHANIEL,[1]) eldest son of JOSEPH and DOLLY (CLARK) PEASE, last of Exeter, Me., and first cousin of the preceding, was born January 29, 1785; married Mary Barker, May 23, 1809, and settled in Exeter, Me., where he died July 2, 1857.

---

*Family Records.

His children were : *

155. 1. LEWIS, b. December 12, 1810. m. Sophia Glover, and resides at Dercham, C. W.
156. 2. JOSEPH, b. March 19, 1813. m. Ann Chapman, and resides at Presque Isle, Me.
157. 3. ANNA C., b. October 27, 1814. m. first, Charles Dearborn. m. second, Ezekiel Andrews, and resides at South Boston, Mass.
158. 4. LOUISA, b. April 24, 1817. m. Otis Pease,† and resides at South Boston, Mass.
159. 5. TAMSON, b. July 20, 1822. Was unmarried in 1867.
160. 6. NATHANIEL, b. June 1, 1829. m. Annette Shaw.
161. 7. IVORY, b. August 25, 1831. d. April 7, 1851.

61.

REV. ALBANA PEASE,[4] (JOSEPH,[3] SAMUEL,[2] NATHANIEL,[1]) brother of the preceding, was born August 15, 1788; married first, Sally Barker; married second Anna Crane, and lived in Exeter, Me., where he died September, 1863. He was a minister of the gospel of the Christian denomination.

His children were: ‡

162. 1. NAOMI, b. March 19, 1810. m. Samuel S. Fifield, and resides at Corinna, Me.
163. 2. SALOME, b. November 13, 1811. m. Samuel S. Smith, and resides at McMinville, Oregon.
164. 3. ALBANA, b. April 15, 1815. m. Eliza A. Rich, and resides at Exeter.
165. 4. OTIS, (twin,) b. April 15, 1815. m. Louisa Pease,§ and resides at South Boston, Mass., a house builder.
166. 5. JOSEPH M., b. 1818. d. an infant.

BY SECOND WIFE:

167. 6. SARAH B., b. June 29, 1820. m. James M. Footman.
168. 7. NANCY, b. November, 1822. m. Louis Cook.
169. 8. DEXTER M., b. March 24, 1825. m. Eleanor Nutt. d. 1852.
170. 9. MARY A., b. 1827. d. young.
171. 10. EMILY, b. 1829. m. Edmund Holmes, and resides at Foxcraft, Me.

---

*Information from members of the family.   †No. 165 of this chapter.
‡Information by Otis Pease, No. 165.   §No. 158 of this chapter.

172. 11. Velzora, b. 1831. m. Rothus Paine, M. D.
173. 12. Mary A., b. 1833. m. Jacob D. Cornish, and resides at Hampton, Me.
174. 13. Roscinda, b. 1835.
175. 14. George F., b. 1842. m. Lizzie Cornish, and resides at Exeter, Me.

62.

McKENZIE PEASE,[4] (Joseph,[3] Samuel,[2] Nathaniel,[1]) brother of the preceding, was born August 15, 1788; married Elizabeth Brown, and resides at Exeter, Me.

His children were : *

176. 1. Cynthia, m. Joseph Robinson, and settled in Exeter, Me.
177. 2. Ann, m. Henry Gale, and resides at Bangor, Me.
178. 3. Elizabeth, m. Abbot, and resides at Stetson, Me.
179. 4. Amanda, m. Jeremiah Damon, and resides at Stetson.
180. 5. Ithel, m., and resides at Belfast, Me.
181. 6. Susan, m. Hall, and settled at Belfast.
182. 7. Urana.

64.

SAMUEL PEASE,[4] (Joseph,[3] Samuel,[2] Nathaniel,[1]) brother of the preceding; married Roxy Hutchins, and resides at Exeter, Me.

His children were : †

183. 1. Elmore, m. Sarah Atwood, and resides at Exeter.
184. 2. Warren, d. young.
185. 3. Hannah, m. Seth Clark, and settled in Stetson, Me.
186. 4. Samuel, m. Shaw, and resides at Exeter.
187. 5. Joel, m. Rosetta Morse, and resides at Corinna, Me.

66.

CLARK PEASE,[4] (Joseph,[3] Samuel,[2] Nathaniel,[1]) brother of the preceding; married Mehitable Brown, and settled in Exeter, Me. He is dead.

His children were : ‡

188. 1. Clarissa, m. William Pullen, and resides at Exeter.
189. 2. Sophia, m. Robshaw.

* Information from Mrs. Andrews, No. 157. † Ibid. ‡ Ibid.

190. 3. SARAH, m. Lorenzo D. Butters, and resides at Exeter.
191. 4. ELIJAH, m.   Pullen, and settled in Exeter.
192. 5. JULIA, m..   Wadson, and settled in Exeter.
193. 6. ELIZABETH.

————oo————

FAMILY OF NATHANIEL.[2]

67.

NATHANIEL PEASE,[4] (ZEBULON,[3] NATHANIEL,[2] NA-
THANIEL,[1]) eldest son of ZEBULON and   PEASE,
last of Parsonsfield, Me., and second cousin of the preceding, was born November 26, 1786; married Olive Townes,
March 21, 1816, and settled in Parsonsfield, Me., where
he died January 25, 1863.   He was a farmer.

His children were:[*]

154. 1. SOPHIA, b. October 16, 1816. m. Amasa Allen, November 10,
1844. d. October 12, 1866.
195. 2. MARY J., b. September 7, 1818. m. Amasa Doe, January,
1840, and resides at South Parsonsfield, Me.
196. 3. USHER P., b. January 29, 1820. m. Juliette Williams, January 12, 1845, and resides at Charlestown, Mass.
197. 4. CLARA T., b. August 21, 1821. m. Uriah Butland, July 4,
1851, and resides at Cambridgeport, Mass.
198. 5. BURLEIGH, b. August 13, 1823. m. Narcissa Pease,[†] November
18, 1857, and resides at Bangor, Me., a lawyer.
199. 6. LORENZO D., b. January 25, 1825. m. Hannah Kilpatrick,
April 10, 1862, and resides at South Parsonsfield, Me.
200. 7. LIZZIE W., b. November 9, 1826. m. Edward Gordon, June 3,
1866.
201. 8. ROXY S., b. March 27, 1828. m. Hiram C. Walker, January,
1856, and resides at Springfield, Ill.
202. 9. JOHN A., b. November 17, 1829. m. Sarah Shaw, May 1, 1854,
and resides at South Parsonsfield.
203. 10. LAVINIA P., b. July 4, 1832, and resides at Boston, Mass.[‡]
204. 11. MARTHA M., b. January 7, 1837.
205. 12. BRADBURY N., b. June 4, 1841. d. February 11, 1843.

* Family Records.
† No. 211 of this chapter.
‡ We are indebted to Miss Lavinia P. Pease for many facts relating to the family
of Nathaniel.[2]

68.

ANDREW PEASE,[4] (ZEBULON,[3] NATHANIEL,[2] NATHANIEL,[1]) brother of the preceding, was born May 13, 1788; married Lavinia Perkins, January 3, 1819, and settled in Parsonsfield, Me. He next resided at Effingham, Me., and last at Bangor, Me., where he died October 18, 1851.

His children were: *
206. 1. SIMEON, b. January 24, 1820.
207. 2 CALVIN, b. April 26, 1822. d. October, 1846.
208. 3. ANNETTE, b. January 16, 1828.
209. 4. MARY, b. July 7, 1836.
210. 5. ADELAIDE, b. July 7, 1841.

69.

ZEBULON PEASE,[4] (ZEBULON,[3] NATHANIEL,[2] NATHANIEL,[1]) brother of the preceding, was born September 2, 1795; married Mary J. Pease,† March 23, 1823, and settled in Freedom, N. H. He died March 23, 1863.

His children were: ‡
211. 1. NARCISSA, b. July 9, 1824. m. Burleigh Pease,§ November 18, and resides at Bangor, Me.
212. 2. ALBION, b. January 22, 1826. d. August 21, 1842.
213. 3. EDWIN, b. April 23, 1827. m. Harriet Smart, August 13, 1847, and resides at Conway, N. H.

———o———

73.

NATHANIEL PEASE,[4] (NATHANIEL,[3] NATHANIEL,[2] NATHANIEL,[1]) only son of NATHANIEL and DOLLY (PEASE) PEASE, and first cousin of the preceding; married, and settled in Freedom, N. H.

*Family Records furnished by Mrs. Pease, No. 211 of this chapter.
†No. 97 of this chapter.
‡Family Records.
§No. 198 of this chapter.

His children were:

214.   1. Alonzo, resides at Freedom, N. H.
215.   2. Anna, married and resides at Lynn, Mass.

———o———

76.

JOSEPH PEASE,[4] (Asa,[3] Nathaniel,[2] Nathaniel,[1])
eldest son of Asa and Sally (Parsons) Pease, and first
cousin of the preceding, was born July 9, 1792; married
Hannah Grace, October 13, 1816, and resided at Tamworth, N. H., where he died October 3, 1846.

His children were: *

216.   1. Susan.
217.   2. Sally.
218.   3. Lydia.
219.   4. Ellen.
220.   5. Parthena.
221.   6. Asa, m.   Lovet, and removed to West Virginia.
222.   7. Sylvester, m.   Lovet, and removed to West Virginia.

79.

JOHN U. PEASE,[4] (Asa,[3] Nathaniel,[2] Nathaniel,[1])
brother of the preceding, was born August 2, 1796; married first, Hetty Crossman, February 10, 1820; married
second, Alvira White, November 28, 1824; married third,
Mrs. Mary Dein, October 8, 1856. He entered the army
in the war of 1812 as a drummer, and marched to Platts-
burgh, N. Y. At the close of the war he received his
land warrant bounty. In 1817 he located a piece of land
in Newfane, Niagara County, N. Y., and settled upon it
where he remained until 1835 when he removed to Syl-
vania, Lucas County, Ohio. At which place he resided in
1867. He has been a merchant and farmer, and four years
county treasurer.

His children were:

223.   1. Hetty C., b. February 10, 1821. m. Reuben F. Wilson, and
resides at Wilson, Niagara County, N. Y.

———

* Information from John U. Pease, Esq.

BY SECOND WIFE:

224. 2. Don Alonzo, b. January 1, 1828. m. Anna E. Anderson, and resides at Toledo, Ohio. He was for several years superintendent of schools in Fremont, Ohio. During the late war he was in the One Hundred and Thirtieth Regiment of Ohio Volunteers Militia.

225. 3. Clarissa B., d. 1842.

226. 4. Frances A., d. 1859.

81.

Dr. NATHANIEL PEASE,[4] (Asa,[3] Nathaniel,[2] Nathaniel,[1]) brother of the preceding, was born August 31, 1801; married first, Martha Parsons, who died 1826; married second, Mary W. Willet, October 26, 1840, and resided at Bridgton, Me., where he died 1867. He was a physician. He had three children by first wife who died young.

His children were: *

227. 1.
228. 2.
229. 3.

BY SECOND WIFE:

230. 4. George.
231. 5. Martha.
232. 6. Mary E.
233. 7. John.
234. 8. Alonzo.
235. 9. Thomas.

———o———

85.

ENOCH PEASE,[4] (Josiah,[3] Nathaniel,[2] Nathaniel,[1]) eldest son of Josiah and Nancy (Parsons) Pease, last of Newfane, N. Y., and first cousin of the preceding; married four wives and was the father of twenty-three children.†

His children were:

236. 1.
258. 23.

---

*Information by John U. Pease, Esq.
10
†Ibid.

89.

NATHANIEL PEASE,[4] (JOSIAH,[3] NATHANIEL,[2] NATHANIEL,[1]) brother of the preceding; married Lucy Barnes, and was the father of three children.*

His children were:

259. 1.
261. 3.

92.

SAMUEL PEASE,[4] (JOSIAH,[3] NATHANIEL,[2] NATHANIEL,[1]) brother of the preceding; married, and died soon afterwards leaving only one child.†

His child was:

262. 1.

———o———

93.

HENRY PEASE,[4] (JOSEPH,[3] NATHANIEL,[2] NATHANIEL,[1]) eldest son of JOSEPH and   (   ) PEASE of New Market, N. H., and first cousin of the preceding; married, and settled in New Market. He is dead.

94.

JOSEPH PEASE,[4] (JOSEPH,[3] NATHANIEL,[2] NATHANIEL,[1]) brother of the preceding; married, and settled in New Market, N. H. He is dead.

95.

JOHN PEASE,[4] (JOSEPH,[3] NATHANIEL,[2] NATHANIEL,[1]) brother of the preceding; married, and resides at New Market, N. H.‡

---

* Information by John U. Pease, Esq.
† Ibid.
‡ I have twice written this man for information concerning his family and brothers but received no response.

96.

HOLLIS PEASE,[4] (JOSEPH,[3] NATHANIEL,[2] NATHANIEL,[1]) brother of the preceding; married, and resides at New Market, N. H.*

———oo———

FAMILY OF BENJAMIN.[2]

103.

JOHN PEASE,[4] (JAMES,[3] BENJAMIN,[2] NATHANIEL,[1]) only son of JAMES and SUSAN (MEAD) PEASE of Meredith, N. H., and second cousin of the preceding, was born about 1798; married first, Betsey Whitcher; married second, Susan Moulton, and settled in Meredith. He now resides at Tamworth, N. H. His children were by first wife.

His children were: †

263. 1. LOVINA, m. Henry A. Gilman.
264. 2. JAMES, m., and resides at Tamworth, N. H.
265. 3. MARY J., m. John Remick.
266. 4. BENJAMIN F., b. March 22, 1829. m. Rebecca A. Locke, and resides at South Boston, Mass.
267. 5. SIMEON.
268. 6. ALMEDA.

———o———

105.

JOHN S. PEASE,[4] (JOSEPH,[3] BENJAMIN,[2] NATHANIEL,[1]) second son of JOSEPH and HANNAH (FOLSOM) PEASE of Meredith, N. H., and first cousin of the preceding, was born March 6, 1801; married Eliza Dow, March 21, 1848. He lived several years in Boston, Mass., but now resides at Meredith, N. H.

His child was:

269. 1. ELLA S., b. August 7, 1854.

---

*I have twice written this man for information concerning his family and brothers but received no response.

† The records of this and the four following families were obtained for this work by Mrs. Mary P. Rogers, No. 121 of this chapter.

109.

JOSEPH F. PEASE,[4] (JOSEPH,[3] BENJAMIN,[2] NATHANIEL,[1]) brother of the preceding, was born October 6, 1808; married Edna Mannahan, and resided at Candia, N. H., in 1867. He had no children.

111.

SIMEON D. PEASE,[4] (JOSEPH,[3] BENJAMIN,[2] NATHANIEL,[1]) brother of the preceding, was born July 7, 1812; married Betsey 'Bachelor, February 2, 1842, and resides at Meredith, N. H.

His children are:

270.   1. ARZEBIA J., b. April 1, 1845.
271.   2. LAURA E., b. February 10, 1847.
272.   3. MARY B., b. November 10, 1849.
273.   4. HANNAH A., b. February 22, 1854.
274.   5. FRANK B., b. December 23, 1855.
275.   6. SIMEON L., b. August 26, 1859.

112.

ROBERT PEASE,[4] (JOSEPH,[3] BENJAMIN,[2] NATHANIEL,[1]) brother of the preceding, was born June 18, 1814; married Lorinda Piper, April 7, 1841, and resides at Holderness, N. H.

His children are:

276.   1. ANNA B., b. October 22, 1842.
277.   2. BENJAMIN F., b. December 26, 1845.

114.

NOAH PEASE,[4] (BENJAMIN,[3] BENJAMIN,[2] NATHANIEL,[1]) only son of BENJAMIN and MARY (CRAM) PEASE, and first cousin of the preceding, was born April 20, 1811; married Betsey M. Prescott, January 1, 1833, and settled in Meredith, N. H., where he died April 29, 1864.

His children were : *

278.   1. BENJAMIN L., b. November 4, 1834, and resides at Chicago, Ill.
279.   2. MARY E., b. November 8, 1836. m. Andrew Rollins, February 28, 1857, and resides at Rollinsford, N. H.
280.   3. SARAH F., b. November 4, 1838. m. Joseph B. Lawrence, November 4, 1858, and resides at Lee, N. H.
281.   4. CHARLES H., d. February 12, 1842.
282.   5. GEORGE D., b. July 11, 1843.
283.   6. EDWIN B., b. July 21, 1847.
284.   7. EMMA J., b. December 12, 1850.
285.   8. ELLA L., b. May 16, 1854.
286.   9. HARRIET C., b. January 31, 1857.   d. May 10, 1854.
287. 10. EDITH L., b. October 21, 1863.

115.

JOHN PEASE,[4] (SIMEON,[3] BENJAMIN,[2] NATHANIEL,[1]) eldest son of SIMEON and MEHITABLE (WEDGWOOD) PEASE of Meredith, N. H., and first cousin of the preceding, was born July 14, 1804; married Sophronia Cram, November 24, 1831, and settled in Meredith. He is dead.

His child was :

288.   1. MARY A., b. August 14, 1845.

119.

MOSES C. PEASE,[4] (SIMEON,[3] BENJAMIN,[2] NATHANIEL,[1]) brother of the preceding, was born August 10, 1817; married first, Betsey M. Ramsey, February 21, 1844; married second, Almira A. Cram, August 25, 1854, and resides at Meredith, N. H.

His children were:

289.   1. AUGUSTUS E., b. November 15, 1844.
290.   2. MARTHA E., b. April 12, 1846.
291.   3. ELLEN W., b. December 15, 1848.
292.   4. LEONETTE, b. August 16, 1853.

BY SECOND WIFE:

293.   5. EDDIE W., b. February 11, 1856. d. in infancy.

*Family Records.

294.   6. CARRIE E., b. June 10, 1858.
295.   7. LUELLA B., b. February 14, 1861.
296.   8. JOHN W., b. July 8, 1863.
297.   9. CHARLES R.

———o———

123.

NATHANIEL PEASE,[4] (NATHANIEL,[3] BENJAMIN,[2] NA-THANIEL,[1]) second son of NATHANIEL and MARY (PERKINS) PEASE, some time of Brighton, and last of Quincy, Ill., and first cousin of the preceding, was born June 10, 1823; married Caroline M. Stone, and resides at Quincy, Ill., a farmer.

His children are:

298.   1. EMILY F., b. January 16, 1853.
299.   2. ALBERT N., b. February 2, 1856.
300.   3. GERTRUDE S., b. November 19, 1859.
301.   4. JAMES F., b. July 27, 1864.

———oo———

FAMILY OF ELIPHALET.[2]

124.

STEPHEN PEASE,[4] (STEPHEN,[3] ELIPHALET,[2] NATHAN-IEL,[1]) eldest son of STEPHEN and SARAH (JOHNSON) PEASE of Cornish, Me., and second cousin of the preceding, was born September 27, 1796; married Mary Cole, and settled in Denmark, Me. He died May 30, 1831.

His children were: *

302.   1. CALVIN, m. first, Sarah Tombs; m. Second, Nancy Skillins, 1859.
303.   2. DANIEL C., m. Nancy Blodgett, 1856. He was killed in the last battle before Petersburg in the war of the rebellion.
304.   3. MARK, m. Rachel Cole, 1849, and settled in Minnesota near St. Anthony.
305.   4. STEPHEN, resides at St. Anthony.
306.   5. ALONZO F., m. first, Eliza Thurston; m. second, Elmira Davis; m. third, Lizzie Landerkin.   d. May 31, 1864.

*Information of this and families No. 125 and No. 128, were furnished us by Mrs. Foster, No. 126 of this chapter.

125.

MARK PEASE,[4] (STEPHEN,[3] ELIPHALET,[2] NATHANIEL,[1]) brother of the preceding, was born September 28, 1798; married first, Joanna Phenix, 1820; married second, Lavinia Morton, 1825, and resides at Jackson, Me.

His children were:

307. 1. LYDIA, m. William B., Pease,* March 27, 1848, and resides at Limerick, Me.

BY SECOND WIFE:

308. 2. ELIPHALET, b. March 15, 1829. m, Harriet Spearing, December 3, 1856, and resides at Thorndike, Me.

309. 3. JOANNA, b. October 11, 1837. m. Joseph H. Rich, April 3, 1862, and resides at Pittsfield, Me.

128.

ELIPHALET PEASE,[4] (STEPHEN,[3] ELIPHALET,[2] NATHANIEL,[1]) brother of the preceding, was born November 12, 1810; married Lois H. Lord, October 17, 1832, and settled in Thorndike, Me.

His children are:

310. 1. VESTA, b. August 9, 1834. d. February 22, 1842.
311. 2. MARY L., b. July 7, 1837. m. Byron L. Carr, October 2, 1868, and lives in Waukegan, Ill.
312. 3. SIMEON, b. February 14, 1842.

————o————

133.

WILLIAM PEASE,[4] (JOHN,[3] ELIPHALET,[2] NATHANIEL,[1]) eldest son of JOHN and MARY (PHENIX) PEASE of Cornish, Me., and first cousin of the preceding, was born May 21, 1806; married Eunice Cole, and resides at Cornish, Me.

His child was: †

313. 1. ROSCOE G., b. June 1, 1831. d. April 27, 1849.

---

*No. 145 of this chapter.

† Information of this and family No. 134, was furnished by Benjamin F. Pease, No. 140 of this chapter.

134.

NATHANIEL PEASE,[4] (John,[3] Eliphalet,[2] Nathaniel,[1]) brother of the preceding, was born November 25, 1808; married Abigail Norton, and resides at East Parsonsfield, Me.

His children were:

314. 1. Mary A., b. February 2, 1837.
315. 2. Harriet, b. May 5, 1840.

140.

BENJAMIN F. PEASE,[4] (John,[3] Eliphalet,[2] Nathaniel[1]) brother of the preceding, was born November 17, 1823; married Rebecca M. Small, May 20, 1848, and resides at Cornish, Me.

His children were: *

316. 1. Roscoe G., b. September 10, 1849.
317. 2. Sarah S., b. February 10, 1851.
318. 3. Carrie B., b. February 15, 1853. d. August 17, 1853.
319. 4. Mary A., b. March 20, 1855.
320. 5. A son, b. August 20, 1857. d. September 12, 1857.
321. 6. John, b. May 17, 1860.
322. 7. Ellen F., b. September 21, 1867.

145.

WILLIAM B. PEASE,[4] (Mark,[3] Eliphalet,[2] Nathaniel,[1]) eldest son of Mark and Sarah (Barker) Pease, of Cornish, Me., and first cousin of the preceding; was born June 29, 1827; married Lydia Pease,† March 27, 1848, and resides at Limerick, Me.

His child is:

323. 1. Sarah B., b. January 14, 1849.

146.

CHARLES H. PEASE,[4] Mark,[3] Eliphalet,[2] Nathaniel,[1]) son of Mark and Rhoda (Allen) (Sawtelle)

---

* Family Records.   † No. 307 of this chapter.

Pease of Cornish, Me., and half-brother of the preceding, was born December 23, 1830; married Rebecca B. Kimball, October, 1852, and resides at Enfield, N. H.

His children are: *

324. 1. WALTER R., b. January 1, 1845.
325. 2. CHARLES F., b. April 12, 1857.
326. 3. REBECCA M., b. January 17, 1860.
327. 4. GEORGE H., b. May 24, 1864.
328. 5. MARK, b. July 12, 1867.

147.

JOHN M. PEASE,[4] (MARK,[3] ELIPHALET,[2] NATHANIEL,[1]) brother of the preceding, was born September 6, 1833; married Lydia A. Marr, and resides at Cornish, Me. He was in the army for the suppression of the rebellion and participated in the battles of Fair Oaks near Richmond, Va.

His child was: †

329. 1. JESSIE B., b. February 25, 1857. d. January 24, 1864.

148.

NATHAN W. PEASE,[4] (MARK,[3] ELIPHALET,[2] NATHANIEL,[1]) brother of the preceding, was born June 4, 1836; married Sarah F. Butterfield, October 10, 1861, and resides at Cornish, Me. He is a photograph artist, and a publisher of stereoscopic pictures of scenes among the White Mountains.

NOTE.

There may be other families of Peases claiming origin in New Hampshire who cannot trace their ancestry in this chapter. A great-grandson of John Pease, Sen., last of Enfield, Ct., named Pelatiah, removed from Enfield and settled in Alstead, N. H., many years ago. It is said he had four sons, viz.: Pelatiah, Jonathan, Noadiah and Oliver. The history of these sons we have not obtained. It is highly probable that some or all of them may have posterity living in New Hampshire now.

---

*Information by Mrs. Mark Pease, wife of No. 59. † Ibid.

CHAPTER X.

CAPTAIN SAMUEL PEASE.

ALLUSION has been made in a previous chapter to Captain Samuel Pease. His history so far as can be ascertained is very brief; but the generous offer of his services to the Governor and Council of the Colony of Massachusetts Bay, and daring bravery displayed in attacking and fighting the armed pirates who infested the New England coast in 1689, merit a brief chapter devoted to his memory in this work. We regret we have been unable to learn anything of his local or family history. We can not find where he lived, or to what family in America he belonged. Mr. S. G. Drake in his history of Boston says he belonged in Salem. We have examined the same sources of information he had and fail to come to his conclusions. All we can learn of his home is that it was in New England. Felt mentions him in his "Annals of Salem," not as we think, however, because he was a resident of the place, but because he was engaged in fighting the pirates who destroyed the commerce of Salem. Nothing is revealed of his history earlier than the summer of 1689.

From a document on file in the office of Secretary of State at Boston, bearing date July 18, 1689, we learn he was then master of the "ship Fortune belonging to his Highness Frederick Carmine, Duke of Courland." At this time he had just returned from a voyage to the islands of Madeira and May. He had taken in a cargo of salt at the island of May with the intention of proceeding directly to the island of Tobago, there to be paid his wages and "cleared" "at liberty to proceed either to Courland or return home to New England." But before leaving May, Captain Pease learned that a French man-of-war had been making havoc with the English merchant vessels in the vicinity of the West Indies, and that the French were determined to take Tobago. He accordingly resolved to take Barbadoes in his way there. Here he learned that great scarcity of provisions prevailed on the island of Tobago, and that the people were about to desert it. Captain Pease then returned to Boston, the place from which he had shipped, and asked of the "Honorable Council" that he might dispose of as much of his cargo of salt as would victual his vessel, and allow him to proceed to the end of his voyage. From the sequel it hardly seems probable that Captain Pease did go on to Tobago afterwards.

During the months of August and September of this year, New England commerce was greatly annoyed with pirates who prowled upon the coast. Captain Samuel Pease volunteered his services to the Colonial Government to go out and break them up. The sloop Mary was fitted out and Captain Pease was commissioned September 30, 1689, to "surprise (and in case of their making resistance) by force of arms to take Thomas Hawkins and Thomas Ponnd, who, with a number of armed men joined with them, had partially seized several vessels belonging to their majesties' subjects."

The sloop Mary sailed out of Boston harbor Friday, October 4; the enemy was found in the vicinity of Martha's Vineyard Sound and attacked the same day. The pirate crew commanded by Thomas Ponnd made a desperate and sanguinary resistance, but the daring bravery and coolness of Captain Pease and his men compelled them to surrender. The struggle cost Captain Pease his life, having received wounds in his arm, thigh and side. His vessel made sail for Newport, R, I., which place it reached

Saturday, October 5. Surgeons were procured to care for the wounded. Here Captain Pease remained until the 11th of October when he was carried to his vessel with the intention of proceeding to Boston. His wounds began bleeding afresh and he was again taken on shore where he died the next day.*

The loss of the noble captain awakened a deep sympathy for his family in the Colonial Government. It sent requests to the different towns in the Province that collections be taken up in the churches for the benefit of his family consisting of a "widow and four orphan children † in low and destitute circumstances." ‡ §

---

*From papers on file in the Clerk's Office of the Supreme Judicial Court at Boston, and printed in the New England Historical and Genealogical Register, Vol. II.

†From the marriage of Martha Pease of Cambridge to Hugh Clark in 1700, and that of Hannah Pease of Cambridge to William Brown who was born 1684, we are inclined to think that a family of Peases may have lived in Cambridge toward the close of the seventeenth century. Possibly it might have been the family of Captain Samuel Pease.

‡From papers on file in the office of the Secretary of State.

§A collection is known to have been taken up for the family of Captain Pease in Dorchester.

CHAPTER XI.

WASHINGTON COUNTY (PA.) PEASES.

WE have in this chapter a family of Peases whose ancestor came directly from Germany.

Nicholas Pees emigrated from Germany in 1773, and settled in Washington County near Cannonsburgh. A brother George came with him but we have no information concerning his history. Our informant states that this ancestor always spelled his name Pees. Many of his descendants have changed the orthography to the common English mode. Nicholas Pees had eight children, viz.:

His children were:

1. NICHOLAS, who d. a young man unmarried.
2. ANDREW.
3. GEORGE.
4. MARY.
5. CATHARINE.
6. ELIZABETH.
7. HANNAH.
8. SUSAN.

SECOND GENERATION.

ANDREW PEES,[2] (NICHOLAS,[1]) served in the Revolutionary War under Washington. He reared a large family of children but their names have not been furnished us.

GEORGE PEES,[2] (NICHOLAS,[1]) brother of the preceding, was born in Germany, July 30, 1770; married Lydia Vaughn, and settled in Washington County, Pa., where he died.

His children were:

1. ANDREW, b. June 4, 1794.
2. REBECCA, b. October 30, 1798. m.   Cook. d. 1830.
3. ZACHARIAH, b. July 15, 1800.
4. JOHN, b. September 18, 1801.
5. ELIZABETH, b. April 25, 1804. m.   Moses. d. January
   30, 1842.
6. NICHOLAS, b. January 30, 1806.
7. MARY, b. November 19, 1807.
8. GEORGE, b. March 10, 1808.
9. JOSEPH, b. December 17, 1811. d. 1850.
10. LYDIA, b. September 14, 1813.
11. JAMES, b. May 10, 1815. d. January 30, 1840.

THIRD GENERATION.

ANDREW PEES,[3] (GEORGE,[2] NICHOLAS,[1]) was born June 4, 1794; married Phebe Cotner, and settled in Washington County, Pa.

His children were:

1. THOMAS.
2. LYDIA A.*
3. ZACHARIAH.
4. JACOB.'
5. MARIAH.
6. ELLEN.
7. JOHN.
8. GEORGE. He served in the army for the suppression of the late rebellion.
9. ANDREW.
10. SUSAN.
11. CLINTON.

* We are indebted to this lady for all the information we possess concerning the Pennsylvania Peeses or Peases.

CHAPTER XII.

MISCELLANEOUS FAMILIES.'

WE have found names of other Peases than those before mentioned which stand associated in New England history or whose names are found in obscure ancient records.

It appears from documents on file in the probate office at Exeter, N. H., that Hannah, daughter of Thomas Walford of New Castle, married a   Pease prior to 1648.* We know of no posterity by this marriage. It has been suggested that Thomas Pease, who purchased by an order an article mentioned in a bill of items presented in court at Portsmouth, N. H., 1682,† may have been a son of this Hannah Pease. As nothing farther can be found of his history in Rockingham County, we think he belonged to Martha's Vineyard and was only transiently in Portsmouth.

The name of Pease is early associated with the history of Newport, R. I. WILLIAM PEASE was a petitioner for a "church of England" at Newport in 1699. It is said he had several children. Among them were two sons, William (history unknown) and Simon. Simon Pease was admitted Freeman from Newport in 1718. In 1729 he was a deputy to the General Assembly. He was a man of considerable wealth and influence and his name is frequently mentioned in the transactions of the General Assembly through a period of many years. He was a petitioner for and one of the incorporators of Brown

*Information furnished the New England Historical and Genealogical Register, Vol. IX., by A. W. Brown, Esq.

†From papers on file in the office of Registry of Deeds at Exeter, N. H.

University in 1764. Simon Pease, Jr., who was admitted Freeman from Newport in 1748 is supposed to have been the son of Simon Pease, Sen. Nothing is known farther of his history.

There lived in Somers, Ct., during the last half of the last century LOT PEASE who was never recognized as belonging to the posterity of the Enfield Peases. The Shakers, whom, with his family of children, he subsequently joined, informed the Rev. David Pease that Lot Pease had said he was of Martha's Vineyard origin. The Hon. Richard L. Pease informs us that he does not recognize his name in the memoranda of his family. Lot Pease was in the French and Indian war. He married at Somers Sarah Mitters, October 10, 1765.

His children were:

1. SAMUEL, b. September 19, 1796. He removed to Watervliet, N. Y., 1788, at the organization of the Shakers in that place, and died there in 1832.
2. JEMIMA, b. December 13, 1788. d. among the Shakers at Hancock, Mass.
3. CALEB, b. June 7, 1771. d. among the Shakers at Enfield, Ct.
4. ELIZABETH.
5. LOT, d. among the Shakers at Enfield.
6. ENOCH. He was a preacher among the Shakers several years. About 1831 he ceased preaching and ceased practicing what he preached. About the same time he left the Shakers with a Shaker sister, married, and went out of the State. He afterwards returned, lived for a time in Scitico, but subsequently purchased a farm in East Longmeadow, where he died. He had one son who died young. It is supposed the posterity of Lot Pease, Sen., has become extinct.

There are several Peases who have emigrated to this country during the present century from Great Britain and Germany. Prominent among them is Mr. William Pease late of New York City. He was born in England about 1800. His father died when he was quite young and he was apprenticed to an organ-builder. He came to this country to put up an organ he had assisted in building and never returned. Not long after he came to America he took up the profession of a teacher of vocal and instrumental music, (chiefly piano-forte,) and as such he has been favorably known in various towns in Massachusetts, New York and Vermont. He has also been organist in the cities of Boston and New York. He was a composer of music and a publisher of a musical work. He married first, Frances Sanford of Belchertown, Mass.; married second, Cornelia Francisco of Newark, N. J. He died in New York City April, 1865.

His children were:

1. WILLIAM E., a merchant and postmaster in Oxford, Mass.
2. EDWARD, a merchant in Worcester, Mass.
3. ELIZABETH F.
4. FRANCES S.

BY SECOND WIFE:

5. AUGUSTUS F., resides in New York City.
6. FREDERICK.
7. CORNELIA.
8. CAROLINE A.
9. CHARLES O., for some time a night clerk in New York City post-office.
10. IDA.
11. MARY.
12. FRANK D.

Another of this class is Mr. Edward Pease, some time of Tariffville, Ct. He was born in Ireland about 1810 of English parents. He came to America in his seventeenth year. The names of his children we are not in possession of. Doubtless there are many instances where names resembling Pease have been mistaken for it in poorly written records, and printed as such in historical and genealogical works. An illustration of this is found in the "History of the Descendants of William Ward of Sudbury." The author of that work married a daughter of this family to "John Pease of Belchertown, born at Brookfield, June 20, 1764," and as the result of this marriage he has names of two generations of children of

12

Peases. After some speculations as to the origin of this family of Peases we wrote to the town clerk of Brookfield and asked for the given name of the father of this John Pease. We were politely informed the father's name was John also. The letter closed with the remark that the name on the town records was spelled Peeso. We then had the explanation, for we had often seen the name of Peeso on the Worcester and Hampshire County Records, and we sometimes should have mistaken it for Peese had we not given it a second glance. As Peese, Peeas, Pees, Peas, Pies, Peis, Peise and Pise are only different orthographies for Pease.*

---

* We have seen all these orthographies either in print or old manuscript records.

INDEX TO GIVEN NAMES.

CHAPTER VI.

New Jersey Peases.

CHAPTER VII.

Martha's Vineyard Peases.

CHAPTER VIII.

Ludlow Peases.

CHAPTER IX.

New Hampshire Peases.

Abigail, 57.
Adelaide, 71.
Albana, 60, 68.
Albert N., 78.
Albion, 71.
Alfred, 65.
Almeda, 75.
Almira, 67.
Alonzo, 72, 73.
Alonzo F., 78.
Amanda, 69.
Andrew, 61.
Ann, 57, 69.
Anna, 63, 72.
Anna B., 76.
Anna C., 68.
Annette, 71.
Arzebia J., 76.
Asa, 58, 58, 60, 62, 72.
Augustus E., 77.
Bathsheba, 57.
Betsey, 61, 62, 63.
Benjamin, 57, 59, 63, 66.
Benjamin F., 66, 76.
Benjamin L., 77.
Bradbury N., 70.
Burleigh, 70.
Calvin, 71, 78.
Caroline, 66.
Carrie B., 80.
Carrie E., 78.
Charles F., 81.
Charles H., 67, 77.
Charles R., 78.
Clara T., 70.
Clarissa, 69.
Clarissa B., 73.
Clark, 60.
Comfort, 60.
Cynthia, 69.
Daniel C., 78.
David, 58.
Dexter M., 68.
Dolly, 59, 60, 61.
Don A., 73.
Dorothy, 58.
Eddie W., 77.
Edith L., 77.

Edwin, 71.
Edwin B., 77.
Eleanor, 57.
Ella L., 77.
Ella S., 75.
Ellen, 72.
Ellen F., 80.
Ellen W., 77.
Elijah, 70.
Eliphalet, 57, 65, 79.
Elizabeth, 58, 69.
Elmore, 69.
Emma J., 77.
Emily, 68.
Emily F., 78.
Enoch, 62.
Frances A., 73.
Frank B., 76.
George, 73.
George D., 77.
George F., 69.
George H., 81.
Gertrude S., 78.
Hannah, 58, 62, 63, 65.
Hannah A., 76.
Harriet, 80.
Harriet C., 77.
Henry, 62.
Hetty C., 62.
Hollis, 62.
Ithel, 69.
Ivory, 68.
James, 59, 75.
James F., 78.
Jessie B., 81.
Joanna, 79.
Joel, 69.
John, 57, 58, 59, 60, 62, 63, 64, 66, 66, 73, 80.
John A., 70.
John M., 67, 67.
John S., 63.
John U., 62, 72.
John W., 78.
Joseph, 58, 58, 59, 59, 60, 61, 62, 68.
Joseph F., 63.
Joseph M., 68.

Josiah, 58.
Judith, 60, 62.
Julia, 70.
Laura E., 76.
Lavinia P., 70.
Leonette, 77.
Lewis, 68.
Lizzie W., 70.
Lorenzo D., 70.
Louisa, 68.
Lovina, 62, 67, 75.
Lucinda, 62, 63.
Lucy, 58, 58.
Lucy B., 62.
Luella B., 78.
Lydia, 58, 62, 72, 79.
Mark, 59, 65, 78, 81.
Martha, 61, 73.
Martha E., 77.
Martha M., 70.
Mary, 58, 59, 59, 63.
Mary A., 64, 66, 67, 68, 69, 77, 80, 80.
Mary B., 76.
Mary E., 73, 77.
Mary J., 62, 66, 70, 73.
Mary L., 79.
Mary P., 65.
McKenzie, 60.
Melville, 66.
Mercy, 66.
Moses C., 64.
Nancy, 59, 59, 60, 60, 62, 65, 68.
Nancy B., 64.
Nancy C., 66.
Nancy J., 67.
Nancy P., 62.
Naomi, 68.
Narcissa, 71.
Nathaniel, 56, 57, 58, 58, 59, 61, 61, 62, 62. 63, 65, 66, 68.
Nathan W., 67.
Noah, 64.
Olive, 67.
Otis, 68.
Parthena, 72.

CHAPTER X.

Captain Samuel Pease.

CHAPTER XI.

Washington County (Pa.) Peases.

CHAPTER XII.

Miscellaneous Families.

INDEX OF SURNAMES

OF PERSONS MARRYING INTO THE PEASE FAMILIES.

A.

Abbott, 69.
Aikin, 24.
Allen, 70, 80.

Anderson, 68, 73.
Andrews, 68.

Ashley, 21.
Atwood, 69.

B.

Barnes, 74.
Bachelor, 76.
Baker, 35.
Barker, 60, 60, 66, 67, 68.
Bartlett, 52, 63.
Barton, 51.

Bates, 51.
Beebe, 50.
Bissel, 34.
Blodgett, 78.
Boggs, 51.
Brown, 21, 33, 69, 69.

Bruce, 33.
Burbank, 67.
Burnham, 24.
Butland, 70.
Butterfield, 62.
Butters, 70.

C.

Cadwell, 32, 51.
Carr, 79.
Chaffee, 51.
Chapin, 32, 52, 53.
Chapman, 67, 68.
Chase, 66.
Church, 50, 62.

Clark, 37, 51, 52, 59, 60, 69.
Cole, 78, 78, 79.
Cook, 68, 85.
Cooley, 50.
Cornish, 69, 69.
Cotner, 85.

Crossman, 72.
Crafts, 51.
Cram, 64, 77, 77.
Crane, 68.
Cummings, 18.
Curtis, 23.

D.

Damon, 69.
Davis, 78.
Dearborn, 68.
Dein, 72.
Denslow, 35.

Derby, 24.
Dewit, 52.
Dillingham, 51.
Doe, 70.

Douglass, 65.
Dow, 75.
Downs, 33.
Drew, 58.

E.

Ellsworth, 35.

Emerson, 24.

F.

Fifield, 68.
Folsom, 63.
Footman, 68.

Foster, 65.
Francisco, 89.

French, 21.
Fuller, 35, 50.

G.

Gale, 69.
Gill, 33.
Gillman, 61, 61, 75.
Glover, 68.

Goodell, 18, 53.
Goodwin, 21.
Gordon, 70.

Grace, 72.
Grant, 65.
Griswold, 35, 66.

H.

Hall, 69.
Hamilton, 53.
Hart, 63.
Haskell, 50.
Hasty, 67.

Healy, 61.
Hickock, 34.
Hill, 52.
Hillyer, 35.
Hobbs, 19.

Holmes, 68.
Hurlburt, 35.
Hutchins, 69.
Hyde, 59.

INDEX OF PERSONS REFERRED TO.

www.ingramcontent.com/pod-product-compliance
Lightning Source LLC
Chambersburg PA
CBHW071351290326
41932CB00045B/1426